Today's Mathematics

PART 1: CONCEPTS AND CLASSROOM METHODS

Stafford Library
Columbia College
1001 Rogers Street
Columbia, Missouri 65216

Tenth Edition

Today's Mathematics

PART 1: CONCEPTS AND CLASSROOM METHODS

James W. Heddens
Professor Emeritus, Kent State University

William R. Speer
Professor, University of Nevada, Las Vegas

WITHDRAWN

John Wiley & Sons, Inc.
New York ▪ Chichester ▪ Weinheim ▪ Brisbane ▪ Singapore ▪ Toronto

V

Acquisitions Editor	Maureen E. Prado Roberts
Marketing Manager	Allison Fichter
Production Services Manager	Jeanine Furino
Production Editor	Sandra Russell
Cover Designer	Kevin Murphy
Production Management Services	Elm Street Publishing Services, Inc.
Cover Image by © W. Yanagida/Photonica	

This book was set in 9/11 Helvetica by Elm Street Publishing Services, Inc. and printed and bound by Courier (Westford), Inc. The cover was printed by Phoenix Color Corp.

The paper in this book was manufactured by a mill whose forest management programs include sustained yield harvesting of its timberlands. Sustained yield harvesting principles ensure that the number of trees cut each year does not exceed the amount of new growth.

This book is printed on acid-free paper. ⊗

Copyright © 2001 by John Wiley & Sons, Inc. All rights reserved.

No part of this publication may be reproduced, stored in a retrieval system or transmitted in any form or by any means, electronic, mechanical, photocopying recording, scanning or otherwise, except as permitted under Sections 107 or 108 of the 1976 United States Copyright Act, without either prior written permission of the Publisher or authorization through payment of the appropriate per-copy fee to the Copyright Clearance Center, 222 Rosewood Drive, Danvers, MA 01923, (508) 750-8400, fax (508) 750-4470. Requests to the Publisher for permission should be addressed to the Permissions Department, John Wiley & Sons, Inc., 605 Third Avenue, New York, NY 10158-0012, (212) 850-6008, E-mail: PERMREQ@WILEY.COM. To order books or for customer service call 1-800-CALL-WILEY (225-5945).

Library of Congress Cataloging-in-Publication Data

Heddens, James W.
    Today's mathematics / James W. Heddens, William R. Speer. — 10th ed.
        p.   cm.
    Includes bibliographical references and index.
    Contents: pt. 1. Concepts and classroom methods—pt. 2. Activities and instructional ideas.
    ISBN 0-471-39144-1 (set: alk. paper)—ISBN 0-471-38794-0 (pt. 1: pbk.: alk. paper)
—ISBN 0-471-38793-2 (pt. 2: pbk.: alk. paper)
    1. Mathematics—Study and teaching (Elementary)   I. Speer, William R., 1946–   II. Title.

QA135.5.H42 2001
372.7—dc21
                                                                                        00-036659

Printed in the United States of America.
10 9 8 7 6 5 4 3 2 1

Preface

The adoption and implementation of contemporary mathematics standards by schools provide children with an unparalleled opportunity to learn mathematical skills and develop an understanding of mathematical processes. At the same time, teachers find themselves faced with new problems, such as how to reorganize instruction to meet higher standards; how to best evaluate mathematics teaching and learning; how to best prepare themselves for dealing with the mathematics content of local, state, and national standards; and how to present the material in the most effective manner.

The value of any mathematics program at any level will be determined by the teacher's ability to understand thoroughly what is to be taught and to present it in the most effective way. The adoption of programs based on analysis of the meaning of concepts and the guided discovery of mathematics through hands-on activities places new demands on teachers. This text represents a major effort to help the teacher meet these demands.

The unique format of *Today's Mathematics* makes it adaptable to a wide range of course syllabi and a variety of student groups. *Today's Mathematics* has been used successfully in both undergraduate and graduate courses in education and mathematics. Specifically, it is designed for use in mathematics methods classes, in "mathematics for teachers" classes, as a tool for in-service work with teachers, and as a valuable personal reference resource for anyone concerned with the mathematics education of children and the development of mathematics teaching. *Today's Mathematics* is designed to aid the teacher in understanding mathematical concepts and relationships commonly found in elementary school programs. The text also assists the teacher in presenting these concepts to children, emphasizing how a given concept is introduced at a particular level and how it is expanded and reinforced at successive levels.

Let's look at the organization of the text to see how this is accomplished. The chapters are arranged in a manner that allows flexibility in their coverage. The Principles and Standards for School Mathematics (2000) are reflected throughout this text. The first three chapters establish the tone of the book and provide an overview of contemporary philosophies and psychologies of learning, teaching, and assessing mathematics. The fourth chapter discusses tools such as calculators, computers, and technologies to enhance learning, teaching, and assessing mathematics. The fifth chapter extends this thinking by identifying and examining the roles of problem solving, decision making, and communication in mathematics. The sixth chapter describes the nature and scope of a beginning mathematics program for the primary grades and the development of number sense and numeration. The remaining chapters deal with the content strands of computation with whole numbers, number theory and systems, algebraic reasoning, fraction and decimal concepts and operations, data handling and analysis, measurement, and geometry.

Changes for the tenth edition of *Today's Mathematics* include revision and reorganization of material into **eighteen chapters that better reflect the vision of mathematics learning, teaching, and assessment as described in the National Council of Teachers of Mathematics *Principles and Standards for School Mathematics* (2000)** and earlier NCTM documents entitled *Curriculum and Evaluation Standards for School Mathematics* (1989), *Teaching Standards for School Mathematics* (1991), and *Assessment Standards for School Mathematics* (1995).

A dramatic and substantive change in the format that continues in the tenth edition is the inclusion of a separate but fully integrated companion text of teacher resources. **Part 1 of the *Today's Mathematics* package, entitled "Concepts and Classroom Methods,"** delineates the underlying theory and principles of sound mathematics instruction. **Part 2, the Student Resource Book entitled "Activities and Instructional Ideas,"** includes a host of **activities for children that**

have been revised to reflect the NCTM grade ranges of preK–2, 3–5, and 6–8. The first three chapters of Part 2 have also been strengthened by the inclusion of:

- a discussion of **changes in content and emphasis in preK–8 mathematics;**
- a listing of the **NCTM standards for grades preK–2, 3–5, and 6–8** and a supporting set of references;
- an example of **a complete NCTM standard.**

A **new chapter** on **Technology Tools for Enhancing Teaching, Learning, and Assessing Mathematics** introduces the teacher to a discussion of the **role of calculators** in the classroom, supported by the complete text of the **NCTM position paper on calculator use,** and a set of **activities** for grades preK–8; and a discussion of the **role of computer technology** in elementary grades, including software, applications, multimedia, and telecommunications (i.e., the Internet and the World Wide Web), supported by the complete text of the **NCTM position paper on technology in the classroom,** and a set of **activities** for grades preK–8.

Part 1 of the text now also includes **Research Snapshots** designed to generate discussion and, perhaps, active research of your own, while Part 2 now has **primary and intermediate sample lesson plans for each content chapter** to aid you in putting research theory into classroom practice.

In addition to the new features of the tenth edition of *Today's Mathematics*, popular features of previous editions have been retained. These include:

- motivational openings for each chapter (with the themes of problem solving, decision making, and the role of communication in mathematics) that focus on **connections to the real world** as well as to other areas of mathematics;
- a **special chapter in Part 2** (Chapter 18) designed to assist student teachers in becoming familiar with some of the practical concerns every teacher faces when making instructional decisions. These aids include a **comprehensive scope and sequence for grades preK–8** that reflects the vision of the NCTM standards, a **comprehensive checklist of mathematical concept clusters,** a variety of **thematic mathematics activity idea-packs,** and a **vignette from the NCTM assessment standards** that is designed to emphasize the importance and **integration of content, teaching, and assessment.**

As the move to identify standards for the improvement of mathematics instruction in the elementary school continues, the importance of understanding mathematics content and methodology cannot be overemphasized. We are certain that you will find that the tenth edition of *Today's Mathematics* continues to contribute to the long-standing tradition of relevance and insight established by previous editions of this text. Combined coverage of both content and methods creates a text that helps student teachers see the relationship between what they teach and how they teach. This interdependent structure helps illustrate the development of elementary school mathematics curriculum from the primary grades through preparation for high school.

All of the features that have contributed to the popularity of previous editions of *Today's Mathematics* have been maintained in this edition. Chapters are consistently structured in the following manner:

- **Chapter objectives and teaching competencies** are identified for each chapter to serve as advance organizers and to set the stage for what should be the major outcomes as a result of completing the chapter.
- Each chapter presents a comprehensive focus on appropriate content and methods for the topics presented.
- An end-of-chapter **glossary** of terminology, symbols, and procedures discussed in the chapter allows the user to quickly review these important aspects of the chapter.
- A complete set of content-oriented **practice exercises** appears in Chapters 5–17. The student teacher can self-check comprehension of the content through use of an appendix with answers to all these exercises.
- A set of revised open-ended **assessment questions corresponding to the teaching competencies in the chapter** is provided for each chapter. These are designed to encourage further **individual and cooperative exploration** and to engage student teachers in discourse and debate centered on various issues raised in the chapter.
- A comprehensive collection of **classroom activities** for use with children in the preK–2, 3–5, and 6–8 grade ranges is provided for Chapters 5–17 in Part 2. These activities, which help the student teacher translate theories and concepts discussed in the chapter, include many experiences with manipulatives and hands-on learning and suggest ways to anchor skills. There are also exercises in each chapter that focus on activities that use **calculators** and **computers** in instruction.
- A collection of up-to-date **references that support the ideas** found in each chapter is also included in Part 2.

The bibliography in Part 2 is drawn from **readily available recent resources** so that student teachers can easily locate additional readings to support and expand their understanding.

SUPPLEMENTS

Continuing a service begun with two previous editions of *Today's Mathematics,* we have revised the **Instructor's Manual** for the tenth edition. For each of the chapters the manual includes:

- an overview of the content
- a list of teaching competencies

- a collection of group or individual activities
- a set of appropriate transparency masters
- a number of multiple-choice discussion questions with detailed analyses of correct and incorrect answers.

We are also pleased to provide a **revised computerized bank of test items** for each chapter of the tenth edition of *Today's Mathematics.* The item bank disk and manual are available for either the IBM PC (and PC-compatible) or the Apple Macintosh series. The bank allows the teacher to create tests by selecting from the existing 60-plus **multiple-choice**, 10 **true-false**, 3 **matching**, 5 open-ended short answer **essay questions**, 3 **short-term performance assessment tasks**, and 3 **long-term performance assessment tasks for each chapter**. Questions can be selected and sorted by the user, so tests can be created for individual chapters, groups of chapters, or the entire book. The teacher can also add questions to any chapter test by appending or replacing existing questions. The teacher can, in addition, build a test bank of his or her own by transferring work from an existing word processing file. The teacher has the option of labeling criteria on each item using any desired scheme such as level of difficulty or objective being tested. Created tests can be stored for future use and can be previewed, edited, scrambled, and printed in different fonts. Of course, an answer key can be printed for any created test.

ACKNOWLEDGMENTS

A special acknowledgment must be given to Marge Speer for her assistance, support, and patience in the preparation of this manuscript.

The authors would also like to express a sincere thank you to:

- Marilyn Sue Ford for translating the vision of the text into sample primary and intermediate lesson plans for each content chapter;
- Jeff Shih for organizing the Research Snapshots in each chapter;
- Juli Dixon for contributing a new chapter focusing on technology tools for enhancing instruction; and
- Virginia Usnick for her input on the geometry chapters and the activities for students in Part 2.

It is also important to reaffirm our appreciation of Daniel Brahier and Christy Falba for the contributions made to the ninth edition of *Today's Mathematics* that have been carried through to the tenth edition.

James W. Heddens   *William R. Speer*

Contents

Chapter 5

Problem Solving, Decision Making, and Communicating in Mathematics   61

Chapter 6

Number Sense, Numeration, and Place Value   83

Chapter 7

Addition and Subtraction of Whole Numbers   113

Chapter 8

Multiplication and Division of Whole Numbers   135

Chapter 15

Measurement   269

Chapter 16

Geometry: Basic Concepts and Structures   287

Chapter 17

Geometry: Polygons and Polyhedra   309

Chapter 18

A Look Back As You Move Ahead   339

Appendix   **341**

Index   **377**

Today's Mathematics

PART 1: CONCEPTS AND CLASSROOM METHODS

Chapter 1

Learning Mathematics

Teaching Competencies

Upon completing this chapter, you will be able to:

■ Describe the vision of mathematics education put forth in the NCTM *Principles and Standards for School Mathematics*.

■ Describe characteristics of an effective contemporary elementary/middle school mathematics program.

■ Contrast characteristics of a contemporary mathematics program with those of a more traditional program, relating the benefits and shortcomings of each.

■ Describe a basic philosophy of teaching mathematics that promotes effective learning.

■ Relate prominent learning theories to classroom mathematics teaching and learning.

■ Describe, in general terms, mathematics content as appropriate for any given grade level, PreK–8.

■ Describe several roles a teacher may play in implementing the NCTM *Principles and Standards for School Mathematics*.

ociety is in constant change, and elementary school mathematics programs must keep pace and, in some sense, contribute to that change. For too many years mathematics programs have been static—unwavering to new demands and challenges. But our contemporary world demands a kind of mathematical knowledge that is very different from that required in the past. A report of the Society for Industrial and Applied Mathematics (1996) listed the mathematical content that mathematicians say they are using in their work. This list included modeling and simulation, probability and statistics, optimization, and discrete mathematics. This is a very different list than one generated 25 years ago (or even 10 years from now). According to the Workforce 2000 report, 70% of the jobs requiring the skills we currently use will be obsolete by 2010! Clearly, the need is greater than ever before for students to learn in a way that ensures that success in the present translates to success in the future.

The Report of the Senior Assessment Panel for the International Assessment of the U.S. Mathematical Sciences (1998) argued that the economic health and the security of the nation has come to depend heavily on mathematics. Today, and even more so in the future, the need is for individuals who can *formulate, define,* and *analyze* significant problems as well as *discover* creative ways to solve them through disciplined imagination.

> *It takes a generation to complete the mathematical education of a single individual. . . . We can no longer afford to sit idle while our children move through school without receiving a mathematical preparation adequate for the twenty-first century. The choices are in front of us. It is time to take action. (National Research Council, 1989, p. 96)*

In previous generations people needed to be able to calculate efficiently and accurately. There is still a need for such skill, but now it is more common to employ technology for lengthy and cumbersome calculations. Calculators are inexpensive, compact, and easily obtainable. In fact, many people carry calculators with them for immediate use when appropriate situations arise. Calculators and computers are, for the most part, readily available to assist people with involved computational demands in our technological society. Consequently, we need to reexamine and redefine the roles of calculators and computers in the classroom as well as the role of arithmetic in the study of mathematics.

An effective elementary school mathematics program must consider a wider range of objectives than just computational skill. Certainly, *skills* necessary for daily life must be taught, but this should be married with the development of *understandings* that free children from mindless rote memorization. A contemporary mathematics program should also attempt to provide a satisfactory foundation for further study and exposure to a cultural and historical perspective of the role of mathematics in our society. To do so requires a firm understanding of mathematics—not simply skill in

mathematics. A healthy combination of skill and understanding offers mathematical power to the learner.

CALLS FOR CHANGE

During the past 40 years, substantial changes have occurred in both teaching strategies and the curricula of elementary mathematics programs. Learning theories—particularly the work of Jean Piaget, Robert Gagné, Jerome Bruner, Zoltan Dienes, and the van Hieles—have greatly informed us on how students learn and influenced how mathematics is taught. The content of elementary mathematics programs is, and should be, constantly evaluated and revised. Such phenomena as the experimental curricular projects of the 1950s and 1960s, "new math," the "back-to-basics" approach, integrated curricula, cooperative learning approaches, and focused attention on problem solving have greatly changed the content and focus of mathematics programs.

A number of reports offering direction for the future have been issued during the past few years. The earliest of these signaled a need for careful examination of past assumptions regarding mathematics education. These reports included *The Underachieving Curriculum: Assessing U.S. School Mathematics from an International Perspective* (1987), *Everybody Counts: A Report to the Nation on the Future of Mathematics Education* (1989), and *America 2000: An Education Strategy* (1991). The discussion and analysis of these and other reports lead to plans of action such as *Standards for All: A Vision for Education in the 21st Century* (1993), *First in the World* (1993), *Foundation for the Future* (1994), *A Perspective on Reform in Mathematics and Science Education—Project 2061* (1996), *What Matters Most: Teaching for America's Future* (1996), *The National Education Goals Report* (1997), and *The Condition of Education* (1998).

It was also during this period that the National Council of Teachers of Mathematics launched three separate landmark publications on mathematics curriculum, teaching, and assessment. In response to the publication of NCTM's *Curriculum and Evaluation Standards for School Mathematics* (1989), the Mathematical Association of America produced *A Call for Change: Recommendations for the Mathematical Preparation of Teachers of Mathematics* (1991). Each of these documents has had widespread influence on mathematics education, and each has been revisited to reflect both the changing needs of society and what we continue to discover regarding how students learn and how we might best contribute to and assess this learning (NCTM 2000, MAA 1998).

The Council of Chief State School Officers (1997), in a study to (1) define and describe state-based frameworks, (2) evaluate the role of frameworks in reform, and (3) assist states in efforts to develop frameworks, reported that nearly all states were developing, revising, and implementing mathematics curriculum frameworks. A report of the major findings of analysis of state standards and assessments (Achieve, 1999) noted that states, as a whole, (1) do not have expectations that are rigorous by international standards, (2) do not have a tightness of alignment between state standards and state assessment tools used to measure attainment of the standards, and (3) do not effectively address the "mile wide and inch deep" phenomenon—covering too many topics in too shallow a fashion as opposed to providing the greatest depth of understanding possible by delving into fewer topics.

State policymakers have, however, taken a lead in supporting systemic reform with challenging expectations and more robust and coherent guidelines in efforts to improve the teaching/learning equation. For example, efforts have been put forth by such state initiatives as Ohio's *Model Competency-Based Mathematics Program* (1990), Virginia's *Mathematics Standards of Learning* (1995), Delaware's *New Directions in Content Standards* (1996), Maryland's *Mathematics: A Curricular Framework* (1997), Illinois's *Learning Standards* (1997), and Nevada's *Mathematics Content and Performance Standards* (1998).

These reports and position papers, as well as others (see additional suggested readings in Chapter 1 of Part 2, the Student Resource Book), have served to raise questions about the content of our mathematics programs, the mathematical performance of our students, and the performance of our mathematics teaching. Some people may brush these reports off as merely the cyclical moaning of longtime critics of education. They are, however, deserving of a closer look and of greater attention from those seeking to improve education.

NATIONAL AND INTERNATIONAL ACHIEVEMENT

The publication of the trends and results of the 1996 National Assessment of Educational Progress (NAEP), in *The 1996 Mathematics Report Card for the Nation and the States* (1997), suggests that national performance in mathematical proficiency for fourth-, eighth-, and twelfth-grade students over the period from 1986 to 1996 did improve. In addition, the 1998 average mathematics score for the ACT and SAT tests continued their upward trend to the highest point in 27 years. Nevertheless, there are some troubling findings that cloud this improvement. Statistically, 100% of the twelfth-grade students demonstrated proficiency with simple arithmetic facts, and 99.9% were proficient with beginning skills and understandings. However, only the eighth-grade students showed an increase in proficiency with moderately complex reasoning and multistep problem solving. Some other trends were identifiable for specific age groups and minorities. Scores for black, Hispanic, and American Indian students remained below those for white students. The gaps between the scores of these subgroups did not change from the earlier assessment. Much work remains to get all students where we want them to be.

The NAEP report also reflected data of an earlier International Assessment of Educational Progress, which measured performance on five topics (geometry, numbers and operations, data analysis/statistics/probability, algebra and functions, and measurement) and three process levels (conceptual understanding, procedural knowledge, and problem solving). U.S. 9- and 13-year-olds scored below the eight-country mean in each area except data analysis/statistics/probability.

Perhaps one of the most significant indicators of the need for reform in mathematics education has come from the analysis of findings from the *Third International Mathematics and Science Study* (1999). The TIMSS study was the most extensive in-depth study of international comparisons of mathematics and science education ever undertaken. Its purpose was to not only examine student achievement in 45 nations at three grade levels—grades 4, 8, and 12—but also to analyze curricula and teaching practices of these countries.

Comparing achievement in the 26 TIMSS countries that participated in fourth-grade testing, the U.S. fourth-grade students were above the international average in mathematics. Comparing achievement in the 41 TIMSS countries that participated in the eighth-grade testing, the U.S. eighth-grade students were below the international average in mathematics. Comparing achievement in the 21 TIMSS countries that participated in the general mathematics twelfth-grade testing, the U.S. twelfth-grade students were significantly below the international average in general knowledge mathematics. Comparing achievement in the 16 TIMSS countries that participated in the advanced mathematics twelfth-grade testing, the U.S. twelfth-grade students were among the lowest in advanced mathematics knowledge. The United States is the only country participating in the full range of TIMSS testing whose mathematics ranking fell from above average at grade 4, to below average at grade 8, to an even more disastrous level in grade 12.

It should be noted that the TIMSS data is not necessarily an indictment of the NCTM standards reform. The TIMSS data was collected in 1995—since the initial set of standards was released in 1989, the students in that study would have had the availability (but not necessarily the opportunity) to experience a standards-based classroom for only 4 or 5 school years. A question to consider is, would this limited exposure to standards-based instruction be a cause of low performance on the part of twelfth graders who may have had a more traditional foundation in their formative elementary and middle school years?

While reasons for the disappointing performance on the TIMSS are difficult to isolate, attempts have been made to describe at least plausible explanations. Most often mentioned is the fact that we have no nationally defined curriculum—a characteristic of many other countries in the study. The study also found that less rigorous content makes up the bulk of our mathematics curriculum and that U.S. teachers try to cover too much material and, consequently, do so in a superficial manner—the opposite of what occurs in high-performing countries. Other reasons often cited include a weak induction process for teachers and very little opportunity for professional interaction with colleagues in teaching.

The main point to be gained from the TIMSS study is not our relative international standing, but what we can learn from others to assist us and our students in achieving higher standards. Whether the messages from TIMSS yield genuine educational reform will depend on the actions of stakeholders at the local, state, and national levels.

The National Sciences Board (NSB) report entitled *Preparing our Children: Math and Science Education in the National Interest* (1999) urged a consensus on a core of knowledge and competency in mathematics and science. The NSB stated that it is both possible and imperative to develop standards that serve the national interest while respecting local responsibility for K–12 teaching and learning. In this report, the NSB offered four recommendations that promote student achievement. These recommendations, generated from research and analysis of best practices, include:

more rigorous standards;
higher expectations that all students can meet these standards;
teachers well prepared in the subjects they are teaching; and
meaningful measures of accountability.

In a report to the Mathematical Sciences Education Board (MSEB), Henry Pollack of Bell Laboratories offered the findings of a study on mathematical expectations of employees in the workplace. Pollack noted that employers want people who:

- have the ability to *set up* problems, not just respond to previously identified ones
- have knowledge of a variety of approaches and techniques to solve problems
- have an understanding of the underlying mathematical features of a problem
- have the ability to work with others to reach a solution to a problem
- have the ability to recognize how mathematics applies to both common and complex problems
- are prepared for open problem situations as opposed to the very few problems that are presented to us in a well-formulated state
- believe in the value and utility of mathematics

Similar characteristics and abilities were identified in a Secretary's Commission on Achieving Necessary Skills (SCANS) report from the U.S. Department of Labor on what work requires of schools.

A moment of reflection on these desired traits and the limited way in which they mesh with the goals and directions of what might be called the "traditional" mathematics preparation of students should raise some clear questions in our minds. For example, *The Mathematics Report Card* (1997) included children's beliefs about mathematics as a discipline. Nationally, 50% of the seventh graders either agreed or strongly agreed that learning mathematics is mostly memorization, while 83% believed that there is always a rule to follow in mathematics. If these are the perceptions of our students, then it becomes clear that they do not embrace the expectations or standards of society for a mathematically literate population.

THE IDENTIFICATION OF STANDARDS

What does it mean to be a mathematics teacher today? What might we believe in, and what might we work toward? How can we better the profession? How can we provide experiences that meet the needs of our students in particular, and of society in general? Perhaps some basic principles or standards would help us to decide.

A **standard** can be thought of as a benchmark or a statement against which a given item or position can be measured or compared. The Bureau of Weights and Measures, for example, has standards that define the various measures that we use. Restaurants and hotels have standards of service that they seek to uphold for their guests. As individuals, we have standards that are reflections of our personal values, philosophy, and way of life. Professions, too, have standards that mirror the vision and values of that profession.

The National Council of Teachers of Mathematics (NCTM), with a membership of more than 100,000 professionals, is an organization devoted to the improvement and promotion of mathematics education. Its mission is to provide vision and leadership in improving the teaching and learning of mathematics so that every student is ensured an equitable standards-based mathematics education and every teacher of mathematics is ensured an opportunity to grow professionally. The Council provides a forum to discuss new educational developments, share innovative classroom experiences, and examine changes taking place in the teaching of mathematics. In addition to several ancillary publications, the Council publishes periodicals for teachers, including *Teaching Children Mathematics* (grades preK–6), *Mathematics Teaching in the Middle School* (grades 5–9), *The Mathematics Teacher* (grades 8–12 and up), and the *Journal for Research in Mathematics Education* (preK–16 and up).

Additional information about the National Council of Teachers of Mathematics, including membership information, publication catalogs, and member services/resources, can be obtained by writing NCTM, 1906 Association Drive, Reston, VA 20191-1593. You may also contact NCTM via email (nctm@nctm.org), the Web (www.nctm.org), fax (703-476–2970), or direct telephone (703-620-9840). NCTM also has a "fax on demand" program that allows you to request faxed copies of items of interest to mathematics educators. This includes information concerning membership, NCTM administration, current issues, resources, position statements, conferences, grants, affiliated group services, and publications. This service can be accessed by calling 1-800-220-8483. The system will ask if you want a complete list of available faxes and can accept requests for up to four documents. Of special interest are the NCTM position statements concerning calculators, early childhood mathematics, evaluation of teacher performance, mathematics for second-language learners, metrication, research, professional development, technology, and mathematics for underrepresented groups.

The NCTM initially published its *Curriculum and Evaluation Standards for School Mathematics* in 1989. These standards were followed by the *Teaching Standards* in 1991 and the *Assessment Standards* in 1995. A major concern of all stakeholders in the education of youth was how to mesh this segregated collection of standards into a cohesive vision. As one answer, the NCTM revisited and revised the 1989, 1991, and 1995 standards into a single document entitled the NCTM *Principles and Standards for School Mathematics* (2000). This document reflects a vision of mathematical literacy necessary in a world that requires understanding and application of problem-solving and decision-making techniques. The main messages of the first three standards documents maintain their relevancy. The new standards document supports the direction and message of the original standards by refocusing, clarifying, and developing connections. The *Principles and Standards for School Mathematics* document also takes into account developments in technology that have occurred since the original standards were released and includes more examples to reinforce the intent and the spirit of the recommendations made.

These standards are important for all mathematics teachers because they have become a primary source for evaluating and driving reforms in mathematics education. Such standards provide significant assistance in the processes of designing, implementing, and evaluating elementary and secondary mathematics programs.

PRINCIPLES AND STANDARDS FOR SCHOOL MATHEMATICS

In order to tackle the realities of today and provide for the expectations of tomorrow, it is essential that students (1) learn to value mathematics, (2) develop confidence in their ability to use mathematics, (3) become problem solvers (as opposed to simply answer finders), (4) learn to communicate mathematically, and (5) learn to reason mathematically. Societal goals for mathematics education must include the development of mathematically literate workers, lifelong learning, opportunity for all, and an informed populace. To accomplish these goals, there must be major shifts in:

Curriculum—allow a deeper study of important mathematics and its uses;

Learning—promote active student engagement with a variety of mathematical tools for solving problems;

Teaching—create a stimulating learning environment in which all students are challenged to reach their full potential; and

Assessment—use assessment that is ongoing and based on many sources of evidence.

The *Principles and Standards for School Mathematics* describes basic tenets or underlying assumptions regarding equity, curriculum, teaching, assessment, and technology for instructional programs in mathematics. These principles endorse a view of what is necessary at the classroom, school, district, and national level for effective mathematics education. The 1989, 1991, and 1995 standards were built on the position that all students can learn mathematics and that teachers play an essential role in helping students understand. The Principles and Standards document goes further by spelling out six central principles that form the foundation on which the standards are built.

The six principles described in the NCTM *Principles and Standards for School Mathematics* (2000) are:

- *Equity.* Excellence in mathematics education requires equity—high expectations and strong support for all students.
- *Curriculum.* A curriculum is more than a collection of activities: it must be coherent, focused on important mathematics, and well articulated across the grades.
- *Teaching.* Effective mathematics teaching requires understanding what students know and need to learn and then challenging and supporting them to learn it well.
- *Learning.* Students must learn mathematics with understanding, actively building new knowledge from experience and prior knowledge.
- *Assessment.* Assessment should support the learning of important mathematics and furnish useful information to both teachers and students.
- *Technology.* Technology is essential in teaching and learning mathematics; it influences the mathematics that is taught and enhances students' learning.

As in previous standards, the *Principles and Standards for School Mathematics* (1998) emphasizes the role of process standards that run through all of the grades. These Process Standards are:

Problem Solving

Instructional programs from prekindergarten through grade 12 should enable all students to—

- build new mathematical knowledge through problem solving;
- solve problems that arise in mathematics and in other contexts;
- apply and adapt a variety of appropriate strategies to solve problems;

Principles

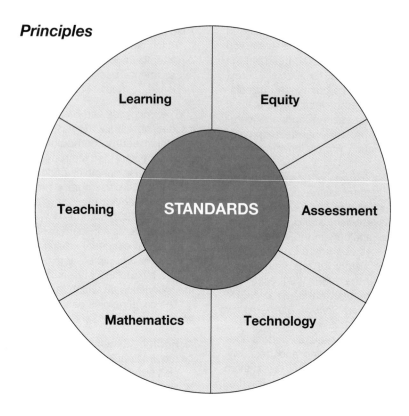

monitor and reflect on the process of mathematical problem solving.

Reasoning and Proof

Instructional programs from prekindergarten through grade 12 should enable all students to—

- recognize reasoning and proof as fundamental aspects of mathematics;
- make and investigate mathematical conjectures;
- develop and evaluate mathematical arguments and proofs;
- select and use various types of reasoning and methods of proof.

Communication

Instructional programs from prekindergarten through grade 12 should enable all students to—

- organize and consolidate their mathematical thinking through communication;
- communicate their mathematical thinking coherently and clearly to peers, teachers, and others;
- analyze and evaluate the mathematical thinking and strategies of others;
- use the language of mathematics to express mathematical ideas precisely.

Connections

Instructional programs from prekindergarten through grade 12 should enable all students to—

- recognize and use connections among mathematical ideas;
- understand how mathematical ideas interconnect and build on one another to produce a coherent whole;
- recognize and apply mathematics in contexts outside of mathematics.

Mathematical Representation

Instructional programs from prekindergarten through grade 12 should enable all students to—

- create and use representations to organize, record, and communicate mathematical ideas;
- select, apply, and translate among mathematical representations to solve problems;
- use representations to model and interpret physical, social, and mathematical phenomena.

In addition to the five process standards, there are five content standards in the *Principles and Standards for School Mathematics* (2000) that address what a student should know. The Content Standards include:

Number and Operations

Instructional programs from prekindergarten through grade 12 should enable all students to—

- understand numbers, ways of representing numbers, relationships among numbers, and number systems;
- understand meanings of operations and how they relate to one another;
- compute fluently and make reasonable estimates.

Algebra

Instructional programs from prekindergarten through grade 12 should enable all students to—

- understand patterns, relations, and functions;
- represent and analyze mathematical situations and structures using algebraic symbols;
- use mathematical models to represent and understand quantitative relationships;
- analyze change in various contexts.

Geometry

Instructional programs from prekindergarten through grade 12 should enable all students to—

- analyze characteristics and properties of two- and three-dimensional geometric shapes and develop mathematical arguments about geometric relationships;
- specify locations and describe spatial relationships using coordinate geometry and other representational systems;
- apply transformations and use symmetry to analyze mathematical situations;
- use visualization, spatial reasoning, and geometric modeling to solve problems.

Measurement

Instructional programs from prekindergarten through grade 12 should enable all students to—

- understand measurable attributes of objects and the units, systems, and processes of measurement;
- apply appropriate techniques, tools, and formulas to determine measurements.

Data Analysis and Probability

Instructional programs from prekindergarten through grade 12 should enable all students to—

- formulate questions that can be addressed with data and collect, organize, and display relevant data to answer them;
- select and use appropriate statistical methods methods to analyze data;
- develop and evaluate inferences and predictions that are based on data;
- understand and apply basic concepts of probability.

The same ten process and content standards are applied in each grade band to link what students should be learning across grades. Consequently, each individual standard includes an explanation and elaboration of key ideas that enable teachers to see what students should know coming to their grade band, what they should learn within that grade band, and where that will later lead. Perhaps most importantly, the *Principles and Standards for School Mathematics* includes research evidence collected since the first set of standards, which demonstrates that a long-term commitment to this vision can lead to improved mathematics teaching and learning.

According to the NCTM:

***The* Principles and Standards for School Mathematics *offers a vision of:*

1. mathematical power for all in a technological society;
2. mathematics as something one does—solve problems, communicate, reason;
3. a curriculum for all that includes a broad range of content, a variety of contexts, and deliberate connections;
4. the learning of mathematics as an active, constructive process;
5. instruction based on real problems; and
6. evaluation as a means of improving instruction, learning, and programs.

To assist the reader, complete statements of all the standards for grades PreK–2, grades 3–5, and grades 6–8 have been placed in Part 2 of *Today's Mathematics*, the Student Resource Book. A sample complete standard, with focus and discussion, has also been included in Part 2.

IMPLEMENTING THE PROCESS STANDARDS

Let us briefly examine the impact of the process standards that are common threads throughout the document. Mathematics is represented as problem solving, reasoning and proof, communication, representation, and as a connection within itself and with other subject areas. These process standards provide a philosophical base for approaching the teaching and learning of all mathematics. If we accept their importance, then they will affect the ways in which we select and organize experiences from the remaining standards.

For example, consider instructional tactics that might be employed for teaching a fourth-grade class the procedure for multiplying 16 times 25. We might resort to a traditional approach in which the teacher "shows and tells" the entire class how to record the algorithmic process. That is, we would write the exercise as:

$$\begin{array}{r} 25 \\ \times\, 16 \end{array}$$

Then we would continue: "Now, multiply 6 times 5 and get 30. Write the 0 below the line under the 6, and write a small 3 above the 2 in 25."

$$\begin{array}{r} 3 \\ 25 \\ \times\, 16 \\ \hline 0 \end{array}$$

"Next, multiply the 6 times the 2 and get 12, and add the 3 to the 12 to get 15. Write this to the left of the 0 below the line. From this point on, forget about that small 3 you wrote above the 2—you don't need it anymore."

$$\begin{array}{r} 25 \\ \times\, 16 \\ \hline 150 \end{array}$$

"Now, multiply the 1 times 5, writing the answer, 5, one place to the left under the 150. Also, multiply the 1 times 2 and write that answer to the left of the 5."

$$\begin{array}{r} 25 \\ \times\, 16 \\ \hline 150 \\ 25 \end{array}$$

"Finally, write the sum of the two partial products under the line, remembering to 'carry,' if necessary, when you add."

$$\begin{array}{r} 25 \\ \times\, 16 \\ \hline 150 \\ 25 \\ \hline 400 \end{array}$$

The above rote steps can be learned through repetition, but the student will possess only the skill to do this particular type of problem—transfer to other problems, even similar ones, will not necessarily occur. Under a rote procedure approach, it would not be unusual to hear a student exclaim, "I know how to do it when they're like this one, but what do I do if a number has 'hundreds' in it?

A different approach to this same computational exercise would take on a dramatically different appearance and spirit if couched in the vision of the standards as represented by problem solving, communication, reasoning, representations, and connections. In such an instance, more consideration would be given to what the exercise actually represents. This vision might be incorporated, to some degree, by placing the exercise in a real-life setting. Rather than just asking for the answer to 16 times 25, we might relate it to determining the cost of purchasing 16 stamps at 25 cents each. Alternatively, we might consider the total number of stamps in an array or sheet of stamps, 16 rows with 25 stamps in each row. Suddenly, our arithmetic exercise has been transformed into a geometric context with the answer representing the area of a rectangle that has dimensions of 16 by 25.

This geometric approach might lead us, in later grades, to recognizing the connection between $(a + b)(c + d)$ and 16×25, both of which can be represented by the sum of four partial products. This can perhaps best be seen by rewriting 16×25 as $(10 + 6)(20 + 5)$ or

$$\begin{array}{r} 20 + 5 \\ \times\ 10 + 6 \\ \hline 120 + 30 \\ 200 + 50 \\ \hline 200 + 120 + 50 + 30 \end{array} \qquad \begin{array}{r} a + b \\ \times\ c + d \\ \hline ad + bd \\ ac + bc \\ \hline ac + ad + bc + bd \end{array}$$

Another tactic might be to emphasize a different interpretation of what "16 times 25" means; that is, "How much is 16 groups of 25?" This latter approach might lead us to think of this same exercise in an alternative form, such as 8 groups of 50 or even 4 groups of 100, thereby encouraging the application of some mental mathematics to solve the exercise.

Even if we chose a strictly paper-and-pencil approach, the discussion that would take place in a contemporary standards-based classroom would differ in emphasis and direction from that of a more traditional classroom. Instead of rote memorization and thoughtless reproduction of meaningless steps in the **algorithm**, or computational procedure, an approach that incorporated the spirit of the standards would continually reflect not only on what was taking place, but also on why. For example, instead of taking "1 times 5 and then 1 times 2 and shifting the answer by one place" as was shown earlier, we would emphasize the multiplication of 25 by 10 to get 250. There are numerous other meaningful reflections that might be made in considering this exercise and others like it.

At this point, it is important to note that although the NCTM *Principles and Standards for School Mathematics* are written in such a way that they can be understood and translated into classroom activities and objectives, they are much more comprehensive than can possibly be conveyed here. For example, the NCTM standards also address evaluation as an integral part of attaining the vision those standards represent. Evaluation is, of course, assessing what students know about mathematics, but it also includes information about how they think about mathematics. Assessment is a constant part of teaching rather than a single act that occurs after teaching. Assessment goes beyond identifying right or wrong responses and requires a more comprehensive view of what is to be evaluated, including student behaviors, curricular choices, and instructional models. Effective assessment demands that we use multiple techniques (e.g., calculators, computers, manipulatives, etc.) and formats (e.g., written, oral, demonstration, etc.) for gathering data as opposed to just traditional paper-and-pencil methods. Finally, assessment, as viewed through the NCTM standards, utilizes standardized achievement test results *as only one of many* indicators of program outcomes and student success.

Our purpose in this chapter is not to offer a detailed discussion of the NCTM *Principles and Standards for School Mathematics*. Because of the volume of material, it is impossible to do a thorough presentation here. Nevertheless, we hope that as you read this text, you will reflect on the intent and vision of mathematics that these standards represent. We urge you to locate a copy and familiarize yourself with this document—a document that has the potential to greatly influence the mathematics learning, teaching, and assessment procedures in our schools today and in the future. The reader is encouraged to purchase a copy of the *Principles and Standards for School Mathematics* from NCTM, 1906 Association Drive, Reston, VA 20191. In Chapters 2 and 3, respectively, you will learn of two earlier landmark companion NCTM standards projects: the *Professional Standards for Teaching Mathematics* (1991) and the *Assessment Standards for School Mathematics* (1995) and of the many ways in which these documents have been incorporated into the recently released *Principles and Standards for School Mathematics* (2000).

DESCRIBING A CONTEMPORARY ELEMENTARY MATHEMATICS PROGRAM

As we begin to explore what an effective elementary school mathematics program consists of, we must ask three fundamental questions: (1) What is mathematics? (2) How do students learn mathematics? (3) What mathematics should students learn?

In the past, mathematics has sometimes been viewed as being synonymous with arithmetic. That is, mathematics was interpreted by many as being limited to the process of completing calculations. Mathematics programs subscribing to this narrow belief were based on **rote memorization** of number facts and routine, mindless computational drill. Contemporary programs stress a broader, yet well-defined, view of mathematics, with an emphasis on understanding fundamental mathematics concepts and the interrelationships among different topics in mathematics and other disciplines. All students need to explore content and applications that extend beyond the solely computational aspect of the arithmetic curriculum. Does this mean that students must no longer memorize basic facts or practice to anchor computational skills? Definitely not! It is essential that students work to develop such skills—the debate is not over "whether" they do this, but "how" they do it. The point is that memorization and drill must be preceded by an understanding of what basic facts mean and why algorithms work. Without this understanding, the pupil has little chance of progressing very far in mathematics or applying the mathematics he or she knows to significant practical problems or applications. An effective elementary school mathematics program emphasizes a marriage between the understanding of mathematical concepts and the development of skills to provide the student with true power in and over mathematics.

Next, let us address how students learn mathematics. If elementary mathematics instruction is to develop creative, mathematical minds, then the methods of presentation and instruction must be examined. For generations, the technique of instruction in mathematics was essentially a three-step process:

1. The teacher told the students what topic they were to learn.
2. The teacher used examples to show how to solve a particular type of example or problem.
3. The students then routinely imitated the given procedure "mechanically" to find answers to a great number of similar examples.

Such a "show-and-tell" approach to teaching mathematics mainly promotes imitation and drill of seemingly meaningless facts and rules. There is not much to be gained in spending countless hours to teach a student HOW to do something that an inexpensive calculator can do more efficiently. This method of instruction reveals little or nothing of the meaning behind the process that the student is imitating. Thousands of people solve problems daily—they "borrow" and "carry" numbers, wonder what to do with remainders, or try to remember which of two fractions in a division exercise is the one to "invert" before multiplying. Such confusion is the natural outcome of learning mathematics by imitation and rote memorization. Picking the correct *rule* from a collection of meaningless rules is not what mathematics learning is about.

Rather than a passive method of mathematics instruction, a contemporary program promotes an *active* learning process—mentally, physically, visually, and emotionally. In this active, guided discovery method, a skilled teacher places students in situations in which each student's actions reveal the extent of his or her reasoning and comprehension of the concepts, definitions, techniques, and processes being explored. Pupils who "think through" mathematics in this way gain more confidence by their own discoveries and observations than by trying to recall imposed memorized rules. They comprehend the reasoning underlying mathematical operations and processes and can apply them in new situations—a true definition of what it means to actually "learn" something.

Using this active interpretation of teaching, children still need to memorize basic facts and develop proficiency in fundamental algorithms for calculation. Also, children still need some practice and drill to anchor skills. Systematic reinforcement should be part of any effective mathematics program. However, such reinforcement must be based on the notion that the student has developed sufficient understanding of the concept prior to practice and, thus, can avoid the purely mechanical application of rules and procedures.

A guided discovery approach relies heavily on **inductive reasoning** (specific examples leading to general rules) rather than **deductive reasoning** (general rules applied to specific examples). For the inductive method, children are asked to solve some examples extending previously learned techniques and then to formulate general statements based on patterns they observe. In effect, students develop their own versions of rules or generalizations (with the teacher's guidance) and then use these to solve other examples. The teacher provides a focus for the children's active discussion, rather than simply showing them which procedure to use in a given situation.

One great advantage of the inductive approach is the freedom children experience in looking for ways to solve mathematical examples. Without teacher-imposed rules to condition or limit their thinking, children are free to find that a given example can be solved in various ways. Thus, pupils discover through their own experience one of the major features of contemporary mathematics: There is often more than one way to arrive at a solution. Children also quickly learn that some problems have more than one correct solution, whereas others have no solution at all. When children are allowed this freedom and are encouraged to use their imaginations without being tied to arbitrary rules and rigid steps, they will learn to seek ways to solve any problem—not just the teacher's way. Even students of apparently lesser ability, guided by a careful and patient teacher, can appreciate the fact that a problem does not necessarily have just one way of being solved. This may, in fact, be a great encouragement to the less imaginative student, who would no longer be baffled and discouraged by trying to remember half-understood rules.

LEVELS OF ABSTRACTION

The issue of different levels of abstraction must also be considered when discussing a guided discovery approach. It is highly unlikely that, when encountering "$126 \div 3$," a student will "discover" the standard abstract algorithm for division, but it is quite likely that the same student will "discover" a means of dividing 126 physical objects into 3 equal groups. The difference, of course, is that the latter is a physical representation of the abstract process asked for in the former. This process of examining concepts at the physical or manipulative level prior to the establishment of abstractions allows the student (and the teacher) to build knowledge by constructing a bridge between the two.

Consider the following unusual scenario to help you understand the importance of levels of abstraction. Suppose you were visited by a creature from another planet, and it became important for you to convey the notion of what a tree is. You would not succeed in communicating any significant meaning by writing the word *tree* on a piece of paper. You'd have to try something other than the abstract word itself. Your success might improve somewhat if you tried to draw a picture of a tree. The stranger would then have a better idea of what a tree actually is, but that understanding would be severely limited by your ability to draw. In any case, even a photograph would leave some misunderstanding about the nature of trees. If you really want to give the stranger a solid foundation for understanding what

a *tree* is, then it would be best to take the stranger outside to see and touch an actual tree.

This is a good analogy for the **levels of abstraction** found in the teaching of mathematics. If you want to teach children about division, you would have little success simply stating a rote rule or procedure. A picture of what takes place when you divide would certainly be more beneficial, but it would still be less effective than actually using physical objects to illustrate the process of dividing a set or collection into equivalent groups. Students are not prepared to learn a concept at the **abstract** or **symbolic** level until they have had sufficient experiences with the concept at the **concrete** or **manipulative** level or, at the very least, at the **representative** or **pictorial** level.

In most cases, a student's approach to an exercise or a problem will be conditioned by his or her own experience. The student may not choose the best or most efficient method to solve a problem if prior experience has not included relevant knowledge. For example, if a student does not understand place value and is called on to complete an addition sentence such as $23 + 41 = \square$, an effective approach would probably be to use counters as a model. In other words, it would be appropriate to count out 23 counters, count out 41 counters, and then combine the two sets and count to determine a total of 64 counters. Another student might recognize that 23 counters are needed at the start and, beginning with 23, count 41 more counters to arrive at a total of 64. The second method could be considered slightly more sophisticated than the first. A third student might recognize 23 on the number line and begin counting from that point. Beginning at 23, this student would count 41 units and arrive at a point named 64. Another student, familiar with place value, might react in this fashion: "Add the tens: $40 + 20 = 60$; add the ones: $1 + 3 = 4$; $60 + 4 = 64$; therefore, my answer is 64." Still another child might arrange the addends vertically, thinking "$3 + 1 = 4$" and write the 4; "$20 + 40 = 60$" and write 60 under the 4; and "$4 + 60 = 64$" and write 64 for the answer.

$$
\begin{array}{ccc}
23 & & 23 \\
+41 & & +41 \\
\hline
4 & \text{or} & 60 \\
+60 & & +4 \\
\hline
64 & & 64
\end{array}
$$

So we have illustrated five different methods for completing the addition sentence $23 + 41 = \square$. How many more can you think of? (You can count on your students to show you many other approaches!) In each of the cases we've shown, the student has had the opportunity to think about the exercise according to a personal level of ability. In this example, each student used the same basic concepts, but at different levels of comprehension and abstraction. It is not our purpose to keep children operating at a primitive level but, rather, to assist them through appropriate experiences to more efficient levels of operation. We can better accomplish this if we

Research Snapshot

What are some of the results of allowing students to construct their own solutions?

Kamii has found that second graders who have been encouraged to do their own thinking since kindergarten are able to invent their own procedures for adding multiplace numbers. They are able to invent procedures for problems such as 35 + 27 written horizontally, vertically, or in any other form on the chalkboard.

In a study where a fourth-grade teacher taught algorithms and then allowed students to invent their own strategies the next year, the students were much more successful when they used invented strategies (Kamii, 1998). Fifteen of the eighteen students that used invented procedures correctly answered 6 + 53 + 185, while the previous year, only three of the sixteen students who used the conventional algorithm gave the correct answer.

Do you think the conventional algorithm is more efficient than students' invented solutions? When a child uses the algorithm to solve a problem correctly, what do you know that the child understands?

Kamii, C., & Dominick, A. (1998). The harmful effects of algorithms in grades 1–4. In L. Morrow, L. & M. Kenney (Eds.). *The teaching and learning of algorithms in school mathematics* (pp. 130–140). Reston, VA: National Council of Teachers of Mathematics.

For additional research briefs, "ERIC Digests" lets you search more than 2,000 short syntheses of research on a range of education topics. The syntheses were produced by the Educational Resources Information Center (ERIC). Check http://ed.gov/databases/ERIC_Digests/index/

structure increasingly abstract connections to already understood concrete and pictorial representations.

Problem-solving activities should be varied and taken from real-life situations so that students do not get the idea that mathematics problems exist only in textbooks. Research in learning theory suggests that the frequent use of physical objects is essential for developing abstract concepts. Children need to manipulate and experiment with models that represent the concept being studied. "Hands-on" and "minds-on" experiences are an important part of developing both skill and understanding in solving practical mathematical problems. Thus, it is no surprise that there is increasing interest in learning center and cooperative learning activities, as well as manipulative materials for the mathematics classroom.

Learning center activities can be used for a variety of purposes—to build readiness for abstract concepts, to provide motivation, to develop problem-solving skills, and to present significant applications of mathematics to practical problems. Students at all levels of ability can profit from learning center experiences, and a folder of activities, such as those found in Part 2 of this text, can be an invaluable aid for the classroom teacher.

Teachers should strive to keep children from developing the idea that problem solving is simply a matter of thrashing about aimlessly until one happens to find a solution. An orderly, systematic, well-thought-out approach should be stressed. The approach used should be selected by applying reasoning and understanding. Children should realize, however, that even with careful selection the "best" method is not always chosen the first time, and they should be encouraged to take various approaches to a given problem when a solution is not readily apparent.

Teachers and pupils should spend time together seeking solutions to problems, rather than the student always attempting to solve problems that the teacher has already solved. Children need to recognize the importance of communicating not only their solutions to others, but also the method of arriving at a solution. Children should be aware that even capable scientists and mathematicians do not have a magical "instant" solution to every problem. It is good for them to know that mathematicians may solve problems, check them, and then go back and look for other approaches when their results indicate that something is wrong. The word *problem* itself indicates that often a solution is not readily apparent—if a solution was readily apparent, then it wouldn't be a problem.

THEORETICAL FOUNDATIONS FOR A CONTEMPORARY MATHEMATICS PROGRAM

Education has developed and grown as a profession through the application and refinement of educational theory. Let us examine briefly some of the major learning theories that influence elementary school mathematics programs and discuss ideas for implementing these theories in your classroom.

It is possible to generalize that a majority of learning theories fall into one of two major categories—the behaviorists and the cognitivists. Any attempt to summarize these positions runs the risk of oversimplification, and this discussion is certainly not intended to be comprehensive. Nevertheless, certain fundamental characteristics can be cited that may assist you in imagining how taking a particular position on any one of these issues can affect the instructional decisions you make as a teacher.

Behaviorists

- Learning is considered to be segmented and linear. Bits and pieces of knowledge and skill are acquired sequentially and in a certain order.
- Instruction is designed to increase competence in terms of goals defined by others (e.g., teachers, administrators, local and state education agencies, etc.).
- Assessment is conducted for the purpose of identifying deficiencies and frequently occurs by means of normative instruments such as standardized tests, which interrupt instruction.

Cognitivists

- Learning is viewed as the processes of incorporating and restructuring. Knowledge and skills are acquired through experiences that add to, interrelate, and change existing perceptions.
- Instruction is a means of facilitating change in the individual. It is designed to assist learners in restructuring goals and the ways in which learners interpret their environment.
- Assessment is conducted to determine the learner's perceptions, strengths, and weaknesses and is designed to serve as part of instruction, not interrupt it.

As you might imagine from these broad statements, it is possible to set up a form of continuum that has "pure" behaviorists on one end and "pure" cognitivists on the other. Throughout this section, a variety of learning theories are discussed briefly. These have not been identified specifically as predominantly falling into either the behaviorist or the cognitivist camp—in fact, very few existing theories lie solely in one camp or the other, but are eclectic variations. As you read the descriptions of each of these theories, give some thought as to where you would place each on this continuum and how the acceptance of a particular theory would affect the climate and demeanor of a mathematics classroom.

An influential theory for interpreting mathematical learning has been that of Jean Piaget, noted Swiss psychologist (Piaget, 1954). Piaget considered the concept of "operation" as fundamental to the development of knowledge. An *operation* requires that the student carry out action on an object and be aware of the consequence of those actions. A student, according to Piaget, has performed an operation only if he or she can reason about the operation. An example would be when a child decides to arrange a set of blocks in order from heavi-

est to lightest and recognizes this feat as an accomplishment of a goal. The action must be internalized and reversible. That is, the child must not merely be repeating someone else's prompting, and the child must recognize that there is a way to return the objects to their original state.

Piaget identified four stages in a learner's development of knowledge. Namely, the *sensorimotor*, *preoperational*, *concrete operational*, and *formal operational* stages. The sensorimotor stage occurs from birth to about age 2, a preverbal and presymbolic stage in which intelligence is defined as the ability to accomplish some task (e.g., to obtain a toy that is lying on a blanket by pulling the blanket). At this stage, the child solves problematic situations by experimentation and action rather than by a purely mental process. In the preoperational stage, which begins at about the age of 2 and continues until about age 7, language is acquired, and the child begins to understand signs and symbols as representations of the real world. However, the child still does not develop knowledge of conservation, the concept that essential properties of things do not change when superficial properties are changed. A classical example of conservation involves two rows of counters, each row spaced differently. A child is asked if the rows contain the same number of objects, fewer objects, or more objects (see the following example).

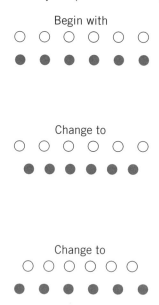

In the first example, the child at the preoperational stage will typically say that there are the same number of counters. In the second, he or she will often say that there are more white counters. In the third, the response will usually be that there are more blue ones. The child at the preoperational stage will display the same sort of faulty reasoning when confronted with other conservation tasks (e.g., number, length, area, volume, etc.).

At the concrete operational stage, stage three of Piaget's theory of development, the child develops logical thought. This stage begins at approximately age 7 (sometimes earlier, sometimes as late as age 9 or 10). At this stage, children can manipulate objects and show logical thinking—they understand conservation and simple logical processes. Finally, at stage four, the formal operational stage, children develop the ability to think abstractly and to make hypotheses. This stage begins at about age 11 or 12—the age of many fifth or sixth graders.

Three important aspects of Piaget's theory of learning are the notions of *disequilibrium*, *accommodation*, and *assimilation*. When an individual encounters information that is either new or contrary to prior knowledge, a person experiences a discord that needs to be resolved. One way of accomplishing this resolution is to incorporate that information as part of that person's view of the world. The individual makes adjustments in the way he or she views the information and its relationship to what he or she already knows by means of accommodation. When successful, the information becomes internalized or assimilated. One might argue that learning could be defined as the recognition of personal disequilibrium, followed by the processes of accommodation and assimilation. Acceptance of such a definition of learning would have a dramatic effect on the nature and design of the classroom experience.

Additional research is still needed with respect to Piaget's work. Even now, there is still some question about whether the rate of progress through the four stages can be accelerated or impeded and, if so, how can this be accomplished? Piaget's theories do, however, suggest important messages for teachers. If most students at the elementary school level have not yet attained the formal operational stage, then we must provide opportunities to explore concepts at manipulative levels and aid in the transition from these models to abstractions. The child must be actively involved in the learning process—physically, visually, mentally, and emotionally. Listening to definitions read by an authority will not lead to the same benefits as forming and reforming a definition through observations. Teachers should strive to provide a stimulating environment for children and encourage them to interact, to experiment, to discover mathematical patterns, to question mathematical processes, and to explore mathematical thinking for themselves.

Lev Semenovich Vygotsky was a Russian child psychologist who completed most of his work in the area of language and thought (Vygotsky, 1962). Like Piaget, he believed that a child learned through sociocultural activity, but Vygotsky did not integrate biological development with cognitive development. He argued, instead, that children transform experiences into knowledge by using prior knowledge—that is, the individual's experience and the history of the culture in which the individual is raised mold cognitive abilities.

Vygotsky suggested that play mediates learning—that play is a risk-free environment, rich in mathematics, science, and language, that allows a child the liberty to make mistakes and provides the motivation to learn from others. An important concept to Vygotskian

theory is the notion of two stages of development, the *zone of actual development* and the *zone of proximal development*. The child's zone of actual development is defined as the stage of development that the child has already achieved, while the zone of proximal development represents the potential developmental level of a child—the point at which a child is capable of participating in guided activities with others. Vygotsky felt that this potential was not revealed by traditional tests, but that the guiding questions of a facilitative instructor or more capable peers would bring about new levels of knowledge.

Another of Vygotsky's main concerns was that of *culturally devised tools*. He was intrigued that culture provides us with ways of dealing effectively with the problems we face through the use of devices as "navigational" equipment. It was his position that not only do these tools make life easier, but that we also increase our intellectual capabilities through their use. Today, Vygotsky would undoubtedly appreciate the huge potential that calculators and computers can play as aids to learning. To a Vygotskian, appropriate interaction with a calculator doesn't destroy your mind—it enriches it.

It is unlikely that you can examine contemporary writings on the subject of learning theories in mathematics (or science) education without encountering a philosophy referred to as *constructivism* (Von Glaserfeld, 1991), sometimes described as an outgrowth of research initiated by Piaget and Vygotsky. In brief, a basic tenet of constructivism is that learners construct their own meaning through continuous and active interaction with their environment. Errors are an important part of this constructive process. Misconceptions are refined and reworked to become alternate conceptions. The notion of a structured controversy becomes a critical factor in the way the learner gains knowledge.

The constructivist epistemology has roots that stretch far back in educational history (Von Glaserfeld, 1991). Socrates is remembered for, among other things, a method of questioning designed to give the student's thoughts and experiences a central role in determining the direction of learning. John Dewey commented on the folly of trying to learn by being told. Dewey wrote:

No thought, no idea, can possibly be conveyed as an idea from one person to another. When it is told, it is to the one to whom it is told, another fact, not an idea. . . . Only by wrestling with the conditions of the problem at first hand, seeking and finding his own way out, does he think. (Dewey, 1974)

Jean Piaget showed constructivist leanings when he emphasized the important role of discovery and free investigation in the learning process. According to Piaget, learning based on the transmission of knowledge from one person to another is "psychologically archaic," and "the goal of intellectual education is not to know how to repeat or retain ready-made truths." For Piaget, knowledge is constructed as students organize their experiences in a manner consistent with prior learning. This is consistent with his notion of disequilibrium, in which competing ideas are refined and revised to be consistent with what the learner knows to be true.

Bodner, in *Constructivism: A Theory of Knowledge* (1986), capsulizes an important defining characteristic of constructivist thought:

> There is no conduit from one brain to another. All teachers can do is disturb the environment. Effective instruction depends on our ability to understand how students make sense of our "disturbances" (stimuli) rather than how we make sense of these stimuli ourselves. Knowledge is constructed by the learner.

An approach to implementing constructivist views in classroom instruction has been described in a model commonly known as the *learning cycle*. This model provides both teacher and learner access to ways to:

1. *engage* and access prior knowledge;
2. *investigate* problems via hands-on and minds-on activities;
3. *develop*, clarify, and construct meaningful explanations;
4. *expand* and apply new understandings;
5. use authentic assessment to judge the new understandings.

Using such a model requires careful planning on the part of the teacher and conscious efforts to avoid being too restrictive in the control of the directions a lesson might take. To avoid lessons that degenerate into "what should we learn now?", a teacher must design an organized but flexible set of investigations that anticipate the various ways that students will perceive the results.

Another theory of learning that has received a great deal of attention is Jerome Bruner's (1968) idea that a child passes through three levels of understanding: *enactive*, *iconic*, and *symbolic*. At the enactive level, the child manipulates objects and in the process develops the ability to conceptualize. At the iconic level, the child can think and reason without manipulating objects. At the symbolic level, the child becomes capable of manipulating symbols and translating experience into language. Bruner's theory suggests that children begin by manipulating concrete, or tangible, objects; generalize a concept or idea based on the manipulation of these materials; and then move to expressing the concept in symbolic form. By means of manipulative models, concepts that might be considered out of reach, if dealt with abstractly, can be explored at the student's level of understanding. The guided discovery method of teaching is based on Bruner's theory in which process is often described as more important than product.

Robert Gagné (1965) discusses what he refers to as the *internal* and *external conditions* of learning. Internal conditions are those conditions that the learner already possesses, which are needed for a successful learning experience. External conditions are those over which the learner has no control (e.g., instructions for activities or exercises). Gagné describes a hierarchy of learning in which he identifies eight steps in the learning process. Each step is discussed with respect to the internal and external conditions of learning. Beginning with the least complex form of learning, the eight steps or types are as follows:

Type 1: Signal learning
Type 2: Stimulus-response learning
Type 3: Chaining
Type 4: Verbal association
Type 5: Multiple discrimination learning
Type 6: Concept learning
Type 7: Principle learning
Type 8: Problem solving

The student is guided step-by-step through a learning experience. The step on which the student is operating is determined by a pretest. Then, when the appropriate subject matter is determined, a sequential program is developed and presented to the learner. The learner moves from the lower levels of learning systematically through concepts and principles to the highest level of problem solving. A great deal of emphasis is placed on prerequisite learning and prerequisite experiences—previous knowledge and activities that are necessary to comprehend the new material. A distinction between Bruner and Gagné can be made in terms of how their theories describe the approach to a concept. For Bruner, the "big picture" is identified globally, and then the pieces are refined. For Gagné, the little pieces are explored before revealing how they interact.

In the late 1950s, Dutch educators Pierre van Hiele and Dina van Hiele-Geldof described a theory of geometry learning that is referred to as the *van Hiele model* (van Hiele, 1986). This theory identified five levels of thinking in geometry. In brief, a learner is presented with appropriate instructional experiences that aid in the progress from one level to the next, with a learner able to achieve a level only by passing through the previous level. First, students are able to recognize shapes (level 0), then they can discover properties of shapes (level 1), and then they can reason informally about the properties of these shapes (level 2). In levels 3 and 4, the learner is able to work with more formal and axiomatic geometric reasoning involving proof. More specifically, the five levels are as follows:

Level 0: The student is able to identify and name geometric figures and shapes such as squares, circles, angles, and line segments based on visual models.
Level 1: The student is able to analyze relationships among various figures and shapes based on component parts, and he or she can discover properties of a set of shapes through hands-on actions such as direct measurement, paper folding, and picture drawing.
Level 2: The student is able to make logical, but informal, arguments that demonstrate connections between properties discovered in levels 0 and 1.
Level 3: The student is able to prove theorems using deductive reasoning and to identify relationships among groups of theorems.
Level 4: The student is able to compare and contrast theorems founded on different basic premises.

You may notice that the van Hiele model of thinking in geometry also seems to use the notion of concrete—representative—abstract stages of development that are so common to other theories. Level 0 clearly reflects a manipulative level that also requires an initial effort of verbal description that becomes more defined as the student passes into level 1. For levels 1 and 2, the student focuses on representative or pictorial models to visualize properties, while in levels 3 and 4, the student has reached a stage where abstract, symbolic reasoning is the common strategy.

Another aspect of the van Hiele model that deserves mention here is the manner in which a student progresses from one level to the next. According to the model, a student must pass through each of five phases at each level. These phases are (1) the information phase (intuitive awareness), (2) the guided orientation phase (teacher-initiated exploring and hypothesizing), (3) the explication phase (verbal or written expression of ideas), (4) the free orientation phase (student-initiated exploring and hypothesizing), and (5) the integration phase (students summarizing and reflecting to bring learnings together). Again, you may notice similarities with the van Hiele model and other learning theories.

THEORY INTO PRACTICE

Translating learning theories into successful classroom practice requires a skillful blending of teaching techniques, content development, and sensitivity to student learning characteristics. We all want to create an environment that is conducive to learning. The problem is, what is conducive? For that matter, what is learning?

The listing of students' previous experiences and the identification of targets for a given grade level provide an important frame of reference for planning the year's instruction. However, they may also mask the challenging variation in student understanding, learning styles, interests, and needs. Within any classroom, there is likely to be a range of intellectual capabilities and interests, as well as an uneven landscape of concept formation, attitudes, and learning habits. Our curriculum should not serve to excuse us from addressing these differences through "teaching to the middle third."

Some students will have acquired their mathematical skills through memorization, others by example and visualization. Part of the class may have a firm grasp of concepts but be weak on skill application. The rest of the class may have the opposite problem. Some individuals will demonstrate a facility for learning new ideas and will readily explore new topics with confidence. Other individuals will be hesitant about new concepts, be reluctant to pose questions, and exhibit doubt and misgivings about their aptitudes for mathematics.

Nonuniform student backgrounds and learning needs call for multiple approaches for developing new ideas and reviewing those previously studied. Some students will understand a particular concept after introduction to a model of that concept. Other students will require multiple examples and/or counterexamples, and still others

will need a formal definition before they fully understand the concept.

For example, some students will distinguish between prime and composite numbers by recognizing that a composite number can be represented by *more than one* rectangular array of dots, while a prime number can be represented by *only one* rectangular array.

Composite (12)

Prime (13)

Other students may more readily understand the concept of a prime number by identifying what it is NOT and comparing this to what it *is* (by counterexample). Still others will be uncomfortable with the concept until they can apply the definition of a prime number as a whole number greater than 1 with only itself and 1 as factors.

Many elementary school children are at the point where they begin to appreciate mathematics as a process and a way of thinking rather than as merely the application of rules and formulas. Some students have sufficient mental maturity to begin to question the why and how of techniques and procedures they may have taken for granted in earlier work. The teacher's task is to encourage this type of thinking at all levels by skillful questioning and by setting an atmosphere of intellectual curiosity.

Students are innately interested in learning new things. By capitalizing on students' expanding interests and growing cognitive abilities, teachers can create situations ripe for hypothesizing and generalizing. Manipulatives, games, calculators, computers, and learning centers offer students opportunities to explore and hone their emerging thinking skills. Problem-solving experiences provide students with the means to learn how to organize information, identify patterns, apply deductive and inductive thinking, and make and check hypotheses.

Activities that do not restrict students' avenues of success to a single route are the key to devising learning experiences that encourage thinking. Students' approaches to and reasoning through learning situations should be as diverse as the students themselves. All students have reached their current levels of achievement by different routes in developing the skills they possess, the attitudes they have acquired, and the modes of thinking on which they rely. The study of mathematics should be a stimulating endeavor that enables students to build from sets of individual experience and that expands their abilities to think mathematically.

Students' perceptions of mathematics and the teacher's ability to correctly read these perceptions play a significant role in instruction. Students who have had difficulty with mathematics in the past will most likely tend to view the subject as a barrier. Efforts to review material with them at the beginning of the school year may meet with resistance and may encourage self-deprecating attitudes. Other students are at the opposite end of this spectrum. Tired of review, these students hunger for new experiences. They may also view mathematics as a wall, of sorts, but for them it is a challenge to get around or over rather than an obstacle blocking their way. For two different reasons, attempts to review at the beginning of the year frequently backfire with both types of students. A teacher who chooses to review rather than explore new topics may find one group of students threatened and the other group bored. Thus, a viable option is the combination of review and extension. The teacher can check competencies and diagnose capabilities with prior content, while also exploring alternative approaches to familiar work. Even simple tasks take on renewed importance if couched in the right situation and explored in an appropriate, sometimes novel, manner.

The building blocks of mathematical understanding are concepts (e.g., comparison, division by distributing equally, and percent as part of a whole). Concepts enable students to bring sense to the operations they perform and provide a framework within which skills are learned and retained. They supply students with the insights necessary to apply and adapt what they know. Students who have a sound conceptual background are capable of thinking and acting mathematically. Students poorly grounded in concepts are often forced to resort to memorization and superficial guesswork in confronting mathematical tasks.

In this respect, teaching mathematics is very much a team activity. Seldom are concepts fully developed during 1 year of instruction. Students progress through stages (concrete, representative, and abstract) in acquiring a full understanding of a concept. Instruction at each successive grade level must build on the ideas previously developed. Assessment of student understanding at any particular grade often reflects the culmination of the efforts of teachers over several grades in building a particular idea. However, important instruction conducted by a teacher during the year may receive relatively little assessment emphasis that year, even

though that instruction may eventually be crucial to whether students comprehend subsequent material.

For these reasons, communication between grade levels is essential to the success of the total program. Teachers must appreciate how their efforts combine and contribute to the success of the program as a whole. A student's image of what mathematics is, how it is best learned, and how it relates to his or her world is not something formed within a given school year—it develops over time. The teachers in a school can aid in this development by presenting a shared and valued perspective only possible through cross-grade communication.

CLOSURE

In this chapter, we introduced you to several aspects of mathematics in contemporary elementary schools. Mathematics education is bringing together new learning theories and materials for creative teachers to use in developing exciting classroom environments. The corresponding chapter in Part 2 of *Today's Mathematics* includes a summary of fundamental concepts and critical ideas for each grade level, preK–8. Embedded in the discussion of each grade level is an outline of important ideas of eight content strands identified by the Ohio Department of Education and the Ohio Council of Teachers of Mathematics in their publication entitled *Model Competency-Based Mathematics Program*. These content strands are patterns, relations, and functions; problem-solving strategies; number and number relations; geometry; algebra; measurement; estimation and mental computation; and data analysis and probability.

Now we are ready to consider an in-depth study on how these mathematics skills are developed with elementary school children. *Today's Mathematics* is designed to aid you now and in the future, in your efforts to reflect the vision of mathematics learning and teaching begun in this chapter and carried throughout the text.

Readers are also encouraged to examine Chapter 18 in Part 2 for additional information on how students learn mathematics.

Terminology, Symbols, and Procedures

Algorithm. A procedure or set of steps to accomplish a given task is an algorithm. For example:

$$
\begin{array}{r}
2 \\
30 \\
200 \\
\hline
23\overline{)5349} \\
4600 \\
\hline
749 \\
690 \\
\hline
59 \\
46 \\
\hline
\textcircled{13}
\end{array}
\quad \text{}232 \quad \text{or} \quad
\begin{array}{r}
232 \\
23\overline{)5349} \\
46 \\
\hline
74 \\
69 \\
\hline
59 \\
46 \\
\hline
\textcircled{13}
\end{array}
$$

The term applies not only to the rules of computation with which most children and adults are familiar but also to the rules followed by devices such as calculators and computers to carry out instructions.

Deductive Reasoning. The process of examining a general rule or set of rules and applying the rules to a specific situation is called *deductive reasoning*. For example, applying the general rule "The product of two negative numbers is always positive" to the specific exercise $(-5)(-7) = \square$ is an example of elementary deductive reasoning.

Inductive Reasoning. The process of examining several specific situations and formulating a general rule that applies for each case is called *inductive reasoning*. The processes of inductive reasoning and guided discovery teaching are used when searching for patterns, comparisons, and similarities in mathematics. For example, noting the pattern in $\frac{2}{4}$; $\frac{4}{8}$; $\frac{6}{12}$; . . . and generalizing that the numerator of $\frac{x}{30}$ would be 15 because, in each specific case, the numerator is half the denominator, is inductive reasoning.

Level of Abstraction. Mathematics can be presented at several levels of abstraction—for example, **symbolically** (using abstract symbols and words), **representatively** (using pictures and visual aids), and **concretely** (using manipulatable physical objects). When introducing a concept, it is often best to begin with a concrete model that aids the student in understanding of the concept. After the child has attached some meaning to the concept through manipulative and pictorial experiences, then symbols may be introduced.

Rote Memorization. The process of memorizing information or rules without an understanding of the principles or meaning underlying the information or rules is called *rote memorization*.

Standard. A standard is a benchmark or statement against which a given item or position can be measured or compared. The NCTM *Principles and Standards for School Mathematics* provides examples that set up a vision of mathematics education for the new millennium.

Teaching Competencies and Self-Assessment Tasks

1. Locate a copy of the NCTM *Principles and Standards for School Mathematics*. Reflect on the need for new standards and new goals discussed in the introduction by reflecting on your own mathematics experiences in the past.

2. Describe what you believe are the defining characteristics of an effective elementary mathematics program.

3. Select a topic from elementary school mathematics and describe activities for that topic at the concrete (manipulative), representative (pictorial), and abstract (symbolic) levels.

4. Describe the importance of having children work with proper materials so that they can discover and generalize about mathematical concepts.

5. Describe a teaching situation that can be used to compare and contrast various teaching methods such as inductive/deductive or guided discovery/lecture.

6. Select two theories of learning. Compare and contrast them as they relate to the teaching and learning of elementary school mathematics. How would these learning theories manifest themselves in a classroom?

7. Locate a copy of the NCTM *Principles and Standards for School Mathematics*. Compare and contrast the set of standards identified for grades PreK–2 with those for grades 3–5 and for grades 6–8.

8. Read the NCTM *Principles and Standards for School Mathematics*, and discuss what role YOU can play in implementing the standards.

References

Achieve. (1999). *Preliminary results of the analysis of state standards and assessments*. East Lansing, MI: TIMSS Center.

American Association for the Advancement of Science. (1989). *Science for all Americans: A Project 2061 panel report on literacy goals in science, mathematics, and technology*. Washington, DC: Author.

American Federation of Teachers. (1997). *Making standards matter, 1997: An annual fifty-state report on efforts to raise academic standards*. Washington, DC: Author.

Bodner, G. M. (1986). *Constructivism: A theory of knowledge*. New York: Wiley.

Bruner, J. S. (1968). *Toward a theory of instruction*. New York: W. W. Norton and Company.

Committee on the Mathematical Education of Teachers. (1991). *A call for change*: *Recommendations for the mathematical preparation of teachers of mathematics*. Washington, DC: The Mathematical Association of America.

Council of Chief State School Officers. (1997). *Mathematics and science content standards and curriculum frameworks: States' progress on development and implementation*. Washington, DC: Author.

Council of Chief State School Officers. (1997). *State indicators of science and mathematics education—1997*. Washington, DC: Author.

Council of Chief State School Officers. (1999). *Improving mathematics education using results from NAEP and TIMSS*. Washington, DC: Author.

Dewey, J. (1974). The child and the curriculum. In R. D. Archambault (Ed.). *John Dewey on education*. Chicago: The University of Chicago Press.

Gagné, R. M. (1965). *The conditions of learning*. New York: Holt, Rinehart & Winston.

Johnston, W. B., & Packers, A. E. (1987). *Workforce 2000*: *Work and workers for the twenty-first century*. Indianapolis, IN: Hudson Institute.

McKnight, C. C., Crosswhite, F. J., Dossey, J. A., Kifer, E., Swafford, J. O., Travers, K. J., & Cooney, T. J. (1987). *The underachieving curriculum*: *Assessing U.S. school mathematics from an international perspective*. Champaign, IL: Stipes Publishing Company.

National Center for Educational Statistics. (1997). *The 1996 mathematics report card for the nation and the states*. Washington, DC: Author.

National Center for Educational Statistics. (1998). *The condition of education*. Washington, DC: Author.

National Commission on Teaching & America's Future. (1996). *What matters most*: *Teaching for America's future*. New York, NY: Author.

National Council of Teachers of Mathematics. (1989). *Curriculum and evaluation standards for school mathematics*. Reston, VA: Author.

National Council of Teachers of Mathematics. (1991). *Professional standards for teaching mathematics*. Reston, VA: Author.

National Council of Teachers of Mathematics. (1995). *Assessment standards for school mathematics*. Reston, VA: Author.

National Council of Teachers of Mathematics. (2000). *Principles and standards for school mathematics*. Reston, VA: Author.

National Research Council. (1989). *Everybody counts: A report to the nation on the future of mathematics education*. Washington, DC: National Academy Press.

National Science Board. (1999). *Preparing our children: Math and science education in the national interest*. Washington, DC: Author.

National Science Foundation. (1998). *Report of the senior assessment panel for the international assessment of U.S. mathematical sciences*. Washington, DC: Author.

Ohio Department of Education. (1990). *Model competency-based mathematics program*. Columbus, OH: Author.

Piaget, J. (1954). *The construction of reality in the child*. New York: Basic Books.

U.S. Department of Education. (1991). *America 2000*. Washington, DC: U.S. Government Printing Office.

U.S. Department of Education. (1993). *Standards for all*: *A vision for education in the 21st century*. Washington, DC: U.S. Government Printing Office.

U.S. Department of Labor. (1991). *What work requires of schools*: *A SCANS report for America 2000*. Washington, DC: U.S. Government Printing Office.

van Hiele, P. M. (1986). *Structure and insight*. Orlando, FL: Academic Press.

Von Glaserfeld, E. (Ed.). (1991). *Radical constructivism in mathematics education*. Dordrecht, The Netherlands: Kluwer Academic Publishers.

Vygotsky, L. S. (1962). *Thought and language*. Cambridge, MA: M.I.T. Press.

Related Readings

For related readings on topics found in this chapter, see the corresponding chapter in Part 2 of *Today's Mathematics*, the Student Resource Book.

Chapter 2

Teaching Mathematics

Teaching Competencies

Upon completing this chapter, you will be able to:

■ Describe the vision of mathematics teaching first put forth in the NCTM *Professional Standards for Teaching Mathematics* and later incorporated into the NCTM *Principles and Standards for School Mathematics*.

■ State characteristics of a positive mathematics classroom environment.

■ Formulate appropriate objectives for mathematics lessons.

■ Suggest appropriate lesson organizations and structures for a given mathematics topic.

■ Describe types of student participation in a mathematics lesson.

■ Write sample lesson plans for a set of specific objectives in mathematics.

n the best of all possible worlds, there is peace and prosperity. The sun seems always to shine, and even when it doesn't, there is a refreshing pleasantness to the rain. The "natural order" of things is seldom disturbed, and, when the occasional unexpected event arises, it is often viewed as a welcome surprise. In this best of all possible worlds, your car always starts, your checkbook always balances, and your students learn all that you have taught.

But, this is not the true nature of the world in which we live. Much of what we enjoy and sometimes take for granted still needs frequent attention. The car doesn't start unless we keep it serviced. The checkbook doesn't balance unless we keep accurate records. And children don't recall ALL that they have been taught, in spite of our best intentions and efforts. We live in a real rather than an ideal world, with mathematics teaching that requires flexibility and ongoing, reflective adjustment to achieve success.

THE NCTM PROFESSIONAL TEACHING STANDARDS

In 1991, the National Council of Teachers of Mathematics (NCTM) issued a publication entitled *Professional Standards for Teaching Mathematics* as a companion document to the previously issued *Curriculum and Evaluation Standards for School Mathematics* (1989). These **professional teaching standards** represented a set of guidelines designed to address the various aspects of professional mathematics teaching. These **standards** were grouped into four major categories— standards for teaching mathematics, for evaluation of teaching, for professional development of teachers of mathematics, and for support and development of mathematics teachers and teaching.

Section 1, the standards for teaching mathematics, dealt with a vision of teaching and learning mathematics that illuminated, supported, and assisted the implementation of the *Curriculum and Evaluation Standards for School Mathematics*. Section 2, standards for evaluation, described the nature and purpose of the evaluation of teaching and the roles that should be played by those involved in this evaluation. The third section of standards focused on guidelines for the preparation of preservice teachers and the continuing education of teachers of mathematics at the K–12 levels. The final section on support and development identified the responsibilities shared by various groups, such as school boards, professional organizations, and policy-makers in government, business, and industry, who help shape the environment in which the teachers teach and the learners learn. Readers who seek a more comprehensive discussion of the full set of teaching standards are encouraged to purchase a copy of the *Professional Standards for Teaching Mathematics* from the National Council of Teachers of Mathematics, 1906 Association Drive, Reston, VA 20191 (1-800-235-7566).

THE NCTM PRINCIPLES AND STANDARDS FOR SCHOOL MATHEMATICS

Following the success of their initial standards efforts, the NCTM released the *Principles and Standards for School Mathematics* (2000), a revision of the curriculum, teaching, and assessment standards into one document. The intent was to make it clear that curriculum, teaching, and assessment are intertwined to a degree greater than that suggested by three separate sets of standards.

Although each of the "big three" (curriculum, teaching, and assessment) deserves elaboration and integration, the scope of this particular chapter requires that we devote most of our attention to focusing on standards for teaching mathematics.

The NCTM standards represent an image of mathematics teaching in which teachers are more proficient in:

- selecting mathematical tasks to engage students' interests and intellect;
- providing opportunities to deepen their understanding of the mathematics being studied and its applications;
- orchestrating classroom discourse in ways that promote the investigation and growth of mathematical ideas;
- using, and helping students use, technology and other tools to pursue mathematical investigations;
- seeking, and helping students seek, connections to previous and developing knowledge;
- guiding individual, small-group, and whole-class work (NCTM, 1991, p. 1).

To assist in accomplishing these goals, the standards for teaching mathematics present an image of what a teacher must know and be able to do in order to teach mathematics effectively.

As outlined in Chapter 1, the *Principles and Standards for School Mathematics* describes six basic tenets or underlying assumptions regarding equity, curriculum, learning, teaching, assessment, and technology for instructional programs in mathematics. These principles endorse a view of what is necessary at the classroom, school, district, and national level for effective mathematics education. Their impact on the teaching process is so vital that they are repeated here for emphasis:

- *Equity.* Excellence in mathematics education requires equity—high expectations and strong support for all students.
- *Curriculum.* A curriculum is more than a collection of activities: it must be coherent, focused on important mathematics, and well articulated across the grades.

■ **Teaching.** Effective mathematics teaching requires understanding what students know and need to learn and then challenging and supporting them to learn it well.

■ **Learning.** Students must learn mathematics with understanding, actively building new knowledge from experience and prior knowledge.

■ **Assessment.** Assessment should support the learning of important mathematics and furnish useful information to both teachers and students.

■ **Technology.** Technology is essential in teaching and learning mathematics; it influences the mathematics that is taught and enhances students' learning.

The teaching standards described in this text are organized and discussed under four broad headings: **tasks**, **discourse**, **environment**, and **analysis**. These headings are descriptive of the kinds of decisions a teacher makes relative to instruction. TASKS are the activities in which a student engages during his or her mathematical development. These might include projects, exercises, constructions, and applications of mathematical content. DISCOURSE is the manner in which teachers and students communicate during tasks—the ways of representing, thinking, and talking about tasks. ENVIRONMENT encompasses the setting for learning. It is the context, both physical and mental, in which the tasks and the discourse come together. ANALYSIS refers to the action of contemplating the interplay of tasks, discourse, and environment. It represents the identification and evaluation of the effectiveness, efficiency, and appropriateness of what the teacher is doing and what the student is learning.

The standards described in the NCTM *Professional Standards for Teaching Mathematics* that refer specifically to the teaching process are described in the following sections.*

Standard 1

Worthwhile Mathematical Tasks

The teacher of mathematics should pose tasks that are based on—

■ sound and significant mathematics;
■ knowledge of students' understandings, interests, and experiences;
■ knowledge of the range of ways that diverse students learn mathematics;

and that

■ engage students' intellect;
■ develop students' mathematical understandings and skills;

*Reprinted with permission from *Professional Standards for Teaching Mathematics*, copyright 1991 by the National Council of Teachers of Mathematics.

■ stimulate students to make connections and develop a coherent framework for mathematical ideas;
■ call for problem formulation, problem solving, and mathematical reasoning;
■ promote communication about mathematics;
■ represent mathematics as an ongoing human activity;
■ display sensitivity to, and draw on, students' diverse background experiences and dispositions;
■ promote the development of all students' dispositions to do mathematics.

Standard 2

Teacher's Role in Discourse

The teacher of mathematics should orchestrate discourse by—

■ posing questions and tasks that elicit, engage, and challenge each student's thinking;
■ listening carefully to students' ideas;
■ asking students to clarify and justify their ideas orally and in writing;
■ deciding what to pursue in-depth from among the ideas that students bring up during a discussion;
■ deciding when and how to attach mathematical notation and language to students' ideas;
■ deciding when to provide information, when to clarify an issue, when to model, when to lead, and when to let a student struggle with a difficulty;
■ monitoring students' participation in discussions and deciding when and how to encourage each student to participate.

Standard 3

Students' Role in Discourse

The teacher of mathematics should promote classroom discourse in which students—

■ listen to, respond to, and question the teacher and one another;
■ use a variety of tools to reason, make connections, solve problems, and communicate;
■ initiate problems and questions;
■ make conjectures and present solutions;
■ explore examples and counterexamples to investigate a conjecture;
■ try to convince themselves and one another of the validity of particular representations, solutions, conjectures, and answers;
■ rely on mathematical evidence and argument to determine validity.

Standard 4

Tools for Enhancing Discourse

The teacher of mathematics, in order to enhance discourse, should encourage and accept the use of—

- computers, calculators, and other technology;
- concrete materials used as models;
- pictures, diagrams, tables, and graphs;
- invented and conventional terms and symbols;
- metaphors, analogies, and stories;
- written hypotheses, explanations, and arguments;
- oral presentations and dramatizations.

Standard 5

Learning Environment

The teacher of mathematics should create a learning environment that fosters the development of each student's mathematical power by—

- providing and structuring the time necessary to explore sound mathematics and grapple with significant ideas and problems;
- using the physical space and materials in ways that facilitate students' learning of mathematics;
- providing a context that encourages the development of mathematical skill and proficiency;
- respecting and valuing students' ideas, ways of thinking, and mathematical dispositions;

and by consistently expecting and encouraging students to—

- work independently or collaboratively to make sense of mathematics;
- take intellectual risks by raising questions and formulating conjectures;
- display a sense of mathematical competence by validating and supporting ideas with mathematical argument.

Standard 6

Analysis of Teaching and Learning

The teacher of mathematics should engage in ongoing analysis of teaching and learning by—

- observing, listening to, and gathering other information about students to assess what they are learning;
- examining effects of the tasks, discourse, and learning environment on students' mathematical knowledge, skills, and dispositions;

in order to—

- ensure that every student is learning sound and significant mathematics and is developing a positive disposition toward mathematics;
- challenge and extend students' ideas;
- adapt or change activities while teaching;
- make plans, both short- and long-range;
- describe and comment on each student's learning to parents and administrators, as well as to the students themselves.

In the NCTM *Professional Standards for Teaching Mathematics*, each of these standards is followed by an elaboration of the statements made above, but, perhaps more illustratively, these standards are laced with "vignettes" or short scenarios designed to model various aspects of specific standards. These often take the form of a lesson in which comments reflecting important points from the standards are included as margin notes. A sample vignette showing the integration of curriculum, teaching, and assessment has been reproduced, with permission from NCTM, in Chapter 2 of Part 2 of this text.

With the publication of the *Principles and Standards for School Mathematics*, NCTM has elected to embed and integrate the material from the earlier *Professional Teaching Standards* and the *Assessment Standards*. Readers who seek a comprehensive discussion of the integration of teaching standards with curriculum and assessment standards are encouraged to purchase a copy of the *Principles and Standards for School Mathematics* from the National Council of Teachers of Mathematics, 1906 Association Drive, Reston, VA 20191 (1-800-235-7566).

DESIGNING MATHEMATICS LESSONS

Sometimes we characterize our efforts to provide an effective and efficient mathematics program as an attempt to reach an ideal—as aiming high or "reaching for the moon." Expanding this analogy, there are a vast number of "impact craters" that influence the shape and the nature of this "moon" we're trying to reach. It is most important that we recognize the control we have over which "craters" we hit, and how hard. Our choice of the approach to a given topic, the role of the textbook, the terminology and language used, the amount of active involvement, and the use of manipulatives are but a few of the factors that require our attention as we plan learning experiences for unique learners.

A *lesson* is the vehicle we use to convey the knowledge, skills, concepts, and values we wish to instill in students. A lesson is a planned learning experience designed (but not necessarily led) by a teacher with input from a variety of resources. A lesson may take many forms and occur in many settings. A lesson might be an informal discussion involving the entire class, or it might be an experiment performed by small groups of students to collect data for analysis and debate. A lesson might occur in the classroom or outside on the school grounds—or at home or at the mall or in the car on a family outing.

Its nature and location aside, every lesson should be designed, implemented, and evaluated in a careful and thoughtful manner. Let us take a look at some of the aspects of lesson preparation that should become a part of the planning process. The reader is advised to also refer to Chapter 2 in Part 2 of this text for additional principles of lesson planning and a sample lesson plan organizational format. Also, each chapter (4–17) in Part 2 includes a complete primary level and a complete intermediate level mathematics lesson plan. These can prove to be valuable resources for "field-testing" your abilities to implement as well as modify existing lesson plans.

In designing a lesson, it is important to research the topic. It is not sufficient to believe that because you are capable of *doing* the mathematics called for in the lesson, you are also capable of *teaching* the underlying mathematics concept. Close examination of the content, possible different approaches, and potential methods of presentation are all central to the planning process. The teacher, whenever feasible, should not rely solely on the direction and organization suggested by the child's text. The teacher's edition, including those from textbook series other than the one used by the children, may prove to be valuable sources of alternative teaching ideas. Books such as this one, written for the preparation of teachers, are rich resources for ideas on alternative curricular, instructional, and assessment approaches. Additional resource materials and activity books published by support companies and independent authors also provide a wealth of ideas to enliven textbook lessons. Subject-specific professional organizations such as the National Council of Teachers of Mathematics (NCTM) and the School Science and Mathematics Association (SSMA), as well as generalist organizations such as the Association for Supervision and Curriculum Development (ASCD), produce curricular and instructional materials designed to supplement ideas the classroom teacher has gleaned from other sources. See Part 2 of this text for a list of names, addresses, and telephone numbers of suppliers of mathematics instruction resource materials.

One of the most important aspects of the planning process centers on the teacher's ability to anticipate— to anticipate the need for materials or models that could help the children meet the objectives of the lesson, to anticipate the questions that children might have but not state, and to anticipate the parts of the lesson that may be the most challenging to teach or the most difficult to understand. Surely, experience has a lot to do with successful anticipation, but this talent is not reserved exclusively for those who have taught for several years. The ability to anticipate is most heavily affected and influenced by the quality and quantity of *objective, reflective thought* that goes into the planning process, not how many years a person has taught.

Teachers must be able to make use of the knowledge they have, but they must also develop the talent of standing aside from their knowledge and examining the content from a naive point of view. Being too close to the content can cause you to miss some important nuances that might help you to identify and comprehend the difficulties that a less experienced student might encounter in the lesson. For example, most adults give little or no thought to the process of finding the value of a collection of pennies and dimes in which like coins might be grouped and then two separate subtotals added to arrive at the total value. How many children recognize the connection between this activity and the process of adding rational numbers expressed as decimals? How many, when questioned how to add decimal numbers, offer a meaningless rule such as "line up the decimal points," when they might just as easily have referred to either the money model emphasizing like coins or a place-value model emphasizing like places? Successful teachers of mathematics combine the thoughts of a child with the thoughts of an adult— successful teachers are adults who have nurtured the ability to observe the world of mathematics through the eyes of a child.

While school districts and state agencies may provide teachers a mandated course of study—topics that must be studied and the grades or courses in which they are to be included—the sequence in which those topics are presented is generally decided by individual schools or, in some cases, by individual teachers. Many teachers simply follow the sequence provided by the adopted textbook, beginning the year with page 1 and vainly attempting to reach the end of the book before they reach the end of the school year. Successful teachers of mathematics are capable of determining whether the textbook's sequence is appropriate for their teaching style, their course of study, and their students' prerequisite skills and experiences. And, if it is not, they should be capable of rearranging the order into one more fitting for their students. Changing the sequence of topics may even provide opportunities to view mathematics not as a collection of unrelated concepts but as a structured, connected body of ideas.

Consider, for example, a fifth-grade teacher planning the start of a new school year who recognizes that many of the students in her incoming class appear to have had little or no instruction in geometry beyond the identification and naming of two- and three-dimensional shapes. She wonders whether looking at "other" mathematics topics through a "geometric lens" would be beneficial to her students. Since the first few weeks of a new academic year are commonly spent reviewing previously taught concepts, she begins to look at the content presented during these weeks to determine how she could use geometry to "cover" these topics. For example, addition and multiplication could be reviewed while exploring concepts of perimeter, area, and volume. Fractions might be revisited through the use of tangrams, emphasizing geometric properties related to part-whole concepts. Problem-solving skills might be developed through a number of hands-on activities involving challenges and investigations in geometry. Having decided to present her curriculum by emphasizing geometric concepts, she "skips" the often regimented and repetitive nature of the first few chapters in her text and moves right into a review couched in the "new" setting of geometry.

After spending a couple of weeks using geometry as a context for review, this teacher may notice that several students who had been low-achievers in previous grades are performing quite well, while some students who had been good mathematics students are now experiencing levels of frustration they had not previously experienced. That is, an emphasis on geometry as an organizer may have changed the "pecking order" in her class. If this is indeed the case, it may be that those students who had had trouble in previous grades may have been more attuned to "spatial" topics than they were to "number" concepts. Their lack of readiness for the arithmetic in earlier grades may have accounted for what might have been labeled as their poor achievement overall.

In addition to the differences in student achievements, the teacher may notice a difference in students' questioning behavior. In the past, many students may have tended to avoid asking questions during mathematics instruction, simply indicating their lack of understanding by saying, "I don't get it." However, under the scenario described above, this teacher might notice that students are actually asking questions; and the questions are coming from all of the students. It may be that, when those who have had an easy time in mathematics encounter topics that are more difficult for them, they are more willing to ask questions than are the low-achievers or are more aware of where they need help and can formulate appropriate questions. When the lower-achieving students see the good mathematics students asking questions, it can become a more socially accepted behavior. The teacher then becomes more excited when this willingness to ask questions invades more "traditional" topics, such as place value and number theory.

A teacher that wonders whether mathematics instruction could be conceived with other content areas as the focus of instruction is one that demonstrates a loyalty to the course of study and, at the same time, a loyalty to his or her ability to create a successful learning experience. It is only natural for such a teacher to wonder what might teaching/learning look like if, for example, probability and statistics was used as a theme for exploring other topics.

CREATING MATHEMATICS OBJECTIVES

When preparing objectives for lessons, teachers must keep in mind the reasons for writing objectives—most notably, to use them as guides THROUGHOUT the planning/teaching/learning/evaluation process. Teachers can use well-conceived, well-written objectives in the planning stages to identify, select, and organize experiences designed to ensure attainment of appropriate outcomes. They can then use these same objectives during the teaching of the lesson to maintain a proper focus and direction for these experiences. Finally, the lesson objectives form a sound basis for judging the effectiveness of both the planning and the teaching as well as the attainment of the learning sought. Meaningful, clearly stated, well-defined objectives are the glue that holds a lesson together. Without them, the smooth transition from planning to implementation to evaluation is lost. In fact, without objectives a teacher is merely passing time with students, hoping that something worthwhile will occur. If you don't know what you're doing, and why you're doing it, does it make any sense to try to do it?

The objectives of any lesson must be prepared with a critical eye toward prerequisite skills and experiences central to the success of a lesson. Teachers must closely examine the content and activities of proposed lessons to determine whether any "assumed learnings" have been clearly identified. For example, an introductory lesson on percents assumes a familiarity with such concepts as ratio and proportion and decimals, to name a few. The teacher must carefully analyze what is to be taught and how it is to be taught rather than simply relying on the textbook approach or on personal familiarity with the content. For a lesson to reach its full potential, the teacher has to attend to the knowledge, skills, experiences, attitudes, and values that the children must possess (and to what level or degree they possess them) prior to exposure to the lesson. By not doing so, the teacher runs the risk of introducing material or ideas into the lesson that only confound or increase the children's confusion and difficulties. See Chapter 18, in Part 2, for a list of Concept Clusters arranged in a hierarchical fashion to help you identify prerequisites for the concepts listed.

In preparing for instruction, it is important for the teacher to distinguish between the GOALS and the OBJECTIVES for a given lesson. A **goal** is usually a broad statement indicating a general outcome to be reached, stated in terms of either the student or the teacher. For example, a goal might be "The student will explore the process of addition with regrouping" or "The teacher will expose the students to three different models for rational numbers." An **objective**, however, should be more narrow in focus, more specific in content, more measurable in some real sense, and couched in terms of the student. For example, a lesson objective might be "The student will use base ten blocks to model the addition of two two-place numbers with regrouping from ones to tens." From these examples, we can see that objectives can be viewed as stepping stones to reach the broader goal.

Some teachers like to include a level of performance or criterion as part of the objective by tacking on a phrase such as ". . . with 80% or better accuracy" or ". . . correctly at least four out of five times." Such additions to objectives are acceptable, but remember that in many instances they are markedly artificial. Why was 80% chosen? Why not 85%? or 89%? Are the reasons for selecting a particular percent cutoff identifiable and rational, or is it just an arbitrary figure deemed to be "high enough"? We suggest that the debate on the level of performance or criterion be resolved by noting that there is a significant difference between an *instructional* objective (which should always *seek* 100% attainment) and an *evaluation* objective (which would *acknowledge* a range of acceptable achievement).

To summarize the distinction made in the previous paragraph, INSTRUCTIONAL OBJECTIVES for a mathematics lesson should be written so that the focus is on the student, not on the teacher. It is essential that a teacher begin any instructional opportunity with the conviction that all students are capable of learning the material. It is never acceptable to BEGIN the teaching process with a stated objective that calls for less than 100% attainment. Isn't it ALWAYS your goal to reach every student? Or do you start out with the notion that you'll be happy if you reach 8 out of 10 students? A teacher must strive for the ideal in each lesson—every student has the potential to comprehend and succeed. An EVALUATION OBJECTIVE, on the other hand, is written as a referent to an "acceptable level" of performance on an assessment AFTER the lesson. In this case, an evaluation objective focuses attention on the real, rather than the ideal. It sets a boundary of performance that was inappropriate when potential was the issue. It is not the case that one form of objective is better than the other, but rather that instructional and evaluation objectives take different forms because they serve different purposes and play their roles at different times of the teaching/learning process.

THE ROLE OF MOTIVATION AND FOLLOW-UP

In addition to meaningful objectives, a lesson plan must also include attention to motivation. The motivation for a particular lesson is so much more than simply a beginning or introductory activity. For example, a teacher could start a lesson by calling for quiet and asking the children to open their books to page 123. This "opening" may get their attention but certainly does nothing to attract their interest in what's about to occur. Alternatively, the teacher could begin a lesson on graphing by simply asking the students to guess how far a toy car would roll down a given ramp. After they guess, the teacher has them try it. Then the teacher moves the ramp to another height, and the students try again. Do the students have an idea about the "best" height for the greatest distance? Can they identify a connection between the height and the distance? Is it always true that a higher ramp yields a greater distance? How could they see this more clearly? At this point, the teacher would be well into the lesson on graphing in an enjoyable and less teacher-oriented manner. Rather than the teacher telling them, "Today, we will do a lesson on graphing" and then continuing with a "lecture-based" format, the teacher with the motivation described above has captured both *attention* and *interest* and has the class considering important questions as a first step to exploring graphing.

In addition to capturing the attention and the interest of the students, an effective motivation should also provide a *reason* for exploring the topic of the lesson and should be tied directly to the content of the lesson in such a way that transition from the motivation to the lesson is nearly seamless. An unrelated game serves little motivational use if it captures attention and interest but does not transfer to the topic at hand. Playing a game as an introductory activity is not a motivation for a lesson unless the game can be directly tied to the objective of the day.

The conclusion of a lesson deserves as much attention as the motivation. All too often teachers end a

---

Research Snapshot

What does research say about the effects of cooperative learning?

Davidson (1985) reviewed approximately eighty studies in mathematics comparing student achievement in whole-class traditional instruction versus cooperative learning. Students in the small-group approaches significantly outscored the control students on individual mathematical performance measures in over 40% of the studies.

Research has shown positive social benefits of cooperative learning as well. Cooperative learning has been shown to increase self-esteem or self-confidence as a learner and to foster intergroup relations including cross-group friendships.

Some of the problems that teachers and students expressed about cooperative learning in mathematics were concerns about covering enough math material, initial problems in forming effective groups, barriers to fostering cooperation among students, and handling the shift in the roles of teacher and student.

How do you think you will organize your groups? What do you think the effect will be on your high-achieving students of using small groups in your classroom? Do you think your high-achieving students will benefit from working in small groups?

Davidson, N. (1985). Small-group learning and teaching in mathematics: A selective review of the literature. In R. Slavin, S. Sharan, S. Kagan, R. Lazarowitz, C. Webb, & R. Schmuck (Eds.). *Learning to cooperate, cooperating to learn* (pp. 211–230). New York, NY: Plenum.

For additional research briefs, "ERIC Digests" lets you search more than 2,000 short syntheses of research on a range of education topics. The syntheses were produced by the Educational Resources Information Center (ERIC). Check http://ed.gov/databases/ERIC_Digests/index/

mathematics lesson by simply asking the children to "do page 123, Exercises 2 through 20, even." Every mathematics lesson should conclude with some attempt to determine the students' level of understanding of the material presented. It is essential that the teacher collect some immediate information regarding the students' understanding of the lesson. It is useless, however, to seek this information by asking, "Does anyone have any questions?" or "Does everyone understand?" Instead, the collection of information about student understanding may best be accomplished by leading a discussion of points central to the day's objective. For example, how do the children respond to both general and specific questions about the activities? How do the children use their own words, orally and in writing, to describe the processes discussed in the lesson? Can the children respond to questions about why the material is important or useful? In addition, the teacher should, whenever feasible, tie the lesson to what was done yesterday and to what will be done tomorrow. Both a look back and a look ahead can help us better understand the present. Note, however, that one of the least-effective ways to "look back" is by opening a lesson with "Who remembers what we did in math class yesterday?" This question is far removed from the concept of motivation!

Finally, on the issue of "do page 123, Exercises 2 through 20, even," it is critical to recognize that practice plays an essential role in learning mathematics. Once students have developed a foundation for practice—that is, once they have a meaningful grasp of the concept—they should work on fully developing the skill. However, the teacher must do more than blindly assign homework or seatwork exercises for the children to complete. At the very least, a teacher should closely examine the textbook exercises one by one to select those that are most appropriate, based on the lesson as taught and on the sort of practice the teacher deems necessary. Each and every assignment should be made with an eye toward student differences in learning styles. Students may best learn through a variety of formats such as individual assignments, learning centers, peer instruction, and cooperative groups. It may be appropriate for some students to practice using concrete manipulatives to illustrate the concepts of the lesson. Others may be ready for more representative models such as pictures or diagrams. Still others may be functioning at the abstract level with numerals and symbols. It cannot be assumed, as is the case when sweeping page assignments are made, that all children are at the same level and have the same needs.

THE EVALUATION OF LEARNING AND TEACHING

Evaluation is one of the most critical aspects of a teacher's responsibilities. At any given point in time, a given student has either learned or not learned a particular intended learning outcome. While there may be such a thing as "partial credit," there is no such thing as "sorta-learned." How can a teacher determine in which category a student falls for each objective?

A first step in determining the answer to the above question lies in knowing what is to be taught—having a clearly identified, specific statement of what is to be learned. Vague objectives beget fuzzy evaluations. If objectives are too general, then it is more likely that a teacher will experience difficulty in assessing the level of understanding of a given student.

If objectives are specific, the evaluation process can be directed toward those specifics. We don't mean to imply that there is no such a thing as partial, or incomplete, learning, but if a student has "partially" learned something, then, by definition, that means that he or she has not yet learned it. Assessment items based on specific competencies will provide evidence of the degree of student learning.

Methods commonly employed to evaluate students include publisher-provided and similar standardized tests. Although these instruments frequently provide data for comparing students, these data are typically not beneficial in identifying *individual* strengths and weaknesses. To gather diagnostic and/or achievement data, teacher-made assessment tools must be woven into the evaluation scheme. This type of assessment should, for example, seek information on different kinds of mathematical thinking and present concepts and procedures in varied settings and contexts.

Paper-and-pencil tests often represent an efficient way of getting the job done. However, some of the critical outcomes in a mathematics program do not easily lend themselves to this form of assessment. Evaluation procedures should reflect this need, matching both teacher purpose and student experiences. For example, the ability to think mathematically can be demonstrated through such actions as being able to approach a problem situation independently by displaying confidence and persistence, that is, a positive **disposition** toward mathematics. This pattern of behavior can be assessed through direct observation to determine if (1) the student makes second and third attempts at solving problems, (2) the student is motivated to learn, (3) the student knows when an answer is reasonable, and (4) the student can determine and communicate methods of solving problems.

Teachers are sometimes reluctant to place weight on observations as an evaluation technique because they feel that observations are subjective, hard to quantify, and difficult to defend. However, observations are a primary means of providing the basis for monitoring and adjusting instruction. Observation can also be a professional evaluation skill when used to assess individuals relative to particular objectives. Evaluative data collected informally through so-called casual observation are often some of the most fruitful. Follow-up questions based on the teacher's perception of student performance are invaluable in formulating judgments. When compared to anticipated learning objectives, this type of subjective evaluation plays an important role in completing the overall evaluation picture.

The importance of measuring the full range of learning outcomes cannot be overstressed. It is essential to assess entry-level knowledge and understanding, including the identification of the small steps necessary for content leaps. Evaluation in mathematics must also include an attempt to measure outcomes in terms of student attitudes, values, and other affective aspects. As a generalization, it sometimes seems that those outcomes that are most important to a student's mathematical understanding and growth are the ones most difficult to assess. A mathematics program that assesses only the most easily measured outcomes will usually find only those outcomes stressed in the classroom. Sadly, the illusion of success on easily measured outcomes may obscure subsequent difficulties students may experience for lack of sound conceptual learning.

(Evaluation issues are discussed more fully in Chapter 3, Assessing Mathematics, which includes information from the *Principles and Standards for School Mathematics* (2000) and the *Assessment Standards for School Mathematics* (1995), the third volume in the trilogy of original standards documents issued by the National Council of Teachers of Mathematics.)

ADJUSTING INSTRUCTION TO MEET NEEDS

The process of intervention is often defined as the identification of alternatives or supplemental action designed to remediate, reinforce, or support student learning relative to specified performance objectives. Simply stated, when some planned educational experience does not lead to a student reaching a desired competency level, then intervention is appropriate. Intervention, then, is based on diagnosis and offers a prescriptive action. Intervention can take the form of different approaches to a topic, including (1) the incorporation of manipulatives that were not present during initial instruction, (2) the use of technology to focus attention on the desired result, (3) different or unusual drill and practice, or (4) learning center opportunities.

The decision to intervene may occur, for example, in the middle of a lesson that doesn't seem to be proceeding on track. A lesson plan is not like a book, in which the print is fixed and unchangeable. Instead, it should allow for, and be receptive to, improvisation to meet "teachable moments" that might arise. Even though there is a general plan and an outline, changes can be made as dictated by "audience reaction." Intervention may be triggered by your observation of students' actions or reactions as you teach. Intervention may also occur after the fact, as patterns on homework or tests suggest the need to approach the topic from another perspective.

Successful classrooms are classrooms in which a variety of types of lessons are utilized. Every lesson, whether it focuses on introducing a new topic or concept, practicing a skill, or reviewing prior knowledge, should contain some aspect of problem solving and decision making. Exploration and manipulation can be used to encourage discovery. This discovery can be guided by the teacher through the careful selection of tasks and subsequent focusing questions. Teacher- and student-led demonstrations can provide material for both open and directed discussions. Writing activities and those that involve collecting, organizing, and recording information can be invaluable in exposing children to mathematics as it is used outside the classroom walls.

Lecture methods and lessons focusing solely on the textbook are typically not appropriate for most students at the elementary/middle school level. Teachers must draw from students' past experiences; continuity is important for both motivation and confidence. There is always much need for exploration and further investigation through simulations, manipulatives, models, calculators, and computers. The final product of a series of lessons must be proficiency with understanding.

Teachers often find that games, calculators, computers, and learning centers allow individual students to go beyond textbook learning to discover special areas of interest in mathematics. A variety of exploration activities that go beyond arithmetic computation can help students expand their understandings of and interests in the processes of mathematics.

For example, reasoning requires interaction, and discussion plays an important role in achieving problem-solving expertise. Therefore, whole-class and small-group settings are important. The teacher must be enthusiastic, motivational, inspirational, supportive of persistent attitudes, nonthreatening, analytical, and able to summarize. Questioning is an all-important art that helps the teacher communicate, focus, direct, and suggest.

Rather than using large-group lectures or discussions exclusively, incorporate other formats such as a small-group cooperative learning environment. Activities should be designed that require the children to work together to reach a desired outcome. Tasks can be shared or decided in such a way that teamwork is encouraged or essential. These alternative approaches to instructional events should be mixed and matched in a fashion that exemplifies the varied nature of the learners, the learning process, and mathematics itself.

CLASSROOM INSTRUCTIONAL AIDS

The use of classroom aids as part of instruction is essential for promoting understanding and skill. Meaningful instruction as well as motivational drill and practice require sound TEACHING AIDS and REVIEW AIDS. The names used to describe these two types of aids are descriptive of their purpose and use. A **teaching aid** is used to assist in the teaching of a concept. A **review aid** is effective in reviewing a concept. A review aid is usually a game or an activity focusing on a concept that has already been introduced and is at least partially understood. The word *review* implies that students already have some degree of competency with the concept but that additional work is necessary to maintain efficiency in associated skills. A review aid can be a learning center activity that students use by themselves or in a small group. It can also be an aid the teacher uses in front of the class to reinforce a concept. A specific example of a review aid might be a board game based on a popular television quiz show such as *Jeopardy* in which the students must state a question that "fits" a given answer.

The primary purpose of a teaching aid is to assist in introducing or explaining a concept. Whereas a review aid focuses on instilling or maintaining a skill, a teaching aid focuses on the meaning or understanding of a concept. A teaching aid seldom takes the form of a game, because games typically require at least basal understanding of the concept being explored. A teaching aid can be used by the teacher for large-group instruction, or it can be a learning center device for individuals or small groups of children. A teaching aid can often be used again at a later date as a review aid. An example of a teaching aid is a set of fractioned circles, perhaps designed to represent pizza slices. These pieces can be used to help a student *understand why* $\frac{3}{4}$ is equivalent to $\frac{6}{8}$ by showing that three of four equal pieces can represent the same amount of pizza as six of eight equal pieces (as long as the pizzas are the same size).

Individual differences in learning styles dictate various teaching styles and approaches. Models and manipulatives often convey understanding in situations where words are not appropriate or sufficient. Manipulatives—so important in the early grades—play an equally critical role throughout the entire preK–12 curriculum (and beyond!). Students should manipulate and explore, using concrete aids (e.g., base ten blocks, fraction pieces, and geoboards), and representative models (e.g., number lines, drawings, charts, and diagrams). Readers are directed to the pamphlet and supplemental manipulatives that have been shrink-wrapped between Parts 1 and 2 as part of the purchase of this text.

Many different manipulative and pictorial aids can be effectively used to illustrate mathematical concepts typically found in a contemporary elementary school mathematics program. Examples of commercially available aids are Cuisenaire rods, pattern blocks, base ten blocks, geoboards, balances, counting blocks, and attribute blocks. Many everyday items, such as spoons, milk cartons, pasta, bread slices, and sponge cubes, can also effectively be used to model concepts and processes. Remember, when introducing concepts, it is important to begin meaningfully at the concrete-manipulative level and then, once the foundation is firm, work toward more efficient methods and processes.

The rates at which students progress from a concrete to an abstract level of understanding differ greatly. Students should continue to use concrete materials as they associate their actions with a manipulative to the corresponding steps of a paper-pencil-and-algorithm. When students have achieved this level of understanding, they should be able to verbalize their

thoughts and write symbolic statements. Without sufficient experiences at the concrete and representative levels, students acquire, at best, only partially understood abstractions.

Teachers are an essential cog to the success of this experience. Both by their modeling and their expectations, teachers lead students to recognize the importance of being able to communicate and demonstrate understanding. By building this awareness, teachers of older students may overcome the students' resistance to manipulatives that is sometimes expressed in the form of "That's kid stuff."

In the past, there has also been some resistance to using the calculator as a classroom tool. Rather than "That's kid stuff," some have felt that calculators are "adult stuff!" That is, they should ONLY be used when you've demonstrated certain abilities without the calculator. On the contrary, calculators, when used properly, can provide excellent *support* for problem-solving experiences and can meaningfully aid in the *development* of concepts.

In fact, calculators (and computers) can provide access to mathematics that students would not otherwise be able to explore. Calculators can provide the means to examine problems that involve arithmetic that is too complex or too time-consuming to be carried out in class with paper and pencil. These kinds of problems may involve numbers from real life ($1.36, $\frac{9}{10}$ a gallon, 3 for $.87, 15.46% interest) or may be whimsical problem situations, such as "How many years old will you be on your billionth (in seconds) birthday?" or "Are there more square inches in a square mile or seconds in a century?" The value of such whimsical questions often lies in the fact that the student, not the calculator, must determine what procedures are necessary to arrive at an answer. Calculators, when used properly, can stimulate, encourage, and help students achieve success in mathematics. They can also help teachers become better teachers.

Among a wealth of other applications, computers are excellent tools for carrying out repetitious tasks. They can quickly provide the output for thousands of trials in a simulation, or they can generate a table of data, enabling the class to check conjectures and search for patterns. Many simulation programs are readily available, whether they be for rolling dice or for identifying the number of cereal boxes needed to gain a set of prizes. Some students may even benefit from the experience of using the random number generation capabilities of a computer and the simple programs to study problems of this kind.

Calculators and computers are not substitutes for learning to think mathematically. Nevertheless, many benefits are derived from using technology appropriately to aid learning. Research that has consistently provided overwhelming evidence of the benefits of calculator and computer use has been accompanied by little evidence of loss of computational skill. Calculators and computers enable students to overcome apprehensions about mathematics, to build self-esteem and confidence, and to learn how to solve problems independently. For these and other sound reasons, teachers are obligated to adjust their instructional styles and patterns to integrate this technology into their classes.

Rather than exploring the role of calculators and computers in the elementary classroom more fully at this time, we ask you to consider the material in Chapter 4 of Parts 1 and 2 and the references throughout the text to suggested uses and applications of calculators and computers.

CLOSURE

Before leaving this chapter, let us return, briefly, to the NCTM standards. Basic assumptions central to these standards are well worth remembering:

1. The goal of teaching mathematics is to help all students develop mathematical power.

2. *What* students learn is fundamentally connected with *how* they learn it.
3. All students can learn to think mathematically.
4. Teaching is a complex practice and, hence, not reducible to recipes or prescriptions (NCTM,1991, p. 21–22).

As you continue through this text and as you continue to develop as a teacher of mathematics, the recognition of, and attention to, the importance of these basic assumptions will keep you focused on your goals.

Readers are also encouraged to examine Chapter 18 in Part 2 for additional information on teaching mathematics, including a grade-by-grade scope and sequence, a concept cluster checklist, a collection of thematic activities across the common topic strands of elementary school mathematics, and a vignette that demonstrates the integration of curriculum, teaching, and assessment.

Terminology, Symbols, and Procedures

Analysis. Analysis is the action of contemplating the interplay of tasks, discourse, and environment.

Discourse. Discourse is the manner in which teachers and students communicate during tasks—the ways of representing, thinking, and talking about tasks.

Disposition. Disposition, as mentioned in the *Professional Standards for Teaching Mathematics*, refers to the willingness to tackle mathematical tasks, to problem solve, and to be flexible in approach.

Environment. Environment encompasses the setting for learning—the physical and mental context in which the tasks and discourse of the classroom come together.

Goal. A goal is usually a broad statement indicating a general outcome to be reached, stated in terms of either the student or the teacher. For example, a goal might be "The student will explore the process of addition with regrouping" or "The teacher will expose the students to three different models for rational numbers."

Objective. An objective, as opposed to a goal, is more narrow in focus, more specific in content, more measurable in a real sense, and couched in terms of the student. For example, an objective might be "The student will use base ten blocks to model the addition of two, two-place numbers with regrouping from ones to tens."

Review Aid. A review aid is effective in reviewing a concept. A review aid is usually a game or an activity focusing on a concept that has already been introduced and is at least partially understood. A review aid can be a learning center activity that students use by themselves or in a small group. It can also be an aid the teacher uses in front of the class to reinforce a concept. A specific example of a review aid might be a board game based on a popular television quiz show such as *Jeopardy* in which the students must state a question that "fits" a given answer.

Standard. A standard is a benchmark or statement against which a given item or position can be measured or compared. The NCTM *Principles and Standards for School Mathematics* is a document that describes standards for curriculum, teaching, and assessing mathematics. A predecessor, the NCTM *Professional Standards for Teaching Mathematics*, set up standards that form a vision of mathematics teaching for implementing the *Curriculum and Evaluation Standards for School Mathematics*.

Tasks. Tasks are the activities in which a student engages during his or her mathematical development.

Teaching Aid. The primary purpose of a teaching aid is to assist in introducing or explaining a concept. Whereas a review aid focuses on instilling or maintaining a skill, a teaching aid focuses on the meaning and understanding of a concept. A teaching aid can be used by the teacher for large-group instruction, or it can be a learning center device. A teaching aid can often be used at a later date as a review aid. An example of a teaching aid is a set of fractioned circles, perhaps designed to represent pizza pieces. These pieces can be used to help a student *understand why* $\frac{3}{4}$ is equivalent to $\frac{6}{8}$ by showing that three of four equal pieces represents the same amount of pizza as six of eight equal, but smaller, pieces (as long as the pizzas are the same size).

Teaching Competencies and Self-Assessment Tasks

1. The NCTM *Principals and Standards for School Mathematics* offers many promises and many challenges for teachers and students of mathematics. Identify and describe what you feel may be the greatest barriers to implementing the vision of this document.

2. What are the major characteristics that you would ascribe to "a positive classroom environment"? Which of these do you, as the teacher, have direct control over? Which are dependent on your students? on the administration? Which are shared responsibilities?

3. In groups of four or five, write instructional objectives for a given mathematics concept; share them with other groups for feedback on clarity and style.

4. Select a mathematics concept to be taught, and discuss what you feel is the most effective presentation to use for children at different grade levels.

5. Give a specific mathematics concept and discuss how provisions can be made for individual differences in a teacher's approach to that concept. Include in your discussion techniques that will elicit various forms of student participation.

6. Select a specific mathematics concept, and examine how several different elementary school textbooks develop the concept. Discuss what you feel are the positive and negative aspects of each presentation.

References

National Council of Teachers of Mathematics. (1989). *Curriculum and evaluation standards for school mathematics*. Reston, VA: Author.

National Council of Teachers of Mathematics. (1991). *Professional standards for teaching mathematics*. Reston, VA: Author.

National Council of Teachers of Mathematics. (1995). *Assessment standards for teaching mathematics*. Reston, VA: Author.

National Council of Teachers of Mathematics. (2000). *Principles and standards for school mathematics*. Reston, VA: Author.

Related Readings and Teacher Resources

For related readings on topics found in this chapter, see the corresponding chapter in Part 2 of *Today's Mathematics*, the Student Resource Book.

Chapter 3

Assessing Mathematics

Teaching Competencies

Upon completing this chapter, you will be able to:

- Describe the vision of mathematics assessment put forth in the NCTM *Principles and Standards for School Mathematics* and the NCTM *Assessment Standards for School Mathematics*.

- State characteristics of worthwhile assessment tasks and techniques.

- State multiple purposes of assessing student progress in the elementary mathematics classroom.

- Compare and contrast standardized and nonstandardized tests that are commonly a part of assessment in elementary/middle schools.

- Describe methods available for teachers to use in assessing student work and student dispositions.

- Design assessment tasks for a given set of objectives in mathematics.

student in a middle-grade mathematics class was asked to simplify the fraction $\frac{16}{64}$. The child immediately answered, "That's easy; it's $\frac{1}{4}$." The teacher smiled at this correct response, seemingly secure with a feeling of having successfully taught the student how to "cancel" when simplifying a fraction. After class, the teacher complimented the student on having successfully rewritten the fraction. The student responded by saying, "Thanks. Really, it WAS easy—all you have to do is to cancel the 6 on the top with the 6 on the bottom, and you have the answer." The teacher probed a little further and asked, "What if the fraction had been $\frac{56}{64}$?" The student said, "Then, we still cancel the 6s, so it would be $\frac{5}{4}$." The teacher then asked, "So, does $\frac{56}{64} = \frac{5}{4}$?" When the student claimed that these must be equal, the smile of satisfaction left the teacher's face, quickly replaced by the recognition that what we believe students have learned is not always the same as what they believe they have learned.

Often, in the classroom, students are able to come up with "answers" that appear to be correct on the surface but do not necessarily imply or reflect a conceptual understanding. Debates have raged as to whether students should simply memorize procedures and be graded on their final answers or whether teachers should emphasize understanding and assign grades based on process as well as final products. Research has indicated that allowing students to construct their own understandings of mathematics initially takes more time but pays much greater dividends in the future. If we agree that teaching involves paying attention to student understanding of processes, then obtaining a picture of what students know becomes a much more complex process than simply asking ten questions on a quiz and grading the answers as "right" or "wrong." If we are to implement the vision of curriculum and teaching addressed in Chapters 1 and 2, then it is clear that we must also change assessment—the ways that we determine how well a student understands the mathematical concepts we are exploring. **Assessment** can be defined as the process of gathering information about student understanding of mathematical concepts, as well as determining the attitudes and beliefs that the student has about mathematics. These attitudes and beliefs, along with a general student willingness to do mathematics, are referred to by the National Council of Teachers of Mathematics (NCTM) as a student's **disposition** toward mathematics. Assessment information is then used to determine student progress for a number of purposes, as discussed later in this chapter.

THE NCTM PRINCIPLES AND STANDARDS FOR SCHOOL MATHEMATICS

Following the success of their initial **standards** efforts, the NCTM released the *Principles and Standards for School Mathematics* (2000), a revision of the curriculum, teaching, and assessment standards into one document. As stated in Chapter 2, the intent was to make it clear that curriculum, teaching, and assessment are intertwined to a degree greater than that suggested by three separate sets of standards. These standards were not intended as a replacement of the earlier works, but as an extension of the spirit and vision of mathematics reflected in the original standards documents. Although each of the three deserves elaboration and integration, the scope of this particular chapter requires that we devote most of our attention to focusing on standards for assessing mathematics.

The NCTM *Principles and Standards for School Mathematics* places emphasis on the integration of six major principles. These principles include the Equity Principle, the Curriculum Principle, the Learning Principle, the Teaching Principle, the Assessment Principle, and the Technology Principle. To assist teachers and other educators in designing a worthwhile assessment system, these principles provide a framework for decisions that need to be made and issues that must be considered in the process of assessment.

ASSESSMENT STANDARDS

In 1995, the NCTM issued a publication entitled *Assessment Standards for School Mathematics*. This document was written as a third companion document to the previously issued *Curriculum and Evaluation Standards for School Mathematics* (1989) and *Professional Standards for Teaching Mathematics* (1991). The assessment document presented a set of guidelines or benchmarks that assisted teachers and other educational decision makers in the development of a meaningful system of assessing student competencies and dispositions. The assessment standards document was divided into two main sections: "Mathematics Assessment Standards" and "Use of the Assessment Standards for Different Purposes."

The first section, "Mathematics Assessment Standards," presented a set of six guidelines regarding the design of assessment programs and techniques. The second section, "Use of the Assessment Standards for Different Purposes," outlined four categories of uses for the results of student assessment and dispositions. The document concluded with a short reflection on what it takes to reform assessment practices in mathematics.

Each section of the assessment standards document is important for educators to explore, but for the purposes of this book we will examine the six assessment standards in particular. For additional information on the assessment standards, contact the National Council of Teachers of Mathematics, 1906 Association Drive, Reston, VA 20191 (1-800-235-7566).

The NCTM assessment standards present a

. . . criteria for judging the quality of mathematics assessments. They are statements about what is valued. Together, they reflect a vision of exemplary mathematics assessment. . . . The Assessment

Standards promote the dynamic and ongoing process of improving mathematics curricula, mathematics teaching, and mathematics assessment. The process involves everyone concerned with mathematics education. These standards for assessment contribute to, and are affected by, the standards for curriculum and the standards for teaching. (NCTM, 1995, p. 9)

The standards outlined in the NCTM *Assessment Standards for School Mathematics* (1995) are the Mathematics Standard, the Learning Standard, the Equity Standard, the Openness Standard, the Inferences Standard, and the Coherence Standard. The *Mathematics Standard* refers to the actual mathematical content that should be assessed in an effective system. The *Learning Standard* refers to the need for assessment to be more than simply gathering data for the purpose of assigning grades. Instead, an effective assessment system is one in which educators use the information to improve classroom instruction and conduct assessments as a part of the classroom routine. The *Equity Standard* refers to the importance of placing high standards of achievement on all students and the need for each student to be given an opportunity to demonstrate mathematical understanding. The *Openness Standard* calls for the sharing of details of assessment by all of the stakeholders. The *Inferences Standard* discusses the inferences, or conclusions, that can be drawn from the analysis of data gathered in assessment procedures. Finally, the *Coherence Standard* refers to the idea that assessment processes should be appropriate for the situation. That is, in the example described at the beginning of this chapter, if the teacher had wanted to assess student understanding of the concept of simplifying fractions, then simply asking for the "answer" to a fraction-simplifying question would not have been sufficient.

The six assessment standards that can be used to judge the quality of an assessment system are described next.*

Standard 1

The Mathematics Standard

Assessment should reflect the mathematics that all students need to know and be able to do.... To determine how well an assessment reflects mathematics that students need to know and be able to do, ask questions such as the following:

- What mathematics is reflected in the assessment?
- What efforts are made to ensure that the mathematics is significant and correct?
- How does the assessment engage students in realistic and worthwhile mathematical activities?

*Reprinted with permission from the *Assessment Standards for School Mathematics*, copyright 1995 by the National Council of Teachers of Mathematics.

- How does the assessment elicit the use of mathematics that is important to know and be able to do?
- How does the assessment fit within a framework of mathematics to be assessed?
- What inferences about students' mathematical knowledge, understanding, thinking processes, and dispositions can be made from the assessment?

Standard 2

The Learning Standard

Assessment should enhance mathematics learning.... To determine how well an assessment enhances learning, ask questions such as these:

- How does the assessment contribute to each student's learning of mathematics?
- How does the assessment relate to instruction?
- How does the assessment allow students to demonstrate what they know and what they can do in novel situations?
- How does the assessment engage students in relevant, purposeful work on worthwhile mathematical activities?
- How does the assessment build on each student's understanding, interests, and experiences?
- How does the assessment involve students in selecting activities, applying performance criteria, and using results?
- How does the assessment provide opportunities for students to evaluate, reflect on, and improve their own work—that is, to become independent learners?

Standard 3

The Equity Standard

Assessment should promote equity.... To determine how well an assessment promotes equity, ask questions such as the following:

- What opportunities has each student had to learn the mathematics being assessed?
- How does the assessment provide alternative activities or modes of response that invite each student to engage in the mathematics being assessed?
- How does the design of the assessment enable all students to exhibit what they know and can do?
- How do the conditions under which the assessment is administered enable all students to exhibit what they know and can do?
- How does the assessment help students demonstrate their best work?
- How is the role of students' backgrounds and experiences recognized in judging their responses to the assessment?
- How do scoring guides accommodate unanticipated but reasonable responses?
- How have the effects of bias been minimized throughout the assessment?

■ To what sources can differences in performance be attributed?

The Openness Standard

Assessment should be an open process. . . . To determine how open an assessment is, ask questions such as these:

■ How do students become familiar with the assessment process and with the purposes, performance criteria, and consequences of the assessment?
■ How are teachers and students involved in choosing tasks, setting criteria, and interpreting results?
■ How is the public involved in the assessment process?
■ What access do those affected by the assessment have to tasks, scoring goals, performance criteria, and samples of students' work that have been scored and discussed?
■ How is the assessment process itself open to evaluation and modification?

The Inferences Standard

Assessment should promote valid inferences about mathematics learning. . . . To determine how well an assessment promotes valid inferences, ask questions such as the following:

■ What evidence about learning does the assessment provide?
■ How is professional judgment used in making inferences about learning?
■ How sensitive is the assessor to the demands the assessment makes and to unexpected responses?
■ How is bias minimized in making inferences about learning?
■ What efforts are made to ensure that scoring is consistent across students, scorers, and activities?
■ What multiple sources of evidence are used for making inferences, and how is the evidence used?
■ What is the value of the evidence for each use?

The Coherence Standard

Assessment should be a coherent process. . . . To determine how coherent an assessment process is, ask questions such as these:

■ How is professional judgment used to ensure that the various parts of the assessment process form a coherent whole?
■ How do students view the connection between instruction and assessment?
■ How does the assessment match its purposes with its uses?

■ How does the assessment match the curriculum and instructional practice?
■ How can assessment practice inform teachers as they make curriculum decisions and determine their instructional practices?

In the NCTM *Principles and Standards for School Mathematics*, the standards and their purposes are elaborated on, often through the use of classroom vignettes or actual samples of student work. These examples are intended to provide a snapshot of what effective assessment looks like, to assist in guiding educators toward the vision of the standards. To provide an indication of the format and style of the NCTM Assessment Standards, a complete statement of Standard 6 and one of the vignettes from the publication have been reproduced, with permission from NCTM, in Part 2 of this text.

PURPOSES FOR ASSESSMENT

In the eyes of too many educators and many members of the general public, assessment is conducted for the sole purpose of yielding data for determining student grades. However, tracking individual student progress in the form of assigning grades is an extremely narrow view of assessment and only one of several purposes for gathering assessment information. In the *Principles and Standards for School Mathematics* document, the NCTM describes four purposes for gathering the information—*monitoring students' progress* as compared with objectives outlined in the mathematics program, *making instructional decisions* to ensure that lessons meet the needs of learners, *evaluating students' achievement* to validate the progress made by individual students, and *evaluating programs* to determine if changes in the mathematics program are needed. This vision of assessment is one in which educators gather information about what students know, what they can do, and what they believe about mathematics for reasons that go beyond "giving grades." The graphic on page 35 illustrates the various purposes of assessment and their results.*

Assessments conducted by the teacher must also be used to directly improve classroom instruction. There should always be a close connection between collected assessment data and classroom instruction. The teacher who uses a variety of methods to gather information about the students' knowledge and dispositions can use these data to influence future lessons. Assessment procedures may be as informal as the teacher listening in on a small-group problem-solving experience or as formal as an extended paper-and-pencil examination. However, whether formal or informal, the data gathered should be used for improving instruction.

---

*Reprinted with permission from the *Assessment Standards for School Mathematics*, copyright 1995 by the National Council of Teachers of Mathematics.

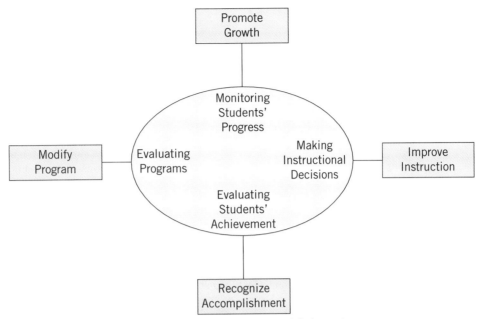

Four purposes of assessment and their results

For example, suppose that a mathematics teacher asks students to write a short entry in a mathematics journal after class each day. After collecting the journals at the end of the week, the teacher discovers that several students have a common misconception about one of the mathematical processes explored that week. The teacher might choose to use the faulty reasoning that appears in the student journals to redirect the class on Monday morning. Since the class may not have asked many questions that week, without the journal information the teacher may not have known that they needed help in a particular area until after a poor performance on a test. In this case, the journal entries were not being written strictly for assigning grades. Instead, they were being used as a method of learning more about what the students think and understand as well as to determine how well they communicate their ideas and what misconceptions, if any, they might hold.

In addition to teacher-collected data for instructional and grading purposes, assessment is often conducted by outside sources, such as school districts issuing competency or standardized tests, states mandating proficiency tests, or commercial/institutional testing services offering examinations for scholarships or college placement. In general, **criterion-referenced tests**, such as local competency examinations, are tests that are tied directly to a school district's curriculum. The student score on a criterion-referenced test is "absolute" in that it may be used to determine whether a student has mastered some set of objectives, rather than to compare the student to others. In contrast, a **norm-referenced test** is an examination that compares student scores to a sample of other students across the country at the same grade level (if grade level is the norming factor used). Scores on norm-referenced tests are "relative" because student progress is compared with the achieve-

ment of other students as opposed to the attainment of certain objectives.

Proficiency tests or "exit exams" are generally examinations that test baseline knowledge that every student in a state, district, or school must possess at a particular grade level. Proficiency tests are often seen as accountability tools for local districts to demonstrate that they are meeting the educational expectations of some governing body at the district, county, state, or even national level.

Proficiency exams might be either norm-referenced or criterion-based—depending on the purpose the exam is designed to serve. Whereas criterion-referenced competency tests are useful for measuring the effectiveness of a local program, the norm-referenced test can be used to give a national comparison of a local program to others at the same grade level. Each type of test has its own strengths and weaknesses and serves a different purpose. All these types of tests are external in that someone other than the teacher has developed, scored, and, in many cases, interpreted them. Consequently, educators need to use caution when using the data collected from various tests. Teachers should no sooner give a grade to a student based on performance on a norm-referenced test than a school district should feel that their program is successful merely because a large number of students are earning A's in their classes. It is, after all, relatively easy to design a set of questions that everyone can answer—just as easy as it is to design a test that few can answer. There's nothing mystical about a percent score—it is merely a reflection of the proportion of correct answers, not an indicator of the difficulty or the challenge found in the question selection.

Teachers also need to use standardized test scores with caution because of the nature of questions that are

Research Snapshot

Are there research programs that relate assessment to instruction?

In Webb's (1992) review of assessment in mathematics education, he describes two programs that integrate assessment with instruction. The programs are based on research about the development of mathematical knowledge.

Cognitively Guided Instruction (CGI) (Carpenter & Fennema, 1988) requires teachers to assess their students' thinking by asking their students to explain how they figured out their answers. The student responses are related to a research-based framework of students' strategies. Based on responses to specific items, the teacher is able to determine a range of problems that the students can solve. In CGI, the instruction is based on the information provided by the assessment.

The Graded Assessment in Mathematics (GAIM) project (Brown, 1988) is focused toward the assessment of the mathematical progress of British students between the ages of 11 and 16. The progress that an average student makes during a year is described using a fifteen-level scheme. Students are assessed in logic, measurement, numbers, space, statistics, algebra, and functions across the fifteen levels. Because students progressed at different rates across different levels, teachers were encouraged to teach and assess more than one level at a time. Teachers devised their own assessment procedures that included oral and practical assessments as well as written items.

How will you balance assessment with instruction? When you spend time assessing your students' knowledge of facts, what do you know about what they understand about mathematics?

Brown, M. (1988). The graded assessment in mathematics project. Unpublished manuscript, King's College, London, U.K.

Carpenter, T. P., & Fennema, E. (1988). Research and cognitively guided instruction. In E. Fennema, T. P. Carpenter, & S. J. Lamon (Eds.). *Integrating research on teaching and learning mathematics* (pp. 2–17). Madison: Wisconsin Center for Education Research.

Webb, N. L. (1992). Assessment of students' knowledge of mathematics: Steps toward a theory. In D. A. Grouws (Ed.). *Handbook of research on mathematics teaching and learning* (pp. 661–683). New York, NY: Macmillan.

For additional research briefs, "ERIC Digests" lets you search more than 2,000 short syntheses of research on a range of education topics. The syntheses were produced by the Educational Resources Information Center (ERIC). Check http://ed.gov/databases/ERIC_Digests/index/

often asked on national tests. It is important to scrutinize a national test by asking, "Does this really measure the teaching that I do in my classroom?" For example, a study by Romberg and Wilson (1989) showed that the six most commonly used standardized achievement tests for eighth graders required problem solving on an average of only 1% of the questions. In the same study, it was noted that 77% of the items centered around computation and estimation skills. If the teacher of the class that took such an exam was creating a classroom environment as described in the *Principles and Standards for School Mathematics*, then it is likely that the class emphasized worthwhile problem-solving tasks. Consequently, the standardized test did not measure what the teacher and the students spent the year trying to develop! In short, teachers should recognize that standardized test scores are only one of many possible measures of student progress and need to be interpreted in the context of the "bigger picture."

We have seen that an effective assessment system must emphasize important mathematics, enhance learning, assure equity, be open, allow for valid inferences to be made, and be coherent. We have also discussed the variety of purposes for assessment and the fact that some assessment data are gathered by teachers for assigning grades and improving classroom instruction, while other data are gathered by a local school district, state, or national testing company for purposes of measuring program effectiveness or providing accountability measures for the public. Now, we turn our attention to specific techniques that teachers can use to gain a broad and multidimensional picture of what their students can do and what their students believe about mathematics.

ASSESSMENT TECHNIQUES

Let us take some time to challenge the traditional view of assessment as synonymous with grading. In light of the previous discussions of the standards for judging the quality of an assessment, think about what we might be missing by making use of the following grading procedure.

Suppose that a teacher has just completed a set of lessons in which the students have been working with the area and perimeter of various polygons. At the conclusion of these lessons, the teacher issues a 20-problem test in which the student is given 10 polygons that require the calculation of area and 10 other polygons for which the perimeter must be determined. The 20 answers are to be written on 20 blanks on an answer sheet. The teacher scores the 20 answers and assigns a percentage grade to each student, based on the number correct. Is the grade that the student receives truly indicative of what the student knows about the concepts of area and perimeter? What does a grade of 75% actually represent? Will this grading process really help the teacher learn about how the students think and where their misconceptions about mathematics lie so that instruction can be improved? Although this grading process is rather typical of traditional testing procedures, it is not consistent with the vision in the standards and the contemporary view of assessment.

On the 20-question test on area and perimeter, is it possible that the student could have a deep understanding of what it means to find area and perimeter but made several calculation errors and, therefore, receive a grade of 75%? Conversely, is it conceivable that the student could have memorized a list of formulas for calculating area and perimeter, cranked out a list of 20 correct answers, but never really had any firm understanding of what the concepts of area and perimeter are all about? The answer to both of these questions is a resounding YES! In this case, unfortunately, the assessment tool issued at the end of the lessons did not attempt to measure understanding. Instead, it focused solely on students' ability to use a formula and find correct numerical answers.

Meaningful assessment tools offer students the opportunity to demonstrate conceptual knowledge that goes well beyond simply putting right answers on blanks on a test paper. Perhaps a more insightful assessment of student learning from these lessons would have been to ask the student to draw a picture of a rectangle whose area is 20 square centimeters and whose perimeter is 24 centimeters. This alternate item would have required the student to relate the concepts of area and perimeter and would have given the teacher a much clearer picture of what the student was able to do.

A student who knows that the teacher will be grading only the 20 answers on the blanks also knows something about what the teacher values—correct answers. The same 20-question test described earlier could be greatly enhanced by eliminating the answer blanks and requiring students to explain their work in writing. This format gives students the message that the teacher values the process that the student used to obtain an answer, not just the answer alone. Knowledge of the process that the student used may be more effective in making inferences about what a student can do than looking only at "final" numerical answers. Consequently, assessment procedures need to be judged on their effectiveness in determining what a student actually knows about the important mathematics. As a result, the conceptual understanding becomes the emphasis, and the teacher becomes much more knowl-edgeable about what the students really know and how they know it.

One technique that can be used effectively in any assessment system is the use of **open-ended** or **free-response questions**. With this type of question, the student is asked to respond by explaining, describing, showing, drawing, or verifying. A variety of student responses are expected, and no two answers in a class will necessarily be exactly alike. Traditional exam items can be rewritten as open-ended questions with some practice. For example, on a third-grade test, a traditional item may have been:

Multiply: 7×12

Instead, the question could be written as follows:

A student has done the multiplication exercise below:

$$\begin{array}{r} 12 \\ \times\ 7 \\ \hline 714 \end{array}$$

Explain the error that the student made. Then, draw a picture that shows that you understand what it means to multiply 7×12.

Worded this way, the student must have a firm grasp of the concept of multiplication to address the question. In the traditional version of the item, only a procedural knowledge of regrouping (sometimes referred to as "carrying") is required to obtain a correct answer.

Since open-ended questions may have multiple solutions or several reasonable ways in which to reach a solution, their use can be extremely powerful in assessing what the student is thinking. However, there are two related issues that must be addressed. First, an open-ended question, by definition, is open to many different responses. It is assumed that the teacher has the mathematical expertise to know a "good" answer from a "bluff." Some students are very skilled at writing long, verbose responses, but a close analysis of the answers may indicate little, if any, mathematical understanding. Simply put, the scoring of open-ended questions is not as easy as the "right or wrong" nature of closed questions and requires that the teacher possess a strong conceptual understanding of what is being assessed.

The second issue that is inherent to open-ended questions is the decision of how to score student responses. If a student assessment is conducted through the use of a worthwhile, perhaps multidimensional, open-ended question, as opposed to 20 fill-in-the-blank questions, then the grading of the response is going to be much different. As a result, many teachers are now using a **rubric** for scoring student responses to open-ended questions. A rubric is a generalized grading scale that is used for assessing student writing on an open-ended item. Many different rubrics are being used by individuals and school districts across the country. In some areas, all the teachers in an entire state are using the same rubric for scoring student work. An example of one school district's rubric for scoring student responses to open-ended questions follows.

4 Complete and Competent

A full and correct response to the question has been given.

Illustrates excellent problem-solving, reasoning, and communication skills.

If open response, the "answers" are all correct.

Work is clearly shown and/or explained.

A minor error, such as incorrect units or rounding, may be present.

3 Basic Competency

A correct response to the question has been given.

Illustrates good problem-solving, reasoning, and communication skills.

If open response, most of the "answers" are correct.

Work is shown/explained.

Some minor mathematical errors or errors in reasoning may be present.

2 Partial Answer

Some of the response to the question may have been omitted.

Illustrates fair problem-solving, reasoning, and communication skills.

A lack of higher-level thinking is evident.

Conclusions drawn may not be accurate.

Some limited understanding of mathematical concepts is demonstrated.

Several mathematical errors or errors in reasoning may be present.

1 Attempted Answer

Problem is copied over but mathematical ideas are never developed.

Problem-solving, reasoning, and/or communication skills are lacking.

Several incorrect calculations may be present.

There is little, if any, mathematical understanding illustrated.

The student has merely made an attempt of some kind.

0 Off-Task or No Response

The response is totally off-task and/or inappropriate.

No evidence of problem-solving, reasoning, or communication skills is shown.

No mathematical understanding is demonstrated at all.

Attempts at "bluffing" may be evident.

No response may have been given at all.

Using this rubric scale, a student response to a question can earn a score from 0 to 4, depending on the strength of the response. Distinctions between scores are not cut-and-dried and as "well-defined" as they are on a true-false examination. Note that scores on a rubric do not necessarily correspond to the traditional notion of "partial credit," in which half of the points are awarded to an answer that is half done. Instead, papers are scored holistically—by looking at the total piece of student work and determining where the response lies on a continuum from, for example, 0 to 4.

Furthermore, a score of 3 using this rubric does not mean 75% correct. Instead, it is a numerical indicator of what the student knows and can do in the problem situation. Would you say that a normal person's temperature was 98.6%? How about a person's golf score as a 78%? These, also, are merely numerical indicators, in these cases of general health or specific ability—they are not percentages.

Teachers in a district that uses a rubric such as the one presented here need to be trained to use it effectively to increase the consistency of scoring student work. Other rubrics being used incorporate a scale from 0 to 2, a scale from 0 to 6, or even a scale from 0 to 10. An example of a quite simple rubric was used by the Mathematical Sciences Education Board (1993) in conducting a pilot of fourth-grade open-ended responses that grouped student answers as high, medium, or low.

Let's take a look at actual student responses to an open-ended question. Students in this third-grade sample were asked to produce a calendar for the month of February, with the first of the month falling on a Sunday, as shown:

S	M	T	W	R	F	S
1	2	3	4	5	6	7
8	9	10	11	12	13	14
15	16	17	18	19	20	21
22	23	24	25	26	27	28

Then, they were to use the calendar to determine how many days make up $\frac{3}{4}$ of the month and to explain how they got their answers. Six samples of actual student responses are displayed on page 39.

Is it possible to score each of these responses as "right" or "wrong"? Are there any samples in which the student got the correct response of 21 but did not appear to understand the concept of taking $\frac{3}{4}$ of a number? Are there any responses in which the student seems to have grasped the concept of taking $\frac{3}{4}$ of a number but produced an incorrect numerical answer? Which students do not understand the concept of $\frac{3}{4}$ at all? If you were using the sample rubric of 0 to 4 described earlier, what scores would you give these papers?

Open-ended questions give the teacher considerably more information about how the student thinks than traditional test items. It takes more effort and experience to learn to score open-ended responses, but the payoff in the long run outweighs the cost, because the teacher gains a clearer picture of each student's reasoning abilities.

Another technique that can be used for the assessment of student knowledge and disposition is a *project* or *investigation*. Projects and investigations are, by nature, long-term activities and often involve teams of students working together on a multifaceted task. Because our world requires workers that are able to serve as members of teams, this type of assessment task is a realistic and authentic measure of how well students can help one another attain a common goal. An example of a project is the following:

How many days make up $\frac{3}{4}$ of the month? __21__

Explain how you know this answer.
I looked aT iT and said ThaT $\frac{3}{4}$ is more Than half of iT so ThaT is how.

(a)

How many days make up $\frac{3}{4}$ of the month? __1__

Explain how you know this answer.
I took 3 - 4 and the dacer was 1

(b)

How many days make up $\frac{3}{4}$ of the month? __21__

Explain how you know this answer.
There are 4 weeks on thiscalender. Each week has 7 days. So I knew that if therewere4 weeks, $\frac{3}{4}$would be 3 of them.So I started at the 1st and counted 3 weeks down,Then I went to the end of the 3rd Week,and it was the 21st

(c)

How many days make up $\frac{3}{4}$ of the month? 12 days

Explain how you know this answer.
I looked at the first four numbers and that was $\frac{1}{4}$ and I did that two more times.

(d)

How many days make up $\frac{3}{4}$ of the month? 3 days

Explain how you know this answer.
because if you had a pie and you could only eat $\frac{3}{4}$ of the pie your taking three pieces out of four that s my answer

(e)

How many days make up $\frac{3}{4}$ of the month? __24__

Explain how you know this answer.
I counted 3 rows on the callender and then I counted how many days were in that 3 rows.

(f)

City planners have been considering installing a new traffic light at the corner of Elm and Front Streets. To make the decision, information is needed about the typical traffic patterns for that intersection. In a team of four students, gather data on typical use of the intersection at various times of the day and week. Then, create a graph or series of graphs on posterboard and make a presentation to the class on your results. Include a recommendation for the city planners, based on your results.

The traffic investigation is a real-world project that models an actual process used by professionals to determine the feasibility of installing, say, a new traffic light. Students have to determine, with the assistance of the teacher, times and means in which to gather sample data about traffic patterns at the intersection. Students may choose to count cars going through the intersection before school, at lunch, after school, and on Saturday or Sunday mornings for several weeks. They may also choose to subdivide the traffic counts into the direction in which the cars are typically traveling and so on. The task of presenting a report to the class is open-ended enough to allow for a variety of possible student responses and conclusions. Students are not necessarily graded for their "answers" or their recommendations. Instead, they are assessed on their ability to work together, to gather data effectively, and to demonstrate an understanding of how to use the data to make an argument.

The teacher's job of assessing a project or investigation is indeed more complex than simply assigning a numerical score to the task based on right answers. Instead, the teacher may devise a form or checklist on which to record information about student work. Such a form may include a space in which to make anecdotal notes on observations of the ability to work together, the strengths/weaknesses of plans to gather the data, the depth of understanding of the key mathematical concepts, the reasonableness of the team's conclusions and recommendations, and the strengths/weaknesses of the student presentations. After all the areas have been assessed, with notes made over a period of time, a final evaluative report that includes comments and a grade for each student can be issued.

Teachers can also gain powerful information about student understandings by conducting informal or formal interviews with the students or by observing the students in teamwork situations. The method of conducting individual interviews, as needed, can be particularly useful for assessment in the primary grades, where the student is likely to be verbal but may, as yet, have limited writing skills. In the interview, the teacher presents the student with a task and asks the student to restate the task and to solve it, explaining by "thinking out loud" as the student works. The teacher can ask questions such as "What does the problem mean to you?", "Do you see a pattern here?", "Have you seen something like this before? When?", and "What do you think would happen if we used a different number here?" Much can be learned by allowing a student to explain a process and answer these types of questions in a one-on-one setting. An anecdotal description of the student's understandings can be written by the teacher and placed in the student file.

Observations of students working individually or in teams can be recorded and used in the assessment of student understandings and dispositions. A teacher can observe to see if students are actively involved, attempting to help others, asking questions, working well with other people, and making effective use of technology and manipulatives. The teacher can also gather information about student dispositions by noting evidence of confidence, flexibility, perseverance, curiosity, reflection, and valuing and appreciating mathematics.

Another valuable technique that can be used to assess student understandings and dispositions is student writing. Students can be asked to maintain a mathematics journal and make entries on a regular basis. For the entries, teachers may wish to give a specific prompt to which students are to respond, or the students may simply be asked to write a reaction to, or a summary of, the important aspects of the day's lesson. The student may wish to comment on a missed homework problem or discuss an example from class that was not clear a few days ago but seems to make sense today.

By regularly collecting the journals, the teacher can gain a broad sense of what the student thinks about mathematics on an individual basis, while also determining whether there are classwide misconceptions that need to be addressed. Research has shown that the power of journaling in mathematics not only lies in helping students address their understanding and communication skills, but that it also positively affects instructional decisions made by the teacher.

A teacher was recently about to begin a series of lessons on probability in the middle grades. Students were asked to think about the following problem:

> Suppose that you were to hold a paper cup at arm's length and let go of it, allowing it to drop to the floor. What is the likelihood or probability that the cup will land on its "top," on its "bottom," or on its "side"?

Students were asked to think about the question and to comment on it in their journals that evening. The next morning, as the teacher gave the class a short quiz on material that was currently under discussion, the journals were collected and briefly scanned by the teacher. Listed below are three samples of actual student entries about the paper cup question.

What are some of the misconceptions about probability that some students in the class appear to have?

Algebra

Jenny   May 9, 1994

The probability would be 1/3 because for each throw the cup it has 3 different ways of landing, upright, down, or on its side. You could also say that it had a 33 1/3% chance.

(a)

Algebra

Nora   May 6, 94

15	65	115
25	75	125
35	85	135
45	95	145
55	105	155

I flipped The cup 15 Times + iT always landed on iTs side, so I guess There's a 100% probability ThaT The cup will land on iTs side

(b)

Algebra

Jason

\# of times out of 200 that landed on side=

||||·|||| ||||·|||| ||||·|||| |||| · |||| ||||·|||| |||| |||| ·
|||| |||| · |||| |||| · |||| |||| · |||| |||| · |||| |||| · |||| |||| · ||||
||||·|||| ||||·|||| ||||·|||| ||||·|||| ||||·|||| ||||

\# of times out of 200 that landed on
bottom = ||

\# of times out of 200 that landed on
top = |||| · |||| |||| · |||| ||||

Probability of landing on side = 87%

Probability of landing on bottom = 1%

Probability of landing on top = 12%

(c)

What types of reasoning are illustrated in these sample responses? How might the teacher use these data to plan a beginning lesson involving a discussion of what probability means? Notice that the writing of journal entries was assigned as a means of collecting diagnostic data on what the students knew before a formal discussion occurred, rather than serving as a grading tool. Journal and log entries can be very powerful in terms of providing the teacher with information about student understanding and the need for specific intervention strategies.

Students may also be asked to react to a prompt in writing several days each week. For example, the fifth-grade teacher may ask the class to "write about what topic you liked the most in mathematics class this week and why you liked it." Or, the teacher may ask the students to complete the statement, "One thing I still don't understand in mathematics is. . . ." These types of questions allow the student to reflect on their own learning, while also serving as data for the teacher to use in determining the direction of future lessons.

The last assessment technique we discuss here is the use of a **portfolio** of student work. A portfolio is a carefully selected collection of samples of student work, including projects, writings, tests, reports, and so on. Portfolios are used to demonstrate the broad range of understanding of mathematics that a student possesses and to indicate growth in understanding and disposition over time. As a collection of items, the portfolio is much more effective in showing what a student knows and can do than any paper-and-pencil test could possibly show on its own. Portfolios have been used effectively in other subject areas, such as art and language arts, for many years, and their use in mathematics has been shown to be equally powerful.

The contents of a portfolio collection are often determined by the students. After all, who is in a better posi-

tion to know what they consider to be evidence of their "best work" than the students themselves? Also, the teacher and student can discuss the contents, as can the student with his or her parents.

The portfolio is more than a random collection of work. Instead, it is a thoughtful selection of work that represents the range of abilities that the student possesses. Teachers who use portfolios in mathematics have commented on the strength of being able to show the actual student work to parents and administrators, over simply being able to show a gradebook filled with numbers. The portfolio, containing such items as photocopies of journal pages, sample tests, a picture of a student project, and an answer to an open-ended question, can visually present evidence of what the student knows, can do, and believes about mathematics.

The evaluation of a student portfolio is not a simple task because no two portfolios will ever look exactly alike. Learning a skill such as word processing is not necessarily an easy task either, but if we recognize the long-term benefits of developing the skill, then we can more readily commit ourselves to learning the technique. With the use of a rubric for scoring portfolios, teachers and students can work together to indicate what the collection should "look" like. The teacher can search the portfolio for evidence of problem-solving strategies, clear communication, thinking and reflection, proper use of terminology and notation, connections to real-world situations, and positive dispositions about mathematics. The teacher can then use the predetermined criteria for determining a holistic grade, if needed. Like the scoring of open-ended questions, a holistic score from a rubric can be assigned, with supporting written comments included as part of the total assessment of the portfolio.

One of the major reasons for designing an effective system of assessment is to help students become better at assessing their own progress, strengths, and weaknesses. In an ideal situation, students should develop such a strong sense of what they understand and what they do not understand that they are aware of their limitations and of areas in which improvement is needed without having to be told by a teacher. Consequently, student self-assessment and reflection should be a part of any assessment program. The self-assessment may take the form of journal or log entries, or it may involve students completing checklists or questionnaires that ask questions such as "How well do you think you contributed to the team effort in your cooperative group this week?" Student self-analysis can then become a part of the portfolio to serve as evidence of the student's ability to reflect on his or her own progress.

This vision of assessment is broad in that it takes in many different methods for gathering information and is not limited to paper-and-pencil tests. The contemporary view of assessment is not simply a method of collecting data on which to base grades for individual students in the classroom. Instead, the process involves the gathering of information through multiple methods for a variety of educational purposes. The data can be useful to the teacher in making instructional decisions. Also, the information may be useful to other parties, such as a principal, school board, or state board of education, in measuring the effectiveness of a program or holding educators and students accountable for their learning.

The contemporary view of assessment is also one of an ongoing, continual process. If the teacher's system of assessing student progress is limited to a Friday afternoon paper-and-pencil test, then that teacher is gaining only a very limited "snapshot" of what the students know, can do, and believe. This traditional form of testing also gives the students a message about what is important in mathematics that appears contrary to our contemporary view of the discipline. Instead, assessment must take place on an ongoing basis, including both formal and informal techniques. The teacher needs to assess student work and attitudes every day to achieve the vision of curriculum and instruction as outlined in the *Principles and Standards for School Mathematics*.

CLOSURE

In conclusion, we revisit the *Assessment Standards for School Mathematics* (1995). The following remarks in the introduction to the document are important to keep in mind:

> *Instead of assuming that the purpose of assessment is to rank students on a particular trait, the new approach assumes that high public expecta-*
> *tions can be set that every student can strive for and achieve, that different performances can and will meet agreed-on expectations, and that teachers can be fair and consistent judges of diverse student performances. Setting high expectations and striving to achieve them are quite different from comparing students with one another and indicating where each student ranks. A constant theme of [the assessment standards] document is that decisions regarding students' achievement should be made on the basis of a convergence of information from a variety of balanced and equitable sources. Furthermore, much of the information needs to be derived by teachers during the process of instruction. Teachers are the persons who are in the best position to judge the development of students' progress and, hence, must be considered the primary assessors of students. However, depending on the purpose, there are other assessors, such as learners who assess their own progress (NCTM, 1995, p. 1).*

As you read the remainder of this text, try to think of rich techniques of assessment that can be used to gather information about what students know, can do, and believe about each of the areas of content we discuss. Reviewing the remarks just described will help you to reach and keep the vision of assessment that has been outlined in this chapter.

Readers are also encouraged to examine Chapter 18 in Part 2 for additional information on assessing mathematics.

Terminology, Symbols, and Procedures

Assessment. Assessment can be defined as the process of gathering information about student understanding of mathematical concepts, as well as determining the disposition that the student has toward mathematics. This information is then used to determine student progress for a number of purposes.

Criterion-Referenced Tests. Criterion-referenced tests are examinations in which the objectives addressed are drawn directly from a local course of study. These tests ordinarily take the form of competency tests and are used to measure the effectiveness of a mathematics program.

Disposition. Disposition refers to the attitudes and beliefs that a student has about mathematics. Disposition includes confidence, flexibility, perseverance, interest, curiosity, inclination to self-reflect, and valuing, applying, and appreciating mathematics.

Norm-Referenced Tests. Norm-referenced tests are examinations in which students are compared to a sample of scores from students at the same age and/or grade level (typically) throughout the country. These tests are used by schools, local districts, or states to compare student performance in one area to normed performance of similar students in other localities.

Open-Ended Question. An open-ended question is a free-response question to which there are usually a variety of possible acceptable answers and/or processes to reach a solution. A major purpose of open-ended questions is to measure student reasoning abilities: The prompts ordinarily ask the student to explain, describe, draw, model, or verify.

Portfolio. A portfolio is a carefully selected collection of samples of student work, including projects, writings, tests, reports, and so on. It is used to demonstrate the broad range of understanding of mathematics that a student possesses. The portfolio can also indicate growth in understanding and disposition over time. The material that goes into a portfolio is usually determined by both the teacher and the student.

Proficiency Test. A proficiency test is an examination that tests baseline knowledge that every student in a state, for example, must possess at some given grade level. Proficiency tests are often seen as accountability tools for local districts to demonstrate that they are meeting the educational expectations of a governing body at the county, state, or even national level.

Rubric. A rubric is a generalized rating scale that is used for assessing student writing on an open-ended item. The criteria and specific scale of rubrics vary, depending on local needs.

Standard. A standard is a benchmark or statement against which a given item or position can be measured or compared. The NCTM *Principles and Standards for School Mathematics* provides examples that set up a vision of mathematics education for the year 2000 and beyond.

Teaching Competencies and Self-Assessment Tasks

1. Discuss how implementation of the NCTM *Principles and Standards for School Mathematics* will help support the vision of the three previous standards documents for curriculum, instruction, and assessment.

2. Examine several elementary school mathematics textbooks and their ancillary materials for teachers. Determine the degree to which the textbooks on the market meet the criteria for effective assessment, as outlined by the NCTM.

3. Why assess? What benefits accrue from a well-thought-out assessment program? What are the advantages and disadvantages of having a consistent or uniform schoolwide assessment framework?

4. Discuss the advantages and disadvantages of using norm-referenced versus criterion-referenced tests. When is one more appropriate than the other?

5. Obtain a set of student responses to an open-ended question. Use the rubric from 0 to 4 presented in this chapter, and give the papers a score based on the stated criteria. In small groups, discuss the difficulties you encountered in scoring the papers.

6. Several different techniques for assessing student progress are described in this chapter. However, most school districts still require teachers to assign a letter grade to a student, based on the student's total performance. Discuss how you might use multiple methods of collecting evidence of student progress but still be able to assign a letter grade for the students in your class.

7. In groups of four or five, write several performance tasks and open-ended questions that would be appropriate for primary, intermediate, and upper elementary/junior high students.

References

Mathematical Sciences Education Board. (1993). *Measuring up*: *Prototypes for mathematics assessment*. Washington, DC: National Academy Press.

National Council of Teachers of Mathematics. (1989). *Curriculum and evaluation standards for school mathematics*. Reston, VA: Author.

National Council of Teachers of Mathematics. (1991). *Professional standards for teaching mathematics*. Reston, VA: Author.

National Council of Teachers of Mathematics. (1995). *Assessment standards for school mathematics*. Reston, VA: Author.

National Council of Teachers of Mathematics. (2000). *Principles and standards for school mathematics*. Reston, VA: Author.

Romberg, T. A., and Wilson, L. (1989). *The alignment of six standardized tests with the NCTM standards*. Unpublished manuscript, University of Wisconsin-Madison.

Related Readings and Teacher Resources

For related readings on topics found in this chapter, see Chapter 3 in Part 2 of *Today's Mathematics*, the Student Resource Book.

Chapter 4

Technology Tools for Enhancing Teaching, Learning, and Assessing Mathematics

Teaching Competencies

Upon completing this chapter, you will be able to:

- Describe the role played by calculators and computers in a contemporary elementary school mathematics classroom as envisioned by the NCTM *Principles and Standards for School Mathematics* and the NCTM *Position Statements on Calculators and Computers.*

- Describe appropriate uses of calculators and computers in the problem-solving process, including the use of Calculator-Based Laboratories and Calculator-Based Rangers.

- Describe features and functions available on calculators commonly used in the elementary school.

- Identify and describe a variety of purposes of educational software and applications software.

- Incorporate contemporary thought on integrating multimedia and telecommunications in classroom instruction.

- State examples of ways the Internet and the World Wide Web can be used in educational settings to locate information of value in everyday life.

he NCTM *Principles and Standards for School Mathematics* acknowledges the important role that technology should play in the mathematical education of youth. A fundamental assumption of these standards, the Technology Principle, states that "Mathematics instructional programs should use technology to help all students understand mathematics and should prepare them to use mathematics in an increasingly technological world" (NCTM, 1998).

Research and experience have clearly demonstrated the potential of calculators and computers to enhance students' learning in mathematics. The cognitive gain in number sense, conceptual development, and visualization can empower and motivate students to engage in true mathematical problem solving at a level previously denied to all but the most talented.

In most real-life situations, we make use of technology to perform the tedious computations that often develop when working with real data in problem situations. Technology can provide a focus on problem-solving processes rather than computations associated with problems, thereby allowing students to gain access to mathematical ideas and experiences that go beyond those levels limited by traditional paper-and-pencil computation.

CALCULATORS IN MATHEMATICS

Calculators have for some time been the focus of considerable discussion among mathematics educators, parents, representatives of the workplace, and others.

Of course, some extreme viewpoints have been represented along with the more frequent moderate opinions. Some have argued that the calculator should not be used in an elementary school classroom until the basic facts have been mastered. Others, citing research that shows the calculator does not pose a threat to skill mastery, suggest that there is no harm—in fact, a considerable amount of good—in introducing the calculator at any point in the curriculum.

Instruction with calculators will extend the understanding of mathematics and will allow all students access to rich, problem-solving experiences. This instruction must develop students' ability to know how and when to use a calculator. Skill in estimation and the ability to decide if the solution to a problem is reasonable are essential adjuncts to the effective use of the calculator.

The aggressiveness of the debate over calculator use has subsided in recent years. Now, the most commonly accepted position is that, when used appropriately, the calculator can be effective at all levels of instruction, including the primary grades. The phrase "used appropriately" implies that the calculator should be used for more than simply checking answers to seatwork or homework papers. The calculator can be incorporated into instruction so that it serves as an aid to understanding concepts.

Consider this: How can we find the square root of a given number, and what does square root mean?

To develop an understanding of square root, do not use the square root key on the calculator. For example, let's locate an approximate square root value for 13.

Research Snapshot

What is the effect of using calculators on children's learning of number concepts and skills?

Groves and Stacey (1998) reported the results of a study of third and fourth graders in the Calculators in Primary Mathematics project, which took place in Australia. Each year, approximately five hundred children participated in the three-year project.

The students with long-term experience with calculators performed better than the students without the calculator experience on a wide range of items, including decimals, negative numbers, and place value in large numbers. They also performed better in mental computation, made more appropriate choices of calculating devices, and were better able to interpret their answers when using a calculator.

Why do you think the calculator-based students in this study did better on noncalculator tasks than those students that relied on paper-and-pencil techniques? How much time in the school curriculum do you think we should devote to paper-and-pencil algorithms?

Groves, S, & Stacey, K. (1998). Calculators in primary mathematics: Exploring number before teaching algorithms. In L. Morrow, L. & M. Kenney (Eds.). *The teaching and learning of algorithms in school mathematics* (pp. 120–129). Reston, VA: National Council of Teachers of Mathematics.

For additional research briefs, "ERIC Digests" lets you search more than 2,000 short syntheses of research on a range of education topics. The syntheses were produced by the Educational Resources Information Center (ERIC). Check http://ed.gov/databases/ERIC_Digests/index/

Since we understand what squaring a number means (a number multiplied by itself), let's use this concept as the starting point for exploring the concept of square root. What are the square numbers "on each side" of 13? We know that $3 \times 3 = 9$ and $4 \times 4 = 16$. That is, 13 is between 9 and 16. So the square root of 13 must be between 3 and 4. Now let's identify the number in the tens place of the square root. The number 13 is closer to the number 16 than it is to 9. So we will select a number a little greater than 3.5, halfway between 3 and 4. Let's try 3.6, and square it. Using the calculator, we find that $3.6 \times 3.6 = 12.96$. Now let's try 3.7: $3.7 \times 3.7 = 13.69$. Since 12.96 is closer to 13 than 13.69, we should try a number a little greater than 3.6. Using the calculator to multiply 3.61×3.61, we find that the square of 3.61 is 13.0321. Continue this estimating process until the square root of 13 is estimated to the number of places needed. A student that explores square root in the fashion described here will have an intuitive base off of which to build. The chances are dramatically increased that this student will have a better understanding of the underlying concept.

The calculator can also be a feedback device, as illustrated in the addition example described here. Round the following numbers to the nearest hundred. After rounding each one, enter the result in the calculator, and press the addition (+) key. When you finish, the number in the display should be 59100.

6137

13490

2856

9720

26882

In this example, the objective is to round numbers to the nearest hundred. The student, not the calculator, must satisfy this objective. That is, the calculator does not perform the task; it merely serves as a self-checking device. If the student does not get a result of 59100 at the end of this exercise, then an error must have occurred, and the student will be made aware of this.

Note, however, that the calculator does not provide information about where the error occurred. This is beneficial in this case: Because there are only five numbers to round and add, the student who has not mastered the objective must now check each number, rather than simply go to the one "marked wrong."

The National Council of Teachers of Mathematics has prepared a position paper on the use of calculators in the mathematics classroom. The full text of that paper is reproduced here with the permission of NCTM.

CALCULATORS AND THE EDUCATION OF YOUTH

The National Council of Teachers of Mathematics therefore recommends the integration of calculators into the school mathematics program at all grade levels.

Appropriate instruction that includes calculators can extend students' understanding of mathematics and will allow all students access to rich problem-solving experiences. Such instruction must develop students' ability to know how and when to use a calculator. Skill in estimation, both numerical and graphical, and the ability to determine if a solution is reasonable are essential elements for the effective use of calculators.

Assessment and evaluation must be aligned with the classroom uses of calculators. Instruments designed to assess students' mathematical understanding and application must acknowledge students' access to, and use of, calculators.

Research and experience support the potential for appropriate calculator use to enhance the learning and teaching of mathematics. Calculator use has been shown to enhance cognitive gains in areas that include number sense, conceptual development, and visualization. Such gains can empower and motivate all teachers and students to engage in richer problem-solving activities.

Therefore, the National Council of Teachers of Mathematics makes the following recommendations:

■ All students should have access to calculators to explore mathematical ideas and experiences, to develop and reinforce skills, to support problem-solving activities, and to perform calculations and manipulations.

■ Mathematics teachers at all levels should promote the appropriate use of calculators to enhance instruction by modeling calculator applications, by using calculators in instructional settings, by integrating calculator use in assessment and evaluation, by remaining current with state-of-the-art calculator technology, and by considering new applications of calculators to enhance the study and learning of mathematics.

■ School districts should provide professional development activities that enhance teachers' understanding and application of state-of-the-art calculator technology.

■ Teacher education institutions should develop and provide preservice and in-service programs that use a variety of calculator technology.

■ Those responsible for the selection of curriculum materials should remain cognizant of how technology—in particular, calculators—affects the curriculum.

■ Authors, publishers, and writers of assessment, evaluation, and mathematics competition instruments should integrate calculator applications into their published work.

■ Mathematics educators should inform students, parents, administrators, school boards, and others of research results that document the advantages of including the calculator as one of several tools for learning and teaching mathematics.

(NCTM Position Statement
on Calculators, July 1998)

The effective use of calculators in the classroom depends largely on the skill, knowledge, and ingenuity of the classroom teacher. The calculator should be considered an essential tool for all students of mathematics and should be an integral part of the mathematics curriculum and not just an appendage for checking calculations already performed. The calculator is especially useful in developing understanding of place value, reversibility, relationships among numbers, operations, decimals, metric measure, prime factoring, composites, changing fractions to decimals, and percentages, as well as for making mathematical estimates. Other uses become apparent as we develop a curriculum that encourages calculator use during instruction.

CALCULATOR FEATURES AND FUNCTIONS

There are many different types of calculators available for classroom use. Unfortunately (or, perhaps, fortunately—when used for exploration and discovery), these various calculators do not all function in exactly the same manner. There are some important differences in available keys and the ways in which operations are handled that make it worthwhile for you to be familiar with the characteristics of the individual calculators being used by your students. Ideally, a classroom set of calculators will alleviate these concerns.

For most elementary school use, the calculator used should be based on **algebraic logic**, that is, the calculator should follow the **order of operation rules for computation**. The calculator should be inexpensive, durable, and accessible to the children, and it should have multiple uses. The keyboard should be of reasonable size, preferably with keys that "click" when they are pressed (some sort of auditory feedback of an input is helpful for many children). The display should be bright, easily readable, and easily seen since several children may share the same calculator. There are two types of calculator displays: LED (light-emitting diode) or the more common LCD (liquid-crystal display). The LCD, by far the most common display type, uses less energy and is easier to read in sunlight or from an angle. The most desirable power source will depend on the facilities available to the teacher. Solar-powered calculators are the most popular and are cheaper than many other models in the long run—in fact, it is a challenge today to find a calculator that is not solar-powered.

Children must learn correct procedures for using the calculator. Proper development of a good foundation will help to avoid confusion at later grade levels. (Proper classroom management of the calculators should also be established early.) Right from the beginning, help children develop appropriate techniques for using the calculator. Watch the display panel and assess the reasonableness of the values that appear on it. When batteries are weak or the calculator is broken (even solar-powered calculators use batteries as backups for memory), wrong answers can appear on the display panel. Have children practice operating the calculator with the opposite hand from the one they use to write. This will allow students to hold a pencil and record

results from the calculations with one hand while using the calculator with the other. Begin each calculator example by pressing the CLEAR (C) or CLEAR ENTRY (CE) key twice. This will prevent extraneous numbers already entered from interfering with the results of the current operation.

Encourage children to learn how to operate the calculator and understand when it would be beneficial and when it would not. The calculator will only do what it is told to do—students must learn to decide what kind of situations require a calculator and how to use the calculator in those situations. Impress on the children that a calculator is only a supplemental tool. It is still important for the children to be able to solve "reasonable" mathematics problems and examples involving calculation without the benefit of a calculator (and to understand how to transfer their skill with these "reasonable" problems to using a calculator for the more "unreasonable" ones).

TOOLS FOR MEASURING MOTION

With the availability and ease of use of motion detectors, teachers are able to lead middle-grade students to an understanding of function and how to interpret continuous graphs. The **motion detector** has been available for use with the **Calculator-Based Laboratory (CBL)** for a number of years. The CBL is a data-gathering device that can be used with several probes to collect different types of data. A CBL with appropriate probes can measure temperature, heart rate, light intensity, and motion, to name just a few of the possibilities.

A perceived complexity of the CBL's use has deterred middle-grade teachers from including the CBL in their repertoire of tools. The **Calculator-Based Ranger (CBR)** was developed in response to teachers' hesitation to use the CBL. The CBR measures motion, exclusively. It can be attached to a TI-73 (a middle school graphing calculator) or to any other Texas Instruments graphing calculator. The CBR collects motion data and sends that data to the calculator to be displayed as a graph or table. A powerful activity that is available as part of the CBR package is to have students "match the graph." Students are given a graph of distance as a function of time. The graph is displayed on the graphing calculator. With a connection to a view-screen panel for the overhead projector, the entire class can see the same graph simultaneously. A student, then, is directed to "match the graph" by walking in front of the CBR motion detector. The student's movement is graphed on the same graph as the original target graph so that the student and the class can compare his or her attempt to match the target. Students should be encouraged to redo their graphs after they discuss with the class how they might walk a more closely related graph. By having students actually "become" or act out a graph, the students gain a different, and perhaps, deeper understanding of the functional relationship of distance and time.

Calculators are widely used at home and in the workplace. As the price of calculators continues to decline, many more children have access to them. Obviously, the calculator boom is a phenomenon that schools cannot afford to ignore. Calculators are not a passing fad. Educators must accept this and provide for instruction in mathematics by making full use of the potential of the calculator as a teaching tool. Increased use of calculators in school will ensure that students' experiences in mathematics will match the realities of everyday life, develop their reasoning skills, and promote the understanding and application of mathematics.

COMPUTERS IN MATHEMATICS

Preparing children to function successfully in the real world is a primary goal of mathematics instruction. Since technology is an ever-growing part of the real world, school systems and teachers have an obligation to teach children how to use that technology to solve problems they face. The fact is that some mathematics becomes more important because technology REQUIRES it; some mathematics becomes less important because technology REPLACES it; and some mathematics becomes possible because technology ALLOWS it (NCTM, 1998).

The responsibility for teaching children to understand and use computers rests almost entirely on the teachers and administrators in our school systems. Unfortunately, some elementary school teachers are unprepared to handle the planning and teaching of computer use and application to children. Some elementary school teachers have never touched a computer, let alone used the computer in their teaching. David Moursand, a well-known computer education expert, has described this situation as one in which "We are asking computer-illiterate teachers to help students become computer literate at a functional level."

The growing placement of computers in classrooms is commonly supported by school administrators, teachers, and parents. If we agree with the assumption that technology is a viable tool of mathematics instruction, then when should computers be introduced into the instructional program? Should technology be introduced in the primary grades, or should we wait until students have mastered certain basic mathematics concepts and skills? Should computers be an integral part of classroom instruction, or should they be reserved for special uses? The range of opinion concerning these and other related questions is indeed broad.

The National Council of Teachers of Mathematics has prepared a position paper on the role of computer technology in the mathematics classroom. The full text of that paper is reproduced here with the permission of NCTM.

THE USE OF TECHNOLOGY IN THE LEARNING AND TEACHING OF MATHEMATICS

The appropriate use of instructional technology tools is integral to the learning and teaching of mathematics and to the assessment of mathematics learning at all levels.

Technology has changed the ways in which mathematics is used and has led to the creation of both new and expanded fields of mathematical study. Thus, technology is driving change in the content of mathematics programs, in methods for mathematics instruction, and in the ways that mathematics is learned and assessed. A vital aspect of such change is a teacher's ability to select and use appropriate instructional technology to develop, enhance, and extend students' understanding and application of mathematics. It is essential that teachers continue to explore the impact of instructional technology and the perspectives it provides on an expanding array of mathematics concepts, skills, and applications.

Therefore, the National Council of Teachers of Mathematics makes the following recommendations:

Every student should have access to an appropriate calculator.

Every mathematics teacher should have access to a computer with appropriate software and network connections for instructional and non-instructional tasks.

Every mathematics classroom should have computers with Internet connections available at all times for demonstrations and students' use.

Every school mathematics program should provide students and teachers access to computers and other appropriate technology for individual, small-group, and whole-class use, as needed, on a daily basis.

Curriculum development, evaluation, and revision must take into account the mathematical opportunities provided by instructional technology. When a curriculum is implemented, time and emphasis must be given to the use of technology to teach mathematics concepts, skills, and applications in the ways they are encountered in an age of ever increasing access to more-powerful technology.

Professional development for preservice and in-service teachers must include opportunities to learn mathematics in technology-rich environments.

(NCTM Position Statement on Technology, 1998)

This position emphasizes that the use of the tools of technology is integral to the learning and teaching of mathematics and that continual improvement is needed in mathematics curricula, instructional and assessment methods, access to hardware and software, and teacher education.

Although the nature of mathematics and societal needs are forces that drive the curriculum, the opportunities that technology presents must be reflected in the content of school mathematics. Curricular revisions allow for the de-emphasis of topics that are no longer important, the addition of topics that have acquired new importance, and the retention of topics that remain important. In the implementation of revised curricula, time and emphasis should be allocated to topics according to their importance in an age of increased access to technology. Instructional materials that capitalize on the power of technology must be given a high priority. The thoughtful and creative use of technology can greatly improve both the quality of the curriculum and the quality of students' learning.

Teachers should plan for students' use of technology in both learning and doing mathematics. The development of ideas should be made with the transition from concrete experiences to abstract mathematical ideas, focusing on the exploration and discovery of new mathematical concepts and problem-solving processes. Students should learn how to use technology as a tool for processing information, visualizing and solving problems, exploring and testing conjectures, accessing data, and verifying their solutions. Students' ability to recognize when and how to use technology effectively is dependent on their continued study of appropriate mathematics content. In a mathematics setting, technology must be an instructional tool that is integrated into daily teaching practices, including the assessment of what students know and are able to do. In a mathematics class, technology ought not be the object of instruction but rather seen as a tool for instruction.

The preparation of teachers of mathematics requires an ability to design technology-integrated classroom and laboratory lessons that promote interaction among the students, technology, and the teacher. The selection, evaluation, and use of technology for a variety of activities such as simulation, the generation and analysis of data, problem solving, graphical analysis, and geometric constructions depend on the teacher. Therefore, the availability of ongoing in-service programs is necessary to help teachers take full advantage of the unique power of technology as a tool for mathematics classrooms. The National Council of Teachers of Mathematics recommends the appropriate use of technology to enhance mathematics programs at all levels. Keeping pace with the advances in technology is a necessity for the entire mathematics community, particularly teachers who are responsible for designing day-to-day instructional experiences for students.

In 1981, only 18% of U.S. public schools had even a single computer for instructional uses. By 1999, 99% of U.S. schools had computers—a total of over eight million machines, twice as many as in 1993. The rapid growth in the number of computers in the schools has placed pressure on teachers to become knowledgeable about computers. The vast majority, if not all, teacher education programs require some structured experience with computers. Teachers must be afforded the time to become familiar with, and develop a degree of confidence with, computers and their uses in the classroom before we can expect technology to be seamlessly integrated with instruction.

INSTRUCTIONAL SOFTWARE IN THE MATHEMATICS CLASSROOM

The focus of the debate over technology in the classroom has switched from the calculator to the computer.

Many of the same arguments have been presented, although the amount of opposition is considerably reduced. In fact, most schools are actively seeking ways to incorporate the computer into their curriculum in all subject areas. The debate that remains centers on the potential educational uses of the computer.

Teachers can begin using computers in the mathematics program by providing commercial software packages. A computer work area should become an important learning center in every elementary school classroom. Do not encourage games for their own sake. Use classroom computers for educational purposes. This can be accomplished by providing your students with software that is appropriate for their needs and your instructional goals and objectives. If your intent is to have students drilled in basic facts, then choose software that will do just that. If your intent is for students to journal about topics in mathematics, then direct students to use word processing software. If the computer is to be used as a discovery tool, then encourage students to explore a particular topic using software designed for this application.

Develop a good filing system to allow easy access to programs needed for particular purposes. Individualizing mathematics will become easier as teachers learn how to change and create programs addressed to specific student needs. The computer can become a record keeper for each child and free the teacher from the tedium of paperwork.

Various types of software programs have been developed and are available to teachers for classroom use. These include but are not limited to the following categories:

drill and practice;
educational game;
simulation;
tutorial;
problem solving;
exploration tool;
records management;
material generation.

These software types are not mutually exclusive, but the majority of available computer programs focus more heavily on one of the applications just listed. It is important for teachers to distinguish between these uses in order to judge the effectiveness and efficiency of a given program. For example, we might examine a program dealing with basic multiplication facts couched in an arcade-like setting and easily categorize this as an educational game. Actually, such a program might be better classified as drill and practice, since the concepts involved are to be memorized and subject to immediate recall.

Similarly, a program that involves estimating various lengths and angles (couched in a golf or artillery game) could be classified as drill and practice although it should really be considered an educational game. In this instance, the game format is used not to drill knowledge-level material, but rather to assist the students in developing estimation skills not subject to immediate recall.

Commercial software that emphasizes the tutorial mode can sometimes be effectively used to provide instruction. The purpose of such software is to assist in the teaching of concepts, although such packages often also include a drill and practice component to check on progress. Tutorial software is frequently used to introduce (or reintroduce) a topic. A student who is new to a school, or one who has been absent for several days, might make good use of a tutorial package to "catch up."

Simulation, problem solving, and exploration tool software packages may be the most valuable of all. These packages are designed to establish an environment for generating and testing hypotheses and looking for patterns. Frequently, the setting is one that is not easily attained in the classroom without the use of a microcomputer. As an example, consider a software package that allows students to "travel" from one planet to the next, collecting data about atmospheres, gravity, surface temperatures, and so on. The student is then free to make conjectures about life on those planets. Exploration tool software might allow a student to look for patterns between the sum of the degrees of the angles in triangles. The software could provide far more examples to use to look for patterns than would be encountered by simply drawing triangles using paper, pencil, and straightedge.

Teachers must become effective software evaluators. Software evaluation techniques and forms are readily available in the literature. First, isolate the purpose of the program. Then compare the purpose with the features of the program with respect to grade level, validity of content, correlation with curriculum, preview options, and instructional design features. Software reviews are often included as monthly columns in mathematics education journals such as NTCM's *Teaching Children Mathematics* and *Mathematics Teaching in the Middle School*. Check out those columns for reviews of software that might be of use to you and your students.

Drill and practice is too often the major use of computers in the classroom. The computer is sometimes used as an expensive electronic worksheet for children. However, more **computer assisted instruction (CAI)** programs are becoming available for classroom use. CAI describes an individualized instructional situation where the student is presented with material by the computer in an interactive mode with systematic evaluation and basic record keeping as integral parts of the software.

Teachers are also using computers for **computer managed instruction (CMI)**. CMI provides the classroom teacher with computer technology to keep records, store test information, and provide prescriptive information to meet individual student needs.

Each teacher needs to experiment with the computer and its uses in the mathematics curriculum in order to develop more effective and efficient techniques. The computer has great educational potential, but we must first learn to use the unique characteristics of the computer to increase the efficiency and effectiveness of mathematics teaching.

APPLICATION SOFTWARE IN THE MATHEMATICS CLASSROOM

Four common and practical tool applications of the computer are to be found in programs that make use of word processing, databases, spreadsheets, and graphics. A word processor, through its editing features, helps students develop confidence in communication by providing a forum for recording ideas removed from the restrictions of linear and rigid thinking. A database, through its searching capabilities, gives students access to patterns and trends in large amounts of data. A spreadsheet, through its formula features, allows students to hypothesize and examine the effect of changing one variable in a multivariable situation. A graphics program, through its drawing capabilities, gives students a vehicle for creative modeling of abstract concepts and geometric principles. All four programs assist students in formulating real-life situations, exploring problem-solving strategies, identifying and verifying hypotheses, communicating findings, and valuing sound decision-making processes.

The application programs available and frequently used by teachers have individual distinctions that make a generic discussion of their operation difficult, at best. Instead of focusing on their idiosyncrasies, let's consider sample activities that make use of the power of these applications as tools for problem solving and patterning.

Word processing programs offer more than the capabilities of a typewriter. Their flexible formatting allows you to move letters, words, phrases, sentences, and paragraphs around easily. Spell-check, find-and-replace, and automatic outline features make this a valuable tool for both students and teachers. Teachers, especially, can make excellent use of the "cut-and-paste" feature of a word processor in preparing lesson plans. The ability to save files for future modification and use is also a real plus. Many word processing programs can incorporate enhancement options such as graphics and different fonts and styles.

Consider the following example of an activity that engages students in the use of a word processor: Have students create a story problem—not the common form of two sentences and a question mark, but a "real" story problem. Using a word processor, the students can refine and extend their creations. Word processors designed for use by children often provide easily accessible graphics that can enhance the story and make it more understandable to beginning readers. Students can seek advice from others to improve the story and motivate the need to help the characters solve their problem. Perhaps students can even work together in creating a story by taking turns writing sentences. When complete, changes and different versions can easily be saved for later discussion. Printouts can form an interactive bulletin board where students are expected to solve the problems they read about. Kid Pix is an example of an application software package that could be used for this purpose.

Database application programs have the advantage of storing a considerable amount of information in a form that makes searching, sorting, and retrieving data an easy process. Teachers can, of course, use a database to store relevant information about their students, such as home address and phone numbers, important special notes about health or diet, or records of assignment completion. Teachers can also use databases to send personalized letters home to parents and students by merging the database with a word processing document. Students can make use of the sorting ability to explore categories and attributes. For example, the teacher can create a database file for each student that includes the number of pets owned, the type of pets, the names of pets, the color of pets, who feeds the pets, etc. Students can then search the files of all classmates to discover the most common pet type, pet name, etc. This information can then be translated to a graph. Tabletop Jr. or Tabletop are examples of database software packages that could be used for this activity.

A **spreadsheet** is often thought of as an electronic accounting pad. Indeed, its greatest power may well lie in calculation. While originally designed for business use as a standard ledger, spreadsheets have become much more flexible and, consequently, more widely used in schools. A teacher can, of course, incorporate the more traditional aspects of a spreadsheet by using it to record and to average student grades, with, for example, weighted scores and/or percentage grades. The teacher can make graphs using this data to chart students' performance over time or in relation to other students' performance on the same assignments. One of the most valuable components to a spreadsheet program is the ability to change numbers or formulas quickly and easily to answer the question of "What if?" An interesting activity that demonstrates this feature is to set up, on the spreadsheet, a restaurant menu with columns for item names, how many of each item ordered, price per item, and the total price. Students can then change the number of items ordered and see the effect of different permutations on the bill. Many integrated software packages, such as Microsoft Word and Clarisworks, incorporate spreadsheets. Many spreadsheet programs have automatic transfer of data to a graph with the push of a button. Students can compare the way data is displayed in a picture graph to a bar graph using graphing software such as The Graph Club. Another commercial program dedicated to spreadsheet and data-graphing explorations is The Cruncher.

A drawing program is also often part of the word processing program, the database, and/or the spreadsheet. For example, **graphics programs** can be used to create banners and signs for bulletin boards, greeting cards for special occasions, or enhancements to other documents. Students can use drawing programs to explore perspective, the two-dimensional/three-dimensional connection, and geometric properties of various shapes. Students can use drawing programs to create a series of graphic images that illustrate a repetitive pattern, such as images of a house, tree, tree, house, tree, and so on. Other students can be asked to determine the pattern, and to continue it. Kid Pix could provide the environment for this activity. A dynamic drawing program could be used to perform transformations such as reflections and then have students move the location of the mirror line to see how it affects the reflected image. The Geometer's Sketchpad is yet another software package that could be used for this type of activity.

MULTIMEDIA IN THE MATHEMATICS CLASSROOM

Multimedia refers to the combination of visual and auditory information controlled by the computer. It can incorporate text, graphics, animation, photography, video, music, and sound. Both the potential of the medium and the applications are diverse. The power of multimedia is the visual image that goes beyond spoken or written words. One embodiment of multimedia is called **hypermedia**. (Originally, hypertext was used to refer to text links while hypermedia suggested links to more visual forms of information.)

Historically, the most common organization for the preservation and presentation of information has been a linear mode. For example, books are typically read from cover to cover, and TV programs are normally viewed from beginning to end. Information can be cross-referenced in a book, but the general layout is still linear and, as such, is confining. Hypermedia provides an escape from the linear presentation of information. Electronic links allow the user to quickly connect to other points of information by clicking on words or graphics, thereby providing a means of making information interactive. One reason compact disc players have replaced vinyl record albums and even cassette tapes is this capability of immediately "jumping" to preferred sections of the music.

CD-ROM discs, similar to music CDs, store vast amounts of information in digital form that can be readily accessed by computer. A single CD-ROM holds about 600 megabytes of data (equivalent to more than 400 high-density floppy disks). Reference CD-ROM titles such as Grolier's Multimedia Encyclopedia or Microsoft's Encarta offer photographs and video clips in addition to text information. The 3-D Atlas CD-ROM provides outstanding visuals and vast amounts of statistical data on ecology, population, and economics, as well as many other categories. Education Development Center's MathFINDER offers a multitude of sample lessons taken from thirty curriculum programs indexed to the NCTM standards. Any of these resources can be effectively used by both students and teachers as research materials in problem solving and project-based inquiries or investigations.

Photography has reached the computer age with the development of **digital cameras**. These are available from a variety of computer and camera manufacturers. Digital cameras are similar to standard cameras in allowing users to take pictures using the familiar point-and-shoot technique. When a digital camera is used, however, the images are captured on a disk, memory chip, or memory card and later downloaded to the computer using preloaded software that allows images to be used immediately. Once downloaded, images can be modified or enhanced and inserted into, for example, a word processing document.

A variety of school applications can be identified for digital photography. As one example, a group of elementary students might be challenged to use the digital camera to take pictures of their environment that reflect the use of patterns, or measurement, or certain aspects of geometry. These images could then be downloaded to lead a discussion of mathematics in our world. A valuable resource for ideas concerning school-based use of digital cameras in the classroom is the Kodak Web site at http://www.kodak.com/US/en/digital/edu/education.shtml

A multimedia learning environment requires a teacher who is comfortable with technology and who is able to integrate that technology into the curriculum. Hypermedia tools can be used by teachers to create classroom applications, but they can also be used as student productivity tools. Students involved in designing their own hypermedia projects, or in using hypermedia programs designed by peers, become actively involved in learning at many levels. A great deal of planning goes into organizing and linking information in meaningful ways. One of the key elements in asking students to develop hypermedia projects is to engage them in peer collaboration during the planning stages of the project.

HyperCard was one of the first programs for creating presentations, interactive stories, nonlinear databases, and multimedia. It is basically a software construction kit designed for nonprofessional programmers. A HyperCard document, called a stack, is made up of a collection of cards. Each card contains a background, and "layers" of information can be added, including graphics, animation, and sound. Buttons are objects that allow user input. For example, clicking on a button may produce a sound, cause text to appear, or move the user to another card.

HyperStudio, another multimedia creation tool, allows for creation of stacks while providing a great deal of on-screen help. Pop-up windows guide the user through the steps of creating buttons and linking them to actions, animations, video, sound, or other cards. A student might use a hypermedia tool to demonstrate understanding of a mathematical concept. For instance, during a unit on quadrilaterals, a student could demonstrate the categorization of different quadrilaterals by making a stack with the first card showing a "family tree" for quadrilaterals. The members of the family tree can be links to other cards that provide justifications for that member's placement in that particular place. Additional links could show examples of those particular quadrilaterals.

A teacher could use a hypermedia tool to showcase collections of students' computer work or scanned paperwork. The teacher could link the work by topic and/or student name and could use the stack for a presentation to other teachers or at an open house.

In addition to curriculum-based topics, hypermedia tools can be used to develop electronic portfolios. This assessment strategy allows for much more information than the paper-based format. Student success can be documented with pictures, sound, video, and work samples. Ideally, the electronic portfolio should include student input when selections are made.

Commonly used hypermedia software:

HyperStudio (Macintosh or IBM) Roger Wagner Publishing 1050 Pioneer Way, Suite P El Cajon, CA 92020 1-800-497-3778	HyperCard (Macintosh) Apple Computer Co. 20525 Mariani Ave. Cupertino, CA 95014 1-800-776-2333
Digital Chisel (Macintosh) Pierian Spring Software 5200 SW Macadam Ave., Suite 250 Portland, OR 97201 503-222-2044	Linkway Live (MS-DOS) IBM, EduQuest 1000 NW 51st St. Boca Raton, FL 33429-1234 408-372-8100

Educational software catalogs and computer stores offer several other titles.

TELECOMMUNICATIONS IN THE MATHEMATICS CLASSROOM

Imagine a giant web covering the globe, connecting thousands of networks of computers and allowing millions of users to access and share information! The **Internet** brings people and information together in a digital world unbound by time and space. Commonly referred to as the "network of networks," the Internet is comprised of thousands of computer networks interconnected around the globe, including many sites located at educational institutions. It began in the 1960s when the U.S. Department of Defense directed the Advanced Research Projects Agency (ARPA) to design a means of preserving communication in the event of a nuclear attack. If all communications were issued from a centralized location, they could be destroyed, so a decentralized network of interconnected computers was designed. Researchers in various universities and laboratories found they could make use of the online communications as a means of sharing information and research findings. Gradually colleges, universities, and organizations began connecting their computers to the network, and, most importantly, they allowed others to access research information and data stored in their computers.

The Internet is primarily used for communicating with people (one-on-one or groups), gathering information, and more recently, conducting business. Teachers can use the Internet as a vast resource for lesson plans and information, and as a means of collaboration and communication. Students also benefit through learning how to gather and share information online.

Electronic mail (e-mail) is one of the most popular uses of the Internet. Communicating with a person in another country is as easy as communicating with a person in the same building. Using e-mail requires access to the Internet, an e-mail software program, and an e-mail address for the recipient of the message. An e-mail message can be addressed to one person or to a group of people.

An e-mail account also allows the user to subscribe to listservs, which are group discussions or interest groups. Classroom-to-classroom connections can be formed through subscribing to mailing lists designed to connect with people around the globe. International Email Classroom Connections (iecc-request@stolaf.edu) is one of many such lists. To subscribe to an e-mail list, a subscription request is sent to the listserv administrative address, usually just, "subscribe LISTSERV NAME," in the message body with a similar message to unsubscribe. To enroll in a listserv discussion on teaching mathematics, you can e-mail majordomo@forum.swarthmore.edu. In the body of your message, type: subscribe math-teach. Your e-mail address will be added to the listserv and information will come to your e-mail account.

Collaboration ideas can be posted through special interest groups or forums such as the Teacher Information Network (TIN), a forum on the America Online commercial network. A project idea typically has a "Call for Collaboration" subject heading and a brief description. Existing online projects can be found in many locations through education forums.

There are also a huge number of Web sites devoted to lesson plan ideas and activities. Among the most notable are TeachNet (http://www.teachnet.com), Collaborative Lesson Archive (http://faldo.atmos.uiuc.edu/TUA_Home.html), and Mathline (http://www.pbs.org/mathline).

As a research tool, the Internet offers databases of information in the form of encyclopedias, magazines, and museums. Unlike traditional materials in text form, digital information on the Internet can be updated at any time. In addition, many electronic references offer sound and video clips as well as text information.

The **World Wide Web**, commonly known as WWW, is a hypertext-based means of accessing and publishing information on the Internet. Web documents, referred to as Web pages, can combine text, graphics, sound, and video, and often contain links to related resources. Links can be words in color text, underlined words, or pictures. Because the Web is composed of digital information, it is constantly evolving and changing. For this reason, Web locations can change or disappear without warning. Also, caution should be taken when using the Web since information available on the Web is not necessarily correct or appropriate for classroom use. The Web is not currently policed for accuracy or content by any external agent.

A **search engine** is used to locate particular topics on the Web. For instance, if you are interested in locating Web sites that focus on travel, you might use a search engine and type in "travel." The search engine would search the Web for travel sites. You would be provided with a list of Web addresses with short descriptions of what you can expect to find at those sites. You could then use the descriptions to choose the sites that might provide information to help your students plan a theoretical trip using a predetermined budget. The broader your topic, the more sites you will likely be given. You could have searched under "travel and Bahamas" to narrow your results. Another benefit of search engines is that you can look up specific companies such as a particular airline company to look up prices of tickets to given locations. Some commonly used search engines are Yahoo!, Excite, and Netscape. Through Netscape, for example, a user can point and click on links to move through information and to explore. Clicking on "Net Directory" brings the user to a database listing of categories.

To access a particular Web page, enter the address or location of the page. A **URL, uniform resource locator**, is the form of the address. For example, http://education.gsfc.nasa.gov/ is the URL for NASA Education Programs, and entering that particular URL brings their home page into view.

An invaluable resource for teachers, AskERIC, can be found by using the URL http://ericir.syr.edu/ and clicking on "Virtual Library." Key areas include ERIC's Lesson Plans, ERIC's Resources, AskERIC's Info-Guides, and AskERIC Toolbox. AskERIC can also be accessed by using the URL http://ericir.syr.edu/. Another relevant site for mathematics educators is NCTM's home page at http://www.nctm.org/. This Web site has access to the *Principles and Standards for School Mathematics* document, information on upcoming meetings, and NCTM educational products and resources.

Other valuable WWW sites for teachers and others include:

Eisenhower National Clearinghouse
    http://www.enc.org

Explorer Math & Science Education Initiative
    http://unite.ukans.edu/

Geometry Center
    http://www.geom.umn.edu

Geometry Forum
    http://forum.swarthmore.edu/

Mathematics History Archive
    http://www-groups.dcs.st-and.ac.uk:80/~history/

Mathematics Problems Internet Center
    http://www.mathpro.com/math/mathCenter.html

Mathematics Virtual Library
    http://euclid.math.fsu.edu/science/math.html

SAMI: Science and Math Initiatives
    http://www.learner.org/sami/

Scholastic Central (Scholastic Network)
   http://www.scholastic.com/

Science and Math Education Resources
   http://www-hpcc.astro.washington.edu/scied/
   science.html

Technical Education Research Center
   (TERC: math./science ed.)
   http://hub.terc.edu

U.S. Department of Education Online Library
   http://www.ed.gov/

Web 66 K–12 WWW
   http://web66.coled.umn.edu/

PBS TeacherSource
   http://www.pbs.org/teachersource/math/

Access to online databases provides entire libraries of information at the user's fingertips. Unfortunately, information does not equal knowledge. Finding ways to organize, use, and share information is vital. For example, students can use statistical data such as that found in the CIA World Fact Book (http://www.odci.gov/cia) to create graphs, make comparisons, and predict trends. Challenge problems and other related bits of mathematics history can be found in various locations such as the SAMI project (http://www.learner.org/sami/).

Several versions of grocery list comparisons, such as the Global Grocery List, have provided opportunities for collaboration and data analysis in a meaningful way for students. The "Let's Compare Prices" activity (http://www.gsn.org/Roger/curr.prices.html) is repeated on a regular basis. A portion of this Web investigation is described below:

> Roger Williams told us the amount he paid for some items when he shopped in Japan. In 1995, Roger sent these prices of things from Japan.
>
>   1.5 liter bottle of Coke is $3.60
>   1 gallon diesel is $3.30
>   2 liters of oil for truck is $16.00
>   A hotel room in Tokyo is $250 per night.
>   A Big Mac with medium Coke and small fries
>   is $7.00.
>   A Big Mac Value Meal costs $9.00.

Classes from around the world can investigate prices for similar products in their locale and report these through the Internet to other participants. Results can then be shared electronically. Classes can compare their information with others and, in the process, discover the variations in currency and economic influences.

WebQuests, similar to, but more detailed than, the activity outlined above, provide a framework for inquiry-based learning on the Web. They often involve having groups of students address engaging problems, using Web sites suggested by the teacher or sites students have themselves discovered to be relevant to the solution of the problem. They can be created for any curriculum area or grade level. According to Robin (1998), each WebQuest consists of the following elements:

an *introduction*, which sets the stage and provides some background information on the problem;
a *task*, which defines the problem-solving goal;
resources, which identify preselected information sites on the Web;
a *process*, which provides guidelines for solving the problem;
guidance, which poses questions and provides directions on how best to use time, resources, and information;
a *conclusion*, which provides closure, evaluation, and a review of the concepts learned.

Novice users can also add online components to their classes by making use of Web sites such as WebCT (http://homebrew1.cs.ubc.ca/webct/) and Blackboard.com (http://www.Blackboard.com/). Without knowing any Web programming language, you can create a "course site" that brings learning materials, class discussions, and even tests online. Other similar tools are available through:

"Web Course in a Box" (http://madduck.mmd.vcu.edu/wcb/wcb.htmlm.)

"Virtual-U Education Systems" (http://kochab.cs.sfu.ca:8000/mkabout.html)

"TopClass" (http://www.wbtsystems.com/index.html)

"Lotus LearningSpace" (http://www.lotus.com/home.nsf/welcome/learnspace)

Benefits of telecommunications and multimedia to teaching and learning become obvious with use. As we expand our use and the way we apply technology, we will explore new ways to develop and deliver educational content. The greatest impact of these technologies may well be the "knocking down of classroom walls," thereby enabling students and teachers to become part of the global community of learners.

COMPUTERS IN THE PROGRAM MODE: HTML

Students and teachers who wish to explore writing code for their own Web pages can do so with very little instruction. After a brief introduction to **hypertext markup language (HTML)**, most middle-grade students can create a simple home page using the "**tags**" (or "commands") that make up the foundation of HTML. One benefit from such an activity is the recognition of the sort of thinking and planning that must go into Web design. A second stems from the problem-posing and solving activity of exploring the tags and what they "do"—and then trying to use commands to accomplish a particular, albeit simple, programming goal.

The following experiment with HTML requires that you have access to a word processing program, such as SimpleText, and access to a **Web browser**, such as

Netscape. First, open up the word processing program and choose a new blank document. Type the following tags exactly as they appear:

```
<html>
<head>
<title>
A Look at HTML and Web Design
</title>
</head>
<body>
Check this program to see how these words got on the
   screen.
</body>
</html>
```

Once you have entered this information, save (to your disk or to the desktop) this document as a text (or text only) file named "First Try." Then, open up your browser and drag the "First Try" file onto the browser's desktop. Once your file is loaded, the browser's title bar should read "A Look at HTML and Web Design" and the page should consist of a simple, plain text statement that reads, "Check this program to see how these words got on the screen."

As you can determine by analysis, each tag has a beginning (denoted by the <descriptive word>) and an end (denoted by </descriptive word>). The HTML tag tells the browser that it is reading HTML commands and script.

In addition to the tags mentioned above, a very basic set of HTML tags includes the following commands. Feel free to try these out and to explore the nature of each and the influence a particular tag or tag placement has on what is displayed on the monitor.

<B>	Bold
<I>	Italics
<U>	Underline
 	Line Break
<Hx>	Text Size (when x = 1, 2, 3, 4, 5, or 6)

If interested, you might then explore other tags, such as <IMG SRC="picture name"> and <A HREF="xx"> and determine how to color the text, how to vary the size and position of the text, how to incorporate pictures on your page, and how to add hypertext links to other Web pages.

It is not, however, necessary to learn any HTML code if you instead choose to make use of an HTML Editor such as:

Netscape Composer
   http://home.netscape.com/download/
      client_download.html?communicator4.04

Claris Home Page
   http://www.claris.com/software/highlights/
      clarispagetrial.html

Adobe PageMill
   http://www.adobe.com/prodindex/pagemill/
      main.html

or Internet Assistant for Microsoft Word
   http://www.microsoft.com/word/Internet/ia/
      default.htm

These WYSIWYG (What You See Is What You Get) editors make creating a Web page no more challenging than creating a word processing document. With these, the user simply types in what is wanted, and the appropriate HTML code is automatically applied. In fact, Internet Assistant allows the user to convert any primitive word processing files created in Microsoft Word into HTML documents ready for the Web.

COMPUTERS IN THE PROGRAM MODE: LOGO

When "lower-cost" microcomputers became available to the education arena, it was common to focus on elements of programming. In their infancy, microcomputers did not come bundled with the wealth of software choices that we now encounter. Instead, it was important, at that time, to learn to "talk" to the computer in order to make it function the way the user wanted. In the elementary school, this need to command the computer was translated into experiences in teaching children to write and run simple computer programs, most often in a language called BASIC (Beginners All-purpose Symbolic Instruction Code). The intent was not so much to teach children how to program a computer as it was to learn what the nature of programming entailed. For example, the process of interpreting the nuances in a BASIC program was used to provide insight into aspects of robotics and how machines follow rules to make decisions.

Logo, a computer language designed to promote problem-solving abilities using a computer, has found some favor in the elementary school curriculum. Logo is a graphic language that can be used for calculations, manipulations of words, writing music, and so forth, as well as for graphics. In the elementary school, it is usually the graphics mode that is explored. The graphics component of Logo is a particularly effective tool for exploring geometric concepts and principles. This aspect of Logo involves immediate reinforcement through the movement of a symbol, referred to as the turtle. Orders are given to the turtle through commands, called "primitives," such as FD 50, RT 90, BK 30, and LT 45, in which the letters represent a directive to the turtle; the number refers to a quantity for that directive (for example, FD 50 might be used to move the turtle forward 50 units). Many different versions of Logo are available. Each version is supported by its own set of primitives, but these differ only slightly in form and in use. Once one version of Logo is mastered, other versions are not difficult to learn.

To command the turtle to draw a square, you might use the following sequence of primitives:

```
FD 50 <RETURN> RT 90 <RETURN> FD 50
<RETURN> RT 90 <RETURN> FD 50 <RETURN>
RT 90 <RETURN> FD 50 <RETURN> RT 90
<RETURN>
```

Most Logo programs have a command, usually CS, to clear the screen and return the turtle to its home position before continuing. A list of some other common Logo commands can be found at the end of this section.

By combining primitives, students can create programs that demonstrate their abilities to observe patterns and make generalizations. "Procedures" are Logo programs that combine several primitives to accomplish a task. For example, the following procedure will yield a square:

```
TO SQUARE
    FD 50
    RT 90
    FD 50
    RT 90
    FD 50
    RT 90
    FD 50
    RT 90
END
```

At first glance this appears to be no less work than simply typing in the primitives. The difference is that we have defined a procedure that will produce a square whenever we type its title. That is, having defined this procedure, to form a square, just type "SQUARE" and the turtle will recall the necessary steps.

Procedures can often be shortened using "loops" that repeat a series of commands. For example, the square defined above could be written as:

```
TO SQUARE
    REPEAT 4 [FD 50 RT 90]
END
```

In this case, the bracketed primitives are carried out four times in succession.

It is also possible to write a procedure that makes use of previously defined procedures. For example, the following yields a drawing resembling a window:

```
TO WINDOW
    REPEAT 4 [SQUARE LT 90]
END
```

It is even possible to write a procedure that makes use of itself. This is called "recursion" and is illustrated by the following example that forms a flower:

```
TO FLOWER
    FD 50
    RT 81
    FLOWER
END
```

Even though this procedure has an END statement, it will continue to run because it calls itself internally. To stop this routine, you'll need to type a stop command.

Logo is most generally known for its usefulness in drawing and problem solving, but it can also be used to print information on the screen. It is possible to define a word and list procedures and to use the word and list

variables in procedures. A Logo word is a set of characters that begins with a quotation mark and ends with a blank space. For example, PRINT "Apple" will cause the computer to output "Apple." A Logo list is a collection of words or lists and must be enclosed in brackets to indicate to the computer that it is a list.

Whatever form and depth of Logo is explored, children will benefit from the exploration, hypothesis formation, and testing, and freedom to discover. Encouraging students to experiment in the Logo environment will result in enthusiasm and interest.

SOME LOGO COMPUTER TERMS

The Logo computer language can provide a powerful motivational tool for exploring such elementary school mathematics topics as geometry, measurement, problem solving, and logical reasoning. With this language, children are encouraged to hypothesize, verify, and generalize.

FD The command to move the turtle forward is FD or FORWARD. It is used in conjunction with a quantity representing millimeters, such as FD 40.

BK The command to move the turtle backward is BK or BACK. It is used in conjunction with a quantity representing millimeters, such as BK 40.

RT The command that causes the turtle to turn right is RT or RIGHT. It is used in conjunction with a quantity representing degrees, such as RT 90.

LT The command that causes the turtle to turn to the left is LT or LEFT. It is used in conjunction with a quantity representing degrees, such as LT 90.

PD The command PD or PENDOWN causes the turtle to draw when it moves.

PU The command PU or PENUP allows the turtle to move without drawing.

PE The command PE or PENERASE erases lines that the turtle moves over.

CG The command CG or CLEARGRAPHICS erases the screen and returns the turtle to its home position.

CLEAN The command CLEAN clears the draw screen but does not move the turtle.

HOME The command HOME will return the turtle to its home position but does not clear the screen.

ST The command ST or SHOWTURTLE puts the computer in the draw mode and causes the turtle to appear on the screen.

HT The command HT or HIDETURTLE makes the turtle disappear.

SS Pressing SS puts the entire screen in the graphics mode and covers up the typed commands. On some versions, the same is accomplished by typing FULLSCREEN.

RW Pressing RW returns the screen to the usual viewing mode that displays the turtle movement and the typing.

REPEAT The REPEAT command is used to have the turtle carry out a command or sequence of commands several times. It is used with a number and a bracketed set of commands, such as REPEAT 4 [FD 40 RT 90].

TO The use of TO, along with a name such as SQUARE, tells the computer that you are about to define a procedure.

END The command END signifies the end of a procedure.

POTS The command POTS prints out the names of the procedures in the workspace.

ERALL The command ERALL erases all of the procedures in the workspace.

ER The command ER or ERASE, when used with a procedure name, erases the procedure from the workspace.

SAVE The command SAVE copies the workspace to a Logo file disk.

SETBG The command SETBG changes the color of the draw screen.

SETPC The command SETPC allows the user to change the color of the turtle's pen.

SETCURSOR The command SETCURSOR allows the user to move the cursor to any point on the text screen.

The goal in examining Logo is to help the student become a better reasoner and problem solver—not a programmer—by analytically examining a series of algorithmic steps. The real benefit is in providing children with an environment in which they can learn to hypothesize how a computer deals with data by making changes in program code and examining the results. Seymour Papert, a mathematician and student of Piaget, was the person most responsible for the development of Logo. His vision was to make the computer "an object to think with," a mental tool for learning based on personal experience (Papert, 1980). This vision can be realized, especially if we don't teach programming for programming's sake, but instead examine Logo programs for valuable problem-solving experiences.

CLOSURE

Calculators are an invaluable tool in the mathematics classroom. The National Council of Teachers of Mathematics and The National Council of Supervisors of Mathematics, among other forward-thinking professional organizations, support the use of calculators in every classroom and at every level of teaching mathematics.

> The widespread impact of technology on nearly every aspect of our lives requires changes in the content and nature of school mathematics programs. In keeping with these changes, students should be able to use calculators and computers to investigate mathematical concepts and increase their mathematical understanding. (NCTM, 1989)

Calculators and computers can become tools of exploration—not replacements for skill, but to enhance understanding. In this light, technology can be used: to assist in choosing the most effective and efficient strategy for solving a problem; to simplify mathematical expressions by making use of order of operations or parentheses; to develop a working description of squaring a number and approximating a square root; to understand the meaning of overflow errors and the benefits of scientific notation; to examine the nature of a limit and a reason for not dividing by zero through dividing a constant by a progressively smaller value; and so on.

In this chapter, we introduced you to several applications of technology for the elementary and middle school classrooms. The influences of technology on the teaching and learning of mathematics are far-reaching. As you read the remainder of this text, think of how you might use computers and/or calculators to lead students to deeper understandings of mathematical concepts.

Terminology, Symbols, and Procedures

Algebraic Logic. Algebraic logic is a sequence of computations that follows the commonly taught rules used for the order of operations for computation.

Calculator-Based Laboratory (CBL). A CBL is a data-gathering device that can be used with several probes to collect different types of data. The data can then be transferred to a graphing calculator to be viewed, described, modeled, and/or manipulated. Data collected with the CBL and the appropriate probes may take the form of temperature, heart rate, light intensity, motion, and pH.

Calculator-Based Ranger (CBR). A CBR is used to collect data describing motion. This data can be transferred to a graphing calculator to be viewed, described, modeled, and/or manipulated.

CD-ROM Disc. CD-ROM discs hold a vast amount of information in digital form that can be readily accessed by computer. A single CD-ROM can store over 400 times more data than a high-density floppy disk.

Computer Assisted Instruction (CAI). Computer assisted instruction describes an individualized instructional situation where the student is presented with material by the computer in an interactive mode with systematic evaluation and basic record keeping as integral parts of the software.

Computer Managed Instruction (CMI). Computer managed instruction provides the classroom teacher with computer technology to keep records and store test information and provides prescriptive information to meet individual student needs.

Database. A database organizes information into fields and records so that the information may be easily searched, sorted, and retrieved.

Digital Camera. Digital cameras are similar to standard cameras in allowing users to take pictures using the familiar point-and-shoot technique. Once the picture is taken, it can be downloaded onto a computer for modification or enhancement and then inserted into a document or sent out on the Internet.

Electronic Mail (e-mail). E-mail is one of the most popular uses of the Internet. Using e-mail requires access to the Internet, an e-mail software program, and an e-mail address for the recipient of the message. E-mail allows the user to send a typed message around the world instantaneously.

Graphics Program. A graphics program can by used to create banners, school flyers, and geometric shapes. Graphic programs are often "connected" to other programs and can be used to enhance documents created within the other programs.

Hypermedia. Hypermedia refers to an electronic environment that allows the user to quickly connect to other points of information that may take the form of text, graphics, music, animation, or digitized audio or video by clicking on words or graphics.

Hypertext Markup Language (HTML). HTML is a computer language used to format and lay out documents so that they can be viewed with a Web browser.

Internet. The Internet comprises thousands of computer networks interconnected electronically around the globe, including many sites located at educational institutions.

Motion Detectors. Motion detectors are used with the Calculator-Based Laboratory (CBL) or as part of the Calculator-Based Ranger (CBR) to measure the movement of an object. That object could be a person walking in front of the sensor, a disk that is swung on a pendulum, or a ball that is bounced.

Multimedia. Multimedia refers to the combination of visual and auditory information controlled by the computer. It can incorporate text, graphics, animation, photography, video, music, and sound.

Order of Operation Rules for Computation. The order of operation rules for computation describes the order in which arithmetic operations are to be performed in a given problem in accordance with algebraic logic. According to these rules, operations within parentheses are to be completed first, then operations with exponents, then multiplication or division as they are encountered from left to right, and then addition or subtraction as they are encountered from left to right.

Search Engine. A search engine is used to locate particular topics on the World Wide Web. Some common search engines are Yahoo!, Excite, and Netscape.

Software Types:

   Drill and Practice. Drill and practice software provides students with skills and/or concepts to be memorized that are subject to immediate recall.

   Educational Game. Educational game software uses a "game" setting to provide the motivation for students to develop skills and/or concepts.

   Exploration Tool. Exploration tool software allows the student to look for patterns that would be difficult to explore without the computer's ability to generate many examples quickly and easily.

   Material Generation. Material generation software can be used to make tests, overhead transparencies, or activity sheets for students. A teacher might use this software to generate several different triangles for students to use to explore angle measures.

   Problem Solving. Problem-solving software allows the student to generate and test conjectures that would not be easy to test without the use of a computer.

   Records Management. Records management software is used to keep records, score test information, and compute grades. This type of software can also be used to generate progress reports to send home to parents.

   Simulation. Simulation software establishes an environment that would not be easily accessible in a classroom. The user is then able to experience consequences to actions that would not be feasible in a live situation.

   Tutorial. The purpose of tutorial software is to assist in the teaching of concepts. It is frequently used to introduce (or reintroduce) a topic.

Spreadsheet. A spreadsheet organizes information into intersecting rows and columns. The most notable feature of the spreadsheet is the facility with which it can be used for calculations.

Tag. A tag is a command that is used to communicate to the Web browser how a document should appear on the Web.

Uniform Resource Locator (URL). A URL is the address or location of a particular Web page and can be used to access that particular Web page.

Web Browser. A Web browser is software used to view the Web. Some examples of Web browsers are Netscape and Microsoft Explorer.

World Wide Web (WWW). The World Wide Web is a hypertext- or hypermedia-based means of accessing and publishing information on the Internet. It is commonly referred to as WWW or the Web.

Practice Exercises for Teachers

Exercises that appear in this location in other chapters are designed as content checks for the reader of this book. Since this chapter (like Chapters 1, 2, and 3) is not centered on mathematics content, per se, there are no practice exercises for teachers given here. Ideas for student classroom activities on the concepts and ideas discussed in this chapter can be found in Part 2 of *Today's Mathematics*, the Student Resource Book. There are also calculator and computer activities included in Chapters 5–17 in Part 2.

Teaching Competencies and Self-Assessment Tasks

1. Locate the standards related to the use of calculators and computers in the NCTM *Principles and Standards for School Mathematics*. Discuss examples of how calculators and computers might be used within a contemporary elementary mathematics classroom to meet each of the standards.

2. Locate at least three elementary or middle school problem-solving activities that incorporate the use of a calculator in the exploration process. Complete the activities and discuss how the calculator enhances each activity.

3. Use the Calculator-Based Ranger's program for matching a graph of distance as a function of time. Try to match the graph you are given by walking in front of the graph. After several attempts, write a short story that describes a child moving from one place to another with stops and other changes in speed and direction. Sketch a graph to match your story.

4. Locate and examine at least two different examples of problem-solving or exploration software. Describe how each might fit within a contemporary elementary curriculum.

5. Locate at least two different elementary-level calculators (one calculator should be a four-function calculator and the other should be a fraction calculator), and explore the features and functions available on each. Write a comparison of the calculators and their uses.

6. Identify at least one piece of software for each of the software types and applications listed in the chapter. State which software fits with which category and provide a justification for your choice. Examples of software types are drill and practice, tutorial, and simulation. Examples of applications are spreadsheets, databases, and word processors.

7. Locate recent articles on incorporating multimedia in elementary mathematics instruction. Report on the ways in which it was used.

8. Locate a dynamic Web site that contains "rich" data and design an elementary-level activity incorporating the data that will require student interpretation and use.

9. Locate and examine at least two Web sites that contain lesson plans for elementary or middle school mathematics.

10. Browse the Web in search of information related to your personal hobbies. Once you have found at least one relevant site, explore the links to that site.

Related Readings and Teacher Resources

For related readings on topics found in this chapter as well as additional material on useful Web sites and software packages, see the corresponding chapter in Part 2 of *Today's Mathematics*, the Student Resource Book.

Chapter 5

Problem Solving, Decision Making, and Communicating in Mathematics

Teaching Competencies

Upon completing this chapter, you will be able to:

- Describe the nature of a "problem" and the problem-solving process.

- State and use a variety of strategies in solving problems.

- Incorporate contemporary thought on integrating problem solving into classroom instruction.

- Describe the role played by logic and reasoning in a contemporary elementary school mathematics classroom.

- State examples of inductive and deductive reasoning that commonly occur in everyday life.

Τ here is an old adage that states, "In our lives, there is nothing certain but death and taxes." Although there may be a hint of truth in that statement, there are many other certainties that we all face. For example, we can all be certain that we will encounter *problems* that influence our lives and that require us to make *decisions* leading to solutions to those problems. Problem solving and decision making are clearly two abilities necessary in day-to-day life. Yet studies such as the National Assessment of Educational Progress and the Third International Mathematics and Science Study continue to indicate that the problem-solving and decision-making abilities of children are sadly lacking. Also, teachers often express a feeling of inadequacy when attempting to teach problem-solving techniques to children. Perhaps if we concentrate on methods of developing our own problem-solving strategies, then our efforts to assist children in improving their performances when they are faced with such tasks will not only increase but be more effective.

The NCTM *Principles and Standards for School Mathematics* identifies five standards that they refer to as "process" standards. These process standards are:

problem solving;
reasoning;
communication;
connections; and
representations.

These process standards reflect major aspects of competency that are essential to increased sophistication with mathematics and its power.

As students learn mathematics, they will develop an increasing repertoire of problem-solving skills, a wide range of mathematical "habits of mind," and increasing sophistication in mathematical argument. Also, students should become proficient at expressing themselves mathematically, both orally and in writing, gain fluency in the language of mathematics and be able to make connections within mathematics and from mathematics to other disciplines. (NCTM, 1998, p. 46)

As you study the material presented in this chapter, consider the foundation it presents and how this impacts your perspective of the material presented in the rest of this book.

THE NATURE OF PROBLEM SOLVING

Before continuing further, we must describe what we mean by the term *problem solving*. In mathematics, we sometimes associate problem solving with word or story problems that we might remember from elementary school textbooks. While such problems do encompass a portion of problem solving, they represent only a very small portion. As it is commonly defined in contemporary mathematics education, **problem solving** describes the process an individual uses to respond to

and overcome obstacles or barriers when a solution or method of solution to a problem is not immediately obvious. Given this context, problem solving is very much an interdisciplinary activity and should not be restricted to a single unit in mathematics. Throughout this book you will find applications of problem solving in all topic areas and suggestions for activities across disciplines.

You may have heard statements such as "$3 + 5 = \square$" referred to as problems. In reality, for most children this is not a problem but is more aptly termed an *exercise*. This distinction is more than a case of semantics. An exercise is typically solved by a collection of prescribed steps, commonly called an *algorithm*, that leads to a solution. A problem, on the other hand, requires greater insight and analysis before an approach to a solution is offered. An example of a problem for a child might be "How many sheets of paper would we need to total a weight equal to 2 pounds?" Certainly, an "exercise" for some people is a "problem" for others—not because the answer is unknown, but rather because a method of determining the answer is unknown. "Solving problems" requires that the learner be involved in decision making whereas "answering exercises" involves applying an algorithm or a set of structured step-by-step procedures.

To clarify the nature of a problem, consider these four examples. First, a "traditional" textbook word problem:

▪ Billy has three apples and Margie has five apples.
   How many more apples does Margie have than Billy?

Second, a multistep textbook word problem:

▪ Marilyn has a square garden bordered by a 36-foot fence.
   If Marilyn wishes to use that same fence to border a 4-foot by 9-foot rectangular garden, will she have enough fence?
   How much fence will be left over?

Third, a nontraditional word problem:

▪ Juli and Ginny are taking turns in a game of darts on the board shown.

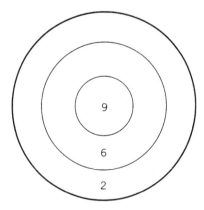

If a game is won with an exact score of 34, what is the fewest number of darts that can be thrown before a winner is declared?

Fourth, a problem situation that you may recognize from your life:

- How much carpet should Jeff purchase to cover the floor?

The first two examples illustrate the important point made about "problems" in the previous paragraph: What is considered a problem by some may simply be an exercise for others. Although many children will quickly recognize that the first example can be solved by subtraction, others will not. Some younger children may even feel that the answer to the question is simply yes, believing that all that was requested was an answer to "Does Margie have more apples?" The second example, however, is more likely to be a problem since an immediate solution or a method of solution is not necessarily evident. Should we divide the 36 by the 4? Should we multiply the 4 and the 9 and see what we get for a product? Even though the problem makes use of knowledge of shape and perimeter, it is not a straightforward application of an algorithm. We must analyze the situation more carefully if we wish to arrive at a meaningful method of answering the question.

In the third example, still another aspect of the nature of a problem is revealed. In this case, not only must we analyze the situation carefully, but we must also be willing to create a method of attack. There is no formula that we can fit—we must apply critical reasoning if we are to succeed without resorting to blind guessing. In this case it is also important to note that even when we discover that 6 is the fewest number of darts that yields a total of 34 (two 9s, two 6s, and two 2s), we must also note that the players are taking turns. Thus a total of 11 darts is the fewest that could be thrown before a winner is declared.

The fourth example is, perhaps, one of the purest forms of a problem. How is this fourth example different from the others? In the first three, the information needed to solve the problem was present in the setting. The problem solver was asked to read the information and then decide if, when, and how to use it. In the fourth case, however, the information needed to solve the problem is not present. In fact, part of the "problem" is deciding what information is important when attempting to find an answer to such a problem. For example, how many rooms do we wish to carpet? Does that include the hallway or entryway? Is money a factor in this decision? Is color? Is availability? These represent only a few of the real-life concerns that we may need to address as we seek a solution. In this last example, as in real life, the question came first, followed by the identification of important information, which, in turn, was followed by the collection and analysis of that information and the application of it to isolate a potential solution.

It is commonly acknowledged that problem solving is a critical aspect of the education (mathematical and otherwise) of our populace and that more emphasis must be placed on developing problem-solving strategies and integrating their application across the curriculum and through the life experiences of children.

The National Council of Teachers of Mathematics has long called for increased attention to problem solving. Nevertheless, an analysis of problem solving as presented in many elementary school textbooks indicates that present teaching is inadequate.

Many elementary school mathematics textbooks and, consequently, some elementary school teachers, mistakenly overemphasize the role of traditional word problems in the development of problem-solving abilities. Some shortcomings common to elementary school mathematics textbooks may include the following:

- Word problems are relegated to a single section at the end of a unit rather than being a constant presence throughout that unit.
- Word problems are used that seem only to require the concepts studied in a particular unit rather than integrating topics from different units and different subjects.
- Word problems tend to focus on one specific interpretation of an operation, such as only "take-away" subtraction or only "partitive" division, thereby narrowing the child's perspective of how these operations can be interpreted in different ways.
- Word problems are written in such a way that children are conditioned to look for "key words" to interpret what to do rather than focusing on finding context clues in the "action" that provides the real context clues in the problem.
- Word problems often oversimplify and trivialize the applications they are intended to demonstrate.

All these observations suggest that we must reexamine the ways in which we approach problem solving in the elementary classroom if we are to truly nurture thinking about mathematics. The last point in the preceding list, although not necessarily more important than the others, is of particular concern. In fact, if we attend to it effectively, we lessen the possibilities that the other weak points will occur.

Applications play a critically important role in the mathematics curriculum. Children need to see and comprehend applications of the concepts they study. Everyday uses of concepts such as estimation, fractions, percents, decimals, ratios and proportions, geometry, measurement, statistics, and probability should receive at least as much attention as the concepts themselves. Applications provide a context in which a given set of skills may be practiced, as well as an opportunity to demonstrate, during motivations and follow-ups, situations in which skills are meaningfully and purposefully used. However, if these applications are presented in one- or two-sentence word problems, they become "unworldly" and artificial. The very aspects that make them interesting in the first place are stripped away.

A word problem that can be solved by simply applying the operation currently being studied is not really a problem. A word problem that only includes information necessary for its solution is not really a challenge. A word problem that requires the child to copy a procedure shown at the top of the page is not really a test of the child's ability to solve a problem. Perhaps we need to direct much, but not all, of our attention away from word problems, as such, and focus on the nature of problems instead.

In life, problems do not come to us with labels. We cannot count on all of Monday's problems to be solvable by dividing. In life, we begin with the question and then collect the information we believe we may need. We then sort out the data that are relevant to the problem, abandoning some information and, perhaps, gathering more. The approach to a solution is not necessarily well formulated; in fact, it may be quite different from the one we used to solve the last problem we considered. It may even be a procedure that we have not tried before.

Careful selection of problems is critical to nurturing successful problem-solving abilities in children. Challenging students to think about mathematics can be difficult. Some students have simply not had to actually think about mathematics in the past. Instead of encouraging a narrow view of problems, consider presenting problems in one or more of the following ways:

- with pictures
- without numbers
- involving manipulatives
- with more than one solution
- with real-world applications
- with no easily identifiable answer
- requiring more time to solve than one mathematics period
- requiring the collection of data
- requiring the following of specific directions
- requiring interpretation of tables and graphs
- requiring a drawing to be made
- with no solution
- with extraneous information
- requiring use of a formula
- involving logic and inference
- requiring inductive or deductive reasoning

Focusing on problem solving helps us to focus a child's attention on generalization. A child's innate curiosity causes him or her to pose questions such as "Why?", "When?", and "How?" Unfortunately, these questions, as common as they may be in the child's mind, often remain unstated. By exploring problem-solving situations, we encounter many opportunities for hypothesizing—for saying "What if?" and examining the consequences.

Ideas are like clay. If you want them to reflect something new and different, you must mold and shape them. It may be necessary to look at things from a new perspective—perhaps inside out or upside down. Hunch playing becomes a valued friend as you learn to try things that you suspect won't lead anywhere, but that may seem to have a shot. You break rules and make rules to eventually reach conclusions that are sound. Unfortunately, students often perceive rules—which are really no more than generalizations—as *merely* ways to get to a correct answer. Without proper guidance, students will neither recognize nor appreciate the role of generalizations in understanding mathematics.

Mathematical thinking is nurtured through problem-solving experiences that do not restrict a child's avenues of success to a single route. Problem solving should be systematic but not rule-bound. Reliance on one method can create difficulty rather than lessen it—instead of trying to solve the problem, the student may simply try to find the "right" way to solve the problem.

By definition, divergence in approach can lead to delightful open-mindedness for alternative solutions. Fascinating discussions can result from considering what is meant by a question and how it might be answered. For example:

- How might a glass be dropped from a height of 10 feet and not break?
- How could we find out how many fish are in a lake?
- What might we need for our trip to the amusement park, and why do we need it?
- What price do we need to charge for the school spaghetti dinner to cover our expenses?

When confronting a problem, some see a challenge and some see a wall. It's the level of anxiety, blended with individual personality traits, that determine the next move. Sometimes just getting started creates a level of frustration that becomes more of a problem than the problem itself. Some students fail to realize that problems are not like exercises—problems are neither straightforward nor quickly answered. Often, problems do not lend themselves to algorithms or prescribed procedures. They require novel approaches and risk taking—the willingness to be wrong during the search for what is right.

Students require three sets of skills to solve problems: *empirical* skills, such as computation and measuring; *application* skills, for handling common situations; and *thinking* skills, for working through situations that are unfamiliar.

A person's ability to solve a problem depends on many factors, such as conceptual style, organizational ability, techniques of processing information, mathematical background, desire for a solution, and confidence in the ability to tackle the problem. Students who seek the "rule to follow" or the "algorithm to use" or the "key words" that tell them what to do will not become proficient problem solvers. To gain power in solving problems, a child must be willing to invest in understanding the problem. The child must learn to unravel the problem before trying to state the answer.

Children need to learn how strategies can help them work through any problem they encounter, including traditional and nontraditional word problems. If textbook word problems are too narrow in scope to require or encourage student thinking, teachers should supplement assignments with problems and investigations that incorporate several strategies in their possible solutions.

Research Snapshot

What are the perspectives of children on what it means to do mathematics in problem-solving classrooms?

Franke and Carey (1997) studied thirty-six first graders from classrooms that reflected the spirit of the reform movement in mathematics education. The children perceived of mathematics as a problem-solving endeavor in which communicating mathematical thinking was an integral part of the task. They assumed a shared responsibility with the teacher for their mathematics learning. The students also explained, justified, and accepted a variety of solution strategies, valuing all solutions equally.

Are these perspectives in line with what you hope your students believe about mathematics? If the students value all solution strategies equally, what will motivate them to progress to more sophisticated strategies?

Franke, M. L., & Carey, D. A. (1997). Young children's perceptions of mathematics in problem-solving environments. *Journal for Research in Mathematics Education*, *28*, 8–25.

For additional research briefs, "ERIC Digests" lets you search more than 2,000 short syntheses of research on a range of education topics. The syntheses were produced by the Educational Resources Information Center (ERIC). Check http://ed.gov/databases/ERIC_Digests/index/

PROBLEM-SOLVING STRATEGIES

First, it is important to approach problem solving with the attitude of meeting an intellectual challenge rather than finishing a menial task. Second, an open-minded initial examination of the problem helps avoid a tunnel-visioned approach to the solution. Be prepared to try unusual ideas and take some risks that might lead to a dead end—often, they don't. Third, persistence, with thought, is often a major ally in problem solving. Take your bearings frequently. Remind yourself of where you are in the problem and what you need to do. Problem solving is not a race with a stopwatch. At times, it pays dividends to stand back and reflect. Fourth, reflection should not only occur during the problem-solving process, but after as well. Look back at the problem and the solution and see if they match. Too often, we end up with an answer that doesn't answer the question asked.

Now let us carefully examine some of the more common strategies children are encouraged to use to help them develop problem-solving techniques. Traditionally, a four- or five-step process was taught: Read the problem, determine what is given, decide what is to be found, and then solve and check. These steps do not really help children solve problems.

To use an analogy, it is true that these steps of problem solving do represent the *route* to a solution, but they do not represent a *map* that will guide us along the route. That is, to solve a problem, we must go through these steps, but *how* do we go through them? Assuming the appropriate reading skills, we can all read the problem, but *how* do we find what is given (especially if either too much, or not enough, is given)? *How* do we decide what is to be found? And *how* do we solve it?

These are the real questions that, if answered, will provide the map for the route.

As useful as the preceding comments might be, we still need to arm the students with strategies that actually help them solve the problem. That is, what tools can students turn to when they feel that they don't know what to do next? Rather than teach them to ask the teacher what to do next, let's teach them to recognize and apply potentially effective strategies. What are some of the **problem-solving strategies** that we can teach children to apply?

Identifying Patterns

Children who have a background in using attribute blocks, classifying, looking for patterns, and extending patterns are definitely ready for solving problems with patterns. This problem-solving strategy can begin in kindergarten and can be extended to all other grade levels.

If we charge $.25 for a ticket for our play, how much should we charge for 2 or 3 tickets? A pattern is developed: If 1 ticket costs $.25, then 2 tickets will cost $.25 + $.25. Three tickets will sell for $.25 + $.25 + $.25. This is a pattern. Now we can put the data into a table, as shown below.

Number of tickets	1	2	3	4	5	6
Price to charge	$.25	$.50	$.75	$1.00	$1.25	$1.50

Now we are beginning to bring the strategy of looking for patterns together with the next strategy to be developed.

Creating Tables and Charts

Learning to organize data into tables and charts is a technique that can help children solve problems. Consider this problem: I want to build a pen for my dog. I would like the dog to have as much play area as possible. In the garage is a roll of fencing that I will use; it is 36 meters long. What should be the dimensions of the pen for the dog? Children should think about the data involved in the problem and organize the information into a table. The pertinent ideas involved are perimeter, length, width, and area. Let us make a table for the problem by systematically entering data into the table. (Other types of tables would also be acceptable.)

Perimeter (in meters)	Length (in meters)	Width (in meters)	Area (in square meters)
36	17	1	17
36	16	2	32
36	15	3	45
36	14	4	56
36	13	5	65
36	12	6	72
36	11	7	77
36	10	8	80
36	9	9	81
36	8	10	80

After the children have made a table, discuss it with them. You will want to use questions such as "Why does the area start to increase?" and "At what point will the area begin to decrease?" The children should discover that the greatest area is obtained when the length and width are the same. The children should generalize that a square will have more area than related rectangles with the same perimeter.

Note that at this point the teacher is discussing with the students the existing concepts and relationships rather than the answer to the problem. Organizing data and using tables are important mathematics problem-solving strategies. The problem begins with a question, and then a technique for solving the problem is developed by using a table. Many examples of this type should be used so children will learn the problem-solving strategy. Use problems that will require the use of many different operations.

Dramatization

For many years, dramatization has been used to help children understand reading lessons, and it represents another strategy that can be applied to problem solving. How many apples are in Tom's box now if Tom began with an empty box and Mary put in 3 apples and George put in 4 apples? Using dramatization, have children take the parts of Tom, Mary, and George and act out the problem.

If the children are functioning at the appropriate level of abstraction, ask them to write *a mathematical sentence* for what they observed: $3 + 4 = \square$. What number correctly completes this number sentence? What is the answer to the problem? Tom now has 7 apples in his box.

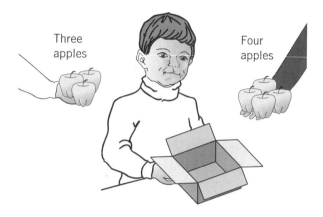

Three apples
Four apples

Make the problems gradually more complicated. All children could participate at once by providing them with coins and challenging them to find out how many different ways they can make 10 cents.

One dime

Two nickels

One nickel
Five pennies

Ten pennies

When developmentally appropriate, children should be encouraged to write mathematical sentences to express the problem-solving situation and to use a complete sentence to answer. This practice will cut down on some of the more careless mistakes.

Make a Drawing or Diagram

Another technique to help children solve mathematical problems is to make a drawing or diagram. Encourage children to make sketches to help them visualize spatial relationships. How many tiles will be needed to place a new floor in a given room? Draw a sketch of the room, and then draw squares to represent the tiles. This will help the children comprehend the concept and develop a technique for solving area problems. Of course, this technique should be used to develop understanding of the concept of area for figures of all shapes. A diagram is also helpful in problems dealing with measurement situations such as "It is twice as far from city A to city B as it is from city B to city C. If all three cities are connected by roads, and if city A is 10 miles from city B, what is the shortest distance possible from city A to city C?" Of course, making a diagram can be utilized in problem-solving situations besides geometry and measurement.

Guess and Check

Another effective problem-solving strategy that can be taught to children is to guess an answer and then check the appropriateness of this answer. Children should be encouraged to make reasonable guesses and not just select a random number. For instance, ask them what single number can be used to make $4 \times \square + \square = 30$? What number belongs in the boxes? Take a guess and then check it. Will the number 4 make the sentence true? Check: $4 \times 4 + 4 = 20$. No. Discuss with the children what they have learned. Why doesn't 4 make the sentence true? Because using 4 gives an answer that is too small. Then what should we try? Do you want to try 5? $4 \times 5 + 5 = 25$. Discuss the guess again. Is the value 5 closer to the correct number? How do you know? What number do you want to try now? Should we try 10? That would be too much. Why? Should we try 6? $4 \times 6 + 6 = 30$. This checks out, so 6 is the number that fits into the box. It's important to note that "guess and check" is really more like "guess, check, and revise your guess from what you've learned."

Estimation

Estimation is a tool that has always had a significant application in problem solving. It may be true in everyday life that we use estimation more frequently than we perform exact computations. Estimation often provides an answer that is sufficient for the question asked. Estimation can also be an effective tool when the numbers are too "messy" to compute an exact answer. Estimation is, at times, the only way to get any answer at all. Estimation also provides a means of determining whether an answer is a reasonable or unreasonable one.

The technological age is placing new emphasis on estimation in the mathematics program. Calculators and computers can calculate much more quickly and efficiently than we can. However, malfunctions of equipment (rare) and poorly selected or incorrectly entered data (more common) are but a few reasons we might arrive at absurd responses from technological devices. Estimation should be used to verify that such computations are, at least, reasonable answers to the problem as we understand it.

For example, suppose that it is late in the evening on the final night of the school play and we wish to know how much money we collected. We're certain that we did well; in fact, we know we sold 321 tickets, but we don't want to take time to count the receipts until morning. If we sold 294 adult tickets at $7.50 each and 27 youth tickets at $4.00 each, how much money was received? Using a calculator, we come up with a total of $1378.50. Does this amount seem reasonable? We can check by using *approximately* 300 adult tickets at $7.00 ($2100.00), and we quickly see that a mistake must have been made with the calculator. (Can you determine what it might have been?)

Let us consider the same problem and the same question, but apply a slightly different interpretation of estimation to help us. As before, we wish to determine about how much we collected, but a calculator is not readily available. Instead, we elect to use numbers that approximate the real situation. That means, for example, that we sold about 300 adult tickets for about $7.00 and about 30 youth tickets for $4.00. Thus we should have about $2220.00 ($2100.00 plus $120.00) when we count the receipts in the morning.

When we approximate numbers, we sometimes use a specific method frequently referred to as *rounding*. This method can take many forms but is most commonly stated as "Five or more, round up; less than five, round down." If, for instance, we strictly followed this rule in our school play problem, we might have rounded the 294 adult tickets to 290 (if rounding to the nearest ten) or to 300 (if rounding to the nearest hundred). We would round the youth tickets to 30 (to the nearest ten) or to 0 (to the nearest hundred).

It is not difficult to imagine how following a specific rounding rule might lead to less-than-desirable approximations. Consider the task that a bank might face in rounding all of its average daily balances to the nearest dollar. Of course, the bank wants to ensure that it does not lose money because of this rounding process. If the computer is programmed to use the "five or more, round up" method, then it is possible that the estimate of total deposits will be more than they actually are. In this case, the bank would end up paying more interest than it is required to pay.

To illustrate this, consider a hypothetical bank that had only four accounts—$16, $28, $45, and $37. If the interest were computed by rounding to the nearest $10, then the bank would be figuring interest on $20, $30, $50, and $40 (a total of $140) instead of on the actual amount of $126. This may not seem like much in this case, but imagine the losses a bank would incur if it followed this procedure for thousands of accounts. A more appropriate alternative rounding "rule" to use in this case might be, "If the amount is even, round up—if odd, round down." This means that roughly half of all accounts will be rounded up, and half down. In our simple example, the rounded total would be $120—a closer estimate to the actual amount. (What other possible rounding "rules" can you create, and in what situations might they be most appropriate or effective?)

Another common rounding strategy is often referred to as "front-end estimation." This method is frequently employed when a range of answers is all that is needed. For example, if we wanted a rough idea of the total cost to repair a car that had $437 damage to the front fender, $223 damage to the side mirror, and $589 to the left side, then we could use front-end estimation to get a low total of $400 + $200 + $500 ($1100) or a high total of $500 + $300 + $600 ($1400).

Solve a Simpler Problem

Our last example in the previous section shows another aspect of estimating in problem solving: Sometimes it makes sense to solve a simpler, related problem when searching for a solution to a more complex problem. In a sense, this strategy involves turning a problem into an exercise (a distinction made earlier in this chapter). In our example, it would have been much more difficult to show the effects of a different rounding technique if we had used real figures from a real bank's files. There would have been too many accounts and too many dollar and cent amounts to deal with easily. The point being made and the reasoning behind it were better explained by creating a simpler situation that mirrored the more challenging real-life one. Often, the use of a simpler, but related, problem will point the way to a method of finding a solution that can be applied to the original problem.

For example, consider the following problem. A person should drink about $2\frac{3}{4}$ liters of water every day. How much water should 5 people take on a $6\frac{1}{2}$-day camping trip? If there is some confusion as to how to approach this, change the figures to 3 liters of water, 5 people, and 6 days, and restate the problem. The use of less intimidating numbers may lighten the perceived level of difficulty of the problem. You may even want to temporarily eliminate some of the additional considerations as you search for a solution method. In this case, for example, how would you find out how much water was needed for just *one* person?

The discussion of the techniques of estimating to solve a problem gives rise to another important concern. Sometimes approximations of an answer are all that we can achieve. Some problem-solving situations do not lend themselves to exact answers. Children need experience with problem situations where approximations are appropriate to estimate an answer. For example, how many jelly beans are in a gallon container? Children could count the number of jelly beans they can place into a half-pint jar and then multiply to approximate the number of jelly beans in a gallon container. If a half-pint container is not available, any small container may be used; count the number of jelly beans in one small full

container, and then count the number of times that the container must be filled to fill the gallon container. Similar estimating techniques can be used to estimate the number of blades of grass on a football field, the number of windows in a skyscraper, or the area of a playground.

Working Backward

Another strategy that can lead us to a solution to a problem is to look at it from another perspective—working backward. The dart game problem we referred to earlier in this chapter offers one example of this technique. Recall that we needed an exact total of 34 to win on this dart board, and that we wanted the fewest number of tosses.

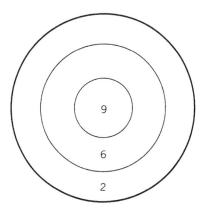

We can begin at the end, that is, with our total of 34 and then subtract the largest amount possible on a toss, 9, to get 25. Is there a way to get 25 that uses another 9? Yes, for example, one 9 and four 4s. Subtract another 9 to get 16. Is there a way to get 16 that uses another 9? No, one 9 means we need 7 more, which we can't get with just 6s and 2s. Therefore, we can throw two darts and get a total of 18 points. Thus we need 16 more points made up of just 6s and two 2s. So the fewest number of darts, by one person, to get exactly 34 is two 9s, two 6s, and two 2s.

Working backward can also be used as an effective strategy in many "logic" problems. Consider a game in which the loser has to double each opponents' chips. After three rounds of the game, you know that each player has 8 chips. You also know that player A lost the first round, player B lost the next round, and player C lost the third round. How many chips did each player have at the start of the game? We begin with the end; that is, we know each player had 8 chips after the third round and that player C lost that round. Thus players A and B must have each had 4 chips at the end of round 2, while player C must have had 16. Since player B lost round 2, we know that before that, player A must have had 2 chips and player C had 8, with B having 14. Finally, since player A lost the first round, we know that the game must have begun with player B having 7 chips, player C having 4, and player A having 13. Now, to check our solution, we play the game as described.

As we hope you have noted by now, you will certainly have greater success in problem solving by "mixing and matching" problem-solving strategies to serve your needs. In the "chip" problem, it might be beneficial to your understanding if you not only work backward but also use objects or a diagram to act it out. This leads us back to perhaps the most effective problem-solving approach of all—*open-minded brainstorming* and *divergent thought* on the part of the problem solver. If we broaden our focus, we are much more likely to identify given and needed information, check for hidden assumptions, and account for all possible answers.

As children develop problem-solving abilities, the teacher must constantly remind them to apply basic ideas in the process of solving problems, as follows:

1. Read the problem several times and restate it to make sure you understand the problem.

2. Think about the relation between the information given in the problem and what is being asked.

3. Translate the problem, if appropriate, into a mathematical sentence that expresses this relation.

4. Check the mathematical sentence with the original problem.

5. Find the solution of the mathematical sentence.

6. Write a sentence that translates the mathematics back into English.

APPROACHING WORD PROBLEMS EFFECTIVELY

For children to develop successful problem-solving techniques, instruction must begin early and be constantly nurtured as each new mathematical concept is introduced and developed. The establishment of problem-solving techniques should begin in the primary grades: First, discuss everyday situations that require mathematics, such as "How many cups will be needed for the children at two tables if there are four children at one table and five at another?" In this way, children will begin to relate mathematics to real-life situations.

As children begin to learn to read, they can be given problems using rebuses. A *rebus* is a picture that is substituted for a word. Study the example:

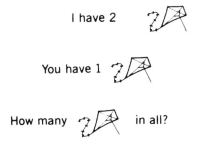

This example should be answered in a complete sentence. A child might print and use a rebus such as:

There are 3 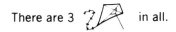 in all.

Make sure that the picture used for a rebus can easily be drawn by children. Do not use animals or other things that are difficult for children to draw. Stickers may also be used as rebuses.

Before beginning word problems with a class, have children read the examples aloud as the other children follow along silently. The children will need to reread each example before they attempt to solve it. A child who is still having difficulty in reading the examples may want to use a cassette recorder with the examples taped as an aid.

In these first steps to solving word problems, have the children develop good habits right from the beginning. Children should read and reread an example before beginning work on paper. If appropriate, ask that an equation be written for each example (even if the word problem is easily solved), and do not accept incomplete answers. You are teaching a technique as well as how to obtain correct answers. For instance, consider this example:

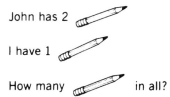

Do not accept a written 3 for the solution to this example. The equation $2 + 1 = \square$ should be written, and the solution should be given as "There are 3 ⬚ in all." Use of this procedure encourages children to think about the reasonableness of their solution. Each solution is a complete spoken or written sentence that must make sense in response to the question the children are trying to answer.

The following examples suggest how mathematical sentences may be written for other word problems:

- Bob has 32 marbles. He wins 17 more marbles in a game. How many marbles does Bob have now?

We can represent the problem as a mathematical sentence this way:

32	+	17	=	□
Original Number of Marbles		Plus the Marbles Won in the Game		Total Number of Marbles

To solve the problem, we must find a solution—in this case another way to say 32 + 17, since our mathematical sentence is an equation.

$$32 + 17 = 49$$

Bob has 49 marbles.

Now look at another example:

■ Bob has a certain number of marbles. He won 23 marbles in a game today. He now has 47 marbles. How many marbles did Bob have before?

What kind of mathematical sentence can we use to represent this story problem? Some pupils might write addition sentences, and others might write subtraction sentences.

$$\square + 23 = 47$$
$$47 - 23 = \square$$
$$\square = 47 - 23$$
$$23 + \square = 47$$

While the first sentence listed best fits the language and action of the problem statement, each of these mathematical sentences is an acceptable representation of the story problem. Examples such as this show the flexibility of thinking and interpretation and the variety of approaches to any problem that contemporary mathematics emphasizes.

Here are two more problems:

■ How many eggs are there in 3 dozen? How many different mathematical sentences can you write for this problem?

$$3 \times 12 = \square$$
$$12 \times 3 = \square$$

If each of 32 children in a class has a desk and they are arranged in rows with 8 children in each row, how many rows of desks are there in the classroom?

How many different mathematical sentences may be written for this problem?

$$32 \div 8 = \square$$
$$32 \div \square = 8$$
$$8 \times \square = 32$$
$$\square \times 8 = 32$$

As children learn to represent word problems as mathematical sentences, the teacher should check their work carefully. Sometimes children have difficulties reading and comprehending the problems, and these difficulties are sometimes incorrectly assumed to be a lack of mathematical ability.

There are many different types of problems for which we must learn to write mathematical sentences. Let's look at more examples. Compare the position of the unknown part in each mathematical sentence and its relation to the action suggested in the English sentence.

1. Jon had three football cards. Lila gave Jon her four football cards. How many football cards does Jon have in all?

    Mathematical sentence: $3 + 4 = \square$

    ■ Answer: Jon has seven football cards in all.

2. Bonnie collects seashells. After Sally gave Bonnie two shells, Bonnie then had eight shells. How many shells did Bonnie have at the beginning?

    Mathematical sentence: $\square + 2 = 8$

    ■ Answer: Bonnie had six shells at the start.

3. Joy had three pencils. George gave Joy the pencils he owed her, and now Joy has eight pencils. How many pencils did George owe Joy?

    Mathematical sentence: $3 + \square = 8$

    ■ Answer: George owed Joy five pencils.

4. Millie had five rings. She gave three of the rings to Sue. How many rings does Millie have left?

    Mathematical sentence: $5 - 3 = \square$

    ■ Answer: Millie has two rings left.

5. Karen had seven pictures made of her teacher. Karen gave some of the pictures to other classmates. When Karen counted the number of pictures she had left, she found three. How many pictures did Karen give away?

    Mathematical sentence: $7 - \square = 3$

    ▌Answer: Karen gave away four pictures of her teacher.

6. Mike had some Matchbox cars. He gave five of the cars to Jon. Mike had four Matchbox cars left. How many Matchbox cars did Mike have at the beginning?

    Mathematical sentence: $\square - 5 = 4$

    ▌Answer: Mike had nine Matchbox cars at the beginning.

7. How many eggs are in four dozen eggs?

    Mathematical sentence: $4 \times 12 = \square$

    ■ Answer: There are forty-eight eggs in four dozen.

8. Ted will need twenty-four balloons for his birthday party. If eight balloons are in a package, how many packages of balloons will Ted need to buy?

    Mathematical sentence: $24 = \square \times 8$

    ▌Answer: Ted will need to buy three packages of balloons.

9. There are thirty-six chairs set up for a play in our classroom. There are four rows of chairs. How many chairs are in each row?

    Mathematical sentence: $36 = 4 \times \square$

    ■ Answer: There are nine chairs in each row.

10. Hank's mother gave him twelve cookies. If Hank shares the cookies equally with two other friends, how many cookies will each of the three boys have?

    Mathematical sentence: $12 \div 3 = \square$

    ▌Answer: Hank and his friends will receive four cookies each.

There are still other types of problems that children must learn to solve. Rather than waiting for the end of a unit of instruction, provide children with opportunities to solve problems each day so that they will begin to develop techniques in solving problems and will maintain those skills.

Another technique that has proven successful is to write a story at the top of a page and then ask a series of questions about the story at the bottom of the page. In such cases, a "story" problem lives up to its billing—it really is a story, rather than just a sentence or two with a question mark at the end. In that sense, these "story" problems are closer to what we actually face in everyday life. For example:

Martha is planning her twelfth birthday party. She will be fifteen years old that day. She wants to invite nine of her friends to share the party with her. Of course she will want to include her three younger brothers, her mother, and her father. Martha would like to give each child three balloons. They will play games at the party. Two teams will be formed to play the peanut relay game, and there will be four teams formed to play Twister. Help Martha plan her birthday party by answering the following questions. Remember to write a mathematical sentence for each example and to write a complete sentence to answer each question.

1. If all of those invited attend the birthday party, how many will be at the party?

2. How many children will attend the party?

3. How many balloons will Martha need?

4. How many children will be on each team when they play the peanut relay game?

5. How many children will be on each team when Twister is played?

6. How many years did Martha not have a birthday party?

7. How tall will Martha be on her fifteenth birthday?

8. How many boys will be at the birthday party?

Note that there are not sufficient data for the children to answer all of the questions: Questions 7 and 8 cannot be answered from the information given.

LOGIC AND REASONING

Problem solving and decision making go very much hand in hand. The analysis of information and the weighing of affecting factors help us decide to take one course of action over another. As the student progresses in mathematics, logic will become increasingly important in his or her mathematical thinking. The student will wonder how one can be sure that a given statement is always true (or false), and will become more and more critical of the reasons that are offered as justification for mathematical statements. Eventually, this will lead to the exploration of the notion of proof, both formal proof and proof by counterexample.

As our society evolves, we need more insight and understanding to comprehend, for instance, statements made by politicians and advertisers. Knowledge of the nature of logical reasoning will provide a sound base for children to analyze claims critically. Children and adults must learn to comprehend true-false statements and recognize fallacious reasoning.

From a very early age, children are exposed to television commercials that use reasoning in their presentations. Consumers must carefully analyze the logic employed in these commercials and other "sales pitches" to ascertain whether fallacious reasoning is being used to sell the product or convince them of its value. For example, students at a young age can be sensitized to the truth or falsity of quantified statements such as, "All of the blocks are red" or "Some of the chairs are being used." As their use of language grows, they can explore the negation of "simple statements" such as the negation of "blue" is "not blue." With increased sophistication they can realize that the negation, or opposite, of "All horses run" is not "No horses run," but instead is "Some horses do not run."

The increased popularity of computers has brought about renewed interest in the study of logic. However, logic is usually not studied as a separate topic in elementary school. Rather, logic is treated as a tool for helping children understand other concepts such as data analysis. In the same spirit, symbolic logic is seldom studied in elementary school, but the underlying principles are explored—at a low level of abstraction.

Logic is implicit in the structural approach used in contemporary elementary programs. Children use logical reasoning more and more as they progress from the primary grades through the intermediate grades and into high school. At the intermediate level, children are more conscious of the way in which statements are related to one another, and they become more clearly aware of how they reason their way to solutions of problems.

THE LANGUAGE OF LOGIC

In everyday speaking and writing, we make frequent use of compound statements. **Compound statements** are formed by joining two **simple statements** with a **connective**. Simple statements are statements such as the following:

1. The sky is clear.
2. It is cold.
3. Grass is green.
4. It is cloudy.
5. It is raining.

Each of these statements contains a noun phrase and a verb phrase.

We can use connectives such as *and, or, if . . . then . . .* and so on, to form compound statements from simple statements. For example, we can use these connectives and the simple statements listed above to form the following compound statements:

- The sky is clear and it is cold.
- It is cold or it is raining.
- If it is raining, then it is cloudy.

These are examples taken from our everyday language. We also have simple statements and compound statements in mathematics. For example, consider these statements:

$$2 < 3 \text{ and } 3 < 4$$
$$2 < \pi \text{ or } 4 < \pi$$
$$\text{If } 7 > x, \text{ then } 8 > x.$$

A compound statement formed by joining two simple sentences with the connective *and* is called a **conjunction**. A conjunction is true if both of its components are true. If either component (or both) is false, the conjunction is considered false.

Consider the compound statement

$$5 + 4 = 9 \text{ and } 6 - 2 = 5$$

Is this statement true or false? Although the first sentence is true, the entire statement is false; the connective *and* requires that *both* of the statements involved be true for the entire statement to be true. What can we say about the following compound statement?

- Rectangles have four sides, and triangles have three angles.

This statement is true, since both of its component statements are true.

A compound statement formed by joining two simple statements with the connective *or* is called a **disjunction**. In everyday speaking and writing, the connective *or* is sometimes used to mean "one or the other, but not both." When *or* is used in this way, it is being used in the exclusive sense. In mathematics the word *or* is always used in the inclusive sense to mean "either or both." If either (or both) of the components of a disjunction is true, the disjunction is true; otherwise the disjunction is false.

Consider these mathematical statements:

$$6 + 22 = 28 \text{ or } 1 - 1 = 1$$
$$5 > 4 \text{ or } 2 > 2$$
$$\frac{4}{8} = \frac{2}{4} \text{ or } \frac{1}{3} > \frac{1}{5}$$

Each of these disjunctions is true, since in each case one or both of the components are true. The following disjunction is false since neither of its components is true:

- Triangles are squares or $5 = 6$.

The next kind of compound statement we consider is the **conditional** statement. Conditional statements are fundamental to mathematics since they provide the language and the logic to evaluate conjectures or hypotheses. A conditional statement is a statement of the form

"If P, then Q" where P and Q are used to stand for component statements. For example, "If it is raining, then it is cloudy."

To discover how conditional statements are judged true or false, let us consider the following promise that one friend might make to another:

- If it rains, then I will drive you home.

Think of a promise that is kept as a true statement and of a promise that is broken as a false statement. Let us consider the possible cases. Suppose it does indeed rain and the person who made the promise does drive his friend home. In this case the promise has clearly been kept. (The statement is true.)

Next, suppose it rains and the person does not drive his friend home. Has the promise been kept or broken? Clearly, it has been broken. (The statement is false.)

Now suppose it does not rain, but the person drives his friend home anyway. Certainly the promise has not been broken, so we may as well say that it was kept. (The statement is true.)

One more possibility remains—the case in which it does not rain and the friend doesn't get driven home. It would not be fair to say that the original promise was broken. (The statement is true.)

Notice that the promise was broken only in the case where the first statement was true and the second statement was false. Thus, we can say that a conditional statement is false only in the case where the first statement (sometimes called the *antecedent*) is true and the second statement (sometimes called the *consequent*) is false. In all other cases it is true.

Conditional statements (sometimes called *implications*) are quite significant; they form the basis for structured reasoning and cause-and-effect arguments. *If-then* statements also play an important role in geometry. For example, "If the base angles of a triangle are equal, then the sides opposite those angles are equal."

All the connectives we have examined are used to join two single statements to form a new, compound statement. The word *not* is also used to obtain one statement from another, called the statement's **negation**. When the word *not* is used for this purpose, it is frequently symbolized by the symbol ~ and written in front of the statement it applies to. Thus we could write, "It is not raining" as

- ~(It is raining)

Notice that some familiar mathematical statements could also be written in a different form with this symbol. Thus, 3 is not less than 2 could be written as

$$\sim(3 < 2)$$

Words such as *some*, *all*, and *none* are called *logical quantifiers*. **Quantifiers** help us express ideas of quantity clearly. The quantifiers *all* and *none* are used to make very sweeping statements to the effect that such and such a thing is true of *every* number or geometric figure. The quantifier *some* is used when we wish to claim the existence of *at least one* thing of a given sort.

("Some real number is equal to its own square," is an example of such a statement.)

A main purpose of logic is judging the validity of arguments. By *argument* we mean a chain of reasoning designed to show that if certain statements called premises are true, then a final statement called the conclusion of the argument is necessarily true. We say that an argument is valid if there is no way for the premises to be true and the conclusion false. If the truth of the conclusion is not guaranteed by the truth of the premises, the argument is invalid.

Consider this argument:

> If it is snowing, then it is cold.
> It is snowing.
> _____
> Therefore, It is cold.

This argument has two premises (the two statements written above the line). The conclusion of the argument is the statement written below the line. Is it possible for the premises to be true but the conclusion false? No. Therefore, the argument is a valid argument. As a matter of fact, every argument similar to this one is valid. Arguments of the form

> If P, then Q
> P
> _____
> Therefore, Q

are valid no matter what statements we may put in place of the letters P and Q.

Now consider this example. Is this a valid argument?

> All dogs are animals.
> Bambi is an animal.
> _____
> Therefore, Bambi is a dog.

Our everyday experience refutes this argument. Since the truth of both premises does not guarantee the truth of the conclusion, we know that the argument is invalid.

What role should logic play in the elementary mathematics program? Mathematical logic is a field of study in its own right. It should be obvious that a child age 4 can speak grammatically correct sentences even though he or she has not studied English grammar. The child will occasionally make mistakes and will need correction, but, eventually the child will become familiar with grammar. This will include inventing sentences, some of them rather complex. Nevertheless, the child will need to know how to make communication clear and consistent with standard English usage. The analogy with logic should be easy to see. A careful teacher can do much to develop a child's capacity for logical reasoning. The child needs many experiences to discover how to avoid faulty reasoning. The teacher may find that some children in grades 5 or 6 are ready for an elementary discussion of compound sentences and quantifiers. Many children will not be ready to consider these abstract concepts explicitly. As always, it is the teacher's job to assess the needs of individual students

and give sensitive guidance based on awareness of these needs.

THE LANGUAGE OF MATHEMATICS

Let's close this chapter by expanding on the notion that logic and logical reasoning are intertwined with mathematics and problem solving to assist us in communicating decisions we make. One of the most important ways in which we communicate with each other is through language. In language arts classes children learn to construct complete, meaningful English sentences. We learn that, to be complete, a sentence must express at least one complete idea. To convey ideas, we learn to use particular patterns of words to form complete sentences.

Mathematics, too, is a form of language and in some respects can be compared with the English language. In English we express ideas by symbols called *words*, which are arranged in patterns to form sentences. In mathematics we express ideas by mathematical symbols, arranged in meaningful patterns called *mathematical sentences*. Just as in English we observe certain conventions in writing sentences, in mathematics, too, we follow certain rules in constructing mathematical sentences.

In general, the language of mathematics uses four categories of symbols: symbols for *ideas* (numbers and elements), symbols for *relations* (which indicate how ideas are connected or related to one another), symbols for *operations* (which indicate what is done with the ideas), and symbols for *punctuation* (which indicate the order in which the mathematics is to be completed).

To express a complete thought, a declarative English sentence requires, as a minimum, a noun phrase and a verb phrase. Consider the sentence "The girl is running." This sentence has both a noun phrase ("The girl") and a verb phrase ("is running"). If we had just said, "The girl," this would not have been a complete sentence, because we would not have been expressing a complete thought (no verb phrase). Similarly, "is running" is not a complete sentence, because these words by themselves do not express a complete thought (no noun phrase).

Mathematical sentences, too, require a particular structure. An examination of various mathematical sentences should suggest ideas about the structure of mathematical sentences in general. Examine the following mathematical sentences carefully:

$$2 + 4 > 5$$
$$\square \div 7 = 2$$
$$\frac{1}{2} + \frac{1}{4} = \frac{3}{4}$$
$$3 \times (n + 4) = (3 \times n) + (3 \times 4)$$

First we examine how these mathematical sentences should be read; then we will study the common characteristics of mathematical sentences.

> $2 + 4 > 5$ is read, "Two add four is greater than five."
> $\square \div 7 = 2$ is read, "What number divided by seven is equal to two?"

$\frac{1}{2} + \frac{1}{4} = \frac{3}{4}$ is read, "One-half add one-fourth is equal to three-fourths."

$3 \times (n + 4) = (3 \times n) + (3 \times 4)$ is read, "Three times the quantity n add 4 is equal to three times n added to three times four."

Is there some common characteristic of these sentences? It should become clear through comparison that each sentence has a particular pattern. *Each sentence consists of two or more names for numbers joined together by a relation symbol.*

Consider the mathematical sentence "2 + 4 = 6." This sentence contains number symbols on the left (an expression composed of two number symbols and an operation symbol, 2 + 4) and a number symbol on the right, 6, joined by a relation symbol, =. But none of these three symbols or expressions forms a sentence by itself, just as neither "John" nor "runs" forms a sentence by itself. However, the expression "2 + 4 = 6" is a mathematical sentence, just as "John runs" is an English sentence, because it expresses a complete thought.

The English sentence "There are seven days in a week" would be classified as true. The sentence "There are 29 days in a week" would be classified as false. In the same way, mathematical sentences can be classified as true or false. The mathematical sentence "7 < 3" would be called false. The sentence "4 = 3 + 1" would be called true.

Suppose someone wrote, "He was president of the United States." This is a complete sentence, but we cannot judge it to be true or false until we know who "he" is. What about the following sentences?

1. Theodore Roosevelt was president of the United States.
2. Mickey Mouse was president of the United States.

Both are complete sentences, and both contain enough information to be judged true or false, since in both sentences a name has been substituted for "he." Thus we can judge sentence (1) to be true and sentence (2) to be false.

Now look at these mathematical sentences:

3. $\square + 7 = 13$
4. $6 + 7 = 13$
5. $14 + 7 = 13$

Sentence (3) is a complete **mathematical sentence**, that is, two number expressions joined by a relation symbol. But we cannot judge the sentence to be true or false until we know what number the placeholder represents. In sentence (4) the number 6 has replaced the placeholder. Thus we have enough information to judge (4) to be true. Sentence (5) is clearly false.

Mathematical sentences that cannot be judged true or false, such as $\square + 7 = 13$, are called **open sentences**. Sentences such as (4) or (5), which contain enough information to be judged true or false, are called **mathematical statements** (or **closed sentences**).

When we write an open mathematical sentence, it is necessary to indicate in some way that a numeral is missing. Very often a frame or placeholder is used to show that one or more numerals are missing. The following are some typical placeholders used in elementary programs:

$$\triangledown \qquad \triangle \qquad \bigcirc \qquad \square \qquad \pentagon$$

The idea of using figures such as these to hold the place of missing symbols in mathematical sentences is developed early in the primary grades. As an introduction to this idea, the teacher can write a simple sentence on a sheet of construction paper:

$$\boxed{2 + 3 = 5}$$

After children have seen this sentence, the teacher cuts out one of the numerals, leaving a box-shaped opening:

$$\boxed{2 + \square = 5}$$

Children can see that numbers (on box-shaped pieces of paper) can be placed in the box to complete the sentence. Sentences such as the following can provide computational drill and familiarize children with placeholders in mathematical sentences:

$\square + 3 = 8$	$7 - 3 = \triangle$
$\bigcirc + 5 = 12$	$8 \div \bigcirc = 4$
$3 + \square = 10$	$3 \times \diamond = 27$

Later, children can examine sentences with missing relation symbols and supply the missing symbols:

$3 + 2 \bigcirc 4 + 1$	$\oslash$ or $\ominus$ or $\otimes$
$14 \div 7 \bigcirc 10 \div 1$	$\oslash$ or $\oslash$ or $\otimes$
$3 \times 7 \bigcirc 2 \times 9$	$\oslash$ or $\oslash$ or $\otimes$

Missing operation signs can be supplied in the same way:

$8 \bigcirc 2 = 10$	$\oplus$
$9 - 7 = 10 \triangle 5$	$\triangle\!\!\!-$
$6 = 9 \triangle 3$	$\triangle\!\!\!-$
$18 \triangle 2 = 12 \triangle 3$	$\triangle\!\!\!\times$

Such exercises provide vital reinforcement of computational skills while teaching the meaning of operations and relations.

As children become familiar with sentences that contain frames, they can be led to see that letters can also be used as placeholders. Letters that are used in this way are called variables; for example, $3 + n = 8$. What numeral can replace n to make the sentence a true statement? (5) As children develop a more sophisticated concept of placeholders, they should understand that when a particular placeholder is used more than once in the same sentence, it represents the same value each time. For example, the open sentence

$$\square + \square = 8$$

indicates that the same numeral is to be used in both boxes:

$$\boxed{4} + \boxed{4} = 8$$

This same concept is also valid in algebra. A given letter represents the same value wherever it occurs in any one problem.

It is interesting to note at this point that some *traditional* elementary arithmetic programs disregarded all mathematical sentences except those using the relation symbol =, "is equal to." Consider, for example, a typical simple story problem:

> If John is 45 inches tall and Jim is 48 inches tall, how much taller is Jim than John?

This problem would usually be solved in the following way:

$$\begin{array}{r} 48 \\ -45 \\ \hline 3 \end{array}$$

"Jim is 3 inches taller than John." This problem, as traditionally introduced, merely involves the translation of an English sentence into a simple subtraction problem. In a contemporary elementary class, the variety of ways of expressing the relations involved should be stressed. The following are some examples of true statements that can be made from the information given in the story problem:

$48 - 45 = 3$	Jim is 3 inches taller than John.
$45 + 3 = 48$	John's height plus 3 inches equals Jim's height.
$48 > 45$	Jim is taller than John.
$45 < 48$	John is shorter than Jim.
$45 \neq 48$	John is not the same height as Jim.

At this point we can begin to classify mathematical sentences according to the relation symbols in the sentences. We have seen sentences of this type called equations. An **equation** is a mathematical sentence in which two expressions are joined by an equal sign:

$$8 - 3 = 4 + 1$$

The equal sign indicates that the expression on the left of the sign names the same number as the expression on the right. In the preceding sentence, $8 - 3$ names the same number as $4 + 1$.

If the expression on the left names a number different from the one on the right, we can use the symbol $\neq$ ("is not equal to") to make a true mathematical sentence. For example, $9 \div 3$ is 3 and $3 \times 4 = 12$. Therefore $9 \div 3$ and 3×4 name two different numbers, and we can write

$$9 \div 3 \neq 3 \times 4$$

We can use the relation symbol > (which means "is greater than") and the symbol < (which means "is less than") to express the relationship with greater precision:

$$9 \div 3 < 3 \times 4$$
$$3 \times 4 > 9 \div 3$$

Sentences of this kind are examples of **inequalities**. We also call $9 \div 3 \neq 3 \times 4$ an inequality.

The inequality symbol ($\geq$) expresses "is greater than or equal to," and the inequality symbol ($\leq$) expresses "is less than or equal to."

$n \geq 5$	n is greater than or equal to five.
$m \leq 10 + 15$	m is less than or equal to ten add fifteen.

Other inequality symbols are the following:

$\not>$	is not greater than
$\not<$	is not less than
$\not\geq$	is not greater than or equal to
$\not\leq$	is not less than or equal to

Here are some sentences that use these symbols:

$4 \not> 5$	Four is not greater than five.
$p \not< 10$	p is not less than 10.
$q \not\geq 5$	q is not greater than or equal to five.
$10 \not\leq 4 + 5$	Ten is not less than or equal to four add five.

The symbols for the two fundamental operations of arithmetic and their inverse operations are also part of the grammar of mathematics:

$+$	addition
$-$	subtraction
$\times$	multiplication
$\div$	division

These symbols indicate operations to be performed but do not, by themselves, form mathematical sentences. They indicate operations to be performed on numbers, not relations between numbers. For example, the expression

$$(4 + 3) - (6 \div 2)$$

indicates several operations to be performed. If these operations are performed, giving $7 - 3$, or 4, we see that we have renamed the original expression. Thus another name for $(4 + 3) - (6 \div 2)$ is 4.

When several operations are to be performed but no symbols are included to indicate the order in which the operations should be accomplished, multiplication and division should be evaluated from left to right and then addition and subtraction from left to right. Children should learn this important order of operations. Consider this example: $2 + 3 \times 4$. If 2 is added to 3 and then multiplied by 4, the answer is 20. If 3 and 4 are multiplied first and then 2 is added, the answer becomes 14. Following the mathematical order of operations, only 14 is the correct answer. So that there can be no mistake in the order of operations, we may choose to use parentheses and write $2 + (3 \times 4)$. However, if we really intend to add 2 and 3 first and then multiply the sum by 4, we should write $(2 + 3) \times 4$; then the answer would be 20.

On a calculator, the above discussion of order of operation takes on new meaning. In evaluating numerical expressions, some calculators commonly found in homes and elementary schools make use of what is referred to as arithmetic logic whereas others employ algebraic logic. A calculator that uses **arithmetic logic** will evaluate an expression in the order in which it is entered. That is, the expression "$3 + 5 \times 6 =$" when keyed into an arithmetic logic calculator will be evaluated as

"48" (3 plus 5 equals 8, and 8 times 6 is 48). An **algebraic logic** calculator will automatically apply the order of operations mentioned in the previous paragraph. With algebraic logic, "3 + 5 × 6 =" will be evaluated as "33" (5 × 6 equals 30 and 3 plus 30 is 33). The algebraic calculator yields 33, the only correct response for the expression "3 + 5 × 6 =".

Use the above discussion to determine whether your calculator uses arithmetic or algebraic logic. You can often tell by just looking at your calculator keys. An algebraic logic calculator contains parentheses keys, ( ), so that the order of operations can be overridden when desired. That is, if you use an algebraic logic calculator with the expression "3 + 5 × 6 =" and you *wanted* to add the 3 and the 5 before multiplying times 6, then you could key in the sequence (3 + 5) × 6 = to get 48. Similarly, if you had an arithmetic logic calculator and *wanted* to multiply the 5 times 6 first, then you would have to revise the expression in your mind first to be "5 × 6 + 3 =" and then key it in that order.

Which type of calculator is preferred? It depends entirely on your intended use. Although used in different ways, both calculators can be effectively used as tools for teaching the order of operations. The decision depends on the approach that you wish to use to demonstrate the need to agree on an order with which to carry out operations.

When a mathematical sentence contains several numbers and several operations to be performed, it is often necessary to indicate the order (other than the usual order of operations) in which the operations are to be performed. To indicate this order, we use punctuation or **grouping symbols**—parentheses, brackets, and braces.

Parentheses are grouping symbols used to indicate which operations are to be performed first. You might interpret parentheses to mean "Do me first." Some teachers prefer to use this expression with children. In the example $7 - 4 - 1 = \Box$, we might write $(7 - 4) - 1 = \Box$, which means that we are to subtract 4 from 7 and then subtract 1 from that difference:

$$(7 - 4) - 1 = \Box$$
$$3 - 1 = \Box$$
$$2 = \Box$$

Or we might write $7 - (4 - 1) = \Box$, which means that we are to subtract 1 from 4 first and then subtract that difference (3) from 7:

$$7 - (4 - 1) = \Box$$
$$7 - 3 = \Box$$
$$4 = \Box$$

In either case the operation to be performed first is indicated within the parentheses.

More than one set of parentheses can be used in the same equation, as in $(7 + 2) - (2 + 3) = \Box$. Again, the operations indicated within the parentheses are to be performed first. The sum of $2 + 3$ is to be subtracted from the sum of $7 + 2$:

$$(7 + 2) - (2 + 3) = \Box$$
$$9 - 5 = \Box$$
$$4 = \Box$$

Later, children will be introduced to another grouping symbol, square brackets, usually printed [ ]. These are used when one or more pairs of parentheses have already been used and another pair might result in confusion. For example, this sentence is a bit confusing to the eye:

$$\left(\frac{1}{4} \times \left(\frac{2}{3} \times 24 \right) \right) \div \frac{2}{3} = \Box$$

It is more clearly written as follows:

$$\left[\frac{1}{4} \times \left(\frac{2}{3} \times 24 \right) \right] \div \frac{2}{3} = \Box$$

The grouping symbols still indicate the order in which operations are to be performed. The operations within the parentheses are usually performed first, then the operations within the brackets.

Some teachers use "rings" or "loops" to reinforce the notion of "Do me first." For example, in the following, we would do the inside loop first, then the outside:

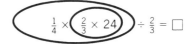

After considerable practice, the loops are replaced by parentheses and brackets.

In exceedingly complicated expressions, we may use parentheses, brackets, and braces as punctuation symbols. For example,

$$500 - (50 \div (2 \times (3 + 5))) = \Box$$

is not nearly as easy to read as

$$500 - \{50 \div [2 \times (3 + 5)]\} = \Box$$

Braces are written as { }. They are used in punctuating number expressions and in naming sets. Context always makes it clear how they are being used in any given situation. Of course, the looping method also works here.

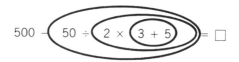

CLOSURE

In this chapter we discussed a number of concerns relative to mathematical problem solving, decision making, and communicating. As you continue to explore other chapters, you will encounter many opportunities to expand on these themes. Remember, the ideas discussed in this chapter are part of the daily diet of mathematics instruction. As teachers, we must recognize and reinforce the importance of having children model and verbalize what we wish them to learn.

Terminology, Symbols, and Procedures

Algebraic Logic. A calculator programmed with an algebraic operating system "knows" to do multiplication and division before addition and subtraction and follows the correct order of operations in simplifying expressions.

Arithmetic Logic. A calculator programmed with an arithmetic operating system automatically simplifies all expressions from left to right, paying no attention to the proper order of operations.

Compound Statement. A compound statement is a statement formed from two or more simple statements by joining these statements with connectives such as *and* or *or*.

Conditional. A sentence of the form "If P, then Q," where P and Q are statements, is a conditional sentence.

Conjunction. A sentence of the form "P and Q," where P and Q are statements, is called a conjunction.

Connective. A connective is a word (or words) used to form compound statements from simpler statements. The familiar connectives are *and*, *or*, and *if . . . then*. . . . The word *not* is sometimes called a connective even though it requires only one statement instead of two. These connectives are denoted by symbols:

- "and" is denoted by the symbol $\wedge$.
- "or" is denoted by the symbol $\vee$.
- "if . . . , then . . ." is denoted by the symbol $\rightarrow$.
- "not" is denoted by the symbol $\sim$.

Disjunction. A sentence of the form "P or Q," where P and Q are statements, is called a disjunction.

Equation. An equation is a mathematical sentence in which two expressions representing the same quantity are joined by an equal sign.

Grouping Symbols. Parentheses ( ), brackets [ ], and braces { } are grouping symbols used to indicate the order in which the operations in a mathematical expression or sentence are to be performed.

Inequality. An inequality is a mathematical sentence in which two number expressions are joined by one of the following relation symbols:

$$> \qquad \ngtr \qquad \leq$$
$$< \qquad \nless \qquad \ngeq$$
$$\neq \qquad \geq \qquad \nleq$$

Examples of inequalities are:

$$2 < 5 + 1 \qquad 2 - 3 \geq 14$$
$$6 \ngtr 9 \qquad 8 + 1 \nleq 3$$

Mathematical Sentence. A mathematical sentence is a sentence that follows a pattern such as the following:

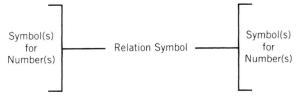

In a mathematical sentence, one number is joined by a relation symbol to another number. For example:

$$3 + 4 = 7$$
$$6 + 13 > 5$$

Mathematical Statement (or Closed Mathematical Sentence). A mathematical statement is a mathematical sentence that contains enough information to be judged true or false. It does not have a placeholder or unknown. It is sometimes called a *closed mathematical sentence*. For example:

$$5 + 4 = 9$$

Negation. The negation of a given statement yields the opposite truth value of the given statement. For example, the negation of "It is red" is "It is not red."

Open Mathematical Sentence. An open mathematical sentence is a mathematical sentence that does not contain enough information to be judged true or false. For example:

$$5 + 4 = \square$$

Problem Solving. Problem solving describes the processes an individual uses to respond to and overcome an obstacle or barrier when a method or solution is not immediately obvious; it must involve more than just applying an algorithm.

Problem-Solving Strategies. A variety of strategies can be used to overcome the barrier between the solver and the solution. These include, but are not limited to, the following:

- restating the problem
- dramatization, or acting out the problem
- estimation
- using a model
- guessing and checking
- making a drawing
- working backward
- solving a simpler, related problem
- constructing a table or graph
- looking for a pattern
- applying a formula
- writing a mathematical sentence

Quantifier. The words *all*, *some*, and *none* are logical quantifiers. These words are used to indicate whether a given sentence is always true, sometimes true, or never true.

Simple Statement. A simple statement is a true or false expression with a noun and verb phrase. For example: It is Tuesday or 12 = 11 + 1.

Practice Exercises for Teachers

These exercises are designed for the reader of this book. While some are suitable for use in the elementary classroom, these examples should not necessarily be assigned to children in this form. Ideas for classroom activities on the concepts and ideas discussed in this chapter can be found in Part 2 of *Today's Mathematics*, the Student Resource Book.

1. Decide which of the problem-solving strategies described in this chapter would be most appropriate, and then use that technique to solve the following problem: A candy factory has a warehouse full of cardboard that has been cut into rectangular regions that measure $8\frac{1}{2}$ inches by 11 inches (the size of a standard sheet of paper). You have been asked to design a box (a bottom and four sides) that will hold the most candy by removing a square from each corner of the cardboard, then folding and gluing the sides. What should the size of the square be so that the box will have the greatest volume for holding candy?

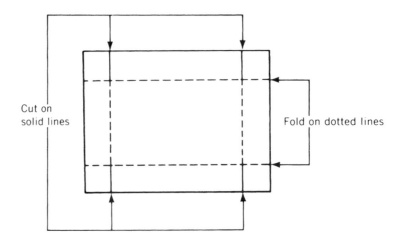

Cut on solid lines   Fold on dotted lines

2. Find all rectangles having the same numerical value for their area and perimeter. Use only whole numbers for measurements. That is, if A = length and B = width, then for what values of A and B does the following equation hold true?

$$A + A + B + B = A \times B$$

3. How many ways can six squares be drawn on a sheet of paper so that, when the figure is cut out, it can be folded into a cube? One example is shown below.

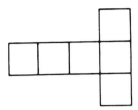

4. Label each of the following as a "true statement," "false statement," "open sentence," or "not a sentence."

   a) $34 = 7$

   b) $7 + 9 \neq 8 - 4$

   c) $3^2 > 1 + 2^2$

   d) $9 \times y \geq 7$

   e) $\square + \triangle > 8$

   f) $12 = [(2 \times 5) - 3] + 1$

   g) $2 + \square > 6$

   h) $18 \div 2 < 3^2$

   i) $6 + (3 + 7) = (6 + 3) + 7$

   j) $n - 3n + 2$

   k) $a^2 + 1 > 2$

   l) $[\diamond \times 2] \div 5$

5. Rewrite each of the following word problems as an open mathematical sentence. Notice that each story problem may be represented in more than one way.

   a) Bobby weighs fourteen pounds more than Edward. Edward weighs fifty-nine pounds. How much does Bobby weigh?
   b) Yesterday there were forty-two children playing at the school playground. Today thirteen more children are playing there. How many children are playing at the school playground today?
   c) Ryan has twice as many football trading cards as Jeff. Ryan has 234 football trading cards. How many football trading cards does Jeff have?
   d) Tommy Tuna weighs 130 kilograms and Barry Barracuda weighs twenty kilograms. How much more does Tommy Tuna weigh than Barry Barracuda?

6. Solve each equation.

   a) $(3 + 4) \times 2 = \square$

   b) $3 + (4 \times 2) = \square$

   c) $(6 + 2) \div 2 = \square$

   d) $6 + (2 \div 2) = \square$

   e) $(3 - 2) + (7 - 1) = \square$

   f) $(\square \times 2) + 3 = 15$

   g) $(2 + 3) + (\square + 7) = 12$

   h) $(2 \times \square) + (3 \times \square) = 20$

7. Solve the following word problem. Be sure to write an appropriate mathematical sentence. Remember to translate the mathematics back into an English sentence for your answer.

   ▪ Mike is three years older than Lila. The sum of their ages is twenty-nine. How old is each?

8. Solve the following word problem.

   ▪ Mary is one year older than four times Tammy's age. Kelly is three times as old as Mary. If Kelly is twenty-seven, how old are Mary and Tammy?

9. Indicate the operation that would most commonly be used to solve each of the following problems.

   a) What will six bicycles cost if one sells for $49.95?
   b) If I buy a new shirt, jacket, and hat, how much will all three items cost?
   c) How much change will I get back from $10.00 if I buy a pair of gloves?
   d) How many balloons will go to each of seven people at my birthday party if I have twenty-eight balloons to distribute equally?

10. Write mathematical sentences for each of the following examples.

    a) If each of the thirty-two students in our classroom brings a quarter for a school charity, how much money will our room contribute?
    b) If we distribute six dozen cookies equally to the twenty-nine members of our class, how many cookies will each person get?
    c) How much change will I receive from a dollar if I buy an ice-cream cone for eighty-seven cents?

11. Identify each of the following statements as simple or compound, and classify each compound statement as a conjunction, disjunction, conditional, or negation.

    a) Jim is tall or Ray is short.
    b) Ice cream melts.
    c) If you stay, then I go.
    d) The hour is late and the air is sweet.
    e) Roses are red.
    f) Smith did it.

12. Tell whether each compound or conditional statement is true or false.

    a) If $(6 < 10)$, then $(5 < 10)$.
    b) $(6 = 5)$ or $(6 > 5)$
    c) $(9 + 1 = 10)$ and $(8 < 7)$
    d) If $(7 < 5)$, then $(7 + 1 < 5 + 1)$.
    e) $(6^2 = 5)$ or $(5^2 = 6)$
    f) If $(\frac{1}{2} = \frac{6}{4})$, then $(0 \neq 1)$.
    g) $(2 < 1)$ and $(1 < 2)$
    h) $(2 < 1)$ or $(1 < 2)$
    i) If $(50 \div 2 = 25)$, then $(7 < 3)$.
    j) $(8 > 1)$ and $(6 > 1)$ and $(0 > 1)$

13. Rewrite each of the following as either a conjunction, a disjunction, or a conditional. (Use words for the connectives.)

    a) Marilyn and Ginny are good students.
    b) I tried the car, but it wouldn't start.
    c) You will succeed provided you try.
    d) Carey or Ryan will call before noon.

14. Identify each of the following sentences as true for all integers x, for some integers x, or for no integers x.

    a) $x > 0$
    b) $x^2 > 0$
    c) $x^2 \geq 0$
    d) $x < x + {}^+1$
    e) $x \geq x - {}^+1$
    f) $x^4 < {}^-1$

15. Which of the following statements are true and which are false?

    a) All isosceles triangles are equilateral triangles.
    b) All squares are rectangles.
    c) Some trapezoids are rectangles.
    d) All squares are quadrilaterals.
    e) All rectangular prisms are cubes.
    f) No triangles are rectangles.
    g) Some right triangles are equilateral triangles.
    h) All quadrilaterals are squares.
    i) No parallelograms are trapezoids.
    j) All isosceles triangles are acute triangles.

16. In the following examples assume that the conditional statement is true.

    a) If Figure C is a square, then Figure C has four sides.
       Figure C is a square.
       What can you conclude?
    b) If Jeff plays basketball, then he will not have time to do his schoolwork.
       Jeff plays basketball.
       What can you conclude?
    c) If it rains, then we will not go on a picnic.
       It is snowing.
       What can you conclude?
    d) If it snows, then we will shovel the sidewalk.
       It is snowing.
       What can you conclude?

17. During class you told your students, "If we finish the chapter by Wednesday, there will be a test on Friday." In which of the following cases would you have broken this promise?

    a) You finished the chapter and gave the test.
    b) You finished the chapter and did not give the test.
    c) You did not finish the chapter but gave the test.
    d) You did not finish the chapter and did not give the test.

Teaching Competencies and Self-Assessment Tasks

1. Discuss how the problem-solving strategies presented in this chapter are different from the techniques you remember learning for solving word problems.
2. Discuss the merits and deficiencies of each of the problem-solving strategies suggested in this chapter. Create sample problems to defend your positions on each strategy.
3. Order the strategies discussed in this chapter according to the degree in which you use them to solve the problems you face. Which strategies do you feel you could make better use of and why?
4. Discuss the roles of the calculator and the computer in developing problem-solving skills.
5. Locate the most recent mathematics results of the National Assessment of Educational Progress or Third International Mathematics and Science Study, and report your findings on U.S. problem-solving attainment to the class.
6. Discuss the relationship that should exist between problem solving in the mathematics program and the entire elementary curriculum. Also, research the relationship between reading and problem-solving ability, and present your findings to the class.
7. Discuss the pros and cons of developing a card file of good word problems. How should such a file be organized? How should it be used in the classroom?
8. Examine at least three elementary school mathematics textbooks, and report on the inclusion of logic—as a separate topic and/or as used within other topics.
9. Report on the appearance of logic in advertising. Locate several examples of both compound and conditional statements, and determine whether the ads have hidden implications or include fallacious reasoning.
10. Identify real-world problems from a child's life (or an adult's life) that lend themselves to more than one of the strategies described in this chapter.
11. (Bonus) Discuss the statement "I always lie." Also, analyze the following situation: A student found a piece of paper. On one side of the paper it read, "The other side is a lie." When the paper was turned over, it read, "The other side is the truth." Could this "logically" be possible?
12. (Bonus) A certain island has two types of inhabitants. One type always tells the truth, and the other type always lies. As you travel down an unfamiliar path, you come to a fork leading in two different directions. One path leads to the village, the other to the caverns. You would like to find out, from the islander standing by the road, which direction leads to the village. What is the ONE (and only one) question that you can ask to be sure of finding your way to the village on the first try?

Related Readings and Teacher Resources

For related readings on topics found in this chapter, see the corresponding chapter in Part 2 of *Today's Mathematics*, the Student Resource Book.

Chapter 6

Number Sense, Numeration, and Place Value

Teaching Competencies

Upon completing this chapter, you will be able to:

■ State anticipated mathematics knowledge that children possess when they enter school.

■ Conceptualize and state appropriate learning experiences for children in a beginning mathematics program.

■ Describe the development of number sense, beginning on the concrete level and moving through the semiconcrete, semiabstract, and abstract levels.

■ Identify the fundamental features of a place-value numeration system.

■ Model numbers using a place-value box and numeral expander.

■ Use standard notation, expanded notation, and exponential notation to express a given number.

■ Describe characteristics of several ancient numeration systems and how those systems compare to our numeration system.

■ Incorporate the principles and structures of numeration and place value in lessons for elementary children.

oung children have creative ideas concerning mathematics and its relationship to their world. They have an inventive quality that, to them, offers a way to acknowledge their interaction with the wonders they uncover every day. Consider the following:

- A young boy used to count without shame
    "one, two, three, four, five, six, then seb-bow."
  Five-and-a-half was his age, he'd exclaim
    even though his birthday was only a month ago.
  To push a game piece a space ahead more
    he'd name the square he was on as "one."
  When playing with a girl who thought her ringfinger WAS four,
    they could count on a game that would never get done.

The children described in the preceding passage use "numberness," counting, and number sense in ways that are not uncommon for children just beginning to explore such concepts. Some children invent names for numbers that make more sense to them. Some children use fraction language long before they possess any meaningful understanding of fraction concepts. Some children have difficulty with one-to-one correspondence and with matching word names for numbers to physical actions. All children, however, need a sound foundation in number sense that requires thoughtful planning and organization on the part of the teacher.

The NCTM lists Number and Operations as the first of the content standards in *Principles and Standards for School Mathematics*.

> Central to this standard is the development of number sense—the ability to decompose numbers naturally, use particular numbers like 100 or $\frac{1}{2}$ as referents, use the relationships among arithmetic operations to solve problems, understand the base-ten number system, estimate, make sense of numbers, and recognize the relative and absolute magnitude of numbers. (NCTM, 2000, p. 32)

A FOUNDATION FOR MATHEMATICS DEVELOPMENT

The mathematics experiences of children beginning school vary tremendously, depending on, for example, the education of their parents, the time the parents devote to their children's education, attendance at preschools, travel experiences, play materials and opportunities, family relationships (older brothers and sisters), television viewing habits, exposure to books, listening to reading by others, and a multitude of other factors. This variance helps define the first mathematical task of any classroom teacher—to assess the mathematics experiences the students have encountered in the past.

A primary mathematics program should begin with the unique mathematics experiences young children have had prior to school, and teachers need to isolate these types of mathematical experiences. For example, children who enter school with counting ability do not necessarily exhibit readiness for mathematics. The child may have simply memorized a series of word names and have little or no concept of the numberness involved.

An effective program should reflect the connections of mathematics to applications in the child's world and should emphasize the integration of mathematics into other subject areas. Situations that develop from the real world should be set up in the classroom. Children may have had any of the following experiences:

using the telephone
earning and spending their own money
correctly setting the table for a meal
recognizing house numbers
playing with toys that incorporate balance and symmetry
tuning the television to a designated channel
playing with a calculator
playing video games
loading software on a home computer
using a computer or typewriter keyboard

These prior experiences, or lack of them, may form a common basis for establishing cooperative groups, setting up workstations, and developing the scope and sequence of a beginning mathematics program.

A theoretical base for a mathematics program can be built on Piaget's learning theory, as well as learning theories by Bruner, Gagné, and others. However, each theorist seems, in one way or another, to support the idea that mathematics should begin in the real world with concrete materials. Children learn through *doing* (and *discussing* what they're doing), so they need many firsthand experiences manipulating, examining, verbalizing, and sharing mathematical ideas. Easily recognizable, familiar materials—such as plastic spoons, forks, paper cups, paper plates, and so forth—should be the main teaching materials. Some specialized educational materials, such as attribute blocks, Cuisenaire rods, base ten blocks, color tiles, pattern blocks, and various forms of physical "counters" can also be used to provide a sound base for development in mathematics.

A beginning mathematics program establishes the foundation of a solid contemporary mathematics program. At one time mathematics focused on the ability to juggle numbers rapidly and accurately. Today's mathematics places greater emphasis on the development of number sense and the recognition and the study of patterns.

> Students with numbers sense naturally decompose numbers, develop and use benchmarks as referents, use the relationships among operations and their knowledge about the base ten numeration system to solve problems, estimate a reasonable result for a problem, and have a disposition to make sense of numbers, problems, and results. (NCTM, 1998, pp. 50–51)

PATTERNS AND OTHER RELATIONSHIPS IN THE PRIMARY CURRICULUM

Numberness and topics related to the development of number sense do not represent the sole focus of a beginning mathematics program. The teacher must also ensure that significant opportunities are provided for interaction with other aspects of the mathematics curriculum. Children should explore such concepts as patterns, measurement, estimation, fractions, and geometry on a regular basis. Of course, this exploration should be carried out at an appropriate level of abstraction, typically at the concrete-manipulative level.

The study of patterns is central to all mathematics learning. If students have developed an appreciation for patterns and can recognize them in different contexts, then transfer of learning will proceed more smoothly. Students who understand the importance of patterns begin to look for patterns in places that others might not look. This leads eventually to reasoning by analogy— that is, a pattern evident in one setting can be used to explain a different situation.

At the primary level, manipulatives such as pattern blocks, attribute blocks, and color tiles are frequently used for pattern making. Patterning usually begins with a teacher-generated concrete pattern that the student is asked to duplicate. This calls for attention to the individual elements of the pattern and a recognition of the order of these elements. This is followed by requests to have the student extend a pattern. Rather than simply duplicating a pattern, the child must now determine what would come next in order to maintain the orderly sequence. Finally, students are asked to create a pattern of their own, usually with concrete objects. At each step of the patterning process, the teacher should emphasize the role of communication and verbalization and justification in describing the pattern and the "rules" the pattern follows.

The study of measurement in the early grades should consist of a wide variety of hands-on experiences in which the children are actively involved in discovering relationships. Initially, attention should be devoted to exploring linear measure using nonstandard units of measure such as "used" pencils or different-length strips of heavy paper such as posterboard. This should initiate a discussion (with the children in the lead—not the teacher) of the need for a standardized unit such as chalkboard erasers or paper clips, which, in turn, should result in the realization of the need for some commonly accepted standardized units such as inches, feet, centimeters, and meters. Children should be given ample opportunity to use these measures to describe objects, both by direct measurement and through estimation prior to direct measurement.

Measurement should not be limited to linear measure and the use of a ruler. The children should also explore simple weight and capacity measurement at this stage through experiences at a sand table, for example. It is important to note, however, that memorization of equivalent measures is not an issue here. The real purpose is to experiment and interact with the measuring process.

Time concepts is another aspect of measurement that deserves attention here. At the primary level, the development of time concepts frequently includes the ability to read a traditional clock to the hour, half hour, and minute. Children are also taught to read the display of a digital clock. (See Chapter 14 for a successful way to introduce young children to reading a clock to the minute.) Days, weeks, months, seasons, and years, and the use of calendars to record these aspects of time passage, are also part of the primary curriculum.

One other use of measurement that receives attention in the primary grades is money. Children learn to recognize the different coins (and bills), begin to associate a particular value with each coin, compare relative values of different coins and sets of coins, and may even begin to explore forming equivalent sets of coins and making change. Readers who desire to explore further discussion of measurement topics at this point are directed to Chapter 14.

Children in the early grades have often formed a notion of fractions before they come to school for the first time. Many children have had the experience of trying to share a group of toy cars or choose half of a candy bar. Because of such real experiences in the child's life, this notion of fraction tends to reflect an idea of sharing that does not necessarily call for equal shares. How else can we explain the child who breaks the candy bar in two pieces to show halves and then, before sharing, inspects the two pieces to see which is the "bigger half"? The idea that a fraction represents equal portions should definitely be part of a primary mathematics program. Considerable use should be made of models, such as circular regions, cut or shaded to demonstrate halves, thirds, and fourths. The children should also be asked to discuss why certain other shadings or cuttings do not represent these fractions. Avoid the temptation to exploit the symbolism at this stage—it is the concept of a fraction, not the symbol for a fraction, that must be the focus here.

Geometric concepts form an integral part of every child's life. Long before children begin formal schooling and apply number concepts to describe things, they explore the world from a geometric standpoint. Objects are thought of, if not described, in terms of such geometric traits as round, curved, flat, pointed, sharp, straight, or crooked. Because the child lives in a three-dimensional world, and because three-dimensional objects can be held and manipulated, a discussion of the traits of such three-dimensional objects as balls, boxes, cylinders, and cones is less difficult than might be imagined. In fact, you may well encounter more difficulty with a discussion of two-dimensional shapes since any model of a two-dimensional shape that we might show a child, even a drawing, is, by its very nature, a three-dimensional model.

Logo, a computer language developed by Seymour Papert of the Massachusetts Institute of Technology, provides a nonthreatening environment for young children to explore geometric concepts. Versions for primary children frequently use single keystrokes on a computer to move a "turtle" (the cursor) around the display while leaving a trail represented by line segments. Check your local computer resources for the availability of Logo in the exploration of geometry.

In any case, take full advantage of the child's natural curiosity and the child's surroundings. The geometry of the environment—shapes and curves in building interiors and exteriors, patterns and designs in sidewalks and gardens, boundaries and angles in playgrounds and games—is a familiar aspect of a child's life that can be drawn on for geometric models. This awareness of the geometry around us not only provides the teacher with a wealth of available teaching aids, but it also illustrates the practical application of geometric concepts and ideas.

Algebra and data analysis are also topics that deserve attention in the primary program. The form of algebra most frequently encountered by a primary child is the algebraic logic present in the language a child uses. For example, just as an adult can express a relationship between two variables as $x = 3y$, a child might express a relationship between two objects by noting that one is above, or inside, or underneath, or next to, or heavier than, or shorter than, and so on. Primary children also encounter seriation activities in which certain tasks or events occur in a certain order. Also, young children begin to explore the notion of consequence through real experiences with conditional events using "if-then" reasoning. Children should encounter classroom scenarios during which they realize that "if this happens, then this will be the result."

Data analysis is yet another form of relationship that young children examine. Most commonly, this analysis occurs in the form of concrete graphing used to compare data collected. For example, during a refreshment break the students might be given a choice of two different fruit drinks. When finished drinking, their choice can be "recorded" by placing their empty cup on the table behind signs indicating the two types. The two concrete bar graphs can then be compared. In such a setting, early explorations of data analysis mirror the kinds of experiences all children encounter as they develop number sense.

In summary, children will enter their formal schooling with a wide variety of experiences and knowledge bases. The successful teacher of the primary age child will attempt to identify these differences and make use of them for cooperative learning, grouping, and other aspects of everyday instruction. This teacher will also emphasize the critically important role of hands-on activities and the equally important need to have children relate the mathematics to their world and to verbalize their discoveries and their understandings.

NUMBER SENSE

Children enter school from a real world in which they have handled real objects. This is the place at which a mathematics program must begin—the concrete level. Giving children tasks based on Piaget's experiments can help determine their developmental levels.

Four activities that seem vital for helping children develop number sense are:

1. sorting or classifying items into groups
2. recognition of the cardinal number of a group
3. one-to-one correspondence, which will help with counting
4. ordering or sequencing of events or ideas.

Sorting is a natural activity. Children sort toys when they place cars in garages, dishes in cupboards, dolls in doll beds, or baseball cards into teams or positions played. At more advanced levels, children must be able to sort through information to select appropriate groups. In mathematics we sort for numbers, least common denominators, prime numbers, factors, geometric shapes, and so on. At beginning levels, sorting leads to the development of the concept of number sense. A child experiences many groups with, say, three elements—three cups, three napkins, three forks, three spoons, three toys. Ultimately the child needs to conceptualize and abstract the common property of "threeness." A child might be shown a red triangle-shaped attribute block and be asked to go to the storage box and find three more triangles or to locate three more red blocks. As time progresses, children can be asked to sort out orally described groups—for example, to locate all of the red triangles or locate all of the small, thin squares.

Attribute blocks are a commonly used manipulative that provide opportunities for children to sort, classify, and to search for and develop patterns that are the basis of all mathematical thinking. Attribute blocks are a set of blocks that have varying identifying characteristics (or *attributes*). Typical attribute blocks might vary in *color*, *shape*, *size*, and *thickness*.

Color	Shape	Size	Thickness
Red Blue Yellow	Square Rectangle Triangle Circle	Large Small	Thick Thin

A first level of activity with any manipulative should be a *free-play period*. During such initial activities, attribute blocks might be randomly distributed to groups of children. The children are usually given no instructions or structuring clues at this time. After they have familiarized themselves through play with the blocks, then ask them to sort the blocks. Typically, they will select color and make piles—for example, one pile of yellow blocks, one pile of blue blocks, and one pile of red blocks. Challenge them to classify the blocks in other ways. *Shape* is very often selected as another way to classify the blocks. Children will probably need to be encouraged to try other classifications based on less obvious attributes such as *size* or *thickness*.

On the next level, start a pattern with the blocks, and allow a child to select the block that "should" be next. For example, lay out the following blocks and ask the child to place the next block:

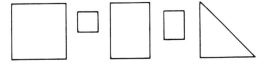

Thus the child must carefully examine the pattern presentation and then decide what attribute block must be placed next to extend the pattern. Often, more than one block could be used to continue the pattern. Have the child verbalize the reason for selecting a particular block. (The activities in Part 2 of this text contain more developmental ideas.)

Cuisenaire rods are a set of wooden or plastic rods based on centimeters and varying in length and color. The rods are *not* scored. Consequently, length is determined by comparing a rod to the unit rod. The rods can be used to sort, classify, develop patterns, develop numberness, and explore many other mathematical concepts.

Color	Size of Rod (in cubic centimeters)
White	$1 \times 1 \times 1$
Red	$1 \times 1 \times 2$
Light green	$1 \times 1 \times 3$
Purple	$1 \times 1 \times 4$
Yellow	$1 \times 1 \times 5$
Dark green	$1 \times 1 \times 6$
Black	$1 \times 1 \times 7$
Brown	$1 \times 1 \times 8$
Blue	$1 \times 1 \times 9$
Orange	$1 \times 1 \times 10$

Initial activities with Cuisenaire rods should involve free play, during which neither teacher-imposed structure nor formal instruction is provided. After the children have become familiar with the rods, then instruction can begin. The children may first organize the rods by separating them by color or by length. The same classification will result either way. Children need many experiences with relationships between the rods. How many red rods does it take to equal the length of one purple rod?

How many different ways can we show a dark green rod?

W	Yellow
Dark green	

Red	Purple
Dark green	

Lt. green	Lt. green
Dark green	

Red	Red	Red
Dark green		

W	W	Red	Red
Dark green			

Children will soon learn that the length of every rod can be shown using other rods.

Note that, in their beginning experiences, the children are developing relationships and do not necessarily associate numbers with the rods. Because of the nature of the rods, a rod's length can be defined many different ways. In one case, the white rod could be defined as one; yet at another time, the red rod could be defined as one. As soon as a unit length is established, this automatically assigns a number value to all other rods. Children should understand the interrelationships among the rods before they associate numberness with the rods. Relationships are developed first, followed by numberness and counting.

The activities in Part 2 of this text contain more developmental ideas. For additional information about using Cuisenaire rods in a beginning mathematics program, research the literature, and locate teachers' manuals specifically designed to direct such a program.

Base ten blocks (shown on next page) are another set of materials that can be used to develop number sense, most often in conjunction with the concepts of place value. As with Cuisenaire rods, the base ten block set has a centimeter cube that can be used to represent one unit. The set also has "long" blocks, much like the Cuisenaire "ten rods," although color is not a factor in the base ten block set. In addition to these blocks, the base ten block set also includes "flat" blocks and large cubes. Similar materials are available for other number bases and are sometimes referred to as **Dienes Multibase Blocks** (see top of next page).

Chapter 4 provides an introduction to the use of these blocks in instruction across the grades.

Zoltan P. Dienes, British educator and creator of the Dienes Multibase Blocks, recommends that the children have free play with the blocks and then move to structured activities from which they can abstract basic mathematical concepts; these concepts should then be examined in many different contexts. Dienes identifies four basic principles on which he structured these blocks:

1. According to the *dynamic principle*, children should be given undirected free play with the blocks before they are given structured activities.

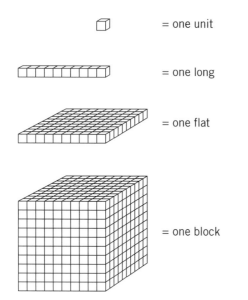

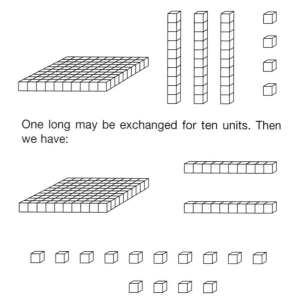

One long may be exchanged for ten units. Then we have:

2. According to the *constructive principle*, children develop constructive thinking intuitively before analytical thinking (before they can make logical judgments). For instance, the children explore what a place-value system is by manipulating the base ten blocks rather than by reasoning out the connection without the benefit of manipulation.

The children should realize that it takes ten units to have as much wood as one long, that it takes ten longs to have as much wood as one flat, and that it takes ten flats to have as much wood as one block. This requires constructive thinking but not analytical thinking (which, according to Dienes, is usually not developed before age 12).

For example, the following figure represents the number 134:

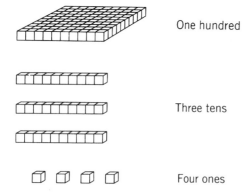

3. According to the *mathematical variability principle*, the relationship among variables can remain constant although the variables themselves are changed. Using the place-value concept exemplified with base ten blocks, you can see that ten longs contain as much wood as one flat and that ten units have as much wood as one long. For example, look at the following arrangement:

4. According to the *perceptual variability principle*, a conceptual structure can remain unchanged when precepts are changed. With base ten blocks, we can use the same conceptual structure of base ten blocks and then substitute with base five or base three blocks. The place-value concept is the same, but the blocks are grouped by fives or by threes.

When used with Piagetian tasks and a constructivist approach to teaching and learning, materials such as attribute blocks, Cuisenaire rods, and base ten blocks will provide a firm foundation on which children can build and develop mathematical thought. The use of collections or groups of objects is a sound and logical way to develop the concept of numbers in gradual stages.

Many contemporary mathematics programs at the elementary school level include, usually in some concrete/pictorial fashion, the concepts of sets. Sets are taught not for their own sake but to provide techniques for introducing and describing fundamental ideals of mathematics. Instead of emphasizing the formal topic of sets that was common in the "New Math" movement of the 1960s, most programs today emphasize *set concepts* by focusing on **groups**, or collections of objects put together for a particular purpose.

By using set concepts, we are able to describe mathematical ideas and operations more clearly and more simply than without them. Groups and grouping are used with children to develop the concept of numbers, as well as classifying, sorting, and ordering. Many educators feel that informal set concepts should be introduced very early, that they help young children form proper number concepts, and that the development of proper number concepts will make more advanced mathematics concepts easier to grasp.

What would you take with you to play golf? What would you buy if you needed dishes to serve eight people? Yes, you would play golf with a *set* of clubs, and you would buy a *set* of dishes. Using these two examples, we can discuss the nature of a set. A **set** can be regarded as any collection or group of things or ideas that are precisely described. The things or ideas that comprise a given set are called the **elements** (or **members**) of the set. A group or collection considered as a set may be composed of ideas, numbers, people, shapes—anything at all. Objects and ideas do not, by themselves, form sets, but they do form sets whenever we choose to link them and think of them as such.

We have often used other words to indicate a set—words such as *team*, *flock*, *herd*, *club*, and *family*. These items indicate that the members of such a set have some common characteristics. A herd would suggest that all the members are elephants (or cattle, or bison, or the like); a team indicates two or more persons playing or working together. However, a set could be made up of elements that have almost nothing in common—a tree, a house, and a car, for example. A set, in mathematics, can be composed of any elements we choose to include. Although items in a set are often related in some obvious way, this is not necessary. The only thing the elements of a set must have in common is membership in the set.

It is extremely important that our groups consist of *distinguishable*, *well-defined* objects. A set or collection is well defined when we can readily tell exactly what elements or objects belong to the set. Consider this example: "all the old homes in the town of Hanover, Illinois." Would this set be clear to everyone? No, because "old" is not precise. One person's idea of what "old" means will not always be another person's idea. Another example might be "all the tall trees in Muir Woods." Again, this is not well defined: "tall" does not have a precise meaning. Is a 7-foot tree tall? A 30-foot tree? A 70-foot tree? We must describe the elements of a group precisely to have a well-defined set or collection. Thus the set of all trees in Muir Woods that are more than 50 feet tall is a well-defined set. The collection of all daisies in Mrs. Smith's yard at 3:00 P.M. today is well defined; the set of all pretty flowers in Mrs. Smith's yard at 3:00 P.M. is not well defined.

We can usually describe a group in several different ways, using several different **levels of abstraction**. We can describe a group by taking real objects and putting them together. For example, a class party requires a decoration committee; the members appointed to that committee are Betty, Jean, and Mary. This group is composed of real elements—people. When we work with real or tangible items, we refer to this as a **concrete** situation. The use of real items on the concrete level will help children relate the mathematics they are about to learn to the real world. For instance, children have had experiences grouping with cookies, toys, and playmates.

A second way to describe a group is by drawing pictures. A group of three chairs could then be represented this way:

Instead of working with real chairs, we use drawings of the chairs to represent the real objects. We call this a **semiconcrete** situation. The semiconcrete level is a representation of a real situation but presents pictures of the real items rather than the items themselves.

A **semiabstract** representation uses tallies to represent elements. A common example of such a representation is ||||| ||. The semiabstract level involves a symbolic representation of a concrete item, but the symbols or pictures do not look like the objects they represent. A number line is commonly used as a semiabstract model. It can be used to picture a situation involving real objects, but the number line doesn't look like the objects it represents.

A group can also be described by using abstract symbols. We might use the letters *a*, *b*, and *c* to stand for the chairs. We can also describe a group by using words—for example, "all presidents of the United States." Are words and symbols as precise as the other means of describing groups? Yes, words and symbols, if used carefully, can be just as precise. However, words and symbols are more abstract than pictures and actual objects. In each case we can clearly and precisely describe the members of a given group. Children reach the **abstract** level when they can understand and use numbers and numerals, without the need to refer to concrete or representative models.

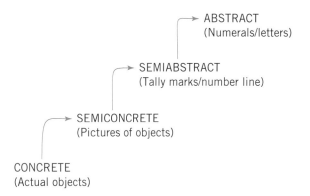

Let us see how sets are used for a progressive development of number concepts.

An initial level of number sense development occurs at the concrete level. In kindergarten and grade 1, the idea of set is developed with real objects. A pack of crayons, a box of pencils, or a bowl of apples can be presented as a **set**. This idea can then be extended to present any collection of different real objects. For example, a pencil, a ball, and a book could be placed together on a desk and described as "the set (or group) of objects on the desk."

On another level, numberness is explored with a group of physical objects that can be represented by drawings (on chalkboard or paper). The use of drawings is more abstract than the use of the objects themselves, so we call this the semiconcrete level. The real objects presented at the concrete level would now be drawn:

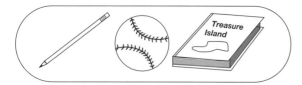

At a higher level, the child is able to match tallies (tally marks or counters such as ice-cream sticks) with the objects of a set. On this semiabstract level, we draw the student's attention away from irrelevant properties of individual elements of the given set and direct attention toward the question "How many?"

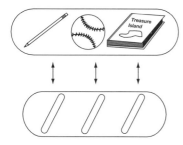

When the child performs such a matching, the emphasis is on discovering whether one group has as many elements as another, although the child is still not using numbers, as such, to make this comparison.

On the highest level, the abstract level, the child matches the elements of a given group with numbers, starting with 1.

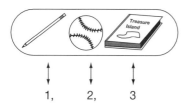

The child comes to understand that the last counting number used in such a matching can be used to tell how many objects are in the given group. Thus the child can speak and write an abstract symbol (a **numeral**) to tell how many (the **number**) objects are in the given set.

Sometimes we are interested not in the objects that compose a set but in only one particular property of the objects. One such property that we might want to consider is the cardinal number. The **cardinal number** of a given set or collection of objects is the number that indicates how many elements the set has. Note that as soon as we use the cardinal number of a set, we are functioning on an abstract level. For example, consider set A:

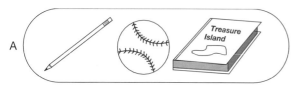

Having matched the objects of the group with the counting numbers, we can say that the number of objects in set A is 3. This is sometimes written as $n(A) = 3$. This

symbolic sentence is seldom, if ever, used with children. When working with young children, we often simply ask, "What is the number of objects in this group?" Usually, we just write 3 beside the group.

The cardinal number of the set above, represented by the numeral 3, is an expression of the number property of the group—in this case, the property of "threeness." This aspect of number sense enables children to discuss groups in terms of number and provides a means by which they can understand the meaning of number. The property of threeness is amplified through comparison of groups. Children are now able to look at groups such as the following in a new way:

While these groups possess many differences, it is evident that all these groups have something in common: the property of "threeness."

Sets can now be compared by comparing their cardinal numbers, that is, by counting and comparing the number of objects in each collection of objects.

The set of **counting numbers** (also referred to as *natural numbers*) can be written as follows:

$$\{1, 2, 3, 4, 5, \ldots\}$$

When there is no final element to a collection, the ellipses (. . .) indicate that the sequence of elements continues in the same manner endlessly.

When we count, we are essentially putting objects into a one-to-one correspondence with counting numbers arranged in the form

$$\{1, 2, 3, \ldots, n\}$$

where n is a counting number. In other words, we match the objects with successive counting numbers, starting with 1. Any set that is either empty or can be counted in this fashion is called a **finite set**. Sets that are not finite are called **infinite sets**. You are probably familiar already with the following mathematical examples of infinite sets:

1. The *counting numbers*:

$$1, 2, 3, 4, 5, \ldots$$

2. The **whole numbers**:

$$0, 1, 2, 3, 4, \ldots$$

3. The *even (whole) numbers*:

$$0, 2, 4, 6, \ldots$$

4. The *odd (whole) numbers*:

$$1, 3, 5, 7, \ldots$$

Each of these is an infinite set (i.e., each continues on and on in the same fashion without end). There is no greatest element in any of these sets.

In the physical world, most groups are finite—in fact, it could be that there are no examples of infinite sets in the physical world. The number of grains of sand on the earth's surface is a staggeringly large number, but these grains form a finite set. One reason we have so much difficulty comprehending the nature of an infinite set is surely because we have no real experience with such a set. When you're weeding a garden on a hot day it seems as though there is always another weed to pull, and yet we know that the number of weeds in the garden, or in the world for that matter, is not infinite!

NUMBER RELATIONS

The child begins at a very early age to make comparisons using terms such as *larger*, *smaller*, *more*, *less*, and so on. Even though a child may not yet be able to count, it is possible to make decisions regarding the size of two groups by matching the elements one-to-one. By doing this, the child can say that one group has more objects than another group. Consider a child presented with two groups of lollipops:

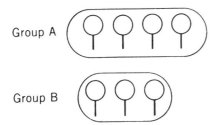

The child will probably choose the group that has more lollipops. By trying to match each object in B with only one object in A, the child sees that there is one lollipop unmatched, or left over, in A. The matching might be done mentally, but on paper it would look like this:

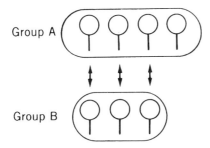

In situations such as this, we realize that children have a background of real experiences in dealing intuitively with nonequivalent sets. It seems only natural to make use of these experiences to further their mathematical knowledge to include unequal as well as equal sets.

A **one-to-one correspondence** between two groups means that each object in the first group is matched with exactly one object in the second group, and each object in the second group is matched with exactly one object in the first group. In a one-to-one correspondence between two sets, there are no elements left over, or left unmatched, in either set.

Two collections that can be placed in one-to-one correspondence are called **equivalent sets**.

$$
\begin{array}{c}
A \quad \boxed{a,\ e,\ i,\ o,\ u} \\
\updownarrow \updownarrow \updownarrow \updownarrow \updownarrow \\
B \quad \boxed{1,\ 2,\ 3,\ 4,\ 5}
\end{array}
$$

Collections A and B are equivalent, because each element in A is matched with exactly one element in B, and no element in either collection is left unmatched. Since they have the same number of elements in one-to-one correspondence, equivalent sets have the same cardinal number.

Let D represent letters in the word *face*, and let E represent the letters in the word *cafe*. Sets D and E can easily be placed in one-to-one correspondence:

$$
\begin{array}{c}
D \quad \boxed{f,\ a,\ c,\ e,} \\
\updownarrow \updownarrow \updownarrow \updownarrow \\
E \quad \boxed{c,\ a,\ f,\ e,}
\end{array}
$$

This shows that sets D and E are equivalent. But even more can be said: Sets D and E consist of exactly the same letters. We can therefore say that set D is not only equivalent to set E: set D is also *equal to* set E. To express the equality in symbols, we write D = E. If two sets are **equal**, they contain exactly the same elements.

Compare these two groups of three children:

$$
\begin{array}{c}
X \quad \boxed{\text{Mary, Betty, Jane}} \\
Z \quad \boxed{\text{Mary, Jean, Joan}}
\end{array}
$$

The elements of set X are not the same as the elements of set Z—Betty and Jane are not identical to Jean and Joan. Set X is not equal to set Z. We write this relation as X ≠ Z, which is read, "Set X is not equal to set Z." Although the elements of sets X and Z are not the same, they can nevertheless be placed in one-to-one correspondence. Therefore set X is equivalent to set Z. We can write this as X ↔ Z, which is read, "Set X is equivalent to set Z." This symbolic notation for equivalent sets is usually not a symbol used in the elementary school program—instead, the symbol for equal sets, =, is sometimes used. The symbols for equal sets, =, and nonequivalent sets, <, >, and ≠, should not be introduced until the concepts underlying the symbols are fully understood.

The ability to count evolves out of manipulating, observing, and conceptualizing numbers. After a strong base is established, children might then be ready to begin writing numerals. Children are usually asked to write numerals under displays of objects.

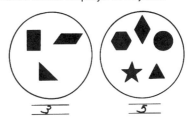

We must emphasize here that you should *not* rush children into writing numerals. Muscular development and fine motor skills of children vary a great deal. Some 5-year-old children will be developed well enough to begin writing numerals, but others will need to wait until they are age 6 or even age 7. Do *not* ask a child to write numerals before he or she has had many opportunities to observe numerals. A child needs to have a mental image of what a numeral looks like in order to write it. Children who have not developed an accurate mental image of the numerals will often write "reversed numerals." In fact, such numeral reversal is not an uncommon occurrence in the written work of primary school children.

Begin teaching children to visualize numerals by using cards with numerals written on them and matching them with groups of objects. Hold the cards in your hand, and with a finger trace the numeral as if you were writing it. You may want to put a small "x" on the numeral showing children where to begin. The goal is to eventually have the children write numerals that are legible and communicate the intended number. The precise duplication of numeral formation is not of greatest concern. The numerals, however, should be legible and look something like these:

Next, have the children trace each numeral with a finger. When you feel the children have the numeral configurations well in mind, they are ready to begin writing. Give the children large sheets of paper without lines. Provide a model of the numeral to be drawn, and ask the child to draw one like the model.

Primary school paper with 1-inch lines and $\frac{1}{2}$-inch guide lines should then be used. Make small reference x's so that the child knows where to begin each numeral. Provide models so that children are less likely to write numerals backward.

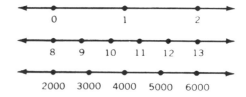

Remember that the cardinal number of a finite group is found by matching the objects of the group with the counting numbers, each object with a separate counting number. As children begin to compare the cardinal numbers of groups, they are ready to expand their idea of number to discover the relations between numbers.

For the cardinal numbers of any two sets A and B, only three relations are possible:

1. A = B: The cardinal number of set A is equal to the cardinal number of set B.
2. A > B: The cardinal number of set A is greater than the cardinal number of set B.
3. A < B: The cardinal number of set A is less than the cardinal number of set B.

The number can then be compared with any other number. Given any two numbers, *x* and *y*, one and only one of the following relations will hold true:

Either $x = y$ or $x > y$ or $x < y$

This fact is sometimes called the **Law of Trichotomy**. The term *trichotomy* comes from the Greek word for *threefold*.

We have presented a logical development beginning with concrete representation of sets and leading to awareness of the possible relations between any two numbers. It is hoped that children will be able to follow through this development rapidly and arrive at a proper understanding of the concept of number.

EXTENDING NUMBERNESS CONCEPTS

Number lines can be used to reinforce and extend students' understanding of relations between numbers. A **number line** is a representation of a geometric line with an arrowhead at each end to indicate that the line continues in both directions:

We mark two points on the line. The first point we label 0, sometimes referred to as the *origin*, and the second point we label 1:

Now we have marked a line segment of one *unit length* on the number line. We can now mark off other congruent line segments (segments having the same measure) on the number line and label these points:

We can establish a unit length on our number line to be any convenient length, provided that on any given number line all unit lengths are equal. Also, we can select any portion of the number line that we wish to use. For example:

In using the horizontal number line, we agree, by conventional use, that numbers of greater value are represented to the right of numbers of lesser value. If the number line is drawn vertically, then the greater value numbers are usually on top. Children can use the number line as another means of examining relations between numbers. For example, on the following number line:

Some of the evident relations are 2 > 1, 3 > 2, 1 < 3, 0 < 2, 3 > 1, and so on.

Remember that the number line represents the semi-abstract level of development. Before you introduce the number line, children should have had experiences on the concrete and semiconcrete levels of development.

Number lines will prove useful for much of a child's mathematical development. In grades 1 and 2 the number line can be used to suggest the concept of ordinal number. Here are two ways of representing a group that consists of a star, a square, a rhombus, a circle, and a hexagon:

In the representation on the left, the objects are jumbled. In the one on the right, they are listed in a certain order: The star is first, the square is second, the rhombus is third, and so on. The numbers we use to tell what position the elements occupy are called **ordinal numbers**. To attach an ordinal number to an element of a set, the objects must be arranged in a definite order, one after another, starting with a certain one. For example, you might ask children to line up for lunch by identifying only certain positions by name—for example, Ann first in line, Dan fourth, Mark sixth, Luke seventh, and John tenth. Allow the class to arrange themselves, "filling in" where appropriate.

Children arrive at school with different backgrounds in number concept development. The task of the teacher is to determine at what level each child is functioning. Some children will be operating on a rote counting level, others will have some comprehension of groups, others will be able to count rationally (use one-to-one correspondence in counting), and others will have a well-developed concept of numbers. Differing backgrounds raise problems that the teacher must solve by individualizing the mathematics program.

PLACE-VALUE NUMERATION

Let us take an imaginary trip to a faraway land. The inhabitants of this place, the Quints, seem friendly enough and engage us in a spirited conversation about our home and about theirs. We soon discover that we enjoy many of the same amusements and suffer many of the same problems. In fact, the further the conversation goes, the more we realize that we live nearly parallel lives—right down to the fact that the Quints also buy their eggs by the dozen. But they claim that they don't buy 12 eggs. Their dozen, they say, is written ㉒, not "12" like ours. They have, it seems to us, an odd way of recording numbers. To write a numeral to represent

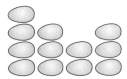

they write ㉒. To count these eggs, they count 1, 2, 3, 4, 5 and draw a loop around that group, or set, and then they count another 1, 2, 3, 4, 5 and draw another loop around that group. They record this process with a 2. Then they count the elements not included in the set—1, 2—and record another 2.

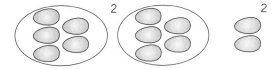

The two 2s are then looped: ㉒. This numeral represents the two sets of five elements and the leftover two elements.

Using this system, how would the citizens of this land record the following quantity?

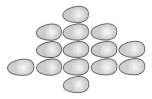

They would count five and draw a loop enclosing that set. They would then count five more and draw a loop around that group. They would find that four elements are left over. They would record the count as ㉔. The 2 stands for two sets of five, and the 4 stands for four ones.

Upon reflection, it appears that the method of counting used in this faraway land is not as strange as it first seemed. We both use "dozens" to describe the way we buy eggs, but when we write our numeral that represents a dozen, we use tens and ones rather than fives and ones. When we count to "24" the numeral we use represents 2 tens and 4 ones, not the 2 fives and 4 ones written by the Quints. But other than the value of the places in the numerals, our system of numeration seems to be the same as the one used by the Quints. We use a decimal place-value system—a system based on grouping by tens.

DECIMAL NUMERATION

The notion of place value is an important idea that is fundamental to whole numbers, integers, and rational numbers expressed as decimals. Understanding the concept of place value is essential to comprehending the computational algorithms we teach. The individual steps of a computational algorithm can often be conveyed meaningfully through the use of a discussion of the algorithm centered on a place-value argument. In general, many teachers do not adequately emphasize place value in their teaching of algorithms. This may lead the student to believe that an algorithm is just a blind application of seemingly arbitrary rules and may contribute to the development of an attitude that mathematics doesn't make sense. Knowledge of the principles of place value gives us power with the numeration system we use. The more students learn about the characteristics and benefits of a place-value system of numeration, the more likely they are to appreciate its superiority, in terms of ease of use, to other types of numeration systems.

Any **place-value numeration system** has a scheme of grouping that is basic to that system. The number of symbols necessary in a particular numeration system is directly related to this basic grouping. For example, in the base ten system there are ten symbols or **digits**:

0, 1, 2, 3, 4, 5, 6, 7, 8, 9

Using these digits, or a combination of these digits, any number, no matter how great or small its value, can be expressed. This is possible because the **decimal system** (or base ten system) uses *place value* and has a special symbol, the zero, for indicating "not any." Zero, as we use it in our numeration system, is a concept that makes our system unique compared to ancient numeration systems.

When we agree that ten is to be the *base* of a numeration system, we are saying that ten is the *basis for grouping* in that system. We can count from 1 to 9 and record this count in the ones column (the first column to the left of the decimal point in the base ten system) with a single digit; when we reach a count of ten, we form a group of ten and express it by a 1 in the next (tens) column to the left. A count greater than 9 but less than 100 must be expressed as a group or groups of ten, and any ones left over are recorded in the ones column.

Children need many experiences grouping and regrouping objects into groups of tens and ones. Place two sheets of paper in front of the children. On one of the sheets print the word *Ones*, and on the other sheet print the word *Tens*. To mimic the place-value arrangement that the children will later use, place the Tens sheet to the children's left and the Ones sheet to the right.

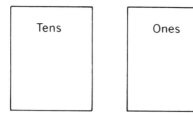

Have the children place plastic spoons on the sheet marked Ones. As they reach nine ones encourage them to think about what we might do when we get ten ones. By focusing on the name of the Tens sheet, children should recognize that whenever ten items (spoons, in this case) are on the Ones sheet, they should be regrouped into one ten on the Tens sheet.

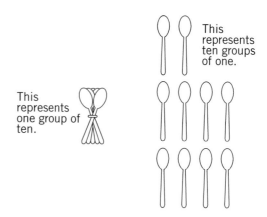

This represents ten groups of one.

This represents one group of ten.

A place-value box may also be used. A place-value box is any box that has compartments labeled corresponding to decimal places. For example:

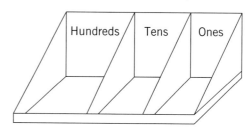

The number 23 can be shown with two groups of tens and three ones. In the place-value box we would place three single spoons in the compartment labeled *Ones*, and we would place two packages of ten spoons each into the compartment labeled *Tens*. We can also show the number 23 by placing three single spoons on a sheet of paper marked *Ones* and placing to the left two packages of ten spoons each on a sheet labeled *Tens*:

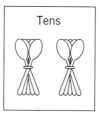
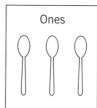

Have the children select numeral cards and place them on the place-value sheets:

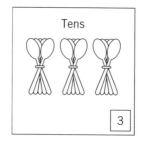
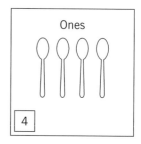

We have already said that ten is the basis for grouping in the decimal system. Now let's examine the regular patterns inherent in this grouping. A group of ten ones becomes 1 ten and 0 ones; a group of ten-tens becomes 1 hundred, 0 tens, and 0 ones; a group of ten hundreds becomes 1 thousand, 0 hundreds, 0 tens, and 0 ones. This can be shown in a large grid made for the children, and they can manipulate groups of objects bundled in ones, tens, or hundreds right on the grid. The children can use a small grid such as the following by placing numeral cards on the grid or using a marking pencil on a grid covered with a clear plastic film:

Thousands	Hundreds	Tens	Ones	
		1	0	Ten ones or one ten
	1	0	0	Ten tens or one hundred
1	0	0	0	Ten hundreds or one thousand

It is evident that whenever we have ten in any group, we move one place to the left and record a one in that column (for one set of ten, one set of one hundred, and so on). Thus a digit in any column represents ten times the value of that same digit in the column to its right. For example, the numeral 1 in the thousands column represents ten times the value of the numeral 1 in the hundreds column. We can rearrange the information in our grid to express this another way:

$10 \times 10 \times 10$	10×10	10	1
Thousands	Hundreds	Tens	Ones

This is an abstract idea—one that is often very difficult for young children to comprehend. Provide physical materials—such as Popsicle sticks and rubber bands—for children to manipulate, and systematically teach, apply, and have children practice the concept of bundling and unbundling. By noting the number of times 10 is used as a factor, we see that each column represents 10 times the value of the column to its right. By the use of exponential notation, we can write this in simpler fashion. We can write a numeral (called an *exponent*) above and to the right of the 10 (in this case, to indicate how many times 10 is used as a factor). We can abbreviate $10 \times 10 \times 10$ by writing 10^3, and 10×10 by writing 10^2. We read 10^3 as "ten to the third power," and we read 10^2 as "ten to the second power." The number 10 can be written as 10^1 (ten to the first power), since 10 occurs only once and is represented by 10×1.

Study the following list of powers of ten. Do you see a pattern that indicates how the number 1 can be written as a power of ten?

$$1000 = 10^3$$
$$100 = 10^2$$
$$10 = 10^1$$
$$1 = 10^?$$

The exponents are decreasing by one as we go down the list, so the exponent that we want is 0; 1 is equal to 10 to the **zero power**: $1 = 10^0$. (In fact, any nonzero number raised to the zero power is equal to 1.) We can

show the values for each column in the grid by using **exponential notation**:

10^3	10^2	10^1	10^0
Thousands	Hundreds	Tens	Ones

In this chart, 10 is called the **base**, and 3, 2, 1, and 0 are called **exponents**. A positive exponent on a numeral indicates the number of times that the base is to be used as a factor:

$$\text{Base} \rightarrow 10^2 \text{ Exponent}$$

A number with an exponent is said to be *raised to a power*; the power is named by the exponent. The powers of ten in the preceding grid are as follows:

10^0 means 10 to the zero power—1. (Except for zero, any number raised to the zero power is equal to 1.)
10^1 means 10 to the first power—10. (Any number raised to the first power is the number itself; so $10^1 = 10$.)
10^2 means 10 to the second power—100. (10^2 means 10 used as a factor two times: $10 \times 10 = 100$.)
10^3 means 10 to the third power—1000; and so on.

To illustrate how exponential notation and place value are related, consider the number 1314. Arrange the numerals in a grid as we did earlier:

10^3	10^2	10^1	10^0
1	3	1	4

In this grid, the place value of each digit is indicated by the power of ten at the top of the column.

$$1314 = (1 \times 10^3) + (3 \times 10^2) + (1 \times 10^1) + (4 \times 10^0)$$
$$= (1 \times 10 \times 10 \times 10) + (3 \times 10 \times 10)$$
$$+ (1 \times 10) + (4 \times 1)$$
$$= (1 \times 1000) + (3 \times 100) + (1 \times 10) + (4 \times 1)$$
$$= 1000 + 300 + 10 + 4$$
$$= 1314$$

Thus we see the relation in our decimal system between place value and exponential notation.

The operations that children perform on numbers are often understood more easily through the use of **expanded notation**, in which numbers are thought of in particular component parts before the operations are performed. These component parts show the place values of the digits in the numerals. A numeral written in expanded notation is called an *expanded numeral*.

Consider the number 2346 written in expanded notation:

1. $2000 + 300 + 40 + 6$

By naming a number in this way, children can see at a glance the makeup of the number in terms of groups of ones, tens, hundreds, thousands, and so on. The preceding expanded notation could also be written as:

2. $(2 \times 1000) + (3 \times 100) + (4 \times 10) + (6 \times 1)$
3. 2 thousands, 3 hundreds, 4 tens, 6 ones
4. $(2 \times 10 \times 10 \times 10) + (3 \times 10 \times 10) + (4 \times 10) + (6 \times 1)$

or, using exponential notation:

5. $(2 \times 10^3) + (3 \times 10^2) + (4 \times 10^1) + (6 \times 10^0)$

Forms (1), (2), and (3) are the most commonly used in the elementary school, with form (3) probably the most meaningful for the elementary child. Forms (4) and (5) tend to be too abstract at this level. Expanded notation helps the child understand the grouping process and to see clearly how the "original" number is actually made up of groups of numbers.

$$2346 = 2000 + 300 + 40 + 6$$
$$= (2 \times 1000) + (3 \times 100) + (4 \times 10) + (6 \times 1)$$

Numeral expanders are excellent devices for children to manipulate and for teachers to demonstrate the meaning of place value. The following are two types of numeral expanders using the number 124:

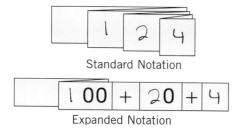

Standard Notation

Expanded Notation

The number 124 can be thought of in many different ways, as the accompanying illustration shows:

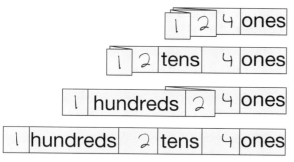

The use of a numeral expander makes it easier to discuss three aspects of numberness essential for interpreting a given numeral: the distinction between place value, face value, and total value when reading a multiplace number. Consider 242. The "2" on the left in this numeral has a face value of 2, its place value is hundreds, and the total value is 200 (2×100). The "2" on the right also has a face value of 2 but its place value is units, so the total value is 2 (2×1). The lesson that children need to learn is that in such a numeral, the 2s don't look different—what makes their value different is the place they occupy. (*Note to the reader*: Information on purchasing numeral expanders and a 24-page teachers' support manual can be obtained by contacting Dr. William Speer via e-mail at speerw@nevada.edu or by writing him at *Today's Mathematics*, John Wiley &

Sons, Inc., Education—College Division, Fifth Floor, 605 Third Avenue, New York, New York 10158.)

As may be evident from the numeral expander examples, sometimes it is less confusing for children if word names for numbers are used instead of just numerals. This seems to be particularly true when discussing subtraction. Study this example written both with words and numerals and with numerals alone:

$46 = $ 4 tens 6 ones	$46 = (40 + 6)$
$\underline{-23} = \underline{-2 \text{ tens } 3 \text{ ones}}$	$\underline{-23} = \underline{-(20 + 3)}$
2 tens 3 ones $= 23$	$20 + 9 = 29$

Children often incorrectly add the numbers in the ones place and subtract the numbers in the tens place (in this case, obtaining a wrong answer of 29).

Let's examine the organization of our base ten number system: U.S. elementary schools most often retain the use of commas to separate the places of the base ten system into "periods." Each period has three places; they are named, right to left, *ones*, *tens*, and *hundreds*. The names *ones*, *tens*, and *hundreds* are repeated in each period along with the period name. Each period has its own name and is used every time we read a number. The international trend in writing large numbers is to replace the commas with spaces—for example, 20 000 instead of 20,000. Since commas are not used in the metric system or in computers or calculators to separate periods within a number, children must be able to read numbers separated by spaces as well as those separated by commas.

Now let us consider the number in the "Period Name" display shown on the next page. (We introduce this as a curiosity and so you can note similarities with place-value names. It is neither necessary nor desirable for children—or even adults for that matter—to learn all these places.)

Each period has a name and a ones, tens, and hundreds place. Study this pattern. To read a decimal number, read the three digits in a period; then give the period name. Continue this process from left to right. Thus the number in the figure would be read, "One hundred twenty-three decillion, four hundred fifty-six nonillion, seven hundred eighty-nine octillion, one hundred twenty-three septillion, four hundred fifty-six sextillion, seven hundred eighty-nine quintillion, one hundred twenty-three quadrillion, four hundred fifty-six trillion, seven hundred eighty-nine billion, one hundred twenty-three million, four hundred fifty-six thousand, seven hundred eighty-nine." Wow! Before returning to reality, you might want to research a number referred to as a *googol*—the name given to a very large number—a "1" with 100 trailing zeros!

Base ten blocks, introduced earlier in this chapter, are excellent materials to use when teaching place-value concepts. For more information about using base ten blocks, we recommend Zoltan Dienes' book *Modern Mathematics for Young Children*.

As discussed previously, the materials for a base ten place-value system are composed of the units shown in the illustration at the bottom of page 97. Note the rela-

hundreds tens ones	hundreds tens ones	hundreds tens ones	hundreds tens ones	hundreds tens ones	hundreds tens ones	hundreds tens ones	hundreds tens ones	hundreds tens ones	hundreds tens ones	hundreds tens ones	hundreds tens ones
{1 2 3},	{4 5 6},	{7 8 9},	{1 2 3},	{4 5 6},	{7 8 9},	{1 2 3},	{4 5 6},	{7 8 9},	{1 2 3},	{4 5 6},	{7 8 9}
Decillions	Nonillions	Octillions	Septillions	Sextillions	Quintillions	Quadrillions	Trillions	Billions	Millions	Thousands	Units

Period Name

tionships that exist among these materials—unit, long, flat, and block (see below).

Although not always apparent to the children using the blocks, renaming numbers using blocks involves a form of Piaget's idea of conservation of volume. Children benefit from manipulating and exchanging blocks so that they maintain the same amount of wood. For example, if a child wants to show the number 123 using base ten blocks, what is the least number of base ten blocks (pieces of wood) the child could have? In this case the child would have 1 flat, 2 longs, and 3 units. Have the child go to the base ten block bank and exchange one of the pieces for an equivalent amount of wood. The child might change 1 long for 10 units. Then he or she would have 1 flat, 1 long, and 13 units. If the child now exchanges 1 long at the bank so that the amount of wood remains constant, then he or she would have 1 flat, 0 longs, and 23 units. This same process can be used so that the amount of wood is always the same but the number and types of pieces vary. A child should see all possible combinations. All possible combinations for 123 units are:

		123 units
	1 long,	113 units
	2 longs,	103 units
	3 longs,	93 units
	4 longs,	83 units
	5 longs,	73 units
	6 longs,	63 units
	7 longs,	53 units
	8 longs,	43 units
	9 longs,	33 units
	10 longs,	23 units
	11 longs,	13 units
	12 longs,	3 units
1 flat,	2 longs,	3 units
1 flat,	1 long,	13 units
1 flat,	0 longs,	23 units

Children should now begin to realize that in each case there is exactly the same amount of wood. The only differences are the type and the number of pieces.

The block, flat, long, and unit can be related to the base ten place-value system. Have the children study the relationships among the blocks and the base ten place-value system.

Ones place	One is equivalent to a unit.
Tens place	Ten is equivalent to a long.
Hundreds place	Hundred is equivalent to a flat.
Thousands place	Thousand is equivalent to a block.

These blocks and pictures of these blocks provide children with many experiences on the concrete, semiconcrete, and semiabstract levels. Children could have more experiences on the semiabstract and abstract levels by using chip trading. In chip trading, a chip of

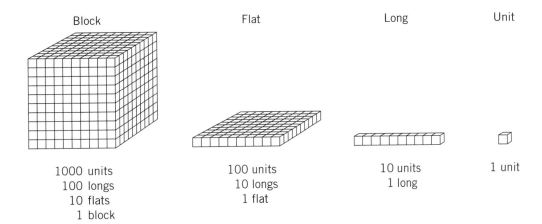

Block	Flat	Long	Unit
1000 units 100 longs 10 flats 1 block	100 units 10 longs 1 flat	10 units 1 long	1 unit

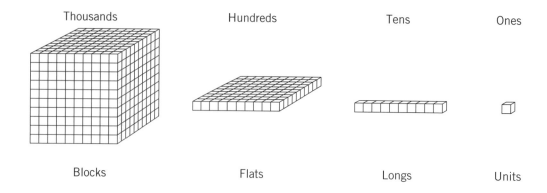

one color is given a value ten times that of another color. Consequently, a collection of, say, 2 blue chips, 4 red chips, and 5 green chips might refer to the number 245, even though there are only 11 chips in all. Often, but not always, chip trading activities incorporate a positional value for the colored chips as shown in the following figure:

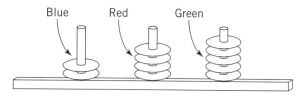

Once children have learned about the base ten system, they may want to apply this knowledge to other systems. This is an appropriate time to introduce them to some of the features of numeration systems used in the past.

ANCIENT NUMERATION SYSTEMS

As human beings mastered their environments and developed organized societies, they found that a major necessity, in addition to language, was a method of counting and recording numbers. From primitive one-to-one matching (notching a stick to keep a tally) to present-day computers, people have created a bewildering variety of ways to count and record numbers.

We tend to take our familiar base ten (decimal) system for granted—so much so, in fact, that we usually fail to understand the full meaning of the numerals we write and of the computations we perform. A brief examination of several historical numeration systems, as well as systems using bases other than ten, might afford a fuller understanding of the measures of our decimal system, such as place value, the zero symbol, and the base of ten. The point here is not the memorization or even the application of other numeration systems, but, rather, an appreciation of the strengths and weaknesses of each.

Obviously we can't study all of the many different numeration systems that have been created and used over the centuries. But we can look at a few examples of additive systems, multiplicative systems, and place-value systems. The ancient Egyptian numeration system is an example of an additive system; the Romans used a modified additive system; the ancient Chinese used a multiplicative system (still in use today); and the Babylonians used a place-value system, although the Babylonian system lacks some of the refinements of our base ten (decimal) system, which of course also uses place value.

Every **numeration system** uses a set of symbols to represent numbers. The following chart shows the symbols used by the ancient Egyptians:

Egyptian Numeral	Number Named	Meaning of Picture Symbol
$\vert$	1	stroke
$\cap$	10	cattle hobble or oxen yoke
ς	100	coil of rope
¶ or 𝟃	1000	lotus plant
𝕁 or ∫	10,000	bent finger
⌒	100,000	tadpole
𝕐 or 𝕐	1,000,000	a god with arms supporting the sky

The ancient Egyptians used an **additive system of numeration** in which the values of numerals were added together regardless of the order in which the numerals were written. For example, the numeral representing 13 could be written as

$$\cap \vert\vert\vert, \ \vert\vert\vert \cap, \ \text{or} \ \vert \cap \vert\vert,$$

Other examples include

$$\varsigma \cap \cap \cap \ \vert\vert\vert\vert\vert = 135$$

$$\cap \cap \cap \cap \cap \cap \cap \cap \cap \vert\vert\vert\vert\vert\vert\vert\vert\vert = 99$$

$$⌒ \ ∫ \ 𝟃 \ \varsigma \cap \vert = 111,111$$

What do you think the major difficulties would be if you had to calculate using the Egyptian system? As you study the following examples, you should begin to appreciate the advantages of calculating with a place-value system instead.

Addition:
$$\text{99} \cap\cap\cap\cap\text{III} + \text{9} \cap\cap\cap\,{}^{\text{III}}_{\text{III}}$$
$$= \quad \cap\cap\cap \;\text{IIIII}$$
$$\text{999} \cap\cap\cap\cap\text{IIII}$$

Subtraction:
$$\text{99} \cap\cap\cap\text{III} - \text{9} \cap\cap\text{IIII} = \text{9}\,{}^{\text{IIII}}_{\text{IIIII}}$$

Do not ask children to calculate in other numeration systems or in other base systems. This system is illustrated here to help students comprehend and appreciate our base ten system. Children who are weak in arithmetic or have little interest in mathematics will not profit from computational practice of this type. It would be much more advantageous to devote teaching time to the study and understanding of computation in our base ten system.

The Egyptian system was based on simple addition, but its symbols represent powers of ten. It did not have a place-value component, and it did not have a symbol for zero. Such a system becomes very clumsy and difficult when greater numbers are involved.

Of all the older systems, the Roman system of numeration is probably the most familiar to us. We still see Roman numerals used for identifying book chapters, clock numerals, formal inscriptions, and even for creating an outline. The Roman system was not a place-value system and did not have a symbol for zero. The most common Roman symbols are as follows:

Roman Numeral	Value of Numeral
I	1
V	5
X	10
L	50
C	100
D	500
M	1000

To find the value of a numeral, the Romans added the values of numerals in much the same way as the Egyptians did:

$$XVI = 10 + 5 + 1 = 16$$
$$LXVIII = 50 + 10 + 5 + 1 + 1 + 1 = 68$$

However, unlike the Egyptian system, the Roman numeration system was not based entirely on simple addition of number values represented by numerals in any order. Although the Roman system did not have place value, numerals of greater value were *usually* placed to the left of the numerals of lesser value:

$$CLXVI = 100 + 50 + 10 + 5 + 1 = 166$$

If a numeral of lesser value was placed to the left of (or preceding) numerals of greater value, this indicated that the lesser value was to be subtracted from the greater value. For example:

$$IX = 10 - 1 = 9$$
$$IV = 5 - 1 = 4$$
$$XCIV = (100 - 10) + (5 - 1) = 94$$

The Chinese continue to use a **multiplicative system of numeration** to indicate number value. This system has symbols to represent the numbers from 1 through 9 and separate symbols for powers of ten. The Chinese symbols and their values are shown in the accompanying table:

Chinese Symbol	Value
一	1
二	2
三	3
四	4
五	5
六	6
七	7
八	8
九	9
十	10
百	100

Repetition of symbols in the Chinese system is avoided by multiplying given numbers by powers of ten. For example, 70 would be written as

七 十

7 x 10 = 70

Research Snapshot

How does the Asian system of naming numbers compare to how English-speaking cultures name numbers?

The Asian system of naming numbers is a complete regular named value system including the tens. That is, 11 is "ten one," and 21 is "two ten one." So in Asian languages, 3 + 9 is "ten two," while in English, it is "twelve." "Ten two" can be thought of as a multiunit, while "twelve" has no connotation of a 10 and a 2.

It is frequently noted that it is more difficult for children from English-speaking countries to construct and use multi-unit conceptual structures. Most English-speaking U.S. first graders, given base ten blocks (tens) and unit counters (ones), make unitary models using only the ones, while most Chinese, Japanese, and Korean first graders use the tens and ones (Miura, Kim, Chang, and Okamoto, 1988). That is, an English-speaking child, when asked to show what the 1 means in the numeral 16, will often pick up one stick instead of the ten sticks that it actually represents.

What are the implications of basing primary mathematics instruction on unitary models? What implications would this have for teaching multiplace operations in your classroom?

Miura, I., Kim, C. C., Chang, C., & Okamoto, Y. (1988). Effects of language characteristics on children's cognitive representation of number: Cross-national comparisons. *Child Development, 59,* 1445–1450.

For additional research briefs, "ERIC Digests" lets you search more than 2,000 short syntheses of research on a range of education topics. The syntheses were produced by the Educational Resources Information Center (ERIC). Check http://ed.gov/databases/ERIC_Digests/index/

Greater numbers could be written this way:

$$(4 \times 100) + (5 \times 10) + 6 = 456$$

The ancient Babylonian civilization was one of the first to develop and use a place-value system. The basic symbol of the Babylonians was a wedge shape. Symbols were inscribed on wet clay tablets with a stylus, and the tablets were then dried. Owing to the dry climate, many of these tablets containing Babylonian cuneiform writing and mathematical symbols have been preserved. The Babylonian place-value system was based on groupings of 60 and multiples of 60; for this reason it is called a *sexagesimal* system. The Babylonian system did not have a symbol for zero until about 200 B.C.

The symbols generally used by the Babylonians were two distinctive wedge-shaped marks, ◄ and ▼. The principal values of these symbols are

| 36,000 | 3600 | 600 | 60 | 10 | 1 |

Obviously, since the same symbol could represent more than one value, there was likely to be some confusion in interpreting numerals. Apparently the Babylonians depended on the context of the numerals to indicate their values. Values from 1 through 9 were noted by simple repetition and addition.

Babylonian Symbol	Value	Babylonian Symbol	Value
▼	1	▼▼▼ / ▼▼▼	6
▼▼	2	▼▼▼▼ / ▼▼▼	7
▼▼▼	3	▼▼ ▼▼ / ▼▼ ▼▼	8
▼▼▼ / ▼	4	▼▼▼ / ▼▼ / ▼▼▼	9
▼▼ / ▼▼	5	◄	10

Place value was indicated by the arrangement of the numerals. In the following examples, the values of the numerals are indicated.

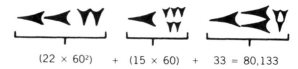

$$(22 \times 60^2) + (15 \times 60) + 33 = 80,133$$

Since the Babylonians did not have a symbol for zero for many centuries, their place-value system was liable to be misread. For example, ◄◄ ▼ could represent 21; or, if the first two symbols were read as 600 + 600, it could represent either 1201 or 1260. Similarly, the number 35 could be written as follows:

$$(3 \times 10) + (5 \times 1)$$

But this could also be interpreted as 2100.

$(3 \times 600) + (5 \times 60)$

A symbol for zero, it seems, is a necessity in an efficient place-value system.

The numeration system that we use today was invented by the Hindus and modified by the Arabs. The Hindu-Arabic system eventually spread through Europe and evolved into our modern **base ten** or **decimal** system of numeration. The efficiency of the decimal system depends on two important features—a symbol for zero and the use of place value. These two features serve to eliminate awkward notation and provide for ease in calculation.

NUMBER BASES OTHER THAN TEN

Many elementary mathematics programs provide an introduction to other numeration systems, including numeration systems having bases other than ten. There are several reasons for examining numeration systems in an elementary mathematics program. First, this creates an awareness of mathematics as part of our cultural history. Also, this demonstrates the possibility of using numeration systems that differ from ours in significant ways.

Many of the basic generalizations made about the base ten system also apply to bases other than ten. Consequently, teaching children about other base systems reinforces the meaning of the structure of our base ten system. Children have an opportunity to apply what they have discovered about one place-value system to new situations. If we teach base five, for example, merely for its own sake or as a curiosity of numbers and do not reinforce the children's knowledge of mathematical structure and number relations in base ten, then we are wasting time that could be put to better use.

Throughout history, various societies have developed different types of numeration systems, or ways of counting and calculating. But the idea of grouping probably occurred when people began to work with large quantities. A basic concept for any place-value system is some method of grouping.

Recall our imaginary trip to a faraway land at the beginning of this chapter. The people we visited counted in a manner similar but clearly different from the way we count. These people, we discovered, were grouping by fives, not tens. Such a system is called a **base five** or **quinary** numeration system. When we calculate using base five (or any base other than base ten), we usually write the name of the base as a subscript to avoid confusion. Thus we could record the two groups of five and four ones as 24_{five}. This is read, "two-four, base five," and means two groups of five and four ones. The reason we don't call this number "twenty-four" is that the word name *twenty-four* actually means two tens and four ones. Examine the accompanying table, which is written in the base five, or quinary, system:

Base-Five Grouping	Base-Five Notation	Base-Five Name
•	1	one
••	2	two
•••	3	three
••••	4	four
•••••	10_{five}	one-zero base five
••••• •	11_{five}	one-one base five
••••• ••	12_{five}	one-two base five
••••• •••	13_{five}	one-three base five
••••• ••••	14_{five}	one-four base five
••••• •••••	20_{five}	two-zero base five
••••• ••••• •	21_{five}	two-one base five
••••• ••••• ••	22_{five}	two-two base five
••••• ••••• •••	23_{five}	two-three base five
⋮	⋮	⋮
••••• ••••• ••••• ••••• ••	42_{five}	four-two base five
••••• ••••• ••••• ••••• •••	43_{five}	four-three base five
••••• ••••• ••••• ••••• ••••	44_{five}	four-four base five

Let's use these basic ideas about grouping to develop an **octal** numeration system. An octal system is a system in which we group by eights. Using this system, how would you count the following elements?

Since we are grouping by eight, we would count 1, 2, 3, 4, 5, 6, 7, 8; draw a loop around this group; and record a 1 to represent one group of eight. There are two left over, so this number would be recorded as a 2. The completed numeral is 12_{eight}. The 1 stands for one group of eight, the 2 stands for two ones, and the subscript reminds us that we are grouping in base eight. How can we record the following items in base eight?

How many groups of eight are there? (Three.) How many ones? (Three.) The number, then, would be recorded as 33_{eight}. Now, examine the octal numeration table on the next page.

Octal Grouping	Octal Notation	Octal Name
•	1	one
••	2	two
•••	3	three
••••	4	four
•••• •	5	five
•••• ••	6	six
•••• •••	7	seven
•••• ••••	10_{eight}	one-zero base eight
•••• •••• •	11_{eight}	one-one base eight
•••• •••• ••	12_{eight}	one-two base eight
•••• •••• •••	13_{eight}	one-three base eight
•••• •••• ••••	14_{eight}	one-four base eight
•••• •••• •••• •	15_{eight}	one-five base eight
•••• •••• •••• ••	16_{eight}	one-six base eight
•••• •••• •••• •••	17_{eight}	one-seven base eight
•••• •••• •••• ••••	20_{eight}	two-zero base eight

Thus we have developed base five and base eight for two-digit numerals. Now let's consider the value of the third place. In base five the first column was used to record the number of ones, and the second column was used to record the number of groups of five. What meaning does a numeral have in the third place? As soon as five ones are counted, they are recorded as 1 in the fives column, or the second place. This indicates one set of five. What happens when we reach five sets of five? Five sets of five are written as 100_{five}. The third column, then, is used to record the number of sets of five-fives (that is, twenty-fives, using our familiar decimal language).

Twenty-fives	Fives	Ones
1	0	0

$100_{five} = 25_{ten}$

100_{five} is equal to 1 set of 25, no sets of 5, and no sets of 1

What does 123_{five} mean? It means one group of five-fives, two groups of five, and three ones, or, translated into base ten, 38_{ten} $(25 + 10 + 3 = 38)$.

What value would the third column have in base eight? The first column is used to record the number of ones and the second column the number of groups of eight. The third column, then, would be used to record the number of groups of eight-eights (8^2 or 64). Eight groups of eight would be written 100_{eight}, which means

one group of eight-eights (64s), no groups of eight, and no ones.

Sixty-fours	Eights	Ones
1	0	0

$100_{eight} = 64_{ten}$

Actually, we use many groupings other than ten on a day-to-day basis; for instance:

- 2 dozen and 3 eggs are 27 eggs or $23_{twelve} = 27_{ten}$
  3 weeks and 4 days are 25 days or $34_{seven} = 25_{ten}$
  1 hour and 8 minutes are 68 minutes or $18_{sixty} = 68_{ten}$
  2 quarters, 1 nickel, and 4 pennies are 59 cents or $214_{five} = 59_{ten}$

A numeration system can be developed using any method of grouping. The base indicates the number of items grouped together. The accompanying table indicates the notation for numeration systems based on various groupings. Note the column for base twelve. How many numerals would be needed for a base twelve numeration system? (Twelve.) We cannot represent all twelve by using base ten numerals, because base ten has only ten one-digit numerals. Consequently we must invent two new symbols. In this case, as is usually the norm, we have chosen to use T and E as one-digit numerals to represent groupings of ten and eleven.

Base Ten	Base Twelve	Base Eight	Base Five	Base Three	Base Two
1	1	1	1	1	1
2	2	2	2	2	10_{two}
3	3	3	3	10_{three}	11_{two}
4	4	4	4	11_{three}	100_{two}
5	5	5	10_{five}	12_{three}	101_{two}
6	6	6	11_{five}	20_{three}	110_{two}
7	7	7	12_{five}	21_{three}	111_{two}
8	8	10_{eight}	13_{five}	22_{three}	1000_{two}
9	9	11_{eight}	14_{five}	100_{three}	1001_{two}
10	T	12_{eight}	20_{five}	101_{three}	1010_{two}
11	E	13_{eight}	21_{five}	102_{three}	1011_{two}
12	10_{twelve}	14_{eight}	22_{five}	110_{three}	1100_{two}
13	11_{twelve}	15_{eight}	23_{five}	111_{three}	1101_{two}
14	12_{twelve}	16_{eight}	24_{five}	112_{three}	1110_{two}
15	13_{twelve}	17_{eight}	30_{five}	120_{three}	1111_{two}
16	14_{twelve}	20_{eight}	31_{five}	121_{three}	10000_{two}
17	15_{twelve}	21_{eight}	32_{five}	122_{three}	10001_{two}
18	16_{twelve}	22_{eight}	33_{five}	200_{three}	10010_{two}
19	17_{twelve}	23_{eight}	34_{five}	201_{three}	10011_{two}
20	18_{twelve}	24_{eight}	40_{five}	202_{three}	10100_{two}
21	19_{twelve}	25_{eight}	41_{five}	210_{three}	10101_{two}
22	$1T_{twelve}$	26_{eight}	42_{five}	211_{three}	10110_{two}
23	$1E_{twelve}$	27_{eight}	43_{five}	212_{three}	10111_{two}
24	20_{twelve}	30_{eight}	44_{five}	220_{three}	11000_{two}
25	21_{twelve}	31_{eight}	100_{five}	221_{three}	11001_{two}

Considering the previous discussion, the numeration table, and our knowledge of the base ten system, we can make the following generalizations about the nature of place-value numeration systems using any base:

1. The first column on the right is always the ones place in any place-value base system.
2. The second column is always used to record the groupings named by the base. In base five the second place is called the *fives* place, in base eight the second place is called the *eights* place, in base ten the second place is called the *tens* place, and so on.
3. The third column is always used to record the number of groupings named by the square of the base. In base five the third place is for the number of groups of five-fives (5^2). In base eight the third place is for the number of groups of eight-eights (8^2). In base ten the third place is for the number of groups of ten-tens (10^2).
4. The numeral that records the number named by the base is always written as 10_{base}. In base five, 10_{five} stands for one group of five. In base eight, 10_{eight} stands for one group of eight.
5. The number of symbols used in any whole-number numeration system is the same as the base of the system. Base five uses five symbols, usually 0, 1, 2, 3, 4. Base eight uses eight symbols, usually 0, 1, 2, 3, 4, 5, 6, 7. Base ten uses ten symbols: 0, 1, 2, 3, 4, 5, 6, 7, 8, 9.

Using these generalizations, we can develop a base two, or **binary**, system. We know that we will need how many symbols? (Two, since we are constructing a base two system.) We know that one of the symbols will have to be a 0. Why? (Because our binary system has place value and requires a symbol to represent "not any.") So let's use the symbols 0 and 1. Let's name the following set in binary notation:

First we want to record the number of ones in the ones place, so we draw a loop around groups of two:

There is 1 one left over to record in the ones column. What will we record in the next column? (The number of sets of two.) How many groups of two are there? (Two.) But the symbol "2" is not a numeral in our base two system. What about the third column? What is recorded there? (The number of sets grouped according to the square of the base, in this case 2^2, or 4.) How many groups of four are there? (One.)

From this diagram, we see that we have one group of four, no groups of two, and one group of one. We can now write the base two numeral as 101_{two}.

In the binary system the values of the places are shown by this diagram:

Sixteen (2^4)	Eight (2^3)	Four (2^2)	Two (2^1)	One

Note that the fourth column is used to record the number of groups of eight and the fifth column the number of groups of sixteen. Drawing on what we have just learned about the binary system, we can now write a table of the binary notations for the first twelve numbers:

Decimal Notation	Binary Grouping	Binary Notation
1	●	1
2	●●	10_{two}
3	●●●	11_{two}
4	●●●●	100_{two}
5	●●●●●	101_{two}
6	●●●●●●	110_{two}
7	●●●●●●●	111_{two}
8	●●●●●●●●	1000_{two}
9	●●●●●●●●●	1001_{two}
10	●●●●●●●●●●	1010_{two}
11	●●●●●●●●●●●	1011_{two}
12	●●●●●●●●●●●●	1100_{two}

Can we now develop a base four system? This time, just for a change, let's invent four new symbols instead of borrowing Hindu-Arabic symbols.

Quantity	Symbol
	◯
●	/
●●	∠
●●●	△
●●●●	/ ◯

In our notation the first column on the right is used to record the number of ones, the second column to record the number of groups of four, and the third column to record the number of groups of four-fours (16).

Sixteens	Fours	Ones	Grouping
		/	●
		∠	●●
		△	●●●
	/	◯	●●●●

(continued next page)

(continued from page 103)

Sixteens	Fours	Ones	Grouping
	/	/	•••• •
	/	∠	•••• ••
	/	△	•••• •••
	∠	○	•••• / ••••
	∠	/	•••• • / ••••
	∠	∠	•••• •• / ••••
	∠	△	•••• ••• / ••••
	△	○	•••• •••• / ••••
	△	/	•••• •••• / •••• •
	△	∠	•••• •••• / •••• ••
	△	△	•••• •••• / •••• •••
/	○	○	•••• •••• / •••• ••••

CLOSURE

Now let us again consider our base ten (decimal) system. It has the same characteristics as systems in other bases. A base ten system must have ten symbols. We use the ten Hindu-Arabic digits:

0, 1, 2, 3, 4, 5, 6, 7, 8

In the first column on the right (or the first column to the left of the decimal point if the number is written as a decimal), we record the number of ones. In the second column (the tens place), we record the number of groups of ten. In the third column (the hundreds place), we record the number of groups of ten-tens (10^2 or 100).

Thus, we see what *place value* means. In a **place-value numeration system**, the *value* a digit represents depends on the *place* of the digit within the numeral.

In subsequent chapters, we will discover that the concept of place value and the structure of our numeration system are critical—in fact, essential—to understanding whole numbers, integers, and rational numbers, as well as the algorithms applied to these number systems.

Terminology, Symbols, and Procedures

Additive System of Numeration. In an additive system of numeration, digits have definite values regardless of the order in which they are written; the value of a numeral is obtained by simply adding the values of the individual symbols that form the numeral. For example, the Egyptian system and, to a more limited extent, the Roman system, were additive systems.

Attribute Blocks. Attribute blocks are a set of blocks that are described by various characteristics, such as color, shape, size, and thickness.

Base. The base of any place-value numeration system is determined by the method of grouping in that system. The **base ten** system groups by *tens*. This means that when we reach a count of nine ones, the next number will be recorded as one group of ten:

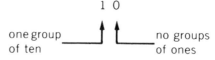

More than nine groups of ten are recorded as one group of 10×10, or 100:

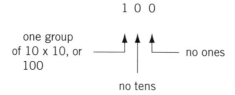

In a **base five** system we group by *fives.* We can count four ones, and the next number is recorded as follows:

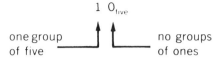

Five sets of five are recorded as follows:

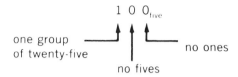

The base two system is sometimes called the **binary** system, the base eight system is called the **octal** system, and the base sixteen system is called the **hexigesimal** system. Each of these has applications in computer technology.

Base Ten Blocks. These are a set of blocks designed to represent one cube, ten cubes, one hundred cubes, and one thousand cubes. These blocks are related to the base ten system of ones, tens, hundreds, and thousands. Similar materials are available for other bases and are referred to as *Dienes Multibase Blocks,* named after Zoltan Dienes, who pioneered their use. Blocks are available for base ten, nine, eight, seven, six, five, four, three, and two.

Cardinal Number. A cardinal number is used to answer the question "How many?" In counting the objects of a finite set, we match the objects one-to-one with counting numbers, and the last (or terminal) counting number named is the cardinal number of the set.

Counting Numbers. The counting numbers (or *natural numbers*) are the numbers 1, 2, 3, . . .

Cuisenaire Rods. Cuisenaire rods are a set of nonscored rods related by color and length. Color is a very important attribute of these rods since they are frequently differentiated by length using the color names; for example, the yellow rod is longer than the red rod.

Decimal System. A decimal system is a place-value numeration system in which ten is the basis for grouping.

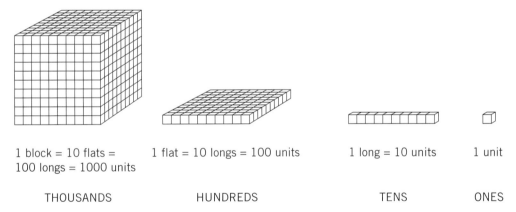

1 block = 10 flats =   1 flat = 10 longs = 100 units   1 long = 10 units   1 unit
100 longs = 1000 units

THOUSANDS   HUNDREDS   TENS   ONES

Dienes Multibase Blocks. See *Base Ten Blocks*.

Digit. Digit is the name given to the basic symbols necessary in a particular numeration system. For example, in the base ten system there are ten basic symbols or digits: 0, 1, 2, 3, 4, 5, 6, 7, 8, 9.

Equal Sets. Equal sets are sets having exactly the same elements. All equal sets are in one-to-one correspondence.

Equivalent Sets. If two sets have the same cardinal number (that is, the same number of elements) even though the elements are not the same, the sets are equivalent. All equal sets are also equivalent sets, but not all equivalent sets are equal sets.

Finite Set. A finite set is an empty set or one that can be put into one-to-one correspondence with a set of the following form:

$$\{1, 2, 3, \ldots, n\}$$

Sets that are not finite are called **infinite sets**. The set of all whole numbers is an infinite set. So is, by the way, the set of all even numbers.

Group. A number of objects put together for a particular purpose is a group.

Law of Trichotomy. For any two numbers *a* and *b*, one and only one of the following relations holds true:

$$a = b \qquad a > b \qquad a < b$$

Levels of Abstraction in Relation to Number. A child progresses through increasingly abstract levels in developing number concepts. *Concrete level*: actual objects—for example, an actual pencil or a ball. *Semiconcrete level*: pictures of objects—for example, a drawing or photograph of a pencil or ball. *Semiabstract level*: matching objects of a group one-to-one with tallies. *Abstract level*: matching the objects of a group with counting numbers to determine the cardinal number of the set.

Multiplicative System of Numeration. A multiplicative system of numeration represents numbers by symbols in which the values of pairs of numerals are multiplied and added. The Chinese system, for example, is a multiplicative system.

Notation. Three ways of expressing a number in base ten are as follows:

Standard Notation:	347
Expanded Notation:	$(3 \times 100) + (4 \times 10) + (7 \times 1)$
Exponential Notation:	$(3 \times 10^2) + (4 \times 10^1) + (7 \times 10^0)$

Standard Notation. The conventional method that we use for writing numbers every day is called *standard notation*. For example, these numbers are written in standard form: 256, 57, 1342.

Expanded Notation. Numbers written in expanded notation are in a form that indicates numerical value and place value in words or by numbers such as 1, 10, 100, or 1000. For example, 275 can be written in expanded notation form as 2 hundreds 7 tens 5 ones or as $(2 \times 100) + (7 \times 10) + (5 \times 1)$.

Exponential Notation. Numbers written in a form that indicates the numerical value are in exponential notation. The place value is expressed in powers of ten. For example, 358 can be written in exponential notation as $(3 \times 10^2) + (5 \times 10^1) + (8 \times 10^0)$.

Number. A number is a concept or idea that indicates *how many*.

Number Line. A number line is a representation of a geometric line with an arrowhead at each end to indicate that the line continues endlessly in both directions. Points are marked to divide the line into sections of equal length, and each point is matched with a whole number. For example:

Numeral. A numeral is an abstract symbol that represents a number.

Numeration System. A system that uses symbols to represent numbers is called a *numeration system*.

One-to-One Correspondence. If each object in a first group is matched with exactly one object in a second group, and if each object in the second group is matched with exactly one object in the first group (so that no object in either group is left over or unmatched), the two groups are in one-to-one correspondence.

Ordinal Number. A number that indicates which position a certain object occupies in a given group is called an *ordinal number*.

Place-Value Numeration System. A place-value numeration system is one in which the value of a digit is determined by its place in the numeral. Examples of place-value systems include the Babylonian system and the decimal system.

Procedure for Reading Any Number in the Base Ten Numeration System.

1. Begin reading the number from the left-hand side.

2. Read the number in the first period on the left; then say the period name.

3. Continue this process one period at a time from left to right until all periods have been read.

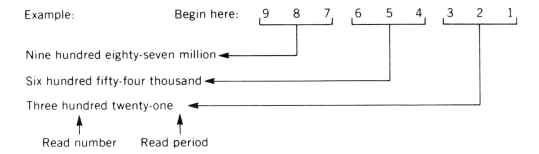

Nine hundred eighty-seven million

Six hundred fifty-four thousand

Three hundred twenty-one

Read number   Read period

Procedure for Translating a Numeral in a Base Other than Ten into a Base Ten Numeral.

1. Set up a place-value grid for the given base.

2. Write the numeral in base ten, using exponential notation.

3. Determine the value of each term in the base ten numeral.

4. Add the numbers obtained in step 3.

    Example: Translate 231_{seven} into a base ten numeral.

    (a)

7^3	7^2	7^1	7^0
343	49	7	1

    (b) $(2 \times 7^2) + (3 \times 7^1) + (1 \times 7^0) = (2 \times 49) + (3 \times 7) + (1 \times 1)$

    (c) $98 + 21 + 1$

    (d) 120_{ten}

Procedure for Translating a Base Ten Numeral into a Numeral in Some Base Other than Ten.

1. Set up a place-value grid showing the value for each place in the grid.

2. Compare the base ten numeral with this place-value grid to determine how many groups are to be counted in each place. For example: Translate 120 into a base seven numeral.

7^3	7^2	7^1	7^0
343	49	7	1

Questions to be considered:

If I have 120 items, can a group of 343 items be made? The answer would be no.

If I have 120 items, can a group of 49 items be made? The answer would be yes. The next question would be, How many groups of 49 would there be? The answer would be two: 2×7^2.

If two groups of 49 are made, how many items are left over? The answer would be that 22 items are left over.

How many groups of 7^1 can be made from the group of 22 items? The answer would be three: 3×7^1.

One item is left over from the 22 items. How many groups of 1 can be made from 1? The answer would be 1: 1×7^0.

Combining this information, we can see that

$$120_{ten} = (2 \times 7^2) + (3 \times 7^1) + (1 \times 7^0)$$
$$= 231_{seven}$$

Set. A set can be thought of as a group of things or ideas that are precisely described.

Whole Numbers. The cardinal numbers of finite sets are called *whole numbers*. The whole numbers are 0, 1, 2, 3, ...

Zero Power. If a number other than 0 is raised to the zero power, the result is equal to 1. For example:

$$1^0 = 1 \qquad 999^0 = 1$$
$$289^0 = 1 \qquad n^0 = 1 \ (n \neq 0)$$

Practice Exercises for Teachers

These exercises are designed for the reader of this book. While some are suitable for use in the elementary classroom, these examples should not necessarily be given to children in this form. Ideas for classroom activities on the concepts and ideas discussed in this chapter can be found in Part 2 of *Today's Mathematics*, the Student Resource Book.

1. Name the level of abstraction a child is using in each of the following situations. Use the labels "concrete," "semiconcrete," "semiabstract," or "abstract."

   a) One child walks around and counts the children present by touching each on the head.
   b) A child holds up five fingers when asked how many members are in the child's family.
   c) A child cuts pictures of shoes out of a catalog and pastes them on a sheet of construction paper to represent a collection of shoes.
   d) A child forms a collection using a ball, a mitt, and a bat.
   e) A child keeps score in a spelling bee by placing tallies on the chalkboard.
   f) A child is asked how many toy cars she has and responds by saying, "five" without counting objects or referring to pictures.

2. Using objects and one-to-one correspondence, make a drawing to show that 7 is less than 9.

3. Construct a number line, and mark an "x" on the first eight counting numbers.

4. Use Cuisenaire rods to answer the following questions.

   a) How many red rods does it take to equal the length of a brown rod?
   b) How many white rods does it take to equal the length of a black rod?
   c) How many light green rods does it take to equal the length of a blue rod?
   d) How many red rods does it take to equal the length of a black rod?
   e) How many red rods does it take to equal the length of an orange rod?

5. State the number of ones, tens, and hundreds for each of the following numbers.

   a) 423   b) 79   c) 382   d) 1365   e) 37   f) 963

   (*Note:* Some textbooks ask children how many tens are in 123 and then make the mistake of stating that the answer is 2; 2 is the digit in the tens place, but there are actually 12 tens in 123.)

6. What digit is in the tens place in 578? How many tens are in the number 578?

7. What digit is in the hundreds place in 2481? How many hundreds are in the number 2481?

8. What digit is in the ones place in 386? How many ones are in the number 386?

9. Using base ten blocks, state the least number of pieces necessary to represent each of the following numbers. Then identify the blocks that should be used.

   a) 214   b) 2496   c) 63   d) 563   e) 731   f) 3867

10. List four important characteristics of our base ten system.

11. Write each of the following numbers three ways, using expanded notation (using words, exponents, and digits).

    a) 197   b) 2496   c) 63   d) 563   e) 731   f) 3060

12. State all the possible ways that base ten blocks can be used to represent the number 123.

13. Write the decimal equivalent of each of the following numerals.

    a)   b)   c)   d) MCCLXXIX

    e)   f)   g) MMDCCCXLIX

14. How you would read or say each of the following numerals?

    a) 35_{eight} b) 87_{nine} c) 40_{five} d) 432_{ten}

15. Explain why it would not be appropriate to read 125_{twelve} as, "one hundred twenty-five, base twelve."

16. Using the following base groupings, name the number represented by the tally marks.

    /////////////////////

    a) _____ eight   b) _____ twelve   c) _____ two

    d) _____ five   e) _____ nine   f) _____ four

17. a) If you wanted to "invent" a base sixteen numeration system, how many basic symbols would you need?

    b) Develop a numeration system with a base of sixteen; then list its first 20 counting numbers.

18. In the numeral 9843, the "4" represents a value how many times the value represented by the "8"?

19. Make a place-value grid showing the first five places in base three, base four, base five, base six, base seven, base eight, base nine, and base twelve. For example, a base two chart would begin with:

Base Two				
		2^2	2^1	2^0
			2	1

20. Using the symbol b for base, use exponents to write a place-value sequence that you can apply to any base system.

21. Write the next five consecutive numerals in the base indicated after each of the following numerals.

    a) 21_{nine} b) 14_{five} c) 101_{two} d) TE_{twelve} e) 10055_{seven}

    f) 535_{eight} g) 1088_{nine} h) 1212_{three} i) 233_{four}

22. Complete the table on page 110 by writing each number in standard notation, in expanded notation, and in exponential notation.

Standard Notation	Expanded Notation	Exponential Notation
101101_{two}		
1234_{five}		
3765_{eight}		
_____ $_{three}$	$(2 \times 100)_{three} + (1 \times 10)_{three} + (2 \times 1)_{three}$	
_____ $_{seven}$	$(6 \times 1000)_{seven} + (4 \times 10)_{seven} + (5 \times 1)_{seven}$	
_____ $_{six}$		$(5 \times 10^3)_{six} + (2 \times 10^2)_{six} + (1 \times 10^1)_{six} + (4 \times 10^0)_{six}$
_____ $_{four}$		$(2 \times 10^2)_{four} + (1 \times 10^1)_{four} + (2 \times 10^0)_{four}$
$12TE_{twelve}$		
_____ $_{nine}$	$(8 \times 1000)_{nine} + (6 \times 100)_{nine} + (4 \times 10)_{nine}$	

23. Complete the table on the next page by counting in each base shown.

24. a) A system for naming numbers in which a digit receives its value from where it is placed is called a _____ system.

   b) The number that indicates the number of objects that can be grouped together in a number system is called the _____.

   c) Any number (except 0) to the zero power is equal to _____.

   d) In any place-value system a numeral may be written in _____ notation, _____ notation, or _____ notation.

   e) In any base system, the basic symbols used to name numbers are called _____.

25. Write in words how each of the following base ten numbers is read.

   a) 3003 b) 606,060 c) 707,700

   d) 345,768,231 e) 1,001,001,001,001 f) 21,478,000

26. Study these numerals written in base nine and base three:

   $578_{nine} = 122122_{three}$

   $483_{nine} = 112210_{three}$

   $56_{nine} = 1220_{three}$

   $3452_{nine} = 1011202_{three}$

   Search for a pattern that will permit you to convert quickly from a base nine numeration system to a base three system without changing to base ten.

Base Ten	Base Nine	Base Eight	Base Seven	Base Six	Base Five	Base Four	Base Three	Base Two
0								
1								
2								
3								
4								
5								
6								
7								
8								
9								
10								
11								
12								
13								
14								
15								
16								
17								
18								
19								
20								
21								
22								
23								
24								
25								

Teaching Competencies and Self-Assessment Tasks

1. Suggest a variety of assessment activities that can be used with young children to determine whether they are ready to begin a formal mathematics program.
2. Discuss the advantages and disadvantages of a structured mathematics program as compared with an incidental mathematics program in kindergarten.
3. Identify "at home" activities that are beneficial for children in developing number readiness.
4. Discuss how a calculator could be used to help young children recognize and discriminate among numerals.
5. Analyze elementary school mathematics textbooks, isolating all instances where place value is used; then make a list of your findings.
6. Conduct a debate regarding what portion of the elementary school mathematics program should be devoted to number systems with bases other than base ten. Why?
7. Describe activities for the concrete, semiconcrete, semiabstract, and abstract levels of developing numberness.
8. Study the learning theory of a particular theorist (such as Piaget, Bruner, or Gagné), and describe the implications of adopting that theory for teaching mathematics in the primary grades.
9. Discuss the importance of developing the concept of one-to-one correspondence in a beginning mathematics program.
10. Research the names for very large and very small numbers in our base ten place-value system of numeration.
11. Make a list of materials that can be used for teaching place value to children. Discuss the comparative benefits and the limitations of each.
12. In this chapter counting numbers were expressed using standard, expanded, and exponential notation. Research how these various forms of notation might be applied to decimal numbers between 0 and 1. How would these forms of notation be used for describing numbers written in bases other than ten?
13. Research an ancient numeration system not described in this book, and present your findings to the class.
14. Make a list of place-value teaching procedures for each of the four levels of development: concrete, semiconcrete, semiabstract, and abstract. Discuss the effectiveness of each procedure as a transition from one level to the next.

Related Readings and Teacher Resources

For related readings on topics found in this chapter, see the corresponding chapter in Part 2 of *Today's Mathematics*, the Student Resource Book.

Chapter 7

Addition and Subtraction of Whole Numbers

Teaching Competencies

Upon completing this chapter, you will be able to:

- State and demonstrate at least two models of the addition process used to develop an understanding of addition and subtraction.

- Model at least three distinct types of subtraction examples, using groups, the number line, and inverse relationships.

- Discuss the use of basic structures and properties to aid children in developing and memorizing basic facts.

- Demonstrate regrouping in addition and subtraction using a place-value box.

- Write a lesson plan for teaching a lesson involving some aspect of addition or subtraction.

young first-grade boy excitedly shouted that he knew how many paper cups would be needed for refreshments for the class party. Although he wasn't exactly sure how to say it, he was so sure he knew the answer that he wrote it on the board. He knew there were 18 girls and 16 boys in the class. All he had to do was add these numbers together. The numeral that he wrote for the answer was 214. It didn't occur to him that this seemed to be an unusual number of paper cups for a class party—probably because the actual problem meant something to him, but the process he used to get an answer did not. He knew he should add 18 and 16, but when he added the 8 and the 6 he got 14 and simply wrote it down:

$$\begin{array}{r} 18 \\ +16 \\ \hline 14 \end{array}$$

Then, when he added 1 and 1 he got 2 and wrote this next to the 14:

$$\begin{array}{r} 18 \\ +16 \\ \hline 214 \end{array}$$

This gave the student the improbable answer of 214 for the sum of 16 and 18! Improbable to us, but not to a child who thoughtlessly applies rote procedures and processes without understanding the underlying concepts.

The NCTM Standards call for a balanced approach to basic computational skills. This balance is achieved by giving appropriate attention to both memorization and understanding. The original NCTM *Curriculum and Evaluation Standards* (1989) stated that students should develop both numbers sense and operation sense and explore relationships among representations of operations, as well as examine and create algorithms and procedures. This theme was expanded in the *Principles and Standards for School Mathematics* as illustrated by the following statement:

> Knowing basic number combinations . . . is essential. Equally essential is computational fluency—having and using efficient and accurate methods for computing. Regardless of the particular method used, students should be able to explain their method, understand that many methods exist, and see the usefulness of methods that are efficient, accurate, and general. (NCTM, 2000, p. 32)

The purpose of this chapter is to help you develop a view of addition and subtraction that includes, but goes beyond, the skill of "getting an answer." You should develop an appreciation of the benefits achieved by focusing attention on both skills and understanding—in other words, on mathematical power. The chapter offers you a repertoire of ideas from which to build your philosophy. How can we best ensure that both skill and understanding develop? Read on.

Previous chapters have suggested techniques for developing both numberness and place value with young children. These two basic ideas form a framework for meaningfully teaching the concepts of addition. Consequently, when teaching addition to children, we must first evaluate the children's readiness. The teacher should evaluate each child's number sense including such specific elements as conservation of number, seriation (ordering of events), one-to-one correspondence, counting ability, recognition of numerals, and writing numerals. Also, research supports the concept that addition should proceed from the concrete level through the semiconcrete, semiabstract, and abstract levels. Two models are commonly used to help children progress through these levels as they develop an understanding of addition: groups of objects and the number line.

Objects taken directly from the child's environment should be used to concretely model number concepts and operation procedures. Teachers will also find that many commercial materials are available for use at the manipulative level—for example, Cuisenaire rods, base ten blocks, pattern blocks, attribute blocks, and number tiles. This text includes a chapter that describes some of these tools for learning, teaching, and assessing and explains selected activities that make good use of these aids. In addition, a set of manipulatives prepared for an overhead projector has been included with the text. Check the resource manuals for each of these materials for more detailed instructions about how to use each of them with children. Also remember that word problems and problem solving should be included in each step of addition concept development. Some suggestions are included in Part 2 of this text, the Student Resource Book.

An addition and subtraction program should begin informally in kindergarten and proceed into a more formal development in grade 1. As we begin the development of the concept of addition, our emphasis must be placed on the concepts and mathematical relationships involved and not on the rote computation aspect. Develop the concept first; then work on memorizing the facts and algorithms. You'll find that students will memorize them more quickly and with greater accuracy when there is a foundation of understanding in place first. In fact, many students will begin to memorize them "on their own" by associating an arrived-at answer with the concrete/manipulative process of getting that answer.

This chapter on teaching addition and subtraction is organized around five basic concepts that must be understood if an individual is to solve any addition or subtraction example in a meaningful way. These five major organizational areas are:

1. understanding the operation
2. the basic facts
3. place value
4. basic structures
5. regrouping.

These areas serve not only as a sound foundation for organizing an addition and subtraction program but also as the basis for valuable review at each subsequent grade level.

MEANING AND MODELS FOR ADDITION

Now let us begin our study by examining two groups of real objects. Using two separate sheets of paper, place two cubes on one sheet and three cubes on the second sheet.

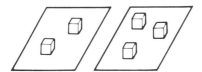

Children now have three available techniques to associate a number with each group. One technique is to simply count the cubes. A second technique is sometimes called *partial counting*. When using partial counting, children recognize the number of cubes in one group and then, beginning with that number, count the number of cubes in the second group. A third technique is to simply associate 2 and 3 with each group, respectively, and to recognize this as a total of 5 (without counting). Children should be encouraged to associate a number with a group of objects without counting, a process called *subitizing*. For groups of about seven or less, children should be able to look at, visualize, and state the total number for each group without having to resort to counting the individual objects in the group.

At this stage of development, begin to associate meaning with the addition symbol (+). Through use, children will associate the addition symbol with the physical act of putting together two (or more) groups of objects.

Ask the children to choose a card with the proper numeral on it that represents the number in each group. Place the numeral card under the proper group of objects. Then place an additional sheet of paper to the right of the groups, and move the two cubes to that sheet. Move the three cubes onto the new sheet, and ask the children how many cubes there are all together. Have one child choose a card with a numeral that describes this new group. It is important to stress that 2 cubes and 3 cubes put together make 5 cubes. Do *not* use 2 cubes, 3 cubes, and then *another*, different set of 5 cubes. Put the 2 cubes together with the 3 cubes to make 5 cubes. To the degree possible, discourage direct counting at this point. Children should begin to associate the numbers 2, 3, and 5 with the process. After they have had many similar experiences, you might then begin to write the addition sentence 2 + 3 = 5 to represent what they saw with the model. Generally, teachers do not provide adequate experiences before requiring children to write numerals. *Do not rush into writing abstract number sentences* — the concept is

more important at this stage than the abstract number sentence.

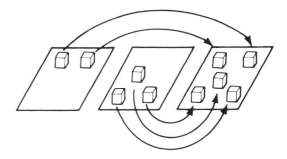

In the operation of addition, the numbers to be added are called **addends**, and the number obtained by adding the addends is called the **sum**.

$$\text{Addend} + \text{Addend} = \text{Sum}$$

or

$$\text{Sum} = \text{Addend} + \text{Addend}$$

The addition operation can be symbolized as:

$$a + b = S$$

or

$$\begin{array}{r} a \\ + b \\ \hline S \end{array}$$

where a and b are the addends and S represents the sum. The addition sentence is read, "Addend add Addend equals Sum," or "Addend plus Addend equals Sum." Addition is a **binary operation** because, even in a series of 5 numbers to add, only two numbers can be added at one time. The sum of 5 is obtained by adding 2 and 3 and is *unique* because no other sum can possibly be obtained using the addends 2 and 3.

Another model that is useful in developing an understanding of addition is the number line. Recall that a number line is a representation of a geometric line, with arrows at each end to indicate that the line extends in both directions. Two points are marked on the number line, and the resulting line segment, representing one unit, is used to mark off other segments equal to one unit. These segments determine a series of points on the line, and the points are then named by placing them in one-to-one correspondence with the whole numbers.

We can use the number line to model addition examples. To illustrate how this is done, let's solve the example 2 + 3 = □. When we use the number line with young children, remember that we always begin modeling at the reference point, zero, sometimes called the *origin*. From zero we measure a segment two units long. From that point we measure a segment three units long and arrive at the point named 5. Thus the number line model shows that 2 + 3 = 5.

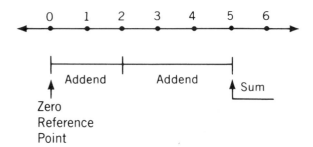

Note that we do not place arrows on the number line segments representing the addends since arrows indicate a direction; direction is not a part of this model until the set of integers (directed numbers) is introduced.

Models using groups and the number line will help children develop an understanding of the addition process. Remember, each of these is a model that achieves the same results as addition but is *not* addition. Counting is *not* addition. Partial counting is *not* addition. Putting objects together is *not* addition. Then what is addition? Addition is the cardinal number of the union of two or more disjoint sets. That's a lofty phrase and shouldn't, of course, be used as stated with children. However, it efficiently describes the nature of addition and the process one might use to arrive at, or to describe, an answer. An alternative description of addition is given below:

> **Addition** is a binary operation performed on a pair of numbers called addends to obtain a unique sum.

To reinforce the basic structure of addition, place each of the terms and symbols for addition on separate cards.

Addend + Addend = Sum

Place the cards randomly in front of the children, and have them arrange the cards in proper order to form an addition sentence. Other cards containing numerals may be placed on the addend and sum cards to relate numbers with the addition sentence.

DEVELOPING BASIC ADDITION FACTS

A family of numbers is often used to help children extend their understanding of addition. A **family of numbers**, in the context of addition, includes all possible combinations of addends that will produce a given sum and should be used for the exploration and development of addition facts but not for memorization of the basic addition facts. As you will discover later in this chapter, there are more effective means for organizing basic facts for memorization.

To model number families, place a group of cubes and two sheets of paper in front of small groups of children and ask them to make all possible combinations of

two groups. The children should record each of their discoveries. For example, 7 cubes might be placed in front of the children, and they would be expected to find all possible combinations for 7.

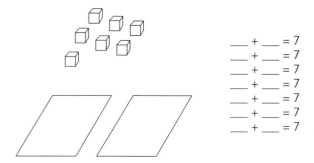

By placing all 7 cubes into two groups, children should discover and write these mathematical relationships:

$1 + 6 = 7$	$6 + 1 = 7$
$2 + 5 = 7$	$5 + 2 = 7$
$3 + 4 = 7$	$4 + 3 = 7$
$7 + 0 = 7$	$0 + 7 = 7$

This set of examples is called the *addition family of seven*.

MEMORIZING BASIC ADDITION FACTS USING STRUCTURES

The teacher should develop the children's understanding of addition by using both groups of objects and the number line as models. When the children are able to generate families of numbers, they are ready to begin memorizing the **basic addition facts**. Basic addition facts must be memorized. To assist children in this process you must help them organize the facts into structures. When you help children organize the basic addition facts, you encourage thinking strategies and an understanding of relationships useful in memorizing the basic addition facts.

> **Basic addition facts** include all combinations of any one-place whole number (addend) added to any one-place whole number (addend) to obtain a one- or two-place sum.

Examples will range from $0 + 0 = 0$ to $9 + 9 = 18$.

Now, let us consider these two groups:

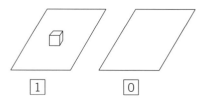

Have the children locate the numeral cards to place under the groups. The numbers that represent the two groups are 1 and 0. Under the addition operation, $1 + 0$ is another name for 1. Thus we can say that $1 + 0 = 1$.

Now let's look at this example:

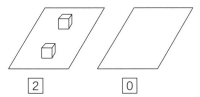

Under the addition operation, the sum of the numbers 2 and 0 is another name for 2. The sum is unique, because the sum obtained for 2 + 0 is always equal to 2.

Now let's consider the following set of addition examples:

2	5	0	0	7	9	0
+0	+0	+8	+3	+0	+0	+4
2	5	8	3	7	9	4

Have the children respond to these questions: "How are all these examples alike? How are the examples different?" After discussing the students' discoveries, what generalizations should children make about the operation of adding the number 0 to another number? The sum of 0 and any other number is always the other number. For this reason, zero is called the **identity element of addition**. Using this basic generalization, children can begin to construct an addition table.

> An **addition table** is an orderly arrangement of columns and rows in which each column and row is headed by an addend and each cell in the table contains a sum.

The following is an incomplete addition table:

Addends

+	0	1	2	3	4	5	6	7	8	9
0										
1										
2										
3										
4						Sums				
5										
6										
7										
8										
9										

(Addends — left side label)

The next table shows the sums in the addition table for all basic addition facts related to the identity element of addition.

Addends

+	0	1	2	3	4	5	6	7	8	9
0	0	1	2	3	4	5	6	7	8	9
1	1									
2	2									
3	3									
4	4					Sums				
5	5									
6	6									
7	7									
8	8									
9	9									

(Addends — left side label)

Note that sums related to the identity element of addition will complete the first row and the first column of the addition table.

Learning the basic addition facts is a two-step process. The first step is to develop the basic facts in a family of numbers, and the second step is to memorize the basic facts when organized in structures. From an understanding of this single generalization about the identity element, children will be able to efficiently memorize 19 basic addition facts.

Now let us carefully examine another basic structure that will help children memorize basic addition facts. We begin with another group model.

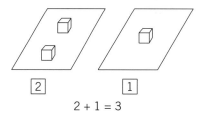

2 + 1 = 3

Now examine the same example, using the number line as a model.

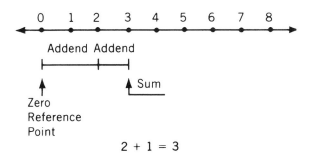

2 + 1 = 3

The expression 2 + 1 is another name for 3. Consider this set of examples:

$$
\begin{array}{cccccc}
3 & 5 & 1 & 1 & 7 & 4 \\
+1 & +1 & +8 & +6 & +1 & +1 \\
\hline
4 & 6 & 9 & 7 & 8 & 5
\end{array}
$$

After the children have solved a number of these types of examples and studied these models, ask them, "How are all these examples alike? How are the examples different?" After a discussion with the children, they should be able to generalize that the sum of any number and 1 is the next greater counting number. If children can count, they can add 1 to a number. These sums fit into the second row and second column of the addition table.

From this "counting" generalization, children should be able to quickly memorize 17 more basic addition facts. Using the two generalizations mentioned so far, the children will have already memorized a total of 36 basic addition facts. Thus, two relatively simple generalizations about adding 0 and adding 1 will help the children memorize more than one-third of the 100 basic addition facts.

Addends

+	0	1	2	3	4	5	6	7	8	9
0	0	1	2	3	4	5	6	7	8	9
1	1	2	3	4	5	6	7	8	9	10
2	2	3								
3	3	4								
4	4	5								
5	5	6			Sums					
6	6	7								
7	7	8								
8	8	9								
9	9	10								

(Addends — left column label)

The application of this process to the basic structure of our number system will help to explain the use of the addition table. For example, use of the **commutative property of addition** will almost cut in half the task of memorizing the basic addition facts. The basic structural property of commutativity for addition can be examined using groups. For example:

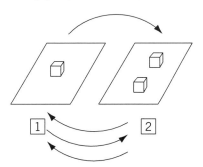

Using groups of cubes on sheets of paper, have children build the addition example $1 + 2 = 3$. Now interchange the two sheets of paper with cubes on them, and have the children write the appropriate addition sentence for the new arrangement: $2 + 1 = 3$. Give the children experience with many similar examples, using sets and number sentences.

We can also use the number line model to demonstrate the commutative property of addition. Using the same example, we can show that $1 + 2 = 2 + 1$ with the following model. The children should model many similar examples.

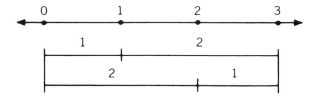

Discuss the two models shown on the number line, compare them to the relationship with the group model, illustrate many different examples, and then have the children generalize the commutative property of addition using words such as, "When you add two numbers, it doesn't matter in what order you add them—you'll still get the same answer."

> The **commutative property** of addition means that the order of two addends does not affect the sum. For example, $2 + 3 = 5$ and $3 + 2 = 5$.

Now let us return to the organization of the basic addition facts for memorization, using basic structures. Children are taught to count by twos long before they begin formal study of the addition of whole numbers. Examine this set of basic addition facts:

$$
\begin{array}{ccccccc}
3 & 2 & 6 & 5 & 2 & 2 & 8 \\
+2 & +7 & +2 & +2 & +4 & +9 & +2 \\
\hline
5 & 9 & 8 & 7 & 6 & 11 & 10
\end{array}
$$

Have the children examine these examples and determine how they are alike and how they are different. Some children may want to use models to help them find likenesses and differences. After a discussion with the children, they should generalize that adding 2 to a number is just like counting by twos. These sums fit into the third row and the third column of the addition table. Also reinforce the commutative property of addition for examples such as $2 + 5 = 5 + 2$.

From this generalization of "skip counting," the children will have memorized an additional 15 basic addition facts. With three generalizations to remember, the children will have memorized 51 basic addition facts—more than half of the facts with only three generalizations.

Addends

+	0	1	2	3	4	5	6	7	8	9
0	0	1	2	3	4	5	6	7	8	9
1	1	2	3	4	5	6	7	8	9	10
2	2	3	4	5	6	7	8	9	10	11
3	3	4	5							
4	4	5	6			Sums				
5	5	6	7							
6	6	7	8							
7	7	8	9							
8	8	9	10							
9	9	10	11							

(Left column labeled vertically: Addends)

Children seem to have less difficulty memorizing basic facts where the two addends are the same number, perhaps because the world in which we live is full of symmetry—5 fingers on each of 2 hands; 9 tires on each side of an 18-wheeler truck; 3 legs on each side of an insect, and so on. Facts with both addends the same are called the *doubles* facts.

This set of examples is made up of doubles:

3	4	5	6	7	8	9
+3	+4	+5	+6	+7	+8	+9
6	8	10	12	14	16	18

This set of sums fits into the addition table on the diagonal; now the addition table will look like this:

Addends

+	0	1	2	3	4	5	6	7	8	9
0	0	1	2	3	4	5	6	7	8	9
1	1	2	3	4	5	6	7	8	9	10
2	2	3	4	5	6	7	8	9	10	11
3	3	4	5	6						
4	4	5	6		8			Sums		
5	5	6	7			10				
6	6	7	8				12			
7	7	8	9					14		
8	8	9	10						16	
9	9	10	11							18

(Left column labeled vertically: Addends)

Immediately following the doubles, we have children memorize basic addition facts called *related doubles*

(sometimes referred to as *near doubles*). Each double has two related doubles (except for 9 + 9).

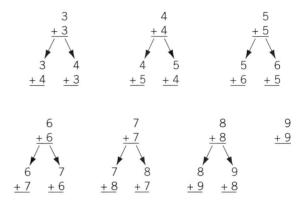

The generalizations become more abstract as we move through the basic addition facts, but the children are also becoming more sophisticated. Memorizing the seven doubles will help the children memorize the twelve related doubles. Since 3 add 4 is one more than 3 add 3, the sum of 3 add 4 will be one more than the sum of 3 add 3. The sums of all related basic facts will be one more than the corresponding double.

Following the structural approach to memorizing the basic addition facts, the students will have efficient techniques for memorizing a total of 70 basic facts. The addition table will now look like this:

Addends

+	0	1	2	3	4	5	6	7	8	9
0	0	1	2	3	4	5	6	7	8	9
1	1	2	3	4	5	6	7	8	9	10
2	2	3	4	5	6	7	8	9	10	11
3	3	4	5	6	7			Sums		
4	4	5	6	7	8	9				
5	5	6	7		9	10	11			
6	6	7	8			11	12	13		
7	7	8	9				13	14	15	
8	8	9	10					15	16	17
9	9	10	11						17	18

(Left column labeled vertically: Addends)

The next set of basic facts to be introduced for memorization are the 10 facts related to "tenness." Let's examine this set of basic facts:

7	4	9	9	5
+9	+9	+6	+3	+9
16	13	15	12	14

This set of addition facts can be related to place value and tenness. As the children have been regrouping by bundling and unbundling groups of ten, the tenness concept is related to this set of facts. For example, consider 9 + 6. Make a group of 9 blocks on the left and a group of 6 blocks on the right. Take 1 block from the group of 6 blocks (making that now a group of 5) and place it with the group of 9 blocks (making it now a group of 10). So, 9 + 6 has become 10 + 5 by "building" a 10. To build a 10, one element is taken from the group other than the group of 9 and is placed with the 9 to make a group of 10. Thus the sum will be a group of 10 and one less than the other addend. Now we have accounted for 80 basic addition facts.

Addends

+	0	1	2	3	4	5	6	7	8	9
0	0	1	2	3	4	5	6	7	8	9
1	1	2	3	4	5	6	7	8	9	10
2	2	3	4	5	6	7	8	9	10	11
3	3	4	5	6	7					12
4	4	5	6	7	8	9	Sums			13
5	5	6	7		9	10	11			14
6	6	7	8			11	12	13		15
7	7	8	9				13	14	15	16
8	8	9	10					15	16	17
9	9	10	11	12	13	14	15	16	17	18

Addends

There are 20 basic facts yet to be memorized. By using the commutative property of addition, we can cut these remaining addition facts to the following 10 facts:

3	3	3	3	4	4	4	5	5	6
+5	+6	+7	+8	+6	+7	+8	+7	+8	+8
8	9	10	11	10	11	12	12	13	14

These facts may be the most difficult addition facts for children to memorize. Do not rush the children into memorizing these facts. Practice just one or two facts per week, but consider both the fact and its commuted form.

Children should memorize basic addition facts *after* they understand the concept of addition and the basic addition structures. However, although memorizing facts is important, it shouldn't take priority over all else. Children should engage in problem-solving experiences, measurement, and geometry, for example, as they continue to build their repertoire of facts.

Regular and systematic practice must be provided to help children memorize the basic addition facts. In general, have the children consider only one classification at a time. For instance, study the identity element of addition for an appropriate period of time and guide the children to realize how easy it is to memorize 19 basic facts. Have the children:

look at the facts
state the facts
listen to the facts
write the facts
visualize the facts
classify the facts.

Aids such as flash cards, cassette tapes, calculators, microcomputers, games, and individual drill activities are potentially valuable in providing a variety of formats for helping children to memorize the basic addition facts.

As the basic facts become more challenging, the children can make use of the associative property of addition, in conjunction with place value.

> The **associative property of addition** states that, when three or more numbers are added, the way in which the addends are grouped does not affect the sum.
> For example, (3 + 6) + 4 = 13 and 3 + (6 + 4) = 13

In the operation of addition, the associative property of addition allows us to combine (or associate) addends with one another in whatever grouping we choose. That is, we can elect to operate on any two addends at a time. For example, we can add 3 + 6 + 4 in either of two ways without changing the order of the addends:

$$(3 + 6) + 4 = 9 + 4 = 13$$
$$3 + (6 + 4) = 3 + 10 = 13$$

(The parentheses tell us how to group or *associate* the addends.) We can consider 3 and 6 and then add 4; or we can choose to associate the 6 and 4 and then add 3 to the sum. Solving the example this way, we might proceed as follows: 6 add 4 is 10, and 10 add 3 is 13. Since 10 is an easy number to build on, it may be simpler for some children to add 3 to 10 than to approach the computation as 3 + 6 = 9 and 9 + 4 = 13. This example may be modeled on the number line.

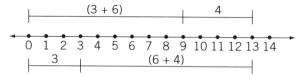

While children are memorizing the basic addition facts and developing an understanding of the associative property, column addition might be introduced. *Column addition* is the addition of three or more addends in one example. Beginning examples should include only one-place numbers, such as:

4		6
3		2
+2	or	+1

Because addition is a binary operation, the first two addends are added, and that sum is then added to the next addend. In the first example, 4 and 3 are addends;

the sum 7 becomes the "unseen number." The unseen number of 7 is then added to the next addend, 2. Thus 7 add 2 is 9. In the second example, 8 is the unseen number, and then 8 and 1 are added to obtain a sum of 9.

Children should be provided with physical models to help them comprehend the concept of column addition. Again, groups and the number line are commonly used as models. Groups of objects can be used on sheets of paper, flannel boards, magnetic boards, or an overhead projector. Children should manipulate many different materials to grasp the underlying concepts of column addition.

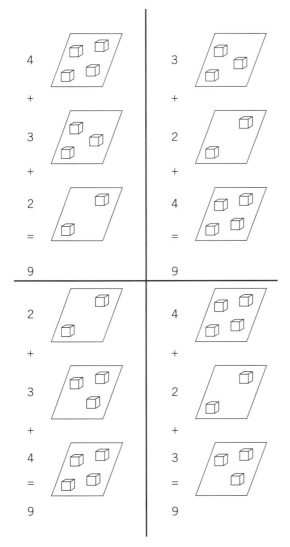

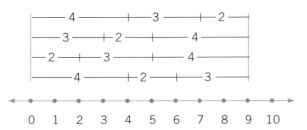

The number line may also be used to effectively show the process of column addition.

Another model that works particularly well for addition, both column and horizontal, is the use of Cuisenaire rods. Note that the following figure shows that 4 + 3 + 2 equals 9, regardless of the order in which the numbers are added:

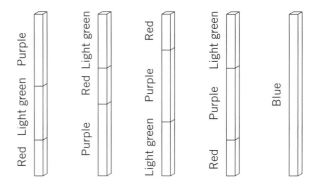

The students are now applying the associative property of addition in the process of finding the sum in column addition. The concept must be extended into more places as children develop their understanding of place value. In fact, extended column addition provides an excellent opportunity to review important concepts of place value.

EXTENDING BASIC ADDITION FACTS USING PLACE VALUE

A logical extension of the basic addition facts is to use multiples of ten. The basic fact of 2 + 3 can easily be extended to 20 + 30. Think 2 + 3 = 5, and relate this basic fact to 2 tens + 3 tens = 5 tens. Plastic spoons can be used to model this concept. Place the two following groups on the overhead projector, and ask the children to state a mathematical sentence that represents placing the two groups together:

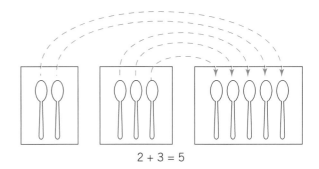

2 + 3 = 5

Hold up a package of 10 plastic spoons. Ask the children, "How many plastic spoons?" Ask the children to watch you carefully as you exchange each plastic spoon in this set with a package of 10 plastic spoons.

Children are now bringing together the concept of place value and the concept of addition. After examining many examples, children should generalize that the basic addition facts are the same regardless of their place value. That is, just as 3 *cows* add 4 *cows* gives a total of *7 cows*, so does 3 *tens* add 4 *tens* give a total of *7 tens*.

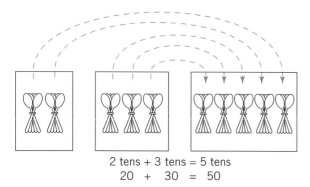

$$2 \text{ tens} + 3 \text{ tens} = 5 \text{ tens}$$
$$20 + 30 = 50$$

Expanded notation provides an efficient method for introducing the addition of numbers having two or more digits. In expanded notation, a number is separated into its component place value parts (hundreds, tens, ones, and so forth). This way children can better see the structure of the numbers and are better able to rename the numbers in a more convenient form.

$$
\begin{array}{ll}
35 = & 3 \text{ tens } 5 \text{ ones} \\
+21 = & 2 \text{ tens } 1 \text{ one} \\
\hline
& 5 \text{ tens } 6 \text{ ones} = 56
\end{array}
$$

Children have studied the basic facts $2 + 3 = 5$ and $1 + 5 = 6$. Their understanding of the basic fact $2 + 3 = 5$ has been extended to 2 tens + 3 tens = 5 tens, which can be written $20 + 30 = 50$.

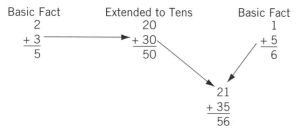

When children have memorized the basic addition facts and understand place value, these two concepts can be brought together to provide the children with the ability to think through examples such as $21 + 35$. The same approach may be used as children move into addition examples with more decimal places.

Now let us examine a three-place addition example, using expanded basic facts and place value.

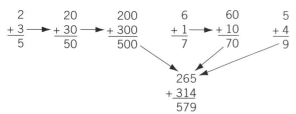

Children need to understand that the basic facts are the cornerstones of success in addition, regardless of the place values involved. Understanding place value

and memorizing the basic addition facts are the prerequisites needed to extend the addition concept. Children with a solid foundation in the concept of addition, the basic addition facts, and place value have a great deal of power with addition.

Children are now in a position to move rapidly forward through addition, without regrouping. Instead of a worksheet with several basic addition examples, all the basic examples of addition facts can be placed together in one example. Carefully study these two sample worksheets:

Traditional Worksheet

Add each example
$$
\begin{array}{llllll}
1.\ \ 2 & 2.\ \ 1 & 3.\ \ 6 & 4.\ \ 3 & 5.\ \ 0 & 6.\ \ 2 \\
\underline{+3} & \underline{+4} & \underline{+0} & \underline{+1} & \underline{+7} & \underline{+4} \\
\\
7.\ \ 8 & 8.\ \ 4 & 9.\ \ 2 & 10.\ \ 1 & 11.\ \ 3 & 11.\ \ 2 \\
\underline{+1} & \underline{+2} & \underline{+1} & \underline{+5} & \underline{+3} & \underline{+6}
\end{array}
$$

Alternative Approach

$$
\begin{array}{l}
1.\quad 216302 \\
\underline{+\ 340174} \\
\\
2.\quad 842132 \\
\underline{+\ 121536}
\end{array}
$$

Note that the practice with specific basic addition facts is the same on both worksheets. Children will have a greater feeling of accomplishment after completing the "alternative approach" worksheet. Children feel that having more places to add makes examples more difficult (although this is not necessarily true, as illustrated above).

REGROUPING IN THE ADDITION PROCESS

One major concept of addition remains to be developed: **regrouping**. If regrouping is introduced on an abstract level, children will often have difficulty with place value when writing the sum. Consider the following example:

$$
\begin{array}{r}
37 \\
\underline{+25}
\end{array}
$$

Children will often obtain a sum of 512—that is, $7 + 5 = 12$ and $3 + 2 = 5$, so $37 + 25 = 512$. Presenting the example on the concrete level or requiring children to write partial sums will go a long way to prevent this error. Preventive action during instruction is better than corrective action after instruction.

Using the place-value box, place 7 single straws in the ones place and three packages of 10 in the tens place. On a sheet of paper in front of the ones place, place 5 single straws; in front of the tens place (on a different sheet of paper), place two packages of 10 straws. Combine the 5 straws with the 7 straws. Ask

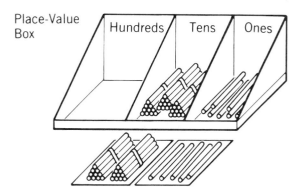

Place-Value Box

Hundreds | Tens | Ones

these questions: "How many straws are now in the ones place? What do you do if you have more than 9 straws in the ones place?" The 12 straws are regrouped into one 10 and two 1s. Place the 2 straws into the ones place. Place a rubber band around the 10 straws to make one group of 10. You have now regrouped 10 ones into one new group of 10. Place the one new group of 10 straws into the tens place; this now makes four groups of 10 straws in the tens place. Then place the two groups of 10 straws on the sheet of paper with the group of 4 tens. There are now six packages of 10 straws in the tens place. Thus we have 62 straws in the place-value box.

Since words alone can be difficult in such contexts, relate the manipulation of tens and ones as in the above example while recording the numbers on the chalkboard or overhead projector. Seven and 5 is 12. What did we do with the 12 when we manipulated the straws? The 12 was regrouped as one 10 and two 1s. The 2 is written in the ones place:

$$
\begin{array}{r}
37 \\
+25 \\
\hline
2
\end{array}
$$

Now combine the tens: the one regrouped ten is combined with the 3 tens and the 2 tens, to obtain a total sum of 6 tens. The 6 is written in the tens place:

$$
\begin{array}{r}
37 \\
+25 \\
\hline
62
\end{array}
$$

If partial sums are recorded, the example would be:

$$
\begin{array}{r}
37 \\
+25 \\
\hline
12 \\
50 \\
\hline
62
\end{array}
$$

When teaching children, teachers generally do not solve enough examples using partial sums so that children can fully comprehend the process this reveals. Provide children with many opportunities for manipulating materials at this point, and have them record these manipulations using partial sums.

The preceding example indicates the sequence of thought that children might follow in learning the oper-

ation of regrouping. Much practice will be necessary before the children should begin to take shortcuts suggested by the teacher. Mastery of the process using concrete models should come first. Based on their understanding of these models, some students will invent their own procedures, such as adding the tens first, then the ones. The constructive nature so common in children can yield many inviting opportunities for the teacher to engage the children in explaining their thinking. Once the children understand the meaning of addition, they can lessen the emphasis on the manipulative steps and write the examples in more abbreviated forms. However, do *not* rush the children through this process. Developing a good foundation will save them time and frustration in the future.

Here is an abbreviated form that children can discover and use:

$$
\begin{array}{r}
^{1}37 \\
+25 \\
\hline
62
\end{array}
$$

These are the familiar forms of the *addition algorithm*. The term **algorithm** refers to the steps and the form of writing we use to solve an exercise. Even though calculators play a much larger role in everyday computation than they once did, children should still demonstrate a high degree of competence with the familiar algorithm. This is not to suggest that we should expend considerable time and effort teaching children to do things that can be and are easily done with a calculator. Rather, students should be able to explain their reasoning during any computation exercise, whether it be paper-and-pencil, mental computation, or calculator-based. When feasible, discourage children from writing the regrouped number above the example so that such "crutches" aren't applied mindlessly. After all, some students don't require a visual "little number" to remember to regroup.

The familiar short form algorithm for addition with regrouping is written:

$$
\begin{array}{r}
37 \\
+25 \\
\hline
62
\end{array}
$$

The regrouping concept needs to be extended into more place values. Regrouping in addition should first be explored from the ones place to the tens place followed by regrouping from the tens place to the hundreds place. As children become proficient with single regrouping, they are ready for double regrouping. Double regrouping includes regrouping from ones to tens and from tens to hundreds within one exercise.

MEANING AND MODELS FOR SUBTRACTION

The development of subtraction should stress the relationship between addition and subtraction. If one operation "undoes" what another operation "does," the "undoing" operation is called the *inverse operation*.

Familiar actions and their inverse actions include unlacing our shoes and then lacing them, or buttoning our shirts and then unbuttoning them. Similarly, we can add and then "unadd" or subtract. That is to say, **subtraction** is the inverse operation of addition.

$$Addend + Addend = Sum$$
becomes
$$Sum - Addend = Addend$$

The process of addition involves finding a missing sum; in subtraction we find a missing addend.

ADDITION	**SUBTRACTION**	
$a + b = \Box$	$a + \Box = S$	$\Box + b = S$

$$\begin{array}{r} a \\ +b \\ \hline \Box \end{array} \qquad \begin{array}{r} S \\ -a \\ \hline \Box \end{array} \qquad \begin{array}{r} S \\ -b \\ \hline \Box \end{array}$$

Understanding addition helps prepare children for subtraction, but some elementary textbooks introduce addition and subtraction at approximately the same time. Research concerning an optimum time to introduce subtraction has been inconclusive. However, introducing addition and subtraction literally *simultaneously* may well lead to confusion. On the other hand, waiting for children to master addition seems to delay subtraction concepts too long.

Readiness for subtraction includes numberness, conservation of number, knowledge of place value, a beginning understanding of the addition concept, and reversibility. The inverse relationship between addition and subtraction is beneficial in teaching subtraction. Since subtraction is the inverse of addition, reversibility concepts (as defined by Piaget) may be one of the most important prerequisites. Children should be tested by using Piagetian tasks to determine their readiness to begin the study of subtraction.

With children, the subtraction concept must be developed from the concrete level with continual progress to the abstract level. As in addition, models used to introduce subtraction concepts frequently include groups of objects and the number line. However, subtraction may prove to be more difficult to teach and to learn because there are at least three different types of subtraction situations to consider.

Some elementary school mathematics textbooks teach children only one type of subtraction, the "take-away" model. If the other types of subtraction situations are not taught to children, they will experience difficulty when they encounter examples such as $4 + \Box = 7$. For this equation, the child seems to ask, "What is needed to add to 4 to get to 7?" In a child's mind, that hardly seems to be a "take-away" question!

Let us first examine the most common conceptualization of subtraction, "take-away" subtraction. If we have 7 spoons and we take away 3 spoons, how many spoons will be left? If children count the 4 spoons that are left, they are not subtracting: they are counting! To prevent counting, you might show the 7 spoons on the

Research Snapshot

What does the research say about the consequences of having students solve multiplace addition problems followed by multiplace subtraction problems?

In Fuson et al.'s (1997) examination of four research projects with a problem-solving approach to teaching and learning multiplace number concepts and operations, the results from two projects suggested that it may be beneficial to intermix multiplace addition and subtraction problems early in instruction.

In the Problem Centered Mathematics Project (PCMP), some children developed an incorrect generalization of an addition solution method to subtraction: they subtracted the tens and then subtracted both ones. In the Children in the Conceptually Based Instruction (CBI) project, students had trouble devising a written method for subtraction because their addition solution method did not generalize to subtraction.

What real-world problem contexts might you use in your classroom if you wanted to teach addition and subtraction problems simultaneously?

Fuson, K. C., Wearne, D., Hiebert, J. C., Murray, H. G., Human, P. G., Olivier, A. I., Carpenter, T. P., & Fennema, E. (1997). Children's conceptual structures for multidigit numbers and methods of multidigit addition and subtraction. *Journal for Research in Mathematics Education, 28*, 130–162.

For additional research briefs, "ERIC Digests" lets you search more than 2,000 short syntheses of research on a range of education topics. The syntheses were produced by the Educational Resources Information Center (ERIC). Check http://ed.gov/databases/ERIC_Digests/index/

overhead projector and then turn the projector off. Have the children watch as you remove some announced quantity of spoons, say, 3. Then, without turning the overhead back on, ask the question, "How many spoons are still on the overhead projector?" After the children have subtracted, turn on the projector and check their response.

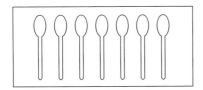

Initially, children see the 7 spoons, and then see 3 spoons physically removed; then they must subtract. They can readily check to see whether they are correct.

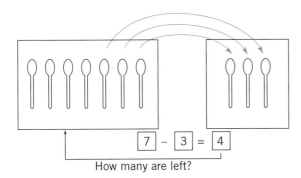

7 − 3 = 4

How many are left?

Although this may be the most familiar form of subtraction, children still need to model many take-away subtraction examples and record each step of the inverse operation in writing. Relate addition with subtraction by combining the two groups of objects that were separated and having children write the addition sentence. Discuss how 3, 4, and 7 are related by addition and subtraction.

Another type of subtraction is "comparison" subtraction. Consider the two following groups:

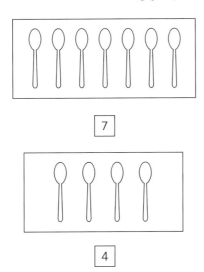

7

4

One set has 7 spoons, and the other has 4 spoons. The teacher can ask either, "How many more spoons does the first group have than the second?" or "How many fewer spoons does the second group have than the first?" One-to-one correspondence can be used to compare the two groups. There is no take-away action in solving this type of subtraction.

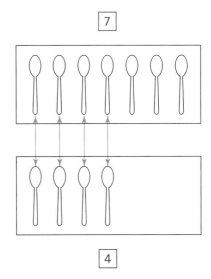

7

4

The difference between the two groups, 7 and 4, is 3, because 3 of the spoons in one set cannot be paired with 3 spoons in the other group. We write 7 − 4 = 3. Comparison subtraction is often seen as more difficult than take-away subtraction because the student must think about two different groups at once and then compare the two groups by using one-to-one correspondence.

The third type of subtraction is frequently referred to as "add-on" or, sometimes, as "missing addend" subtraction. Look at the following group and ask, "How many more spoons are needed to have 7 spoons in all?"

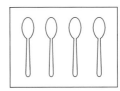

This may be difficult for children because they must think of the number 7 and compare the 4 spoons that they see with the number 7. The missing addend can also be obtained by counting beginning with 5 and, as spoons are placed, counting 6 and 7. Three spoons were added: 4 + 3 = 7 or 7 − 4 = 3.

Children need many experiences on the concrete level with each type of subtraction. Some teachers choose to teach only one type of subtraction at a time, believing that after children become effective with one type of subtraction, then they are ready to move on to the next type. After the various types of subtraction have been taught and the children can function effectively with each type, teachers then provide mixed practice with all types. Other teachers may elect to expose the children to all types from the onset, with emphasis on the real-world action that accompanies each type of subtraction. That is, these teachers would engage the children in problem situations in which the particular type of subtraction would be called for by the action needed to solve the problem.

Here are examples: "take-away"—if you have 7 cookies and you eat 4 of them, how many do you have left?; "comparison"—if you have 7 cookies and I have 4 cookies, how many more do you have than me?; and "missing addend"—if you have 4 cookies, how many more do you need to have 7 cookies? Each of these problems has a known addend and a sum, and is seeking a missing addend—the context of the problem determines which type of subtraction is appropriate. The most important consideration, however, is that the children have ample experiences in acting out all types of subtraction using manipulative models. This forces acknowledgment that the process of subtraction may require different interpretations of the same abstract subtraction sentence.

Using these interpretations of subtraction, children are then ready to understand a working definition for subtraction. Remember that subtraction is *not* counting either forward or backward. Remember that "take-away" is not synonymous with subtraction but only one of the possible forms subtraction may take. Then what is subtraction?

> **Subtraction** is an operation performed on a sum and one addend to obtain a missing addend.

DEVELOPING BASIC SUBTRACTION FACTS

The children are now ready to use the same addend and sum cards for subtraction sentences that they used with addition sentences. In order to help children recognize the reversibility of addition and subtraction, children should have many experiences relating an addition sentence to a subtraction sentence and relating a subtraction sentence to an addition sentence.

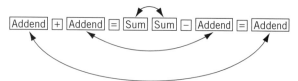

Many elementary school mathematics programs successfully use the number line as a model for developing an understanding of all types of subtraction. Consider the example $7 - 4 = \square$. Because 7 is the sum and 4 is an addend, we can write $4 + \square = 7$. Then subtraction is modeled just as addition was. Children know that all modeling on the number line should begin at the reference point, zero. Draw a line segment from 0 to 4 for the known addend. On the number line locate the point that corresponds to the sum, 7. Now use a dotted line

and draw a line segment from 4 to 7. This dotted line segment represents the missing addend $\square$. How long is the dotted line segment? It is three units long.

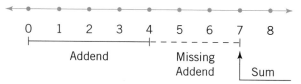

This way we can see that the missing addend is 3. Therefore $4 + 3 = 7$, so $7 - 4 = 3$.

At this stage of development, children should be able to look at two groups and write four related mathematical sentences. For example:

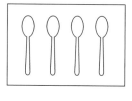   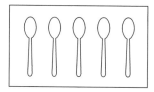

$4 + 5 = 9$ $9 - 4 = 5$
$5 + 4 = 9$ $9 - 5 = 4$

If children have memorized the basic addition facts, then they also know, or at least have a good jump on, the basic subtraction facts. What is a basic subtraction fact?

> A **basic subtraction fact** is a one- or two-place sum subtract a one-place addend to obtain another one-place addend.

For example, if children have memorized $4 + 5 = 9$ and if they understand the inverse relationship between addition and subtraction, then they should see that the solution to $4 + \square = 9$ is 5. Can you discover another way to express this inverse relationship?

$$9 - 4 = \square \quad \text{or} \quad \begin{array}{r} 9 \\ -4 \\ \hline \square \end{array} \quad \text{or} \quad \begin{array}{r} 4 \\ +\square \\ \hline 9 \end{array}$$

The table of basic addition facts can be used to solve subtraction exercises. Consider $7 - 4 = \square$. In this example, 7 is the sum, 4 is the known addend, and the box indicates the missing addend. In the addition table, the addends are located in the top row and in the left-hand column. Locate the known addend 4 in the top row, and look down the column until you come to the sum 7. Now look to the left along the row containing 7 until you come to the missing addend, 3, in the left-hand column. Clearly, $7 - 4 = 3$.

Sometimes children need a guide to help them locate a specific example in the addition table. Make a guide by cutting two strips from a sheet of transparent acetate. Use rubber cement to connect the two strips at a 90° angle. Cut a square for the product where the two strips overlap.

Addends

+	0	1	2	3	4	5	6	7	8	9
0	0	1	2	3	4	5	6	7	8	9
1	1	2	3	4	5	6	7	8	9	10
2	2	3	4	5	6	7	8	9	10	11
3	3	4	5	6	7	8	9	10	11	12
4	4	5	6	7	8	9	10	11	12	13
5	5	6	7	8	9	10	11	12	13	14
6	6	7	8	9	10	11	12	13	14	15
7	7	8	9	10	11	12	13	14	15	16
8	8	9	10	11	12	13	14	15	16	17
9	9	10	11	12	13	14	15	16	17	18

(A d d e n d s)

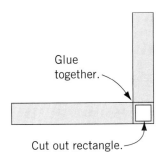

Glue together.

Cut out rectangle.

When placed on a basic fact table, the answer will be displayed through the cut-out square.

The basic subtraction facts must be developed, organized into a table, and then memorized. This sequential procedure for teaching subtraction is much like that for addition. Teachers report that organizing basic subtraction facts into a structural or conceptual approach that children understand (much like we did for addition) is helpful to students trying to memorize the basic subtraction facts.

MEMORIZING BASIC SUBTRACTION FACTS USING STRUCTURES

Now let us begin by considering this set of basic subtraction facts:

$$
\begin{array}{cccccccccc}
0 & 1 & 2 & 3 & 4 & 5 & 6 & 7 & 8 & 9 \\
\underline{-0} & \underline{-1} & \underline{-2} & \underline{-3} & \underline{-4} & \underline{-5} & \underline{-6} & \underline{-7} & \underline{-8} & \underline{-9} \\
0 & 0 & 0 & 0 & 0 & 0 & 0 & 0 & 0 & 0
\end{array}
$$

Students should again look for likenesses and differences. They should generalize much as they did when learning addition and note that when a number is subtracted from itself, the missing addend (the answer) is 0. With this conclusion, children will have memorized 10 of the 100 basic subtraction facts.

Examine this set of basic subtraction examples:

$$
\begin{array}{ccccccccc}
1 & 2 & 3 & 4 & 5 & 6 & 7 & 8 & 9 \\
\underline{-0} & \underline{-0} & \underline{-0} & \underline{-0} & \underline{-0} & \underline{-0} & \underline{-0} & \underline{-0} & \underline{-0} \\
1 & 2 & 3 & 4 & 5 & 6 & 7 & 8 & 9
\end{array}
$$

Following an observation-based procedure, the children should be encouraged to examine these examples for likenesses and differences. Children should notice that when 0 is subtracted from a number, the other number is the same as the missing addend (the answer). Another 9 basic facts have now been memorized. Thus, using only two basic structure ideas, children can memorize 19 basic subtraction facts.

As numberness and number sequencing were developed with the children, we noted which number comes after a certain number and which number comes before a certain number. What number is just before 6? Children can use the number line as a model to help them. This idea will help them to memorize this set of basic subtraction facts:

$$
\begin{array}{ccccccccc}
2 & 3 & 4 & 5 & 6 & 7 & 8 & 9 & 10 \\
\underline{-1} & \underline{-1} & \underline{-1} & \underline{-1} & \underline{-1} & \underline{-1} & \underline{-1} & \underline{-1} & \underline{-1} \\
1 & 2 & 3 & 4 & 5 & 6 & 7 & 8 & 9
\end{array}
$$

These examples can be considered neighbors, as the children look for likenesses and differences. When 1 is subtracted from a number, the number that precedes it is the missing addend (the answer). Nine more basic facts have been memorized for a total of 28. More than one-fourth of the basic subtraction facts have now been memorized.

Extending the idea of neighbors a little further, we can consider this set of examples:

$$
\begin{array}{cccccccc}
3 & 4 & 5 & 6 & 7 & 8 & 9 & 10 \\
\underline{-2} & \underline{-3} & \underline{-4} & \underline{-5} & \underline{-6} & \underline{-7} & \underline{-8} & \underline{-9} \\
1 & 1 & 1 & 1 & 1 & 1 & 1 & 1
\end{array}
$$

Again, after the children have studied the examples, encourage them to conclude that when a number just before a given number is subtracted, the missing addend (the answer) is 1. Eight more basic subtraction facts have been memorized, making a total of 36 that have been memorized (more than one-third of all basic subtraction facts).

Now review counting by twos with the children. This concept will help them to memorize this set of basic subtraction facts:

$$
\begin{array}{cccccccc}
4 & 5 & 6 & 7 & 8 & 9 & 10 & 11 \\
\underline{-2} & \underline{-2} & \underline{-2} & \underline{-2} & \underline{-2} & \underline{-2} & \underline{-2} & \underline{-2} \\
2 & 3 & 4 & 5 & 6 & 7 & 8 & 9
\end{array}
$$

Using the number line, the children can realize that subtracting 2 yields the same result as skip-counting by two backward on the number line. This is the third row of the subtraction and addition table. These 8 examples with the 36 already memorized make a total of 44 basic subtraction facts that have been memorized.

Related to the previous set of subtraction facts is the following set of facts:

$$
\begin{array}{ccccccc}
5 & 6 & 7 & 8 & 9 & 10 & 11 \\
\underline{-3} & \underline{-4} & \underline{-5} & \underline{-6} & \underline{-7} & \underline{-8} & \underline{-9} \\
2 & 2 & 2 & 2 & 2 & 2 & 2
\end{array}
$$

These numbers are two apart on the number line, so the missing addend (the answer) is 2. This will help children memorize 7 more basic facts. Now 51 basic subtraction facts have been memorized.

The children have studied the doubles with respect to basic addition facts. Now relate the doubles to the subtraction facts. This set of facts is:

$$
\begin{array}{ccccccc}
6 & 8 & 10 & 12 & 14 & 16 & 18 \\
\underline{-3} & \underline{-4} & \underline{-5} & \underline{-6} & \underline{-7} & \underline{-8} & \underline{-9} \\
3 & 4 & 5 & 6 & 7 & 8 & 9
\end{array}
$$

After careful examination, the children should see that the given addend is the same as the missing addend (the answer). Seven more basic subtraction facts have been memorized, for a total of 58.

The next set of subtraction facts to consider is:

$$
\begin{array}{cccccc}
12 & 13 & 14 & 15 & 16 & 17 \\
\underline{-9} & \underline{-9} & \underline{-9} & \underline{-9} & \underline{-9} & \underline{-9} \\
3 & 4 & 5 & 6 & 7 & 8
\end{array}
$$

After studying these examples, the children should discover that the missing addend is one greater than the number in the ones place of the sum. This generalization will help the children to memorize 6 more basic facts, for a total of 64.

Consider this set of facts with a difference of 9:

$$
\begin{array}{cccccc}
12 & 13 & 14 & 15 & 16 & 17 \\
\underline{-3} & \underline{-4} & \underline{-5} & \underline{-6} & \underline{-7} & \underline{-8} \\
9 & 9 & 9 & 9 & 9 & 9
\end{array}
$$

In subtraction, when the numbers in the ones place are neighbors and the lesser number is on top, the missing addend is 9. This makes another 6 basic subtraction facts, so at this point the children should have 70 basic facts memorized. Encourage the children to examine carefully the last 30 basic subtraction facts that must be memorized and to use whatever they discover will help them. All children do not need the same methods to help them memorize the facts. The basic subtraction facts remaining to be memorized are:

$$
\begin{array}{ccccccccc}
7 & 8 & 9 & 10 & 11 & 9 & 10 & 11 & 12 \\
\underline{-3} & \underline{-3} & \underline{-3} & \underline{-3} & \underline{-3} & \underline{-4} & \underline{-4} & \underline{-4} & \underline{-4} \\
4 & 5 & 6 & 7 & 8 & 5 & 6 & 7 & 8
\end{array}
$$

$$
\begin{array}{ccccccccc}
11 & 12 & 13 & 13 & 14 & 15 & 7 & 8 & 9 \\
\underline{-5} & \underline{-5} & \underline{-5} & \underline{-6} & \underline{-6} & \underline{-7} & \underline{-4} & \underline{-5} & \underline{-5} \\
6 & 7 & 8 & 7 & 8 & 8 & 3 & 3 & 4
\end{array}
$$

$$
\begin{array}{ccccccccc}
9 & 10 & 11 & 10 & 11 & 12 & 13 & 11 & 12 \\
\underline{-6} & \underline{-6} & \underline{-6} & \underline{-7} & \underline{-7} & \underline{-7} & \underline{-7} & \underline{-8} & \underline{-8} \\
3 & 4 & 5 & 3 & 4 & 5 & 6 & 3 & 4
\end{array}
$$

$$
\begin{array}{ccc}
13 & 14 & 15 \\
\underline{-8} & \underline{-8} & \underline{-8} \\
5 & 6 & 7
\end{array}
$$

This last set of 30 basic facts is often more challenging for children. Give them 1 or 2 of these basic facts to memorize at a time. Teachers sometimes tend to require too much memorization too rapidly. The organization suggested in this chapter has proved suc-

cessful, even with children suffering from certain severe learning difficulties.

EXTENDING BASIC SUBTRACTION FACTS USING PLACE VALUE

After understanding place value, subtraction as the inverse of addition, and the basic subtraction facts, children should be ready to explore how to extend the basic subtraction facts. Help the children relate the following two examples, much as we did for addition:

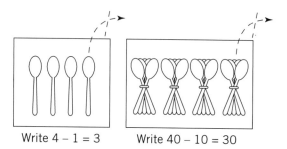

Write 4 − 1 = 3   Write 40 − 10 = 30

Children should generalize that the basic subtraction facts apply, regardless of the decimal place. Children who understand place value and who have memorized basic facts can apply this knowledge to solve two-place subtraction examples successfully.

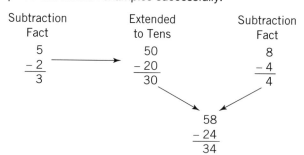

Subtraction examples can also be written in another form:

$$
\begin{array}{rl}
64 = & 6 \text{ tens } 4 \text{ ones} \\
\underline{-12} = & \underline{-1 \text{ ten } \ 2 \text{ ones}} \\
& 5 \text{ tens } 2 \text{ ones} = 52
\end{array}
$$

$$
\begin{array}{rl}
57 = & 5 \text{ tens } 7 \text{ ones} \\
\underline{-23} = & \underline{-2 \text{ tens } 3 \text{ ones}} \\
& 3 \text{ tens } 4 \text{ ones} = 34
\end{array}
$$

$$
\begin{array}{rl}
45 = & 4 \text{ tens } 5 \text{ ones} \\
\underline{-31} = & \underline{-3 \text{ tens } 2 \text{ ones}} \\
& 1 \text{ ten } \ 4 \text{ ones} = 14
\end{array}
$$

Do not write the examples like this:

$$
\begin{array}{rl}
64 = & 60 + 4 \\
\underline{-12} = & \underline{-10 + 2}
\end{array}
$$

Children will subtract the number in the tens place and add the number in the ones place, because they see the addition sign in the middle of the subtraction example. This is a poor teaching procedure that, potentially, will cause the children to subtract only the 10 and not the 2. Instead, use place-value names until children internalize them. That is, the expanded form might be read as "6 tens and 4 ones subtract 1 ten and 2 ones." Even a correct abstract form, shown here,

$$64 = 60 + 4$$
$$-12 = -(10 + 2)$$

will likely cause confusion about what should be added and what should be subtracted.

Practice exercises for children can be placed together to make one large example, as demonstrated with addition. For instance, study the two following samples to learn how the first 5 basic facts are combined into one example:

Solve each.

1. 7	2. 5	3. 6	4. 3	5. 8
-4	-1	-2	-0	-5

6. 9	7. 4	8. 1	9. 2	10. 8
-6	-3	-0	-2	-7

Solve each.

1. 75638
    -41205

2. 94128
    -63027

All children can proceed this way, including children who are experiencing difficulty learning mathematics. As mentioned in the addition section, children think that the more digits an example has, the more difficult it is, which is not necessarily true. Children can develop a feeling of accomplishment from solving examples with more digits. The children are just applying the concepts of subtraction and place value and the basic facts to examples with more decimal places. Actually, no new teaching is necessary.

The notion of inverse operation is an important aspect of basic mathematical structure; it is essential to understanding elementary arithmetic. Also, the basic properties of subtraction should be examined. Using manipulative materials, children can explore the ideas of basic structures and generalize that:

1. Subtraction is not commutative:

$$8 - 6 \neq 6 - 8$$

2. Subtraction is not associative:

$$(8 - 4) - 2 \neq 8 - (4 - 2)$$

3. Subtraction does not have an identity element:

Even though $7 - 0 = 7$,
it is not true that $0 - 7 = 7$

REGROUPING IN THE SUBTRACTION PROCESS

The trend in contemporary classrooms is to use the term *regroup* to describe the process that has been called (and still is, in some circles) *carry and borrow*. The word regroup seems more descriptive of the process that we are trying to describe. The manipulation and concept are the same for addition and subtraction: 10 ones are changed (or "regrouped") to be one group of 10, and one group of 10 is changed (or "regrouped") to be 10 ones. The terminology will help to relate the two ideas, but it is only a process of regrouping taught as one reversible concept, not as two separate concepts.

Before introducing subtraction examples that require regrouping, it is a good idea to review expanded notation and the concept that a number can be named in many ways. The children should use some type of counters, such as Popsicle sticks, and demonstrate each name for a number. The number 372, for example, can be written as:

3 hundreds	7 tens	2 ones
or		
2 hundreds	17 tens	2 ones
or		
2 hundreds	16 tens	12 ones
or		
2 hundreds	15 tens	22 ones

and so on.

The use of Numeral Expanders, as described in Chapter 6, will assist greatly here.

When beginning subtraction with regrouping, children will often subtract the lesser number from the greater number, regardless of the position of the numbers in the example. For instance, children might think that

$$\begin{array}{r} 71 \\ -28 \\ \hline 57 \end{array}$$

Since 8 cannot be subtracted from 1, children will often subtract 1 from 8. This type of response indicates that the children do not really understand the meaning of subtraction and that the children were likely *told how* to regroup on the abstract level. If children are encouraged to explore on the concrete level, they will not be as likely to make this type of error. It is better to anticipate the children's difficulties and prevent them from occurring than to try to correct the misconceptions later. Now let's carefully examine the regrouping process in subtraction.

How would a child subtract 27 from 53, beginning on the concrete level? Using a place-value box and the "take-away" model, start with 53 counters and have the students remove 27 counters.

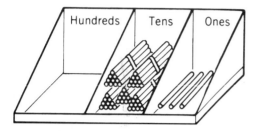

To remove 7 ones, the student must regroup one pack of 10. A student cannot remove 7 counters from the ones place without regrouping 1 ten to 10 ones. This is the same way a child must think in order to understand regrouping in the written algorithm for subtraction. Children need many concrete examples before they can begin to record their ideas using the algorithm.

Next, have the students use place value to rewrite this example:

$$53 = \quad 5 \text{ tens } 3 \text{ ones}$$
$$-27 = -2 \text{ tens } 7 \text{ ones}$$

The children should see that they cannot subtract yet, since the number of ones in the first line of the example is less than the number of ones in the second line. Children with a weak understanding of subtraction will not recognize this difficulty and will subtract the lesser number from the greater regardless of the position of the numbers. Continually relate to the concrete model, using the place-value box as we have pictured. To overcome the difficulty, 5 tens 3 ones can be regrouped as 4 tens 13 ones:

$$53 = \quad 4 \text{ tens } 13 \text{ ones}$$
$$-27 = -2 \text{ tens } \ 7 \text{ ones}$$
$$\quad\quad 2 \text{ tens } \ 6 \text{ ones} = 26$$

Children need to model and record the results of many examples.

Children who have been taught regrouping from the concrete level to the abstract level will be able to apply the concept to more places and manipulate counters to understand the regrouping.

$$323 = \quad 3 \text{ hundreds } \ 2 \text{ tens } \ 3 \text{ ones}$$
$$-156 = -1 \text{ hundred } \quad 5 \text{ tens } \ 6 \text{ ones}$$

$$= \quad 2 \text{ hundreds } 11 \text{ tens } 13 \text{ ones}$$
$$= -1 \text{ hundred } \quad 5 \text{ tens } \ 6 \text{ ones}$$

Place value and expanded notation can be used to develop an understanding of regrouping. After children understand regrouping, it should be easy for them to see the relationship of these concepts to the mental processes involved in using the short subtraction algorithm with which we wish them to become familiar:

$$\begin{array}{r} 323 \\ -156 \\ \hline 167 \end{array}$$

Children who have been taught this way will not need to write regrouped numbers above the examples. Children who understand the concept will not need these "crutches"; children with a weak or poorly developed understanding may, however, need additional help.

Children who have a sound understanding of regrouping will also have little difficulty with zeros in subtraction. Consider the example 700 − 256. Traditionally, this type of example required double regrouping:

$$\begin{array}{r} {}^6\llap{7}{}^7\llap{9}0{}^1 0 \\ -2\ 5\ 6 \\ \hline 4\ 4\ 4 \end{array}$$

If we think of the number 700 as 70 tens and 0 ones, we need only one regrouping. Study this example. Note that no markings are placed above the example.

$$700 = 70 \text{ tens } 0 \text{ ones} = 69 \text{ tens } 10 \text{ ones}$$
$$-256 = 25 \text{ tens } 6 \text{ ones} = 25 \text{ tens } \ 6 \text{ ones}$$
$$\quad\quad\quad\quad\quad\quad\quad\quad\quad\quad 44 \text{ tens } \ 4 \text{ ones}$$
$$= 4 \text{ hundreds } 4 \text{ tens } 4 \text{ ones} = 444$$

Other children might approach this exercise by subtracting the 200 from the 700 and then deal with how to take away the remaining 56. As stated earlier, many invented mental strategies can and should be explored along with the more common, traditional algorithms.

It is of historical interest that many other algorithms have been used for addition and subtraction. You may be interested in doing research on the Austrian method and the method of complementary subtraction. Consider what might be probable advantages and disadvantages of these other algorithms.

CLOSURE

In summary, there are five major concepts that a student should understand to assist him or her in solving any *addition* example:

1. The student must understand what the process of addition means.
2. The student must understand the basic addition facts and have them memorized.
3. The student must understand place value and be able to relate place-value concepts to addition. This allows the student to extend the basic addition facts to many-place numbers.
4. The student should understand the basic structures or properties (for example, the commutative property and the identity element) as applied to addition.
5. The student must understand the concept of regrouping and be able to relate the regrouping concept to addition.

There are also five major concepts that a student should comprehend to assist him or her in solving any *subtraction* example:

1. The student must understand the various interpretations of subtraction.
2. The student must comprehend the basic subtraction facts and have them memorized.
3. The student must understand place value and relate place-value concepts to the inverse operation of subtraction.
4. The student must understand that the basic structures or properties of addition (for example, commutativity) do not apply to subtraction.
5. The student must understand the concept of regrouping as it applies to the subtraction process.

The major concepts of addition and subtraction have been organized into the following convenient table:

	Addition	Subtraction
Understanding the operation	$A + A = S$	$S - A = A$
Basic facts	100 basic facts	100 basic facts
Place value	Same as for subtraction	Same as for addition
Structures	Commutative property, associative property, identity element of addition, and so on	Properties do not apply to subtraction.
Regrouping	Change ones to tens, and so on.	Change tens to ones, and so on.

Terminology, Symbols, and Procedures

Addend. Each of the two numbers to be added in an addition example is called an *addend*.

Addition. The operation of addition is a binary operation performed on a pair of numbers called *addends* to obtain a unique sum. While not defined for children as such, the operation can be defined abstractly as follows: If a and b are any two whole numbers, and if A and B are sets such that $n(A) = a$ and $n(B) = b$, then $a + b$ is, by definition, the cardinal number of the union of sets A and B; that is, $a + b = n(A \cup B)$, where $A \cup B$ is the union of sets. Addition may be symbolized as:

$$\text{Addend} + \text{Addend} = \text{Sum} \quad \text{or} \quad \begin{array}{r} \text{Addend} \\ + \text{Addend} \\ \hline \text{Sum} \end{array}$$

Addition is read, "Addend add Addend equals Sum" or "Addend plus Addend equals Sum"; that is, $2 + 3 = 5$ is read, "Two add three equals five" or "Two plus three equals five."

Addition Table. An addition table is an orderly arrangement of columns and rows. Each row and column is headed by an addend, and each cell in the table contains a sum.

Algorithm. An algorithm is the form in which mathematical computations are written and solved, showing the steps necessary to solve them. Several types of algorithms can exist for one example, such as a short algorithm and a long algorithm. For example:

Horizontal Algorithm

$$2 + 3 = 5$$

Vertical Algorithm

$$\begin{array}{r} 8 \\ + 5 \\ \hline 13 \end{array}$$

Long Algorithm

$$\begin{array}{r} 67 \\ + 48 \\ \hline 15 \\ 100 \\ \hline 115 \end{array}$$

Short Algorithm

$$\begin{array}{r} 67 \\ +48 \\ \hline 115 \end{array}$$

Basic Addition Facts. Basic addition facts include all combinations of one-place whole numbers (addends) added to one-place whole numbers (addends) to obtain a one- or two-place sum. There are 100 basic addition facts.

Basic Subtraction Facts. Basic subtraction facts include all combinations of one-place whole numbers (addends) subtracted from one- or two-place whole numbers (sums) to obtain a one-place whole number (addend). There are 100 basic subtraction facts.

Binary Operation. The two fundamental operations on numbers (addition and multiplication) are often referred to as *binary operations*, because computation is done with only two numbers at one time.

Family of Numbers. All the possible combinations of whole number addends that will produce a given sum are called a *family of numbers* for that sum. For example:

- The family of five is $0 + 5$, $1 + 4$, $2 + 3$, $3 + 2$, $4 + 1$, and $5 + 0$.

Identity Element of Addition. Zero (0) is the identity element of addition, since the sum of any number and zero is always that number. For example:

$$6 + 0 = 6 \quad 9 + 0 = 9 \quad 4 + 0 = 4$$

Properties of Addition. The properties of addition discussed in this chapter are:

1. Addition is **associative**. For any whole numbers a, b, and c:

$$(a + b) + c = a + (b + c)$$

2. Addition is **commutative**. For any whole numbers a and b:

$$a + b = b + a$$

Regrouping. Regrouping is the process used in changing a group of ten to ten groups of one or changing ten groups of one to one group of ten. For example:

47 can be regrouped from 4 tens 7 ones to 3 tens 17 ones;
2 tens 16 ones can be regrouped as 3 tens 6 ones.

Subtraction. Subtraction is defined as the inverse operation of addition. It is a binary operation performed on a sum and one addend to obtain the missing addend. Subtraction is symbolized as:

$$\text{Sum} - \text{Addend} = \text{Addend} \quad \text{or} \quad \begin{array}{r} \text{Sum} \\ - \text{Addend} \\ \hline \text{Addend} \end{array}$$

Sum. A sum is the result of adding two or more addends.

Practice Exercises for Teachers

These exercises are designed for the reader of this book. While some are suitable for use in the elementary classroom, these examples should not necessarily be given to children in this form. Ideas for classroom activities on the concepts and ideas discussed in this chapter can be found in Part 2 of *Today's Mathematics*, the Student Resource Book.

1. Create a number line diagram to solve these examples. Label the addends and sum for each.

   a) $5 + 4 = \square$ b) $3 + 2 = \square$ c) $1 + 6 = \square$ d) $8 + 7 = \square$
   e) $9 - 4 = \square$ f) $7 + \square = 11$ g) $8 - 2 = \square$ h) $15 - 9 = \square$

2. Use the addition operation and its inverse to write four related sentences using each of the given numbers.

   a) 4, 7, 11   b) 9, 2, 7   c) 6, 13, 7   d) 31, 75, 44

3. Write two subtraction sentences suggested by each of these addition sentences.

   a) $8 + 9 = \square$ b) $4 + 9 = \square$ c) $\square = 53 + 39$ d) $7 + 6 = \square$

4. Name the two basic facts and the expanded basic fact that will help children solve each of the following two-place addition examples:

   a) $18 + 31 = \square$ b) $26 + 31 = \square$ c) $73 + 15 = \square$ d) $52 + 45 = \square$

5. Rewrite each of the following examples in expanded notation and solve.

   a)   18   b)   247   c)   73   d)   364
      +41   +532   +25   +213

6. Solve each of the following examples with regrouping. Show each step of the regrouping process.

   a)   37   b)   61   c)   73   d)   219   e)   378
      +49   +54   +88   +466   +154

   f)   56   g)   346   h)   459   i)   521   j)   832
      +29   −83   −272   −146   −398

7. Use expanded notation to calculate each of the following sums. Show your work in horizontal form, and name the property of addition that justifies each step. (The purpose of this exercise is to help teachers understand the mathematics underlying the algorithm. Do not ask children to solve examples in this manner.)

   a)   37   b)   276   c)   48
      +28   +49   +75

8. Solve each subtraction example, using renaming and only one regrouping and with no "borrow marks" written above the example.

   a)   500   b)   802   c)   900
      −273   −367   −258

9. Using the words *addend* and *sum*, write four related addition and subtraction sentences.

10. Describe how the subtraction example shown below might be solved using take-away, comparison, and missing addend models.

$$54 - 18 = \square$$

Teaching Competencies and Self-Assessment Tasks

1. What prerequisite skills and concepts are needed for the development of the addition concept? the subtraction concept?

2. According to Piagetian theory, when should a child be ready to understand subtraction?

3. Discuss how Cuisenaire rods and base ten blocks can be used in developing addition and subtraction concepts.

4. Discuss the pros and cons for each model used in this chapter to develop an understanding of the addition and subtraction operations.

5. Research the literature, and then discuss effective techniques for encouraging children to memorize the basic addition and subtraction facts.

6. Discuss the likenesses and differences between how addition and subtraction are presented in this chapter and how you remember learning these operations.

7. What types of materials can be used with children to develop the concepts of addition and subtraction?

8. Research the literature for alternative ways to add and subtract, and then compare and contrast the different methods (e.g., low-stress algorithms, Austrian method of subtraction, and the equal additions method).

9. Some textbooks suggest that addition and subtraction should be taught simultaneously; others recommend that subtraction be taught after addition. Take a stand and support your position.

Related Readings and Teacher Resources

For related readings on topics found in this chapter, see the corresponding chapter in Part 2 of *Today's Mathematics*, the Student Resource Book.

Chapter 8

Multiplication and Division of Whole Numbers

Teaching Competencies

Upon completing this chapter, you will be able to:

- State as well as physically demonstrate four different models that can be used to develop an understanding of the process of multiplication.

- Use four different models to demonstrate and describe two types of division (measurement and partition).

- Use a model that represents multiplication or division, and demonstrate regrouping with multiplication and division using a place-value box.

- Write examples to demonstrate the basic properties of multiplication.

- Develop a teaching sequence for multiplication and division.

hildren encounter multiplication and division concepts long before they begin the formal study of such notions. A kindergarten child might be asked to share a box of 18 crayons with two other friends so that all three children have the same number of crayons. A first grader might begin a hide-and-seek game by closing his or her eyes and skip-counting by fives (or twos or tens). A group of second graders might want to determine how many cans of food they will collect for the holiday food drive if each of the 25 children in the class brings in 4 cans. A third grader might notice the pattern of floor or ceiling tiles in the classroom and wonder how many tiles there are in all. In each case, a student has an opportunity to explore a practical application of multiplication and/or division concepts. In each situation, the child can determine the answer in a way that lends meaning to the concept, rather than shrouding the concept in rules and rote procedures.

The National Council of Teachers of Mathematics (NCTM) has responded to the call for reform in the teaching and learning of mathematics by publishing the *Principles and Standards for School Mathematics* (2000). This chapter on multiplication and division incorporates both the organization and the spirit suggested by these NCTM standards. More emphasis must be placed on development of understanding and thinking skills, and less emphasis on repetitive practice and drill. The calculator and computer should receive greater emphasis as our culture moves forward in a knowledge-centered society. Teachers must be willing to experiment with new techniques and media to accomplish more effective mathematics teaching.

Chapter 7 carefully examined the teaching of addition and its inverse operation, subtraction, to children. In this chapter we examine the operation of multiplication and its inverse operation, division. The basic format for teaching multiplication and division is similar to that used for teaching addition and subtraction.

MEANING AND MODELS FOR MULTIPLICATION

Readiness for multiplication and division includes an understanding of numberness to at least thousands; place value of at least ones, tens, and hundreds; conservation of number; reversibility; and addition and subtraction as inverse operations. This readiness has been developed in Chapters 1 through 7, so we can now develop an understanding of the operation of multiplication and its inverse operation, division.

> **Multiplication** is a binary operation performed on two numbers to obtain a unique result. The numbers we multiply are called *factors,* and the result of the multiplication is called a *product.*

For example, in the mathematical sentence

$$3 \times 4 = 12$$

the numbers 3 and 4 are the **factors**, and 12 is the **product**.

$$\text{Factor} \times \text{Factor} = \text{Product}$$
$$3 \quad \times \quad 4 \quad = \quad 12$$

Now let's carefully examine how to introduce children to multiplication. The first step in teaching multiplication to children is to develop an understanding of the operation. An understanding of the operation is developed from the concrete level to the abstract level using a variety of models. We will use four models to develop an understanding of multiplication—groups of objects, arrays, number lines, and repeated addition. Let us begin to develop an understanding by examining each multiplication model as we would develop them with children. Remember that children must do the actual manipulating to function on the concrete level.

The approach to multiplication using groups resembles the approach we used for addition. Suppose we want to find the product of three groups of 4. The children should be asked to make three separate groups with 4 items in each group. To illustrate this idea, select three groups with 4 objects in each. For example:

The first factor, 3, tells us the number of groups; the second factor, 4, tells us how many objects should be in each group. The product, 12, is the total number of objects. This model would be read, "Three groups of four is twelve." The mathematical sentence $3 \times 4 = 12$ is then related to the model, and the reading of "three groups of four is twelve" is related to reading the sentence as "three times four is twelve." The difference between addition and multiplication is that in multiplication, each group must have the same number of items. The multiplication symbol, $\times$, must be related to "groups of" in the mathematical sentence.

Since children have already studied addition, the model of successive addition can be introduced to help the children realize why three groups of four is twelve. We can obtain the same results by placing the three groups together much as we did in addition. We can think of 3×4 in terms of addition, but remember that *repeated addition is not multiplication*. Repeated addition is only a model to help children develop an understanding of multiplication.

$$3 \times 4 = 4 + 4 + 4 = 12$$

Therefore, we can think of this example as $4 + 4 + 4 = 12$, or 3 groups of 4 is 12, or $3 \times 4 = 12$. Using multiplication, we write $3 \times 4 = 12$ (read, "Three times four is equal to twelve").

Similarly, we can find the product of 4 × 5.

$$4 \times 5 = 20$$

Here we have four groups with 5 objects in each group. We can read this, "Four groups of five equals twenty." The addition sentence that helps explain that 4 × 5 equals 20 is 5 + 5 + 5 + 5 = 20. Remember that if a child adds 4 fives, the child is adding, not multiplying. This only helps the child to realize that four groups of 5 is really twenty. The multiplication sentence, 4 × 5 = 20, is read, "Four times five equals twenty."

Now let's examine another extremely useful model for multiplication: an array. A child's real-life experiences include many examples of objects arranged in an array format. For example, the desks in many classrooms, the seats in many movie theaters, the tiles on many floors or ceilings, the partitions in an egg carton, or the individual blocks of candy in a Hershey's chocolate bar.

> An **array** is an arrangement of objects or symbols into orderly rows and columns.
>
> *   *   *   *   *
> *   *   *   *   *
> *   *   *   *   *

This array would be called a 3-by-5 array. The child should use the eye movement developed in learning to read and begin at the upper left-hand corner. The child's eye moves across, visualizing one group of five down to two groups of five, and then down to three groups of five. Thus a child would think of this array as three groups of five, and it would be read, "three groups of five." The product of the number of rows and the number of columns in an array is always equal to the number of objects or symbols in the array. Thus, to discover that 3 × 5 = 15, the child can count the objects or symbols in a 3-by-5 array or use successive addition (5 + 5 + 5) to obtain the product.

Arrays can be helpful for developing basic facts and properties for multiplication. For example, a 2-by-4 array can be turned on its end to form a 4-by-2 array. This can be done to show that 2 × 4 = 4 × 2.

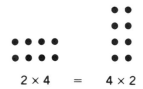

$$2 \times 4 \quad = \quad 4 \times 2$$

This example illustrates that the multiplication of whole numbers is commutative. This certainly seems reasonable, since multiplication of whole numbers can be considered in terms of repeated addition (i.e., addition of equal addends).

As another example of commutativity, consider that 3 × 2 = 6 could mean 2 + 2 + 2 = 6. It is easy to illustrate the commutative property of multiplication by simply turning an array on its end. In the array pictured here, the total number of objects is six in both cases:

The grouping or physical arrangement is different, but the product is the same. Whether two groups of three or three groups of two are used, the total number involved is six. This is the commutative property of multiplication.

> The **commutative property of multiplication** means that the order of two factors does not affect the product.
> For example, 3 × 2 = 6 and 2 × 3 = 6,
> or $a \times b = c$ and $b \times a = c$

It is important to emphasize that under the commutative property of multiplication, it is the *product* that is the same. For example, if you work 3 hours for $10 per hour you will earn $30 (3 × 10 = 30). Note that if you work 10 hours for $3 per hour you will still earn $30 (10 × 3 = 30). Are the two jobs the same? Which would you choose if they involved the same skill and effort? The product in each case is $30 but the situations are different. Many more examples of the commutative property of multiplication should be presented to children in the same fashion.

Multiplication can also be examined using the number line. Let's look at the example 3 × 4 = 12 and show it by modeling on the number line, using repeated addition.

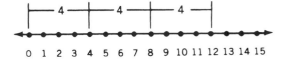

We begin to model at the origin, zero, and mark off four units, which puts us at the place named by 4. From this point, we mark off another four units; and from that point, named by 8, we mark off four more units. This puts us at the point labeled 12. Therefore, 4 + 4 + 4 = 12 and 3 × 4 = 12. The same procedure, of course, can be used to show that 4 × 3 = 12, thus illustrating again the commutative property of multiplication.

With young children, always begin modeling on the number line at the origin, zero. In this example we mark off three units, starting at zero, which puts us at the point named by 3. From that point, we mark off another three units; from that point (6), we mark off three more units; and from that point (labeled 9), we mark off another three units. Now we have arrived at the product of 12. Thus this model illustrates that four groups of three modeled on the number line is $4 \times 3 = 12$. You should provide children with many experiences modeling multiplication on the number line. This will also reinforce the commutative property of multiplication.

The *Cartesian product* can also be used as a model for multiplication; however, it is not recommended for elementary school children unless you use concrete objects or pictorial representations. This model is more difficult for students to comprehend at the abstract level, so a symbolic approach should be reserved for more mature children (about middle school level).

Consider one group of 2 sweaters and one group of 3 pairs of pants. How many color combinations of sweaters and pants are possible?

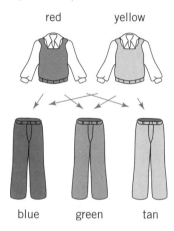

The red sweater, *r*, may be worn with each pair of pants to give the following color combinations:

$$(r, b) \qquad (r, g) \qquad (r, t)$$

The yellow sweater, *y*, may also be worn with each pair of pants. Thus we have three more possible combinations:

$$(y, b) \qquad (y, g) \qquad (y, t)$$

The group of all color combinations is shown in the following table:

	Sweaters	
	red	yellow
Pants		
blue	(r, b)	(y, b)
green	(r, g)	(y, g)
tan	(r, t)	(y, t)

Each time we match a sweater with pants, we obtain an ordered pair. For example, (*r*, *t*) is the ordered pair obtained by matching the red sweater with the tan

pants. The set of all ordered pairs obtained by matching the elements of sweaters with the elements of pants is called the **Cartesian product** of the set of sweaters and the set of pants. This set of ordered pairs is denoted by A × B (read, "the Cartesian product of A and B").

Note that when we use a table to display the possible combinations of 2 sweaters and 3 pairs of pants, an array is generated. In this case we have a 3-by-2 array that provides six different combinations.

We have identified five models that can be used for multiplication: groups of objects, arrays, number lines, repeated addition, and Cartesian products. These models can help children discover and develop an understanding of multiplication. None of these models is likely to solve all a child's difficulties in understanding multiplication. The teacher should be flexible and sensitive and must vary the models to suit the needs of the children in each class.

DEVELOPING AND MEMORIZING BASIC MULTIPLICATION FACTS

How are these models used to help children understand multiplication? Let's deal with groups as an example of a model. Place three sheets of paper on a desk; on each sheet of paper place 2 cubes, small toys, or plastic eating utensils.

Then ask these questions:

How many groups are there?
How many items are in each group?
How many items are there all together?

In this case there are three groups with 2 items in each group, so there are 6 items all together. Thus we can say that three groups of two is six.

$$3 \text{ groups of } 2 = 6$$
$$3 \times 2 = 6$$

Children need to view many groups of materials and to say, discuss, and write multiplication sentences. The overhead projector is an excellent tool for presenting groups and arrays to children. Use small rectangles of colored plastic on an overhead projector for each group, and place plastic spoons or forks as items on each group. Arrays can be made on overhead transparencies by pasting circular disks in columns and rows. Gummed disks also work well on worksheets.

Do not begin with two groups of 2, because 2 add 2 gives the same result as 2 times 2. Use base ten blocks, Cuisenaire rods, attribute blocks, pattern blocks, and other materials. Consult the specific manuals designed to help teachers use the materials.

Make multiplication arrays on sheets of paper, using gummed dots. Roll up the sheets of paper. As the students unroll each array, they can develop the multiples for any given number.

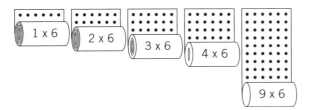

> **Multiples** of a given number include all products obtained by multiplying the set of whole numbers by a given factor.

For example, the multiples of 4 are obtained by multiplying 4 by 0, 1, 2, 3, 4, 5, . . . So, the multiples of 4 are 0, 4, 8, 12, 16, 20, . . .

Now children can begin to generate the multiples of a number by using groups as models. Generating the multiples of 2 using groups as models is illustrated here as an example:

	1 group of 2	1 x 2 = 2
	2 groups of 2	2 x 2 = 4
	3 groups of 2	3 x 2 = 6
	4 groups of 2	4 x 2 = 8
	5 groups of 2	5 x 2 = 10
	6 groups of 2	6 x 2 = 12
	7 groups of 2	7 x 2 = 14
	8 groups of 2	8 x 2 = 16
	9 groups of 2	9 x 2 = 18

Skip-counting helps children learn to generate the multiples of a number. Practice counting by twos, then by fives. Try having the children skip-count by threes while they are looking at a number line. Use a calculator with automatic memory to practice skip-counting by fours by punching the "4" key followed by the "+" key and then punch the "=" key several times in a row. Use this method to practice skip-counting by many different numbers. Children need many experiences generating multiples of a given number. Remember that a multiple is a product obtained by multiplying a whole number by a given factor. Applying the definition to a given factor of 6, we multiply 6 by 0, 1, 2, 3, 4, . . . This procedure must be followed very carefully. Note that the first factor changes but the second factor remains constant. In this example, we continually add another group of 6 and generate the multiples for 6.

Whole Numbers as Factors	Factor	Multiples
0	6	0
1	6	6
2	6	12
3	6	18
4	6	24
5	6	30
6	6	36
7	6	42
8	6	48
9	6	54
10	6	60
● ● ●	● ● ●	● ● ●

By using appropriate models, children should be able to develop the basic facts of multiplication and organize them into a multiplication table. Ten factors are written on the horizontal axis and on the vertical axis. The products associated with these factors are placed in the table.

Factors

×	0	1	2	3	4	5	6	7	8	9
0										
1										
2										
3										
4										
5										
6										
7										
8										
9										

Factors

There are 10×10 or 100 possible pairs of one-place factors and 100 possible products in the table. The children must memorize 100 basic multiplication facts. Two things must be done: The basic multiplication facts must be developed and then memorized.

> The basic multiplication facts include all one-place factors multiplied by all one-place factors to obtain a one- or two-place product.

We begin here with the development of the basic multiplication facts that do not involve zero as a factor, because if we do use zero as a factor, how can we show zero groups of three on the concrete level? It may also be just as difficult for the children to comprehend three groups of zero as a beginning example.

The children can use groups of objects, successive addition, arrays, and the number line to discover facts such as $2 \times 3 = 6$, $3 \times 2 = 6$, $4 \times 2 = 8$, $2 \times 4 = 8$, $3 \times 4 = 12$, and $4 \times 3 = 12$. As the children discover basic facts, help them to become aware of the basic structure of multiplication. (Commutativity is especially helpful.) Arrays, as we have already mentioned, can be very convincing models for illustrating the commutative property of multiplication.

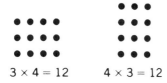

$$3 \times 4 = 12 \qquad 4 \times 3 = 12$$

When the students have had sufficient experience with nonzero factors, they should begin the exploration of exercises that have zero as the second factor. Groups are perhaps the most useful model for introducing multiplication facts such as $2 \times 0 = 0$ and $4 \times 0 = 0$. Two empty boxes would be an acceptable model for two $2 \times 0 = 0$; four empty boxes could model $4 \times 0 = 0$.

$$4 \times 0 = 0 + 0 + 0 + 0 = 0$$

When the children have used arrays or other models to discover the commutative property of multiplication, then they can use this property to discover that:

$$0 \times 2 = 0$$
$$0 \times 3 = 0$$
$$0 \times 4 = 0$$
and so on

The children need to generalize that the product of 0 and any other factor is 0. This is known as the **zero property of multiplication**. For all numbers n:

$$n \times 0 = 0$$
$$0 \times n = 0$$

This generalization allows the completion of one entire row and one entire column of the multiplication table:

Factors

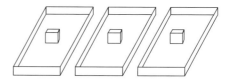

×	0	1	2	3	4	5	6	7	8	9
0	0	0	0	0	0	0	0	0	0	0
1	0									
2	0									
3	0									
4	0									
5	0									
6	0									
7	0									
8	0									
9	0									

(Factors)

A similar approach can be used to develop the identity element for multiplication. Three groups of 1 can be modeled with three boxes and one block in each box.

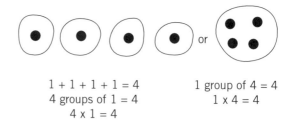

By applying the basic property of commutativity, we see that $1 \times 3 = 3$. Successive addition will also help children understand the relationship between addition and multiplication and the commutative property.

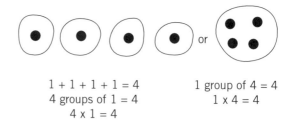

$1 + 1 + 1 + 1 = 4$	1 group of 4 = 4
4 groups of 1 = 4	$1 \times 4 = 4$
$4 \times 1 = 4$	

Again, by applying the basic property of commutativity, we see that $1 \times 4 = 4$. The children can now make the generalization that the product of 1 and any other factor is equal to the other factor. The number 1 is thus defined as the *identity element of multiplication*. The **identity property for multiplication** states that for any number a:

$$a \times 1 = a$$
$$1 \times a = a$$

Factors

×	0	1	2	3	4	5	6	7	8	9
0	0	0	0	0	0	0	0	0	0	0
1	0	1	2	3	4	5	6	7	8	9
2	0	2								
3	0	3								
4	0	4								
5	0	5								
6	0	6								
7	0	7								
8	0	8								
9	0	9								

(F a c t o r s)

related examples by relating multiplication and place-value concepts. Two groups of 3 can be modeled as:

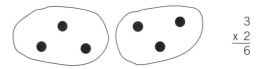

$$\begin{array}{r} 3 \\ \times\,2 \\ \hline 6 \end{array}$$

Now exchange each element in each group with a package of ten. The model now becomes:

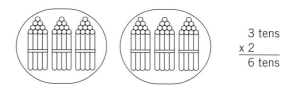

$$\begin{array}{r} 3 \text{ tens} \\ \times\,2 \\ \hline 6 \text{ tens} \end{array}$$

Children can easily count to verify that two groups of 3 is 6 and two groups of 3 tens is 6 tens. So two groups of 30 is 60. From many of these related models, children should generalize what happens in each case. The basic fact is the same in both examples: $2 \times 3 = 6$. The only difference is the place value. This concept is known as *expanding the basic facts*. By using place value, we expand the basic fact of $2 \times 3 = 6$ into $2 \times 30 = 60$. Children should generalize that the basic facts are the same regardless of place value.

The children need to generate the multiples for 2, 3, 4, 5, 6, 7, 8, and 9 and enter the products into the multiplication table. The children will eventually be able to construct the entire multiplication table of basic facts. When the students have memorized 55 of the basic multiplication facts in the table, they will know the remaining 45 facts because of the commutative property of multiplication. (The symmetry resulting from the commutative property is indicated here by shading.)

$$\begin{array}{r} 3 \\ \times\,2 \\ \hline 6 \end{array} \qquad \begin{array}{r} 30 \\ \times\,2 \\ \hline 60 \end{array}$$

You might want to review place value with the children before developing this lesson.

The multiplication table could be expanded to include an indefinite number of products, but it would then become large, awkward, and difficult to use. Instead, given an understanding of the properties of multiplication and the basic multiplication facts, a **multiplication algorithm** can be developed for solving multiplication examples that involve greater numbers.

Before we continue the development of multiplication with children, let us examine some other properties of this operation. We have already studied the commutative property of multiplication. Now, let's consider the associative property of multiplication. Multiplication is a binary operation; this means that it can be performed on only two numbers at one time. This gives us the freedom to associate factors in different ways for greater ease in computation. Consider the associative property of multiplication, and note its effective application in this example:

Factors

x	0	1	2	3	4	5	6	7	8	9
0	0	0	0	0	0	0	0	0	0	0
1	0	1	2	3	4	5	6	7	8	9
2	0	2	4	6	8	10	12	14	16	18
3	0	3	6	9	12	15	18	21	24	27
4	0	4	8	12	16	20	24	28	32	36
5	0	5	10	15	20	25	30	35	40	45
6	0	6	12	18	24	30	36	42	48	54
7	0	7	14	21	28	35	42	49	56	63
8	0	8	16	24	32	40	48	56	64	72
9	0	9	18	27	36	45	54	63	72	81

(F a c t o r s)

EXPANDING BASIC MULTIPLICATION FACTS THROUGH PLACE VALUE

As soon as children understand place value and the operation of multiplication, they can solve a great number of related examples. For instance, if they understand that $3 \times 2 = 6$, then they should be able to solve these

$$(29 \times 25) \times 4 = 29 \times (25 \times 4)$$

The parentheses tell us how to associate the factors. Obviously, the student who does not learn to look for shortcuts will multiply 29×25 and then multiply the product by 4.

Research Snapshot

Are there alternatives to teaching the formal multiplication algorithm?

Baek (1998) observed six classrooms in grades 3–5 in which teachers never taught students formal algorithms to solve multidigit multiplication problems, but instead encouraged students to solve problems in different ways and to invent algorithms.

The multiplication problems were usually given to the students as word problems. The students solved them individually or in small groups. The children then shared their invented algorithms, compared them, and discussed the mathematical meaning underlying their inventions. The invented algorithms demonstrated the students' understanding of multiples of ten and number sense. The algorithms were classified developmentally according to the main schemes that the students used to solve the problems.

How can you, as a teacher, help your students develop their own invented algorithms and how can you help them move to more sophisticated algorithms?

Baek, J. (1998). Children's invented algorithms for multidigit multiplication problems. In L. Morrow & L. & M. Kenney (Eds.). *The teaching and learning of algorithms in school mathematics* (pp. 151–160). Reston, VA: National Council of Teachers of Mathematics.

For additional research briefs, "ERIC Digests" lets you search more than 2,000 short syntheses of research on a range of education topics. The syntheses were produced by the Educational Resources Information Center (ERIC). Check http://ed.gov/databases/ERIC_Digests/index/

$$
\begin{array}{r}
29 \\
\times 25 \\
\hline
145 \\
58 \\
\hline
725
\end{array}
\qquad
\begin{array}{r}
725 \\
\times 4 \\
\hline
2900
\end{array}
$$

However, an observant student who understands the associative property of multiplication will rethink the example $(29 \times 25) \times 4$ as $29 \times (25 \times 4)$ and, consequently, reason that $25 \times 4 = 100$, and then that $29 \times 100 = 2900$. Using the associative property of multiplication to look at an example this way, we can see the kind of efficiency and understanding that a good mathematics program stresses.

In this example, we used a specific instance of the associative property:

$$(29 \times 25) \times 4 = 29 \times (25 \times 4)$$

In general:

The **associative property of multiplication** means that when three or more factors are to be multiplied, the grouping of the factors does not affect the product.

For example, $(8 \times 2) \times 5 = 8 \times (2 \times 5)$,
or $(a \times b) \times c = a \times (b \times c)$

Let's look at an example that uses both the commutative and associative properties of multiplication: $60 \times 21 \times 5$.

$$
\begin{aligned}
(60 \times 21) \times 5 &= 60 \times (21 \times 5) \quad \text{Associative property} \\
&= 60 \times (5 \times 21) \quad \text{Commutative property} \\
&= (60 \times 5) \times 21 \quad \text{Associative property} \\
&= 300 \times 21 \qquad\quad \text{Multiplication (renaming)} \\
&= 6300
\end{aligned}
$$

Do *not* ask children to label each statement of an exercise; we have done so here only to illustrate the properties being used. Children should examine many exercises before they begin to calculate. If they can see that a property will help them to simplify an exercise, they should use that property. In this case, the use of two properties has simplified the exercise.

Use of basic structural properties achieves another worthwhile objective: It keeps children from believing that there is only one way to solve a mathematics exercise. Since mathematics uses a highly disciplined approach to problem solving and since there is often only one answer to a given problem, it is easy for children to believe that there is only one approach to a correct solution. This mistaken belief is one of the greatest enemies of insight, creativity, and intelligence in problem solving. Students must learn to seek from the many possible paths the best approach for a given situation. They must be released from narrowly channeled patterns of thought and allowed to develop their own critical and analytical abilities.

Another fundamental property of operations on whole numbers is the distributive property of multiplication over addition. This simply means that an example such as 3×23 can be thought of as $3 \times (20 + 3)$ and can be written as $(3 \times 20) + (3 \times 3)$. The steps in the calculation are then much simplified:

$$3 \times 23 = 3 \times (20 + 3) = (3 \times 20) + (3 \times 3)$$
$$= \quad 60 \quad + \quad 9$$
$$= \quad 69$$

Inspection of this statement reveals that our multiplication algorithm depends on the distributive property of multiplication over addition. Every multiplication example having two or more places can be solved using the distributive property over addition (or subtraction). Essentially, in multiplication we express one of the factors as the sum of two or more addends. For instance, in the previous example, 3×23, we rename 23 as $(20 + 3)$. We then find the partial products and the final product by applying the distributive property, just as we did in the previous example.

Many elementary school mathematics textbooks inappropriately introduce the distributive property of multiplication over addition with two one-place numbers. For example, 2×8 can be solved as $2 \times (2 + 6) = (2 \times 2) + (2 \times 6) = 4 + 12 = 16$. The distributive property can be applied, but the children will see no need for this property, since we expect them to memorize the product of 2×8. So, do not introduce the distributive property of multiplication over addition until the children are ready to multiply a two-place number by a one-place number.

Now consider another exercise: $2 \times 42 = \square$. In this case, we can set up our multiplication as follows:

$$
\begin{array}{r}
42 \\
\times\ 2 \\
\hline
4 \rightarrow (2 \times 2) \\
+80 \rightarrow (2 \times 40) \\
\hline
84 \rightarrow (2 \times 42)
\end{array}
$$

We are renaming the number 42 as groups of tens and groups of ones. Then we can state the example as $2 \times (40 + 2)$. The distributive property allows us to express this multiplication in another form: $(2 \times 40) + (2 \times 2)$. Carrying out these operations gives us $80 + 4$, or 84. The product is the same as that obtained by using the multiplication algorithm.

Showing the multiplication step-by-step in expanded notation can be helpful for guiding children to a clear understanding of the operation.

$$
\begin{array}{r} 42 \\ \times\ 2 \\ \end{array}
\quad\blacktriangleright\quad
\begin{array}{r} 40 + 2 \\ \times\quad\quad 2 \\ \end{array}
\quad\blacktriangleright\quad
\begin{array}{r} 40 + 2 \\ \times\quad\quad 2 \\ \hline 80 + 4 = 84 \\ \end{array}
$$

$$
\begin{array}{r} 42 \\ \times\ 2 \\ \end{array}
\quad\blacktriangleright\quad
\begin{array}{r} 42 \\ \times\ 2 \\ \hline 4 \\ 80 \\ \end{array}
\quad\blacktriangleright\quad
\begin{array}{r} 42 \\ \times\ 2 \\ \hline 4 \\ 80 \\ \hline 84 \\ \end{array}
$$

Our numeration system is a place-value system. Thus the shorter algorithm (the standard algorithm) represents a brief and accurate method of performing the operation. In other words, multiplying 2 ones by 2 in the ones place gives us 4 ones, which is recorded in the ones column. Then, multiplying 4 tens by the 2 in the ones place gives us 8 tens. The 8 is written in the tens column to the left of the 4 in the ones column. The alignment of the numbers in the vertical algorithm is efficient because of our place-value numeration system and the distribution of multiplication over addition.

Suppose a child wants to multiply 28×4. Using the distributive property, the child can make the example easier to solve by breaking up one of the factors into another grouping. Considering our decimal system of numeration, the child might write $4 \times (20 + 8)$. This is grouped in terms of tens and ones. (This is not necessarily the most efficient arrangement, however.) The child would then think $(4 \times 20) + (4 \times 8) = 80 + 32 = 112$. Or the child might group in this manner: $4 \times (25 + 3)$. In this case the child would think $(4 \times 25) + (4 \times 3) = 100 + 12 = 112$. Adding to the number 100 is clearly a simple matter; it is also clear that 4×25 is 100. Familiarity with our money system (a decimal system) makes it easier for children to multiply such combinations.

> The **distributive property of multiplication** over addition means that the product of a number and a sum can be expressed as a sum of two products. For example: $4 \times (20 + 3) = (4 \times 20) + (4 \times 3)$, or $a \times (b + c) = (a \times b) + (a \times c)$.

The concepts of the zero property of multiplication and the identity element of multiplication can be put together to help children multiply by 1, 10, 100, and so on. After working many examples, children should generalize that multiplying by 10 changes the place value by one place. In other words, we move the numeral one place to the left, and place a zero in the ones place. Study these examples:

$$
\begin{array}{ll}
2 \times 10 = 20 & \quad 10 \times 2 = 20 \\
10 \times 7 = 70 & \quad 7 \times 10 = 70 \\
10 \times 4 = 40 & \quad 4 \times 10 = 40
\end{array}
$$

Children should be provided much oral practice in multiplying by 10. Then the teacher should extend the idea into more places, and multiply two- and three-place numbers by 10.

$$
\begin{array}{rl}
1 \times 5 = & 5 \\
10 \times 5 = & 50 \\
1 \times 12 = & 12 \\
10 \times 12 = & 120 \\
10 \times 234 = & 2340
\end{array}
$$

Apply the same two concepts to numbers multiplied by 100: $1 \times 5 = 5$, $10 \times 5 = 50$, $100 \times 5 = 500$. After doing numerous examples, children can generalize that multiplying by 100 changes the place value by moving the numeral two places to the left, and zeros are placed in the tens and ones places.

For a sound understanding of multiplication involving factors with two or more digits, the children will need to be familiar with the distributive property of multiplication over addition. Arrays are another excellent device for helping children to discover this property.

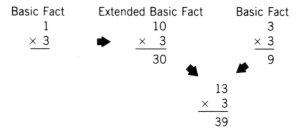

$$3 \times 12 \qquad (3 \times 10) \quad + (3 \times 2)$$

Introduce the distributive property of multiplication over addition as the class begins to study multiplication of a two-place number by a one-place number.

Consider this example: $3 \times 13 = \square$. The number 13 can be named in many ways. In this case, let's use (10 + 3) because place value is useful in the multiplication algorithm. If the distributive property is used, children can apply basic multiplication facts to find the product:

$$
\begin{aligned}
3 \times 13 &= 3 \times (10 + 3) &&\text{Renaming 13}\\
&= (3 \times 10) + (3 \times 3) &&\text{Distributive property}\\
&= \quad 30 \quad + \quad 9 &&\text{Multiplication (renaming)}\\
&= \quad 39 &&\text{Addition (renaming)}
\end{aligned}
$$

The solution to this example can best be written as follows:

$$
\begin{array}{ccc}
\begin{array}{r} 13 \\ \times\ 3 \\ \hline \end{array}
&
\begin{array}{l} 1 \text{ ten } 3 \text{ ones} \\ \times \qquad 3 \\ \hline 3 \text{ tens } 9 \text{ ones} = 39 \end{array}
&
\begin{array}{r} 13 \\ \times\ 3 \\ \hline \end{array}
\end{array}
$$

Encourage children to look for the relationships that exist within the examples. For instance, the preceding example can be thought of as follows:

Basic Fact
$$\begin{array}{r} 1 \\ \times\ 3 \\ \hline \end{array}$$

Extended Basic Fact
$$\begin{array}{r} 10 \\ \times\ 3 \\ \hline 30 \end{array}$$

Basic Fact
$$\begin{array}{r} 3 \\ \times\ 3 \\ \hline 9 \end{array}$$

$$\begin{array}{r} 13 \\ \times\ 3 \\ \hline 39 \end{array}$$

The children have memorized the basic multiplication facts, so they should know the basic facts in this example: 3×1 and 3×3. The basic fact 3×1 has been expanded to 3×10. The two examples 3×10 and 3×3 are put together using the concept of place value to get the example 3×13.

Consider the example $3 \times 23 = \square$. The number 23 can also be named as (20 + 3). Again, the students can apply the distributive property:

$$
\begin{array}{ccc}
\begin{array}{r} 23\ = \\ \times\ 3\ = \\ \hline \end{array}
&
\begin{array}{l} 2 \text{ tens } 3 \text{ ones} \\ \times \qquad 3 \\ \hline 6 \text{ tens } 9 \text{ ones} = 69 \end{array}
&
\begin{array}{r} 23 \\ \times\ 3 \\ \hline 69 \end{array}
\end{array}
$$

Renaming using expanded notation can also help to develop the concept of multiplication with three-place factors:

$$
\begin{array}{ccc}
\begin{array}{r} 124\ = \\ \times\quad 2\ = \\ \hline \end{array}
&
\begin{array}{l} 1 \text{ hundred } 2 \text{ tens } 4 \text{ ones} \\ \times \qquad\qquad 2 \\ \hline 2 \text{ hundreds } 4 \text{ tens } 8 \text{ ones } = 248 \end{array}
&
\begin{array}{r} 124 \\ \times\ 2 \\ \hline 248 \end{array}
\end{array}
$$

Another form of algorithm can be used when an understanding of multiplication has been developed through expanded notation.

$$
\begin{array}{r}
121 \\
\times\ 3 \\
\hline
3 \to (3 \times\quad 1) \\
60 \to (3 \times\ 20) \\
300 \to (3 \times 100) \\
\hline
363
\end{array}
$$

Use the longer forms of the multiplication algorithm to develop understanding. When the children are ready to develop the skill, use the short algorithm. Children should have the opportunity to apply their knowledge of basic structure and of the algorithm to two-place multiplication.

A good beginning example might involve an even ten (10, 20, 30, and so on). Consider the example $10 \times 12 = \square$. The identity element of multiplication has been developed:

$$
\begin{array}{cc}
\begin{array}{r} 3 \\ \times\ 1 \\ \hline \end{array}
&
\begin{array}{r} 4 \\ \times\ 1 \\ \hline \end{array}
\end{array}
$$

The basic facts have been expanded into

$$
\begin{array}{cc}
\begin{array}{r} 30 \\ \times\ 1 \\ \hline \end{array}
&
\begin{array}{r} 40 \\ \times\ 1 \\ \hline \end{array}
\end{array}
$$

Spend time with the children now to help them understand the place-value concepts involved at this point.

$$
\begin{array}{cccc}
\text{If} & \begin{array}{r} 12 \\ \times\ 1 \\ \hline 12 \end{array}
& \text{Then} & \begin{array}{r} 12 \\ \times\ 10 \\ \hline 120 \end{array}
\end{array}
$$

$$
\begin{array}{cccc}
\text{If} & \begin{array}{r} 12 \\ \times\ 2 \\ \hline 24 \end{array}
& \text{Then} & \begin{array}{r} 12 \\ \times\ 20 \\ \hline 240 \end{array}
\end{array}
$$

After the children understand the concept of multiplying by an even ten, then two examples that children can already solve may be put together. Consider the example $12 \times 14 = \square$. The two examples prerequisite to solving 12×14 are 2×14 and 10×14. Both of these examples have been taught. Now you must help the students to bring these two ideas together into one example:

$$
\begin{array}{cc}
\begin{array}{r} 14 \\ \times\ 2 \\ \hline 28 \end{array}
&
\begin{array}{r} 14 \\ \times\ 10 \\ \hline 140 \end{array}
\end{array}
$$

$$
\begin{array}{r}
14 \\
\times\ 12 \\
\hline
28 \\
140 \\
\hline
168
\end{array}
$$

Note that in each method for solving this example, the answer has been obtained by taking the sum of four different products: (2×4), (2×10), (10×4), and (10×10). This idea must then be expanded into other decimal places. Children must be able to analyze multiplication examples and recognize all the different basic multiplication examples that make up the examples.

REGROUPING IN MULTIPLICATION

There is still another major concept that must be developed for multiplication: **regrouping** (sometimes called *carrying*). The term *regrouping* is used here because it applies to addition, subtraction, multiplication, and division; we do not need to introduce *carrying* and *borrowing* as two different concepts if we introduce *regrouping* and use it with all the operations. The term *regrouping* is used to indicate when a number is renamed from one place value to another.

The following example illustrates the development of regrouping in the multiplication algorithm:

$$\begin{array}{r} 24 \\ \times 3 \\ \hline \end{array}$$

A child might think and write:

$$\begin{array}{r} 24 \\ \times 3 \\ \hline 12 \\ 60 \\ \hline 72 \end{array}$$

In this particular case, the child thought 3×4 and wrote 12 and then thought 3×20 and wrote 60; the two partial products were then added. There was no regrouping involved in finding the sum of 12 and 60. Nevertheless, examples of this type are prerequisite to understanding the regrouping concept. Rewriting the example using tens and ones is another excellent activity:

$$\begin{array}{rcr} 24 & & 2 \text{ tens} \quad 4 \text{ ones} \\ \times 3 & = \times & 3 \\ \hline & & 6 \text{ tens} \quad 12 \text{ ones} \end{array}$$

This is the beginning of readiness for regrouping:

6 tens 12 ones
6 tens (1 ten 2 ones)
7 tens 2 ones = 72

If the child thinks 3×4 is 12 and then thinks of 12 as 1 ten and 2 ones, the child is regrouping. Regrouping was used at the stage where 12 was regrouped as 1 ten and 2 ones and the 1 ten was regrouped with the tens.

Regrouping is also used in the following example:

$$\begin{array}{r} 48 \\ \times 2 \\ \hline 96 \end{array}$$

In multiplying 2×8 to get 16, we record the 6 in the ones place and regroup 1 ten. Multiply 2×40 or 2×4 tens (do not just say 2×4) to get 8 tens, add the regrouped number of 1 ten with 8 tens, and record the 9 in the tens place.

Another regrouping example is:

$$\begin{array}{rcl} 268 & = & 2 \text{ hundreds 6 tens 8 ones} \\ \times 26 & = \times & 2 \text{ tens 6 ones} \\ \hline & & 48 \quad (6 \times \quad 8) \\ & & 360 \quad (6 \times \quad 60) \\ & & 1200 \quad (6 \times 200) \\ & & 160 \quad (20 \times \quad 8) \\ & & 1200 \quad (20 \times \quad 60) \\ & & \underline{4000} \quad (20 \times 200) \\ & & 6968 \end{array}$$

When multiplying 6×8 to get 48, we record 8 in the ones column and regroup the 4 (40). When multiplying 6×60 to get 360, we record 6 in the tens column and regroup the 3 (300). The "carried" or regrouped numbers are written in the proper place and added to the sum. Note that the regrouped figure is *not* written above the example. If children need to record the regrouped number as a crutch, teach them to write it below the example, *where it has real meaning*.

The familiar short algorithm, however, omits the extra steps that show how we regroup:

$$\begin{array}{r} 268 \\ \times 26 \\ \hline 1608 \\ \underline{5360} \\ 6968 \end{array}$$

When the concept of regrouping is taught, a great deal of practice must be provided. The concept should be extended into more decimal places so that children can multiply at least a two-place number times a three-place number with multiple regroupings. In society today, we commonly use a calculator or microcomputer to multiply many-place numbers. But the consumer of mathematics must be able to understand the concept and estimate the reasonableness of the answer provided by the calculator or computer.

At this level of development all the basic ideas of multiplication have been taught:

1. The student must understand what multiplication means.
2. The student must understand the basic multiplication facts and have them memorized.
3. The student must understand place value and multiplication of greater numbers.
4. The student must understand the structures of multiplication (the commutative property of multiplication, the associative property of multiplication, the zero property of multiplication, the identity element of multiplication, and the distributive property of multiplication over addition). There are other properties, but these are the properties usually taught and used in elementary school.
5. The student must understand the concept of regrouping as it applies to multiplication.

The concepts thus developed must be applied to many different examples; children should practice and review them. Electronic devices can be used with children for drill and practice of these concepts. Computer software is available, but teachers must carefully evaluate the software to make sure that the practice is appropriate for each child. Children in upper grades can write simple computer programs or programs for calculators such as the TI-73 to solve mathematics exercises.

MEANING AND MODELS FOR DIVISION

Division has the same sort of inverse relationship to multiplication that subtraction has to addition.

> **Division** is an operation performed on two numbers to obtain a unique result. The number we divide is called a product, and both the number we divide by and the result of the division are called factors.

Division "undoes" what multiplication "does"; we might use the term "unmultiply" to indicate division. Teaching the basic ideas of division should parallel the teaching of multiplication. The concepts of subtraction can also be used to advantage here. Traditional mathematics programs have not placed sufficient emphasis on division as the inverse operation of multiplication. The understanding of division has often been neglected, because so much emphasis has been placed on memorizing the algorithm and developing the skills of computation. Also, research tells us that division has the most difficult algorithm to teach, although it is not the most difficult operation to understand.

To develop children's understanding of division, instruction should begin on the concrete level. A mathematics program that tries to teach division on the abstract level focuses on rote calculation, and not on the meaning of division as representing an inverse relationship to multiplication. Models that might be used to introduce division include groups of objects, arrays, number lines, and successive subtraction. Let's carefully examine each of these models as we develop an understanding of division.

Consider a group of 6 plastic spoons:

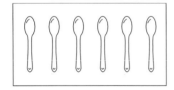

We can ask the children, "How many groups of 2 spoons can we make from a group of 6 plastic spoons?"

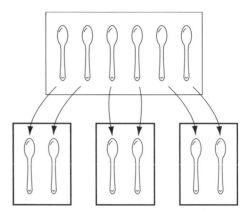

By moving the plastic spoons and making groups of 2 spoons, children see that they can make three groups. A group of 6 plastic spoons can be separated into three groups of 2. We can write:

$$\begin{array}{r} 3 \\ 2\overline{)6} \\ -6 \\ \hline 0 \end{array}$$

We could have asked a different division question about the 6 plastic spoons: "If the 6 plastic spoons are separated into two groups, how many spoons will be in each group?" Again, children must be able to manipulate the plastic spoons into two groups.

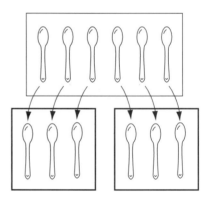

These are the two interpretations used to teach division to children. Notice that both interpretations represent a solution to the example "six divided by two," and yet these interpretations are visually and procedurally quite different.

Now let us consider the use of arrays in division. The following array has a total of 8 dots, but a sheet of paper is covering part of the array. We can ask, "How many dots are in each row?"

Number of rows $2\overline{)8}^{\,4}$ How many in each row? Total amount

There are 4 dots in each row. After the children think about the example and decide that there are 4 dots in each row, they can remove the sheet of paper and check to see whether they are correct.

An array can be used in another way: Use the same procedure as in the previous example, but this time use the sheet of paper to cover part of the columns. We can ask, "How many dots are in each column?" The example will be written the same, but the labels will be different. There are 4 dots in each column. After the children have discussed the example and reached a conclusion, the sheet of paper can be removed, and the children can check to see whether they are correct.

We have examined division by using both groups of objects and the array model to develop an understanding of the concept. Now let's study the number line as a model for division. We will look again at the example $2\overline{)8}$ (i.e., 8 divided by 2 or 8 ÷ 2) and model this on the number line:

We begin at the origin, zero, and mark off two units, which puts us at the point marked 2. From the point named 2, we mark off another two units; from that point, named 4, we mark off two more units. We continue marking off two-unit segments until we reach 8. Now we can see that there are four segments, each two units long, in eight. Therefore $8 - 2 = 6$, $6 - 2 = 4$, $4 - 2 = 2$, and $2 - 2 = 0$ (or $8 ÷ 2 = 4$), because 2 has been subtracted four times from 8. Thus, successive subtraction can also be used to model $8 ÷ 2 = 4$.

The children have learned that $4 \times 2 = 8$ and that 4 and 2 are factors and 8 is the product. Begin with multiplication examples written on a sheet of paper; use a pair of scissors to cut out one of the factors. Now ask the question, "What number was on the piece of paper that has been cut out?"

$$2 \times \boxed{} = 8$$

Since division is the inverse operation of multiplication, we can think of division in terms of finding a missing factor. Thus the example $12 ÷ 3 = \square$ can be thought of as $3 \times \square = 12$. The example $12 ÷ 3 = \square$ can be (and should be) written in other equivalent forms. For example:

$$3\overline{)12}^{\,\square} \quad \text{or} \quad \frac{12}{3} = \square \quad \text{or} \quad \frac{12}{\square} = 3$$

$$3 \times \square = 12 \quad \text{or} \quad \square \times 3 = 12$$

$$\text{or} \quad 12 = \square \times 3 \quad \text{or} \quad 12 = 3 \times \square$$

It is important for children to recognize division when it is written in any of its many different forms. Children should be able to rewrite any of these examples into a form that they can use to calculate the missing factor.

If a factor times a factor equals a product, then division can be thought of as an operation in which a product divided by a factor equals a factor.

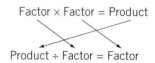

Provide the children with cards that have the words *factor*, *factor*, and *product* and the symbols ×, ÷, and = printed on them. Have the children construct a multiplication sentence with the cards. Then have the children rearrange the cards into a division sentence. Children should observe the multiplication sentence being changed into an inverse division sentence, and they should notice how the product moves to the other side of the equation.

As mentioned earlier in this section, two interpretations of division must be developed with children: *measurement division* and *partition division*.

Measurement division seems to be more easily understood by children, so it is usually taught first. Consider the following example: If a person has 12 cookies and wishes to put them into "packages" of 3 cookies for sale at a bake sale, how many packages can be made?

The person can take the 12 cookies and then place 3 cookies into a first package, 3 cookies into a second package, and so on until the cookies are distributed.

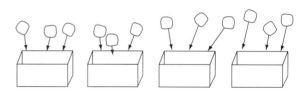

Measurement division begins with a product and then asks the questions, "How many groups of a certain number can be made?" or, in this case, "How many groups of 3 can be made from 12?" This can be written as:

$$3\overline{)12}^{\,4}$$

Therefore, measurement division begins with a product and the number of objects in each group. We must find the number of groups.

$$\text{Factor} \times \text{Factor} = \text{Product}$$
$$\square \quad \times \quad 3 \quad = \quad 12$$

Partition division is commonly taught after measurement division. Even though the physical act of dividing by the partitive method is easy for one- and two-place numbers—that is, physically distributing a collection of things by dealing them out one at a time to a given number of groups is not challenging for 24 divided by 3—the extension of this to situations involving larger numbers can be exhausting.

Let's consider a simple example to make a point. If a person has 12 cookies and wishes to put them into 3 packages with the same number in each package, how many cookies will each package receive?

It would *not* make sense to use the measurement model or successive subtraction to solve this type of division example. If a person has 12 cookies, he or she cannot subtract 3 "packages." Instead, it *does* make sense to put the 12 cookies into 3 packages by dealing them out to the packages one at a time.

Therefore, partition division begins with a product and the number of groups. We must find the number of items in each group.

Factor × Factor = Product

3   ×   □   =   12

Children need many experiences with models of group separation, arrays, number lines, and successive subtraction to develop an understanding of division. Both measurement and partition division must be modeled and developed. The terms **dividend**, **divisor**, and **quotient** also need to be developed because of their relatively common use in the classroom, on tests and, sometimes, in real-life situations.

Factor	Quotient
Factor)Product	Divisor)Dividend

DEVELOPING AND MEMORIZING BASIC DIVISION FACTS

Basic division facts exist, just as basic subtraction facts do. However, when children thoroughly understand multiplication and the inverse relationship, they already know all basic division facts.

The multiplication table should also be used for the basic division facts. Locate the given factor in the top row; then move down that column until you locate the product. Move to the left in that row; the first number is the missing factor. To use the table with the example

$6 \div 2 = \square$, find the factor 2 in the top row of the table. Move down the 2 column until the product 6 is located. Now move to the left, and you will find the missing factor, 3.

Factors

	x	0	1	2	3	4	5	6	7	8	9
	0	0	0	0	0	0	0	0	0	0	0
	1	0	1	2	3	4	5	6	7	8	9
F	2	0	2	4	6	8	10	12	14	16	18
a	3	0	3	6	9	12	15	18	21	24	27
c	4	0	4	8	12	16	20	24	28	32	36
t	5	0	5	10	15	20	25	30	35	40	45
o	6	0	6	12	18	24	30	36	42	48	54
r	7	0	7	14	21	28	35	42	49	56	63
s	8	0	8	16	24	32	40	48	56	64	72
	9	0	9	18	27	36	45	54	63	72	81

Sometimes children need a guide to help them locate a specific example in the multiplication table. Make a guide by cutting two strips from a sheet of transparent acetate. Use rubber cement to connect the two strips at a 90° angle. Cut a square for the product where the two strips overlap.

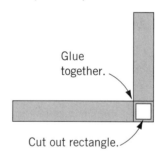

Glue together.

Cut out rectangle.

When placed on a basic fact table, the answer will be displayed through the cut square.

Difficulties arise if we attempt to divide by zero. Consider the sentence $5 \div 0 = \square$. If we rewrite this sentence as a multiplication sentence with a missing factor, we obtain:

$$0 \times \square = 5$$

There is no whole number that we can use in the box to make the sentence true. Regardless of which whole number n we put in the box, the product will be 0, so the resulting sentence will be false.

$$0 \times \square = 5$$
$$0 \times n = 5$$
$$0 = 5 \qquad \text{False}$$

An even stranger situation results when we attempt to divide zero by itself. The sentence $0 \div 0 = \square$ could be rewritten as $0 \times \square = 0$. What whole number will make this sentence true? Any whole number! There is no unique number that can be considered the quotient for $0 \div 0 = \square$. Each time we attempt to divide by zero, we encounter this dilemma. *Teachers must be careful not to tell children that any number divided by itself equals 1.* Zero divided by zero is an exception to this statement. Therefore, we either leave division by zero undefined, or else we say that *division by zero is not possible.*

After acquiring an understanding of division, children should be given ample practice in the basic division facts, to learn to calculate efficiently. Again, you might want to obtain software practice programs for your computer to provide the necessary practice of the basic division facts. Many examples similar to the following should be provided for practice:

$$6 \times \square = 24 \qquad 2 \times \square = 4 \qquad \square \times 3 = 12$$
$$\square \div 6 = 3 \qquad 8 \div 2 = \square \qquad 10 \div \square = 2$$
$$2\overline{)6} \qquad\qquad 5\overline{)15} \qquad\qquad 3\overline{)9}$$

REMAINDERS IN DIVISION

Now, let's consider the notion of remainders in division. What is the missing factor in the example $2\overline{)7}$? Three different answers might be given, and all could be considered correct:

If the example refers to 2 sticks of gum that sell for 7 cents, how much will 1 stick of gum cost? This example of 7 divided by 2 has an answer of 4. At the store the child will pay 4 cents per stick of gum. There is no remainder in this case. One-half is not a remainder, because the child can't pay in half cents.

If the example refers to 7 children forming 2 teams, with the same number of children on each team, how many children will be on each team? This example of 7 divided by 2 is 3; there will be 3 children on each team and one person left over to referee the game.

If the example refers to 7 candy bars to be equally shared by 2 children, the question becomes, "How much candy will each child receive?" In this case the answer is 3 and $\frac{1}{2}$ candy bars for each child; there is no remainder.

Children need to understand that remainders are handled in different ways, depending on the situation. We do not really know what the solution to $2\overline{)7}$ is until the example has been placed in context. From the context of an example, we choose one of three ways to handle a remainder:

1. Drop the leftover part.
2. Raise the answer to the next number.
3. Place the leftover part as a fraction of the missing factor.

We do *not* recommend that children be taught to write a missing factor as "3 r 1." What is the meaning of "r 1"? This is only a mechanical way to write a response so that the student's paper will be easier for the teacher to grade. The real meaning of a remainder is not apparent if "r 1" is used. Expose children to the three types

of situations that give rise to a remainder in real-life situations and have the children label or describe any existing remainder in a way that emphasizes the appropriate interpretation.

After solving examples of this type, the teacher can introduce an example involving division with a remainder using the method of successive subtraction. For example, $19 \div 4 = \square$:

$$
\begin{array}{rl}
19 & \\
\underline{-4} & \quad (1) \\
15 & \\
\underline{-4} & \quad (2) \\
11 & \\
\underline{-4} & \quad (3) \\
7 & \\
\underline{-4} & \quad (4) \\
3 &
\end{array}
$$

We can see that there are 4 fours in 19, with a remainder of 3. This example can also be shown using the number line as a model:

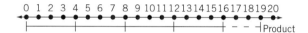

Beginning at the origin, zero, we mark off successive segments of four units each and recognize that there are three units left over. In fact, the number line is an excellent way to introduce the notion of remainder interpreted as a fraction. In the above example, we were successively subtracting groups of 4. On our last step we would only be able to subtract a part of a group of 4, namely 3 of 4. Another way to write this leftover as a part of a group of 4 would be as a ratio of 3 parts to 4 total, or $\frac{3}{4}$.

EXPANDING BASIC DIVISION FACTS THROUGH PLACE VALUE

After studying the basic facts and solving a number of simple examples such as these, the children will be ready to extend the basic division facts. Using $6 \div 2$ and groups, we can think of 6 objects separated into groups of 2. How many groups of 2 can we make from one group of 6?

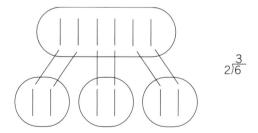

Six elements can be separated into three groups of 2.

Using the same example but substituting bundles of ten for each object, we can ask, "How many groups of 2 can we make from a group of 6 bundles (6 tens)?"

$$\frac{3\text{ tens}}{2\overline{)6\text{ tens}}} \quad \text{or} \quad \frac{30}{2\overline{)60}}$$

Six bundles of 10 can be separated into two groups of 3 bundles of 10. Thus, just as 6 elements can be separated into two groups of 3, 60 elements can be separated into two groups of 30. Children should be given many such examples extending the basic division facts.

After extending the basic division facts, children are ready to study division of a two-place number by a one-place number. Consider 69 divided by 3. The children have solved:

$$\begin{array}{r} 2 \\ 3\overline{)6} \\ -6 \\ \hline 0 \end{array}$$

and extended the basic fact to:

$$\begin{array}{r} 20 \\ 30\overline{)60} \\ -60 \\ \hline 0 \end{array}$$

They have also solved:

$$\begin{array}{r} 3 \\ 3\overline{)9} \\ -9 \\ \hline 0 \end{array}$$

Now these two examples can be put together so that the children can solve $3\overline{)69}$. Addition, multiplication, and subtraction examples are solved by beginning on the right-hand side; children need to know that the standard division algorithm is begun on the left-hand side. First give them simple examples that they already know how to solve.

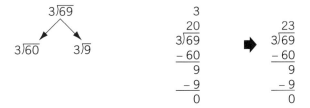

Children should then solve each of the following examples:

$$2\overline{)6} \quad 2\overline{)60} \quad 2\overline{)600} \quad 2\overline{)8} \quad 2\overline{)80} \quad 2\overline{)4}$$

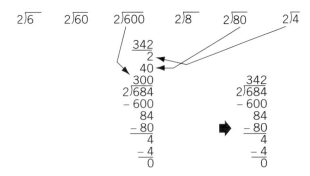

Again, children must learn to analyze division examples so that they can see the simple examples that they

know how to solve within the more complex examples. After solving division examples of a two-place number divided by a one-place number, the teacher must extend the division concept into two-place or many-place products divided by one-place factors. Examples with and without remainders should be considered.

The **division algorithm** and techniques of estimating quotients must be developed with children. Let us examine the example $7\overline{)247}$ and develop the algorithm using the partition division model. In this model, 247 objects would be "shared" or partitioned equally in seven groups. How many would be in each group? The task of using manipulatives to answer this question would be a bit overwhelming, but it would be beneficial to go through the process at least once to impress the need for a quicker, more efficient algorithm.

Using a place-value box and the partition model, we would begin the example with the following arrangement:

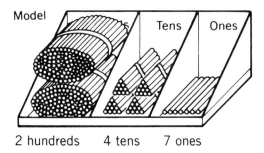

2 hundreds   4 tens   7 ones

To "share" these equally among seven groups, it would be useful to rearrange them (regroup them) as 24 tens and 7 ones.

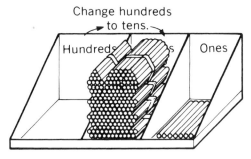

24 groups of ten   7 ones

Now, the 24 tens can be put into seven groups with 3 tens in each group and 37 (3 tens and 7 ones) left over. Consequently, we have "3 tens" as part of our answer to the original question, but we must deal with the remaining 37 objects.

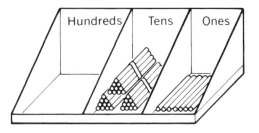

These can be renamed as 37 ones.

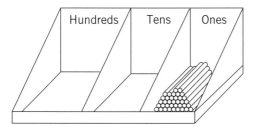

Thus we need to partition these 37 leftovers into seven groups. We are able to do so by putting 5 in each group and having 2 left over. To complete our answer, we note that we were able to share the 247 objects evenly in seven groups with 3 tens and 5 ones in each group (35) with 2 left over.

Children need a great deal of practice using tangible materials and relating them to the development of the division algorithm. Mastery of one-digit division is essential before beginning two-digit division.

Now consider this example:

$$15\overline{)349}$$

Outside the four walls of the classroom, division is couched in a real setting. The answer to whether a problem represents a partition or measurement situation is easily determined by context. However, when presented as purely abstract division exercises—a reality only in the school setting—such examples are more easily understood using the measurement model. That is, how many groups of 15 can be made from 349? Estimation and mental mathematics can help us find appropriate trial quotients. Here we need to know how many multiples of 15 can be subtracted from 349. Can 100 fifteens be subtracted from 349? No, because $100 \times 15 = 1500$, which cannot be subtracted from 349. Can 10 fifteens be subtracted from 349? Yes, because $10 \times 15 = 150$, which can be subtracted from 349. Can a greater multiple be subtracted? Yes; 20 fifteens can be subtracted: $20 \times 15 = 300$.

$$\begin{array}{r} 20 \\ 15\overline{)349} \\ -300 \quad (20 \times 15) \\ \hline 49 \end{array}$$

How many fifteens can be subtracted from 49? We try 3:

$$\begin{array}{r} 23 \\ 3 \\ 20 \\ 15\overline{)349} \\ -300 \quad (20 \times 15) \\ \hline 49 \\ -45 \quad (3 \times 15) \\ \hline 4 \end{array} \quad \text{or} \quad \begin{array}{r} 23 \\ 15\overline{)349} \\ -300 \\ \hline 49 \\ -45 \\ \hline 4 \end{array}$$

$$349 = (23 \times 15) + 4$$

Thus we see that there are 23 fifteens in 349, with a remainder of 4.

Consider another example: $34\overline{)856}$. How many groups of 34 can be made from 856 things?

Can one group be made? Yes. $1 \times 34 = 34$
Can ten groups be made? Yes. $10 \times 34 = 340$
Can one hundred groups be
   made? No. $100 \times 34 = 3400$,
   too much since we only have 856.

Thus the first estimate must be in the tens place. How many tens are in 856? Compare 34 with 85. The first estimate would be 2, so that is placed in the tens place, representing 20.

$$\begin{array}{r} 2 \\ 34\overline{)856} \\ -68 \\ \hline 176 \end{array}$$

How many groups of 3 can be made out of 176 things?

Can one group be made? Yes. $1 \times 34 = 34$
Can ten groups be made? No. $10 \times 34 = 340$

Therefore this estimate must be placed in the ones place. Comparing 3 with 17, the best estimate is 5.

$$\begin{array}{r} 25 \\ 34\overline{)856} \\ -68 \\ \hline 176 \\ -170 \\ \hline 6 \end{array}$$

The more accurately a pupil estimates the trial quotient, the shorter the actual computation will be. For instance, inaccurate estimates make the following example unnecessarily long:

$$\begin{array}{r} 25 \\ 1 \\ 4 \\ 10 \\ 10 \\ 27\overline{)691} \\ -270 \quad (10 \times 27) \\ \hline 421 \\ -270 \quad (10 \times 27) \\ \hline 151 \\ -108 \quad (4 \times 27) \\ \hline 43 \\ -27 \quad (1 \times 27) \\ \hline 16 \end{array}$$

Now the same example is shown with more accurate estimates:

$$\begin{array}{r} 25 \\ 5 \\ 20 \\ 27\overline{)691} \\ -540 \quad (20 \times 27) \\ \hline 151 \\ -135 \quad (5 \times 27) \\ \hline 16 \end{array} \quad \text{or} \quad \begin{array}{r} 25 \\ 27\overline{)691} \\ -540 \\ \hline 151 \\ -135 \\ \hline 16 \end{array}$$

These examples are provided to help teachers visualize the steps through which children progress as they learn to divide. It is *not* suggested that children write each step.

Children's comprehension of division begins with real-world experiences from which we help them visualize, understand, and record. The basic facts of division must be memorized. Establishing place value, then making the estimate of a trial quotient, is an aid for children in dividing. Much practice of division is necessary as children progress and learn new concepts.

As we carefully examine the teaching of division to children, we note again that there are five major ideas that students must understand to solve any division example:

1. The student must understand what division is.
2. The student must understand the basic division facts and have them memorized.
3. The student must understand place value and be able to relate the place-value concept to division.
4. The student must understand that division has no basic structures, in that it is not commutative or associative.
5. The student must understand the concept of regrouping as it applies to division.

CLOSURE

The nature and role of computation is rapidly changing in our technological world. The form and frequency of our encounters with computation are influenced by the ways in which we process information in our society. While it is hard to imagine a world in which computation is unimportant, it is not hard to imagine one in which it is important to know when (or whether) to use alternative means of determining an answer to a computational exercise. It's not hard to imagine such a world because we live, work, and play in that world now. The calculator, as one example, is an integral part of day-to-day life and cannot be (nor should it be) ignored as one of the tools for computation. Estimation, as another example, is something that we do on a daily basis, often without stopping to acknowledge the value of our abilities to estimate length, amount, capacity, weight, etc. Students need to explore and determine the appropriate time to use paper-and-pencil algorithms, mental computation, estimation and rounding, and calculators. Instruction in computation must make allowances for that.

Terminology, Symbols, and Procedures

Array. An array is an orderly arrangement of objects or symbols into rows and columns. An array with m rows and n columns (where m and n are whole numbers) is called an m-by-n array.

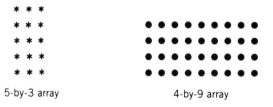

5-by-3 array   4-by-9 array

Cartesian Product. If A and B are any two sets, then the Cartesian product, A × B, is the set of all ordered pairs (*a*, *b*) whose first elements are members of A and whose second elements are members of B. For example, if A = {*p*, *q*, *r*} and B = {*h*, *k*}, then:

$$A \times B = \{(p, h), (p, k), (q, h), (q, k), (r, h), (r, k)\}$$

Division Algorithm. The division algorithm is the numerical process that is applied to a dividend and a divisor to obtain a quotient. The following is an application of this algorithm:

```
        54
         4
        50
   23)1242              23)1242
     -115  (50 × 23)      -115
        92                   92
      -92  (4 × 23)         -92
         0                    0
```

(54 × 23) = 1242

Division, Dividend, Divisor, and **Quotient.** Division is the basic operation performed on a product and a factor to obtain the second factor. The given product in a division example is frequently called the *dividend*; the known factor (the number by which we divide) is frequently called the *divisor*; and the result of performing the operation is frequently called the *quotient*. For example:

$$5 \times \square = 15 \quad \text{or} \quad 15 \div 5 = \square$$
$$5 \times 3 = 15 \qquad 15 \div 5 = 3$$

Division is the inverse operation of multiplication; that is, division "undoes" what multiplication "does." If a number is first multiplied and then divided by the same nonzero quantity, the number is left unchanged. For example:

$$7 \times 4 = 28 \qquad 28 \div 4 = 7$$
$$\text{or}$$
$$(7 \times 4) \div 4 = 7 = (7 \div 4) \times 4$$

Factor. The numbers that are multiplied in a multiplication example.

Identity Property for Multiplication. The product of 1 and any other factor is always the other factor. The identity element for multiplication is 1.

$$1 \times a = a$$
$$a \times 1 = a$$

Multiple. A multiple is a product obtained by multiplying a whole number by a given factor. For example, the multiples of 4 are created as follows:

Whole Numbers as Factors	Given Factor	Multiples of 4
0	4	0
1	4	4
2	4	8
3	4	12
4	4	16
• • •	• • •	• • •

Multiplication. Multiplication is a binary operation on whole numbers that matches with any two whole numbers (called *factors*) a unique whole number (called the *product*). While not defined for children as such, the operation can be defined abstractly as follows: If a and b are any two whole numbers, and if A and B are sets such that $n(A) = a$ and $n(B) = b$, then $a \times b$ is, by definition, the cardinal number of the set $A \times B$; that is, $a \times b = n(A \times B)$, where $\times$ is the Cartesian product.

The product of two whole numbers can be obtained by using many models: groups of objects, successive addition, arrays, Cartesian products, or the number line.

Multiplication Algorithm. The multiplication algorithm is the numerical process that is applied to two factors to obtain a product. The following is an application of this algorithm:

$$
\begin{array}{r}
54 \\
\times\, 23 \\
\hline
12 \quad (3 \times 4) \\
150 \quad (3 \times 50) \\
80 \quad (20 \times 4) \\
1000 \quad (20 \times 50) \\
\hline
1242
\end{array}
$$

Product. The product is the result obtained in a multiplication example.

Properties of Division. Division of whole numbers has the following properties:

1. Division is not commutative. For example:

$$12 \div 3 \neq 3 \div 12$$

2. Division is not associative. For example:

$$(24 \div 4) \div 2 \neq 24 \div (4 \div 2)$$

3. Division is distributive only if the distribution is on the *left* of the division sign, not if it is on the right:

$$(20 + 8) \div 4 = (20 \div 4) + (8 \div 4)$$
$$24 \div (2 + 4) \neq (24 \div 2) + (24 \div 4)$$

Properties of Multiplication. The properties of multiplication discussed in this chapter are:

1. Multiplication is **commutative**. For any whole numbers a and b:

$$a \times b = b \times a$$

2. Multiplication is **associative.** For any whole numbers a, b, and c:

$$(a \times b) \times c = a \times (b \times c)$$

3. Multiplication is **distributive** over addition (and subtraction). For any whole numbers a, b, and c:

$$a \times (b + c) = (a \times b) + (a \times c)$$
$$(b + c) \times a = (b \times a) + (c \times a)$$
$$\text{and}$$
$$a \times (b - c) = (a \times b) - (a \times c)$$
$$(b - c) \times a = (b \times a) - (c \times a)$$

Regroup. To regroup is to convert a unit from one place value to another place value, keeping the value of the number constant but changing the grouping. For instance, the number 42 can be regrouped to 3 tens and 12 ones; the number 42 remains constant, but "4 tens and 2 ones" is renamed "3 tens and 12 ones."

Zero Property of Multiplication. The product of 0 and any other factor is always 0.

Practice Exercises for Teachers

These exercises are designed for the reader of this book. While some are suitable for use in the elementary classroom, these examples should not necessarily be given to children in this form. Ideas for classroom activities on the concepts and ideas discussed in this chapter can be found in Part 2 of *Today's Mathematics*, the Student Resource Book.

1. Use the multiplication example $3 \times 4 = \square$ to sketch a model using

   a) groups of objects   b) arrays   c) number line

   d) ordered pairs   e) successive addition

2. Draw an array for each of the following examples.

   a) $4 \times 2 = 8$ b) $3 \times 6 = 18$ c) $2 \times 3 = 6$ d) $5 \times 3 = 15$

3. Draw arrays to show a model for $3 \times 6 = 6 \times 3$.

4. Write a multiplication sentence for each of the following arrays.

5. Model 6×4 on a number line.

6. Show how successive addition can verify that $4 \times 5 = 20$.

7. Write a multiplication sentence for each given example; then write a related inverse sentence.

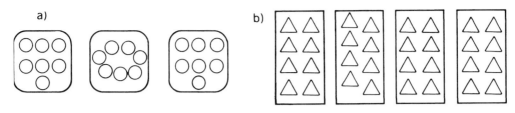

8. Use a number line model to show each of the following division examples.

   a) $18 \div 3 = \square$ b) $12 \div 4 = \square$ c) $16 \div 8 = \square$ d) $11 \div 3 = \square$

9. Write two inverse sentences for each given sentence.

   a) $7 \times 8 = \square$ b) $72 \div 9 = \square$ c) $108 \div 9 = 12$

   d) $8 \times 23 = 184$ e) $221 \div 17 = 13$ f) $124 \times 9 = 1116$

10. Solve each of the following sets of examples.

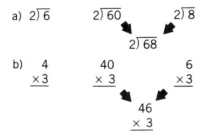

11. We have used the distributive property of multiplication over addition. We can also use the distributive property of multiplication over subtraction. Study the general statement; then solve the following examples by using the general statement as a guide:

$$a \times (b - c) = (a \times b) - (a \times c)$$

   a) 6×97 b) 7×48 c) 4×98 d) 3×1998

12. Show how successive subtraction can verify that $48 \div 6 = 8$.

13. On a sheet of graph paper 24 squares wide and 36 squares long, demonstrate that 24×36 is 864; use the distributive property of multiplication over addition to explain your model.

14. Using graph paper, demonstrate how you can verify that the answer to $448 \div 14$ is 32.

Teaching Competencies and Self-Assessment Tasks

1. Discuss the prerequisite knowledge that is necessary to understand and model multiplication and division.
2. Discuss reasons that might be offered to explain why division is the more difficult operation for children to learn.
3. Create word problems to demonstrate the distinction between measurement and partition division.
4. Research the work of John Napier, and make a report on the use of "Napier's bones" in teaching multiplication.
5. Research three methods of estimating quotients to two-place division examples, and discuss the merits and disadvantages of each. These methods are often referred to as the apparent method, the increase-by-one method, and the round-off method.
6. Discuss the notion of remainder in division and the advantages and disadvantages of expressing the remainder in various ways.
7. Discuss objections to writing the zero to the right of the ones place when multiplying a number by another number having a zero in the ones place. For example:

$$\begin{array}{r} 23 \\ \times\,40 \\ \hline \end{array} \qquad\qquad \begin{array}{r} 23 \\ \times\,40 \\ \hline \end{array}$$

8. Demonstrate why it is impossible to divide by zero.
9. Discuss how the calculator can be integrated into the teaching of multiplication and/or division.
10. Locate the results of the most recent International Mathematics and Science Study or a recent National Assessment of Educational Progress in Mathematics report related to multiplication and division. Discuss the implications of these results.
11. Discuss the likenesses and differences between teaching multiplication and division.

Related Readings and Teacher Resources

For related readings on topics found in this chapter, see the corresponding chapter in Part 2 of *Today's Mathematics*, the Student Resource Book.

Chapter 9

Number Theory and Number Systems

Teaching Competencies

Upon completing this chapter, you will be able to:

- Classify counting numbers as prime/composite or even/odd.

- State the Fundamental Theorem of Arithmetic and write the prime factorization of any given counting number.

- Describe and calculate the least common multiple and the greatest common factor for a given set of counting numbers.

- State and explain the rules for divisibility by given counting numbers.

- Describe the process of adding, subtracting, multiplying, and dividing integers and rational numbers.

- State the relationships between the system of real numbers and its subsystems.

- Develop lessons for children that relate the structure of number theory and number systems in a meaningful way.

et's begin this chapter with a number riddle. Play along, following each direction as you go. Ready?

- Choose any whole number between 1 and 10.
- Add 3 to that number.
- Multiply the resulting sum by 9.
- Find the sum of the individual digits of the product.
- If the sum is greater than 10, then find the sum of these digits.
- Subtract 5 from the resulting sum.

Now, continue by following these steps.

- Translate your final number above into a letter of the alphabet using this code: A = 1, B = 2, C = 3, D = 4, and so on.
- Give the name of a country in Western Europe that begins with that letter.
- Give the name of an animal that begins with the letter that ends the country name.
- Give the name of a color that begins with the letter that ends the animal name.

At this point, turn to page 180 and look at the print at the bottom of the page.

It is quite likely that the authors of this book were able to predict the color, animal, and country that you came up with as a result of picking a random number between 1 and 10. How is this possible? After all, you chose the number to start this off. You might have picked the number 4, or 7, or 9. Perhaps you should go back to the start and choose another number and see how it works out this time. We'll wait. . . .

How did you do this time? Same answer? Was it just chance that the arithmetic led you to 4, which translates to "D," and hence to Denmark (since Denmark is the only country in Western Europe that begins with "D")? A check of the steps reveals that in the third step you multiplied a number by 9. You may recall (or you can easily verify) that when you multiply any whole number by 9, the sum of the digits of the resulting product will always be some multiple of 9. If you did get a multidigit multiple of 9, you were then asked to add those digits. Eventually you will get to just 9. Then, when you subtract 5, you will get 4—the number that you were asked to translate into a letter. Since everyone gets a 4, everyone is "forced" to use a "D." After exhausting your knowledge of Western European countries and settling for Denmark, you almost surely will choose kangaroo (or, perhaps, koala) as the animal—there just aren't that many animals beginning with "k" that come immediately to mind. The selection of kangaroo leads to orange, while the selection of koala might likely lead to aqua.

So, some things that first appear to be unlikely are not always so when mathematics is applied. Surprising results can be explained with mathematics, and, per-

haps, even appreciated more for their elegance. Amaze your friends with mathematics!

In this chapter we look more closely at several aspects of a structural approach to teaching mathematics. Mathematical structures provide a solid foundation for building power with mathematics—not just the ability to process algorithms. Here we consider some of the most efficient approaches to understanding numbers and their factors.

The NCTM *Principles and Standards for School Mathematics* (2000) embeds the discussion of number theory and number systems in the process standards (Problem Solving, Reasoning and Proof, Communication, Connections, and Representations) and, most notably, in the content standards for Number and Operation and Algebra.

The content standard for Number and Operations in grades preK–12 states that:

Instructional programs from prekindergarten through grade 12 should enable all students to—

- understand numbers, ways of representing numbers, relationships among numbers, and number systems;
- understand meanings of operations and how they relate to one another;
- compute fluently and make reasonable estimates.

The content standard for Algebra in grades preK–12 states that:

Instructional programs from prekindergarten through grade 12 should enable all students to—

- understand patterns, relations, and functions;
- represent and analyze mathematical situations and structures using algebraic symbols;
- use mathematical models to represent and understand quantitative relationships;
- analyze change in various contexts.

We hope that, as a result of the examination of number structure as presented in this chapter, each teacher will recognize the importance of a thorough understanding of operations on whole numbers, integers, and fractional numbers (a term commonly reserved for fractions greater than zero). The information in this chapter is essential background for every elementary classroom teacher—not solely for those that teach these concepts.

THE LANGUAGE OF NUMBER THEORY

Before delving into the main subject of this chapter, let's review some of the language commonly used in discussing multiplication of whole numbers as presented in many elementary mathematics programs today. (See Chapter 8 for further details.) Let's begin by naming the parts of a mathematical sentence involving multiplication:

$$2 \times 3 = 6$$

In this sentence the 2 and the 3 are called **factors**, and the 6 is called the **product**. We also say that:

2 is a *factor* of 6
3 is a *factor* of 6
6 is the *product* of the *factors* 2 and 3
6 is a *multiple* of 2
6 is a *multiple* of 3

When we say that 6 is a multiple of 2, we mean that we can multiply 2 by some whole number factor to get 6 as a product. Each time we multiply 2 by a whole number, we get a multiple of 2. Thus the multiples of 2 are 0, 2, 4, 6, 8, 10, and so on. The multiples of 5 are 0, 5, 10, 15, 20, 25, and so on. In the primary grades we often have children count by 2s, by 3s, by 5s, and by 10s, a practice often referred to as "skip counting." When children do this, they are naming multiples of 2, multiples of 3, multiples of 5 and multiples of 10. This experience provides a foundation for developmentally appropriate skill building that will later assist the children in the understanding and memorization of multiplication facts.

As early as the primary grades, a child learns that a number such as 7 can be named in many ways. For example, usually beginning with addition, children learn that $2 + 5 = 7$ and $3 + 4 = 7$. Later, they note that $9 - 2 = 7$ and $12 - 5 = 7$. Still later, they begin to recognize that each of the following is another name for 12:

$11 + 1$	2×6
$15 - 3$	$24 \div 2$
3×4	$36 \div 3$

We use the words **product expression** to talk about names, such as 3×4 and 2×6, that involve multiplication (or finding a product). In other words, 3×4 and 2×6 are product expressions for 12.

As we saw in Chapter 8, a product expression with two factors can be pictured by a **rectangular array**. For example, we can picture the product expression 3×4 as this array:

• • • •
• • • •
• • • •

We call this a *3-by-4 array*. The first number tells how many rows (3), and the second number tells how many columns (4).

We can use any of several different product expressions to represent the number 12. Some examples are:

• • • • • • • • • • • •   • • • • • •   • • • •
                                  • • • • • •   • • • •
                                                       • • • •

     1 x 12   2 x 6   3 x 4

Each of these product expressions for the number 12 has been expressed here as a rectangular array. This

means that they can be expressed as an orderly arrangement of one or more rows and columns. Any whole number can be represented by a rectangular array having only one row. That is, an array for the number 15 could be a 1-by-15 array.

In the case of the number 6, there are two product expressions containing two factors (plus two more that are omitted because of the commutative property):

     1 x 6   2 x 3

We have formed rectangular arrays with 12 objects (1×12, 2×6, and 3×4) and with 6 objects (1×6 and 2×3). Now let's consider other numbers:

Number	Product Expression	Array
14	1×14	• • • • • • • • • • • • • •
	2×7	• • • • • • • • • • • • • •
20	1×20	• • • • • • • • • • • • • • • • • • • •
	2×10	• • • • • • • • • • • • • • • • • • • •
	4×5	• • • • • • • • • • • • • • • • • • • •

But what happens in the case of the number 13? With 13 objects or symbols we can form a rectangular array of only a single row (1×13) or a single column (13×1):

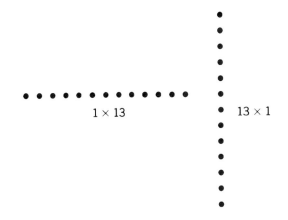

     1 × 13   13 × 1

What other numbers can be represented *only* by a rectangular array of a single row or column?

Examining the following table, we find that 2, 3, 5, 7, and 11 also can be represented only by single rows or single columns.

Number	Product Expression	Array
2	1 × 2	• •
3	1 × 3	• • •
4	1 × 4	• • • •
4	2 × 2	• • • •
5	1 × 5	• • • • •
6	1 × 6	• • • • • •
6	2 × 3	• • • • • •
7	1 × 7	• • • • • • •
8	1 × 8	• • • • • • • •
8	2 × 4	• • • • • • • •
9	1 × 9	• • • • • • • • •
9	3 × 3	• • • • • • • • •
10	1 × 10	• • • • • • • • • •
10	2 × 5	• • • • • • • • • •
11	1 × 11	• • • • • • • • • • •

What about a greater number—for example, 30?

1 x 30

2 x 15

3 x 10

5 x 6

From this brief examination we can draw several conclusions:

1. A product expression for a number is another name for the number itself. For example, product expressions for 12—that is, 1 × 12, 12 × 1, 2 × 6, 6 × 2, 3 × 4, and 4 × 3—are different ways of naming 12.
2. Every whole number greater than 1 can be named by at least one product expression: 1 times the number itself (and, by using the commutative property, the number itself times 1).
3. Many numbers can be named by more than one product expression. For example, 4, 6, 8, 9, 10, 12, 14, 20, and 30 can all be named by more than one product expression.

From our review of the language of multiplication, we know that the numbers making up a product expression are called *factors*. We know that many of the numbers we've discussed have more than two factors. For example, we can name the set of all factors of 12: {1, 2, 3, 4, 6, 12}. But many numbers have only two factors: 1 and the number itself. The only factors of 11, for example, are 1 and 11.

THE SIEVE OF ERATOSTHENES

Another way of examining numbers in the light of their factors comes to us from ancient Greece. Eratosthenes, a famous geographer of the third century B.C., first devised the method that has come to be called the *sieve of Eratosthenes*. The following arrangement of numerals is one example of a pattern for a sieve:

	2	3	4	5	6	7	8	9	10
11	12	13	14	15	16	17	18	19	20
21	22	23	24	25	26	27	28	29	30
31	32	33	34	35	36	37	38	39	40
41	42	43	44	45	46	47	48	49	50
51	52	53	54	55	56	57	58	59	60
61	62	63	64	65	66	67	68	69	70
71	72	73	74	75	76	77	78	79	80
81	82	83	84	85	86	87	88	89	90
91	92	93	94	95	96	97	98	99	100

To begin our examination of the sieve, let us recall our discussion of rectangular arrays. The number 2 can be represented by a rectangular array of a single row or column only. The product expression for 2 is 1 × 2, but every multiple of 2 (other than 2 itself) can be represented by rectangular arrays with more than a single row or column.

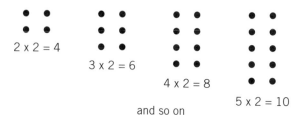

2 x 2 = 4

3 x 2 = 6

4 x 2 = 8

5 x 2 = 10

and so on

Now, referring to the table, or sieve, circle the numeral 2, and cross out all the other multiples of 2 (i.e., 4, 6, 8, 10, . . . , 100).

Next, consider 3. You will recall that 3 can be represented by only a single row or column array: the only factors of 3 are 1 and 3. Multiples of 3 (other than 3 itself), however, can be represented by rectangular arrays with 3 columns. On the sieve, circle the 3, and then cross out all other multiples of 3 (6, 9, 12, 15, 18, . . . , 99). You will notice that many of the multiples of 3 have already been crossed out, because some multiples of 3 are also multiples of 2—for example, 6, 12, and 18.

The next consecutive numeral not already circled or crossed out is 5. Circle the 5, and cross out all other multiples of 5 (10, 15, 20, 25, . . . , 100). Again, you will notice that many of the multiples of 5 have already been crossed out, because some multiples of 5 are also multiples of 2 or 3—for example, 30 and 60.

The next numeral not crossed out is 7. Circle the 7, and cross out all other multiples of 7 (14, 21, 28, . . . , 98).

The next numeral not crossed out is 11. Circle the 11, and cross out all other multiples of 11 (22, 33, 44, . . . , 99). You will observe that all the multiples of 11 (other than 11 itself) have already been crossed out.

②	③		⑤		⑦			
⑪		13				17		19	
		23						29	
31						37			
41		43				47			
		53						59	
61						67			
71		73						79	
		83						89	
						97			

At this point, what generalizations could you make about the multiples of 13? (All multiples of 13, other than 13 itself, have already been crossed out.)

You will notice that there are still some numerals on the chart that have not been crossed out. What generalization could you make about the arrays that illustrate these numbers? (In each case the array consists of either a single row or a single column. We cannot form any other rectangular arrays for these numbers.) For each of these numbers, what are the only factors? (For each number, the only factors are 1 and the number itself.) Make a list of the numerals on the chart that are not crossed out (2, 3, 5, 7, 11, 13, 17, 19, 23, 29, 31, 37, 41, 43, 47, 53, 59, 61, 67, 71, 73, 79, 83, 89, and 97). These whole numbers are greater than 1 and have only 1 and themselves as factors; they are called **prime numbers**. Whole numbers greater than 1 that have whole number factors other than 1 and themselves are called **composite numbers**.

What do you notice that is common to all prime numbers except 2? (They are all odd.) This is true because every even number has 2 as a factor, so every even number greater than 2 has a factor other than

itself and 1. Note, however, that not all odd numbers are prime. For example, 23 is prime, but 33 is not.

We have now examined the structure of certain numbers in two ways—by making arrays of physical objects or symbols and by marking off multiples of certain numbers on a chart. Comparing the results of these two approaches, what conclusions can we draw? The prime numbers (the numbers still visible on the chart—the ones that were not crossed off the sieve) are numbers that can be represented in an array by only one row or one column of physical objects or symbols. What can we say about the factors that make up the product expressions of these numbers? (The only factors these numbers have are 1 and the numbers themselves.)

We have not included the number 1 in this discussion because the number 1 is unique. It is a factor of every number ($2 = 1 \times 2$, $3 = 1 \times 3$, $15 = 1 \times 15$, $189 = 1 \times 189$, and so on) and is called the *identity element for multiplication*. To say that 1 is a factor of a number, then, does not really tell us much about the number. By definition, *the number 1 is neither prime nor composite.* (It is sometimes called a *generator*.) Remember that any number greater than 1 that has only 1 and the number itself as factors is a prime number. Any whole number greater than 1 must therefore be either prime or composite (nonprime). Using arrays and the sieve of Eratosthenes, we have sorted the set of whole numbers between 2 and 100 inclusive into prime and composite numbers.

A further remark on the work of Eratosthenes explains the term *sieve*. Working with numerals arranged on a parchment sheet, Eratosthenes physically punched out all the multiples of 2, except for 2 itself, leaving holes in the parchment. The multiples of 3, except for 3 itself, were cut from the sheet in the same way; then the multiples of 5, and so on. The result was a sheet on which only the prime numbers remained. This parchment filled with holes where the composite numbers had dropped through closely resembled a sieve.

We can discover interesting patterns in number charts by placing varying amounts of numbers in the rows or columns. Let us look at the pattern that develops when the numbers are placed into a chart with six columns.

Where are the prime numbers located? Will a prime number ever appear in the column headed by 4 or 6? Justify your response.

Encourage students to further study the table on the next page. Where are the multiples of two located? the multiples of three? the multiples of five? of seven? of 11? Look for patterns and improve communication skills by describing these patterns to others.

FACTOR TREES

We have found that every composite number can be renamed as a product expression other than 1 times the number. For instance, 24 can be renamed using any of the following product expressions:

1	②	③	4	⑤	6
⑦	8	9	10	⑪	12
⑬	14	15	16	⑰	18
⑲	20	21	22	㉓	24
25	26	27	28	㉙	30
㉛	32	33	34	35	36
㊲	38	39	40	㊶	42
㊸	44	45	46	㊼	48
49	50	51	52	(53)	54
55	56	57	58	(59)	60
(61)	62	63	64	65	66
(67)	68	69	70	(71)	72
(73)	74	75	76	77	78
(79)	80	81	82	(83)	84
85	86	87	88	(89)	90
91	92	93	94	95	96
(97)	98	99	100	(101)	102

2×12
3×8
4×6

This can also be shown in another way:

Example (a): Example (b): Example (c):

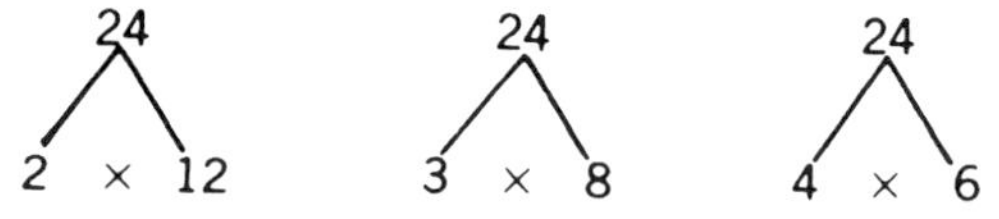

In example (a), we know that 12 can be renamed as 2×6 or as 3×4, so example (a) can be extended in two possible ways:

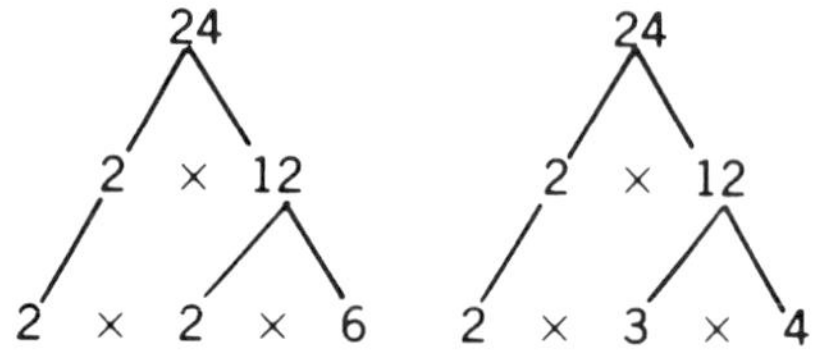

We can see in these two cases that 6 and 4 are both composite numbers, but each can be factored in only one way (excluding 1 as a factor):

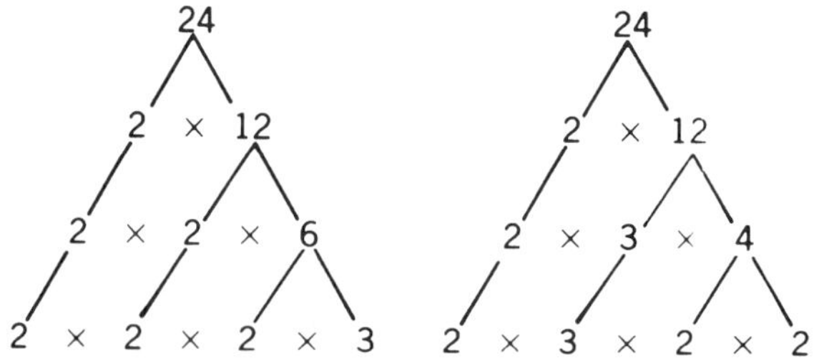

We see now that every number named in the last row is a prime number. Because of the shape of these particular diagrams, they are sometimes referred to as *factor trees*.

In example (b), we know that 8 can be expressed only as 2×4. Hence we have the following factor tree:

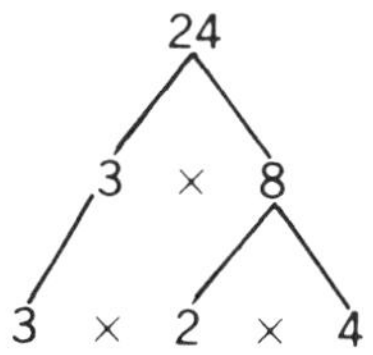

Examining the last row of this factor tree, we find the composite number 4, which can be named by the product expression 2×2:

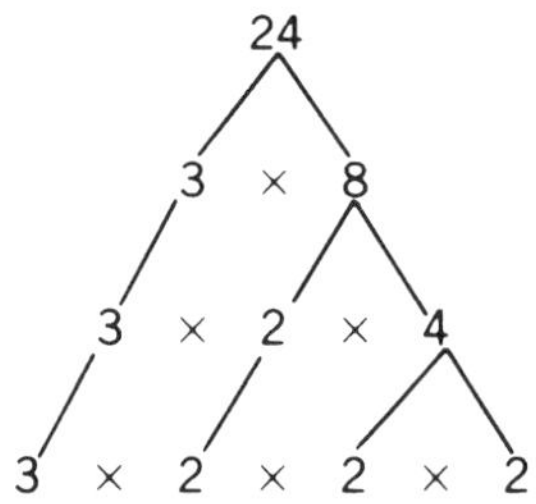

By examination we see that every number named in the last row is now a prime number.

In example (c), both 4 and 6 are composite numbers and can be shown by the product expressions 2×2 and 2×3, respectively. The following factor tree results:

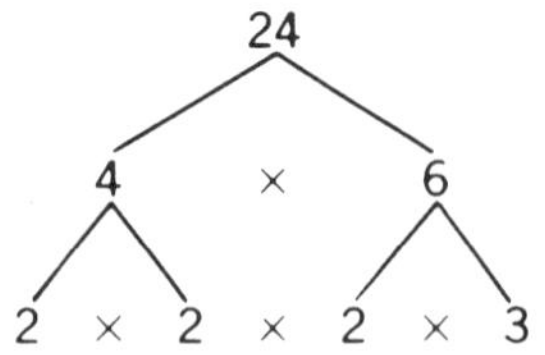

Since every number named in the last row is a prime number, the factor tree is complete.

Now examine the last row of each of the factor trees:

Example (a):	$2 \times 2 \times 2 \times 3$ or
	$2 \times 3 \times 2 \times 2$
Example (b):	$3 \times 2 \times 2 \times 2$
Example (c):	$2 \times 2 \times 2 \times 3$

You will notice that in each example the final result is a product expression for 24 in which each factor is a prime number. Furthermore, each product expression uses the same set of factors. Because of the commutative property of multiplication, the fact that they are arranged in a different order is not important.

Now examine another number, 18, and the appropriate factor trees:

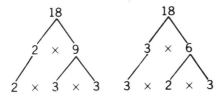

Notice that whether we use 2 × 9 or 3 × 6 as the first product expression, the last product expression in each factor tree is composed of the same set of factors. Again, the fact that they are arranged in a different order is not significant.

Factor trees for the number 36 look like these:

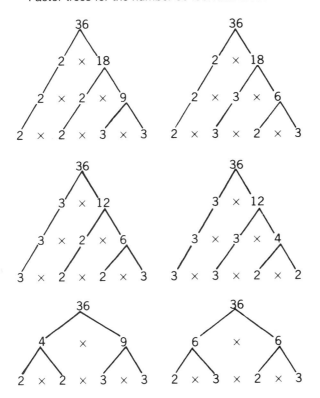

We see that the factor trees *appear* to be a bit different from each other. Nevertheless, the same set of factors is found in the last product expression of all the trees. Can there ever be more than one set of factors in the last row of the factor trees for a particular number? (No.) This important conclusion is formally known as the *Fundamental Theorem of Arithmetic*.

> The **Fundamental Theorem of Arithmetic** states that, except for the order of the factors, a composite number can be expressed as a product of prime numbers in one and only one way.

PRIME FACTORIZATION

When a composite number is expressed as a product of prime numbers, we often refer to this as **prime factorization**, or complete factorization. The following are some examples of prime factorization:

$$45 = 3 \times 15 \qquad 42 = 2 \times 21$$
$$ = 3 \times 3 \times 5 \qquad = 2 \times 3 \times 7$$

$$50 = 2 \times 25 \qquad 56 = 2 \times 28$$
$$ = 2 \times 5 \times 5 \qquad = 2 \times 2 \times 14$$
$$ = 2 \times 2 \times 2 \times 7$$

$$72 = 2 \times 36$$
$$ = 2 \times 2 \times 18$$
$$ = 2 \times 2 \times 2 \times 9$$
$$ = 2 \times 2 \times 2 \times 3 \times 3$$

Notice that the prime factorization of a number is found when each factor in the final product expression is a prime number.

Now let us investigate some practical applications involving prime factors. Many times, in different mathematical contexts, it is helpful to factor numbers into primes. For example, we can use prime factorizations when we write fractions in simplest form and when we find least common denominators (see Chapters 11 and 12). Thus, we may choose to use prime factorization to factor a number in the most efficient manner.

To decide whether any given number is prime or factorable, we apply a successive division test. First we attempt to divide the given number by the least prime number, 2; then we use successively greater prime divisors. For example, let's test 92:

$$2 \overline{)92}$$
$$2 \overline{)46}$$
$$23$$

By starting with the divisor 2, it quickly becomes evident that 92 can be factored by 2, since we obtain a quotient and a zero remainder. That is, 92 divided by 2 is 46. Now, 46 is also divisible by 2. Remember that in testing each quotient, we always begin with the least prime number, 2, as the divisor. The next quotient, 23, we find is not divisible by 2, 3, 5, 7, 11, 13, or 19. It is a prime number, so our factoring is complete. The prime factorization of 92 is thus shown to be 2 × 2 × 23. By the inverse relationship of division and multiplication, we know that a divisor and a quotient can be expressed in a related multiplication form as two factors. In the preceding example, the divisor 2 and the quotient 46 are factors of 92 in the related multiplication equation 2 × 46 = 92. Similarly, 2 and 23 are factors in the multiplication equation 2 × 23 = 46.

Now try a number with more factors, 468:

$$2 \overline{)468}$$
$$2 \overline{)234}$$
$$3 \overline{)117}$$
$$3 \overline{)\ 39}$$
$$13$$

In this case the divisor 2 is effective in the first two steps, but the quotient 117 cannot be divided by 2. Our next step, then, is to see if 117 is divisible by the next prime number, 3. It is, so the division is performed, and the new quotient obtained is 39. Obviously, 39 is not divisible by 2, since it is an odd number. However, it is divisible by the next prime number, 3. Since the quotient 13 is prime, this is as far as our factoring can be carried. The prime factorization is a combination of *all* the divisors *and* the final quotient. (Divisors are, of course, also factors.) The following expression shows the prime factorization of 468:

$$2 \times 2 \times 3 \times 3 \times 13$$

Because some greater numbers are prime, much time can be wasted attempting to find divisors (other than 1 and the numbers themselves) for greater numbers that are, in fact, prime. However, there is an aid that can save us some time. We should try only divisors that are *not* greater than the square root of the number being tested. The *square root of a given number* is the number that when multiplied by itself yields that given number. For example, 5 is the square root of 25, because $5 \times 5 = 25$. In general, *N* is called the *square root* of *P* if $N \times N = P$.

Let's consider the number 97 and test it for factorization, beginning with the least prime number as a divisor. The number 97 is obviously not divisible by 2, because 97 is not an even number. It is also not divisible by 3. Next we try the divisors 5 and 7, still unsuccessfully. There is no reason to try any greater primes as divisors. The square root of 97 is less than 10 (since $10 \times 10 = 100$), and 7 is the greatest prime divisor that isn't greater than this square root. If we bothered to test any prime number greater than 7, the square would be 121 (11×11) or greater. Consequently, checking for divisibility by 2, 3, 5, and 7 is sufficient for us to conclude that 97 must be prime.

Students should understand the reasons we do not attempt to use divisors greater than the square root of the number involved, but do *not* ask children to merely apply a rote rule. To illustrate the reasoning, let us consider what happens when a divisor is selected. For example:

$$\underline{2)24} \\ 12$$

We see that factors appear in pairs. As soon as one number is used as a divisor, a second number appears as a quotient. When 24 is divided by 2, another factor, 12, appears automatically. For a moment let's consider all pairs of factors of 24: 1×24, 2×12, 3×8, and 4×6. Notice that in each case a greater factor is paired with a lesser factor.

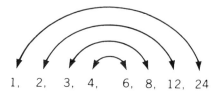

Clearly, if no lesser number (other than those listed) is a factor of 24, then no greater number is a factor either. We see that 4 is the greatest factor we need to divide into 24 to list all the factors of 24 (if we have already divided by 1, 2, and 3). Hence, generalizing from the example of 24 to all whole numbers, we need to consider only the lesser numbers as divisors—that is, numbers that aren't greater than the square root of the number under consideration.

Note that the square root of 24 lies between the square root of 16 and the square root of 25:

$$\sqrt{25} = 5 \qquad 5 \times 5 = 25 \\ \sqrt{16} = 4 \qquad 4 \times 4 = 16$$

Because $25 > 24$, we do not need to test any divisors greater than 4 to obtain *all* the factors of 24.

Consider the number 100.

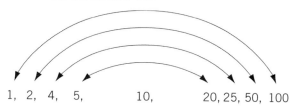

1, 2, 4, 5, 10, 20, 25, 50, 100

If we divide 100 only by factors of 100 up to and including the square root of 100 (10), we will obtain all the factors of 100. What is our procedure for finding the prime factorization of 100?

1. Begin by trying the least prime number, 2, as a divisor:

$$\underline{2)100} \\ 50$$

2. We can divide by 2 again, since the quotient, 50, is an even number:

$$\underline{2)100} \\ \underline{2) \ 50} \\ 25$$

3. This quotient is not divisible by 2 or by the next prime number, 3; but it is divisible by the prime number 5:

$$\underline{2)100} \\ \underline{2) \ 50} \\ \underline{5) \ 25} \\ 5$$

4. Our prime factorization of 100 is now complete, since the quotient 5 is prime:

$$2 \times 2 \times 5 \times 5$$

With large numbers it is extremely helpful to use only prime number divisors that are less than the square root of the dividend. For example, consider the number 469. Is this a prime number? If not, what is its prime factorization?

Our first step is to determine the greatest prime number that we need to try as a divisor. To determine this, we need to find only the square root, or the approximate square root, of 469. We know that $20 \times 20 = 400$. What are the prime numbers closest to 20? They are 19 and 23. Since $23 \times 23 = 529$ (and $529 > 469$), we know that 19 is the greatest prime number we need to try as a divisor.

Dividing 469 by primes (beginning, as always, with 2), we find that 2, 3, and 5 will not divide 469 evenly. The next prime number is 7, which does divide 469 evenly:

$$7\overline{)469}$$
$$67$$

Because 469 is not a multiple of 2, 3, or 5, neither can the number 67 be a multiple of 2, 3, or 5. By trying 7, 11, 13, 17, and 19 as divisors, we find that 67 is prime. Or, because the square root of 67 is approximately 8, we find that we have tested as far as is necessary with a divisor of 7. In either case, 67 is prime, and the prime factorization of 469 is 7×67.

Now let us test 73. We know that the square root of 73 lies somewhere between 8 and 9, because $8 \times 8 = 64$ and $9 \times 9 = 81$. The greatest prime divisor to test, then, is 7.

Is 73 divisible by 2? (No)
Is 73 divisible by 3? (No)
Is 73 divisible by 5? (No)
Is 73 divisible by 7? (No)

Any attempt to go further in division is unnecessary, because the next prime, 11, is greater than the square root of 73. The number 73, then, is prime.

To factor numbers completely and efficiently:

1. We should understand prime factors.
2. We should have a systematic approach to factorization.
3. We should have some simple rules for determining whether or not a number is divisible by the most common prime numbers.

DIVISIBILITY "RULES"

The sieve we discussed earlier in this chapter can be used to help children derive simple tests of divisibility for the numbers 2, 3, and 5. By inspecting the multiples of 2, 3, and 5, children can discover the structural peculiarities of any number divisible by 2, 3, or 5. First, by examining the multiples of 2, children can see that the digit in the ones place is always 0, 2, 4, 6, or 8. Only whole numbers ending in one of these digits are divisible by 2. In other words, only even numbers are multiples of 2 (that is, divisible by 2).

Next, children should inspect the multiples of 3. A more complex development becomes apparent here. After some inspection, it may be noticed that any number divisible by 3 is a number whose digits add up to another number that is divisible by 3. For example, consider the following:

Number	Sum of Digits	Factors of Numbers
12	$1 + 2 = 3$	3×4
15	$1 + 5 = 6$	3×5
18	$1 + 8 = 9$	3×6
21	$2 + 1 = 3$	3×7
24	$2 + 4 = 6$	3×8
27	$2 + 7 = 9$	3×9
96	$9 + 6 = 15$	3×32
168	$1 + 6 + 8 = 15$	3×56
4035	$4 + 0 + 3 + 5 = 12$	3×1345

In each case the sum of the digits is divisible by 3 and the original number is also divisible by 3. On the other hand, any number the sum of whose digits is not a multiple of 3 is not itself divisible by 3. This can be verified by examining such numbers as 11, 13, 14, 76, and 371.

Finally, children should inspect the multiples of 5. Every number that is divisible by 5 contains 0 or 5 in the ones place:

$$2 \times 5 = 10$$
$$3 \times 5 = 15$$
$$4 \times 5 = 20$$
$$5 \times 5 = 25$$
$$6 \times 5 = 30$$
$$7 \times 5 = 35$$
$$8 \times 5 = 40$$
$$9 \times 5 = 45$$
$$10 \times 5 = 50$$

and so on

Any whole number that doesn't end with 0 or 5 is not divisible by 5—for example, 11, 17, and 134. These simple rules of divisibility can be very helpful. Children learn more about number sense and number structure by applying such tests than by going through the more cumbersome and time-consuming process of division by trial and error.

To become proficient at certain aspects of mental mathematics and estimation, it is often helpful to be able to recognize certain patterns and structures in numbers. For instance, it is sometimes helpful to be able to determine whether one number is a factor of another without the use of potentially lengthy or time-consuming computation. If a calculator is handy, this would be an excellent time to put it to use, but what can be done if a calculator is not readily available?

A potentially useful technique for children is to understand and use the divisibility rules. Children should be able to determine rather quickly if a given number is divisible by another number. Children need a great deal of guidance and focus as they discover and use divisibility rules. Examples need to be carefully examined, and children should discuss how the examples are alike and how they are different.

Let us summarize divisibility. When we say that a given counting number is **divisible**, we mean that it can be divided by a counting number divisor so that there is a zero remainder. Look at the following examples. We say that 9 is divisible by 3 because we obtain a zero remainder:

$$
\begin{array}{r}
3 \\
3 \overline{)9} \\
\underline{-9} \\
0
\end{array}
$$

In the following example:

$$
\begin{array}{r}
2 \\
3 \overline{)7} \\
\underline{-6} \\
1
\end{array}
$$

we say that 7 is not divisible by 3 because when 7 is divided by 3 we have a nonzero remainder—in this case, 1.

Now let us summarize the divisibility rules. We have already systematically explored divisibility by 2, 3, and 5. To develop other divisibility rules, use the following procedure: Use a calculator to identify numbers that are multiples of (and thus divisible by) 9. Find at least ten such numbers and list them. Examine the list, looking for some common pattern or trait that the numbers share. With focused attention you may note that, in each case, the sum of the digits of the number is divisible by 9. Check this with many other examples. A similar procedure can be used to discover other divisibility rules for 4, 6, and 8. Use this procedure, and have the children check a sample of numbers so that they can justify the divisibility rules.

1. Any even number is divisible by 2. Two is a factor of any even number, and a 0 is obtained as a remainder.
2. A number is divisible by 3 if the sum of the digits is a multiple of 3. We know that 144 is divisible by 3 because by adding the digits 1, 4, and 4, we obtain a sum of 9, and 9 is divisible by 3.
3. A number is divisible by 4 if the last two digits, taken together as a number, are evenly divisible by 4. The number 328 is divisible by 4 because 28 is divisible by 4; therefore 328 is divisible by 4.
4. A number is divisible by 5 if there is either a 0 or a 5 in the ones place.
5. A number is divisible by 6 if the number is divisible by both 2 and 3. The number 546 is even; therefore it is divisible by 2. It is divisible by 3 because $5 + 4 + 6 = 15$, and 15 is divisible by 3. Therefore 546 is divisible by 6 because it is divisible by both 2 and 3.
6. A number is divisible by 8 if the last three digits, taken together as a number, are divisible by 8; 9864 is divisible by 8 because 864 is divisible by 8.
7. A number is divisible by 9 if the sum of the digits is divisible by 9. The number 756 is divisible by 9 because $7 + 5 + 6 = 18$, and 18 is divisible by 9.
8. A number is divisible by 10 if there is a 0 in the ones place.

Note that these are not *rules* in the sense that they must be committed to memory. In fact, some teachers ask children to memorize them in a rote manner and, consequently, the children forget them and lose the point of what divisibility is all about. The divisibility rules should instead be treated as interesting investigations. They are merely useful observations of number structure and applications of number sense.

Research Snapshot

What are the consequences of memorizing the divisibility rules without conceptually understanding them?

In a study of 21 preservice elementary school teachers, Zazkis and Campbell (1996) found that many of the teachers were procedurally oriented and considered the divisibility rules procedurally as well.

In the absence of conceptual understanding, many of the teachers misapplied and overgeneralized the divisibility rules when they did not have rules to use. The results suggest that for these teachers, insufficient emphasis has been placed on a meaningful understanding of divisibility.

What could you do in your classroom to promote the development of a conceptual understanding of divisibility?

Zazkis, R., & Campbell, S. (1996). Divisibility and multiplicative structure of natural numbers: Preservice teachers' understanding. *Journal for Research in Mathematics Education, 27*, 540–563.

For additional research briefs, "ERIC Digests" lets you search more than 2,000 short syntheses of research on a range of education topics. The syntheses were produced by the Educational Resources Information Center (ERIC). Check http://ed.gov/databases/ERIC_Digests/index/

LEAST COMMON MULTIPLES AND GREATEST COMMON FACTORS

Every composite number has been shown to have a unique prime factorization. We can use this fact to help us find other information about numbers. For example, it is often very useful to know the greatest common factor (GCF) of two numbers.

The ideas of GCF and LCM (least common multiple) are used extensively to develop concepts about operations on **fractional numbers**. They are mentioned in this chapter because of their relation to prime factors. The practical applications shown in subsequent chapters will be of interest to the teacher and of great importance throughout the study of rational numbers.

Let's first examine the concept of greatest common factor (GCF).

> The **greatest common factor (GCF)** of two or more given numbers is the greatest number that will divide evenly into the numbers.

Consider the numbers 24 and 36. What is the greatest common factor of these two numbers?

Perhaps the easiest way to approach this question is to break the question down into three parts:

1. What are the factors of 24 and the factors of 36?

2. What are the common factors of 24 and 36?

3. Which is the greatest of the common factors of 24 and 36?

What are the factors of 24? (1, 2, 3, 4, 6, 8, 12, and 24) What are the factors of 36? (1, 2, 3, 4, 6, 9, 12, 18, and 36) The common factors of 24 and 36 are 1, 2, 3, 4, 6, and 12. Twelve is the greatest factor common to both 24 and 36.

We can also find the greatest common factor of 24 and 36 by using prime factorization. To do this, we first write prime factorizations for 36 and 24:

$$36 = 2 \times 2 \times 3 \times 3$$

$$24 = 2 \times 2 \times 2 \times 3$$

By inspecting these factorizations, we can select each factor that is common to both numbers. Clearly, $2 \times 2 \times 3$ appears in both sets of factors. Since each number is "built" with these factors, each of the numbers is divisible by these factors. Thus the greatest common factor (GCF) of 36 and 24 is $2 \times 2 \times 3$, or 12.

The previous development of prime factorization and factor trees should clarify why the method described here leads to the determination of the GCF. You will recall that a number can be factored (with factor trees) into successive product expressions until the prime factorization is reached. For example:

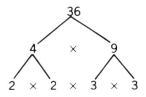

Note that any factor or combination of factors expressed in the last line of the preceding factor tree is a divisor of 36. From this list of factors (2, 2, 3, 3), we can take any two, three, or four factors and multiply them together to find another factor, one that is greater than any of the single factors listed. In this case we discover the following factors:

$$2$$
$$3$$
$$2 \times 2 = 4$$
$$2 \times 3 = 6$$
$$3 \times 3 = 9$$
$$2 \times 2 \times 3 = 12$$
$$2 \times 3 \times 3 = 18$$
$$2 \times 2 \times 3 \times 3 = 36$$

By drawing a factor tree to discover the prime factorization, we found that $24 = 2 \times 2 \times 2 \times 3$. From the list of factors (2, 2, 2, 3), we can take any two, three, or four factors and multiply them together to find other factors that are greater than the single factors listed. Thus we discover the following factors:

$$2$$
$$3$$
$$2 \times 2 = 4$$
$$2 \times 3 = 6$$
$$2 \times 2 \times 2 = 8$$
$$2 \times 2 \times 3 = 12$$
$$2 \times 2 \times 2 \times 3 = 24$$

By comparing the set of factors of 36 and the set of factors of 24, we can see that the greatest number that is a factor of both 36 and 24 is 12 (or $2 \times 2 \times 3$).

As well as finding the greatest common factor of two numbers, we can also find the least common multiple (LCM) of two numbers. What do we mean by least common multiple? First, we know that a *multiple* of any number is evenly divisible by that number. For instance, the multiples of 2 (0, 2, 4, 6, 8, 10, . . .) can all be divided evenly by 2. Second, when we say *common multiple*, we are speaking of a number that is a multiple for each of at least two numbers. For example, 24 is a common multiple of 12 and 8 because it can be divided evenly by either 12 or 8. Third, when we speak of the *least common multiple*, we mean the least nonzero number that is a multiple of all the numbers being considered.

> The **least common multiple (LCM)** of two or more given numbers is the least nonzero number that is a multiple of each of the given numbers.

Now let us find the least common multiple of 24 and 36. We can begin by listing multiples of each number until we find a common multiple. The multiples of 24 are:

0, 24, 48, 72, 96, 120, 144,
168, 192, 216, and so on

The multiples of 36 are:

0, 36, 72, 108, 144, 180,
216, 252, and so on

By careful examination of the multiples of these two numbers, we find that some of the common multiples of 24 and 36 are:

0, 72, 144, 216, . . .

Thus the least common nonzero multiple of 24 and 36 is 72.

Another method for finding the least common multiple for two (or more) numbers is to use Cuisenaire rods as a concrete, manipulative model. To find the LCM for 6 and 9, make two separate rod trains, one of multiples of 6 and the other of multiples of 9. Compare these trains and make note when the two trains are of equal length.

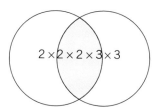

For example, in the figure you'll see that the two trains "match" at 18. The least common multiple of 6 and 9 is 18.

Now let's find the least common multiple for 24 and 36 by using the more abstract method of prime factorization:

$$36 = 2 \times 2 \times 3 \times 3$$
$$24 = 2 \times 2 \times 2 \times 3$$

Since a multiple of a number must contain that number, it must also contain the prime factorization of that number. This stands to reason, since the prime factorization is the basic structure or composition of the number. Hence we can conclude that a multiple of a number must, at the very least, include the prime factorization of that number. Now we want to construct a multiple of both 36 and 24. This must contain the prime factorizations of both 36 and 24 to be a common multiple:

$$36 = 2 \times 2 \times 3 \times 3$$
$$24 = 2 \times 2 \times 2 \times 3$$

The LCM must contain $2 \times 2 \times 3 \times 3$ to accommodate 36, and it must contain $2 \times 2 \times 2 \times 3$ to accommodate 24. By comparing the two product expressions, we see that, in addition to the factors in the product expression for 36 ($2 \times 2 \times 3 \times 3$), we need an additional 2 to make sure that the prime factorization of 24 is included.

Clearly, then, the least common multiple of 24 and 36 must be $2 \times 2 \times 3 \times 3 \times 2$, or 72.

Notice that the least common multiple contains the prime factorizations of both 36 and 24 ($2 \times 2 \times 3 \times 3$) $\times$ ($2 \times 2 \times 2 \times 3$), but it is not simply the product of 36 and 24. If a factor appears in both numbers, then it must appear in the LCM only as often as it appears in the number (of the two numbers) in which it appears most often. For example, the factor 2 appears twice in 36 ($2 \times 2 \times 3 \times 3$), and three times in 24 ($2 \times 2 \times 2 \times 3$); therefore, it must appear exactly three times in the LCM. In the same way, the factor 3 appears once in 24 ($2 \times 2 \times 2 \times 3$) and twice in 36 ($2 \times 2 \times 3 \times 3$); therefore, it must appear exactly twice in the LCM. Clearly, 72 ($2 \times 2 \times 2 \times 3 \times 3$) is the least number that contains three 2s and two 3s as factors.

The relationship between LCM and GCF can be more clearly seen in the following diagram:

$2 \times 2 \times 2 \times 3 \times 3$

The loop on the left encircles the factors of 24 while the loop on the right contains the factors of 36. Examination of the intersection of these two circles (i.e., the factors they have in common) yields the GCF, while the union of the two circles is the LCM.

In this chapter we have examined only number theory applicable to the elementary school mathematics program. Some children will become interested in number theory and will want to do additional study on their own. There are many other aspects of number theory that children might find interesting. These include such topics as figurate numbers, perfect numbers, amicable numbers, Pythagorean triples, and Fibonacci numbers, to name but a few.

NUMBER SYSTEMS

In previous chapters we examined various aspects of our number system. We began with numberness associated with concrete objects; then we moved to the study of abstract numbers. After that we looked at some of the various sets of numbers that make up our mathematics system.

Numberness in the elementary school mathematics program is based on a logical organization that begins with the numbers we call the *counting numbers* or the *natural numbers*. You should recall that **counting numbers** begin with 1 and continue with 2, 3, 4, 5, and so forth, in that pattern. We symbolize the counting numbers {1, 2, 3, 4, 5, . . .}.

The next logical set of numbers we consider is the set of **whole numbers**—that is, the counting numbers with the inclusion of 0. The whole numbers are symbolized {0, 1, 2, 3, 4, 5, . . .}. Note that one new element, 0, has been included to expand the set of counting numbers to the system of whole numbers. The following diagram illustrates the relation between counting numbers and whole numbers:

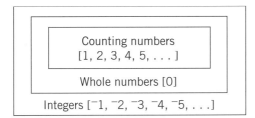

This figure shows that whole numbers *include* all counting numbers.

Another set of numbers we will examine in this chapter is the set of integers. Counting numbers and whole numbers are included in the set of integers. We now show the counting numbers as positive numbers {⁺1, ⁺2, ⁺3, ⁺4, ⁺5, . . .}. Zero is included as an integer. By extending the number line to the left, we see that there is a logical need for negative numbers. So, we can name three sets of numbers that make up the integers: counting numbers, negative numbers (that is, the opposites of the counting numbers), and zero. (Negative numbers will be explained in more detail later.) We can show the relationship among the numbers with the following diagram:

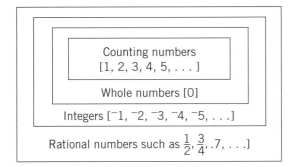

The system of numbers can now be extended to include rational numbers. **Rational numbers** may be written in two different forms—fractions and decimals. Since counting numbers, whole numbers, and integers are rational numbers, we can extend the diagram of the number system as follows:

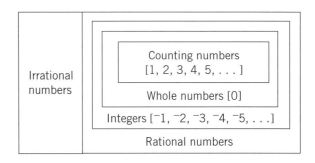

In this chapter we will also briefly examine **irrational numbers**. We will show that irrational numbers are not related to counting numbers, whole numbers, integers, or rational numbers, so they are set off to one side.

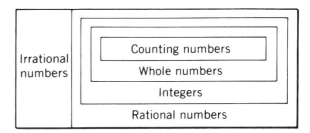

All of these systems of numbers make up the *real number system*, as shown in the following figure:

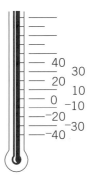

Let's consider the system of integers and some approaches that might be used to convey important aspects of this system to elementary school children.

As we worked with whole numbers, we found that the sum of any two whole numbers is a whole number, but sometimes the difference between two whole numbers is not a whole number. Consider, for example, $3 - 4 = \square$. There is no whole number that satisfies this equation. Thus we need another kind of number to solve examples such as this.

The call for a number system that includes numbers less than zero is answered by the use of negative numbers. Many children are familiar with real-life situations that can be represented by integers such as: above/below sea level and upper floors/subbasements in buildings. To explore this concept, let's take a look at a familiar number line that we all use in our everyday lives—a thermometer.

Essentially, a thermometer is a number line with equivalent divisions on both sides of the zero point.

We see that zero is the reference point (origin) on this thermometer and that numerals are marked at regular (equal) intervals to indicate temperature. Many of us are familiar with readings such as 25°, 32°, 59°, and 89°. But what about midwinter readings, or readings on a deep-freeze thermometer, such as 10 below zero or 15 below zero? Temperatures below zero, when recorded in the newspaper, are written as −10° and −15° and, technically, should be read, "negative 10 degrees" and "15 below zero." You should not refer to temperature below zero as "minus 10 degrees" since "minus" refers to the operation of subtraction, not to a relative position on a number line.

Can we, on our number line, mark and label points to show the part of the number line that corresponds to the below-zero readings of a thermometer?

Obviously, we must distinguish between the numerals written on the "negative side" of the zero and those written on the "positive side." One way of doing this is to place a sign (–) in front of any numeral written on the negative side of 0 to indicate that it represents a number *less than zero*:

A number represented by a numeral with this sign is called a *negative number*, and the sign (⁻) is called a *negative sign*. The numerals written on the positive side of the zero represent positive numbers, and a positive number is sometimes written with a positive sign (⁺) placed in front of it (for example, ⁺10 or ⁺20). Numerals written without signs are understood to represent positive numbers. The number zero is neither positive nor negative. Numbers that are named by numerals with signs to indicate that the numbers named are positive (⁺) or negative (⁻) are called **directed numbers**. Notice that the positive and negative signs are often raised to avoid confusion with signs for addition (plus, +) and subtraction (minus, –). Pupils should not mistakenly think of the raised ⁺ (positive) and ⁻ (negative) signs as operation signs. The raised ⁺ and ⁻ signs are part of the names of the numbers. When positive and negative numbers are first introduced to children, it is best to place the ⁺ sign with every positive number under discussion. Later, children will recognize that positive numbers can sometimes be written with the ⁺ understood.

Some individuals read ⁻2 as "minus two" and ⁺2 as "plus two." When the terms *minus* and *plus* are associated with positive and negative numbers, children confuse the concept of integers with the operations of addition and subtraction. This is why, in Chapter 7, we suggested reading the + sign as "add"; now with integers we will read the ⁺ sign as "positive." The ⁻ sign with integers will be read as "negative." The difficulties that children experience in developing an understanding of integers are usually caused by confusion over the language used for the signs.

Examine the following number line diagram:

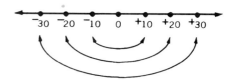

Notice that the points labeled ⁺20 and ⁻20 are the same distance from zero, but that one is to the right of zero, while the other is to the left of zero. We call such pairs of numbers *opposites* or *additive inverses*. In general, if two points are the same distance from the zero point, but on opposite sides of the zero point, the numbers that correspond to these points are called **opposites**. Thus ⁺10 and ⁻10 are opposites, as are ⁺5 and ⁻5, ⁺3 and ⁻3, and so on. So that every number will have an opposite, it is customary to say that *zero is its own opposite*.

A number is an **integer** if it is a whole number or the opposite of a whole number. We can indicate the integers as follows:

$$\{\ldots, \ ^-4, \ ^-3, \ ^-2, \ ^-1, \ 0, \ ^+1, \ ^+2, \ ^+3, \ ^+4, \ \ldots\}$$

The integers that are greater than zero form the *positive integers*:

$$\{^+1, \ ^+2, \ ^+3, \ ^+4, \ ^+5, \ \ldots\}$$

The integers that are less than zero form the *negative integers*:

$$\{^-1, \ ^-2, \ ^-3, \ ^-4, \ ^-5, \ \ldots\}$$

The number 0 is an integer, but it is considered to be neither positive nor negative.

We have seen that we can represent the integers on the number line. On the following number line, locate the point named by ⁺5. As we have just seen, the 5 indicates how many unit lengths the number is from zero, and the ⁺ indicates the direction.

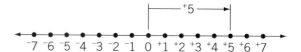

Considering the line segment that begins at zero on the number line, the arrow indicates the direction (the *sign* of the number), and the length indicates the number of unit lengths from zero (the *value* of the number regardless of its sign). This line segment stands for the value ⁺5.

Consider the value ⁻2. The negative sign indicates direction, and the 2 indicates magnitude. **Magnitude** (or **absolute value**) refers to the length of the line segment in unit lengths—that is, the distance the point is from zero. Note that distance is always positive; thus absolute value is always positive. The absolute value of a number x is symbolized by $|x|$. The absolute value of 5 is 5 ($|5| = 5$) and the absolute value of ⁻2 is 2 ($|^-2| = 2$).

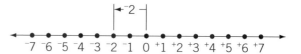

This line segment stands for $^-2$ because it is two units long and has a negative direction. Remember that, starting at zero, we move left from zero to indicate negative numbers, and right from zero to indicate positive numbers. The point $^-2$, however, has an absolute value of 2 because it is a distance of two units from zero.

Using the number line, children have learned number relations in whole numbers and in fractional numbers. They have found that, beginning with zero, numbers increase in value to the right on the number line. This is, of course, still valid when the negative integers are located on the number line.

$$^-7 \quad ^-6 \quad ^-5 \quad ^-4 \quad ^-3 \quad ^-2 \quad ^-1 \quad 0 \quad ^+1 \quad ^+2 \quad ^+3 \quad ^+4 \quad ^+5 \quad ^+6 \quad ^+7$$

Since children have already learned relations such as $4 > 2$, $5 < 7$, $3 > 0$, and so on, it is not difficult to extend this concept to include negative integers. Any number on the number line is greater than any number to its left, as we have seen. So, on the preceding number line, we see that $^-1 > {}^-2$, $^-3 > {}^-7$, $0 > {}^-1$, $^-2 > {}^-3$, $^-1 > {}^-10$, and so on. This extension of children's knowledge of relations on the number line is consistent and logical. The evident truth of statements such as $^+1 > {}^-7$, seen on the number line, will help children understand the meaning of negative integers. A number is still greater than any number named to its left on the number line. However, zero is not a "beginning" point now but a point of reference between positive and negative numbers. The set of integers extends endlessly to the right and to the left of zero.

To further clarify the meaning of $^-8 < {}^+1$, for example, the familiar analogy of being in debt, or "in the hole," could be mentioned. If Mr. Smith owes $8 and Mr. Friedlund has $1, who has more money? Mr. Friedlund does because Mr. Smith is $8 in debt, or has $^-8$ dollars, while Mr. Friedlund has $^+1$ dollar.

The positive integers have the properties of the whole numbers with which the children are familiar, but numbers should be labeled with the $^+$ sign when the set of integers is being explored. In a short time, pupils will be familiar enough with integers to consider positive integers without labeling them $^+$ when they are named.

The addition (and subtraction) of integers can be modeled effectively using chips of two different colors. For example, let us say that blue chips are used to represent positive numbers and red chips are used to represent negative numbers. Then, $^-5 + {}^+6 = \square$ can be shown as a pile of 5 blue chips and a pile of 6 red chips. To find the sum, combine the two piles into one. To interpret the value of this new pile, match blue and red chips in pairs until you can no longer do so. These pairs represent "zeros" (according to the property of opposites). In this exercise, one red chip would be left, representing $^+1$, the answer to $^-5 + {}^+6 = \square$.

It may be beneficial to look at this color chip approach in terms of a subtraction of integers exercise. Consider, for example, $^+6 - {}^-3 = \square$. Begin with a pile of 6 red chips to represent $^+6$. To subtract $^-3$ you would need to remove 3 blue chips from this pile. Since there

aren't any blue chips in this pile, you can put some in by putting in 3 blue *and* 3 red (that is, add "0" to the pile in the form of $^-3 + {}^+3$). Now the pile contains 3 blue chips that can be removed, leaving a total of 9 red. These 9 red chips represent $^+9$, the answer to $^+6 - {}^-3 = \square$.

Now let's look at some examples of addition of integers modeled on the number line. In each of the following examples, find the indicated sum.

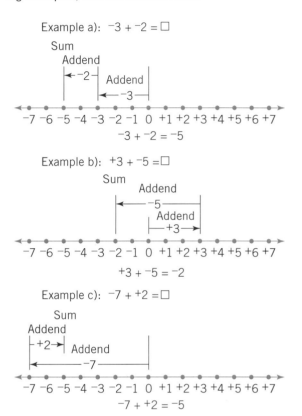

Example a): $^-3 + {}^-2 = \square$

$^-3 + {}^-2 = {}^-5$

Example b): $^+3 + {}^-5 = \square$

$^+3 + {}^-5 = {}^-2$

Example c): $^-7 + {}^+2 = \square$

$^-7 + {}^+2 = {}^-5$

In each example, all the arrows are drawn according to the magnitude and direction indicated in the equation. Generalizing from these examples, we see that if we wish to represent sums of positive and negative numbers as moves on the number line, we can observe the following procedure:

1. Starting at zero on the number line, draw an arrow so that its length in unit lengths equals the first addend to be added. The direction in which the arrow is drawn corresponds to the sign of the number (left for $^-$ and right for $^+$).

2. Starting from the end of the first arrow (and just above it), draw an arrow so that its length in unit lengths equals the second addend to be added. The direction in which the arrow is drawn corresponds to the sign of the number.

3. The point on the number line where the second addend ends names the sum. The resultant is always the sum of an addition example, and it is read from the end of the arrow that names the second addend. It is named by a point on the number line.

You will readily see that, if we add two integers that are opposites, we get zero for the sum. For example, $^+4 + ^-4 = 0$:

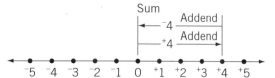

The arrow for the first addend ($^+4$) takes us to $^+4$, and the arrow for the second addend ($^-4$) brings us back to zero. If we read the point at the end of the second arrow, we find the sum to be zero. Nevertheless, it should be clear from the diagram that $^+4 + ^-4 = 0$. Similarly, the sum of any two opposites is zero:

Addend		Addend		Sum
$^+7$	+	$^-7$	=	0
$^-9$	+	$^+9$	=	0
$^+12$	+	$^-12$	=	0
		and so on		

The fact that any two opposites have a sum of zero is often referred to as the **addition property of opposites**.

Besides the addition property of opposites, what other properties exist for addition of integers? Using number line models, it is easy to see that addition of integers has all the basic properties that we found for whole numbers and fractional numbers:

1. Addition of integers is *commutative*.
2. Addition of integers is *associative*.
3. Zero (0) is the *additive identity element* for the operation of addition on the integers.

At this point we will leave it to you to draw number line models to convince yourself that these properties do indeed hold true.

From the number line diagrams, it is easy to see that the sum of two positive integers must be positive: $^+3 + ^+5 = ^+8$, $^+6 + ^+7 = ^+13$, and so on. It is equally clear that the sum of two negative integers must be negative: $^-2 + ^-3 = ^-5$, $^-7 + ^-1 = ^-8$, and so on. What about the sum of a positive integer and a negative integer?

Consider this example: $^+8 + ^-4 = \square$. The property of opposite numbers tells us that $^+4 + ^-4 = 0$. We can use the concept of opposites and the number line to find a solution:

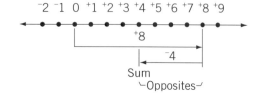

Let us look at another example: $^+3 + ^-9 = \square$.

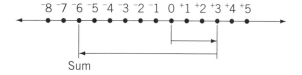

Another example: $^+10 + ^-7 = \square$.

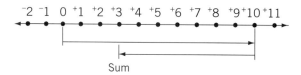

And another: $^-17 + ^+19 = \square$.

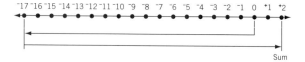

Locate where the opposites are apparent in each example.

Notice that integers, like other numbers, can be renamed in many different ways. For example, we can rename 12 as $11 + 1$, $10 + 2$, $9 + 3$, and so on. We can, in the same manner, rename $^-12$ in different ways: $^-11 + ^-1$, $^-10 + ^-2$, $^-9 + ^-3$, and so on. We could also rename $^-12$ as $^-13 + ^+1$.

Now, let's look at the inverse operation of subtraction in relation to the set of integers. Subtraction, we know, is the inverse operation of addition.

	Addend		Addend		Sum
	6	+	8	=	14
	Sum		Addend		Addend
	14	–	6	=	8
or	14	–	8	=	6

Let's examine the way in which the inverse operation of subtraction is performed using the number line. Consider $^+4 - ^+2 = \square$. We can rewrite the example in the form $^+2 + \square = ^+4$. Draw an arrow that is two units long and points to the right (the positive direction) to represent the first addend. The arrow for the second addend, which is the missing addend, must go from the tip of the first arrow to the point representing $^+4$ (the sum). Draw this arrow, using a dotted line to indicate that it represents the missing addend.

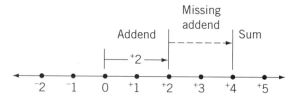

What integer does the dotted arrow represent? Since it is two units long and points in the positive direction, it represents $^+2$. The missing addend is therefore $^+2$. Thus:

Sum		Addend		Addend
$^+4$	–	$^+2$	=	$^+2$

Consider this example: $^-5 - ^+3 = \square$. This example can be rewritten in the form $^+3 + \square = ^-5$. This example can also be modeled on the number line by beginning at the reference point, 0, and pointing the arrow of the addend 3 in a positive direction. Next locate the point $^-5$, which is the sum. We know that the missing addend must begin at the end of the first addend and end at the sum. The number line model can be drawn in the following way:

The diagram shows that $\square = {}^-8$. Therefore:

$$^-5 - {}^+3 = {}^-8$$

Look at the following subtraction examples, which have been rewritten and solved:

Subtraction	Rewritten	Solution
$^+4 - {}^+2 = \square$	$^+2 + \square = {}^+4$	$\square = {}^+2$
$^+4 - {}^+1 = \square$	$^+1 + \square = {}^+4$	$\square = {}^+3$
$^+4 - \ \ 0 = \square$	$0 + \square = {}^+4$	$\square = {}^+4$
$^+4 - {}^-1 = \square$	$^-1 + \square = {}^+4$	$\square = {}^+5$
$^+4 - {}^-2 = \square$	$^-2 + \square = {}^+4$	$\square = {}^+6$

These five examples have been rewritten to illustrate the generalization that subtracting a number gives the same result as adding its opposite. However, do *not* push this generalization as a rule to be rotely remembered and repeated by children. It should be viewed as merely an observation that they might discover and make:

$^+4 - {}^+2 = \square$	$^+4 + {}^-2 = \square$	$\square = {}^+2$
$^+4 - {}^+1 = \square$	$^+4 + {}^-1 = \square$	$\square = {}^+3$
$^+4 - \ \ 0 = \square$	$^+4 + \ \ 0 = \square$	$\square = {}^+4$
$^+4 - {}^-1 = \square$	$^+4 + {}^+1 = \square$	$\square = {}^+5$
$^+4 - {}^-2 = \square$	$^+4 + {}^+2 = \square$	$\square = {}^+6$

The concept of subtracting integers closely parallels subtraction of whole numbers. The number line has been used as a model to help develop an understanding. Inverse sentences have been used to help children comprehend the existing relationships. After the children have had many experiences with subtraction as related to integers, they should begin to look for patterns to help them generalize. Teachers should not rush the children by pushing them into generalizing prematurely. Generalizations should be based on patterns observed through a wide variety of examples.

We mentioned earlier that addition of integers has all of the properties of addition of whole numbers and fractional numbers. What properties does subtraction have? When we studied subtraction of whole numbers, we found that it was neither commutative nor associative. The same is true for subtraction of integers. For example $^+2 - {}^+4 = {}^-2$, but $^+4 - {}^+2 = {}^+2$; therefore $^+2 - {}^+4 \neq {}^+4 - {}^+2$, which is enough to show that subtraction is not commutative. Can you devise a counterexample to show that subtraction is not associative?

So far we have found two properties that subtraction of integers does *not* have. (Subtraction of whole numbers did not have these properties, either.) An important property that subtraction of integers *does* have is that

for any integers a and b, $a - b$ is also an integer. In the system of whole numbers, there is no way to subtract a greater number from a lesser one, but in the system of integers, this is possible.

Let us turn our attention now to multiplication of integers. The process used to multiply two nonnegative integers is the same as the process used to multiply whole numbers. For instance:

Factor		Factor		Product
$^+3$	$\times$	$^+2$	$=$	$^+6$
0	$\times$	$^+5$	$=$	0
$^+6$	$\times$	$^+7$	$=$	$^+42$
$^+1$	$\times$	$^+8$	$=$	$^+8$

and so on

Multiplication examples such as 2×4 can be interpreted to mean "two sets of four." We can model the example on the number line:

If we interpret $^+2 \times {}^+4$ as two jumps of $^+4$ in a positive direction, we arrive at $^+8$. Following the same logic, we can interpret $^+2 \times {}^-4$ as two jumps of $^-4$ in the negative direction. Thus we see that $^+2 \times {}^-4 = {}^-8$.

Using the commutative property of multiplication, we can change $^+2 \times {}^-4 = {}^-8$ to $^-4 \times {}^+2 = {}^-8$.

Statements such as $^+3 \times {}^+5 = {}^+15$ and $^+3 \times {}^-5 = {}^-15$ can be illustrated on the number line if we use the idea of repeated addition.

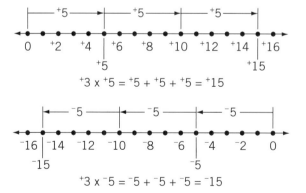

$$^+3 \times {}^+5 = {}^+5 + {}^+5 + {}^+5 = {}^+15$$

$$^+3 \times {}^-5 = {}^-5 + {}^-5 + {}^-5 = {}^-15$$

However, a number line approach to multiplication examples in which both factors are negative is awkward, at best. The movement on the number line is not as "natural" and easily interpreted as the preceding examples. Probably the best approach is to use patterns and generalizations.

Patterns are helpful for children to justify the results of multiplication of integers. Now let's look at the operation of multiplication using negative numbers and looking for patterns. Consider the following examples:

Factor		Factor		Product
$^+3$	$\times$	$^+5$	$=$	$^+15$
$^+2$	$\times$	$^+5$	$=$	$^+10$
$^+1$	$\times$	$^+5$	$=$	$^+5$
0	$\times$	$^+5$	$=$	0
$^-1$	$\times$	$^+5$	$=$	$?$
$^-2$	$\times$	$^+5$	$=$	$?$
$^-3$	$\times$	$^+5$	$=$	$?$

Examining the pattern found here, we discover that the product becomes five less every time the first factor becomes one less. If this pattern is extended to include the last three examples in the series above, we get negative products:

$^-1$	$\times$	$^+5$	$=$	$^-5$
$^-2$	$\times$	$^+5$	$=$	$^-10$
$^-3$	$\times$	$^+5$	$=$	$^-15$

A similar approach can be used to discover how to define multiplication when the second factor is negative and the first factor is positive. Look for the pattern in these examples:

Factor		Factor		Product
$^+5$	$\times$	$^+3$	$=$	$^+15$
$^+5$	$\times$	$^+2$	$=$	$^+10$
$^+5$	$\times$	$^+1$	$=$	$^+5$
$^+5$	$\times$	0	$=$	0
$^+5$	$\times$	$^-1$	$=$	$?$
$^+5$	$\times$	$^-2$	$=$	$?$
$^+5$	$\times$	$^-3$	$=$	$?$

Examining the pattern, we see that the first factor is the same in all the examples. The second factor is decreasing by one, and the product is decreasing by five. If this pattern continues, the last three examples will give negative products:

$^+5$	$\times$	$^-1$	$=$	$^-5$
$^+5$	$\times$	$^-2$	$=$	$^-10$
$^+5$	$\times$	$^-3$	$=$	$^-15$

We can generalize from these examples by saying that the product of a positive integer and a negative integer is the same as the product of two positive integers, except that the sign of the product is negative.

Now consider the following examples:

Factor		Factor		Product
$^-4$	$\times$	$^+3$	$=$	$^-12$
$^-4$	$\times$	$^+2$	$=$	$^-8$
$^-4$	$\times$	$^+1$	$=$	$^-4$
$^-4$	$\times$	0	$=$	0
$^-4$	$\times$	$^-1$	$=$	$?$
$^-4$	$\times$	$^-2$	$=$	$?$
$^-4$	$\times$	$^-3$	$=$	$?$

We can discover a pattern here: Every time the second factor becomes one less, the product becomes four greater. Extending this pattern to include the last three examples in the series, we get positive products:

$^-4$	$\times$	$^-1$	$=$	$^+4$
$^-4$	$\times$	$^-2$	$=$	$^+8$
$^-4$	$\times$	$^-3$	$=$	$^+12$

We can generalize from these examples by saying that the product of two negative numbers is the same as the product of two positive numbers.

This examination of the multiplication of negative numbers has revealed that the product of a negative number and a positive number is negative, and that the product of two negative numbers is positive. Of course, the product of two positive numbers is positive. Therefore, we can observe the following steps in the multiplication of signed numbers:

1. Determine the value of the product, regardless of its sign, by multiplying the two factors as though they were both positive.
2. Determine the sign of the product. If the factors have identical signs (both positive or both negative), the sign of the product is positive. If the factors have different signs (one positive and the other negative), the sign of the product is negative.

Multiplication of integers, like multiplication of whole numbers, is a binary operation. Multiplication of integers has the same basic properties that we found for multiplication of whole numbers: It is commutative, associative, and distributive over addition. The number $^+1$ is the identity element for multiplication of integers.

Now, let's examine the operation of division with respect to integers. Consider the following multiplication examples and the division examples that have been derived from them:

Factor		Factor		Product		Product		Factor		Factor
$^+3$	$\times$	$^+4$	$=$	$^+12$		$^+12$	$\div$	$^+4$	$=$	$^+3$
$^-3$	$\times$	$^+4$	$=$	$^-12$		$^-12$	$\div$	$^-3$	$=$	$^+4$
						$^-12$	$\div$	$^+4$	$=$	$^-3$
$^-3$	$\times$	$^-4$	$=$	$^+12$		$^+12$	$\div$	$^-4$	$=$	$^-3$

We know that the multiplication examples are correct, because we have just examined multiplication with integers. We also know that the division examples are correct, because we discovered in Chapter 8 that the operation of division can be interpreted as the inverse operation of multiplication. Examining the division examples and generalizing from them, we see that we can observe the following steps when dividing one number by another:

1. Determine the value of the quotient, regardless of its sign, by performing the indicated division as though both the divisor and the dividend were positive.
2. Determine the sign of the quotient. If the divisor and dividend have the same signs (both positive or both negative), the sign of the quotient is positive. If the divisor and dividend have different signs (one positive and the other negative), the sign of the quotient is negative.

Division with negative numbers can also be modeled on the number line. However, this is considerably more complex than the development of multiplication and would not prove useful to an elementary-level pupil.

The system of integers was formed as an extension of the system of whole numbers. For each whole number greater than zero, we include the opposite negative number. By including numbers less than zero with our system, we were able to label an infinite set of points to the left of zero on the number line.

Now let us consider the system of fractional numbers and form a larger system by including the opposites of all the fractional numbers. When we do this, we obtain a system of numbers that includes not only $\frac{1}{2}$, $\frac{3}{7}$, $\frac{4}{5}$, $\frac{9}{8}$, and so on, but also numbers such as $-\left(\frac{1}{2}\right)$, $-\left(\frac{3}{7}\right)$, $-\left(\frac{4}{5}\right)$, $-\left(\frac{9}{8}\right)$, and so on. This larger system of numbers, consisting of all the fractional numbers and their opposites, is called the system of *rational numbers*. The rational numbers can also be thought of as all quotients $\frac{a}{b}$, where a is an integer and b is a nonzero integer. (Notice the similarity between this last statement and the definition of a fractional number as the quotient $\frac{a}{b}$ of a whole number and a counting number.)

The system of numbers called *rational numbers* can be written in two different forms—as fractions or decimals.

Let's look at a number line on which some of the points have been labeled with rational numbers expressed as fractions.

We know that the point halfway between 0 and $^+1$ is $^+\left(\frac{1}{2}\right)$. Then, from our knowledge of opposites, the point halfway between 0 and $^-1$ is $^-\left(\frac{1}{2}\right)$. The point named $^+1$ could be named as $^+\left(\frac{1}{1}\right)$, $^+\left(\frac{2}{2}\right)$, and so on. Then, in the same way, we could rename $^-1$ as $^-\left(\frac{1}{1}\right)$, $^-\left(\frac{2}{2}\right)$, and so on. So it should be clear that every rational number has an opposite. That is, $^+\left(\frac{1}{2}\right) + ^-\left(\frac{1}{2}\right) = 0$, $^+\left(\frac{2}{3}\right) + ^-\left(\frac{2}{3}\right) = 0$, and so on.

Operations with signed rational numbers follow the same patterns that we discovered among the integers.

$$^+2 + ^+3 = ^+5 \qquad ^+\left(\frac{1}{2}\right) + ^+\left(\frac{1}{3}\right) = ^+\left(\frac{5}{6}\right)$$
$$^-3 \times ^-2 = ^+6 \qquad ^-\left(\frac{1}{2}\right) \times ^-\left(\frac{1}{4}\right) = ^+\left(\frac{1}{8}\right)$$
$$^+8 \div ^-2 = ^-4 \qquad ^+\left(\frac{1}{2}\right) \div ^-2 = ^-\left(\frac{1}{4}\right)$$
$$^+2 - ^+5 = ^-3 \qquad ^+\left(\frac{1}{8}\right) - ^+\left(\frac{3}{8}\right) = ^-\left(\frac{1}{4}\right)$$

Of course, rational numbers can be named in many ways. For example:

$$^+\left(\frac{1}{4}\right) = ^+\left(\frac{2}{8}\right) = ^+\left(\frac{3}{12}\right) = ^+\left(\frac{4}{16}\right) \text{ and so on}$$

Also:

$$^+\left(\frac{1}{4}\right) = \frac{^+1}{^+4} = \frac{^-1}{^-4} = \frac{^-2}{^-8} \text{ and so on}$$

Similarly:

$$^-\left(\frac{2}{3}\right) = \frac{^-2}{^+3} = \frac{^+2}{^-3} = \frac{^+10}{^-15} \text{ and so on}$$

A full discussion of all the fundamental operations as they apply to rational numbers is presented in Chapters 11, 12, and 13. It will probably come as no surprise that in the system of rational numbers these fundamental operations enjoy all of the properties that they had in the systems studied earlier. You will perhaps find it helpful to convince yourself of this fact by testing each property with specific examples.

We have now extended our number line in the negative direction, thus increasing the number of points with which we are familiar. If we take any two points on the number line that represent rational numbers, there is always another point between them that represents another rational number. This third number is necessarily greater than one of the first two numbers and less than the other; that is, the third number is necessarily intermediate in value between the first two. Consider, for example, the points labeled 0 and 4. Between them we find points labeled 1, 2, and 3, to name just a few. Consider the points labeled 0 and 1. Between them we find points labeled $\frac{1}{2}$, $\frac{1}{4}$, and $\frac{5}{8}$, again naming just a few.

We can also perform this process without benefit of the number line. For example, between the rational numbers $\frac{1}{4}$ and $\frac{3}{4}$ we find such other rational numbers as $\frac{1}{2}$ and $\frac{5}{8}$. The fact that we can always perform this process is due to the *property of density for rational numbers*.

The **Property of Density for Rational Numbers** states that between any two rational numbers there exists a third rational number of intermediate value.

Not all number systems possess this density property. The whole numbers, for example, do not possess density. By way of illustration, consider the whole numbers 11 and 12; there is no third whole number that falls between 11 and 12. The rational numbers, however, do possess the property of density. Given any two rational numbers, we can always find a third rational number between them. Another way of illustrating this property is to add the two given numbers and divide the sum by 2. For example, given $\frac{1}{5}$ and $\frac{2}{5}$, we know that $\frac{3}{10}$ is between them:

$$\frac{1}{5} + \frac{2}{5} = \frac{3}{5} \quad \text{Adding the two numbers}$$
$$\frac{3}{5} \div 2 = \frac{3}{10} \quad \text{Dividing the sum by 2}$$

Of course, there are also many other rational numbers between $\frac{1}{5}$ and $\frac{2}{5}$.

If you divide some integer by any other nonzero integer, your result will always be a member of the rational number system. That is, any rational number can always be rewritten as the quotient of two integers. There are, however, some numbers that cannot be written as the quotient of two integers. These are called *irrational numbers* and, of course, they are not part of the rational number system. Examples include decimal numbers that neither terminate in a fixed number of places nor repeat a set of digits endlessly. For example, .25, .34, and .666666 . . . are rational numbers because their decimal form either terminates or repeats. However, consider, for example, .12112111211112111112 . . . . This is an irrational number because it is a nonterminating, nonrepeating decimal. It is nonrepeating because each successive 2 has one more 1 immediately preceding it than the preceding 2. Another irrational number is the square root of 2, the number that when multiplied by itself equals 2. The Greek mathematician Pythagoras, or, as some believe, his followers, proved some 2400 years ago that the square root of 2 is not a rational number.

There are also negative irrational numbers; for example, the opposite of the square root of 2, which we write as $-\sqrt{2}$, is an irrational number.

Putting together the rational numbers and the irrational numbers gives us a system called the set of **real numbers**. One of our goals has been to show how number systems are expanded step-by-step and how each move to a larger system allows us to add new numbers and, in many cases, new properties to the previous number system. This development of numberness evolved from practical applications and continues in the fields of pure and applied mathematics. As one example, the extension of the real number system to include a set of numbers called *imaginary numbers* occurred BEFORE there was an application for them in the real world. Only later was it determined that imaginary numbers "behave" in a manner suitable for describing alternating current in electricity.

CLOSURE

We have now considered several different kinds of points on the number line. The easiest method for developing the relationships between the different systems of numbers that we have considered is to draw a diagram, as was shown earlier in the chapter and repeated here. This diagram shows the set of real numbers (the most comprehensive of the systems we have considered) broken down successively into the different kinds of numbers that make up the systems of numbers.

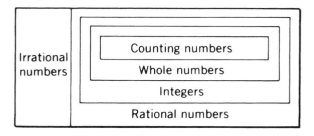

The teaching of the structure of the real number system is begun in grade 1 with the concept of number developed from the real world and leading into the counting numbers. Children are gradually introduced to different number systems through extension of those already encountered. It is not uncommon for children to have explored up to and including the system of real numbers by the time they complete grade 8.

Terminology, Symbols, and Procedures

Addition Property of Opposites. This property states that any two opposites when added have a sum of zero.

$$^{+}3 + {}^{-}3 = 0$$
$$^{+}a + {}^{-}a = 0$$

Composite Number. A composite number is a whole number greater than 1 that has whole number factors other than 1 and itself.

Counting Numbers. The system of counting numbers are the numbers 1, 2, 3, . . . The counting numbers are sometimes referred to as the set of *natural numbers*.

Directed Numbers. Directed numbers are numbers that are expressed by a numeral and a positive ($^{+}$) or negative ($^{-}$) sign. Examples of directed numbers are $^{+}4$, $^{-}15$, $^{-}.714$, $^{+}\frac{3}{5}$, and $^{-}\sqrt{2}$.

Divisible. A number is said to be divisible by another number if a zero is obtained as a remainder when the number is divided by the other number.

Factorization (or **Factoring**). Factorization is the process of expressing a whole number as the product of whole numbers greater than or equal to 1.

Factors. Factors are two or more numbers that, under the operation of multiplication, result in a single, unique number (called the *product*). A first number is a factor of a second number if the first divides evenly into the second. For example, 2 and 3 are factors of 6.

Fractional Number. *Fractional number* is a generalized name commonly reserved for describing fractions greater than zero. That is, fractional numbers are positive and form a subset of the rational numbers.

Fundamental Theorem of Arithmetic. The Fundamental Theorem of Arithmetic states that, except for the order of the factors, a composite number can be expressed as a product of prime numbers in one and only one way. That is, every composite number has a unique factorization into primes.

Greatest Common Factor (GCF). The greatest common factor (GCF) of two whole numbers is the greatest whole number that is a factor of each of the two numbers.

Integers. The integers consist of the counting numbers (positives), their opposites (negatives), and zero.

Irrational Numbers. Irrational numbers are all the real numbers that are not rational. For example, the square root of 2 (that is, the number that when multiplied by itself yields 2) is an irrational number.

Least Common Multiple (LCM). The least common multiple of two whole numbers is the smallest (least) nonzero number that is a multiple of both numbers.

Magnitude (or **Absolute Value**). The magnitude or absolute value of a number is its value without a positive or negative sign. On a number line, it is the unit length of the line segment regardless of direction.

Opposites. Opposites are pairs of numbers corresponding to points on the number line that are equidistant from the zero point, but in different directions from zero. For example, $^+3$ and $^-3$ are opposites. The sum of any pair of opposites is equal to zero. For example, $^+3 + ^-3 = 0$.

Prime Factorization. Prime factorization is the process of expressing a composite number as the product of prime numbers only. For example, $2 \times 2 \times 3 \times 3$ is the prime factorization of 36.

Prime Number. A prime number is a whole number greater than 1 that cannot be expressed as the product of two lesser whole numbers (each greater than 1). A prime number has only two factors, itself and 1. The number 1 is by definition neither prime nor composite. The first ten prime numbers are 2, 3, 5, 7, 11, 13, 17, 19, 23, and 29.

Product. A product is the single, unique number that results from the operation of multiplication on two or more numbers (called *factors*).

Product Expression. A product expression for a number is an expression composed of two or more factors expressed as a multiplication operation. For example, 2×3 is a product expression for 6.

Property of Density for Rational Numbers. This property states that between any two rational numbers there exists a third rational number of intermediate value.

Rational Numbers. The rational numbers are all numbers that can be expressed as the quotient of two integers. Both fractional numbers and the integers themselves are rational numbers. (Don't forget that a number cannot be expressed with zero in the denominator.)

Real Numbers. The real numbers are all numbers that can be represented by points on the number line. The set of real numbers includes all rational numbers (positive numbers, negative numbers, and zero) and all irrational numbers.

Rectangular Array. A rectangular array is an array that has one or more rows and one or more columns. The following are arrays:

Whole Numbers. The whole numbers contain zero and the counting numbers; thus the whole numbers are 0, 1, 2, 3, . . .

Practice Exercises for Teachers

These exercises are designed for the reader of this book. While some are suitable for use in the elementary classroom, these examples should not necessarily be given to children in this form. Ideas for classroom activities on the concepts and ideas discussed in this chapter can be found in Part 2 of *Today's Mathematics*, the Student Resource Book.

1. List all of the whole number factors for each of the following numbers.

   a) 8   b) 17   c) 24   d) 100   e) 10

2. List all possible product expressions containing exactly two factors for each of the following numbers.

   a) 12   b) 27   c) 48   d) 100   e) 10

3. Draw all the possible rectangular arrays for each of the following numbers.

   a) 9   b) 11   c) 10   d) 4

4. List the prime factors for each of the following composite numbers.

   a) 8   b) 14   c) 36   d) 80   e) 41

5. Factor each of the following composite numbers completely (into prime factors).

   a) 28   b) 78   c) 38   d) 92   e) 110

6. Use the principles of divisibility to determine whether each of the following numbers is divisible by 2, 3, or 5.

   a) 99   b) 831   c) 615   d) 118,590   e) 458

7. Twin primes are two prime numbers that have exactly one composite number between them. For example, 3 and 5 are considered to be twin primes. Name all the twin primes between 4 and 100.

8. Determine the greatest common factor for each of the following pairs of numbers.

   a) 372 and 390   b) 168 and 714   c) 340 and 390   d) 80 and 84

9. Determine the least common multiple for each of the following pairs of numbers.

   a) 36 and 60   b) 20 and 42   c) 8 and 14   d) 9 and 15

10. Study the following number sentences:

$$4 = 2 + 2$$
$$6 = 3 + 3$$
$$8 = 5 + 3$$
$$10 = 7 + 3 = 5 + 5$$
$$12 = 7 + 5$$

What kind of numbers do the numerals on the left side of the equal signs represent? Are the addends on the right side of the equal signs prime numbers? Can you formulate a statement that relates this information in the form of a general conjecture?

11. Study the following.

$$2^2 = 4, \text{ which has divisors } 1, 2, 4$$
$$3^2 = 9, \text{ which has divisors } 1, 3, 9$$
$$5^2 = 25, \text{ which has divisors } 1, 5, 25$$
$$7^2 = 49, \text{ which has divisors } 1, 7, 49$$
$$11^2 = 121, \text{ which has divisors } 1, 11, 121$$

See if you can devise a general formula that summarizes the apparent pattern. Use your formula to determine the divisors of 169.

12. A number is called *perfect* if it is the sum of all the numbers (except itself) that divide it. For example, 6 is a perfect number because $6 = 1 + 2 + 3$, where 1, 2, and 3 are divisors of 6. Find another perfect number between 6 and 35.

13. Name six different number systems, and list several subsets of each.

14. Name the opposite of each of the following numbers.

   a) $^{+}2$ b) $^{-}3$ c) 0
   d) $^{-}\frac{1}{4}$ e) $^{-}\frac{2}{3}$ f) $^{+}217$
   g) $^{-}43$ h) $^{-}47$ i) $^{+}73$
   j) $^{-}49$ k) $^{-}\frac{7}{8}$ l) $^{-}\frac{14}{23}$

15. Draw a number line model for each of the following examples, and name the sum.

   a) $^{+}3 + {}^{-}2 = \square$ b) $^{-}5 + {}^{+}2 = \square$
   c) $^{-}4 + {}^{-}5 = \square$ d) $^{+}7 + {}^{-}3 = \square$
   e) $^{+}6 + {}^{+}2 = \square$ f) $^{-}8 + {}^{+}5 = \square$
   g) $^{-}2 + {}^{-}4 = \square$ h) $^{+}1 + {}^{-}6 = \square$

16. Solve each of the following addition examples.

    a) $^-43 + {}^+17 = \square$ b) $^-57 + {}^-78 = \square$ c) $^+61 + {}^-56 = \square$
    d) $^-83 + {}^+69 = \square$ e) $^+47 + {}^+34 = \square$ f) $^-92 + {}^-89 = \square$
    g) $^-68 + {}^+73 = \square$ h) $^-37 + {}^-53 = \square$ i) $^+48 + {}^-84 = \square$

17. Draw a number line model for each of the following examples, and name the missing addend.

    a) $^+7 - {}^-8 = \square$ b) $^-4 - {}^-3 = \square$
    c) $^-6 - {}^+2 = \square$ d) $^-9 - {}^+3 = \square$
    e) $^-1 - {}^-8 = \square$ f) $^+4 - {}^-7 = \square$

18. Solve each of the following subtraction examples.

    a) $^-24 - {}^-42 = \square$ b) $^-51 - {}^+68 = \square$
    c) $^+23 - {}^-19 = \square$ d) $^-73 - {}^+91 = \square$
    e) $^+86 - {}^-27 = \square$ f) $^+39 - {}^+93 = \square$

19. Using the rules for multiplying integers, solve each of the following examples.

    a) $^+7 \times {}^-9 = \square$ b) $^-8 \times {}^+6 = \square$ c) $^-9 \times {}^-6 = \square$
    d) $^-43 \times {}^-17 = \square$ e) $^-32 \times {}^-23 = \square$ f) $^-47 \times {}^-18 = \square$
    g) $^-68 \times {}^+42 = \square$ h) $^+53 \times {}^+65 = \square$ i) $^-85 \times {}^-19 = \square$
    j) $^-39 \times {}^+17 = \square$ k) $^+74 \times {}^-51 = \square$ l) $^-67 \times {}^+37 = \square$

20. Solve each of the following division examples.

    a) $^-48 \div {}^+6 = \square$ b) $^+72 \div {}^+9 = \square$ c) $^-63 \div {}^-7 = \square$
    d) $^-42 \div {}^-7 = \square$ e) $^-69 \div {}^-3 = \square$ f) $^-144 \div {}^+6 = \square$
    g) $^-72 \div {}^-4 = \square$ h) $^+84 \div {}^-12 = \square$ i) $^+98 \div {}^-14 = \square$
    j) $^-204 \div {}^-34 = \square$ k) $^-208 \div {}^+26 = \square$ l) $^+378 \div {}^-42 = \square$

21. Solve the following examples selected from the system of real numbers.

    a) $^+\frac{3}{4} \times {}^-\frac{7}{8} = \square$ b) $^-\frac{5}{6} \div {}^-\frac{2}{3} = \square$ c) $^-.8 \times {}^-.06 = \square$
    d) $^-.96 \div {}^+1.2 = \square$ e) $^-\frac{3}{5} + {}^-\frac{5}{9} = \square$ f) $^+7.8 - {}^-.21 = \square$
    g) $^+\frac{7}{8} - {}^+\frac{2}{3} = \square$ h) $^-3.41 + {}^+2.9 = \square$ i) $^-\frac{5}{8} \times {}^-\frac{4}{15} = \square$
    j) $^-1.84 \div {}^+2.3 = \square$ k) $^+2.03 - {}^+1.45 = \square$ l) $^+\frac{9}{13} + {}^-\frac{2}{7} = \square$

22. Suppose that we use letters to designate the following systems of numbers we have studied.

    A = counting numbers   E = rational numbers
    B = whole numbers   F = irrational numbers
    C = integers   G = real numbers
    D = fractional numbers

    a) Which of these contain all of the others in the list?
    b) Which of these does *not* contain A?
    c) Which of these contain E?
    d) Which of these are contained in E?
    e) Which of these have $^-\left(\frac{2}{3}\right)$ as an element?
    f) In which is division by zero possible?

Teaching Competencies and Self-Assessment Tasks

1. Draw a picture using arrays to show why 21 is not considered to be a prime number but 13 is prime. Relate the argument using arrays to the abstract definition of a prime number as "a number greater than 1 with only 1 and itself as factors."

2. Discuss why 1 is not a prime number.

3. Identify at least two methods of convincing children that zero is an even number.

4. Discuss how a student might know whether a sum will be even or odd without actually adding the addends.

5. Discuss the collection of numbers having an odd number of factors. Make a generalization about these numbers.

6. A child has some blocks with values of either 2, 3, 5, or 7 written on them. You don't know how many blocks the child has, but you do know that the product of the values of the blocks is 126. What are the values of the individual blocks? How many blocks does the child have?

7. Describe the relationship between least common multiple (LCM) and least common denominator (LCD). In what way is this relationship similar to the relationship between greatest common divisor (GCD) and greatest common factor (GCF)? In what way is it different?

8. A student excitedly states that there is a relationship between the least common multiple (LCM) and greatest common factor (GCF) of two numbers and the two numbers themselves. If you multiply the LCM and GCF of two numbers, you get the same product as when you multiply the two numbers. Does this always work? How would you explain this?

9. What is the least (smallest) whole number that is divisible by 1, 2, 3, 4, 5, 6, 7, 8, and 9? How do you verify this?

10. If you have determined that 35,694 is divisible by 9, how can you *quickly* tell if 49,653 is divisible by 9? What about 96,534? 56,349? 69,345? 6,345?

11. Use both the number line and the "chip-matching" method to illustrate addition and subtraction of integers. Compare the advantages and disadvantages of these two methods of modeling integer operations.

12. Describe the relationship of the integers to the operation of subtraction. What problems are encountered by using the "take-away" model of subtraction for integers on a number line? Does the "missing addends" model suggested in this chapter work for whole numbers? Discuss the advantages and disadvantages of using only one approach to modeling subtraction for all number systems.

13. Using a reference book, locate the height of the tallest mountain in the world (Mt. Everest) and the depth of the deepest ocean (Pacific Ocean—Mariana Trench). Which of these varies most from sea level? Relate the discussion to integers.

14. Locate a copy of Dr. Marijane Werner's book, *Teaching the Set of Integers to Elementary School Children*. Discuss the variety of suggested teaching techniques.

15. Some mathematics educators suggest that, following the structures of mathematics, integers should be taught before rational numbers. Each member of the class should take a stand either supporting or rejecting this statement, and debate the question in class.

16. Examine standardized achievement tests for children. Itemize the number of examples related to each system of numbers defined in this chapter. Discuss the appropriateness of the distribution of examples.

17. Discuss the points on the number line in relation to the rational numbers, irrational numbers, and integers.

18. Define the terms *integers*, *rational number*, and *real numbers*.

19. Locate and describe materials that can be used for the concrete development of number theory.

20. Examine elementary school mathematics textbooks. How and when are integers introduced? Have a class discussion on the merits of teaching integers in the elementary classroom.

21. Research the literature, and provide evidence to support teaching integers to elementary school children.

22. Discuss the dot pictures that can be drawn for square numbers and triangular numbers and the relationships between these dot pictures and the patterns they represent.

23. Locate and study Goldbach's Conjecture; then present your findings to the class.

Related Readings and Teacher Resources

For related readings on topics found in this chapter, see the corresponding chapter in Part 2 of *Today's Mathematics*, the Student Resource Book.

AN ORANGE KANGAROO IN DENMARK
(OR, PERHAPS, AN AQUA KOALA IN DENMARK)
(See the riddle at the beginning of this chapter)

Chapter 10

Algebraic Reasoning: Generalizing Patterns and Relationships

Teaching Competencies

Upon completing this chapter, you will be able to:

- Formulate a definition of algebraic reasoning and describe several purposes for the need to develop algebraic reasoning in elementary school mathematics programs.

- Outline the major algebra concepts that are developed throughout a child's elementary school experiences.

- Give examples of the types of experiences that children in elementary school might have that will help them develop algebraic thinking.

- Explain how early explorations of patterns can lay a foundation for the study of more abstract algebra concepts.

- Demonstrate how to use concrete materials to illustrate equation-solving and expression-simplifying processes.

- Explain the rule for a pattern by using multiple representations, including a verbal pattern, a table, a graph, or an algebraic expression or equation.

- Describe the development of the use of variables in elementary school mathematics programs.

- Design instructional activities that promote algebraic thinking in ways appropriate for elementary school children.

O ne train leaves New York at 3:30 P.M. and another leaves Chicago at 4:15 P.M. If the first train is traveling at a speed of 55 mph. . . ." Had enough yet? Think back to your experiences with learning algebra. What do you remember? Many adults recall taking an algebra course in grade 9 that included the study of solving equations, factoring, and working with complicated fraction expressions. It may have also involved the solving of "different types" of word problems, from age and coin and mixture problems to questions about trains traveling in different directions at different speeds.

From a contemporary view of elementary school mathematics, we view the development of algebraic thought as a meaningful and gradual process, requiring exposure to a variety of algebra-related problems every year that a child is in school. If we believe that the development of number sense is important enough to include in the curriculum every year to develop it over time, then algebraic reasoning should be included in the curriculum every year to develop it over time as well. The key is to present activities to children that are developmentally appropriate as they construct an understanding of algebra.

THE CONTENT OF ALGEBRA

Algebra can be thought of as the process of generalizing, abstracting, and representing functions and relationships. It can also be viewed as the study of mathematical structure and as a language for conveying and applying that structure. Algebra can further be thought of as a language that explores unknowns, placeholders, formulas, relationships, and generalizations.

The NCTM *Principles and Standards for School Mathematics* (2000) describes a vision of algebra that should be developed for all children in grades preK–8 as follows:* Instructional programs from prekindergarten through grade 12 should enable all students to—

■ understand patterns, relations, and functions;
■ represent and analyze mathematical situations and structures using algebraic symbols;
■ use mathematical models to represent and understand quantitative relationships;
■ analyze change in various contexts.

This algebra standard acknowledges the importance of students' exploring patterns and relationships as a foundation for algebraic thinking. The fundamental elements of the algebra standard are reflected in the following expectations for the grade levels of PreK–2, 3–5, and 6–8.

Algebra Standard

PreK–2 Expectations

In prekindergarten through grade 2 all students should—

* Reprinted with permission from the *Principles and Standards for School Mathematics*, copyright 2000 by the National Council of Teachers of Mathematics.

■ sort, classify, and order objects by size, number, and other properties;
■ recognize, describe, and extend patterns such as sequences of sounds and shapes or simple numeric patterns and translate from one representation to another;
■ analyze how both repeating and growing patterns are generated;
■ illustrate general principles and properties of operations, such as commutativity, using specific numbers;
■ use concrete, pictorial, and verbal representations to develop an understanding of invented and conventional symbolic notations;
■ model situations that involve the addition and subtraction of whole numbers, using objects, pictures, and symbols;
■ describe qualitative change, such as a student's growing taller;
■ describe quantitative change, such as a student's growing two inches in one year.

Grades 3–5 Expectations

In grades 3–5 all students should—

■ describe, extend, and make generalizations about geometric and numeric patterns;
■ represent and analyze patterns and functions, using words, tables, and graphs;
■ identify such properties as commutativity, associativity, and distributivity and use them to compute with whole numbers;
■ represent the idea of a variable as an unknown quantity using a letter or a symbol;
■ express mathematical relationships using equations;
■ model problem situations with objects and use representations such as graphs, tables, and equations to draw conclusions;
■ investigate how a change in one variable relates to a change in a second variable;
■ identify and describe situations with constant or varying rates of change and compare them.

Grades 6–8 Expectations

In grades 6–8 all students should—

■ represent, analyze, and generalize a variety of patterns with tables, graphs, words, and, when possible, symbolic rules;
■ relate and compare different forms of representation for a relationship;
■ identify functions as linear or nonlinear and contrast their properties from tables, graphs, or equations;
■ develop an initial conceptual understanding of different uses of variables;
■ explore relationships between symbolic expressions and graphs of lines, paying particular attention to the meaning of intercept and slope;
■ use symbolic algebra to represent situations and to solve problems, especially those that involve linear relationships;

Research Snapshot

What does research say about the experiences of teachers that follow NCTM reform documents and focus the teaching of algebra on conceptual understanding, using functions to develop the concept of variables?

In a case study of a ninth-grade teacher of introductory algebra, Haimes (1996) found that the actions of the teacher in the implementation of the "function" curriculum did not reflect the intended teaching approach of the curriculum. The intended curriculum emphasized conceptual understanding and process skills, promoting problem solving, applications, and the use of student-centered activities. The teacher focused on curriculum content coverage and emphasized rules and procedures using teacher-centered pedagogy.

The teacher's beliefs about algebra and teaching algebra were the most powerful influences on her teaching. Her own prior experiences as a student and a teacher reinforced the importance of methods and procedures.

Do the results of this study surprise you? Would your answer change if the mathematics content area that was taught were not algebra?

Haimes, D. H. (1996). The implementation of a "function" approach to introductory algebra: A case study of teacher cognitions, teacher actions, and the intended curriculum. *Journal for Research in Mathematics Education*, 27, 582–602.

For additional research briefs, "ERIC Digests" lets you search more than 2,000 short syntheses of research on a range of education topics. The syntheses were produced by the Educational Resources Information Center (ERIC). Check http://ed.gov/databases/ERIC_Digests/index/

- recognize and generate equivalent forms for simple algebraic expressions and solve linear equations;
- model and solve contextualized problems using various representations, such as graphs, tables, and equations;
- use graphs to analyze the nature of changes in quantities in linear relationships.

A contemporary view of algebraic thinking is that it should not be a topic relegated solely to a high school course. Instead, algebraic reasoning is a gradual process of developing the use of algebra across grade levels. The teacher should utilize activities that allow students to make connections among major aspects such as:

1. patterns and models
2. variables
3. exponents
4. graphing
5. functions

At the elementary level, the use of concrete discovery should be emphasized over abstract algorithms, and numerous teaching activities should be used across the grade levels. If prerequisite material is considered and if the content is presented in a manner that is developmentally appropriate, then even the youngest school children can grasp the underlying concepts of algebra. This thinking is not entirely new, however. Barber (1932), for example, argued for the inclusion of algebra topics in the elementary and middle grades more than 70 years ago!

ALGEBRA IN PROBLEM SOLVING

Let us turn our attention to the types of activities that allow for the development of algebraic thinking in the elementary grades.

Consider the following problem:

- A teacher administers a 5-question true-false quiz to a class. Suppose that a student had been absent for several days and simply guessed on each quiz item. How likely is it that the student would get all 5 questions correct?

A number of approaches can be used to solve this problem. First, each student in the class might simply take a piece of paper, number it from 1 to 5, and randomly place a T or an F by each number. Then, by comparing student responses to the teacher's answer key, the class can count the number of times that a student "answered" all of the questions correctly. This experimental approach can be used to provide a basis on which to explore the problem in a more theoretical manner.

A second approach to this problem would be for a student to make a systematic list of all of the possible answer keys. By taking five slips of paper with "T" written on one side and "F" written on the other, a student can arrange and rearrange them on a desk and record the various keys (different combinations) that could be formed. For example:

Students should determine a strategy for systematically laying out the pieces to ensure that all of the keys are listed. For example, they might begin by listing all of the answer keys that have only one True answer (e.g., TFFFF, FTFFF, FFTFF, FFFTF, and FFFFT) and then move on to those keys that have exactly two true answers, and so on.

A third approach to this problem might involve the use of the strategy of solving the simpler problem. In this case, the student might ask, "What if the quiz only had one question?" In this case, the quiz would have only two possible keys—T or F. If the quiz had two questions, then four keys could be formed—TT, TF, FT, or FF. A quiz with three questions would have eight keys. (Can you list them?) Then, noticing a pattern, a table could be constructed to represent the data collected so far:

Number of Quiz Items	Number of Answer Keys
1	2
2	4
3	8

At this point, students might notice two things: (1) the number of answer keys doubles with each new quiz item added, and (2) the numbers in the "Number of Answer Keys" column are all powers of two. An interesting discussion should occur as students explain why the number of answer keys appears to double each time. Looking at this in a different way, each time a new item is added, the list of answer keys would include all of the previous keys with a "True" added to the end of each key and all of the previous keys with a "False" added to the end of each key—exactly twice as many as there were at the beginning.

Using this logic and extending the pattern, students can determine that the number of possible answer keys for a 4-item quiz would be 16, and for a 5-item quiz, it would be 32. Therefore, the chances of guessing all 5 items correctly is $\frac{1}{32}$—about 3% of the time. At this point, the students could take the data and put it into a graphical form, as follows:

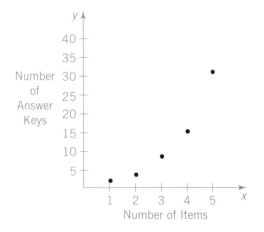

Notice that the values on the x-axis represent the number of items on the quiz, and the y-values represent the possible number of answer keys that can be constructed. Students should recognize that the graph does not represent a **linear function** (the points do not lie in a straight line) and that as x-values get larger, the y-values get larger at a greater rate each time.

This same notion is central to understanding how compound interest works: The amount of money earned from interest on an investment in the first few years may be relatively small, but after 20 or 30 years, the interest can make the initial investment grow to a surprisingly large amount. For example, an investment of $5,000 at 9% interest compounded annually will earn only $450 in the first year but will grow to over $28,000 in 20 years and over $66,000 in 30 years. Solving problems involving compound interest is likely to be less confusing in high school if the student has had experiences with problems such as the Answer Key problem in elementary school.

If students recognize that the "Number of Answer Keys" column is a power of two, then they may be able to generalize the formula for "x" items on the quiz.

Number of Quiz Items	Number of Answer Keys	Power of Two
1	2	2^1
2	4	2^2
3	8	2^3
x	y	2^x

By making this variable representation, students can quickly determine not only the solution to the original problem, but they can also generalize the solution for quizzes with even more questions. For example, the chances of guessing all 10 items correctly on a true-false quiz is less than 1 in 1000, and the chances of guessing all 20 items correctly on a true-false quiz is less than 1 in 1,000,000!

Similarly, the student can generalize the result to the following "new" problem:

> Suppose that the teacher decided to give a 5-question multiple-choice quiz instead, with each item having 5 possible choices. How likely would it be to guess all 5 of these answers correctly?

In this case, the student could decide to simply compute 5^5 to find that there are 3125 possible answer keys. Students will see that the benefit of the algebraic solutions of graphing and writing an equation such as $y = 2^x$ is that the solutions can be used to generalize the problem and, consequently, solve other, related problems. The systematic construction of a table is often an integral part of the generalization process.

Let's consider how this problem parallels the content strands suggested previously. Solving the Answer Key problem called for the systematic listing of quiz items and numbers of answer keys to determine a pattern and to develop a mathematical model. When the pattern was generalized into the expression 2^x, a variable expression was developed. A **variable** is a symbol that represents a number or set of numbers in an expression or an equation. This particular problem also dealt with the proper use of exponents. Also, the data from the table was translated into a series of points that could be graphed.

Finally, the Answer Key problem involved a function, $y = 2^x$. A **function** is a rule that assigns exactly one value in a set to a given value in another set. In our case, for example, "2" was associated with "4," since 2 questions generate 4 answer keys. Similarly, "5" is associated to "32," in that a 5-item quiz produces 32 possible answer keys. We could say, therefore, that the number of answer keys "is a function of" the number of items on the quiz. When we describe functions, we discuss how changes in one value bring about changes in the other value, a basic concept that is fundamental to the study of algebra.

Furthermore, a function generally consists of an **independent variable** and a **dependent variable**. The value of the dependent variable "depends on" the value of the independent variable. In our example, the dependent variable would be the number of answer keys because it depends on the number of items asked on the quiz.

The preceding problem allows children to design multiple representations, including verbal, using a table, drawing a graph, and writing an equation with variables. In summary, a problem that is rich in mathematical content can be used to develop the type of algebraic thinking described in NCTM's *Principles and Standards for School Mathematics*.

PROMOTING ALGEBRAIC THINKING IN THE LOWER ELEMENTARY GRADES

In the primary grades, it is important that children develop a sense of "if this happens, then the result will be . . ." as they work toward developing basic patterning skills. Linking literature to mathematics, teachers can make use of children's books that describe situations such as, "Cats have fur. Fluffy is a cat. So . . . ," which allows children to consider a given condition and draw conclusions based on it. Additional information on the nature and development of logical reasoning can be found in Chapter 5.

The analysis of simple patterns is also critical to the development of algebraic thinking in the early primary years. Reasoning skills are being developed anytime a child works with a set of manipulatives and creates a pattern that another student must extend and explain. For example, using play money, a child might lay out the following sequence on her desk:

A partner might explain, for example, that a dime might come next because the pattern quarter—dime—dime—quarter seems to have been established. Not only should students become proficient at naming the next term in a sequence, but they should also be required to verbalize the pattern that has been recognized (e.g., "If a quarter is laid down, then two dimes always come next, so the next coin in this pattern has to be a dime").

With the use of concrete materials, children can also generate patterns that connect algebra with other content areas. For example, a child has an oyster cracker that is the shape of a hexagon and lays it on the desk. The perimeter of the cracker is 6 units, as it has 6 equal sides "exposed." Have the child then place two and then three of the crackers side-by-side so that the crackers share a side, as shown in the figure. The child should continue to determine the perimeter of the figure.

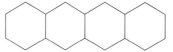

Students should be able to count to determine that the distance around one cracker is 6 units, but when two are joined together, the total perimeter is 10 units. They should notice and be able to communicate that the perimeter is not 12 units, because two of the sides are touching one another and are no longer part of the perimeter of the shape. Taking the data from several examples and putting it into a table yields the following result:

Number of Crackers	Perimeter
1	6
2	10
3	14
4	18

The children should then be asked to predict the perimeter of a shape that is made up of five or ten crackers. They should recognize that the "rule" being applied here is that each cracker adds 4 to the perimeter. This rule by which the "Perimeter" changes as the "Number of Crackers" changes describes the function in this problem. We would say that the perimeter is a function of the number of crackers. The number of crackers is the independent variable, and the perimeter is the dependent variable, although we would not generally use this terminology with elementary school children.

Functions can be explored in other ways in the lower grades. Have students draw a vertical line down the center of a blank piece of paper and lay cubes on each side of the line—8 cubes on the left side and 5 cubes on the right, as shown:

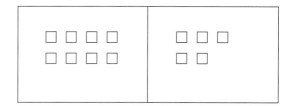

Children should be challenged to "compare what you see on the two sides of the line." Responses might include the following:

- ■ The right side is three less than the left.
- ■ The right side is the left side minus three.
- ■ The left side is three more than the right.

- The left side is the right side plus three.
- The number of cubes on the left is greater than the number of cubes on the right.
- The number of cubes on the right is less than the number of cubes on the left.

Now ask the children to place 4 cubes on the left and 1 cube on the right. They should recognize this as another example of the same rule. Then you can ask the children to tell how many cubes would be on the right if there were, for example, 7 cubes on the left. During this exploration, children are attempting to apply an observed rule and extend it to other situations—a key concept in the study of algebra.

The data for the number of cubes can also be put into a table:

Number on the Left	Number on the Right
4	1
5	_____
6	_____
7	_____
8	5
_____	8

Children can be encouraged to identify and apply a rule to fill in the blanks in the table. Eventually, children should be encouraged to use variables to express a rule describing the relationship, such as $L = R - 3$ or $R + 3 = L$, where R is the number on the right, and L is the number on the left.

The issue of getting children comfortable with the use of variables at the lower grades is not to be taken lightly. A recent study showed that nearly 9 out of 10 ninth graders could "solve" the equation $\square - 6 = 9$, but when the problem was expressed as $x - 6 = 9$, only half of the same students could find the value of x! In other words, it was not the difficulty of the problem but the unfamiliarity with variable notation that scared off even high school students. Children need exposure to working with variables throughout their academic careers to avoid the development of an attitude that algebra is too difficult.

Algebraic thinking can also be promoted while working with basic addition facts. Suppose that a child were to be given a family of facts, such as the "7 family." All of the facts that make up the 7 family can be systematically listed: $0 + 7, 1 + 6, 2 + 5, 3 + 4, 4 + 3, 5 + 2, 6 + 1,$ and $7 + 0$. Then, each of these facts can be viewed as coordinates of points that can be graphed. The points are $(0, 7), (1, 6), (2, 5), (3, 4), (4, 3), (5, 2), (6, 1),$ and $(7, 0)$. Placing these points on a coordinate grid would yield a graph similar to the one at the top of the next column.

Children should be asked to describe what they see. They should note that the points are linear—that is, if connected they form a straight line. Children can explore other families, such as the families of 5s or 12s, to list them in order and graph the facts to find out if they are also linear. They can also discuss the fact that $3 + 4$ and $4 + 3$ represent different points on the graph

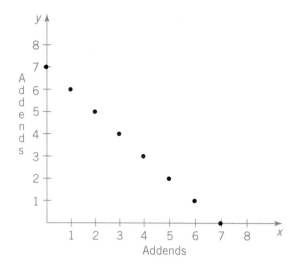

but yield the same result. Finally, children can make a list of the "fact families" and the number of facts in each family to form a table such as this:

Fact Family	Number of Facts	
0	1	$(0 + 0)$
1	2	$(1 + 0, 0 + 1)$
2	3	$(2 + 0, 1 + 1, 0 + 2)$
3	4	$(3 + 0, 2 + 1, 1 + 2, 0 + 3)$
4	5	$(4 + 0, 3 + 1, 2 + 2, 1 + 3, 0 + 4)$

Children can use this table to predict the number of facts in, say, the 10 family and then list them to verify their conjecture. Finally, children can generalize the result to determine that for the "n" family, $n + 1$ facts can be listed.

Similar patterns can be explored in the upper primary grades by exploring multiplication and looking at factors of given numbers. The point here is that some very powerful algebraic skills can be developed in the context of exploration of what we consider "basic facts" in mathematics. In the process, children get additional practice with basic facts and may be more likely to memorize those facts that are a challenge more effectively and efficiently.

Another technique frequently used in elementary school for the study of functions is the **function machine**. A function machine can easily be constructed by taking cardboard and cutting a circle and a square with small slits above and below each shape as shown:

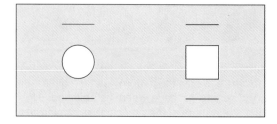

Also, several strips of heavy stock paper should be made so that they can be inserted in the slits and slid behind the cut-out shapes. Then, numbers should be written on the strips so that, for example, when the circle shows a "3," the square displays a "5," and when the circle shows a "6," the square displays an "8." This construction is called a *function machine* because it displays pairs of numbers—the one showing through the circle is the input, and the one displayed through the square is the output.

The role of the student is then to explain a rule that the machine is following to make each input into an output. For the example described above, a rule might be that "the square is the circle number plus two." By using several strips, a teacher can challenge a class or small group of children to determine a rule that makes the input value into the output. The function machine helps children to analyze functions and patterns and to become familiar with the use of variables to describe the models.

By engaging in activities like the ones described in this section, children in the lower elementary grades gain considerable exposure to and practice in algebraic thinking. Developmentally appropriate methods allow children to reason and communicate patterns through the use of activities that utilize concrete materials. These early experiences then set the tone and lay the groundwork for more advanced algebraic reasoning problems in the upper elementary and middle grades.

ENHANCING ALGEBRAIC THINKING IN THE UPPER ELEMENTARY AND MIDDLE GRADES

In the upper elementary grades, children explore and extend the notions of patterns, variables, exponents, graphing, and functions. The problems posed continue to emphasize the reasoning that is involved in representing problems in a variety of ways. Children should become more familiar with the use of variables and should also explore functions that are nonlinear. Simple equation-solving processes and mathematical properties should also be developed in these grades. In this section, we will explore some examples of the problems and teaching strategies that can be used in the upper elementary and middle grades.

Consider the following problem:

▪ Each student in the class is given a rectangular piece of paper. Ask the students, "How many rectangles do you see?" Then, have them fold the paper in half, and repeat the question. Have them put one more fold in the paper, and ask the question again. Finally, have them fold the paper a third time, and ask the question one last time. Record the data in a table and predict how many rectangles you would be able to count if the paper were folded ten times.

Of course, the piece of paper with no folds forms one rectangle. After folding the paper one time, there are three rectangles—the original rectangle and two,

smaller rectangles. Folding the paper again, the sheet would look like this:

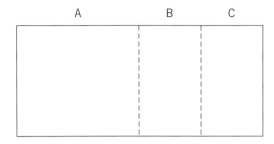

How many rectangles do you see? If you take each of the pieces A, B, and C by themselves, there are three rectangles. Then, there is a rectangle that contains both A and B and one that contains both B and C. Finally, there is the rectangle with which we started, the one made up of all three—this gives a total of six rectangles. Now, suppose you fold the paper one more time so that there are three folds and four "sections" formed. You should find ten rectangles. (Did you?)

The collected data can be placed in a table, as shown:

Number of Folds	Number of Rectangles
0	1
1	3
2	6
3	10

After putting the data in the table, allow students to predict how many rectangles would be formed after a fourth fold by asking them to verbalize any patterns that they see. Typically, children recognize that the difference between 1 and 3 is 2; the difference between 3 and 6 is 3; and the difference between 6 and 10 is 4; so they speculate that the next number in the sequence might be 5 greater, or 15. Ask them to fold the paper once more and count the rectangles to verify their conjectures.

At this point, children should have worked with the pattern of numbers enough to be able to use a calculator to determine the number of rectangles formed when the paper has ten folds. As was discussed earlier in this chapter, students can then take the values in the table and plot them on a graph, with the x-axis representing number of folds and the y-axis representing the number of rectangles, as shown on the next page.

When asked to describe what they see, children should acknowledge that the graph is not linear because the y-value increases by more and more each time the x-value is increased. Finding the equation of a function that is nonlinear is much more difficult than for linear functions. At the upper grades, children should be challenged to determine the equation that relates the x- and y-values in the table and on the graph. In this case, the equation is rather complicated, $y = \frac{(x+1)(x+2)}{2}$, but careful and deliberate analysis of the table or graph may lead students to it.

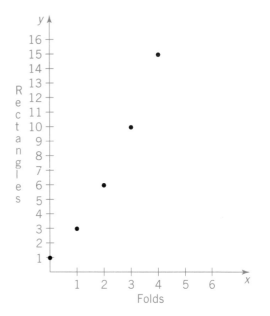

This paper-folding problem allows students to explore a nonlinear set of data points through a hands-on procedure that is used to generate a table. Subsequent discussions can center on drawing a graph and looking for patterns to determine an equation for the function. As with the True-False Quiz problem discussed earlier in this chapter, the paper-folding puzzle emphasizes the multiple representations of a function and gives students practice in going back and forth between raw data, a table, a graph, and an equation, all of which describe the function.

Students in the upper elementary grades should also begin to develop equation-solving processes through informal means. One way to explore equation solving is to present a situation such as the following to students:

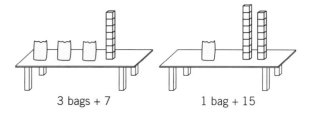

| 3 bags + 7 | 1 bag + 15 |

Students are told that:

1. There are an equal number of cubes on each table.
2. There are an equal number of cubes in each bag.

Unfortunately, we don't know how many cubes are on each table, because we can see only those that are not in the bags. The problem is to determine how many cubes must be in each bag.

There are a number of ways in which students might solve this problem. The most common is to compare the stack of 7 cubes on the left table to the stack of 15 cubes on the right and to deduce that there are 8 more cubes "showing" on the right-hand table. Since each bag has the same number of cubes, the 8 "extra"

cubes on the right must be balanced with the cubes in two of the bags on the left. We know that each bag contains the same number of cubes, so each bag must contain 4 cubes, and the problem is solved.

In symbols, this problem could have been written as:

$$3x + 7 = x + 15$$

Traditionally, in a first-year algebra course, we solve this type of problem by using the following procedure:

$3x + 7$	$= x + 15$		$3x + 7$	$= x + 15$
$3x + 7 - x = x + 15 - x$			$3x + 7 - 7 = x + 15 - 7$	
$2x + 7$	$= 15$	OR	$3x$	$= x + 8$
$2x + 7 - 7 = 15 - 7$			$3x - x$	$= x - x + 8$
$2x$	$= 8$		$2x$	$= 8$
x	$= 4$		x	$= 4$

This method does yield a result for the number of cubes in each bag but requires a much higher level of abstraction to follow the procedure. By using the bags and cubes, children explore the processes involved with equation solving long before they actually put a pencil to paper and "solve for x."

One of the most powerful manipulatives for exploring equations and expressions is a set of **algebra tiles**. A set of algebra tiles typically contains at least three different shapes with the following dimensions and values:

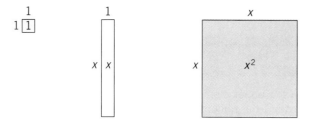

This concrete representation uses an area model—the area of the small square with dimensions 1 by 1 is 1; the rectangle has dimensions 1 by x and an area of x; and the large square has dimensions x by x and an area of x^2. With these tiles, a number of algebraic processes can be readily illustrated.

Suppose that students were to solve the following equation:

$$4x + 5 = 3x + 9$$

They would begin by using a mat with a line drawn down the center representing the equals sign. With the algebra tiles, they would represent the quantities shown on each side of the line:

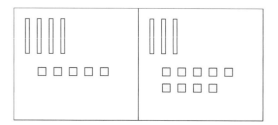

Because both sides of the paper are "in balance," students may remove any tiles they wish from each side, provided that they keep both sides in balance by removing the same number from each side. In a very concrete way, they can "remove" 5 squares and 3 rectangles from each side of the sheet, leaving a rectangle on the left side and 4 squares on the right. Therefore, the "*x*" tile stood for 4 tiles, and *x* = 4 is the solution to the equation.

Suppose that the problem had been the following:

$$2(x + 3) = 10$$

In this case, the students would lay out the tiles on their mats as shown:

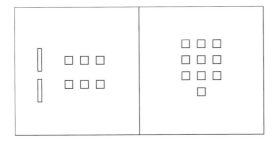

In laying out the tiles on the mat, students meaningfully apply one of the most important mathematical structures used in algebra—the distributive property, described in Chapter 8. Clearly, 2(*x* + 3) means to repeat *x* + 3 twice and results in a total of 2*x* + 6 (and children don't need to be told this as a rule in algebra). After the tiles are laid out, the children can remove 6 squares from each side and complete the problem by splitting the remaining squares on the right into two piles, since they represent two "*x*" values:

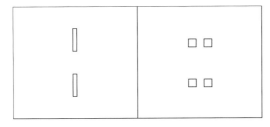

Again, if the student were to use a purely symbolic method of solving this equation, it would look like this:

$$2(x + 3) = 10$$
$$2x + 6 = 10$$
$$2x + 6 - 6 = 10 - 6$$
$$2x = 4$$
$$x = 2$$

But younger children still operating at a concrete-operational stage can solve the same problem with algebra tiles. Later, students can draw pictures of their tiles as they move from the concrete to the pictorial stage, and eventually, the tiles can give way to pure symbolic manipulation. More advanced students who are working with positive and negative numbers can use tiles of

two different colors—one to represent positives and one to represent negatives—and use similar hands-on methods to solve algebraic equations. Some sets of algebra tiles also come with tiles that represent another variable, "*y*," as well as y^2 and *xy*.

When solving equations by using algebra tiles, it is extremely important that students verbalize throughout the process what they are doing and why they are doing it. They should be saying, "I am trying to find what number the *x* tile equals, so, I need to get the *x* tile by itself on one side of the line." This focuses the student on the goal of symbolic equation manipulation before a move from the concrete level to the pictorial and the abstract level is made.

Algebra tiles can also be useful for teaching children how to multiply expressions that involve variables. An effective way to represent a multiplication fact such as 4 × 5 is to picture a rectangle that is 4 units by 5 units, having an area of 20 square units:

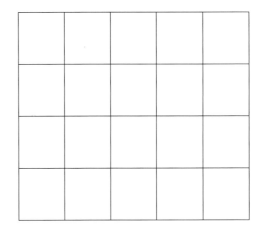

Also, children may have already had experiences with modeling the multiplication of two-digit numbers with base ten blocks. For example, the following model shows the four multiplications that are required to determine 12 × 14:

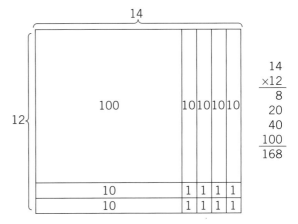

$$12 \times 14 = (10 \times 10) + (2 \times 10) + (4 \times 10) + (2 \times 4)$$
$$= 100 + 20 + 40 + 8$$
$$= 168$$

Similarly, children can explore the multiplication of **polynomials** by using an area model. A polynomial is the sum of one or more algebraic expressions that are sometimes referred to as monomials or terms. Examples of polynomials include $y + 6$, $-7 + 3n$, $x^2 + 4x - 2$, $3x + 5y + 1$, and so on. Suppose that the child needed to multiply $(x + 5)$ and $(x + 3)$. In this case, the tiles would be arranged so that a rectangle is formed whose length is $x + 3$ and whose height is $x + 5$, as shown:

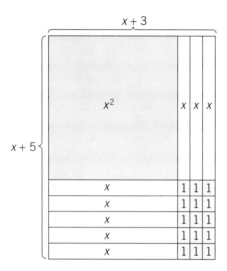

In high school algebra many of us memorized this procedure for multiplying polynomials as the FOIL method—First $(x \cdot x)$, Outside $(x \cdot 3)$, Inside $(5 \cdot x)$, and Last $(5 \cdot 3)$—without having any idea why the method required these four multiplications. By using the algebra tiles, students can make a connection not only to area but to previous learning about multiplying two-digit numbers. There is no need to memorize an abstract procedure here because the process in algebra is a logical extension and abstraction of something that children should already know from the study of arithmetic multiplication.

Children can also explore number puzzles by using their algebra tiles. Suppose that a teacher asks the class the following:

■ Think of a number. Add 5 to the number. Double the result. Subtract 4 from this answer. Divide by 2. Subtract the number that you started with. I can read your mind—your final number is 3!

Actually, the final number will always be 3, and students will quickly realize this. But why? What is going on here? By using algebra tiles and then symbol manipulation, students can model the problem-solving process. The sequence of six steps with algebra tiles, shown at the top of the next column, parallels the steps in the puzzle and illustrates why the result must be 3.

Children will realize that the puzzle can be analyzed through the use of a concrete model, and they can be challenged to design their own puzzle that will always result in a particular answer.

By dealing with larger numbers that don't lend themselves to the use of algebra tiles, students can be led to

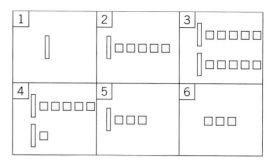

the use of symbols and pencil-and-paper algebra skills to explore them. Consider this problem:

■ Write down the month in which you were born. Multiply the number by 10. Add 20 to the result. Multiply this answer by 10. Add 165. Now, add your age to the result. Subtract 365. The result should be a number that contains the month of your birth, followed by your age.

This is another example of a procedure that "always works." Can you use your knowledge of algebra to determine why?

Upper-grade children should also have experiences interpreting a variety of functions displayed as graphs. Real-life phenomena are often recorded as data points and graphed, and the skill of analyzing the graphical data is important to the development of algebraic thinking. Consider the graph below:

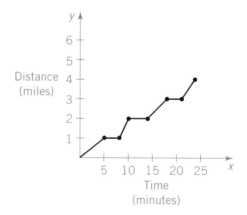

In the graph above, the trip of a person driving a car from their driveway to the grocery store is represented. The x-values represent the total amount of time, and the y-values display the distance from home.

Students should be asked to interpret the graph—that is, to explain what is going on in the trip. For example, they should be able to determine that horizontal line segments in the graph represent time spent without moving, perhaps at a traffic light or in congested traffic. They should also be able to determine that steeper line segments mean that the car traveled a given distance in less time; therefore, the car was moving faster. This discussion can lead to an informal understanding of the slope of a line representing a rate of change.

A common misconception the children may have is to interpret the graph as showing the car "driving up hills," rather than to think in terms of distance traveled in a given amount of time. It is a worthwhile exercise for children to begin with a graph and give examples of the coordinates of points on the graph. Often, mathematics textbooks overemphasize the conversion of sets of points into graphs and ignore the reverse process. A student's elementary school background should include a balance of both. A connection can also be made to literature: Children can be asked to write a story about the trip to the grocery store that the graph represents.

CLOSURE

By the time a student has completed the upper elementary and middle grades, the foundation should be firmly established for the formal study of algebra from a more symbolic standpoint. In the past, it was not unusual for the content of a "typical" ninth-grade algebra book to be considered 90% "new" material to the student, whereas the majority of the content at the junior high level was considered to be "review topics." As a result, students in high school were often frightened by algebra, which they saw as disconnected and unrelated to previous experiences. In the contemporary view of algebra, the content is seen as a continuous process, developing algebraic thinking across grade levels.

In 1992, a conference on Algebra for the Twenty-first Century was conducted by the NCTM. The general consensus of the participants who attended that conference was that with the advance of technology and our increased understanding of how children learn, algebra cannot continue to be taught as a separate high school course, as has been the case for decades. The conference proceedings list the following eight "big ideas" of algebra that need to be developed throughout a student's K–12 experience.

Representation *of patterns, relationships, situations, number sequences with table/graph/matrices and the ability to explore interrelationships between representations*

Language—*appreciation of symbols; precision of symbolic representations; modeling*

Sense of Symbol Use *in modeling contextual cases; different meanings/uses of variables as a name, as changing quantity, as a placeholder; equivalence of expressions; formulas; write expression, sentences for various situations (linear, quadratic, inverse, exponential, periodic)*

Graphing—*exploration of/comparison of situations that produce linear, quadratic, inverse, exponential, periodic patterns/shapes; structure of number system; connection between graph and solution*

Applications of Patterns—*critically analyze data, sequences, shapes; investigate graphically and symbolically*

Expressions and Equations—*solving equations and inequalities; finding and recognizing equivalent functions*

Structure of Algebra—*appreciation of the structure; parallelism with structure of number systems (properties)*

Proof and Logic—*derivations; connections with geometry (NCTM, 1992, pp. 63–64)*

Proficiency with using these "big ideas" demands that students have experiences with problems requiring algebraic thinking at all grade levels, preK–12. It has been estimated that 75% of all current jobs require a basic proficiency in algebra and geometry. This statistic alone suggests that we need to establish a goal that every student will develop algebraic thinking. Algebra should not and cannot continue to exist as a stand-alone course for high school students. By using developmentally appropriate means, students can establish their ability to work with patterns, variables, exponents, graphing, and functions throughout their elementary school experience. Algebra is for *all* students.

Terminology, Symbols, and Procedures

Algebra. Algebra is a mathematics content area that involves the study of patterns and models, variables, exponents, graphing, and functions. Algebraic thinking requires the abstraction and generalization of patterns by using a variety of representations (tables, graphs, and equations, for example).

Algebra Tiles. Algebra tiles are manipulatives that help children to visualize polynomial operations and solve equations. The tiles are based on an area model and generally include many of the following pieces:

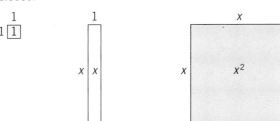

For older students, algebra tiles often come in two colors, one to represent positive numbers and one to represent negative numbers.

Dependent Variable. In an algebraic equation, the dependent variable is the symbol whose value relies on the value of another variable in order to be determined. For example, in the equation $y = 3x - 5$, the value of y depends on the value of x. So, we refer to y as the *dependent variable*.

Function. A function is a rule that assigns exactly one value in a set to a given value in another set. For an equation such as $y = 2x + 1$, we say that "y is a function of x" in that the y-value can be determined only after we know the x-value.

Function Machine. A function machine is a teacher-constructed device that can be used to help children find a "rule" for how an input value is transformed into an output value. The rule that is found is referred to as the *function*.

Independent Variable. In an algebraic equation, the independent variable is the symbol whose value determines the value of another variable in the equation. For example, in the equation $y = 3x - 5$, the value of y cannot be determined unless a value for x is stated first. So, we refer to x as the *independent variable*.

Linear Function. A linear function is a relationship between two sets in which the graphical representation results in a set of points that all lie on a line.

Polynomial. A polynomial is the sum of one or more monomials or terms. Examples of polynomials include the following: $y + 6$, $3n - 7$, $x^2 + 4x - 2$, $3x + 5y + 1$, and so on.

Variable. A variable is a symbol that represents a number or set of numbers in an expression or an equation.

Practice Exercises for Teachers

These exercises are designed for the reader of this book. While some are suitable for use in the elementary classroom, these examples should not necessarily be given to children in this form. Ideas for classroom activities on the concepts and ideas discussed in this chapter can be found in Part 2 of *Today's Mathematics*, the Student Resource Book.

1. Solve each of the following equations for x.

   a) $2x - 3 = 5x + 9$
   b) $4(x + 2) = -6 + 2x$
   c) $1 - 5x = -14$
   d) $3x + 7 - 2x + 1 = 7 - x$
   e) $8 - 2(x + 5) = 3(2x - 4) + 12$

2. Find a function rule for each of the following tables and determine whether the function is linear or nonlinear.

a) x	y		b) x	y		c) x	y
3	8		2	5		0	1
5	10		4	9		2	5
6	11		7	15		4	17

3. Draw a picture of algebra tiles arranged to represent each of the following equations.

   a) $2x + 3 = 7$
   b) $5x + 6 = 1 + 3x$
   c) $3(x + 3) = x + 4$
   d) $2 + 4(2x + 1) = 6$
   e) $x^2 + 4x + 1 = 2x + 3$

4. In this chapter, the following puzzle was posed: "Write down the month in which you were born. Multiply the number by 10. Add 20 to the result. Multiply this answer by 10. Add 165. Now, add your age to the result. Subtract 365. The result should be a number that contains the month of your birth, followed by your age." Use algebra symbols to show why this "trick" always works. Explain what is happening.

5. Use drawings of algebra tiles to visualize and to simplify each of the following products.

    a) $(x + 3)(x + 4)$
    b) $(x + 1)(x + 5)$
    c) $(2x + 5)(x + 2)$
    d) $(x + 1)^2$
    e) $(3x + 1)(2x + 2)$

6. A tennis tournament involves 20 participants in a round-robin play-off. In other words, each participant must play the other 19 competitors exactly once.

    a) How many games must be played to complete the tournament?
    b) Use the strategy of solving the simpler problem to make a table, find a pattern, and extend the pattern to find the total number of games that need to be played.
    c) Write an equation that relates the number of games played to the number of competitors.
    d) Which variable is independent and which variable is dependent in this problem?

7. Suppose that you invest some money in the bank and leave it there over a period of many years, allowing the interest to compound each year (i.e., the interest earns interest). Find the amount of money in the bank for each of the following cases.

    a) $1000 invested at 7% for 40 years
    b) $10,000 invested at 8% for 30 years
    c) $7500 invested at 6.5% for 25 years
    d) $1 invested at 5% for 200 years
    e) $500 invested at 10% for 18 years

8. The graph below represents the height that a projectile launched from a pad is above the ground.

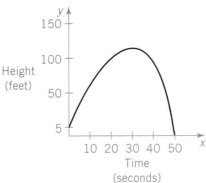

    a) What is the maximum height reached by the projectile?
    b) Why is the "starting" point at (0, 5), rather than (0, 0)?
    c) How many seconds is the projectile in the air?
    d) How high is the projectile after 45 seconds?
    e) Write three more questions that could be asked about this graph.

9. Suppose that a new video store opens in your neighborhood. You have a choice between two plans for rental of tapes, as follows:

    Plan A: You pay an annual membership fee of $20, and each video rental costs $1.50.
    Plan B: There is no annual fee, but the cost of each video rental is $2.75.

    Compare the two plans. Which plan would you choose and why? How did you use algebraic thinking to answer the questions?

10. Explain a rule describing each of the following sequences of numbers.

    a) 1, 3, 5, 7, 9, . . .
    b) 1, 4, 9, 16, 25, . . .
    c) 5, 10, 8, 13, 11, 16, 14, . . .
    d) 1, 2, 3, 5, 7, 11, 13, . . .
    e) 2, 7, 17, 37, 77, . . .

11. Suppose that *T* stands for the price of a cassette tape, and *D* stands for the cost of a compact disc. Write an equation relating these variables for each of the following situations.

   a) A compact disc costs $4 more than a cassette tape.
   b) A cassette tape costs $3.50 less than a compact disc.
   c) On sale, the cost of a cassette tape is half the cost of a compact disc.
   d) Two compact discs cost $1 more than three cassette tapes.
   e) Four cassette tapes and a compact disc cost $43 altogether.

Teaching Competencies and Self-Assessment Tasks

1. Discuss the difference between the traditional view of "algebra as a one-year, high school course" and the contemporary view of "algebraic thinking as a strand of elementary school mathematics."
2. List the five content strands often associated with the study of algebra and describe an activity that would help children develop their knowledge of each strand at both the lower elementary level and the upper elementary level.
3. To what degree can equation solving be explored in the lower primary grades? Explain how you might do this.
4. When a piece of paper is folded in half, the new piece is two layers thick, and when folded a second time, the piece becomes four layers thick. Using a piece of paper, determine how many times it can be folded until it becomes impossible to fold it in half again. Then, represent this problem as a function in three forms: a table, a graph, and an equation relating the number of folds to the number of layers.
5. Examine the NCTM *Principles and Standards for School Mathematics* on Algebra. What role does pattern recognition and description play in the development of algebraic thought?
6. Locate a middle school mathematics textbook and find a chapter that deals with solving equations. Discuss the degree to which concrete methods are emphasized to assist students in learning what it means to solve an equation.
7. Explain how two-colored algebra tiles can be used to solve an equation such as $3(x - 4) + 5 = 8 - 2x$.
8. When children use manipulatives extensively to explore algebra, as described in this chapter, assessment in the traditional paper-and-pencil sense becomes irrelevant. Explain how you might assess your middle school students' understanding of multiplying polynomials as they work with algebra tiles.
9. Research the literature to explore how children develop a sense of the use of variables. Then describe the types of experiences that children need in elementary school to prepare them to work with variable expressions with confidence.
10. Identify several real-life situations in which you use algebraic thinking. Which content strands within the area of algebra seem to be used the most in these situations?
11. Choose another content strand, such as measurement or probability. Describe how you might pose a problem or series of problems involving measurement or probability that will develop algebraic thinking in your students as they explore the problem.
12. Locate several elementary mathematics textbooks. You are likely to see entire chapters devoted to geometry or fractions but not to algebra. Page through these books and find examples—if there are any—of algebraic thinking being promoted in other contexts.

Related Readings and Teacher Resources

For related readings on topics found in this chapter, see the corresponding chapter in Part 2 of *Today's Mathematics*, the Student Resource Book.

Chapter 11

Rational Numbers Expressed as Fractions: Concepts

Teaching Competencies

Upon completing this chapter, you will be able to:

- Use at least three models to develop an understanding of nonnegative rational numbers expressed as fractions.

- Describe alternative sequences to teaching fraction concepts.

- Describe prerequisite knowledge, skills, and understandings to be achieved before a formal study of operations on rational numbers expressed as fractions.

- Demonstrate an understanding of various fraction concepts and terminology.

- Develop the concept of fraction in a meaningful way for students.

Three children were bragging about how much pizza they had eaten at a friend's party. They each felt that they had eaten more pizza than anybody else and were determined to prove it any way they could. Jeff stated that he had eaten 4 pieces and that he knew that was more pieces than anyone else had eaten—so he should be the winner! Marge only ate 3 pieces of an 8-piece pizza, but they were bigger pieces than Jeff's—so she should be the winner! Ryan ate $\frac{1}{2}$ of a small pizza, also only 3 pieces, but $\frac{1}{2}$ of a pizza is more than $\frac{3}{8}$ of a pizza—so he should be the winner! What do YOU think? Perhaps more importantly, what do you think children would think? And why?

This story illustrates how fractional parts can be misinterpreted and can lead to confusion. Children often focus attention on *parts* to the exclusion of the *whole*. Students must realize that a fraction means little without reference to a whole unit associated with that fraction. For example, it may come as a surprise that a half does not always equal a half, especially if the former refers to half of a dollar and the latter refers to half of a dime. Unless you have a reference to what the whole is, it is difficult, at best, to compare two or more fractions. A sound foundational understanding of important, but often overlooked, fraction concepts will provide students with a base for meaningful communication about fractions in their world.

A FRACTIONAL PART OF THE HISTORY OF FRACTIONAL NUMBERS

In reviewing the early history of number development, we find that the growth and extension of number ideas is directly related to the increasing complexity of civilization. In much the same way that limited tallying or matching became insufficient, so eventually did whole numbers alone not satisfy human needs. It became necessary to describe parts of whole things or parts of groups of things. Fractions are often, but not exclusively, described as parts of a "broken" whole. The word *fraction* is derived from the Latin *frangere*, meaning "to break."

Early applications of fraction concepts were, by our standards, quite awkward. Ancient Egyptians, with a few exceptions, employed only unit fractions—fractions whose numerators were one and whose denominators varied (but were never zero). To express a given non-unit fraction, they added together the required unit fractions. For example, the fraction $\frac{5}{8}$ was expressed as $\frac{1}{2} + \frac{1}{8}$, whereas $\frac{5}{6}$ would be expressed as $\frac{1}{2} + \frac{1}{3}$. The difficulties involved in such a system are obvious, especially when you consider that the ancient Egyptians were also hampered by cumbersome numerals (see Chapter 6). The symbol used for a fractional number was the hieroglyph $\bigcirc$, which was placed over a numeral that indicated the number of parts into which the whole was divided:

$$\overset{\bigcirc}{||||} = \frac{1}{4} \qquad \overset{\bigcirc}{\cap\cap I} = \frac{1}{21} \qquad \overset{\bigcirc}{\text{P}} = \frac{1}{100}$$

The Babylonian numeration system was vastly superior to that used by the Egyptians, which may help account for many Babylonian advances in astronomy and construction. Theirs was a sexagesimal system (that is, it was based, like their system of whole numbers, on groupings of 60). The many possible factors and multiples of 60 (2, 3, 4, 5, 6, 10, 12, 15, 20, 30, 60, 120, 180, and so on) greatly facilitated work with fractions. The denominator in a Babylonian "fraction" was a factor or multiple of 60, while the numerator, in contrast to the Egyptian system, was allowed to vary. The symbols used for fractional numbers, however, were extremely complicated.

In Roman society and culture, fractions were used largely in commerce. The Romans used denominators that were based on 12 and multiples of 12, and names were given to twelfths and twenty-fourths of whole things, these parts of the whole becoming subunits. By using subunits, they avoided the use of fractions in computation, much the same as we do today by choosing to say "one ounce" rather than "one-sixteenth of a pound."

The development of our familiar representation of fractional numbers comes from Hindu mathematicians, who began the convention of writing one numeral *over* another: $\frac{2}{3}$. The incorporation of the **fraction bar** separating the numerator from the denominator was an Arabic device that was not generally used in the Western world until the late Middle Ages.

Today, the place of rational numbers expressed as fractions (and decimals) and the rationale for exploring them in the curriculum are changing. Because of the increasing role of technology in our society (calculators and computers almost exclusively use decimal notation), and other factors such as an increased use of the decimal-based metric system for measurement, some elementary mathematics programs are teaching rational numbers expressed as decimals BEFORE teaching rational numbers expressed as fractions. When the teaching strategy is based on the concrete level and models, the sequences "fraction then decimal" or "decimal then fraction" can be easily interchanged. However, when the teaching of fractions and the teaching of decimals are overly dependent on one other, it may be more difficult to change the teaching sequence. We believe that Chapters 9, 10, 11, 12, and 13 in this text can be easily interchanged with only a few minor alterations.

RATIONAL NUMBERS—A DEFINITION AND DESCRIPTION

Rational numbers are commonly expressed in two different forms—as fractions or as decimals. This chapter deals with rational numbers expressed as fractions.

A **rational number** is any number that can be written in the form of $\frac{a}{b}$, where a is any integer and b is any nonzero integer.

Fractional numbers are positive rational numbers written in fraction form; **fractions** are the symbols that we use for writing fractional numbers. Thus, three-fourths is a rational number. When this number is written in fraction form, we call it a fractional number, and the symbol used to represent the fractional number, $\frac{3}{4}$, is called a fraction. Some texts do not make a distinction between fractional numbers (positive rationals) and rational numbers (positive and negative rationals).

Children may enter school with the mistaken notion that one-half means "one of two pieces." We do not usually cut food items exactly in half: We tend to cut them in two similar, but not identical, pieces, and children always take the "larger" piece. When children say they will take the larger piece, they may be demonstrating an unacceptable understanding of the notion of one-half—or, perhaps, they understand the concept well and recognize that the cutting REALLY didn't produce one-half. If it did, they wouldn't care which piece they received.

Because whole numbers are a subset of rational numbers (that is, all whole numbers are also rational numbers), students know a great deal about rational numbers BEFORE they begin formal study. Too often we don't take full advantage of the whole-number knowledge base in designing and implementing approaches to fraction concepts. Sadly, it is not too uncommon to hear the study of fraction concepts prefaced by an announcement that "we're going to do something unlike what we've done with whole numbers." Relations between whole numbers and fractions should be explored, not hidden.

Parents divide candy bars or apples "in half" for children and introduce them to ideas underlying the concept of fractions at a very early age. The task then becomes helping the students develop a more refined meaning and a sound understanding of the appropriate use of rational numbers and fractions.

Fractions can be thought of as more than "part of a whole object." Fractions can also be viewed as an indicated division. For example, the fraction $\frac{3}{4}$ can be thought of as 3 divided by 4. However, indicated division is generally explored more abstractly and should not be introduced at this time.

Fraction Models

There are basically three different models that can be used to develop students' understanding of fractions: regions, sets, and number lines. Either circular and/or rectangular regions are customarily used in modeling the concept of fractions. For example:

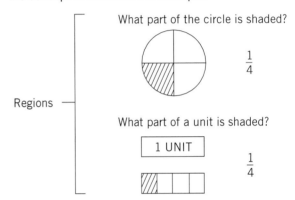

Research Snapshot

What knowledge do elementary school students bring to the classroom about fractions?

In a study of 8 sixth-grade students where instruction was designed to build on informal knowledge, Mack (1990) found that students possessed a rich store of informal knowledge of fractions that was based on partitioning units and treating the parts as whole numbers.

Informal knowledge is the applied, real-life knowledge that students themselves construct and that they bring to problem-solving situations. Their informal knowledge was initially determined to be disconnected from their knowledge of fraction symbols and procedures, but over the course of the study, the students were able to relate their informal knowledge to fractions and symbols in meaningful ways. For example, all of the students constructed meaningful algorithms for converting improper fractions to mixed numerals when they solved subtraction problems with regrouping.

The use and knowledge of rote procedures often interfered with students' attempts to build on their informal knowledge.

What problem-solving contexts could you use to help your students build on their informal knowledge of fractions?

Mack, N. (1990). Learning fractions with understanding: Building on informal knowledge. *Journal for Research in Mathematics Education*, 21, 16–32.

For additional research briefs, "ERIC Digests" lets you search more than 2,000 short syntheses of research on a range of education topics. The syntheses were produced by the Educational Resources Information Center (ERIC). Check http://ed.gov/databases/ERIC_Digests/index/

What part of the set of dots is shaded?

Sets

$\frac{1}{4}$

What part of the number line is marked?

Number
line
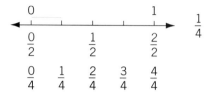
$\frac{1}{4}$

Materials such as Cuisenaire rods, base ten blocks, pattern blocks, and fraction bars or circles are excellent tools for assisting students in understanding basic fraction concepts. Cuisenaire rods may be used either with or without a referencing number line. Carefully examine teachers' manuals for each set of materials; these manuals give specific directions and describe effective activities for using these manipulative materials to develop fraction concepts. You will also find ideas and activities for their use in professional journals such as *Teaching Children Mathematics*.

Let us carefully examine each of the three common models—regions, groups of objects, and number lines—as we discuss fractions.

THE "REGIONS" MODEL FOR FRACTIONAL NUMBERS

The teacher should present the concept of fractions by having children manipulate physical models showing a whole and fractions of that whole. Most commonly, either rectangular regions or circular regions (or both) are used as physical models.

Let's examine rectangular regions first. Usually we start with a *basic unit* or *unit region*, such as the region pictured, often cut from posterboard or felt that has been divided into congruent parts. Congruent parts are parts that have the same size and shape. For example, let this rectangular region be the basic unit, or unit region:

BASIC UNIT OR UNIT REGION

If we wish to identify the shaded part of the basic unit with a fractional number, that number is one-half, which can be written $\frac{1}{2}$. In this case, the 2 denotes the number of equal (congruent) pieces into which the basic unit is divided. The 1 denotes how many of these two equal (congruent) pieces we are concerned with at the moment. For practice, children can be asked to recognize equal parts of regions and name the parts, or they can color appropriate physical models. In these physi-

cal models children can, by counting, identify the part of each region that is shaded, name the appropriate fractional number, and write the corresponding fraction.

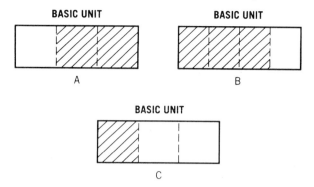

In A, two of three equal parts are shaded; the corresponding fraction is $\frac{2}{3}$. In B, three out of four equal parts are shaded; this can be represented by the fraction $\frac{3}{4}$. In C, one part out of three equal parts is shaded; the appropriate fraction is $\frac{1}{3}$.

As an extension of this activity, children can be asked to shade or color given parts of regions—for example, one-sixth of the following circular region:

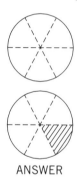

ANSWER

What fraction names the shaded part of this circular region? $\left(\frac{1}{6}\right)$ Or, one-half of the following region:

We should emphasize that this can be done in several ways; three possible ways are indicated here.

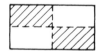

These examples stress the fact that fractions can be used to indicate parts of a whole. In each of the drawings two out of four congruent regions have been shaded. Thus, we can write the fraction $\frac{2}{4}$. The 4 is the **denominator** of the fraction; in this case, it tells us into how many equal parts the whole has been separated. The name *fourth* is assigned to each of the four pieces. The word *denominator* comes to us from the Latin word *nomen*, which means "to name." Thus the denominator functions as the "namer" of the number of congruent parts into which a unit has been separated.

In the fraction $\frac{2}{4}$, the 2 is the **numerator**. In the examples shown, the numerator tells us how many of these equal pieces we are considering. In this case we have considered two of the pieces, each called *fourths*. The numerator of the fraction is the number that expresses how many of the equal pieces we are considering. In the fraction $\frac{2}{4}$, the 2 and the 4 are called the *terms* of the fraction.

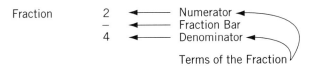

Now let us examine fractions using circular regions. The following illustration represents a unit:

Children should use a template to cut circular regions from a piece of paper and then subdivide these circular units into fractions—$\frac{1}{2}$, $\frac{1}{4}$, and $\frac{1}{8}$—by folding, and then cutting. Since it is very difficult to fold a circular region into thirds, you may want to provide a template for thirds and any other fractional parts you want the children to make. Give each child an envelope in which to place the fractions of the circular regions. At the early stages of concept development it might be beneficial to color-code the fraction pieces for ease of sorting. It should be noted, however, that color-coding can also be a disadvantage since it may lessen attention to the attributes of fractions that *really* matter—one-half isn't one-half because it's green! That is, two pieces match, not because they are the same color, but rather because they are the same size.

Once the children have made these fraction kits, discuss how the fractional parts of the unit relate to the whole. Two equivalent pieces are called *halves*. If we consider one of the pieces, then we would call that piece *one-half*, written in fraction form as $\frac{1}{2}$. The numerator 1 tells us how many pieces we are considering, and the denominator 2 tells us the name of the pieces.

Consider a circular region separated into four equivalent pieces.

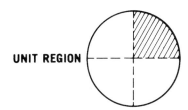

Because the unit is separated into four equivalent pieces, we name each piece *one-fourth*. The one piece that is shaded would be represented by the fraction $\frac{1}{4}$ because we are considering one of the four pieces. If two are shaded, we write $\frac{2}{4}$ because two of the pieces we call fourths are shaded.

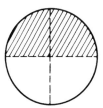

Notice that the shaded region is the same size as one-half of the region. That is, $\frac{2}{4}$ is the same size as $\frac{1}{2}$. Although it is too early in the development of fraction concepts to discuss equivalent fractions abstractly, it is not too early to begin the foundation of the concept, and an important foundation is the notion of comparing the two fractions with a common unit region.

If three parts are shaded, we write $\frac{3}{4}$ because three of the pieces we name fourths are being considered.

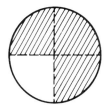

It is important to note that there may be advantages to using circular regions either early in the child's development of the concepts of fractions or when difficulties or misunderstandings seem to arise. When a fractional part of a circular region is displayed, the child can more readily *visualize* a whole circular region and make a mental comparison. If a fractional part of a rectangular region is used, then there is no ready mental image of the whole. The child will need to refer to an actual model of the whole before comprehending. To ensure your own understanding of this observation, trace the figures shown, and show the circular fraction "piece" to a friend and ask for a fraction name for that piece. Then show the rectangular piece and ask the same question.

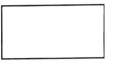

Most will say "one-fourth" for the circular piece. For the rectangular fraction "piece," most will say that they need to know how big the original unit is before they can give an answer. Note—they assumed that the first piece was part of a circle when it may actually have been part of a semicircle. In that case, it would represent one-half, not one-fourth. Until we know for certain what the unit is, we run the risk of falling victim to assumption.

Once children have had many experiences using *both* rectangular and circular regions to help them understand fractions, then introduce fractional parts of other shapes. For example, $\frac{1}{2}$ of this region is shaded:

and $\frac{3}{4}$ of this region is shaded:

Emphasize that the *shape* of a region does not influence the fraction—the number of equal pieces into which that region is divided does.

THE "GROUPS OF OBJECTS" MODEL FOR RATIONAL NUMBERS

Children should also have an opportunity to develop an understanding of fractional numbers by working with groups of objects, the second model we will use. To establish a firm understanding of fraction concepts, children must actually manipulate materials. When these manipulatives are groups of objects, fractions can be used to name parts of the groups.

Consider the following group of six objects:

By separating the group into two equal subgroups and considering one of those subgroups, we consider one-half of the original group. A loop can be drawn around one-half of the group, or one-half of the objects can be colored, to indicate the fractional number $\frac{1}{2}$.

Many other fractional numbers can be represented in the same way:

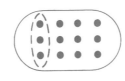

In the first picture above, we can separate the 12 dots into four equal subgroups by considering only columns of dots. Then, by drawing a loop around one of the columns, we represent the fractional number $\frac{1}{4}$. In the second picture, we can separate the 8 dots into four equal subgroups by considering only rows of dots. Then if we enclose one of the rows with a loop, the number $\frac{1}{4}$ is again represented. Similarly, the third picture illustrates $\frac{1}{3}$.

Suppose that now, however, we consider the dots individually, not as rows or columns. Again taking the preceding group of 12 dots, let's consider the dots independently of the column that was enclosed. We can do this by enclosing each of the dots of that column individually:

In this way we illustrate the number $\frac{3}{12}$, since there are 12 dots and we are separately considering 3 of them. Notice that in both cases exactly 3 dots out of the 12 are under consideration, but that in one case we are illustrating the number $\frac{1}{4}$, while in the other we are illustrating $\frac{3}{12}$. Evidently, $\frac{1}{4}$ and $\frac{3}{12}$ are equivalent fractions. Why? Compare the two figures below:

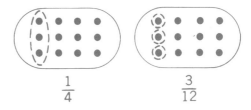

$$\frac{1}{4} \qquad\qquad \frac{3}{12}$$

In a similar fashion we can demonstrate that $\frac{1}{4} = \frac{2}{8}$ and that $\frac{1}{3} = \frac{3}{9}$.

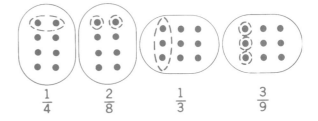

$$\frac{1}{4} \qquad \frac{2}{8} \qquad \frac{1}{3} \qquad \frac{3}{9}$$

It is very important to emphasize that the unit here is the *entire* group by drawing a loop around it. Otherwise, children may focus their attention on each of the individual elements of the group rather than the group itself. Without this attention, a student might easily believe that $\frac{4}{8}$ is "bigger" than $\frac{3}{6}$ instead of correctly interpreting that $\frac{4}{8}$ of one unit may be more than $\frac{3}{6}$ of a different unit.

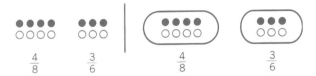

Children should make a number of representations to help them identify two distinct concepts:

1. A fraction may represent part of a whole.
2. A fraction may represent part of a group.

THE "NUMBER LINE" MODEL FOR RATIONAL NUMBERS

Now let us reiterate that a fraction is a number that can be written in the form $\frac{a}{b}$ in which a and b are integers (where b is not zero). Of course, fractions can also be written as decimals: For example, .1 and $\frac{1}{10}$ represent the same number.

A third model may be used to help us understand fractions: the number line. We can ask, "How do fractions fit in with the numbers we have already studied on the number line?" So far we have matched equally spaced points on the number line with whole numbers (the numbers 0, 1, 2, 3, . . .):

But what about points that are located *between* the whole number points? Are there numbers to match with these points? We will find that many of these "in-between" points can be matched with fractional numbers.

When we considered the whole numbers under the operation of division, we found that division is not closed for this set. That is, when you divide one whole number by another, you don't always get a whole number as an answer. We discovered division examples in which the missing factor could not be expressed as a whole number. By way of illustration, consider $4 \div 5 = \square$. This example indicates the need for another set of numbers if we are to find answers for examples such as this—there is no whole number that "fits" in the box.

We may note another indication of the need for fractional numbers as we attempt to express measurement more accurately. Using a ruler in a practical application, we seldom arrive at a measurement of an exact number of inches. A method of expressing measurements that includes parts of inches, parts of feet, parts of cups, and parts of pounds is provided by using the set of fractional numbers.

As we continue to make use of the metric system of measurement, there will be less need for the use of fractions in measurement. The metric system is based on a decimal relationship. Measurements in the metric

system are recorded most commonly in decimal form—for example, in tenths, hundredths, or thousandths (.1, .01, or .001). There will, however, always be a place for reference to "simple" fractions in measurement settings, such as $\frac{1}{2}$, $\frac{3}{4}$, $\frac{2}{3}$ and even $\frac{5}{12}$ and $\frac{3}{16}$, but the need and advantages of considering fractions such as $\frac{3}{29}$ or $\frac{15}{37}$ have all but disappeared. If application is one test of the usefulness of fractions, then these awkward fractions can easily be replaced by those more common—after all, the procedures used would be identical.

Before developing fractional numbers on the number line, children should be familiar with the way we illustrate basic operations with whole numbers on the number line. Draw a number line and indicate a reference point on it. Let's label that point "0," calling it *zero*. Now select another point, anywhere on the line (usually to the right of zero), and label that point "1." Using this segment from 0 to 1 as a standard unit, mark off additional line segments equal in length to the standard unit. Each point should be matched with one of the whole numbers.

Now, let's play a game and pretend that we are at the point named 0. If we make a jump of one unit to the right, where do we land? We land at the point named 1. If we make another jump of one unit to the right, where do we land this time? We land at the point named 2. Now, starting at 2, if we take a jump of one unit to the left, where do we land? We land back at 1.

But suppose that we are now getting tired and, when we jump to the left, we do not make it all the way back to 0 but land at the point labeled "A."

How can we name this point where we have landed? Every point on the number line that we have seen so far has had a name. What do you think the name of this point should be? We have found that point A is equidistant from 0 and 1. The length of the line segment between 0 and A is the same as the length of the line segment between A and 1. The segment that we have defined as one unit for this particular number line has been divided by point A into two segments of equal length. How can we express this idea? We can express it by the notation $\frac{1}{2}$. Of the two equivalent segments between 0 and 1, we are one of the two segments away from 0. The notation $\frac{1}{2}$ expresses this fact. Another name for point A, therefore, is $\frac{1}{2}$.

Now suppose that we are at the point named by $\frac{1}{2}$ and jump to the point named by 1. How far are we then from the starting point 0? How many one-half units separate us from 0? Clearly, we are two one-half units from the starting point. This is expressed by the fraction $\frac{2}{2}$. We divide the whole into two equivalent parts and consider them both:

If we now start at 1 and jump another one-half unit to the right, where do we land? (Halfway between 1 and 2). How many one-half units are we away from 0? (Three). We can express this fact by the fraction $\frac{3}{2}$, which can be interpreted to mean that, if we divide each unit length into two equivalent parts, we are considering three of the resulting one-half-unit segments.

We can continue in this way, naming each whole number and each point halfway between any pair of whole numbers. The resulting collection of points names the set of halves.

What is another name for 1? Two halves, $\frac{2}{2}$, is another name for 1, because $\frac{2}{2}$ and 1 name the same point on the number line. What is another name for 2? Four halves, $\frac{4}{2}$, is another name, because $\frac{4}{2}$ and 2 name the same point.

KNOWLEDGE AND UNDERSTANDINGS PRIOR TO OPERATIONS

There are a number of experiences focusing on foundational skills and understandings of rational numbers expressed as fractions that must be an integral part of instruction BEFORE students are introduced to the formal study of the addition, subtraction, multiplication, and division of rational numbers. A teacher who adjusts instruction to emphasize attention to these prerequisites will provide an excellent base for expansion later. Students need to understand the meaning of fractions, model fractions in several ways, generate equivalent fractions, simplify fractions, compare fractions, and order fractions. Once students have these prerequisites in hand, the study of operations on fractions becomes a matter of applying these understandings rather than searching, often aimlessly, for the "correct rule" to apply when adding, subtracting, multiplying, or dividing.

To explore fully the conceptual base for fractions, some common terminology is essential for communicating ideas. At this point, it is not necessary that this terminology be either formal or definitional. You'll find that children often invent language that conveys meaning better than the words that we use as adults. For example, "bottom-nator" is certainly a more vividly descriptive term than *denominator*, although, of course, not preferred. If you accept this child-developed, personalized language and complement it with the more widely accepted terminology, you'll find students will begin to adopt the appropriate words they read and hear.

A fraction, such as $\frac{3}{2}$, in which the numerator is greater than or equal to the denominator, is called an **improper fraction**. Thus, $\frac{3}{2}$, $\frac{7}{5}$, $\frac{6}{6}$, and $\frac{13}{8}$ are improper fractions. A **proper fraction** is one in which the numerator is less than the denominator. Examples of proper fractions are $\frac{2}{3}$, $\frac{4}{5}$, $\frac{3}{8}$, and $\frac{24}{25}$. Rather than risk giving children the impression that there is something "wrong" with fractions that have been labeled as "improper," some programs have initially made use of children's invented language such as "top-heavy" to describe improper fractions, followed by the more formal term at a later date.

There are many names for any point on the number line. For the number 1, we have written the symbols 1 and $\frac{2}{2}$; for the number 2, we have written 2 and $\frac{4}{2}$. Is there another way we can write $\frac{3}{2}$, $\frac{5}{2}$, and other fractional numbers in which the numerator is greater than the denominator? Consider the point labeled $\frac{3}{2}$. This point is one-half unit $\left(\frac{1}{2}\right)$ to the right of 1, so another way to indicate $\frac{3}{2}$ is $1 + \frac{1}{2}$, or $1\frac{1}{2}$. If the expression $1 + \frac{1}{2}$ is rewritten as $\frac{2}{2} + \frac{1}{2}$, which clearly equals $\frac{3}{2}$, it becomes obvious that $1 + \frac{1}{2}$ and $\frac{3}{2}$ are different names for the same number. Now consider the fraction $\frac{5}{2}$. By looking at the number line, we find that the point named by $\frac{5}{2}$ is one-half unit $\left(\frac{1}{2}\right)$ to the right of 2. This point, therefore, can be indicated by $2 + \frac{1}{2}$, or $2\frac{1}{2}$. If $2 + \frac{1}{2}$ is rewritten as $\frac{4}{2} + \frac{1}{2}$, which is clearly equal to $\frac{5}{2}$, it becomes evident that the symbols $\frac{5}{2}$ and $2\frac{1}{2}$, $\left(\text{or } 2 + \frac{1}{2}\right)$ are merely different names for the same number. Numerals such as $1\frac{1}{2}$, $3\frac{1}{2}$, and $6\frac{1}{2}$ (for $\frac{3}{2}$, $\frac{7}{2}$, and $\frac{13}{2}$, respectively) are called **mixed numerals**. In this form, we combine, or mix, a numeral naming a counting number and a numeral naming a fraction.

The mixed form for writing fractional numbers gives us another way of naming the numbers represented on the number line:

But remember, $1\frac{1}{2}$ can also be expressed as $\frac{3}{2}$:

$$1\frac{1}{2} = 1 + \frac{1}{2}$$
$$= \frac{2}{2} + \frac{1}{2}$$
$$= \frac{3}{2}$$

Circular regions should also be used to develop the concept of mixed numerals. Consider three of the pieces that we have named half of a circle:

We can write $\frac{3}{2}$ as a fraction for these regions. By rearranging the regions we can easily see that we have one and one-half circular regions.

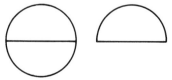

Children need many experiences in manipulating regions that they have cut from paper and included in their fraction kits. They also must be put into situations that require them to *verbalize* the relationships shown by the fraction pieces. The language and terms the children use in communicating about fractions are not, at this early stage, as critical as the awareness and identification of important fraction concepts.

We can also develop the concept of mixed numerals using rectangular regions:

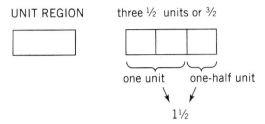

Children can rearrange the pieces to see why $\frac{3}{2}$ and $1\frac{1}{2}$ are names for the same number. Children should be given the opportunity to discover relations between the set of halves and other numbers on the number line. They may make the generalization that, when we add parts by moving to the right on the number line, the denominators remain the same and the numerators are added the way whole numbers are added. Children have had experience in counting by ones, fives, and tens. Now the opportunity is provided for them to count by halves: $\frac{1}{2}, \frac{2}{2}, \frac{3}{2}, \frac{4}{2}, \frac{5}{2}$, and so on (or $\frac{1}{2}$, 1, $1\frac{1}{2}$, 2, $2\frac{1}{2}$, and so on). The patterns in the set of halves should become clear.

Now let's develop the set of fourths, again using a number line. Each unit-long line segment is divided into four segments of equal length.

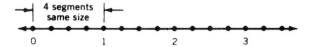

If the segment between 0 and 1 is divided into four equivalent parts, what can we name one of these parts? We can name it *one-fourth*. Thus, we can label the first point to the right of zero on the number line above as $\frac{1}{4}$, or one-fourth. Similarly, we can label the second point $\frac{2}{4}$, or two-fourths; the third point $\frac{3}{4}$, or three-fourths; and the fourth point $\frac{4}{4}$, or four-fourths. Thus:

We can continue in this manner indefinitely, naming the set of fourths:

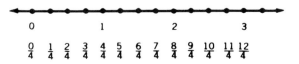

It is evident now that another name for 1 is $\frac{4}{4}$. Similarly, another name for 2 is $\frac{8}{4}$. We can also use other names to designate the points on the number line that represent fractional numbers greater than 1; we can use mixed numerals to designate these points. For example, the point labeled $\frac{5}{4}$ can be renamed with the mixed numeral $1\frac{1}{4}$, and the next point can be designated $1\frac{2}{4}$ instead of $\frac{6}{4}$.

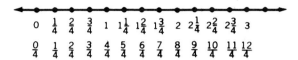

Now let's represent the set of halves and the set of fourths on the same number line. We should encourage children to discover as many relations as possible.

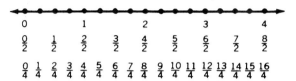

What are some other names for 1? ($\frac{2}{2}$ and $\frac{4}{4}$) After children have examined the point named by 1, they should be able to make the generalization that when any counting number (1, 2, 3, 4, and so on) appears as both numerator and denominator, the resulting fraction is another way to name 1. Thus there are infinitely many fraction names for 1.

$$\frac{1}{1}, \frac{2}{2}, \frac{3}{3}, \frac{4}{4}, \cdots$$

Similarly, children should discover many ways to write 2, 3, 4, 5, and other counting numbers as fractions. The children may then be ready to draw the following important conclusion: Because every whole number can be named by a fraction with a whole-number numerator and a counting-number denominator, *every whole number is also a fractional number*. Thus the set of whole numbers is a subset of the set of fractional numbers. That is, the fractional numbers include all of the whole numbers.

The point named by 1 can be indicated by either $\frac{1}{1}$ or $\frac{2}{2}$ because these are merely different names for the same point ($\frac{1}{2} = \frac{2}{2}$). Children should then be shown that $\frac{1 \times 2}{1 \times 2} = \frac{2}{2}$ and $\frac{1 \times 3}{1 \times 3} = \frac{3}{3}$. The important thing for children to recognize here is that in each example the same factor is used in the numerator and in the denominator. Moreover, $\frac{1}{2}$ and $\frac{2}{4}$ name the same number ($\frac{1}{2} = \frac{2}{4}$), and the relation $\frac{2 \times 1}{2 \times 2} = \frac{2}{4}$ is thus valid. We call fractions that name the same number **equivalent fractions**.

Despite the appearance of the abstract notation, emphasis should be placed on the notion of actually multiplying a number by 1, written in the form $\frac{a}{a}$ ($a \neq 0$), rather than using the wording, "Multiply both the top and the bottom by the same number." This wording may yield a correct answer, but children tend to see it as only an arbitrary rule with no foundation in their prior knowledge of multiplication by 1.

The concept of equivalent fractions can also be presented by using regions. For example:

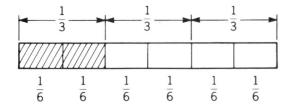

This basic unit is divided into thirds and has also been divided into sixths. The shaded part of the unit region is $\frac{2}{6}$ of the entire region (two parts out of a total of six). But the shaded part is also $\frac{1}{3}$ of the entire unit region. When $\frac{2}{6}$ is renamed as $\frac{1}{3}$, we say that it is in **simplest form**. A fraction is in simplest form if the numerator and the denominator have no common factors other than 1. For example, we have seen that $\frac{2}{6} = \frac{1}{3}$.

$$\frac{2}{6} = \frac{1 \times 2}{3 \times 2}$$
$$= \frac{1}{3} \times \frac{2}{2}$$
$$= \frac{1}{3} \times 1$$
$$= \frac{1}{3}$$

We use the phrase *simplest form* rather than the more traditional *reduce to lowest terms*. To children, the term *reduce* means "to make smaller," but the fraction is really still the same size and represents the same amount. We are actually writing a fraction in a form that is easier to comprehend. Students are not just mechanically following an algorithm: They are developing the concept of renaming fractions. In the fraction $\frac{2}{6}$, the numerator and the denominator have the factor 2 in common; therefore $\frac{2}{6}$ is not in simplest form. The fraction $\frac{1}{3}$, however, is expressed in simplest form because the numerator and the denominator share no common factors except 1.

Combining regions to form a chart is an excellent way to develop students' concept of equivalent fractions and the relationships among fractional numbers. Children can discover visually that any fraction has many names. For example, we know that $\frac{1}{2} = \frac{2}{4} = \frac{4}{8}$. A child can discover this by manipulating materials or by using a chart such as this one:

Unit	1						
Halves	$\frac{1}{2}$				$\frac{1}{2}$		
Fourths	$\frac{1}{4}$		$\frac{1}{4}$		$\frac{1}{4}$		$\frac{1}{4}$
Eighths	$\frac{1}{8}$	$\frac{1}{8}$	$\frac{1}{8}$	$\frac{1}{8}$	$\frac{1}{8}$	$\frac{1}{8}$	$\frac{1}{8}$ $\frac{1}{8}$

In this chart the unit interval is represented in four different ways: At the top it is represented by a single rectangular region, labeled 1 because it spans the entire interval. Below this the unit interval is represented by two rectangular regions; these are labeled $\frac{1}{2}$ be-

cause each region spans only one-half of the interval. Next the unit interval is represented by four rectangular regions, each labeled $\frac{1}{4}$ to indicate that it spans only one-fourth of the interval. Finally, there are eight congruent rectangular regions, each labeled $\frac{1}{8}$.

By shading some of the regions on the chart, children can see that fractional numbers can be renamed in various ways:

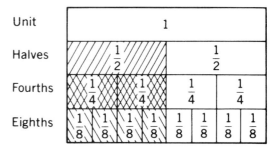

For example, in this chart, there are eight rectangular regions labeled $\frac{1}{8}$. Four of these have been shaded. This fact can be indicated by the fraction $\frac{4}{8}$, the denominator, 8, indicating the total number of regions, and the numerator, 4, indicating the number of these regions that are shaded. Considering the rectangular regions labeled $\frac{1}{4}$, we see that an equal area has been shaded. There are four regions labeled $\frac{1}{4}$, two of which have been shaded. This fact is indicated by the fraction $\frac{2}{4}$. Clearly, $\frac{4}{8}$ and $\frac{2}{4}$ are equivalent fractions. Now considering the rectangular regions labeled $\frac{1}{2}$, we see that an equal area has again been shaded. There are two regions labeled $\frac{1}{2}$, only one of which has been shaded. The fraction $\frac{1}{2}$ indicates this fact. Obviously, $\frac{1}{2}$ is equivalent to $\frac{2}{4}$ and $\frac{4}{8}$ $\left(\frac{1}{2} = \frac{2}{4} = \frac{4}{8}\right)$. Other charts can be made that illustrate equivalent fractions. For example, the following chart illustrates the equivalence of $\frac{1}{3}$, $\frac{2}{6}$, and $\frac{4}{12}$ $\left(\frac{1}{3} = \frac{2}{6} = \frac{4}{12}\right)$:

Unit	1											
Thirds	$\frac{1}{3}$				$\frac{1}{3}$				$\frac{1}{3}$			
Sixths	$\frac{1}{6}$		$\frac{1}{6}$		$\frac{1}{6}$		$\frac{1}{6}$		$\frac{1}{6}$		$\frac{1}{6}$	
Twelfths	$\frac{1}{12}$	$\frac{1}{12}$	$\frac{1}{12}$	$\frac{1}{12}$	$\frac{1}{12}$	$\frac{1}{12}$	$\frac{1}{12}$	$\frac{1}{12}$	$\frac{1}{12}$	$\frac{1}{12}$	$\frac{1}{12}$	$\frac{1}{12}$

Practice with these charts to help clarify the meaning of equivalent fractions and to build a foundation for examining methods of finding equivalent fractions. Now let's construct a chart that includes all denominators from 2 to 10. A chart such as the one at the top of the next page emphasizes the fact that increasing the value of the denominator, while leaving the numerator unchanged, reduces the value of the fraction.

On such a chart, equivalent fractions can be found and comparisons can be made among fractions of different values. For example, we see that $\frac{1}{2} = \frac{2}{4} = \frac{4}{8}$. In this way rows of equivalent fractions can be determined:

$$\frac{1}{2} = \frac{2}{4} = \frac{3}{6} = \frac{4}{8} = \frac{5}{10}$$
$$\frac{2}{3} = \frac{4}{6} = \frac{6}{9}$$

Furthermore, the relation between fractional numbers such as $\frac{1}{3}$ and $\frac{1}{7}$ can readily be seen:

$$\frac{1}{3} > \frac{1}{7} \quad \text{or} \quad \frac{1}{7} < \frac{1}{3}$$

A similar chart to the one discussed above can be made using the manipulatives known as Cuisenaire rods. In this case, use the orange rod and two white rods end-to-end. This will form the unit length. Now, for this arrangement, $\frac{1}{2}$ would be represented by a dark green rod, $\frac{1}{3}$ by a purple rod, $\frac{1}{4}$ by a light green rod, $\frac{1}{6}$ by a red rod, and $1\frac{1}{2}$ by a white rod. ($\frac{1}{5}$, $\frac{1}{7}$, $\frac{1}{8}$, and $\frac{1}{10}$ cannot be shown because no existing rod or combination of rods represents these fractional parts of a unit made up of 12 subsections.)

The number line can also be used to model equivalent fractions. For instance, we can show the truth of the statement $\frac{1}{2} = \frac{2}{4}$ by using the number line. In the following illustration the unit segment is divided into two segments of equal length:

Similarly, the segment between 0 and $\frac{1}{2}$ is separated into two equivalent parts, and the segment between $\frac{1}{2}$ and 1 is also divided into two equivalent parts. Thus the unit segment has been separated into four equivalent parts, and the point $\frac{1}{2}$ (or $\frac{2}{4}$) is two of the $\frac{1}{4}$ units from 0.

Notice that $\frac{1}{2}$ and $\frac{2}{4}$ each name the same point and that $\frac{1 \times 2}{2 \times 2} = \frac{2}{4}$. This is an application of the identity element for multiplication, which states that any number multiplied times 1 is the number itself, $a \times 1 = a$. Of course, we can substitute any equivalent name for 1—for example, $\frac{2}{2}$ or $\frac{3}{3}$. If $a = \frac{1}{2}$ in the mathematical sentence $a \times 1 = 1$, then we write $\frac{1}{2} \times 1 = \frac{1}{2}$. Also, because $\frac{2}{2}$ is another name for 1, we can write $\frac{1}{2} \times \frac{2}{2} = \frac{1}{2}$ or $\frac{1 \times 2}{2 \times 2} = \frac{2}{4} = \frac{1}{2}$. Similarly, because $\frac{3}{3}$ is another name for 1, we can also write $\frac{1}{2} \times \frac{3}{3}$ $= \frac{1}{2}$ or $\frac{1 \times 3}{2 \times 3} = \frac{3}{6} = \frac{1}{2}$. By using the identity element this way, we can find many different names for any point on the number line.

$$\frac{1}{4} = \frac{1}{4} \times \frac{2}{2} = \frac{1 \times 2}{4 \times 2} = \frac{2}{8}$$
$$\frac{1}{4} = \frac{1}{4} \times \frac{3}{3} = \frac{1 \times 3}{4 \times 3} = \frac{3}{12}$$
$$\frac{1}{4} = \frac{1}{4} \times \frac{5}{5} = \frac{1 \times 5}{4 \times 5} = \frac{5}{20}$$

We realize that children have not yet formally studied multiplication of fractions. However, we feel that they can explore relationships among the fractions to justify that fractions can be renamed by means of the identity element of multiplication. Children should have an opportunity to discover many names for any point on the number line. They will want to expand their concept of fractions to include other fractions such as thirds, sixths, and eighths.

The number line is an excellent device for developing the order of fractions. Children should discover that the numerators of the set of halves follow the same pattern as the counting numbers; that the denominators are the same, 2, in every case; and that any fraction named on a traditional number line is greater than (>) each fraction to its left and is less than (<) each fraction to its right. When two fractions are compared, one of three possible relations between them will hold true: One fraction is equal to (=), is greater than (>), or is less than (<) the other. Using the number line, children can begin to see relationships among fractions that do not name the same number.

When several sets of related fractions appear on one number line, children can readily tell which one of any two fractional numbers is greater. They should acquire experience in writing statements such as $\frac{1}{2} < \frac{3}{4}$. This statement is read, "One-half is less than three-fourths." The statement $\frac{1}{2} > \frac{1}{3}$ is read, "One-half is greater than one-third."

As discussed earlier, mathematicians read the symbol < as "is less than" and the symbol > as "is greater than." With young children the phrase "is more than" may be clearer at first than "is greater than"; children have experienced situations in which one child has more marbles or more pieces of candy than another. In any case, avoid referring to one fraction as "smaller than" another because it is possible that $\frac{1}{2}$ is really smaller than $\frac{1}{4}$, if we are referring to different unit sizes. Teachers should introduce the correct terminology in its proper place, and children will come to understand this terminology by using it. In working with whole numbers, children learn that, as they move to the right on the traditional number line, the numbers become greater, and, as they move to the left, the numbers become less. Fractional numbers, of course, follow the same pattern.

Teachers should provide many opportunities for children to show the relation between two fractional numbers by placing the proper sign between two fractions. Using placeholders between fractions as shown, have children fill in the correct relation symbol:

$$\frac{1}{4} \bigcirc \frac{3}{4} \qquad \frac{1}{4} \oslash \frac{3}{4}$$
$$\frac{1}{8} \bigcirc \frac{2}{4} \qquad \frac{1}{8} \oslash \frac{2}{4}$$
$$\frac{3}{4} \bigcirc \frac{7}{8} \qquad \frac{3}{4} \oslash \frac{7}{8}$$
$$\frac{3}{2} \bigcirc \frac{11}{8} \qquad \frac{3}{2} \oslash \frac{11}{8}$$

If you prefer, a blank line can be used between the two fractions, and the student can be asked to fill in the correct phrase: "is greater than," "is less than," or "is equal to."

Another way to look at a fraction is as a number obtained when an integer is divided by an integer other than zero. No rational number is named by $\frac{2}{0}$ (or $\frac{3}{0}$, $\frac{4}{0}$, and so on), because $\frac{2}{0}$ indicates division by zero. Zero, however, can be renamed by a fraction. Zero divided by any counting number is zero; $\frac{0}{2} = 0$, $\frac{0}{3} = 0$, $\frac{0}{27} = 0$, and so on.

Every whole number is a part of the set of fractional numbers, since every whole number can be considered the result of dividing some whole number by a counting number. For example, every whole number is equal to itself (a whole number) divided by one (a counting number). Look at the following examples:

$$2 = 4 \div 2 \quad \text{or} \quad 2 = \frac{4}{2}$$

But not every fraction is an element of the set of whole numbers—for example, $\frac{1}{3}$, $\frac{2}{13}$, and $\frac{5}{14}$.

All mixed numerals name fractions because all whole numbers can be written as fractions. For example:

$$2\tfrac{1}{7} = 2 + \tfrac{1}{7}$$
$$= (1 + 1) + \tfrac{1}{7}$$
$$= \left(\tfrac{7}{7} + \tfrac{7}{7}\right) + \tfrac{1}{7}$$
$$= \tfrac{14}{7} + \tfrac{1}{7}$$
$$= \tfrac{15}{7}$$

A number line showing equivalent fractions is a useful aid in preparing to develop the four basic operations with respect to fractional numbers.

Children can be asked to begin at zero and move a jump of $\frac{2}{4}$ to the right. An additional jump of $\frac{1}{4}$ will end at $\frac{3}{4}$. Thus we conclude that $\frac{2}{4}$ add $\frac{1}{4}$ is $\frac{3}{4}$, or $\frac{1}{2}$ add $\frac{1}{4}$ is $\frac{3}{4}$.

Regions can also be used to introduce children to the foundations of adding and subtracting fractions. First, discuss the use of regions to model equivalent fractions. Have the children lay out one-half of a circular region and find how many fourths can be placed on top to completely cover half the region.

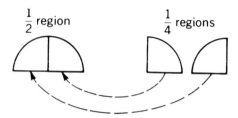

How many $\frac{1}{8}$ circular regions may be placed on top of the $\frac{1}{2}$ region? Continue this process until children realize that $\frac{1}{2} = \frac{2}{4} = \frac{4}{8} = \frac{5}{10}$, and so forth.

Next, instead of having the children place one region on top of the other, have them place it adjacent to the other. The following examples show that $\frac{1}{2} + \frac{1}{4} = \frac{3}{4}$ and $\frac{1}{6} + \frac{2}{6} = \frac{3}{6}$:

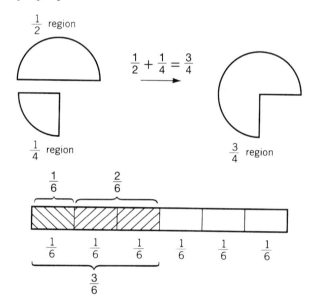

CLOSURE

Before beginning a more rigorous or formal study of operations on fractions, a child *must* have a solid grasp, as measured by both action and word, of the many foundational concepts discussed in this chapter. Careful and deliberate attention to the prerequisite knowledge, skills, understandings, and experiences described in this chapter will result in significant benefits in later instruction. With such a foundation, as we shall see in the next chapter, the learning of operations on rational numbers is greatly aided, and the time spent attaining understanding and skill is greatly lessened.

Terminology, Symbols, and Procedures

Denominator. The denominator of a fraction is the number below the fraction bar, indicating the number of equivalent pieces into which a unit is being divided. For example, the denominator of $\frac{5}{7}$ is 7, reflecting that some unit, or group of objects viewed as a unit, has been divided into seven equal parts.

Equivalent Fractions. Equivalent fractions are fractions that name the same number. For example, $\frac{2}{3}$, $\frac{4}{6}$, and $\frac{8}{12}$ are equivalent fractions $\left(\frac{2}{3} = \frac{4}{6} = \frac{8}{12}\right)$.

Fraction. A fraction is a numeral of the form $\frac{a}{b}$ where a and b are integers and $b \neq 0$.

Fraction Bar. The line segment drawn horizontally between the numerator and the denominator is the fraction bar. It can also be represented by a slanted segment (/), but this is sometimes reserved for noting a ratio.

Improper Fraction. An improper fraction is a fraction in which the numerator is greater than or equal to the denominator, such as $\frac{7}{5}$, $\frac{3}{3}$, and $\frac{6}{2}$.

Mixed Numeral. A mixed numeral is a numeral, such as $2\frac{3}{4}$, that consists of a whole number and a fraction. That is, $2\frac{3}{4}$ is an abbreviated form of $2 + \frac{3}{4}$.

Numerator. The numerator of a fraction is the number above the fraction bar, indicating how many "pieces" we are considering. For example, the numerator in $\frac{5}{7}$ is 5, reflecting that some unit, or group of objects viewed as a unit, has been divided into seven equal parts and that we are considering only five of those seven parts.

Proper Fraction. A proper fraction is a fraction in which the numerator is less than the denominator, such as $\frac{2}{3}$, $\frac{1}{2}$, and $\frac{7}{8}$.

Rational Number. Any number that can be written in the form $\frac{a}{b}$, where a is any integer and b is any integer other than zero, is a rational number.

Simplest Form. The simplest form is the form in which a fraction is written when the numerator and the denominator have no common factors other than 1. For example, $\frac{2}{3}$, $\frac{6}{7}$, and $\frac{5}{8}$ are fractions written in simplest form. The fraction $\frac{4}{12}$ is NOT in simplest form.

Practice Exercises for Teachers

These exercises are designed for the reader of this book. While some are suitable for use in the elementary classroom, these examples should not necessarily be given to children in this form. Ideas for classroom activities on the concepts and ideas discussed in this chapter can be found in Part 2 of *Today's Mathematics*, the Student Resource Book.

1. Shade part of each of the following regions as suggested by the given fraction.

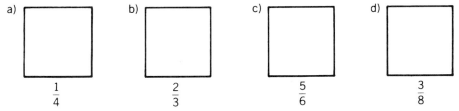

2. Shade part of each of the following groups as indicated by the given fraction.

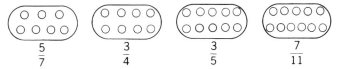

3. Shade part of each of the following regions as suggested by the given fraction.

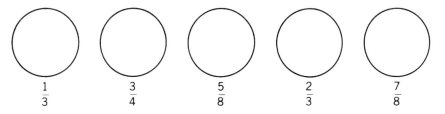

4. Make a number line from 0 to 2; locate and label each of the following fractions.

$$0, 1, 2, \frac{1}{2}, \frac{1}{3}, \frac{1}{4}, \frac{2}{3}, \frac{3}{4}, \frac{2}{2}, \frac{4}{2}, \frac{2}{4}, \frac{1}{6}, \frac{2}{6}, \frac{4}{6}, \frac{3}{6}, \frac{5}{6}, \frac{4}{3}, 1\frac{1}{2}, 1\frac{1}{3}, \frac{5}{3}, 1\frac{2}{3}$$

5. Place each of the following groups of fractions in order from least to greatest.

a) $\frac{1}{6}, \frac{1}{2}, \frac{1}{4}, \frac{1}{5}, \frac{1}{3}, \frac{1}{7}, \frac{1}{9}, \frac{1}{8}$ b) $\frac{3}{5}, \frac{1}{5}, \frac{2}{5}, \frac{5}{5}, \frac{4}{5}, \frac{6}{5}$

c) $\frac{3}{6}, \frac{1}{3}, \frac{4}{6}, \frac{1}{6}, \frac{5}{6}, \frac{3}{3}$ d) $\frac{5}{8}, \frac{1}{3}, \frac{3}{8}, \frac{2}{3}, \frac{3}{4}, \frac{1}{4}, \frac{1}{8}, \frac{4}{4}$

6. Place the correct relation symbol (<, =, and >) or phrase ("is less than," "is equal to," and "is greater than") between each of the following pairs of fractions to make a true statement.

a) $\frac{1}{10} \bigcirc \frac{2}{10}$ b) $\frac{3}{4} \bigcirc \frac{3}{8}$ c) $\frac{3}{8} \bigcirc \frac{2}{3}$ d) $\frac{1}{2} \bigcirc \frac{5}{12}$

e) $\frac{2}{3} \bigcirc \frac{5}{6}$ f) $\frac{11}{8} \bigcirc \frac{5}{4}$ g) $\frac{5}{8} \bigcirc \frac{3}{4}$ h) $\frac{3}{14} \bigcirc \frac{6}{28}$

7. Write each of the following as a fraction in simplest form.

a) $\frac{8}{12}$ b) $\frac{4}{16}$ c) $\frac{18}{32}$ d) $\frac{15}{18}$

e) $\frac{16}{24}$ f) $\frac{125}{5}$ g) $\frac{91}{161}$ h) $\frac{34}{51}$

8. Write each of the following mixed numerals as a fraction.

a) $3\frac{3}{5}$ b) $5\frac{3}{10}$ c) $1\frac{7}{8}$ d) $3\frac{1}{7}$

e) $4\frac{1}{2}$ f) $16\frac{3}{8}$ g) $5\frac{2}{5}$ h) $7\frac{1}{7}$

9. Fill in the blanks in the following lists of equivalent fractions. Keep the denominators in increasing order.

a) $\frac{1}{2}$, _____, _____, $\frac{4}{8}$, _____, _____, _____

b) $\frac{3}{8}, \frac{6}{16}$, _____, _____, _____, _____, _____

c) $\frac{5}{7}$, _____, $\frac{15}{21}$, _____, _____, _____, _____

10. Complete the following explanation of why the fraction $\frac{3}{5}$ is equivalent to $\frac{21}{35}$.

If a rectangular region is divided into 5 regions of the same size, we can shade _____ (how many?) of these regions to represent $\frac{3}{5}$. If each of the 5 regions into which the original region is divided is itself divided into 7 equivalent regions, then the original rectangular region will have been divided into $5 \times$ _____equivalent regions. The portion that was shaded will then consist of _____ $\times 7$ of these smaller regions. Thus the portion of the original rectangular region that is shaded can also be represented by the fraction $\frac{21}{35}$. Since $\frac{21}{35}$ and $\frac{3}{5}$ both indicate what portion of the original region is shaded, we can conclude that $\frac{21}{35}$ and $\frac{3}{5}$ are _____ fractions.

11. Use reasoning similar to that in Exercise 10 to argue that $\frac{4}{7}$ is equivalent to $\frac{400}{700}$.

12. Write each of the following improper fractions as a mixed numeral.

a) $\frac{29}{5}$ b) $\frac{17}{4}$ c) $\frac{37}{7}$ d) $\frac{24}{9}$ e) $\frac{43}{12}$

f) $\frac{31}{4}$ g) $\frac{49}{9}$ h) $\frac{19}{5}$ i) $\frac{25}{13}$ j) $\frac{44}{9}$

13. Mark each of the following statements true or false.

a) The number represented by $1\frac{2}{7}$ can be named with a proper fraction.

b) It is incorrect to call $2\frac{2}{3}$ a fractional number, because it is the sum of a whole number and a fractional number.

c) Every improper fraction names a number that is either greater than or equal to 1.

d) Every mixed numeral can be rewritten as an improper fraction.

e) The number $\frac{10}{5}$ is a fraction but not a whole number.

f) Every proper fraction names a number greater than 0.

g) Every proper fraction names a number less than 1.

h) An infinite number of fraction names are possible for the number 1.

Teaching Competencies and Self-Assessment Tasks

1. Set up an experiment to compare the use of circular regions versus rectangular regions in exploring a fraction concept. What are the advantages and disadvantages of one over the other? How do other shapes fit into this discussion?

2. Make a set of number line overlays for the overhead projector, illustrating fractions marked on the number line. Demonstrate the use of the number line transparencies to your class.

3. Research the use of the following materials to introduce fraction concepts in the elementary grades. Present your findings to the class.
  a) Cuisenaire rods   b) pattern blocks   c) base ten blocks   d) graph paper

4. Examine the fraction curriculum scope and sequence in several elementary school text-books and discuss with your peers the similarities and differences among the content, sequence, and approaches found in these programs.

5. In preparation for a discussion on which should be taught first (rational numbers expressed as decimals or rational numbers expressed as fractions), separate a page into columns. In one column list the advantages and disadvantages of teaching decimals first and in the second column list the advantages and disadvantages of teaching fractions first. Compare the lists and debate the findings.

6. Discuss how pure discovery and guided discovery can be effectively used in introducing fractions to children.

7. Prepare a collection of readiness activities that can be used in the elementary grades, especially at the primary level, as a foundation for the formal introduction of fractions.

8. When fractional parts of a group are being considered, is it necessary that the number of objects in the group always be some multiple of the denominator of the fraction being considered? For example, if you wish to find one-fifth of a group of objects, must the number of objects in the group be a multiple of five? Is it possible to find one-third of a group of five? Can this be shown on the following group?

How about on this group?

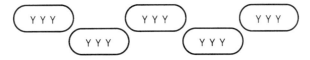

What difficulties arise from such a discussion in a classroom, and how do you overcome them?

9. Fractions should be introduced on the concrete level and then carried through the semi-concrete, semiabstract, and abstract levels. Discuss manipulative materials, commercial and teacher/student-made, that can be used at various levels of student development.

10. Identify and discuss situations that a teacher can create in the primary classroom to involve children with fractions from their real-world experiences.

11. Discuss how problem solving would be incorporated into the study of fractions. How might the notion of communication be incorporated? reasoning? connections? Describe examples of each in the preK–2, 3–5, and the 6–8 curriculum.

Related Readings and Teacher Resources

For related readings on topics found in this chapter, see the corresponding chapter in Part 2 of *Today's Mathematics*, the Student Resource Book.

Chapter 12

Rational Numbers Expressed as Fractions: Operations

Teaching Competencies

Upon completing this chapter, you will be able to:

■ Use regions, groups, number lines, and other models to develop an understanding of addition, subtraction, multiplication, and division of fractions.

■ Describe an appropriate instructional sequence for addition, subtraction, multiplication, and division of fractions.

■ Use commonly employed algorithms for addition, subtraction, multiplication, and division of fractions.

■ Use the least common denominator and the greatest common factor, as well as fundamental numerical properties, as tools in calculating with fractions.

■ Design lessons for children that incorporate meaningful models for exploring operations on rational numbers expressed as fractions.

C onsider the following drawing of an arrangement of Cuisenaire rods that uses the dark
green rod to represent one unit. What does
the picture reveal to you? What fraction concepts can be seen in this picture? What relationships
between the rods can you find? Before reading on, see
if you can use the drawing to make some specific statements about the many names for 1, equivalent fractions,
comparing fractions, mixed numerals, improper fractions, and even adding and subtracting fractions with
unlike denominators!

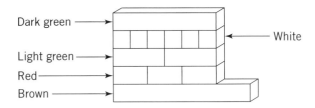

Dark green ⟶
Light green ⟶
Red ⟶
Brown ⟶
⟵ White

Ready? Close examination of the picture should reveal that one unit (the dark green rod, in this case) can
be represented by $\frac{6}{6}$, $\frac{3}{3}$, and $\frac{2}{2}$. Look closely: $\frac{2}{6}$ (two of the
white rods) is equal to $\frac{1}{3}$ (one of the red rods): $\frac{2}{6} = \frac{1}{3}$.
Notice that $\frac{2}{3}$ (two of the red rods) is greater than $\frac{1}{2}$ (one
of the light green rods): $\frac{2}{3} > \frac{1}{2}$. The brown rod is clearly
more than one unit—in fact, it is $\frac{8}{6}$ (the same length as
eight of the white rods), or $\frac{4}{3}$ (the same as four of the red

rods), or $1\frac{1}{3}$ (the same as one dark green and one red):
$\frac{8}{6} = \frac{4}{3} = 1\frac{1}{3}$. Finally, it can easily be seen that $\frac{2}{3}$ (two red
rods) is greater than $\frac{1}{2}$ (one light green rod). How much
greater? That is, how much of a difference in length is
there between $\frac{2}{3}$ and $\frac{1}{2}$ as shown in the drawing? Do
you see that the difference is one white rod $\left(\text{i.e., } \frac{1}{6}\right)$? So,
$\frac{2}{3} - \frac{1}{2} = \frac{1}{6}$. Quite a fraction feast from such a small drawing! Imagine what might be illustrated using other
arrangements of Cuisenaire rods!

Approaches using regions, groups, and number
lines, as well as Cuisenaire rods, base ten blocks, pattern blocks, and other manipulative materials, can help
to develop students' understanding of operations on
fractions. Locate and study teachers' manuals and support books and articles that will provide assistance as
you instruct children using such materials.

In Chapter 11 we used models of regions, groups,
and number lines as techniques to help students
develop an understanding of rational numbers written in
fraction form. After the children have developed an
understanding of rational numbers, as reflected by their
grasp of the topics discussed in Chapter 11, they are
ready to address the operations of addition, subtraction, multiplication, and division as applied to fractions.
A strong understanding of whole numbers and operations with whole numbers forms the base for developing operations with fractions. Many of the concepts and

Research Snapshot

*If children are encouraged to create their own ways to solve problems, can they invent their own algorithms for oper-
ations with fractions?*

Along with two fifth-grade teachers, Huinker (1998) investigated this question. Rather than directly teaching algorithms as presented in the textbooks, the research team focused the class on developing meaning for fractions operations. They began with word problems to give their students a context in which to use objects and pictures to make
sense of fraction concepts and operations. Students were encouraged to share their solution strategies with each
other while the teachers would focus on making connections between the various representations.

The students were able to invent algorithms for adding, subtracting, multiplying, and dividing fractions, and there
were many positive results in allowing students to invent their own algorithms. Some of them include:

■ The students were interested in solving and posing word problems with fractions.
■ They were flexible in their choice of strategy for solving both fraction word problems and computation exercises.
■ They were more accustomed to discussing their mathematical thinking and reasoning.

How will you make use of fraction models in support of allowing your students to create their own representations?

Huinker, D. (1998). Letting fraction algorithms emerge through problem solving. In L. Morrow & L. & M. Kenney (Eds.). *The
teaching and learning of algorithms in school mathematics* (pp. 170–182). Reston, VA: National Council of Teachers of
Mathematics.

For additional research briefs, "ERIC Digests" lets you search more than 2,000 short syntheses of research on a range
of education topics. The syntheses were produced by the Educational Resources Information Center (ERIC). Check
http://ed.gov/databases/ERIC_Digests/index/

structures of whole numbers can be directly applied to operations on fractional numbers.

The binary operations of addition and multiplication and the inverse operations of subtraction and division can be extended to fractions so that fundamental numerical properties are preserved. Addition and multiplication remain **commutative** and **associative**; multiplication is still **distributive** over addition; and 0 and 1 continue to be the **identity elements** for addition and multiplication, respectively. Once children grasp the idea that the operations and structure already studied extend naturally to fractions, they have learned a great deal about the system of fractional numbers. This recognition of shared properties also helps children see the connections and relationships between things too often viewed as having little or nothing to do with each other—operations on whole numbers and operations on rational numbers.

ADDITION OF FRACTIONAL NUMBERS

Let's begin our study by examining the addition of fractional numbers. The following figures illustrate the use of rectangular regions in modeling addition of fractional numbers. We choose to begin with fractions with like denominators because the addition process involving such fractions most closely resembles the process of addition with whole numbers. A fraction chart (as illustrated in Chapter 11) is an excellent device for children to use in exploring addition. For example:

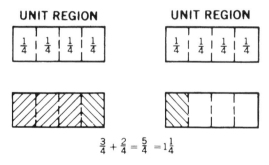

$$\frac{3}{4} + \frac{2}{4} = \frac{5}{4} = 1\frac{1}{4}$$

The two unit regions are both divided into fourths. Each small region therefore represents $\frac{1}{4}$. Suppose we want to add $\frac{3}{4}$ and $\frac{2}{4}$. To represent $\frac{3}{4}$ in the diagram, we shade 3 of the smaller regions; to represent $\frac{2}{4}$, we shade 2 more regions. This gives us a total of 5 regions that are shaded, each one representing $\frac{1}{4}$. We can indicate 4 of these regions as $\frac{4}{4}$, which equals 1. Since the region remaining represents $\frac{1}{4}$, we can represent the sum of the 5 shaded regions by the numeral $\frac{5}{4}$—that is, $\frac{4}{4} + \frac{1}{4}$ or $1\frac{1}{4}$. (Note that this example presents an opportunity to reinforce the equivalency of the improper and mixed numeral form of writing a given fraction.)

Circular regions should also be used as models of units to illustrate addition of fractions. Consider the same example using "equal" circular regions as unit models. Using fraction kits, each child should model the example:

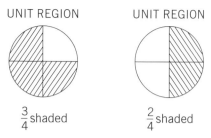

$\frac{3}{4}$ shaded $\frac{2}{4}$ shaded

The 2 circular unit regions shown above have been separated into fourths. Each small region then represents $\frac{1}{4}$ of the circular unit region. If we wish to add $\frac{3}{4}$ and $\frac{2}{4}$, we shade $\frac{3}{4}$ of one circular unit region and $\frac{2}{4}$ of a second circular unit region; then we combine the shaded regions.

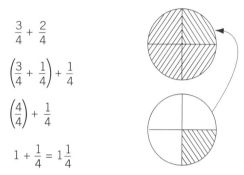

$$\frac{3}{4} + \frac{2}{4}$$

$$\left(\frac{3}{4} + \frac{1}{4}\right) + \frac{1}{4}$$

$$\left(\frac{4}{4}\right) + \frac{1}{4}$$

$$1 + \frac{1}{4} = 1\frac{1}{4}$$

Note that by moving one of the fourths to the first region, we can form one complete unit, and $\frac{1}{4}$ of a unit is left over. So the result of adding $\frac{3}{4}$ and $\frac{2}{4}$ must be $1\frac{1}{4}$. (A point made in Chapter 11 is worth repeating here: When we use circular units, a student's ability to visually see the completion of a whole unit is much more obvious, especially compared to the use of rectangular units.)

The same example can also be illustrated with groups as follows:

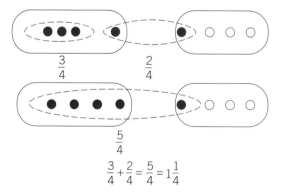

$$\frac{3}{4} + \frac{2}{4} = \frac{5}{4} = 1\frac{1}{4}$$

Each group of 4 dots represents a unit, and each individual dot represents $\frac{1}{4}$. To represent $\frac{3}{4}$ we draw a loop around 3 dots, and to represent $\frac{2}{4}$ we draw a loop around 2 more dots. This gives us a total of 5 dots that have been enclosed, indicating a value of $\frac{5}{4}$ or $1\frac{1}{4}$. We can represent this by drawing a loop around all 5 dots, as shown.

We have used rectangular regions, circular regions, and groups to model addition of fractions; we can also use the number line. Remember that children have already modeled addition on the number line using whole numbers. We can use the number line to develop children's understanding of addition of fractions. Consider $\frac{3}{4} + \frac{1}{4} = \square$, for example.

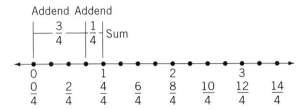

Children should have no difficulty finding the point on the number line that names $\frac{3}{4}$ and, since this is addition, jumping one-fourth of a unit to the right. To start at $\frac{3}{4}$ and jump one-fourth $\left(\frac{1}{4}\right)$ of a unit to the right puts us at the point labeled $\frac{4}{4}$. We know, of course, that $\frac{4}{4}$ is another name for 1. Therefore:

$$\frac{3}{4} + \frac{1}{4} = \frac{4}{4} = 1$$

Some children may wonder about the example $\frac{1}{4} + \frac{3}{4} = \square$. They may start at $\frac{1}{4}$ and jump three-fourths $\left(\frac{3}{4}\right)$ of a unit to the right.

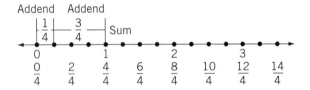

These children will write:

$$\frac{1}{4} + \frac{3}{4} = \frac{4}{4} = 1$$

From these two examples some children might conclude that since $\frac{3}{4} + \frac{1}{4} = 1$ and $\frac{1}{4} + \frac{3}{4} = 1$, then $\frac{3}{4} + \frac{1}{4} = \frac{1}{4} + \frac{3}{4}$. This example hints at the existence of the commutative property for addition of fractional numbers. Here is an excellent chance for children to apply the basic structure that they have previously learned for whole numbers to test a hypothesis for rational numbers.

Consider this example: $\frac{3}{8} + \frac{7}{8} = \square$.

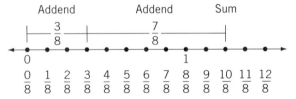

Locate $\frac{3}{8}$ on the number line; then jump, or count, $\frac{7}{8}$ unit (seven-eighths of a unit) to the right. This puts us at $\frac{10}{8}$. But $\frac{10}{8}$ has another name. We have passed the point named by 1 and moved another $\frac{2}{8}$ unit (two-eighths of a unit) to the right. Another name for $\frac{10}{8}$, then, is $1\frac{2}{8}$. Since $\frac{2}{8}$ can also be renamed in simplest form as $\frac{1}{4}$, another name for $\frac{10}{8}$ is $1\frac{1}{4}$.

$$\frac{3}{8} + \frac{7}{8} = \frac{10}{8}$$
$$= \frac{8}{8} + \frac{2}{8}$$
$$= 1 + \frac{2}{8}$$
$$= 1 + \frac{1}{4}$$
$$= 1\frac{1}{4}$$

(Children are not usually asked to record each of these steps. The steps are shown here for the teacher's benefit to aid the discussion of the process.)

After many examples, children should be able to generalize: To add fractional numbers with like denominators, we add the numerators as we would add any pair of whole numbers and keep the same denominator. We may want, as in the preceding example, to express the sum as a mixed numeral and to write it in simplest form $\left(e.g., \frac{2}{8} = \frac{1}{4}\right)$ for greater clarity.

Children can discover how to add using mixed numerals while they are learning to add fractional numbers with like denominators. Consider the example $\frac{4}{3} + \frac{5}{3} = \square$.

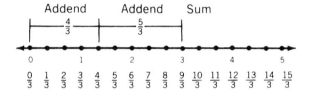

Locate $\frac{4}{3}$ on the number line; from this point jump $\frac{5}{3}$ units to the right. This puts us at the point named by $\frac{9}{3}$, so $\frac{4}{3} + \frac{5}{3} = \frac{9}{3}$. This can also be expressed with mixed numerals: $1\frac{1}{3} + 1\frac{2}{3} = 3$, since $\frac{4}{3} = 1\frac{1}{3}$ and $\frac{5}{3} = 1\frac{2}{3}$ and $\frac{9}{3} = 3$. Therefore, If we were given the example $1\frac{1}{3} + 1\frac{2}{3} = \square$, we could approach it by first translating it into improper fraction form, then solving it, and finally translating it back into mixed-numeral form.

There is, however, a more direct method for solving examples written in mixed-numeral form. We know that $1\frac{1}{3}$ can be expressed as $1 + \frac{1}{3}$ and that $1\frac{2}{3}$ can be expressed as $1 + \frac{2}{3}$. Thus $1\frac{1}{3} + 1\frac{2}{3} = \square$ can be rewritten as $\left(1 + \frac{1}{3}\right) + \left(1 + \frac{2}{3}\right) = \square$. We can then solve the example as follows:

$$1\frac{1}{3} + 1\frac{2}{3} = \left(1 + \frac{1}{3}\right) + \left(1 + \frac{2}{3}\right) \quad \text{Renaming}$$
$$= (1 + 1) + \left(\frac{1}{3} + \frac{2}{3}\right) \quad \text{Commutative and associative}$$
$$= 2 + \frac{3}{3} \quad \text{Renaming}$$
$$= 2 + 1 \quad \text{Renaming}$$
$$= 3 \quad \text{Renaming}$$

(Remember: This drawn-out written form illustrates how we want children to *think* of examples. It is not recommended that you require children to write each of these steps out.) Thus we can add mixed numerals by adding their whole number parts separately ($1 + 1 = 2$), then adding their fractional parts separately ($\frac{1}{3} + \frac{2}{3} = \frac{3}{3}$), and, if necessary, rewriting the sum ($2 + \frac{3}{3} = 3$).

Regions can also be used as models to help children understand how to add mixed numerals. You can see that three one-thirds equals 1 unit, that $\frac{4}{3}$ is $\frac{1}{3}$ more than a unit, and that $\frac{5}{3}$ is $\frac{2}{3}$ more than 1 unit. When we put them together, there are 2 and $\frac{3}{3}$ or a total of 3 units.

1 unit			1 unit			1 unit		
$\frac{1}{3}$	$\frac{1}{3}$	$\frac{1}{3}$	$\frac{1}{3}$	$\frac{1}{3}$	$\frac{1}{3}$	$\frac{1}{3}$	$\frac{1}{3}$	$\frac{1}{3}$

$$\frac{4}{3} \quad + \quad \frac{5}{3} \quad = \frac{9}{3} = 3$$

Experiment using circular regions as a model or using Cuisenaire rods, base ten blocks, or any other manipulative material as models. Children should be encouraged to experiment with a number of different models to assist them as they generalize concepts.

Children have little difficulty adding fractions with like denominators. Addition of fractions with unlike denominators, however, may be more difficult (depending on how the topic is approached). Gradually move into unlike denominators by beginning with examples that have unlike but *related* denominators. Examples of these would include $\frac{1}{3} + \frac{1}{6}$. In this case, one of the denominators of the given fractions turns out to be the common denominator. After children become proficient with unlike but related denominators, move on to examples with unlike but *unrelated* denominators, such as $\frac{1}{3} + \frac{1}{4}$. Note that, in this case, neither of the given denominators is the common denominator for the two fractions. Next, examples such as $\frac{1}{4} + \frac{1}{6}$ may be studied. In this last case, the two denominators do share a common factor (2), but neither denominator is the common denominator.

How can we add fractions when the denominators of the addends are unlike? Consider the example $\frac{1}{3} + \frac{5}{6} = \square$. Let's use a number line model:

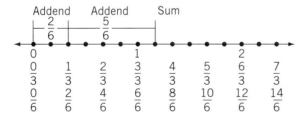

Locate $\frac{1}{3}$ on the number line. We can see that $\frac{1}{3}$ has another name, $\frac{2}{6}$. After locating $\frac{1}{3}$ (or $\frac{2}{6}$), we can add $\frac{5}{6}$ by moving $\frac{5}{6}$ units (five-sixths of a unit) to the right, which brings us to the point named by $\frac{7}{6}$. The fact that $\frac{1}{3}$ can be rewritten as $\frac{2}{6}$, which has the same denominator as $\frac{5}{6}$, should suggest another way of obtaining the sum $\frac{7}{6}$.

$$\frac{1}{3} + \frac{5}{6} = \frac{2}{6} + \frac{5}{6}$$
$$= \frac{7}{6} \text{ or } 1\frac{1}{6}$$

Note that, as emphasized in Chapter 11, the child who is well versed in the prerequisite of writing equivalent fractions should encounter little or no difficulty here.

The example $\frac{1}{3} + \frac{5}{6} = \square$ may also be modeled using rectangular regions.

1 unit					
$\frac{1}{3}$		$\frac{1}{3}$		$\frac{1}{3}$	
$\frac{1}{6}$	$\frac{1}{6}$	$\frac{1}{6}$	$\frac{1}{6}$	$\frac{1}{6}$	$\frac{1}{6}$

Separate the region into thirds and sixths, since those are the denominators of the two fractions to be added. The student can easily see that $\frac{2}{6}$ is another name for $\frac{1}{3}$. When $\frac{1}{3}$ is put with $\frac{5}{6}$, we see that we have $\frac{1}{6}$ more than 1; thus, we have $\frac{7}{6}$.

1 unit					
$\frac{1}{3}$	$\frac{1}{6}$	$\frac{1}{6}$	$\frac{1}{6}$	$\frac{1}{6}$	$\frac{1}{6}$

$$\frac{1}{3} \quad + \quad \frac{5}{6} \quad = \frac{7}{6} = 1\frac{1}{6}$$

This will be a simple step for many children if models have been used to develop a basic understanding of what rational numbers expressed as fractions really are. An understanding of the generation of sets of equivalent fractions and renaming fractions are also necessary. We cannot stress too often the importance of developing an understanding through models. If more emphasis is placed on developing an understanding of fraction concepts, less time (and even less effort) will be needed to develop an understanding of operations with fractions.

After studying equivalent fractions, children should not have difficulty with addition of fractions having unlike denominators. They can apply knowledge they already have to find equivalent fractions with common denominators. In general, if two fractional addends have unlike denominators, we can rename one (or both) of the addends so that the denominators are the same; then we find the sum of these fractions in the usual manner. Consider $\frac{1}{3} + \frac{1}{6} = \square$.

$$\frac{1}{3} + \frac{1}{6} = \frac{2}{6} + \frac{1}{6} \quad \left(\text{since } \frac{1 \times 2}{3 \times 2} = \frac{2}{6}\right)$$

We may prefer to express our answer, $\frac{3}{6}$, in simplest form, usually the most convenient way to name fractions. Reviewing simplest form briefly, we know from number line models that $\frac{3}{6} = \frac{1}{2}$. At this point of development you may wish to review simplifying fractions and renaming fractions using the identity element of multiplication. We can multiply a fraction by 1 without affecting its value.

$$\frac{1}{2} \times 1 = \frac{1}{2} \times \frac{3}{3}$$
$$= \frac{1 \times 3}{2 \times 3}$$
$$= \frac{3}{6}$$

The inverse of this is also true. We can divide a fraction by 1 without changing the value of the fractional number. Thus:

$$\frac{3}{6} = \frac{3 \div 3}{6 \div 3} = \frac{1}{2}$$

Now let us consider addition of unlike and unrelated fractions. How can we add $\frac{1}{4}$ and $\frac{1}{3}$? Begin with models to help children understand why a common denominator is important and how a common denominator can be found. If circular regions are used as models, we can place $\frac{1}{4}$ of a unit circle with $\frac{1}{3}$ of a unit circle, but the children probably do not know what fraction name to use to describe this new region.

By placing other parts of circular regions on top of these 2 regions, children should discover that twelfths would fit. After much experimentation, children should develop a systematic technique to solve examples of this type.

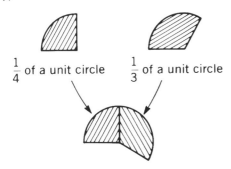

$\frac{1}{4}$ of a unit circle $\frac{1}{3}$ of a unit circle

What part of a circular region is this?

Before fractional numbers such as $\frac{1}{4}$ and $\frac{1}{3}$ can be added (or subtracted), a common denominator must be found that is divisible by each of the two original denominators—it must be a multiple of each of the denominators. In the case of $\frac{1}{4} + \frac{1}{3} = \square$, the common denominators are 12, 24, 36, 48, or, for that matter, any nonzero multiple of 12. Any one of these common denominators could be used in adding the two fractional numbers; however, it is typically most convenient to use the **least common denominator (LCD)** (12, in this case).

Finding the least common denominator is actually a simple extension of the process of finding the **least common multiple (LCM)** of the denominators. In fact, a student that comprehends finding the LCM can readily make the connection to finding an LCD—the multiples found in the LCM process are simply used as denominators in the LCD process. When the *least* common multiple is used as the common denominator, it is usually easier for us to express our answer in simplest form.

Consider the example suggested earlier: $\frac{1}{4} + \frac{1}{3}$. One readily understood method of identifying the least common multiple (i.e., the denominator) is to break the process into three steps:

1. List several of the *multiples* of each of the numbers in order:

    Multiples (nonzero) of 4: 4, 8, 12, 16, 20, 24, 28, . . .

    Multiples (nonzero) of 3: 3, 6, 9, 12, 15, 18, 21, 24, . . .

2. Find those multiples that are *common* to both lists:

    4, 8, 12, 16, 20, 24, 28, . . .
    3, 6, 9, 12, 15, 18, 21, 24, . . .

3. Simply select the *least* of these common multiples. This choice will be the least common multiple, and, when expressed as a denominator, it will be the least common denominator.

Another method of determining the least common multiple (LCM) is by factoring the denominators "completely"—that is, by factoring them into prime factors:

$$\frac{1}{4} = \frac{1}{2 \times 2}$$
$$\frac{1}{3} = \frac{1}{3}$$

The LCM can be constructed from the prime factorizations of the denominators. First, the LCM must have 2×2 as a factor in order for it to be a multiple of 4:

$$LCM = 2 \times 2 \times \, ?$$

The "2×2" ensures that the LCM is divisible by 4, and the question mark indicates that there may be other factors. Next, we know that the LCM must contain the factor 3 in order to be divisible by 3:

$$LCM = 2 \times 2 \times 3$$

Now it is apparent that the LCM we have constructed is divisible by both 4 and 3. So, $2 \times 2 \times 3$, or 12, is the least common multiple of 3 and 4 and, hence, the least common denominator of thirds and fourths.

The least common multiple can always be built by factoring the denominators into prime factors and then finding the least number that is a multiple of both denominators. Let's consider another example:

$$\frac{1}{6} + \frac{1}{8} + \frac{1}{3} = \square$$

Factor the denominators completely:

$$\frac{1}{6} = \frac{1}{2 \times 3} \qquad \frac{1}{8} = \frac{1}{2 \times 2 \times 2} \qquad \frac{1}{3} = \frac{1}{3}$$

Now build the least common multiple of 6, 8, and 3. The LCM must contain 2×3 in order to be divisible by 6:

$$LCM = 2 \times 3 \times \, ?$$

It must also contain $2 \times 2 \times 2$ to be divisible by 8. That is, the LCM must contain 2 as a factor three times. But since we have already recorded 2 as a factor once (LCM = $2 \times 3 \times$?), it is necessary to record it only twice more for the LCM to accommodate divisibility by 8:

$$LCM = 2 \times 3 \times 2 \times 2 \times \, ?$$

Finally, the LCM must contain the factor 3 so that it can be divided by 3. But 3 has already been indicated as a factor (LCM = $2 \times 3 \times 2 \times 2 \times$?), so it shouldn't be recorded again. Thus we have identified the LCM as:

$$2 \times 3 \times 2 \times 2 = 24$$

The basic structure that we have studied shows that multiplying a number by the **identity element for multiplication**, 1, does not change the value of the number ($a \times 1 = a$). We have also learned how to name 1 by using fractions such as $\frac{2}{2}, \frac{3}{3}, \frac{4}{4}, \frac{5}{5}$, and $\frac{6}{6}$. Therefore, any fraction can be multiplied by an equivalent value of 1 (any fraction whose numerator and denominator are identical, other than 0) without changing the value of the fraction. With this in mind, let's return to our original example and find the sum.

$$\frac{1}{6} + \frac{1}{8} + \frac{1}{3} = \square$$

$$\frac{1}{6} = \frac{\square}{24} \rightarrow \frac{1 \times \square}{6 \times \square} = \frac{\square}{24} \rightarrow \frac{1 \times 4}{6 \times 4} = \frac{4}{24}$$

$$\frac{1}{8} = \frac{\square}{24} \rightarrow \frac{1 \times \square}{8 \times \square} = \frac{\square}{24} \rightarrow \frac{1 \times 3}{8 \times 3} = \frac{3}{24}$$

$$\frac{1}{3} = \frac{\square}{24} \rightarrow \frac{1 \times \square}{3 \times \square} = \frac{\square}{24} \rightarrow \frac{1 \times 8}{3 \times 8} = \frac{8}{24}$$

We have now found equivalent fractions for each fraction in the original example. Since these new fractions have a common denominator, we can easily find the sum by adding their numerators.

$$\frac{4}{24} + \frac{3}{24} + \frac{8}{24} = \frac{15}{24}$$

$$\frac{15}{24} = \frac{15 \div 3}{24 \div 3} = \frac{5}{8}$$

Now let's consider another example: $\frac{3}{8} + \frac{5}{6} = \square$. First we must find the least common denominator for $\frac{3}{8}$ and $\frac{5}{6}$—that is, the least common multiple (LCM) of 8 and 6.

$$\frac{3}{8} = \frac{3}{2 \times 2 \times 2}$$

$$\frac{5}{6} = \frac{5}{2 \times 3}$$

$$\text{LCM} = 2 \times 2 \times 2 \times ? \quad \text{(The LCM is divisible by 8.)}$$

$$= 2 \times 2 \times 2 \times 3 \quad \text{(The LCM is also divisible by 6.)}$$

$$= 24$$

Then we must rename $\frac{3}{8}$ and $\frac{5}{6}$ as fractions having the common denominator of 24.

$$\frac{3}{8} = \frac{\square}{24}$$

$$\frac{3}{8} \times 1 = \frac{\square}{24}$$

What equivalent fraction can we use for 1 in this example? Since $\frac{3}{8} \times \frac{3}{3} = \frac{9}{24}$, we can use $\frac{3}{3}$ to make the denominator 24.

$$\frac{5}{6} = \frac{\square}{24}$$

$$\frac{5}{6} \times 1 = \frac{\square}{24}$$

What equivalent fraction can we use to represent 1 this time? We can use $\frac{4}{4}$ to make the denominator 24.

$$\frac{5}{6} \times \frac{4}{4} = \frac{20}{24}$$

Now we can use these conversions to add:

$$\frac{3}{8} + \frac{5}{6} = \frac{9}{24} + \frac{20}{24}$$

$$= \frac{29}{24}$$

$$= \left(\frac{24}{24} + \frac{5}{24}\right)$$

$$= 1 + \frac{5}{24}$$

$$= 1\frac{5}{24}$$

The concept of finding common denominators must be extended to mixed numerals. Begin with examples such as $1\frac{1}{2} + \frac{1}{3}$; then move to examples with two mixed numerals, such as $1\frac{1}{2} + 4\frac{1}{3}$. Then, move on to examples that will require renaming, such as $3\frac{4}{5} + 2\frac{3}{4}$.

SUBTRACTION OF FRACTIONAL NUMBERS

Subtraction of fractional numbers can be introduced shortly after beginning addition. Regions, groups of objects, and number lines may be used as models for subtraction as well as addition. The children should manipulate the pieces in their fraction kits, or pieces from the fraction chart, pattern blocks, or Cuisenaire rods before attempting to use the more abstract number line.

Let's model the example $\frac{3}{4} - \frac{1}{4} = \square$ using regions. The unit has been separated into fourths, and we begin with 3 one-fourths $\left(\frac{3}{4}\right)$. One-fourth may be taken away from the $\frac{3}{4}$, leaving $\frac{2}{4}$. Another name for $\frac{2}{4}$ is $\frac{1}{2}$.

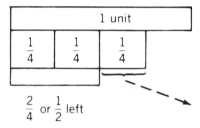

Regions can also be used to model subtraction of fractions according to the missing addend (or the comparison) method first discussed in Chapter 7. Rather than taking away one-fourth, we can place a region representing one-fourth on top of a region representing three-fourths. The question then becomes, "What do we need to add to the one-fourth to equal the three-fourths?"

Through use of the number line (using whole numbers), children should realize that subtraction is the inverse operation of addition and that we can use the number line to model subtraction. Consider this example:

$$\frac{3}{4} - \frac{1}{4} = \square$$

We could also use the idea that subtraction is the inverse of addition and rewrite the subtraction example $\frac{3}{4} - \frac{1}{4} = \square$ as $\frac{1}{4} + \square = \frac{3}{4}$. The addition example can then be solved on a number line as follows:

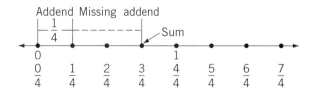

Therefore, $\square = \frac{2}{4} = \frac{1}{2}$; so $\frac{3}{4} - \frac{1}{4} = \frac{1}{2}$. Notice that $\frac{2}{4}$ is renamed as $\frac{1}{2}$. This is possible because $\frac{2}{4}$ and $\frac{1}{2}$ are equivalent fractions. We rename $\frac{2}{4}$ as $\frac{1}{2}$ to express the answer in simplest form.

After working through several examples directed to students' understanding of the process, children should be able to make some generalizations about subtraction of fractions.

1. To subtract fractional numbers, represent them by fractions having like denominators.
2. Then, subtract the numerators in the same way that whole numbers are subtracted.
3. The denominator of the difference is the same as the common denominator found in step 1.
4. The answer is usually written in simplest form for convenience.

Now consider another example: $\frac{5}{8} - \frac{3}{8} = \square$. Again using the idea that subtraction is the inverse of addition, we can think of $\frac{5}{8}$ as the sum and $\frac{3}{8}$ as the known addend. What is the missing addend? The example could be rewritten $\frac{3}{8} + \square = \frac{5}{8}$. The example can then be modeled on a number line as follows:

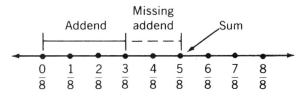

We find that the missing addend is $\frac{2}{8}$. Another name for this is $\frac{1}{4}$. Notice that $\frac{2}{8}$ in simplest form is $\frac{1}{4}$, or

$$\frac{2 \div 2}{8 \div 2}$$

Therefore, $\frac{5}{8} - \frac{3}{8} = \frac{2}{8} = \frac{1}{4}$.

We can use a similar method to subtract $\frac{7}{8}$ from $\frac{19}{8}$.

Mark the known addend, $\frac{7}{8}$, and then locate the sum, $\frac{19}{8}$. The missing addend is found to be $\frac{12}{8}$ but another name for $\frac{12}{8}$ is $\frac{2}{3}$. That is, $\frac{12}{8} \div \frac{4}{4} = \frac{3}{2}$ or $1\frac{1}{2}$. How would you also use regions to model this example?

$$\frac{19}{8} - \frac{7}{8} = \frac{12}{8}$$
$$= \frac{3}{2}$$
$$= 1\frac{1}{2}$$

Children should apply fundamental knowledge of addition to the subtraction of fractions to discover how a problem such as the following can be solved:

$$\frac{7}{8} - \frac{3}{4} = \square.$$

They should recall that it is useful for fractions to have like denominators before computation (addition or subtraction) is performed. In this case, one of these fractions should be renamed. We can rename $\frac{3}{4}$ as $\frac{6}{8}$. The example can now be solved.

$$\frac{7}{8} - \frac{3}{4} = \frac{7}{8} - \frac{6}{8}$$
$$= \frac{1}{8}$$

This example, of course, can also be solved using the number line as a model:

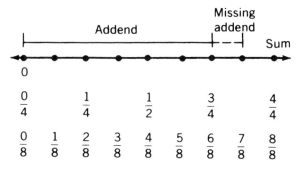

Again, the answer is clearly $\frac{1}{8}$.

Now let's consider a slightly more complex example:

$$\frac{11}{12} - \frac{5}{8} = \square$$

By applying knowledge of least common multiples, children should be able to factor both denominators and find the LCM:

$$\frac{11}{12} = \frac{11}{2 \times 2 \times 3}$$
$$\frac{5}{8} = \frac{5}{2 \times 2 \times 2}$$

Then they should build the LCM by using the factors of 12 and 8. The LCD is thus $2 \times 2 \times 3 \times 2$, or 24. Finally, they should rename $\frac{11}{12}$ and $\frac{5}{8}$ and perform the indicated subtraction.

$$\frac{11}{12} = \frac{11 \times 2}{12 \times 2} = \frac{22}{24}$$
$$\frac{5}{8} = \frac{5 \times 3}{8 \times 3} = \frac{15}{24}$$
$$\frac{22}{24} - \frac{15}{24} = \frac{7}{24}$$

We can solve each of these subtraction examples by using regions or sets. Let's demonstrate the region and set approaches in solving the example $\frac{7}{8} - \frac{7}{16} = \square$. Consider the following unit region, which has been divided into 16 parts (subregions) to illustrate eighths and sixteenths:

UNIT REGION

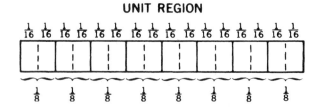

We can represent $\frac{7}{8}$ by shading 7 of the 8 regions that illustrate eighths. We can represent $\frac{7}{16}$ by shading 7 of the 16 regions that illustrate sixteenths. To represent $\frac{7}{8} - \frac{7}{16}$, however, the shaded region indicating $\frac{7}{16}$ must be entirely contained within the shaded region indicating $\frac{7}{8}$ (because we are subtracting $\frac{7}{16}$ from $\frac{7}{8}$), so the regions indicating $\frac{7}{8}$ and $\frac{7}{16}$ must be shaded differently:

UNIT REGION

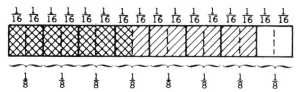

In this unit region, the difference between $\frac{7}{8}$ and $\frac{7}{16}$ is indicated by the part of the region shaded only once. This region contains 7 smaller regions illustrating sixteenths; therefore it represents $\frac{7}{16}$. So $\frac{7}{8} - \frac{7}{16} = \frac{7}{16}$.

Now let's approach this example using groups. Consider the following group of 16 dots:

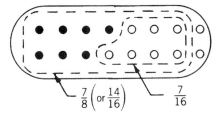

If this group represents 1 unit, then each individual dot represents $\frac{1}{16}$ unit, and each column of dots represents $\frac{1}{8}$. Now, if we enclose seven of the eight columns with a loop, the 14 enclosed dots illustrate the fractional number $\frac{7}{8}$. If we draw another loop around 7 of these dots (already enclosed), we illustrate $\frac{7}{16}$ (since there are 16 dots in the entire group and 7 of them are enclosed by this second loop). The difference between $\frac{7}{8}$ and $\frac{7}{16}$ is indicated by all the dots enclosed by the first loop but not by the second. In the following figure, these dots are shaded:

Because there are 7 dots shaded (out of a total of 16 dots in the group) and since each of the dots represents $\frac{1}{16}$, the difference between $\frac{7}{8}$ and $\frac{7}{16}$ is clearly $\frac{7}{16}$, or $\frac{7}{8} - \frac{7}{16} = \frac{7}{16}$.

Often we need to work with mixed numerals. For example, solve $5\frac{7}{8} - 4\frac{5}{8} = \square$. It is not difficult to extend our understanding of subtraction to include mixed numerals. Our approach here is very similar to that used for addition with mixed numerals:

$$5\frac{7}{8} = 5 + \frac{7}{8}$$
$$-4\frac{5}{8} = -\left(4 + \frac{5}{8}\right)$$
$$\overline{\qquad\qquad 1 + \frac{2}{8}}$$
$$= 1 + \frac{1}{4}$$
$$= 1\frac{1}{4}$$

Note that with the two addition symbols, one in front of the $\frac{7}{8}$ and one in front of the $\frac{5}{8}$, some children are likely to subtract the whole numbers and then add the fractions. To lessen this possibility, you may wish to replace the addition symbol with the word *and* so that instead of "$5 + \frac{7}{8}$," you have "5 and $\frac{7}{8}$." If, however, you

feel that the addition symbol is a must in this situation, then call children's attention to the parentheses, and explain that both the whole number and the fraction must be subtracted. That is, we write mixed numerals as the sum of whole numbers and fractional numbers. Then we subtract whole numbers to obtain the whole-number difference and fractional numbers to obtain the fractional-number difference. Notice that we write the fractional-number difference in simplest form.

In subtraction with mixed numerals, it is important to develop an understanding of renaming. For instance, consider the following subtraction example:

$$3\frac{1}{4}$$
$$-2\frac{3}{4}$$

In such cases, even though the fractions already have a common denominator, we cannot simply subtract the numerators. Therefore, we must find another way of expressing $3\frac{1}{4}$ so that we can subtract $2\frac{3}{4}$ from it.

$$3\frac{1}{4} = 3 + \frac{1}{4}$$
$$= (2 + 1) + \frac{1}{4}$$
$$= \left(2 + \frac{4}{4}\right) + \frac{1}{4}$$
$$= 2 + \left(\frac{4}{4} + \frac{1}{4}\right)$$
$$= 2 + \frac{5}{4}$$
$$= 2\frac{5}{4}$$

By renaming 3 as $2 + 1$ and expressing 1 as $\frac{4}{4}$, we can rewrite $3\frac{1}{4}$ as $2\frac{5}{4}$ and proceed with subtraction.

$$3\frac{1}{4} = 2\frac{5}{4}$$
$$-2\frac{3}{4} = -2\frac{3}{4}$$
$$\overline{\qquad = \frac{2}{4} = \frac{1}{2}}$$

Note that the series of written steps shown here is usually not to be recorded by students with such detail. It is important, however, that these same steps be demonstrated many times through physical models such as regions or number lines. The children must *see* that $3\frac{1}{4}$ has been renamed as $2\frac{5}{4}$. This should not be left to the abstract form only. Consider, for example, the pictorial representation of $3\frac{1}{4} - 2\frac{5}{4} = \square$.

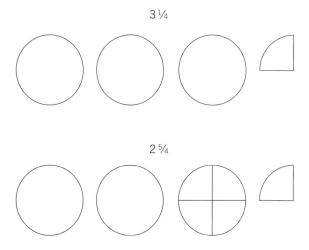

In this representation, one of the 3 wholes in $3\frac{1}{4}$ has been cut into fourths so that $3\frac{1}{4}$ is now represented by 2 wholes and a total of 5 fourths—that is, $2\frac{5}{4}$.

Another example of this kind, presented abstractly, is $8\frac{1}{6} - 3\frac{5}{6} = \square$.

$$
\begin{aligned}
8\frac{1}{6} &= \quad 8 + \frac{1}{6} = 7 + \left(\frac{6}{6} + \frac{1}{6}\right) &&= \quad 7 + \frac{7}{6} \\
-3\frac{5}{6} &= -\left(3 + \frac{5}{6}\right) = && \quad \underline{-\left(3 + \frac{5}{6}\right)} = \underline{-\left(3 + \frac{5}{6}\right)} \\
&&& \quad\quad 4 + \frac{2}{6} \\
&&&= \quad 4 + \frac{1}{3} \\
&&&= \quad\quad 4\frac{1}{3}
\end{aligned}
$$

Now let's examine another example:

$$
\begin{aligned}
7\frac{3}{8}\\
-2\frac{3}{4}
\end{aligned}
$$

First, we should obtain a common denominator. Because $\frac{3}{4} = \frac{6}{8}$, we can rename $2\frac{3}{4}$ as $2\frac{6}{8}$.

$$
\begin{aligned}
7\frac{3}{8} &= \quad 7\frac{3}{8} \\
-2\frac{3}{4} &= -2\frac{6}{8}
\end{aligned}
$$

Now we should find another way to name $7\frac{3}{8}$ so we can easily subtract the numerators;

$$
\begin{aligned}
7\frac{3}{8} &= 7 + \frac{3}{8} \\
&= (6 + 1) + \frac{3}{8} \\
&= \left(6 + \frac{8}{8}\right) + \frac{3}{8} \\
&= 6 + \left(\frac{8}{8} + \frac{3}{8}\right) \\
&= 6 + \frac{11}{8} \\
&= 6\frac{11}{8}
\end{aligned}
$$

Now we can solve the example:

$$
6\frac{11}{8} - 2\frac{6}{8} = 4\frac{5}{8}
$$

In general, the difference between two fractions named by mixed numerals can be determined in the following way:

1. Find a common denominator for the fractional number parts, if necessary.
2. Rewrite the first mixed numeral, if necessary, so that the numerators of the fractional number parts can be subtracted.
3. Find the difference between the whole-number parts of the two numbers.
4. Find the difference between the fractional-number parts of the two numbers.
5. Express the difference in simplest form.

We have used the number line, physical models, and groups of objects to develop the operations of addition and subtraction with respect to fractional numbers. We must emphasize that we are extending "old" ideas—not teaching new ones. We are helping children discover how to apply the operations and basic structure they

have already studied and learned about whole-number operations to a new situation: operations with fractions.

MULTIPLICATION OF FRACTIONAL NUMBERS

In this chapter we have so far examined the operations of addition and subtraction with respect to fractional numbers. Now let's consider multiplication. To help establish a pattern of reasoning, we begin with examples in which a fractional number is multiplied by a whole number. As is the case with other operations, children should work with a variety of models to develop understanding of the processes involved in multiplying fractions.

Multiplication of whole numbers, with which children are quite familiar at this stage, always results in a product that is either equal to or greater than either of the original factors. When children begin to apply the operation of multiplication to fractional numbers, they will, for the first time, find that a product may be less than both factors.

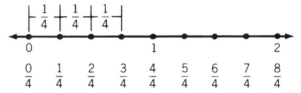

Look at the number line above and the example $3 \times \frac{1}{4} = \square$. We think of the example as meaning three groups with $\frac{1}{4}$ in each group. If we start at the point named 0 and make three jumps to the right, each jump $\frac{1}{4}$ of a unit in length, where do we land? We land at the point named $\frac{3}{4}$. By using the number line in this way, we can show the product, $3 \times \frac{1}{4}$, to be equal to $\frac{3}{4}$.

$$
3 \times \frac{1}{4} = \frac{3}{4}
$$

This example can also be written as follows:

$$
\left(\frac{3}{1}\right) \times \left(\frac{1}{4}\right) = \frac{3}{4}
$$

As we will discuss later, you should not be too quick to use this form of notation. Meaning is more important than symbolism at this developmental stage.

Now let's look at another example.

$$
6 \times \frac{2}{3} = \square
$$

On the number line we can model $6 \times \frac{2}{3}$ with 6 line segments, each $\frac{2}{3}$ of a unit in length, placed end-to-end.

In doing so, we find that the resulting line segment is 4 units long. Thus the product of 6 and $\frac{2}{3}$ is shown to be 4.

$$
\begin{aligned}
6 \times \frac{2}{3} &= \frac{2}{3} + \frac{2}{3} + \frac{2}{3} + \frac{2}{3} + \frac{2}{3} + \frac{2}{3} \\
&= \frac{12}{3} \\
&= \frac{4}{1} \\
&= 4
\end{aligned}
$$

On the same number line we can also show $\frac{2}{3} \times 6$. This can be pictured as $\frac{2}{3}$ of a line segment 6 units long. If the segment from 0 to 6 is divided into three parts, each 2 units long, $\frac{2}{3} \times 6$ is represented by two of these parts, or a total of 4 units.

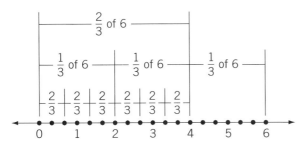

In this way the **commutative property of multiplication** is clearly illustrated:

$$6 \times \frac{2}{3} = \frac{2}{3} \times 6$$

The number line can be used as a teaching aid, without undue difficulty, to illustrate multiplication examples in which one of the factors is a whole number. The number line is not the best model, however, to explain situations in which neither factor can be written as a whole number—for example, $\frac{2}{3} \times \frac{4}{5} = \square$ and $\frac{7}{21} \times \frac{2}{9} = \square$. To illustrate examples like these, we can make good use of a region model.

To explore the way in which regions are used to illustrate multiplication of fractional numbers, let's first look at the example $6 \times \frac{2}{3} = \square$ again.

UNIT REGION

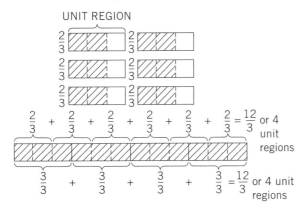

This illustration indicates the way in which multiplication can be modeled as repeated, or successive, addition. Thus:

$$6 \times \frac{2}{3} = \frac{2}{3} + \frac{2}{3} + \frac{2}{3} + \frac{2}{3} + \frac{2}{3} + \frac{2}{3}$$
$$= \frac{12}{3}$$
$$= 4$$

We can count the number of shaded parts (one-thirds) and see that there are 12 one-thirds, $\frac{12}{3}$. Another name for $\frac{12}{3}$ is 4.

$$\frac{12}{3} = \frac{3}{3} + \frac{3}{3} + \frac{3}{3} + \frac{3}{3}$$
$$= 1 + 1 + 1 + 1$$
$$= 4$$

But, as stated earlier, the repeated addition model is not the most appropriate for exercises such as $\frac{1}{2} \times \frac{1}{3}$. A different approach to the use of regions is called for when the product of two fractions is involved.

A valuable device to teach multiplication of fractions is a *unit square*, a square with each side one unit long. The unit square may be subdivided into smaller squares. Let us examine the following models:

UNIT SQUARES

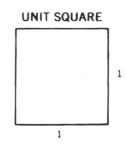

This unit square is divided into 100 smaller squares.

This unit square is divided into 144 smaller squares.

By strategically placing a colored rubber band across a unit card, we can illustrate $\frac{1}{2}$ of the card, $\frac{1}{4}$ of the card, or several other fractions. Using rubber bands and the unit card, let's consider this example:

$$\frac{1}{2} \times \frac{1}{3} = \square$$

First we construct a unit square.

UNIT SQUARE

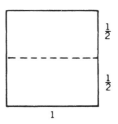

Next we divide the unit square horizontally into halves.

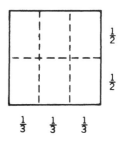

Then we divide the unit square vertically into thirds.

Examining the unit square, we see that it has been partitioned into 6 congruent regions. To show the result of $\frac{1}{2} \times \frac{1}{3}$, we shade any $\frac{1}{3}$ of the unit square (shading one direction); then we shade either the lower or the upper $\frac{1}{2}$ of the unit square (shading a different direction). By observation we can see that one part of the unit square has been shaded twice. The double-shaded region indicates the product of $\frac{1}{2}$ and $\frac{1}{3}$.

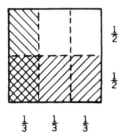

Comparing the double-shaded region with the total square, we see that one of the six parts (smaller regions) has been shaded twice. This leads us to the conclusion that $\frac{1}{2} \times \frac{1}{3} = \frac{1}{6}$. The same diagram, or one similar to the following, can be used to illustrate $\frac{1}{3} \times \frac{1}{2} = \frac{1}{6}$. This is another example of the commutative property of multiplication.

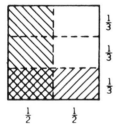

Now let's see how we can use the same reasoning to find the product of two fractions whose values are both greater than 1.

$$\frac{3}{2} \times \frac{4}{3} = \square$$

First we construct a unit square, dividing the square horizontally into halves and vertically into thirds. We divide the square into halves and thirds because they are the fractional parts being considered (indicated by the denominators) in this particular example.

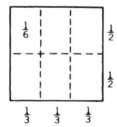

Notice that the square is now divided into six congruent parts. Since we have established our unit square, we can extend it horizontally and vertically to form a region that is $\frac{3}{2}$ by $\frac{4}{3}$ in size. We do this because $\frac{3}{2}$ and $\frac{4}{3}$ are the two factors being considered.

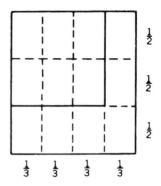

Again, notice that each small region is actually $\frac{1}{6}$ of a unit square. In this case we have more small regions than are necessary to make up one unit square. In fact, there are 12 small regions, or $\frac{12}{6}$ of a unit square. Since $\frac{12}{6}$ is another name for 2, we can see that there are actually enough small regions to complete two unit squares. Consequently, $\frac{3}{2} \times \frac{4}{3} = \frac{12}{6} = 2$. (*Note:* It might be advantageous to use centimeter graph paper for this model rather than unit square cards. A unit can be marked off on part of the graph paper. Then, when it comes time to "add on" to the unit square, you will be able to do so by enlarging the boundary of the unit square on the graph paper.)

After children have solved many examples of this kind and have developed an understanding of multiplication of fractions, the more familiar algorithm for multiplying fractions can be introduced. Children should be led to generalize for themselves that when multiplying two fractions, they can multiply the numerators of the two factors to obtain the numerator of the product, and multiply the denominators of the two factors to obtain the denominator of the product. The last two examples can be solved using this algorithm as follows:

$$\frac{1}{2} \times \frac{1}{3} = \frac{1 \times 1}{2 \times 3} = \frac{1}{6}$$

$$\frac{3}{2} \times \frac{4}{3} = \frac{3 \times 4}{2 \times 3} = \frac{12}{6} \text{ or } 2$$

In each case we get the same answer that we obtained by using regions. Notice that after we have determined the numerator and denominator of the product, we may wish to rewrite the product in another form (as an equivalent fraction or as a whole number, for instance). In the second example, the product $\frac{12}{6}$ can be rewritten as 2. Since whole numbers and fractional numbers named by mixed numerals can be expressed in fraction form, we can find the product of any two fractional numbers by means of the algorithm.

$$6 \times \frac{2}{3} = \frac{6}{1} \times \frac{2}{3} \qquad\qquad 3 \times \frac{1}{4} = \frac{3}{1} \times \frac{1}{4}$$

$$= \frac{6 \times 2}{1 \times 3} \qquad\qquad\qquad = \frac{3 \times 1}{1 \times 4}$$

$$= \frac{12}{4} \text{ or } 3 \qquad\qquad\qquad = \frac{3}{4}$$

$$2\frac{1}{2} \times \frac{1}{3} = \frac{5}{2} \times \frac{1}{3} \qquad\qquad 2 \times 5 = \frac{2}{1} \times \frac{5}{1}$$

$$= \frac{5 \times 1}{2 \times 3} \qquad\qquad\qquad = \frac{2 \times 5}{1 \times 1}$$

$$= \frac{5}{6} \qquad\qquad\qquad\qquad = \frac{10}{1} \text{ or } 10$$

We can now generalize that to multiply any two fractions (whole numbers are understood as having the denominator 1), the following steps should be performed:

1. Multiply the numerators of the factors to obtain the numerator of the product.
2. Multiply the denominators of the factors to obtain the denominator of the product.
3. If desired, rename the product (as an equivalent fraction or whole-number numeral, for example).

> If $\frac{a}{b}$ and $\frac{c}{d}$ are any two fractions such that $b \neq 0$ and $d \neq 0$, then
> $$\frac{a}{b} \times \frac{c}{d} = \frac{a \times c}{b \times d}$$

After completing a multiplication example, it may be necessary to simplify the product. For instance:

$$\frac{2}{3} \times \frac{3}{4} = \frac{2 \times 3}{3 \times 4} = \frac{6}{12} = \frac{1 \times 6}{2 \times 6} = \frac{1}{2}$$

It may be much easier if the example is simplified before multiplying. Consider the example $\frac{2}{3} \times \frac{3}{4}$ again.

$$\frac{2}{3} \times \frac{3}{4} = \frac{2 \times 3}{3 \times 2 \times 2} \quad \text{Factor}$$
$$= \frac{3 \times 2 \times 1}{3 \times 2 \times 2} \quad \text{Rewrite}$$
$$= \frac{3}{3} \times \frac{2}{2} \times \frac{1}{2} \quad \text{Rewrite}$$
$$= 1 \times 1 \times \frac{1}{2} \quad \text{Rename}$$
$$= \frac{1}{2}$$

Factor the numerator and denominator completely. Look for values of 1. Thus you have simplified the example prior to multiplication.

$$\frac{5}{6} \times \frac{3}{10} = \frac{1 \times 5 \times 3}{2 \times 3 \times 5 \times 2}$$
$$= \frac{1 \times 3 \times 5 \times 1}{2 \times 3 \times 5 \times 2}$$
$$= \frac{1}{2} \times 1 \times 1 \times \frac{1}{2}$$
$$= \frac{1}{4}$$

Before going on to division of fractions, let's look at the example $\frac{1}{2} \times \square = 1$. Clearly, $\square = 2$ (or $\frac{1}{2}$), since $\frac{1}{2} \times \frac{2}{1} = \frac{2}{2} = 1$. If we work through some additional examples like this one, we begin to see a pattern emerge:

$$\frac{1}{5} \times \square = 1 \rightarrow \square = \frac{5}{1} \quad \therefore \frac{1}{5} \times \frac{5}{1} = 1$$
$$\frac{4}{7} \times \square = 1 \rightarrow \square = \frac{7}{4} \quad \therefore \frac{4}{7} \times \frac{7}{4} = 1$$
$$\frac{5}{3} \times \square = 1 \rightarrow \square = \frac{3}{5} \quad \therefore \frac{5}{3} \times \frac{3}{5} = 1$$
$$\square \times \frac{11}{4} = 1 \rightarrow \square = \frac{4}{11} \quad \therefore \frac{4}{11} \times \frac{11}{4} = 1$$

In each of these examples, we discover a pair of fractional numbers whose product is equal to 1. (Recall that the number 1 is the identity element for multiplication of whole numbers. We shall see a little later in this chapter that 1 is also the identity element for multiplication of fractions.) Two fractions whose product is 1 are called **reciprocals** or **multiplicative inverses** of each other. For instance, the last three examples show that the reciprocal (or multiplicative inverse) of $\frac{4}{7}$ is $\frac{7}{4}$, that the reciprocal of $\frac{3}{5}$ is $\frac{5}{3}$, and that the reciprocal of $\frac{4}{11}$ is $\frac{11}{4}$. We also observe that for the fractions in each of these examples, the numerator of the first fraction

equals the denominator of the second, and the denominator of the first equals the numerator of the second.

Is it possible to use this idea to find reciprocals? Let's see. If we interchange the numerator and denominator in the fraction $\frac{2}{3}$, we obtain $\frac{3}{2}$. Is $\frac{3}{2}$ the reciprocal of $\frac{2}{3}$? That is, is $\frac{3}{2} \times \frac{2}{3}$ equal to 1? Yes, because $\frac{3 \times 2}{2 \times 3} = \frac{6}{6} = 1$. Is it always true that if $\frac{a}{b}$ is a fraction, then its reciprocal is $\frac{b}{a}$? We might ask this question in a slightly different way: Is it true, for every fraction $\frac{a}{b}$, that $\frac{b}{a} \times \frac{a}{b} = 1$? The answer is yes, provided neither a nor b is equal to zero. (Why must we exclude these cases?)

> If $\frac{a}{b}$ is any fraction such that $a \neq 0$ and $b \neq 0$, then
> $$\frac{a}{b} \times \frac{b}{a} = 1$$

Thus we have the following procedure for finding the reciprocal (or multiplicative inverse) of a nonzero fractional number:

1. Express the given number in fraction form.
2. Interchange the numerator and denominator of the fraction in step 1. The result is the reciprocal (or multiplicative inverse) of that fraction.

What is the reciprocal of $2\frac{3}{8}$? Use the procedure suggested. First, write the mixed numerals in fractional form:

$$2\frac{3}{8} = 2 + \frac{3}{8} = \frac{16}{8} + \frac{3}{8} = \frac{19}{8}$$

Second, interchange the numerator and denominator of the fraction $\frac{19}{8}$. This gives the fraction $\frac{8}{19}$. Clearly, $\frac{8}{19}$ is the reciprocal of $2\frac{3}{8}$ since $2\frac{3}{8} \times \frac{8}{19} = \frac{19}{8} \times \frac{8}{19} = \frac{152}{152} = 1$.

Returning to our discussion of multiplying fractions. Let's consider the multiplication example $3 \times 2\frac{1}{2} = \square$. We might choose to solve this example by expressing the factors in fraction form and multiplying as we would any two fractions.

$$3 \times 2\frac{1}{2} = \frac{3}{1} \times \frac{5}{2} \quad \text{Renaming}$$
$$= \frac{3 \times 5}{1 \times 2} \quad \text{Procedure for multiplying with fractions}$$
$$= \frac{15}{2} \quad \text{Multiplication}$$
$$= \frac{14}{2} + \frac{1}{2} \quad \text{Renaming}$$
$$= 7 + \frac{1}{2} \text{ or } 7\frac{1}{2} \quad \text{Renaming}$$

However, there is another way of solving this example if we remember that a mixed numeral names the sum of a whole number and a fraction. That is, $2\frac{1}{2}$ can be written as $2 + \frac{1}{2}$.

$$3 \times 2\frac{1}{2} = 3 \times \left(2 + \frac{1}{2}\right) \quad \text{Renaming}$$
$$= (3 \times 2) + \left(3 \times \frac{1}{2}\right) \quad \text{Distributive property of multiplication over addition}$$
$$= 6 + \frac{3}{2} \quad \text{Multiplication}$$
$$= 6 + \left(\frac{2}{2} + \frac{1}{2}\right) \quad \text{Renaming}$$
$$= 6 + \left(1 + \frac{1}{2}\right) \quad \text{Renaming}$$
$$= (6 + 1) + \frac{1}{2} \quad \text{Associative property}$$
$$= 7 + \frac{1}{2} \quad \text{Addition}$$
$$= 7\frac{1}{2} \quad \text{Renaming}$$

Therefore, $3 \times 2\frac{1}{2} = \frac{7}{2}$.

As with other examples of this type, the intermediate steps need not be recorded with such detail by children—indeed, they shouldn't be. Instead, it is sufficient for them to note, "Three times two and one-half is equal to three times two added to three times one-half, or six added to three-halves, or seven and one-half."

Now let's try another example: $3 \times 7\frac{1}{8} = \square$. We *could* choose to rewrite the first number as $\frac{3}{1}$ and the second as $\frac{57}{8}$ and then multiply these two fractions. Instead, let's examine the exercise as, perhaps, a more meaningful statement. We might then solve this, as described in the previous paragraph, by mentally renaming the second number as the sum of a whole number and a fraction. This allows us to interpret $3 \times 7\frac{1}{8}$ as three groups of 7 (21) and three groups of $\frac{1}{8}$ $\left(\frac{3}{8}\right)$, for a total of $21\frac{3}{8}$.

Apply the same reasoning described in the preceding examples, with a challenging twist, to solve $4\frac{1}{2} \times 6\frac{1}{4} = \square$.

Teaching multiplication of numbers named by mixed numerals is really no more than an extension of what has been taught previously. Multiplication with mixed numerals should provide an opportunity for children to apply basic structure and discover how to solve new, but related, examples.

DIVISION OF FRACTIONAL NUMBERS

Now let's examine the inverse operation of multiplication, division, with respect to fractions. This is often as challenging a topic for children to master as it is for teachers to develop in a meaningful manner. Actually, division of fractions is not very relevant to everyday life. Try, for example, to create a "real-life" story problem, meaningful to an elementary school child, that involves the division of two fractions. (Be careful with recipe examples: Most of these involve either the division of a fraction by a whole number or the multiplication of two fractions—not the division of a fraction by a fraction.)

Recall that the operation of division on whole numbers was defined as the process of finding a missing factor (Chapter 8). Let's apply this definition of division to the set of fractions. Consider the example $\frac{1}{4} \div \frac{1}{2} = \square$. The definition of division suggests that we can rewrite this example as the multiplication sentence $\frac{1}{2} \times \square = \frac{1}{4}$. Written in this form, the example asks us to find a number that will yield a product of $\frac{1}{4}$ when multiplied by $\frac{1}{2}$.

The example can also be expressed as follows:

$$\frac{1 \times \diamond}{2 \times \triangle} = \frac{1}{4}$$

Because we know that $1 \times 1 = 1$, the numerator of the missing factor is clearly 1. Since we know that $2 \times 2 = 4$, the denominator is 2. Therefore, the answer is $\frac{1}{2}$.

$$\frac{1 \times 1}{2 \times 2} = \frac{1}{4} \qquad \frac{1}{2} \times \frac{1}{2} = \frac{1}{4} \quad \text{or} \quad \frac{1}{4} \div \frac{1}{2} = \frac{1}{2}$$

Consider the example $\frac{3}{4} \times \square = \frac{6}{16}$. It can be expressed in this form:

$$\frac{3 \times \diamond}{4 \times \triangle} = \frac{6}{16}$$

The answer here is $\frac{2}{4}$, which can be renamed as $\frac{1}{2}$.

$$\frac{3}{4} \times \frac{2}{4} = \frac{6}{16} \quad \text{or} \quad \frac{3}{4} \times \frac{1}{2} = \frac{3}{8}$$

This procedure has been successful so far, but some examples might become very difficult if no alternative procedure were available. Consider the example $\frac{3}{7} \times \square = \frac{5}{9}$, which can be rewritten as follows:

$$\frac{3 \times \diamond}{7 \times \triangle} = \frac{5}{9}$$

Three times what number equals 5, and seven times what number equals 9? This method gives us a very cumbersome answer.

$$\frac{1\frac{2}{3}}{1\frac{2}{7}}$$

How can children begin to comprehend the meaning of such a fraction? How can they possibly translate it into something with more meaning for them? We clearly need another method for division of fractions.

The meaning of the inverse operation of division, as related to rational numbers expressed as fractions, may be thought of in another way. The children are familiar with the symbol $\overline{)}$, which they have learned to interpret as division; they are also familiar with division of whole numbers. With these two ideas as prerequisite learnings, children are ready for the division of rational numbers expressed as fractions. Parallel the discussion of the division of whole numbers with the division of fractions. First, review a whole-number example such as, "What does $2\overline{)6}$ mean?" This example can mean that we have 6 things and we want to know how many groups of 2 can be made.

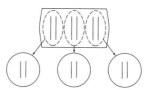

Three groups of 2 can be made from 6 things.

If we have six eighths, how many groups of two eighths can we make?

$$\frac{3}{2 \text{ eighths} \,\overline{)\,6 \text{ eighths}}}$$
$$\underline{6 \text{ eighths}}$$

$$\frac{6}{8} \qquad\qquad 2\overline{)\,\dfrac{6}{8}}\,\dfrac{3}{}$$

One group of $\frac{2}{8}$ One group of $\frac{2}{8}$ One group of $\frac{2}{8}$

On the concrete level, by using sectors of a circle, we can show that there can be three groups of $\frac{2}{8}$ each made from a group of $\frac{6}{8}$. Thus $\frac{6}{8} \div \frac{2}{8} = 3$. Alternatively, consider the figure that follows. To help interpret $\frac{1}{3} \div \frac{1}{6}$ = □, we could use pattern blocks with the yellow hexagon representing one whole unit. Then, a blue rhombus has a value of $\frac{1}{3}$ and a green triangle has a value of $\frac{1}{6}$. To determine the answer to $\frac{1}{3} \div \frac{1}{6}$, we need to determine how many groups of $\frac{1}{6}$ there are in $\frac{1}{3}$. Clearly, there are two groups of $\frac{1}{6}$ in $\frac{1}{3}$. Thus, the answer to $\frac{1}{3} \div \frac{1}{6}$ = □ is 2.

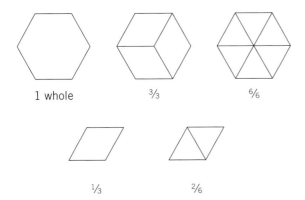

Let's compare another division example using fractions with an example using whole numbers, specifically $9 \div 3$ and $\frac{9}{10} \div \frac{3}{10}$.

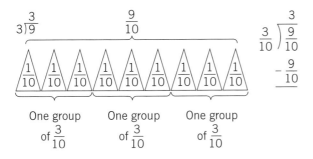

Thus we can see that there are three groups of $\frac{3}{10}$ in $\frac{9}{10}$.

Sometimes an example does not divide evenly. For instance:

$$
\begin{array}{r}
4\frac{1}{2} \\
2\overline{)\ 9} \\
\underline{-8} \\
1
\end{array}
$$

Now relate this example to $\frac{2}{10}\overline{)\frac{9}{10}}$.

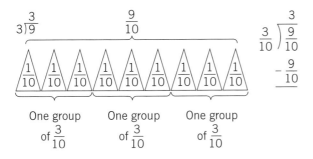

Thus:

$$
\begin{array}{r}
4\frac{1}{2} \\
\frac{2}{10}\overline{)\ \frac{9}{10}} \\
\underline{-\frac{8}{10}} \\
\frac{1}{10}
\end{array}
$$

The $\frac{1}{10}$ is $\frac{1}{2}$ of a group of $\frac{2}{10}$.

In developing an alternative method for division of fractions, we *must* understand the meaning of division by 1. Consider this example:

$$\frac{5}{3} \div 1 = \frac{5}{3}$$

From this example and others like it, we can generalize that any fraction divided by 1 is equal to the number itself. That is, division by 1 leaves any fraction unchanged. Now we are prepared to develop another method for dividing fractions.

Let's reconsider the following example:

$$\frac{5}{9} \div \frac{3}{7} = \square$$

We know that $\frac{5}{9} \div \frac{3}{7}$ can be written in complex fraction form as

$$\frac{\frac{5}{9}}{\frac{3}{7}}$$

Since the identity element for multiplication, 1, is a valid concept in the set of fractions, just as it is in the set of whole numbers, we can multiply

$$\frac{\frac{5}{9}}{\frac{3}{7}}$$

by 1 and by doing so translate the examples into a new form:

$$\frac{5}{9} \div \frac{3}{7} = \frac{\frac{5}{9}}{\frac{3}{7}} = \frac{\frac{5}{9}}{\frac{3}{7}} \times 1$$

$$= \frac{\frac{5}{9} \times \frac{7}{3}}{\frac{3}{7}}$$
We know that the reciprocal of the denominator $\frac{3}{7}$ is $\frac{7}{3}$, and if we multiply any number by its reciprocal the result is 1. Thus we choose here to multiply the fractional number $\frac{\frac{5}{9}}{\frac{3}{7}}$ by $\frac{\frac{7}{3}}{\frac{7}{3}}$ (another name for 1).

$$= \frac{\frac{5}{9} \times \frac{7}{3}}{\frac{3}{7} \times \frac{7}{3}}$$

$$= \frac{\frac{5}{9} \times \frac{7}{3}}{1} \quad \text{(The product of reciprocals is 1.)}$$

$$= \frac{5}{9} \times \frac{7}{3} \quad \text{(Division by 1)}$$

In this manner the example $\frac{5}{9} \div \frac{3}{7}$ = □ has been rewritten as $\frac{5}{9} \times \frac{7}{3}$ = □. So, we have translated the division example into a multiplication example (which we already know how to solve) by changing the division sign into a multiplication sign and by replacing the fraction after the operation sign $\left(\frac{3}{7}\right)$ with its reciprocal $\left(\frac{7}{3}\right)$. Thus we can determine the quotient for $\frac{5}{9} \div \frac{3}{7} = \square$.

$$\frac{5}{9} \div \frac{3}{7} = \frac{5}{9} \times \frac{7}{3}$$
$$= \frac{5 \times 7}{9 \times 3}$$
$$= \frac{35}{27}$$

Intermediate steps could have been omitted in the determination of the answer, because they are unnecessary. Whenever one fraction is to be divided by another, we can bypass these steps by inverting the second fraction and multiplying (instead of dividing).

If $\frac{a}{b}$ and $\frac{c}{d}$ are any two fractions such that $b \neq 0$ and $c \neq 0$, then

$$\frac{a}{b} \div \frac{c}{d} = \frac{a}{b} \times \frac{d}{c}$$

It is important to note that children should not be directed to such abstract rules during initial instruction. It is not necessarily easy for children to understand division of fractions; only after they have developed such an understanding should they use shortcuts—and even then, they should know what they are doing and be able to verbalize what is taking place. It is counterproductive to expose them to shortcuts such as "invert and multiply" until they have demonstrated some understanding of division of fractions using models. In general, mathematical shortcuts should not be presented without first exploring an adequate explanation of their use, purpose, and why they work.

CLOSURE

We have carefully examined some basic structures (properties) related to addition, subtraction, multiplica-

tion, and division with fractions. Regarding the properties of fractional numbers, we find the following:

1. Fractions are commutative with respect to addition and multiplication but *not* with respect to subtraction and division.
2. Fractions are associative with respect to addition and multiplication but *not* with respect to subtraction and division.
3. The number 0 is the identity element for addition with fractions. The number 1 is the identity element for multiplication with fractions.
4. Multiplication is distributive over addition and subtraction for the set of fractions.
5. Division is *not distributive* over addition or subtraction for the set of fractions.

Student facility with operations on fractional numbers is not as critical as it was once thought to be. Students will find, however, that fraction algorithms will serve them well as they explore algebra and other advanced topics in their mathematical development. Ratio and proportion, percents, probability, polynomial expressions, linear and quadratic equations, and the slope of lines and curves are but a few of the areas where students will again encounter the material found in this chapter. Perhaps we should not overemphasize the role of computations with fractional numbers, but we shouldn't underestimate it either. Certainly, the concepts underlying operations involving rational numbers are fundamental to success in mathematics.

Terminology, Symbols, and Procedures

Addition of Fractions Having Like Denominators. Add the numerators in the same manner that all whole numbers are added. The denominator remains the same. For example,

$$\frac{3}{8} + \frac{2}{8} = \frac{5}{8}$$

In general: $\frac{a}{b} + \frac{c}{b} = \frac{(a + c)}{b}$

Addition of Fractions Having Unlike Denominators. Rewrite the fractions as fractions having a common denominator (the least common denominator may be the easiest to use). Then add as usual. For example:

$$\frac{3}{4} + \frac{5}{8} = \frac{6}{8} + \frac{5}{8} = \frac{11}{8} \text{ or } 1\frac{3}{8}$$

Addition of Fractions with Mixed Numerals Having Like Denominators. Add the whole-number parts; then add the fraction parts. The fraction in the answer should usually be expressed as a proper fraction in simplest form. For example:

$$\begin{array}{r} 1\frac{3}{7} \\ +3\frac{5}{7} \\ \hline 4\frac{8}{7} \text{ or } 5\frac{1}{7} \end{array}$$

Associative Property of Addition. Addition of fractions is an associative operation. For any fractions $\frac{a}{b}$, $\frac{c}{d}$, and $\frac{e}{f}$ (where $b \neq 0$, $d \neq 0$, and $f \neq 0$):

$$\left(\frac{a}{b} + \frac{c}{d}\right) + \frac{e}{f} = \frac{a}{b} + \left(\frac{c}{d} + \frac{e}{f}\right)$$

Subtraction of fractional numbers is not associative:

$$\left(\frac{a}{b} - \frac{c}{d}\right) - \frac{e}{f} \neq \frac{a}{b} - \left(\frac{c}{d} - \frac{e}{f}\right)$$

Associative Property of Multiplication. Multiplication of fractions is an associative operation. For any fractions $\frac{a}{b}$, $\frac{c}{d}$, and $\frac{e}{f}$ (where $b \neq 0$, $d \neq 0$, and $f \neq 0$):

$$\left(\frac{a}{b} \times \frac{c}{d}\right) \times \frac{e}{f} = \frac{a}{b} \times \left(\frac{c}{d} \times \frac{e}{f}\right)$$

Division of fractional numbers is not associative:

$$\left(\frac{a}{b} \div \frac{c}{d}\right) \div \frac{e}{f} \neq \frac{a}{b} \div \left(\frac{c}{d} \div \frac{e}{f}\right)$$

Commutative Property of Addition. Addition of fractions is a commutative operation. For any fractions $\frac{a}{b}$ and $\frac{c}{d}$ (where $b \neq 0$ and $d \neq 0$):

$$\frac{a}{b} + \frac{c}{d} = \frac{c}{d} + \frac{a}{b}$$

Subtraction of fractional numbers is not commutative:

$$\frac{a}{b} - \frac{c}{d} \neq \frac{c}{d} - \frac{a}{b}$$

Commutative Property of Multiplication. Multiplication of fractions is commutative. For any fractions $\frac{a}{b}$ and $\frac{c}{d}$ (where $b \neq 0$ and $d \neq 0$):

$$\frac{a}{b} \times \frac{c}{d} = \frac{c}{d} \times \frac{a}{b}$$

Division of fractional numbers is not commutative:

$$\frac{a}{b} \div \frac{c}{d} \neq \frac{c}{d} \div \frac{a}{b}$$

Distributive Properties. In the set of fractional numbers, multiplication is distributive over addition and over subtraction.

$$\frac{a}{b} \times \left(\frac{c}{d} + \frac{e}{f}\right) = \left(\frac{a}{b} \times \frac{c}{d}\right) + \left(\frac{a}{b} \times \frac{e}{f}\right) \text{ and } \left(\frac{c}{d} + \frac{e}{f}\right) \times \frac{a}{b} = \left(\frac{c}{d} \times \frac{a}{b}\right) + \left(\frac{e}{f} \times \frac{a}{b}\right)$$

$$\frac{a}{b} \times \left(\frac{c}{d} - \frac{e}{f}\right) = \left(\frac{a}{b} \times \frac{c}{d}\right) - \left(\frac{a}{b} \times \frac{e}{f}\right) \text{ and } \left(\frac{c}{d} - \frac{e}{f}\right) \times \frac{a}{b} = \left(\frac{c}{d} \times \frac{a}{b}\right) - \left(\frac{e}{f} \times \frac{a}{b}\right)$$

Division is distributive over addition and subtraction from the right, but not from the left:

$$\left(\frac{c}{d} + \frac{e}{f}\right) \div \frac{a}{b} = \left(\frac{c}{d} \div \frac{a}{b}\right) + \left(\frac{e}{f} \div \frac{a}{b}\right) \text{ but } \frac{a}{b} \div \left(\frac{c}{d} + \frac{e}{f}\right) \neq \left(\frac{a}{b} \div \frac{c}{d}\right) + \left(\frac{a}{b} \div \frac{e}{f}\right)$$

$$\left(\frac{c}{d} - \frac{e}{f}\right) \div \frac{a}{b} = \left(\frac{c}{d} \div \frac{a}{b}\right) - \left(\frac{e}{f} \div \frac{a}{b}\right) \text{ but } \frac{a}{b} \div \left(\frac{c}{d} - \frac{e}{f}\right) \neq \left(\frac{a}{b} \div \frac{c}{d}\right) - \left(\frac{a}{b} \div \frac{e}{f}\right)$$

Identity Element for Addition. The number 0 is the identity element for addition. For any fractional number $\frac{a}{b}$ (where $b \neq 0$):

$$\frac{a}{b} + 0 = \frac{a}{b} \text{ and } 0 + \frac{a}{b} = \frac{a}{b}$$

Identity Element for Multiplication. The number 1 is the identity element for multiplication. For any fractional number $\frac{a}{b}$ (where $b \neq 0$):

$$\frac{a}{b} \times 1 = \frac{a}{b} \text{ and } 1 \times \frac{a}{b} = \frac{a}{b}$$

Least Common Denominator (LCD) and Least Common Multiple (LCM). To find the least common denominator (LCD) of two fractions, find the least common multiple (LCM) of their denominators. To find the LCM of two denominators, list the multiples of the denominators in order, identifying the multiples that are common to the lists and then choosing the least of these common multiples. We can also find the LCM of two denominators by factoring them completely (prime factorization) and taking the smallest whole number that contains all the factors of each denominator. For example:

$$\frac{3}{4} = \frac{3}{2 \times 2}$$

$$\frac{5}{8} = \frac{5}{2 \times 2 \times 2}$$

$$\text{LCM} = 2 \times 2 \times ? \text{ (The LCM is divisible by 4.)}$$

$$= 2 \times 2 \times 2 \text{ (The LCM is also divisible by 8.)}$$

$$= 8$$

$$\therefore \frac{3}{4} = \frac{6}{8} \text{ and } \frac{5}{8} = \frac{5}{8}$$

Procedure for Dividing Two Numbers Expressed in Fraction Form. To divide one number expressed in fraction form by another number expressed in fraction form, multiply the first number by the reciprocal of the second number. For example:

$$\frac{1}{7} \div \frac{1}{3} = \frac{1}{7} \times \frac{3}{1} = \frac{3}{7}$$

This procedure should not be shared with children before appropriate experience and understanding of the reasons why this yields a correct quotient.

Procedure for Multiplying Two Numbers Expressed in Fraction Form. To multiply two numbers expressed in fraction form, multiply the numerators of the two numbers to obtain the numerator of the product, and multiply the denominators of the two numbers to obtain the denominator of the product. For example:

$$\frac{2}{3} \times \frac{1}{5} = \frac{2 \times 1}{3 \times 5} = \frac{2}{15}$$

This procedure should not be shared with children without appropriate experience and understanding of the reasons why this yields a correct product.

Reciprocal (or **Multiplicative Inverse**). The reciprocal or multiplicative inverse of any nonzero number is the number whose product with the given number is 1. If a nonzero fraction is expressed in fraction form, interchange the numerator and denominator to find the reciprocal. For example, if we interchange the numerator and denominator of $\frac{3}{4}$, we get $\frac{4}{3}$; the reciprocal of $\frac{3}{4}$ is indeed $\frac{4}{3}$, since $\frac{3}{4} \times \frac{4}{3} = \frac{12}{12} = 1$.

Subtraction of Fractions Having Like Denominators. Subtract the numerators in the same way that whole numbers are subtracted. The denominator remains the same. For example, $\frac{5}{9} - \frac{1}{9} = \frac{4}{9}$. In general:

$$\frac{a}{b} - \frac{c}{b} = \frac{(a-c)}{b}$$

Subtraction of Fractions Having Unlike Denominators. Rewrite the fractions as fractions having a common denominator (the least common denominator may be easiest to use). Then subtract as explained for like denominators. For example:

$$\frac{3}{4} - \frac{5}{8} = \frac{6}{8} - \frac{5}{8}$$
$$= \frac{1}{8}$$

Subtraction of Fractions Named by Mixed Numerals Having Like Denominators. Subtract the whole-number parts; then subtract the fraction parts. For example:

$$6\frac{4}{5}$$
$$-2\frac{1}{5}$$
$$\overline{4\frac{3}{5}}$$

In cases where the new numerators cannot be readily subtracted, it may be necessary to rename the first of the two mixed numerals before subtracting. For example:

$$9\frac{2}{5} = \left(8 + \frac{5}{5}\right) + \frac{2}{5} = 8 + \left(\frac{5}{5} + \frac{2}{5}\right) = 8\frac{7}{5}$$
$$-5\frac{4}{5} = -\left(5 + \frac{4}{5}\right) \qquad\qquad\qquad = -5\frac{4}{5}$$
$$\qquad\qquad\qquad\qquad\qquad\qquad = 3\frac{3}{5}$$

Practice Exercises for Teachers

These exercises are designed for the reader of this book. While some are suitable for use in the elementary classroom, these examples should not necessarily be given to children in this form. Ideas for classroom activities on the concepts and ideas discussed in this chapter can be found in Part 2 of *Today's Mathematics*, the Student Resource Book.

1. Write an addition sentence for each of the following models.

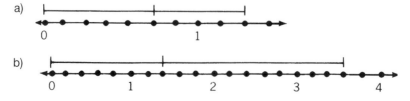

c)

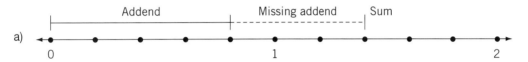

2. Complete the table; write all answers in simplest form.

Addends

A d d e n d s	$+$	$\frac{5}{12}$	$\frac{1}{12}$	$\frac{7}{12}$	$\frac{11}{12}$	$\frac{1}{4}$	$\frac{17}{12}$	$\frac{2}{3}$	$\frac{5}{6}$	$\frac{2}{5}$	$\frac{1}{2}$	$\frac{1}{3}$	$\frac{3}{4}$	$\frac{1}{7}$
	$\frac{3}{12}$													
	$\frac{3}{4}$													

3. Solve each of the following examples and model each with number lines and regions.

   a) $\frac{3}{16} + \frac{7}{16} = \square$ b) $\frac{6}{7} + \frac{5}{7} = \square$ c) $\frac{7}{8} + \frac{3}{8} = \square$ d) $\frac{2}{9} + \frac{7}{9} = \square$

4. Consider the following numbers as denominators. Find the LCM for each group of denominators.

   a) 4, 6   b) 15, 12   c) 8, 12   d) 3, 5, 9   e) 6, 15, 10

5. Write a subtraction sentence for each of the following models.

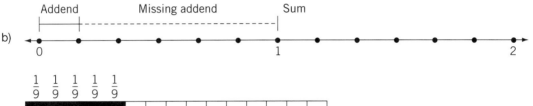

a)

b)

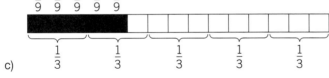

c)

6. Solve each of the following examples. Model each one on the number line and with regions.

   a) $\frac{4}{5} - \frac{3}{10} = \square$ b) $\frac{7}{8} - \frac{3}{4} = \square$ c) $\frac{5}{6} - \frac{1}{3} = \square$ d) $\frac{2}{3} - \frac{1}{4} = \square$

7. Model each of the following multiplication examples on the number line.

   a) $3 \times \frac{1}{4} = \square$ b) $4 \times \frac{2}{5} = \square$ c) $5 \times \frac{2}{3} = \square$

   d) $6 \times \frac{1}{2} = \square$ e) $8 \times \frac{5}{6} = \square$ f) $5 \times \frac{3}{4} = \square$

8. Model each of the following multiplication examples by using regions.

   a) $\frac{1}{2} \times \frac{3}{4} = \square$ b) $\frac{2}{3} \times \frac{1}{4} = \square$ c) $\frac{2}{5} \times \frac{1}{6} = \square$

   d) $\frac{5}{6} \times \frac{1}{8} = \square$ e) $\frac{3}{8} \times \frac{4}{5} = \square$ f) $\frac{2}{3} \times \frac{4}{5} = \square$

9. Solve each of the following division examples by using a drawing.

   a) $\frac{2}{9}\overline{)\frac{8}{9}}$ b) $\frac{1}{4}\overline{)\frac{3}{4}}$ c) $\frac{5}{11}\overline{)\frac{10}{11}}$ d) $\frac{1}{4}\overline{)\frac{3}{8}}$ e) $\frac{2}{3}\overline{)\frac{5}{6}}$ f) $\frac{4}{5}\overline{)\frac{4}{3}}$

10. Name the reciprocal of each of the following numbers.

   a) $\frac{3}{5}$ b) $\frac{1}{4}$ c) $\frac{5}{6}$ d) $\frac{9}{5}$

   e) 17   f) $2\frac{1}{4}$ g) $6\frac{7}{8}$ h) $3\frac{4}{9}$

11. Solve the following examples by rewriting each one in the form $\left(\frac{a}{b}\right)/\left(\frac{c}{d}\right)$. Then multiply the numerator and denominator by the reciprocal of $\frac{c}{d}$.

a) $\frac{2}{9} \div \frac{8}{9} = \square$ b) $\frac{3}{4} \div \frac{1}{4} = \square$

c) $\frac{10}{11} \div \frac{5}{11} = \square$ d) $\frac{3}{8} \div \frac{1}{4} = \square$

e) $\frac{5}{6} \div \frac{2}{3} = \square$ f) $\frac{4}{3} \div \frac{4}{5} = \square$

12. Suppose that $\frac{x}{z}$ and $\frac{y}{z}$ represent two fractional numbers. Complete each of the following statements by supplying the correct relation symbol ($=$, $<$, or $>$).

a) If $x < y$, then $\frac{x}{z} \bigcirc \frac{y}{z}$

b) If $x = y$, then $\frac{x}{z} \bigcirc \frac{y}{z}$

c) If $x > y$, then $\frac{x}{z} \bigcirc \frac{y}{z}$

13. If a, b, c, and d are any counting numbers and $a \times d < b \times c$, then $\frac{a}{b} < \frac{c}{d}$. This fact enables us to compare two fractional numbers by comparing products of counting numbers. Use this test to decide which is the lesser of each of the following pairs of fractional numbers.

a) $\frac{13}{27}, \frac{27}{55}$ b) $\frac{71}{81}, \frac{18}{21}$ c) $\frac{6}{17}, \frac{23}{67}$

14. Solve each of the following examples.

a) $\left(\frac{3}{4} \times \frac{5}{6}\right) \div \frac{2}{3} = \square$ b) $\left(\frac{7}{8} \div \frac{4}{5}\right) \times \frac{1}{2} = \square$

c) $\frac{2}{5} \times \left(\frac{2}{3} \div \frac{3}{4}\right) = \square$ d) $\frac{5}{7} \div \left(\frac{4}{9} \times \frac{2}{5}\right) = \square$

15. Internally simplify each of the following examples before multiplying.

a) $\frac{7}{9} \times \frac{3}{8} = \square$ b) $\frac{4}{5} \times \frac{15}{28} = \square$ c) $\frac{6}{7} \div \frac{4}{5} = \square$ d) $\frac{8}{9} \div \frac{4}{18} = \square$

e) $\frac{5}{6} \div \frac{20}{21} = \square$ f) $\frac{3}{11} \times 2\frac{4}{9} = \square$ g) $2\frac{5}{6} \div 3\frac{1}{4} = \square$ h) $1\frac{3}{8} \times 4\frac{2}{3} = \square$

16. If a room measures $12\frac{1}{2}$ feet by $11\frac{3}{4}$ feet, how many square yards of carpeting will be needed to cover the entire floor?

Teaching Competencies and Self-Assessment Tasks

1. Identify teaching materials and aids that can be used to teach children operations with fractions. What are the most effective means of developing children's understanding of operations on fractions?

2. Discuss the important concepts that children must comprehend before the teacher should introduce division with fractions.

3. Defend the importance of learning the operations with fractions as we increase the use of metric measure, calculators, and computers.

4. Describe the difficulties that children encounter when attempting to use most calculators and computers for operations on fractions.

5. Discuss the relationships between ratios and fractions. How are they alike? How are they different? Compare and contrast the standard algorithm for adding fractions to an algorithm for adding ratios.

6. Discuss the relationship between regrouping with whole numbers and regrouping using fractions. How are they alike? How are they different?

7. Make a list of instances where the identity element of multiplication is used with fractions. How important is the identity element of multiplication in operations with fractions?

8. What are the advantages and disadvantages of allowing children to develop and use their own fraction kits? Should the kits be made with circular or rectangular regions (or both)?

Related Readings and Teacher Resources

For related readings on topics found in this chapter, see the corresponding chapter in Part 2 of *Today's Mathematics*, the Student Resource Book.

Chapter 13

Rational Numbers Expressed as Decimals: Concepts and Operations

Teaching Competencies

Upon completing this chapter, you will be able to:

- Use base ten blocks, regions, money, the number line, and other models to develop an understanding of decimals and operations on decimals.

- Write any given rational number in fraction form, decimal form, or expanded notation and describe situations in which one form may be more useful or appropriate than another.

- Perform operations and inverse operations on numbers expressed in decimal form.

- Express numbers in scientific notation.

- Use ratio and proportion to describe problem situations and to solve percentage problems.

- Rewrite any terminating or repeating decimal in fraction form.

- Design lessons that incorporate meaningful models for rational numbers expressed as decimals.

Why are decimal numbers so widely used in science, industry, commerce, and in applications involving the metric system, calculators, and computers? Why is it that rational numbers expressed as fractions do not play a greater role in such situations? A major reason is that decimal numbers provide a convenient and efficient form of rational numbers for both comparison and computational purposes. The use of rational numbers expressed as decimals permits the application of the place-value notation used for whole numbers to be extended to rational numbers.

MODELS THAT GIVE DECIMALS MEANING

A beginning step in teaching children rational numbers expressed as **decimals** is to develop an understanding of what a given decimal number represents. Several models can be used with children. Let's begin to develop an understanding of decimals by using base ten blocks.

Review whole-number place-value concepts at this point. With whole numbers, children understand the value of the base ten blocks as illustrated:

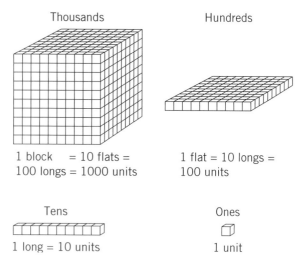

Thousands   Hundreds

1 block   = 10 flats =   1 flat = 10 longs =
100 longs = 1000 units   100 units

Tens   Ones

1 long = 10 units   1 unit

At this stage of development, children should have had many experiences with base ten blocks in learning the concept of place value applied to whole numbers.

Now let's redefine the values of the blocks. Base ten blocks are always defined in terms of the block that is being used to represent the ones place. When a particular block is defined as being one unit, the other blocks of a base ten set are defined accordingly. Begin by using a block defined as one unit.

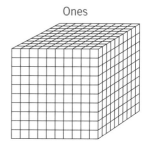

Ones

Then discuss with the children the relationships among the blocks, as tenths, hundredths, and thousandths are defined. If a large block is defined to be equal to one, then a flat is one-tenth of a large block because one block is equivalent to ten flats. A long is one-tenth of a flat because there are ten longs in a flat. And, a cube is one-tenth of a long because there are ten cubes in a long.

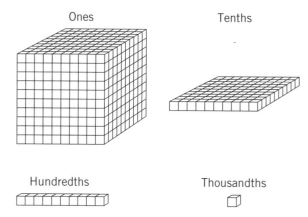

Ones   Tenths

Hundredths   Thousandths

More commonly, and more "naturally," teachers choose to use the flat block to represent 1 when discussing decimal numbers. In such case, a long is one-tenth of a flat and a cube is one-hundredth (one-tenth of one-tenth). This assignment allows the teacher the advantage of using the flat as 100 cubes when discussing whole numbers and a cube as one-hundredth of a flat when considering decimal numbers. Also, ten longs are equivalent to a flat, so a long is one-tenth of a flat.

Children need to manipulate the blocks, see the new relationship, extend the place-value chart, and discuss the extension of the place-value system. This is not a new concept for the children: It only extends a concept developed in earlier grades. If decimals are introduced before fractions, then the use of base ten blocks and the concept of place value provide an excellent procedure for introducing rational numbers expressed as decimals.

Another material that should be used with children is a graph paper model of decimal numbers. Graph paper models are more dependent on fractions than are base ten blocks. Let's examine the models and their usefulness for introducing students to decimals.

If students have worked with fractions, they should understand fractions representing tenths and hundredths. Graph paper is an effective way to illustrate $\frac{1}{10}$ and $\frac{1}{100}$ (and, consequently, .1 and .01).

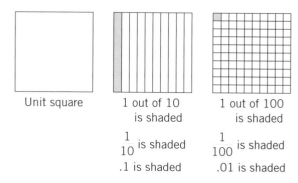

Unit square   1 out of 10   1 out of 100
                 is shaded   is shaded

                 $\frac{1}{10}$ is shaded $\frac{1}{100}$ is shaded

                 .1 is shaded   .01 is shaded

Circular regions can be used in a similar manner.

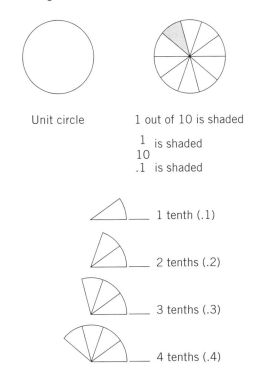

Unit circle   1 out of 10 is shaded

$\frac{1}{10}$ is shaded

.1 is shaded

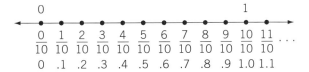

___ 1 tenth (.1)

___ 2 tenths (.2)

___ 3 tenths (.3)

___ 4 tenths (.4)

Students may have modeled many fractions on the number line. After doing halves, thirds, fourths, fifths, sixths, and eighths, students will find it easy to model tenths on a number line.

$$
\begin{array}{ccccccccccccc}
0 & & & & & & & & & & 1 & & \\
\frac{0}{10} & \frac{1}{10} & \frac{2}{10} & \frac{3}{10} & \frac{4}{10} & \frac{5}{10} & \frac{6}{10} & \frac{7}{10} & \frac{8}{10} & \frac{9}{10} & \frac{10}{10} & \frac{11}{10} & \cdots \\
0 & .1 & .2 & .3 & .4 & .5 & .6 & .7 & .8 & .9 & 1.0 & 1.1 &
\end{array}
$$

While graph paper and regions can be very useful when discussing decimals, let's return to the place-value approach and examine it further. The concept of place value is fundamental to an understanding of decimals. So that students may be able to discover the meaning of decimals for themselves, it is necessary for them to examine and make use of place value.

PLACE VALUE—A FOUNDATION FOR DECIMALS

Let's examine a procedure that might be used to teach understanding of decimals. Write a numeral for a three- or four-place whole number on the chalkboard. Label the place-value name above each numeral. Using a heuristic approach, review the relation between each value of the places. For example:

The children's responses to each of these questions should be that each place value is 10 times the place value on its right.

Now, using the same procedure, compare the value of each place to the value of the place to its immediate right.

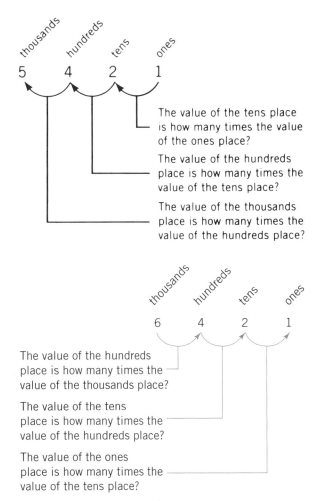

The value of the tens place is how many times the value of the ones place?

The value of the hundreds place is how many times the value of the tens place?

The value of the thousands place is how many times the value of the hundreds place?

The value of the hundreds place is how many times the value of the thousands place?

The value of the tens place is how many times the value of the hundreds place?

The value of the ones place is how many times the value of the tens place?

The answers to each of these 3 questions should be that the place value on the right is $\frac{1}{10}$ of the place value on its immediate left.

These questions merely reflect the place-value understanding that children should have already developed in exploring whole numbers. Now ask the children to imagine that there is a place to the *right* of the ones place. What relationship might exist between the ones place and this *new* place? Permit the children to discuss their ideas about this new place.

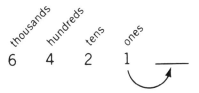

The students should respond that, assuming that the same pattern continues, the value of the new place should be $\frac{1}{10}$ that of the value of the ones place. From their understanding of fractions, the children know that $\frac{1}{10} \times 1 = \frac{1}{10}$. Therefore, we agree to call this new place the *tenths place*. What about the next place to the right of the tenths place? What relation exists between this new place and the tenths place? The value of this new place should be $\frac{1}{10}$ the value of the tenths place. Since

$\frac{1}{10}$ of $\frac{1}{10}$ is $\frac{1}{100}$, we can name this place the *hundredths place*. Using the developing pattern, we can continue this procedure to find the values of as many decimal places as we wish to examine.

All the places to the right of the ones place represent fractional parts of 1, so we need a way to indicate this fact. We do this with a **decimal point**, our reference point to indicate the separation of whole-number values from fractional-number values in a decimal (base ten) numeral. The decimal point is marked between the ones place and the tenths place.

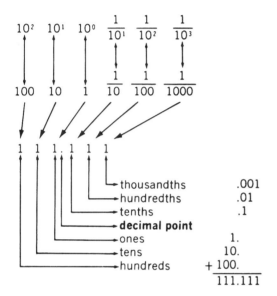

Take a moment to continue this place-value scheme to both the left and the right. Name, for example, the first six places to the right of the decimal point. Using the pattern developed, you should be able to name each of these places and, in so doing, see clearly the structure and meaning of the *decimal system* of notation.

Money should also be used to develop an understanding of tenths and hundredths. Place a 1-dollar bill in the ones place; then, a dime is $\frac{1}{10}$ of a dollar, and a penny is $\frac{1}{100}$ of a dollar. A dime is written as .10, and a penny is written as .01.

Ones

Dollar

Tenths

Dime

Hundredths

Penny

Discuss money with the children, and relate the writing of money values to the place-value system. Using money can be particularly useful in comparing the relative value of different one- and two-place decimals and in beginning discussions of addition and subtraction of decimals.

Numeral expanders can also be used to help children understand decimal notation (see the discussion of numeral expanders in Chapter 6). To use a numeral expander to explore place value, put the numeral expander that has the zeros printed on it in front of you. Make sure that the small section of the numeral expander is on the left and that the longer sections are on the right. (This is the opposite of the way that the numeral expander is placed for whole numbers.) Using the special marking pencil, mark a large dot, so that everyone in the classroom can see it, in the lower left-hand corner of the small section. This dot will be used as the decimal point.

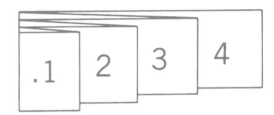

On each of the next three panels with zeros printed on them, mark a large dot in the lower left-hand corner. Also, write a large numeral on each of the four panels.

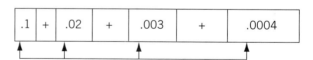

When the numeral expander is ready for use with decimals in expanded form, it will look like this model. Note that four decimal points have been written on the expander—one on the tenths panel, one on the hundredths panel, one on the thousandths panel, and one on the ten-thousandths panel.

Now, use the prepared numeral expander with the decimal points marked. Hold the numeral expander as illustrated, so that the tenths and hundredths places face the students.

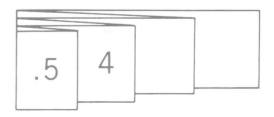

Next, fold back the thousandths and ten-thousandths places so that they do not show. Now the tenths and hundredths places can be expanded by unfolding these two places.

Have the students write the number in standard notation when the expanded notation is shown and in expanded notation when the standard notation is shown.

Children are Shown	Children Write
.4 + .07	.4 + .07 = .47
.2 + .09	.2 + .09 = .29
.36	.36 = .3 + .06
.23	.23 = .2 + .03

When the children have a firm understanding of tenths and hundredths, they are then ready to consider additional places. Use similar procedures to develop standard notation for tenths, hundredths, thousandths, and ten-thousandths. The numeral expander will help children understand the standard and expanded notation for these four places.

[Note: Information on purchasing two plastic numeral expanders (one with zeros and the other with word names for place values), a 24-page teacher's booklet, and an erasable marking pencil can be obtained by contacting Dr. William Speer, Curriculum and Instruction, ms-3005, University of Nevada, Las Vegas, Nevada 89154-3005.]

EXPONENTIAL NOTATION

In our discussion of the structure of place-value numeration systems, we saw that every whole number can be renamed in several ways. For example, 427 can be written in *expanded notation*:

$$427 = 400 + 20 + 7$$

We can also write 427 using **exponential notation**:

$$427 = (4 \times 10^2) + (2 \times 10^1) + (7 \times 10^0)$$

Can all decimal numerals be written in similar alternative forms? Yes, this is possible. Consider, for example, the numeral 23.56; we can rewrite it in expanded notation as follows:

$$23.56 = 20 + 3 + .5 + .06$$

We can continue and write the numeral in several other forms:

$$
\begin{aligned}
23.56 &= 20 + 3 + .5 + .06 \\
&= 20 + 3 + \tfrac{5}{10} + \tfrac{6}{100} \\
&= (2 \times 10) + (3 \times 1) + \left(5 \times \tfrac{1}{10}\right) + \left(6 \times \tfrac{1}{100}\right) \\
&= (2 \times 10^1) + (3 \times 10^0) + \left(5 \times \tfrac{1}{10^1}\right) + \left(6 \times \tfrac{1}{10^2}\right)
\end{aligned}
$$

Children in the intermediate grades should be able to rewrite decimal numerals in these alternative forms to demonstrate an understanding of place value in decimal numerals. Some children in the middle grades may be ready to use negative exponents to write decimals in yet another form. If the children understand the meaning of negative integers, you might use the patterns in the following chart to help the children discover the meaning of 10^{-1}, 10^{-2}, and so on:

Decimal	Exponential Notation
1000	10^3
100	10^2
10	10^1
1	10^0
.1	$10^?$
.01	$10^?$
.001	$10^?$

Children should be familiar with the way exponential notation is used in the first four rows of the chart. What exponents should we use to complete the pattern in the right-hand column of powers of ten? We observe that as we go down the right-hand column, the exponents decrease by 1 each time. If this pattern continues, what exponent should we use to replace the first question mark? Yes, $^-1$ (the integer that is 1 less than 0). What integer should replace the second question mark? Clearly the answer is $^-2$ since $^-2$ is the integer that is 1 less than $^-1$. What integer should replace the third question mark? Yes, $^-3$. In this way the children can discover the following about negative exponents:

$$
\begin{aligned}
10^{-1} &= \;.1 = \tfrac{1}{10} \quad \text{or} \quad \tfrac{1}{10^1} \\
10^{-2} &= \;.01 = \tfrac{1}{100} \quad \text{or} \quad \tfrac{1}{100^2} \\
10^{-3} &= .001 = \tfrac{1}{1000} \quad \text{or} \quad \tfrac{1}{1000^3}
\end{aligned}
$$

From these and similar facts the children should be able to make the generalization that for any whole number *n*:

$$10^{-n} = \tfrac{1}{10^n}$$

Expanded notation and powers of ten that involve negative exponents can be used to reinforce ideas about place value. For example:

$$
\begin{aligned}
34.1 &= 30 + 4 + .1 \\
&= (3 \times 10) + (4 \times 1) + \left(1 \times \tfrac{1}{10}\right) \\
&= (3 \times 10^1) + (4 \times 10^0) + (1 \times 10^{-1}) \\
234.12 &= 200 + 30 + 4 + .1 + .02 \\
&= (2 \times 100) + (3 \times 10) + (4 \times 1) + \left(1 \times \tfrac{1}{10}\right) + \\
&\quad \left(2 \times \tfrac{1}{100}\right) \\
&= (2 \times 10^2) + (3 \times 10^1) + (4 \times 10^0) + \\
&\quad (1 \times 10^{-1}) + (2 \times 10^{-2}) \\
764.123 &= 700 + 60 + 4 + .1 + .02 + .003 \\
&= (7 \times 100) + (6 \times 10) + (4 \times 1) + \left(1 \times \tfrac{1}{10}\right) + \\
&\quad \left(2 \times \tfrac{1}{100}\right) + \left(3 \times \tfrac{1}{100}\right) \\
&= (7 \times 10^2) + (6 \times 10^1) + (4 \times 10^0) + \\
&\quad (1 \times 10^{-1}) + (2 \times 10^{-2}) + (3 \times 10^{-3})
\end{aligned}
$$

(*Note:* Do not ask children to write out these steps. These are here primarily to help *you* understand the concepts. Teachers should be able to understand and write these steps. This use of expanded notation should further clarify the meaning of decimals in our number system—a *base ten* or *decimal system*.)

ADDITION WITH DECIMAL NUMBERS

Children that have studied fractions, place value, and addition of whole numbers should find that adding decimal numbers is merely an extension of prior knowledge. Let's look at an addition example involving decimals by comparing it to regions of a circle. Using tenths of a circle, let's explore the example .2 + .3 = □. The students that understand basic addition know that:

2 tenths + 3 tenths = 5 tenths

We can write:

$$.2 + .3 = .5 \quad \text{or} \quad \begin{array}{r} 2 \text{ tenths} \\ +3 \text{ tenths} \\ \hline 5 \text{ tenths} \end{array} \quad \text{or} \quad \begin{array}{r} .2 \\ +.3 \\ \hline .5 \end{array}$$

Now, let's look at the same example modeled on the number line, illustrated just like any other addition example.

0 .1 .2 .3 .4 .5 .6 .7 .8 .9 1.0 1.1

Begin at 0, the origin. Mark off an addend of 2 tenths, then mark off an addend of 3 tenths, and you arrive at the point we call the sum, which, in this case, is 5 tenths. Therefore .2 + .3 = .5.

Another approach to the addition of decimals uses a logical extension of the process of adding whole numbers and does not require prior experience with adding fractions. Base ten blocks can be a valuable manipulative device for illustrating the addition process as it applies to decimals. To do this, define the value of the blocks (as was done earlier in this chapter) so that the flat block represents 1, or one whole. The long block would then be one-tenth of the flat block, and the cube block would be one-hundredth of the flat block. Using this scheme, the addition example 1.45 + .7 would appear as shown at the top of the next column.

By putting the blocks together and "adding" similar blocks, we can easily see that the result would be 1 flat block, 11 longs, and 5 cubes. The 11 longs could be renamed as 1 flat block and 1 long. Therefore, the total can be renamed as 2 flat blocks, 1 long, and 5 cubes. A variety of exercises such as this should be used, both with and without the notion of renaming.

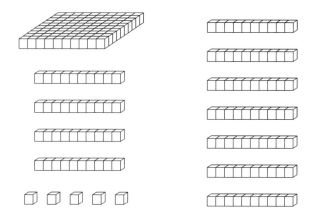

When adding whole numbers, similar place values are added. That is, ones are aligned in the ones column, tens in the tens column, and so on. The same idea applies to addition of decimals. Tenths are added to tenths and are aligned in the tenths column; hundredths are added to hundredths and are aligned in the hundredths column; and so on. If the children understand place value and similar terms, they should then understand that, in the addition of decimals, the decimal points are aligned. The meaning of place value should be reviewed and stressed as often as necessary when introducing children to rational numbers in decimal form.

If the child has had prior experience with adding fractions, then you may wish to take advantage of this knowledge. Consider another addition example:

$$\frac{3}{10} + \frac{4}{10} = \frac{7}{10}$$

After the study of fractions, this example should not prove to be too challenging. We know from our examination of decimals that we can rewrite these fractions as follows:

$$\begin{array}{r} \frac{3}{10} = .3 \\ +\frac{4}{10} = +.4 \\ \hline \frac{7}{10} = .7 \end{array}$$

Thus another way to add $\frac{3}{10}$ and $\frac{4}{10}$ is to rewrite these fractions as decimals.

$$\begin{array}{r} .3 \text{ (three-tenths)} \\ +.4 \text{ (four-tenths)} \\ \hline .7 \text{ (seven-tenths)} \end{array}$$

Take another example:

$$\frac{23}{100} + \frac{14}{100} = \frac{37}{100}$$

Another way of stating this example is:

$$\begin{array}{r} .23 \\ +.14 \\ \hline .37 \end{array}$$

A longer example illustrates the procedure more clearly:

$$.234 \; = \; \frac{234}{1000} = \frac{2340}{10,000} = \; .2340$$

$$.1742 = \; \frac{1742}{10,000} = \frac{1742}{10,000} = \; .1742$$

$$\underline{+.11 \quad = + \; \frac{11}{100} = \frac{1100}{10,000} = \underline{+.1100}}$$

$$\frac{5182}{10,000} = \; .5182$$

(Again, do not ask children to write out these steps.)

By working through a number of similar examples, children should soon realize why decimal points are aligned in addition and subtraction. Alignment of decimal points is comparable to finding a common denominator, as we saw in the preceding example. A shorter analysis of the example is shown below. Notice the use of zeros in illustrating place value.

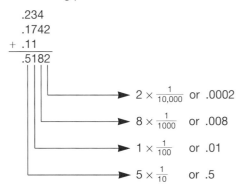

$$
\begin{array}{r}
.234 \\
.1742 \\
+ \;.11 \\
\hline
.5182
\end{array}
$$

$2 \times \frac{1}{10,000}$ or   .0002

$8 \times \frac{1}{1000}$ or   .008

$1 \times \frac{1}{100}$ or   .01

$5 \times \frac{1}{10}$ or   .5

Notice that in the hundredths column we obtain a sum of .11, or $\frac{11}{100}$. We record the .01 $\left(\frac{1}{100}\right)$ in the hundredths column and add the 0.1 $\left(\frac{1}{10}\right)$ to the tenths column; we add this .1 to the .4 and indicate the sum, .5, in the tenths column.

Consider this example: .8 + .6 = □. We can solve this example as follows:

$$
\begin{array}{r}
.8 \\
+.6
\end{array}
$$

We know that $\frac{8}{10} + \frac{6}{10} = \frac{14}{10} = 1\frac{4}{10}$ or $1 + \frac{4}{10}$. Therefore:

$$
\begin{array}{r}
.8 \\
\underline{+.6} \\
1.4
\end{array}
\quad \text{or} \quad (1 + .4)
$$

After working many such examples involving decimals, children should discover that the decimal points are always aligned in addition and, more important, that numerals must be expressed with their proper place value just as in addition of whole numbers. If children know the basic addition facts and can relate fractions and decimals, they should have very little difficulty with addition of decimals. The basic structure of whole numbers and fractional numbers is merely applied in a "new" way.

SUBTRACTION WITH DECIMAL NUMBERS

From a knowledge of addition, children should be able to formulate some generalizations concerning subtraction of decimals. They should explore the subtraction of decimals using models, such as circular regions.

Let's consider an example: .5 − .3 = □. Once again, base ten blocks are effective as a model for subtraction (with or without renaming). This manipulative approach to .5 − .3 = □ can be accomplished using either the take-away or the missing addend interpretation of subtraction shown below. (For this particular exercise, we'll use flats as representing one-tenth of a large block.)

Of course, circular regions can also be used. In this case, each pie-shaped piece represents one-tenth of a circular region.

When using the number line as a model, we always begin at 0. In the example .5 − .3 = □, the .3 is an addend and .5 is the sum. From 0 we mark the addend .3 and then mark the sum .5. What is the missing addend?

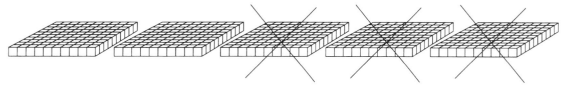

Take-Away Model

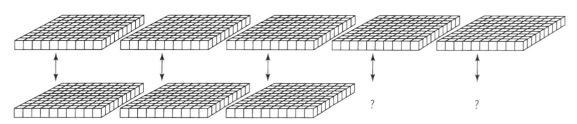

Missing-Addend Model

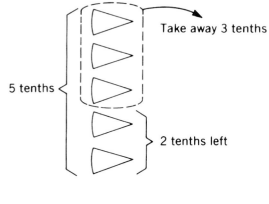

Take away 3 tenths

5 tenths

2 tenths left

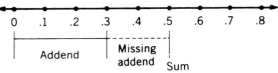

| Addend | Missing addend | |
| 0 .1 .2 .3 .4 .5 .6 .7 .8 | | Sum |

Thus we can see that .5 − .3 = .2.

Children should discover that the decimal points are always aligned in subtraction and that the numbers must be expressed with their proper place value, just as in addition of decimals. This is illustrated in these examples:

$$\frac{7}{10} - \frac{3}{10} = \frac{4}{10} \qquad \begin{array}{r} .7 \\ -.3 \\ \hline .4 \end{array}$$

$$\frac{29}{100} - \frac{12}{100} = \frac{17}{100} \qquad \begin{array}{r} .29 \\ -.12 \\ \hline .17 \end{array}$$

Another example illustrates conversion of fractions with unlike denominators:

$$\begin{array}{r} .73 = \frac{73}{100} = \frac{73}{100} \rightarrow .73 \\ -.4 = -\frac{4}{10} = -\frac{40}{100} \rightarrow -.40 \\ \hline \frac{33}{100} \qquad .33 \end{array}$$

Again, alignment of decimal points is associated with finding a common denominator. By aligning tenths under tenths, we are subtracting numbers named with like denominators.

$$\begin{aligned} .73 - .4 &= (.7 + .03) - .4 \\ &= (.7 - .4) + .03 \\ &= .3 + .03 \\ &= .33 \end{aligned}$$

$$\begin{aligned} .73 - .4 &= \left(\frac{7}{10} + \frac{3}{100}\right) - \frac{4}{10} \\ &= \left(\frac{7}{10} - \frac{4}{10}\right) + \frac{3}{100} \\ &= \frac{3}{10} + \frac{3}{100} \\ &= \frac{30}{100} + \frac{3}{100} \\ &= \frac{33}{100} \\ &= .33 \end{aligned}$$

After exploring a number of similar examples and developing place-value generalizations, children should be provided with practice exercises until the process is

clear. Students need practice in subtraction involving "ragged" decimals and decimals with more places, as in these examples:

| 27.4 | 42.78 | 74.2 | 80 |
| − 3.5 | −17.2 | −38.176 | −29.63 |

These exercises give the students the opportunity to compare and contrast the benefits of using fraction notation, base ten blocks, expanded notation, and regrouping. Such exercises also provide the teacher with an opportunity to evaluate the students' knowledge of basic subtraction facts and knowledge of place value.

MULTIPLICATION WITH DECIMAL NUMBERS

Now, let's consider multiplication of decimals. Begin with models on the concrete level. Consider the example $3 \times .2 = \Box$. What does this mean? It means you have three groups with 2 tenths in each group. If ▷ represents 1 tenth of a circle, then you have 2 of these in each of three groups.

By observation we can conclude that three groups of 2 tenths will equal 6 tenths. We write:

$$3 \times .2 = .6 \quad \text{or} \quad \begin{array}{r} 2 \text{ tenths} \\ \times 3 \\ \hline 6 \text{ tenths} = .6 \end{array} \quad \text{or} \quad \begin{array}{r} .2 \\ \times 3 \\ \hline .6 \end{array}$$

The same example can also be modeled on a number line.

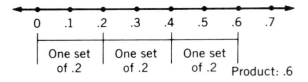

| One set of .2 | One set of .2 | One set of .2 |
| 0 .1 .2 .3 .4 .5 .6 .7 | | Product: .6 |

Thus $3 \times .2 = .6$.

Another approach to teaching multiplication with decimals is to have children make use of what they have learned about multiplication with fractions. Suppose we are given a multiplication example where both factors are written as decimals. Rewrite the decimals as fractions; multiply as usual; and the result will be the product expressed in fraction form. Rewrite this fraction as a decimal; this gives the answer for the original example expressed in decimal form.

Let's look at an example that is solved using this procedure. Suppose we wish to solve the example $2.7 \times .3 = \Box$.

1. Use place-value and basic properties to help rewrite the decimals as fractions.

$$\underbrace{2.7 \times .3}_{\text{Decimals}} = 2\tfrac{7}{10} \times \tfrac{3}{10}$$

$$= \left(2 + \tfrac{7}{10}\right) \times \tfrac{3}{10}$$

$$= \left(\tfrac{20}{10} + \tfrac{7}{10}\right) \times \tfrac{3}{10}$$

$$= \underbrace{\tfrac{27}{10} \times \tfrac{3}{10}}_{\text{Fractions}}$$

2. Using the fraction form, multiply as usual according to the short-form algorithm (i.e., numerator times numerator, denominator times denominator).

$$\tfrac{27}{10} \times \tfrac{3}{10} = \tfrac{27 \times 3}{10 \times 10}$$

$$= \tfrac{81}{100}$$

3. Rewrite the fraction obtained in step 2 as a decimal to get the final answer.

$$\tfrac{81}{100} = .81$$

Therefore, $2.7 \times .3 = .81$

Now, let's use the same procedure to solve $14.5 \times 2.17 = \square$.

1. Write the example in fraction form.

$$14.5 \times 2.17 = 14\tfrac{5}{10} \times 2\tfrac{17}{100}$$

$$= \left(\tfrac{140}{10} + \tfrac{5}{10}\right) \times \left(\tfrac{200}{100} + \tfrac{17}{100}\right)$$

$$= \tfrac{145}{10} \times \tfrac{217}{100}$$

2. Multiply.

$$\tfrac{145}{10} \times \tfrac{217}{100} = \tfrac{145 \times 217}{10 \times 100}$$

$$= \tfrac{31,465}{1000}$$

3. Rewrite the answer in decimal form.

$$\tfrac{31,465}{1000} = 31.465$$

Therefore, $14.5 \times 2.17 = 31.465$

Children who understand and practice this procedure are not as likely to encounter the difficulty of not knowing "where to put the decimal point." Eventually the children can make the transition to the usual short-form algorithm for multiplying decimal numbers:

$$
\begin{array}{r}
16.2 \\
\times .357 \\
\hline
1134 \\
8100 \\
48,600 \\
\hline
5.7834
\end{array}
$$

$\tfrac{162}{10} \times \tfrac{357}{1000} = \tfrac{57,834}{10,000}$

tenths × thousandths = ten-thousandths

Tenths times thousandths gives ten-thousandths, so the final digit in the answer should occupy the ten-thousandths place. After practice with several examples of this sort, the children can be led to *discover* that to determine the location of the decimal point, we count to see how many digits are to the right of the decimal points in the factors.

This method will provide children with insight into the meaning of multiplication of decimals. When pupils come to *understand* multiplication of decimals thoroughly and discover that they can determine the location of the decimal point by counting the number of places in the factors, then they can make use of this particular shortcut.

DIVISION WITH DECIMAL NUMBERS

Division of decimals can also begin with models. Let us examine $2\overline{).6}$. What does it mean? It could mean that 6 tenths are to be separated into two groups. Suppose that $\triangleright$ represents 1 tenth of a circular region. Then:

6 tenths

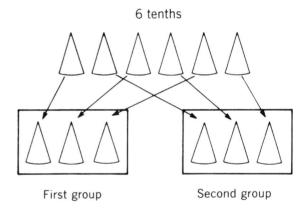

First group   Second group

Thus, when 6 tenths are separated into two groups, there are 3 tenths in each group.

$$\begin{array}{r} .3 \\ 2\overline{).6} \end{array}$$

We can also use the number line to demonstrate. Mark off the product (.6), and then separate this line segment into 2 equivalent segments.

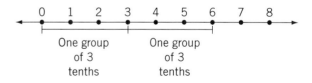

There are two groups of .3 in .6.

$$\begin{array}{r} .3 \\ 2\overline{).6} \end{array}$$

Now, consider .6 divided by .2. That is, $2\overline{).6}$. This can be interpreted to mean that we have a product of .6 and want to make groups of .2. How many groups of .2 can we make from a group of .6?

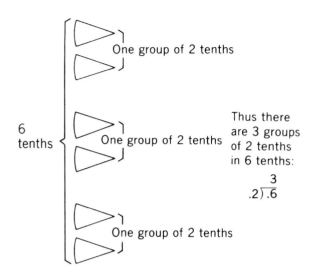

6 tenths

One group of 2 tenths

One group of 2 tenths

One group of 2 tenths

Thus there are 3 groups of 2 tenths in 6 tenths:

$$.2\overline{)\,.6}^{\,3}$$

We can also use the number line. Mark off a product of 6 tenths, and then mark off groups of 2 tenths from 0 until you reach 6 tenths.

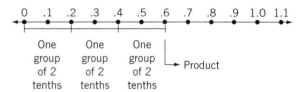

0 .1 .2 .3 .4 .5 .6 .7 .8 .9 1.0 1.1

One group of 2 tenths   One group of 2 tenths   One group of 2 tenths   → Product

There are three groups of .2 in .6:

$$.2\overline{)\,.6}^{\,3}$$

Now, consider an example such as $\frac{.8}{.4} = \square$. We know that we can multiply the numerator and the denominator by the same number to get an equivalent fraction (that is, we can multiply by 1 in the form of $\frac{a}{a}$, where $a \neq 0$). In this case let's multiply by $\frac{10}{10}$.

$$\frac{.8}{.4} \times \frac{10}{10} = \frac{8}{4} = 2$$

What about an example such as $\frac{.84}{.21} = \square$? We can multiply $\frac{.84}{.21}$ by $\frac{100}{100}$, which is another name for 1.

$$\frac{.84}{.21} \times \frac{100}{100} = \frac{84}{21} = 4$$

Let's relate this to the long division format: $.21\overline{)\,.84}$. In this case we should multiply both the product and the known factor by 100 to obtain a whole-number divisor.

$$21\overline{)\,84}^{\,4}$$

In this way we rationalize by using the traditional short-cut process of "moving" the decimal point in long division to obtain a whole-number divisor. By multiplying *both* the dividend and the divisor by 100, we are actually multiplying the entire indicated division by 1, in the form of $\frac{100}{100}$. Connect this procedure to the use of common denominators for division of rational numbers expressed in fraction form.

RELATING DECIMALS AND FRACTIONS

Now we are ready to take a closer look at the relation between decimals and fractions in the form $\frac{a}{b}$. We have said that any fractional number, $\frac{a}{b}$, can be thought of as a quotient obtained from the division of a whole number a by a counting number b. This can also be stated another way: A fractional number is any number y that satisfies an equation of the form $b \times y = a$, where a is a whole number and b is a counting number. For such an equation, the solution can be expressed either as $y = a \div b$ or as $y = \frac{a}{b}$. Thus the fraction $\frac{a}{b}$ means the same thing as $a \div b$. That is, $\frac{6}{2}$ is the same as $6 \div 2$, and $\frac{.6}{.2}$ is the same as $.6 \div .2$.

We have seen that any fraction whose numerator is a whole number and whose denominator is a power of ten (1, 10, 100, 1000, and so on) can be easily expressed as a decimal. What about other fractions? Are all other fractions easily expressed with denominators of powers of ten? Consider the fraction $\frac{1}{4}$.

$$\frac{1}{4} = \frac{1}{4} \times 1$$
$$= \frac{1}{4} \times \frac{25}{25}$$
$$= \frac{25}{100}$$
$$= .25$$

We could also find the decimal for $\frac{1}{4}$ by recalling that $\frac{1}{4}$ means 1 divided by 4 (1 ÷ 4).

$$
\begin{array}{r}
.25 \\
4\overline{)1.00} \\
-8 \\
\hline
20 \\
-20 \\
\hline
0
\end{array}
$$

In view of this, let's ask, "What is the decimal name for $\frac{5}{8}$?"

$$\frac{5}{8} = \frac{5}{8} \times \frac{125}{125}$$
$$= \frac{5 \times 125}{8 \times 125}$$
$$= \frac{625}{100}$$
$$= .625$$

We chose $\frac{125}{125}$, another name for 1, because 125 is the least number that when multiplied by 8 will give a product in the denominator that is a power of ten: $8 \times 125 = 1000$.

But since $\frac{5}{8}$ can be interpreted as the indicated division, 5 divided by 8, let's examine the division form.

$$
\begin{array}{r}
.625 \\
8\overline{)5.000} \\
-4\,800 \\
\hline
200 \\
-160 \\
\hline
40 \\
-40 \\
\hline
0
\end{array}
$$

The decimal for $\frac{5}{8}$, then, is .625 (six hundred twenty-five thousandths).

What are the decimal names for the following common fractions?

a) $\frac{3}{8}$ b) $\frac{4}{5}$ c) $\frac{3}{4}$

a) $\frac{3}{8} = \frac{3}{8} \times \frac{125}{125} = \frac{375}{1000} = .375$

or

```
    .375
8)3.000
 -2 4
    60
   -56
    40
   -40
     0
```

b) $\frac{4}{5} = \frac{4}{5} \times \frac{2}{2} = \frac{8}{10} = .8$

or

```
    .8
5)4.0
 -4 0
    0
```

c) $\frac{3}{4} = \frac{3}{4} \times \frac{25}{25} = \frac{75}{100} = .75$

or

```
    .75
4)3.00
 -2 8
    20
   -20
     0
```

Note that in many cases the division method is far simpler to use, as in this example: $\frac{21}{32}$.

```
      .65625
32)21.00000
  -19 2
    1 80
   -1 60
      200
     -192
       80
      -64
      160
     -160
        0
```

We can readily discover that certain fractions, when renamed as decimals, do not terminate but yield a quotient that repeats endlessly. An example is $\frac{1}{3}$.

```
    .333 . . .
3)1.000
```

We put three dots (called an *ellipsis*) after the third digit in the quotient to show that the pattern continues in the same way—an endless succession of 3s. We can never get a remainder of zero, regardless of how many places we calculate in the quotient.

Observe the result in performing the indicated division in $\frac{3}{7}$, or $3 \div 7$. We obtain the quotient .42857142857. . . . Again, we can never obtain a zero remainder, regardless of how many places we calculate in the quotient. Notice that in this quotient a particular sequence of numerals occurs repeatedly: the sequence 428571. A fractional number whose quotient repeats a particular sequence of digits is called a **periodic** or **repeating decimal**. A repeating decimal is often indicated by a bar over the digits that repeat—for example, $.\overline{428571}$. . . . All fractions whose decimal forms do not terminate are periodic. (Although we do not prove this here, it may be an interesting challenge for you to pursue.) Thus, we see that fractional numbers named in decimal form give either repeating decimals (in which one or more digits repeat endlessly) or **terminating decimals** (in which the quotient terminates—that is, eventually has a zero remainder).

We can easily determine whether the decimal for a fraction terminates or repeats by inspecting the prime factorization of its denominator.

Fraction	Prime Factorization of Denominator	Decimal
$\frac{1}{4}$	2×2	.250 or .25
$\frac{1}{2}$	2	.50 or .5
$\frac{1}{10}$	2×5	.10 or .1
$\frac{1}{20}$	$2 \times 2 \times 5$	.050 or .05
$\frac{1}{50}$	$2 \times 5 \times 5$	.020 or .02

Notice that each prime factorization listed in the preceding table contains only factors that are also factors of 10, the base of our number system. Fractions whose denominators, when factored into primes, contain only 2s and 5s as factors form terminating decimals.

Let's examine some fractions whose denominators contain factors other than 2s and 5s.

Fraction	Prime Factorization of Denominator	Decimal
$\frac{1}{3}$	3	.333 . . .
$\frac{1}{6}$	2×3	.1666 . . .
$\frac{1}{12}$	$2 \times 2 \times 3$	.08333 . . .

These fractions contain, in the prime factorization of their denominators, factors other than 2 or 5. Fractions of this kind form repeating decimals. Note that we usually round off repeating decimals such as .333. . . . We *sometimes* refer to this as simply .33, but it very important to recognize that .33 is only an approximation, not an exact value for the number .333. . . .

Decimal fractions can be indicated on the number line in the same manner as whole numbers or common fractions.

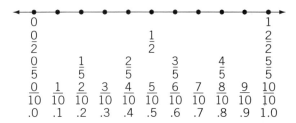

Note that points on the number line are now named in decimal form. We can see that:

$$\frac{1}{5} = \frac{2}{10} = .2$$
$$\frac{1}{2} = \frac{5}{10} = .5$$
$$1 = \frac{2}{2} = \frac{5}{5} = \frac{10}{10} = 1.0$$
and so on

Other number lines can be drawn that show other decimal names. For example:

The number line is an extremely useful device for demonstrating order relationships between different decimals—for example, to show that .5 > .375 and that .125 < .625. It is also useful for showing the decimal equivalents of common fractions, as was the case on the preceding number line. How would we locate the point named by a repeating decimal? This is not difficult if we have a method for converting a repeating decimal into a fraction.

You might approach the task of relating fractions to repeating decimals by asking children to explore patterns generated through performing the indicated division that certain fractions represent. For example, using a calculator (or paper and pencil, if you prefer) calculate the decimal equivalent for $\frac{1}{9}$. The indicated division yields .1111. . . . (Note that depending on your calculator, you may get eight 1s preceded by a decimal point. This is only an approximation. The actual answer is a decimal number with repeating 1s. This can be verified by the paper-and-pencil method if need be.) If you calculate the decimal equivalent for $\frac{2}{9}$ you'll get .222 . . . for an answer. Can you predict the decimal equivalent for $\frac{3}{9}$ (or $\frac{1}{3}$)? What about $\frac{7}{9}$? Conduct a similar experiment for $\frac{1}{7}, \frac{2}{7}, \frac{3}{7}, \frac{4}{7}$, and so on.

An algebraic approach can also be used to convert a repeating decimal to an equivalent fraction. Let's examine how this is done by writing the periodic decimal $.\overline{63}$ as a fraction. If we let n equal the repeating decimal .636363 . . . , we can find the value of $100 \times n$ by multiplying .6363 by 100.

$$n = .63\overline{63} \ldots$$
$$100 \times n = 63.63\overline{63} \ldots$$

Now, we subtract the first of these two equations from the second.

$$\begin{array}{r} 100 \times n = 63.636363\ldots \\ - \quad n = (\quad .636363\ldots) \\ \hline 99n = 63 \end{array}$$

We find that if $99 \times n = 63$, then $n = \frac{63}{99}$. Translating this into simplest form, we find that $n = \frac{7}{11}$. We can now write the repeating decimal .636363 . . . as the fraction $\frac{7}{11}$.

Now try converting .333 . . . and $.037\overline{037}$ . . . into fraction form. First multiply .3333 . . . by 10 and .037037 . . . by 1000. (Notice that in the first example the single digit 3 is repeated, so we multiply the decimal by 10^1, or 10. But in the second example, three digits, .037, are repeated, so we multiply the decimal by 10^3, or 1000.) After proceeding as before to solve these two examples (getting $\frac{1}{3}$ and $\frac{1}{27}$ for answers), we can draw some generalizations for changing periodic decimals into fraction form:

1. Assign an unknown (such as n) to represent the repeating decimal.
2. Multiply the equation in step 1 by some power of 10 so that the decimal point is shifted to the right as many places as there are digits that repeat.
3. Subtract the equation in step 1 from the equation in step 2.
4. Solve the new equation obtained in step 3; write the solution as a fraction.

Apply these generalizations to the periodic decimal $.015\overline{015}$. . . .

1. Let $n = .015\overline{015} \ldots$
2. Multiply the equation in step 1 by 1000 so that the decimal point is moved three places to the right (since there are three digits, 015, in the repeating period).

$$1000 \times n = 015.015\overline{015} \ldots$$

3. Subtract the equation in step 1 from the equation in step 2.

$$\begin{array}{r} 1000 \times n = 015.015\overline{015}\ldots \\ - \quad (n = \quad .015\overline{015}\ldots) \\ \hline 999 \times n = 15 \end{array}$$

4. Solve the equation obtained in step 3.

$$n = \frac{15}{999} = \frac{5}{333}$$

SCIENTIFIC NOTATION

We have shown that in our number system we can name numbers in many ways. One of the ways we found earlier to rename numbers is by using expanded notation. For example, 123 can be written as 100 + 20 + 3. We might also choose to express 123 in terms of powers of 10.

$$(1 \times 10 \times 10) + (2 \times 10) + 3$$

Consider another way to name 123. If we are multiplying two 10s together, we can use exponential notation, as we did in discussing place value (see Chapter 6). Thus we can write 10^2 for 10×10 (the 2 as it is used here is called an *exponent*). Using exponential notation, we write 123 as follows:

$$123 = (1 \times 10^2) + (2 \times 10^1) + (3 \times 10^0)$$

There are many other ways of using exponents in naming 123. For example:

$$12.3 \times \quad 10 \quad \text{or} \quad 12.3 \times 10^1$$
$$1.23 \times \quad 100 \quad \text{or} \quad 1.23 \times 10^2$$
$$.123 \times 1000 \quad \text{or} \quad .123 \times 10^3$$

If the number 123 is expressed as 1.23×10^2, it is said to be expressed in scientific notation. The following table shows some numbers expressed in scientific notation:

Number	Scientific Notation
24	2.4×10^1
324	3.24×10^2
1324	1.324×10^3
12,000	1.2×10^4
140,000	1.4×10^5
1,750,000	1.75×10^6

Examine these numbers expressed in scientific notation. What generalization can we make about writing numerals in this way? In **scientific notation**, a number is always expressed as some number equal to or greater than 1 and less than 10 that is multiplied by 10 raised to a certain power. For example, 24 is expressed in scientific notation as 2.4 (a number greater than 1 and less than 10) multiplied by 10^1, or 2.4×10^1. Similarly, the number 140,000 is expressed as 1.4 (again, a number greater than 1 and less than 10) multiplied by 10^5, or 1.4×10^5. Because 10^5 equals 100,000 we have:

$$1.4 \times 10^5 = 1.4 \times 100,000$$
$$= 140,000$$

Scientific notation, as the name suggests, is an efficient way for people in technical fields to express and work with very large quantities. The following table lists some astronomical distances expressed in scientific notation:

Planet	Distance from the Sun (in miles)
Mercury	$3.6 \ \times 10^7$
Venus	6.71×10^7
Earth	9.29×10^7
Mars	1.42×10^8
Jupiter	4.83×10^8
Saturn	8.86×10^8
Uranus	1.78×10^9
Neptune	2.79×10^9
Pluto	3.67×10^9

Just as numbers representing great quantities can be expressed conveniently in scientific notation, so can numbers representing very small quantities. We have examined fractional parts expressed in decimal form and, earlier, the use of negative exponents to name fractional parts. Now, let's examine the use of scientific notation to express very small numbers. First, we have seen that $\frac{1}{10}$ can be expressed as .1 or 10^{-1}. (Remember that 10^{-1} means $\frac{1}{10^1}$ or $\frac{1}{10}$, since any number raised to the first power is equal to the number itself.) Then $\frac{1}{100} = .01 = \frac{1}{10^2}$. Again, 10^{-2} means $\frac{1}{10^2}$ or $\frac{1}{100}$. If we continued in this way, we could make a chart such as the following:

Fraction	Decimal	Scientific Notation
$\frac{1}{10}$	.1	1×10^{-1}
$\frac{1}{100}$	.01	1×10^{-2}
$\frac{1}{1000}$	.001	1×10^{-3}
$\frac{1}{10,000}$	.0001	1×10^{-4}
$\frac{1}{100,000}$	.00001	1×10^{-5}
$\frac{1}{1,000,000}$	.000001	1×10^{-6}
$\frac{1}{10,000,000}$	.0000001	1×10^{-7}
$\vdots$	$\vdots$	$\vdots$

The pattern is evident. Now, let's simply apply our knowledge of scientific notation to this sequence. In scientific notation we express a number as the product expression of a number between 1 and 10, and 10 raised to some power. For example, 300,000 is expressed as 3×10^5. How could we express $\frac{3}{100,000}$? This rather awkward fraction could be rewritten as follows:

$$3 \times 10^{-5}$$

The relation of this numeral to the fraction form is:

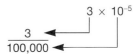

Now, suppose you wished to express the time required for a computer to perform one addition operation. Some older computers require 115 nanoseconds per processing step. This would be written as .000000115 or, in fraction form, as $\frac{115}{1,000,000,000}$ (115 billionths). Scientific notation, 1.15×10^{-7}, is a much simpler way of referring to and using this number.

RATIO, PROPORTION, AND PERCENT

Many elementary school mathematics programs introduce and teach the concept of ratio in conjunction with rational numbers expressed as fractions. We have chosen to introduce ratios at this point in the mathematics program as a means of reviewing fraction ideas and as a vehicle for teaching percents. The concept of ratio is another aspect of rational numbers that is useful in solving a variety of examples.

Look at a problem such as this:

> Balloons are sold at the rate of 2 balloons for 5¢.
> How many balloons can you buy for 10¢?

This problem can be interpreted this way: "Two balloons for five cents" suggests a fixed rate (a comparison between two numbers), which we can call a **ratio**. If this ratio is constant, we should be able to find out how many balloons we can buy for 10 cents or 20 cents, or how much it would cost to buy 4 balloons or 6 balloons.

One way we can express the ratio of balloons to cents is 2:5 (2 balloons for 5 cents). A somewhat more convenient notation is the familiar fraction form:

$$\frac{2}{5} \leftarrow \text{(two balloons)} \atop \leftarrow \text{(five cents)}$$

Young students need to manipulate real objects so that they can easily see and then understand this relationship. For example:

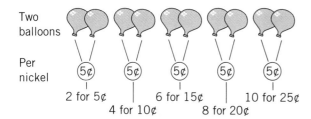

Now, suppose we want to find the number of balloons we can buy for 10 cents. If "two balloons for 5 cents" can be expressed as a ratio, $\frac{2}{5}$ (often read "two to five" in this context), then there is some number of balloons that we can buy for 10 cents. Suppose we let n stand for the number of balloons we can buy for 10 cents. Then we can write:

$$\frac{n}{10} \leftarrow (n \text{ balloons}) \atop \leftarrow \text{(ten cents)}$$

Thus, we see that we can buy 2 balloons for 5 cents, 4 balloons for 10 cents, and so on. We can write $\frac{2}{5}, \frac{4}{10}, \frac{6}{15}, \frac{8}{20}, \frac{10}{25}, \ldots$. These are *equivalent ratios* because each ratio expresses the same relationship: The relationship 2 to 5 is the same as the relationship 4 to 10, and so on.

An equation of two equivalent ratios, such as $\frac{2}{5} = \frac{n}{10}$, is called a **proportion**. When the problem is stated in this way, we can see that if $\frac{n}{10}$ is equal to $\frac{2}{5}$, then the numerator and denominator of $\frac{2}{5}$ must be multiplied by 1 in the form of $\frac{a}{a}$, where $a \neq 0$, to obtain $\frac{n}{10}$. The form of $\frac{a}{a}$ in this case is $\frac{2}{2}$ because the denominator, 5, must be multiplied by 2 to get 10, and so must the numerator, 2, be multiplied by 2. The value of n, then, is clearly 2×2, or 4. We can buy 4 balloons for 10 cents.

$$\frac{2}{5} = \frac{4}{10}$$

Helping students look for patterns is an excellent technique for locating missing numbers in a proportion. Let's examine ratio patterns in several different ways:

Research Snapshot

What mathematical knowledge is needed to develop children's concepts of ratio and proportion?

In a study of a fifth grader, Lo and Watanabe (1997) found that the following mathematical knowledge was useful in the development of the concepts of ratio and proportion:

- number structures, such as multiples and divisors
- a conceptual basis of multiplication and division
- familiarity with a variety of multiplication and division situations
- meaningful multiplication and division algorithms,
- the integration of this knowledge with rational number concepts

The authors also suggest that ratio and proportion instruction should start with situations that are meaningful for students.

What kinds of mathematical experiences do you think would help children develop more sophisticated understandings of ratio and proportion?

Lo, J., & Watanabe, T. (1997). Developing ratio and proportion schemes: A story of a fifth grader. *Journal for Research in Mathematics Education, 28*, 216–236.

For additional research briefs, "ERIC Digests" lets you search more than 2,000 short syntheses of research on a range of education topics. The syntheses were produced by the Educational Resources Information Center (ERIC). Check http://ed.gov/databases/ERIC_Digests/index/

Relationship between Denominator and between Numerators

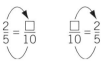

$$\frac{2}{5} = \frac{\square}{10} \qquad \frac{\square}{10} = \frac{2}{5}$$

Since one denominator is twice the other, the corresponding numerator must be twice the other.

Relationship between Numerator and Denominator

$$\frac{4}{8} = \frac{\square}{2} \qquad \frac{4}{8} = \frac{1}{\square}$$

Since the numerator is one-half of the denominator in one ratio, it must be one-half in the other.

Since the denominator is twice as large as the numerator in one ratio, it must be twice as large in the other.

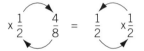 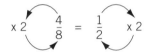

As we mentioned, when two equivalent ratios are expressed as an equality, they form a proportion. A proportion is a mathematical sentence.

$$\frac{2}{5} = \frac{4}{10}$$

This proportion is read, "Two is to five as four is to ten." Because a ratio always expresses a relation between two quantities, this proportion means, "Two balloons for five cents indicates the same price ratio as four balloons for ten cents."

If we use notation of the form *a:b* to express the ratios, then the proportion $\frac{2}{5} = \frac{4}{10}$ would be written 2:5 = 4:10. Some textbook authors prefer to use the symbol :: in place of the equal sign (=) when ratios are expressed in the form *a:b*. The proportion would then be written 2:5::4:10. Such symbolism serves more to confuse elementary school children than to enlighten them, however. We want to exploit the connections between ratios and fractions—not hide them in abstractions that aren't needed until much later.

We can, by use of the ratio method, find the cost of any number of balloons or the quantity of balloons we can buy for any given amount of money.

$$\frac{2}{5} = \frac{4}{10} \leftarrow \begin{cases} 2 \text{ balloons for } 5¢ \\ 4 \text{ balloons for } 10¢ \end{cases}$$

Therefore, $\frac{2}{5} = \frac{40}{100}$ ← 40 balloons for 100¢

Establish a pattern with children by first setting up a table to find the cost of 2, 4, 6, 8, . . . balloons.

Number of Balloons	Cost
2	5¢
4	10¢
6	15¢
8	20¢
10	25¢
12	30¢
14	35¢
⋮	⋮

Children can see that the ratio is always $\frac{2}{5}$ and that different proportions can be set up.

$$\frac{2}{5} = \frac{4}{10} \qquad \frac{2}{5} = \frac{8}{20} \qquad \frac{2}{5} = \frac{14}{35} \qquad \text{and so on}$$

A ratio is an expressed relation between two numbers: 2 tickets for \$3 $\left(\frac{2}{3.00}\right)$ or 3 cans of juice for 99¢ $\left(\frac{3}{99}\right)$. A proportion is a statement of equality for two ratios:

$$\frac{2}{5} = \frac{4}{10} \qquad \frac{3}{7} = \frac{21}{49} \qquad \frac{1}{3} = \frac{4}{12}$$

There is an interesting property commonly used in solving proportions: If two equivalent ratios are written in fraction form, then the two products formed by multiplying the numerator of one fraction by the denominator of the other are equal. In symbols we can say:

$$\text{If } \frac{a}{b} = \frac{c}{d}, \text{ then } a \times d = c \times b$$

To see why this is always true, multiply both sides of $\frac{a}{b} = \frac{c}{d}$ by the product of the denominators ($b \times d$).

$$\frac{a}{b} \times (b \times d) = \frac{c}{d} \times (b \times d)$$

$$\frac{a \times (b \times d)}{b} = \frac{c \times (b \times d)}{d}$$

$$\frac{(a \times d) \times b}{b} = \frac{(c \times b) \times d}{d}$$

$$(a \times d) \times \frac{b}{b} = (c \times b) \times \frac{d}{d}$$

But $\frac{b}{b} = 1$ and $\frac{d}{d} = 1$, so the last equation simplifies to:

$$(a \times d) \times 1 = (c \times b) \times 1$$
$$\text{or}$$
$$a \times d = c \times b$$

The products $a \times d$ and $c \times b$ are often called *cross products*, because they are formed according to this scheme:

$$\frac{a}{b} \Longleftarrow = \Longrightarrow \frac{c}{d}$$

Use simpler proportions and patterns to assist students in the discovery of cross products. Provide students with many examples of simple proportions such as $\frac{1}{2} = \frac{2}{4}$, $\frac{1}{3} = \frac{2}{6}$, $\frac{2}{3} = \frac{6}{9}$, and so on. Encourage students to look for patterns in the relationships between the numerators and the denominators. Challenge the students to look for a relationship or pattern that yields 4 = 4 (for the first pair) or 6 = 6 (for the second) or 18 = 18 (for the third).

Let's solve some proportions by using both patterns and the cross-product method. Consider this example: "Suppose 3 waitresses can serve a total of 17 tables. How many waitresses are needed to serve 51 tables?" This problem can be expressed by the following proportion:

$$\frac{3}{17} = \frac{w}{51}$$

Looking for patterns, we might recognize that $17 \times 3 = 51$.

If the denominator of the second ratio is 3 times the denominator of the first ratio, then the numerator of the second ratio must be 3 times the numerator of the first ratio.

$$\frac{3}{17} \times 1 = \frac{w}{51}$$
$$\frac{3}{17} \times \frac{3}{3} = \frac{w}{51}$$
$$\frac{3}{17} \times \frac{3}{3} = \frac{9}{51}$$

Using the cross-product method, we find that:

$$3 \times 51 = w \times 17 \quad \text{or} \quad w \times 17 = 153$$

Therefore,

$$w = 153 \div 17 \quad \text{or} \quad w = 9$$

Thus, 9 waitresses are needed to serve 51 tables, if 3 waitresses are needed for 17 tables.

Comparing the two techniques for solving ratio examples, we find using patterns to be simpler if one term of a proportion is a multiple of another term of the proportion. The following example also points out the importance of clearly identifying the specific relationship that the ratio is intended to convey:

If a class has 4 boys and 6 girls, then how many boys would we expect in a class of 30 students?

The temptation might be strong to set up the following proportion and solve for *n*:

$$\frac{4}{6} = \frac{n}{30}$$

However, careful consideration of the problem should suggest that the ratio of boys to *classmates* should be expressed by $\frac{4}{10}$, not $\frac{4}{6}$. That is, there are 10 classmates and this question asks for a comparison of the number of boys to the number of classmates, not to the number of girls. Therefore, the problem should be solved by the following proportion:

$$\frac{4}{10} = \frac{n}{30}$$
therefore, $n = 12$

Consider a common example of ratio in action: "Marilyn Sue kept a record of the number of hits for the total official times at bat. She found that she had 8 hits

for 40 times at bat. At this rate, how many hits should she have for 45 times at bat?" The example can be expressed by the following proportion:

$$\frac{8}{40} = \frac{h}{45}$$

Use of the cross-product method gives:

$$8 \times 45 = h \times 40 \quad \text{or} \quad h \times 40 = 360$$

Therefore,

$$h = 360 \div 40 = 9$$

Thus Marilyn Sue can expect 9 hits out of 45 times at bat. This is a representation of Marilyn Sue's hitting ability. How might we compare her hitting with the hitting of another player?

In studying baseball facts, the following information was gathered:

Player	Hits	Times at Bat	Ratio
Mary Ann	6	24	$\frac{6}{24}$
Cecelia	4	10	$\frac{4}{10}$
Tom	3	30	$\frac{3}{30}$
Dan	5	25	$\frac{5}{25}$
Jim	2	8	$\frac{2}{8}$

Which player has the best batting average? A batting average is calculated by comparing the number of hits to the number of official times at bat. It is very difficult to simply compare the ratios for these players to determine the best batter because each ratio is based on a different number of times at bat. To compare the batting averages, we may choose to rewrite the ratios so that they all have the same second term or denominator. For convenience, let's select 100 as a common denominator.

Player	Ratio	Rewritten Ratio
Mary Ann	$\frac{6}{24}$	$\frac{25}{100}$
Cecelia	$\frac{4}{10}$	$\frac{40}{100}$
Tom	$\frac{3}{30}$	$\frac{10}{100}$
Dan	$\frac{5}{25}$	$\frac{20}{100}$
Jim	$\frac{2}{8}$	$\frac{25}{100}$

Now that the ratios have been written with a common denominator, 100, we can compare them and can easily see that Cecelia has the best batting average and Tom has the poorest. Ratios that have a common denominator of 100 are often called *percentages*. The symbol for percent is %. The word **percent** comes from the Latin *per centum*, meaning "for a hundred." By percent we mean "per hundred," or "parts of a hundred." Thus, 1% means "one per hundred" or "one out of every hundred" $\left(\frac{1}{100} \text{ or } .01\right)$; 25% means "twenty-five per hundred," or "twenty-five out of every hundred"

$\left(\frac{25}{100}\right.$ or .25); and 50% means "fifty per hundred," or "fifty out of every hundred" $\left(\frac{50}{100}\right.$ or .50).

An effective way of modeling percent is to use base ten blocks, specifically, the flat block as 1 whole, or 100%. Long blocks can then be used to signify 10%, and small cubes to represent 1%. We can easily show that 50% equals $\frac{1}{2}$ by showing that 5 longs are the same as one-half of a flat.

Another related, but perhaps more readily available, method is to use graph paper with 100 squares to represent 100%. Yet another model for developing children's understanding of percentage is a hundreds board. Use a heavy cardboard square and divide it into 100 smaller squares.

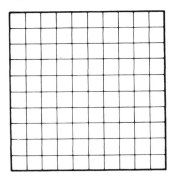

Children may want to draw on graph paper by marking off 10-by-10 squares. By definition, the entire card represents 100%—that is, all of the squares.

In the square on the left, 1 small square is shaded. We can see that $\frac{1}{100}$ of the square is shaded. Changing the fraction to a decimal, we see that .01 of the square is shaded. Each small square on the card is 1%. In the center square, 10 small squares are shaded; $\frac{10}{100}$ of the large square is shaded. The fraction $\frac{10}{100}$ is another name for $\frac{1}{10}$. Thus we can say that .1, .10, or 10% of the center square is shaded. A rubber band or ribbon could be stretched around the large square to illustrate 10%. The square on the right has a rubber band up two rows from the bottom. This card shows 20% below the rubber band and 80% above the rubber band.

Students need to work with other shapes and objects to understand the concept that all of something is 100%. For example:

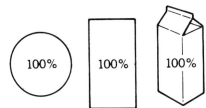

What percentage of each following region is shaded?

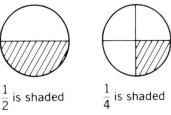 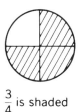

$\frac{1}{2}$ is shaded	$\frac{1}{4}$ is shaded	$\frac{3}{4}$ is shaded
$\frac{50}{100}$ is shaded	$\frac{25}{100}$ is shaded	$\frac{75}{100}$ is shaded
50% is shaded	25% is shaded	75% is shaded
.5 is shaded	.25 is shaded	.75 is shaded

We have seen that .01, $\frac{1}{100}$, and 1% are three names for the same number (one one-hundredth). Similarly, the number seventeen one-hundredths can be represented as a decimal, as a fraction, or as a percent: .17, $\frac{17}{100}$, or 17%. Each of these numerals can be thought of as expressing a ratio (17 per 100).

Several different ways may be used to express each comparison—a fraction, a ratio, a decimal, or a percent. For example, we say that $\frac{1}{2}$, $\frac{50}{100}$, .50, and 50% are equivalent. We often have the need to name the likelihood of an event in a probability situation, such as tossing a coin for heads or tails, by using fractions $\left(\text{say, }\frac{1}{2}\right)$, percent (say, 50%), and decimals (say, .5). The following table shows some equivalent names for percents:

Fractions	Ratios	Decimals	Percents
$\frac{1}{2}$	$\frac{50}{100}$	.50	50%
$\frac{1}{4}$	$\frac{25}{100}$	.25	25%
$\frac{1}{3}$	$\frac{33\frac{1}{3}}{100}$	$.33\frac{1}{3}$	$33\frac{1}{3}\%$
$\frac{1}{8}$	$\frac{12\frac{1}{2}}{100}$	$.12\frac{1}{2}$	$12\frac{1}{2}\%$
$\frac{3}{4}$	$\frac{75}{100}$	.75	75%

When one form or name for percent is known, how do we find the other forms? One of the basic structures of mathematics that we must use is the identity element of multiplication. Consider a pack of gum that contains 5 sticks. If a child is chewing 2 sticks of gum, what part or percent of the pack is the child chewing? Since the child is chewing 2 sticks out of a pack of 5, we would say that the child is chewing $\frac{2}{5}$ of the pack. How can we find the ratio for $\frac{2}{5}$ that has a denominator of 100? We know that $\frac{2}{5} \times 1 = \frac{2}{5}$, and that 1 has many names, such as $\frac{2}{2}, \frac{3}{3}, \frac{4}{4}, \ldots$ What value for 1 should we select so that the denominator of the original ratio, $\frac{2}{5}$, becomes 100? Since $5 \times 20 = 100$, we should select $\frac{20}{20}$ as the form for 1 to use here. Now, since $\frac{2}{5} \times 1 = \frac{2}{5}$ and $1 = \frac{20}{20}$, we write: $\frac{2}{5} \times \frac{20}{20} = \frac{40}{100}$. Thus the fraction $\frac{2}{5}$ can be written as an equivalent ratio of $\frac{40}{100}$. From our study of decimals we know that $\frac{40}{100}$ can be written as .40 and that .40 can be written as 40%.

Some fractions have denominators that are not factors of 100. How are these fractions changed to ratios, decimals, and percents? Either of the two techniques learned earlier in this chapter may be applied in this situation. You know that the fraction bar can also mean "divide," so we can change a fraction to a decimal by dividing the numerator by the denominator. We also know that when an element is missing in a proportion, we can find it by using the cross-product method.

For example, consider the fraction $\frac{5}{6}$. We see that 6 is not a factor of 100. Using the first method, we divide the numerator by the denominator.

$$.83\frac{2}{6} = .83\frac{1}{3} = 83\frac{1}{3}\%$$
$$\frac{5}{6} = 6\overline{)5.00}$$

Thus we say that $\frac{5}{6}$ equals $83\frac{1}{3}\%$ Now let's consider the cross-product method.

$$\frac{5}{6} = \frac{n}{100}$$
$$5 \times 100 = n \times 6$$
$$500 = n \times 6$$
$$500 \times \frac{1}{6} = n \times 6 \times \frac{1}{6}$$
$$\overset{250}{\cancel{500}} \times \frac{1}{\underset{3}{\cancel{6}}} = n$$
$$250 \div 3 = n$$
$$83\frac{1}{3} = n$$

Thus:

$$\frac{5}{6} = \frac{83\frac{1}{3}}{100} = .83\frac{1}{3} = 83\frac{1}{3}\%$$

Ratio and proportion play a major role in the study of percentage. In more traditional mathematics programs, three rather mechanical approaches to percentage problems were commonly taught. Today a single, more meaningful approach is usually presented. By defining percent as parts of a hundred, we eliminate the tedious, mechanical formula requiring children to move decimal points back and forth and to drop and add percent signs. The following examples use the ratio approach to percent:

Example a):   20% of 10 = □
Example b):   □% of 10 = 2
Example c):   20% of □ = 2

Consider Example a), 20% of 10 = □. In some programs, 20% is expressed as $\frac{20}{100}$ or 20 per 100. Therefore, 20% of some number (in this case, 10) can be expressed by equivalent ratios: 20 per 100 is equivalent to some number n per 10.

$$\frac{20}{100} = \frac{n}{10} \quad \text{or} \quad \frac{n}{10} = \frac{20}{100}$$

The numerator and denominator of $\frac{n}{10}$ must both be multiplied by the same number to get $\frac{20}{100}$. Since the denominator, 10, must be multiplied by 10 to get 100, the numerator, n, must also be multiplied by 10 to get 20.

$$n \times 10 = 20$$
$$n = 2$$

Thus n is equal to 2:

$$\frac{2}{10} = \frac{20}{100}$$

and 20% of 10 = 2.

Now, consider Example b), □% of 10 = 2. We can solve examples of this kind by recognizing that the percent is not known but can be expressed as some part, n, of 100. We see that 2 out of 10 is equivalent to some part, n, of 100.

$$\frac{n}{100} = \frac{2}{10} \quad \text{or} \quad \frac{2}{10} = \frac{n}{100}$$

The value of n is clearly 20, and $\frac{20}{100}$ can be expressed as 20%.

$$20\% \text{ of } 10 = 2$$

Finally, let's look at Example c, 20% of □ = 2. This example should be written as follows:

$$\frac{20}{100} = \frac{2}{n} \quad \text{or} \quad \frac{2}{n} = \frac{20}{100}$$

We can determine the value of n by examining the proportion in terms of equivalent fractions. The value of n is thus shown to be 10.

Simple examples involving percent, such as those just given, are often more easily understood in the elementary grades when interpreted by means of proportions (equivalent ratios). Moreover, since ratio can be a rather complex topic, it is not elaborated at this point but is introduced to children in terms of a familiar topic—equivalent fractions.

Ratio is just one method taught to children to solve percentage problems. Let's examine another method. After children have used models such as graph paper and have an understanding of the meaning of percentage, then a formula method may be introduced. In the formula method, students must learn to identify the rate, base, and percentage. Consider this example:

$$20\% \text{ of } 40 = 8$$

■ The rate here is 20%.
The base here is 40.
The percentage here is 8.

The formula the student must learn is $r \times b = p$, which stands for "rate times base equals percentage."

Consider the following problem:

■ Sam correctly solved 60% of the 30 mathematics examples on the last test. How many examples did Sam solve correctly?

In this problem, 60% is the rate, 30 is the base, and the percentage needs to be found. Substitute the values in the percentage formula, and solve the example. Remember that we may express 60% as .60 to help us "keep track" of the decimal point when calculating.

$$r \times b = p$$
$$.60 \times 30 = p$$
$$18.00 = p$$

Therefore, Sam solved 18 examples correctly.

Let's change the example to illustrate another case of percentage.

> On a mathematics test, Sam solved 18 out of 30 examples correctly. What percentage of the mathematics examples did Sam solve correctly?

In this problem, 30 is the base, 18 is the percentage, and we are to find the rate. Now we can substitute the values in the percentage formula and solve for the rate.

$$r \times b = p$$
$$r \times 30 = 18$$

When given a product and a factor, the student should understand how to solve the example.

$$\square \times 30 = 18$$
$$\square = \frac{18}{30} = \frac{3 \times 6}{5 \times 6} = \frac{3}{5} \times \frac{6}{6}$$
$$\frac{3}{5} \times 1 = .60$$
$$.60 = 60\%$$

Thus, Sam solved 60% of the mathematics examples correctly.

If Sam solved 60% of the examples correctly and he solved 18 correctly, how many examples are on the entire mathematics test? The rate is 60%, which can be written as .60. The percentage is 18. Substituting these values in the percentage formula $r \times b = p$, we get:

$$r \times b = p$$
$$.60 \times b = 18$$

The product is 18, and .60 is a factor.

$$b = \frac{.60}{18}$$
$$\text{so, } b = 30$$

There are a total of 30 examples on Sam's mathematics test.

CLOSURE

With continuing emphasis on place value and understanding of our number system, there is no reason children should approach decimals with the idea that decimals are something completely isolated from concepts that they have already discovered and used. What children should discover is the relationships of decimal numbers to the structure of our number system. When they begin to recognize that operations with decimals can be more convenient in many situations than operations with fractions, they will realize the importance of decimal notation and facility with decimal operations.

We leave this chapter with an interesting example of ratios, fractions, decimals, and percent that conveys the importance of their relationships to each other.

Jeff and Ryan are two baseball players. In one month Jeff gets 20 hits in 25 at bats (20 for 25), and Ryan gets 19 hits in 25 at bats (19 for 25). Clearly, Jeff is the better hitter for that month, even if only by one hit. In the next month neither player gets much playing time due to injuries. Still, Jeff continues to do a little better than Ryan, getting 3 hits in 10 at bats (3 for 10) while Ryan gets 1 hit in 5 at bats (1 for 5). How is it, then, since Jeff had better averages both months, that Ryan has the better average overall (20 for 30 versus 23 for 35)?

Problems such as this one can bring about new discussion on what a ratio represents and how it may be different from a fraction.

Terminology, Symbols, and Procedures

Decimal. A fractional number may be expressed in several ways. We have found that fractions such as $\frac{2}{10}$, $\frac{3}{100}$, $2\frac{24}{1000}$, and so on, whose denominators are powers of 10, may be rewritten (using a decimal point) in a form called *decimal form*. For example:

$$\frac{2}{10} = .2 \qquad \frac{3}{100} = .03 \qquad 2\frac{24}{1000} = 2.024$$

Fractions whose denominators are not powers of 10, such as $\frac{3}{4}$, $\frac{5}{8}$, and $\frac{4}{7}$, can also be changed to a decimal form. These examples are often treated as indicated divisions (3 ÷ 4, 5 ÷ 8, and 4 ÷ 7). This division technique is used to change a fraction to a decimal.

Decimal Point. The decimal point is a mark (.) that is used (in the base ten system) when recording numbers to separate the whole-number parts of numbers from the fractional-number parts. For example, consider the mark (.) in 29.05.

$$29.05$$

$$29 \longleftarrow \quad \longrightarrow \frac{5}{100}$$

Where there is no whole-number part, for example, $\frac{32}{100}$, we write .32 (or 0.32).

Exponential Notation. Exponential notation permits us to represent powers of numbers by means of superscripts (or raised numerals). In exponential notation, a number is represented in terms of another number taken as a factor a specified number of times. The first number is called the *base*, and the superscript is called the *exponent*. The absolute value of the exponent indicates how many times the base is used as a factor. In the example 10^5, the base is 10 and the exponent is 5.

$$10^5 = (10 \times 10 \times 10 \times 10 \times 10)$$

Percent. Percent means a certain number of hundredths. For example, 25 percent, written 25%, means either 25 out of 100, $\frac{25}{100}$, twenty-five hundredths, or .25.

Periodic (or **Repeating**) **Decimal.** A periodic or repeating decimal is a decimal in which some digit or series of digits repeats endlessly. In .0575757 . . . or $.0575\overline{57}$, for example, the three dots indicate that an endless number of digits follow, and the bar over the last 57 indicates that this pair of digits is repeated endlessly. Every fraction can be expressed as either a terminating decimal or a periodic decimal.

Proportion. A proportion is a mathematical sentence stating that two ratios are equal. For example:

$$\frac{2}{5} = \frac{4}{10} \qquad \frac{n}{3} = \frac{16}{12}$$

Ratio. A ratio is a comparison between two numbers. The ratio of two to five, for example, is written as 2:5 or $\frac{2}{5}$.

Scientific Notation. A number that is expressed as some number equal to or greater than 1 and less than 10, and multiplied by a power of 10, is said to be expressed in scientific notation. For example, 82,000,000 is expressed in scientific notation as 8.2×10^7.

Terminating Decimal. A terminating decimal is a decimal that can be written with a finite number of digits: for example, .315 or .7590452.

Practice Exercises for Teachers

These exercises are designed for the reader of this book. While some are suitable for use in the elementary classroom, these examples should not necessarily be given to children in this form. Ideas for classroom activities on the concepts and ideas discussed in this chapter can be found in Part 2 of *Today's Mathematics*, the Student Resource Book.

1. Write 346.128 in expanded form.

2. Translate each of the following decimals into a fraction.

   a) 2.1896   b) .003201   c) $.12\overline{12}$ d) $.46\overline{46}$
   e) .88 . . .   f) .25   g) $.35\overline{8}$ h) $.072\overline{072}$

3. Translate each of the following fractions into a decimal.

   a) $\frac{4}{7}$ b) $1\frac{12}{13}$ c) $\frac{8}{11}$ d) $\frac{11}{12}$ e) $\frac{5}{15}$ f) $\frac{2}{3}$

4. Is it possible that there is a fraction with a whole-number numerator and a counting-number denominator that, when changed to a decimal, is neither terminating nor repeating? How can you be sure of your answer?

5. Complete the indicated operation in each of the following examples.

   a) $2.34 + 17.1 + .0234 + .123$ b) $43.7 - 12.684$
   c) 7.43×2.1 d) $6.2\overline{)8.928}$

6. Solve each of the following problems by using ratios.

   a) Tomato juice is on sale at 3 cans for 97 cents. How much must you pay for a dozen cans?
   b) Mr. Shih's class is going to the art museum. If 5 children can ride in each car, how many cars are needed to carry all 35 children in the class?
   c) If 100 centimeters measures the same length as 1 meter, how many centimeters are needed to measure the same length as 3 meters?
   d) If 1 kilometer is approximately .6 mile, how many kilometers will measure the same length as 1 mile?

7. Solve each of the following problems by using ratios and proportions.

   a) A chair that normally sells for $150.00 has been marked down to sell for $100.00. What is the percent of discount?

b) The price for unleaded gasoline has increased at a particular station from 112.9 cents per gallon to 125.9 cents per gallon. What percent of increase has there been at that station?

c) In a fourth-grade class, 10% of the children received perfect scores on an arithmetic test. If 33 children received perfect scores, how many children took the test?

d) At Boulder City Elementary School, 56% of the students walk to school every day. How many students walk to school if there are 500 pupils in the school?

e) At Greenspun School, 391 children attended the school play. If this is 17% of the number of children in the school, what is the total number of children who attend Greenspun School?

8. Use the percentage formula to solve each of the problems in the previous exercise. Describe how the solutions differ.

9. Express each of the following with an ordinary base ten numeral:

a) 9.38×10^5 b) 2.37×10^4 c) 4.66×10^9 d) 5.3×10^6
e) 8.31×10^{-2} f) 3.641×10^{-6} g) 2.2×10^{-3} h) 4.681×10^{-5}

10. Express each of the following numbers in scientific notation.

a) 7300   b) 24,000,000   c) 8,900,000,000
d) 123   e) 16,432   f) 437.56

11. Change each of these fractions, $\frac{1}{3}$, $\frac{5}{7}$, and $\frac{6}{13}$, to decimals. How often does the sequence of digits repeat? Formulate a general principle that will allow you to predict the maximum number of decimal places that can occur before a digit is repeated. (*Hint:* Be sure to consider the denominator of each of the examples.)

12. How might you use a 10-by-10 square cut from graph paper to show that $\frac{1}{2}$ and $\frac{1}{2}\%$ are different concepts?

13. Translate each of the following fractions into a percent.

a) $\frac{7}{8}$ b) $\frac{9}{11}$ c) $\frac{3}{15}$ d) $\frac{7}{13}$ e) $\frac{3}{4}$ f) $\frac{8}{9}$

Teaching Competencies and Self-Assessment Tasks

1. Examine a number of elementary school mathematics textbooks at different grade levels; compare and contrast the techniques for introducing decimals to children.

2. What homemade or commercial teaching aids are effective in developing an understanding of decimals?

3. Discuss the use of decimals in society today. Which is more useful, decimals or fractions? Why?

4. List the advantages of using decimals instead of fractions with a calculator or a computer.

5. Compare the common characteristics of a specific operation on decimals with that same operation on whole numbers.

6. Discuss why, when dividing 1 by 6, some calculators might display .1666666 and others .16666667. What is the "real" value, and how do we write it?

7. Compare the pencil-and-paper algorithm for multiplying the following factors to one using the scientific notation representation of the factors.

a) 24×57 b) $34,000 \times 2800$ c) $809,000 \times 45,600,000$
d) 2.3×34.675 e) $0.0003 \times .00405$

8. Discuss the similarities and differences between ratios and fractions. Is it possible to add ratios meaningfully? If so, is adding ratios the same as adding fractions?

9. Debate whether .9999 . . . is equal to 1, or simply very close to 1. Structure your debate to use the decimal equivalents of $\frac{1}{3}$ and $\frac{2}{3}$ and the fact that $\frac{1}{3} + \frac{2}{3} = \frac{3}{3}$, or 1.

10. Discuss the prerequisite knowledge necessary for studying concepts and operations on decimals.

11. Discuss useful evaluation techniques for assessing the understanding of decimals on the concrete level.

12. Discuss the advantages of teaching decimals before fractions and teaching fractions before decimals.

Related Readings and Teacher Resources

For related readings on topics found in this chapter, see the corresponding chapter in Part 2 of *Today's Mathematics*, the Student Resource Book.

Chapter 14

Data Analysis: Graphs, Statistics, and Probability

Teaching Competencies

Upon completing this chapter, you will be able to:

- Define the terms *range*, *mean*, *median*, and *mode* and calculate these measures for a given collection of data.

- Construct graphs (frequency polygons, histograms, bar graphs, line graphs, pictographs, or circle graphs) for a given set of data.

- Construct stem-and-leaf plots and/or box-and-whisker plots from real-life data collections.

- Determine the possible outcomes in a simple probability experiment and the probability that certain events will occur.

- Describe ways in which statistics and probability are used in real life and identify ways in which statistics and probability might be misused or misinterpreted.

- Use Pascal's Triangle and/or geometric arguments to calculate probability.

- Design instructional activities that reflect the NCTM *Principles and Standards for School Mathematics* by incorporating data gathering, handling, and interpretation in a manner appropriate for elementary school children.

he amount and type of information available to us is expanding daily. To obtain maximum benefit from this data explosion, it is essential that we develop efficient and effective means of organizing, analyzing, and interpreting information. Clearly, data handling and analysis have extensive applications in the physical and biological sciences, the social sciences, and business. Computer manufacturers, for example, use statistics to assess and project the buying habits of the population: How many computers should be produced this year to meet public demand? What portion of the population will purchase home computers? What portion of the businesses in the United States will use computers for inventory control? What portion of the computer business can each manufacturer expect to capture this year? These, and similar questions in other industries, are being asked every day. Statistics helps people find answers to such questions by making available intelligent methods for organizing and handling limited amounts of data in order to make predictions. **Statistics** is the analysis of numerical and qualitative data to determine the relationships that exist among the data (such as central tendencies, dispersion, or scatter).

The NCTM *Principles and Standards for School Mathematics* recognizes and emphasizes the role played by data analysis in the mathematical literacy of children (and adults).

Instructional programs from pre-kindergarten through grade 12 should enable all students to—

- formulate questions that can be addressed with data and collect, organize, and display relevant data to answer them;
- select and use appropriate statistical methods to analyze data;
- develop and evaluate inferences and predictions that are based on data;
- understand and apply basic concepts of probability.

According to NCTM, "A thorough grounding in statistics and probability provides tools and ways of thinking that will be useful throughout students' lives. Because some things children learn in school seem to them predetermined and rule-bound, it is critical that they also learn that some problems involve solutions that depend on assumptions and have some degree of uncertainty" (NCTM, 1998, p. 71). Students, in fact all of us, stand to benefit from the ability to deal intelligently and rationally with assumption, variation, and uncertainty.

A CHILD'S VIEW OF STATISTICS

Children in the elementary grades will benefit from an introduction to basic concepts of data handling and analysis. Teaching problem solving, beginning in kindergarten, helps to create a foundation on which basic statistical concepts can be developed. Acquaintance with methods of gathering and organizing data should be a part of each child's mathematical experience. In most

cases, work with elementary statistics can be tied quite naturally to activities in science, social studies, sports, and so on, to give insight into the relevance of mathematics and real-world applications in many different areas.

Let's think about the number of children assigned to a "typical" elementary classroom. The number, of course, varies from one classroom to another and from one part of the country to another. Suppose we were able to list all the classrooms across the nation as well as the numbers of students assigned to these classrooms. We would then have a complete collection of information. **Data** are such collections of numerical facts. (*Data* is the plural form, whereas *datum* is singular.)

The total *population* for the data we are considering would be enormous. In view of the size of the population, we would do better to work with only a subset or *sample* of the population. In selecting a sample with which to work, we must be careful to ensure that the sample will have characteristics similar to those of the total population. Careful selection of the sample is important in any situation where statistics is being used to illustrate a point or support an argument. The sampling technique will vary with the type of study being conducted and the questions to be answered, but it is essential that it yield a representative sample of the population from which it is drawn.

Let us return to our example of classroom size as described by the number of students in a classroom. Once we have collected the data we need about the numbers of students in the classrooms, we must have some way to put these data in a useful form. In other words, we must *organize* the data. One way to organize data is to arrange them in a tabular form. For example, suppose we have obtained data on the 21 classrooms in Cortland School. In this school there are 3 classrooms for each grade level, K through 6. The data collected are listed in the table by grade, teacher, and number of students.

K	Mrs. Forde	27
K	Ms. Usnicki	26
K	Mrs. Dixxon	29
1	Ms. Lits	34
1	Mr. Shih	33
1	Mrs. Mose	32
2	Miss Friedlund	30
2	Mr. Brahier	29
2	Mrs. Toady	31
3	Ms. LoTadams	29
3	Ms. Paske	32
3	Ms. Close	31
4	Ms. Nocigar	36
4	Mrs. Sanderson	34
4	Mrs. Short	35
5	Ms. Thin	32
5	Mr. Wide	31
5	Mrs. Hopkins	33
6	Mr. Brumbaugh	28
6	Mr. Hynes	29
6	Ms. Falba	27

Our interest is focused on the number of children in each classroom. Thus the data in the table might be further organized as follows:

Children per Classroom	Tally	Number of Classrooms
36	I	1
35	I	1
34	II	2
33	II	2
32	III	3
31	III	3
30	I	1
29	IIII	4
28	I	1
27	II	2
26	I	1

This table gives the specific number of children in various classrooms and tells how many classrooms contain that number of children. The number of classrooms containing a given number of students might be referred to as a frequency. A **frequency** tells us how many times a particular datum occurs.

MEASURES OF CENTRAL TENDENCY IN DATA

Depending on the purpose for collecting data, we may be interested in the *dispersion* or scattering of the data, or in its *central tendencies*. One measure of dispersion is the **range**. The range of the data from the table in the preceding section is from a low of 26 students per classroom to a high of 36 students per classroom. The range is also commonly thought of as the difference between the least and the greatest measure. In our example, the range would be 10. At times, the range can be a useful measure. However, because it merely reflects the difference between the high and the low measures and tells us nothing about the positions of "inner data points," unusually high or low bits of datum, called *outliers*, may render this statistical descriptor practically useless.

The most common measure of central tendency is the **mean**. The mean for the situation we are considering would be the number of students per classroom if the school population were evenly distributed, with the same number of students in each classroom. The mean is also referred to as the **arithmetic mean** or, sometimes, simply as the **average**. (Although *any* measure of central tendency can legitimately be called an average, we will restrict the use of that term here to be equiva-

lent to the mean.) What is the average number of students per classroom at Cortland School? We can calculate the mean by adding the measures and dividing by the number of measures.

$$\frac{\text{Sum of measures}}{\text{Number of measures}} = \text{Mean or average}$$

In our example the mean is the sum: 27 + 26 + 29 + 34 + 33 + 32 + 30 + 29 + 31 + 29 + 32 + 31 + 36 + 34 + 35 + 32 + 31 + 33 + 28 + 29 + 27, divided by 21 (the number of classrooms). When we add the above measures, we get a sum of 648. Dividing this by the total number of classes, we get an average of nearly 31 students per class.

$$\text{Therefore, the average} = \frac{648}{21},$$
or about 31 children per classroom

The mean can be thought of as the numerical balancing point for a set of data. If the students could be easily transferred from one class to another, without regard for grade level, then all classes would be balanced at about 31 students per classroom. Note that the actual computed average for this set of data is 30.857142 . . . , or 30 students with 18 students left over. Certainly, in this particular case, an approximate average is quite usable. Note that, for these data, the actual computed average is not the same as any of the individual class enrollments. Sometimes, the average of a collection of data will be found within that data (e.g., the average of 3, 4, 8, and 15 is 8), but sometimes, as in the preceding classroom enrollment example, the average will not actually be one of the data points. One thing is certain, however: The average must always fall within the extremes of the data.

As a rule, the mean is a good measure for describing the central tendency of a collection of data. It is most reliable when the range of the data is not too great. If the range is great, the mean may be misleading. For example, if one of the classrooms in Cortland School had contained 100 children, the mean would have been almost 34 children per classroom, when actually, the figure of 31 is a better description of the situation in the school than a figure of 34. To overcome the difficulties that arise from atypically or unusually large or small extreme measures, we can use a different measure of central tendency known as the median. When the data are listed in order of size, the **median** is the middle measure. To find the median class size for Cortland School, we can again use the frequency table.

Since the number 11 is halfway between 1 and 21, we can count down from the top (or up from the bottom) to find the middle measure. We find that the eleventh measure, or median, for this set of data is 31. If we consider our earlier hypothetical situation in which one classroom had 100 children instead of 35, the median would still be equal to 31. Note that this one extreme measure may have a great effect on the mean or average, but little or no effect on the median. But knowing how to find the median is not valuable unless you also know when to use it.

Research Snapshot

What does research say about children's notions of what is representative or average?

Mokros and Russell (1995) interviewed 21 students from grades 4, 6, and 8 to examine their notions of average. Five predominant approaches to solving the open-ended problems were found. Two of the approaches taken by the students did not recognize the notion of values being representative (average as the mode, average as an algorithmic procedure) while the other three approaches embodied an idea of representativeness (average as what is reasonable, average as midpoint, average as a mathematical point of balance).

The youngest students in the study who viewed the average as the mode did not treat the data set as an entity, but as a list of values of numbers. Their idea of representativeness was limited to the mode, or the value with the "most" data.

To help develop children's knowledge of representativeness, the authors encourage giving students opportunities to describe and compare data sets, to compare different concepts of the "middle," and to introduce other measures of central tendency, such as the median, that connect with emerging concepts.

What specific data sets from the students' real-life experiences might you suggest as being appropriate to the developmental and experiential level of children within the elementary grade levels of preK–2, 3–5, and 6–8?

Mokros, J., & Russell, S. J. (1995). Children's concepts of average and representativeness. *Journal for Research in Mathematics Education, 26,* 20–39.

For additional research briefs, "ERIC Digests" lets you search more than 2,000 short syntheses of research on a range of education topics. The syntheses were produced by the Educational Resources Information Center (ERIC). Check http://ed.gov/databases/ERIC_Digests/index/

This points out that the best measure of central tendency to use in a given situation depends on the distribution of the measures. If the measures are rather close together, with no notably extreme cases, then the mean is likely to be an appropriate measure of central tendency. If there are one or two scores that are extremely high or extremely low, the more appropriate measure of central tendency to use is probably the median.

A third measure of central tendency is the **mode**, the measure that occurs most often in a set of data—that is, with the greatest frequency. The mode at Cortland School is 29 students per classroom, because more classrooms have that number of students than any other number of students. If a sample has *two* measures that occur with the same frequency (and more than all the others), then the distribution is said to be *bimodal*. A set of data could have many modes.

ORGANIZING AND INTERPRETING DATA

One approach to introducing children to the measures that we apply to data is to begin with concrete graphs. These are graphs made by using real objects to represent, say, preferences or choices. Children might be asked to choose their favorite fruit drink and to show each choice by stacking the cups behind labels for each flavor, thereby forming a "real" graph. Alternatively, you might use photographs or children's drawings of their pets arranged into a "graph" by putting the pictures side by side next to a label indicating the pet type.

Teachers commonly take individual pictures of the students in their classrooms and then use these pictures throughout the year to form "snapshot bar graphs" of month of birth, height, or other identifiable and distinguishing characteristics such as favorite pets, number of siblings, or amount of television watched each week. Other materials that might be used to form a graph include strings of paper clips made to specified lengths as well as buttons or inexpensive plastic disks glued to posterboard to match given criteria. Students can also use stacking cubes to form the bars of a bar graph or stretch a length of rope or yarn across the front of the room off of which cards (or student pictures) representing data points may be hung.

A **graph** is one of the most convenient devices for organizing and presenting data. Well-constructed graphs make it easy to present a great deal of information, literally at a glance. Graphs give a view of the shape of the data that is difficult, if not impossible, to get in other ways. One great advantage in using a graph to analyze data is the visual impact that many graphs have. This quick conveyance of information is a prime reason newspapers and other popular press make heavy use of graphs—they present a lot of information in a little space.

Let's look at a graph showing the enrollments for the 21 classrooms at Cortland School. The kind of graph shown in the following illustration is called a **histogram**:

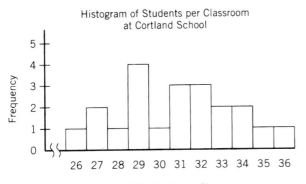

Histogram of Students per Classroom at Cortland School

Graphs are essentially pictures designed to illustrate relationships among data so that the reader can easily interpret the data shown. A graph must have a title and be labeled in such a way as to indicate clearly to the reader what the graph is attempting to describe. The histogram is only one of several different types of graphs. The type of graph one should select depends on the data collected and how that data can best be presented to the reader.

Let's look at a **frequency polygon**, another type of graph. The following frequency polygon was made by connecting the midpoints of the tops of the bars in the histogram of the students per classroom at Cortland School.

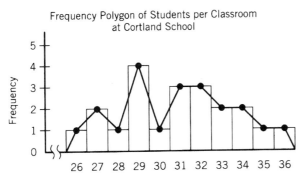

Frequency Polygon of Students per Classroom at Cortland School

Note the similarities and differences between a histogram and frequency polygon. A histogram is more often called a **bar graph**, while a frequency polygon is commonly referred to as a **line graph**.

Let's take a closer look at a bar graph. A bar graph may be oriented either horizontally or vertically. The bars should be all the same width to avoid the potential misunderstanding that the area of the bar is somehow more important than its height. Using the bar graph at the top of the next column, we can compare the amount of money collected by each grade in Cortland School.

At a glance you can tell which class collected the most money, which class collected the least, and which classes collected the same amount.

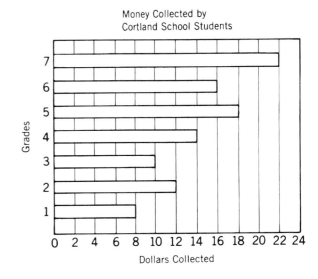

Money Collected by Cortland School Students

Sometimes several bar graphs are combined to make either a *side-by-side multiple bar graph* or a *stacked bar graph*. A side-by-side bar graph is commonly used to compare two different groups of data on the same characteristics. For example, the graph below illustrates residence hall versus off-campus housing preferences for college freshmen, sophomores, juniors, and seniors.

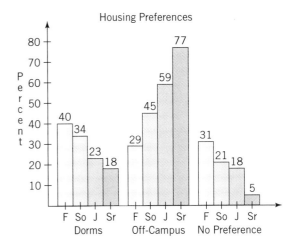

Housing Preferences

A stacked bar graph is often used to show how two or more parts make up a whole bar. As an example, consider the graph at the top of the next page that shows gender preferences for different colors. Note that the individual bars are composed of two distinct sections. To interpret these graphs you must realize that one section is literally stacked on the other, as opposed to two stacks beginning at zero.

Bar graphs are suited to *discrete* data—that is, data that are noncontinuous, distinct, countable, and separate from other information, such as the number of pets in a household, the different colors of cars in a parking lot, or the number of people that like particular types of music.

We can make a line graph by taking the bars off a bar graph and connecting the center point of each bar.

Color Preferences

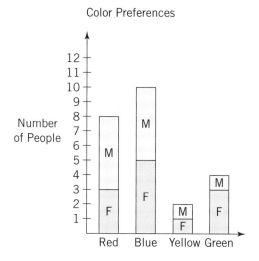

This method *might* be used to change the money bar graph shown on page 257 into a line graph. However, a line graph is more suited to *continuous* data such as temperature change or a person's height over a period of time—that is, data that do not change by "jumps" but by a constant, "fluid" process. A line graph can, for example, show fluctuation, such as the change in temperature illustrated in the following graph:

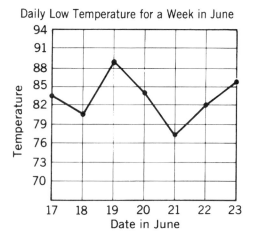

One of the major difficulties in constructing a line graph is the selection of a proper scale for one or both of the axes. The scale, of course, must be able to accommodate the collected data. To do this, the scale must provide for the variance between greatest and least values to be graphed, and it must reflect the degree of accuracy required. Let us examine the growth of a seedling. Each morning at 9:00 A.M. a class measures the height of a bean plant. The data are then placed on a graph as shown at the top of the next column.

The horizontal and vertical axes serve as the reference points for the graph. The horizontal axis is the reference line for the days of the week. The vertical axis is the reference line for the height of the plant. Note that the scale is marked in centimeters and that the height is approximated for each day.

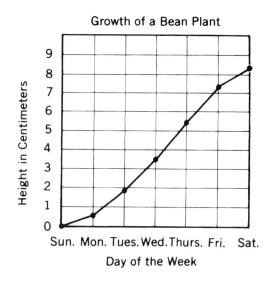

Consider the exact same information plotted on exactly the same graph, with one very notable exception—the vertical axis in the graph below has a scale of decimeters (1 decimeter = 10 centimeters).

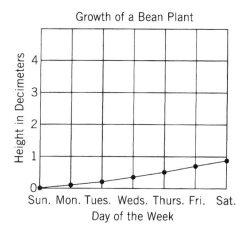

Notice that if you quickly glanced at this graph, you might come to a very different conclusion about the growth rate of the seedling than you would have from the first graph. Data, and the graphs resulting from the data, must be carefully handled and interpreted. Too often data can be manipulated in correct but misleading ways to show whatever point the designer of the graph wants to emphasize.

As mentioned earlier, young children often create "graphs" using real objects, such as drink cups stacked on a table or a chalkboard tray to show the children's preferences in juice flavor. In this activity, each cup represents one vote for a particular flavor. If we drew a picture of such a physical graph (such as that at the top of the next page) and let each cup represent several children's choices, then we'd have a natural extension to graphing as it develops in the upper elementary grades.

When an actual concrete graph using real objects is drawn representatively it is commonly referred to as a pictograph. A **pictograph** is a graph in which pictures

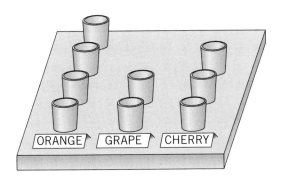

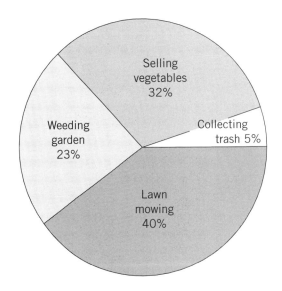

represent values; for instance, a picture of a car may represent a certain number of cars sold. Numbers are commonly rounded off for convenience. For example, in the following pictograph, the symbol 🚗 represents 100 cars; thus, 🚗 represents 50 cars. This pictograph has a title, a scale, and pictures representing the number of cars sold.

Cars Sold by Brahier Agency, 1996–1999

🚗 = 100 cars

Year

1999 🚗 🚗 🚗 🚗 🚗 🚗

1998 🚗 🚗 🚗 🚗 🚗 🚗 🚗

1997 🚗 🚗 🚗 🚗 🚗 🚗

1996 🚗 🚗 🚗 🚗 🚗 🚗 🚗 🚗

The first line of the pictograph represents the Brahier Agency car sales for 1999. There are $5\frac{1}{4}$ units shown on the line, each unit representing 100 cars. Multiplying $5\frac{1}{4}$ times the scale of 100 indicates that the Brahier Agency sold approximately 525 cars during the year 1999. The second line of the graph indicates that $6\frac{1}{2}$ 100-car units were sold during 1998. Multiply $6\frac{1}{2}$ by 100; this indicates that the Brahier Agency sold approximately 650 cars in 1998. Using the same procedure to interpret the number of cars sold during 1997 and 1996, we find that approximately 600 cars were sold in 1997 and approximately 800 in 1996.

A **circle graph** can be used similarly, with sectors of a circle representing percentages of the data being studied. The following circle graph shows the data in the table concerning John's earnings in a week:

Money Earned by John in a Week			
	Money Earned	Percent of Earnings	Measure of Sector
Lawn mowing	$12.00	40%	40% of 360° = 144°
Weeding garden	7.00	23%	23% of 360° = 83°
Selling vegetables	9.50	32%	32% of 360° = 115°
Collecting trash	1.50	5%	5% of 360° = 18°
Total earned	$30.00		

A circle graph is typically very easy to read, because one can see at a glance the relative value of each item shown. However, to construct such a graph, students need to have some understanding of both angular measurement and percentage.

Stem-and-leaf plots are an efficient and relatively easy way of displaying and comparing raw data. These are commonly used when the data can be represented by numbers over a range of tens and ones (or hundreds and tens, thousands and hundreds, etc.). Individual measures are preserved in the display of a stem-and-leaf plot, but the manner in which the data are recorded shows the "shape" of the entire set. Consider the following data representing the distances achieved (in meters) in a softball throwing contest:

73, 30, 57, 45, 33, 33, 38, 74, 62, 30, 35, 62, 56, 46

As listed, it is difficult to make any quick statements about the data and measures of central tendency. If these raw data are organized into a stem-and-leaf plot, then certain aspects become more visible. In the following figure, the *stem* is the digit in the tens place of each number, and the *leaves* are the digits in the ones place. For example, the second "row" of the figure represents two scores, 45 and 46, while the fourth row represents two scores that are the same, 62. The first row represents six scores. What are they? What is the lowest score?

Softball Throwing Contest Results (in meters)

Stem	Leaf
3	0 0 3 3 5 8
4	5 6
5	6 7
6	2 2
7	3 4

It's relatively easy to see the individual data points in such an arrangement, but you also can quickly see the range (30 to 74) and any modes (30, 33, and 62). You can quickly count to get the median (45.5, halfway between 45 and 46), and you get an approximate sense of the mean (a little less than 50).

Side-by-side stem-and-leaf plots are an excellent way of comparing two distinct sets of raw data. Such arrangements often appear as shown below. Examine the following stem-and-leaf plot. What conclusions can you draw about the data?

Test Score Comparisons

Fourth Grade					Third Grade				
	6	7	8	|5|	2	4			
		4	6	|6|	1	7	8		
			4	|7|	5	5	5	7	8
		5	7	|8|	0	0	2	2	8
2	3	3	5	8	|9|	3	4		

(*Note:* In a side-by-side stem-and-leaf plot, the center column is the leading digit. Consequently, the first row for fourth grade has scores of 56, 57, and 58, while the first row for third grade is 52 and 54.)

Box-and-whisker plots are another visual means of displaying the range, quartiles, mean, and distribution of a data set. Such graphs are usually reserved for upper grades due to their more complex construction than stem-and-leaf plots. Nevertheless, we can benefit from examining data in this manner. The data from the preceding softball throwing example have been arranged into a box-and-whisker plot here:

**Softball Throwing Contest Distance Summary
(in meters)**

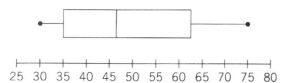

Close examination of the graph shows that the data split into four distinct sections, called quartiles. When the data are arranged in numerical order, *quartile* is the name given to each successive one-fourth of the data. The "box" in the graph represents the two middle quartiles (the middle 50% of the scores), and the "whiskers" show the lower and upper quartiles (the lowest 25% of the scores and the highest 25% of the scores, respectively). The box and whiskers give you a quick picture of the shape of the data. For example, at a glance you can see that the scores of the entire data set lie approximately between 30 and 75. You can also see that 25% of the scores are between 30 and 35 and that the middle 50% of the group have scores falling between 35 and approximately 62. The vertical line in the box represents the median, about 46. What other pieces of information can you glean from a box-and-whisker plot?

TAKING A "CHANCE"

Graphs are not only valuable in providing visual models of data; they can also be used for conjecture. For example, a graph representing temperatures throughout the year for a given location can be used to predict temperatures for next year's vacation. In this sense, graphs may be used as an introduction to informal probability notions.

The concept of probability is part of our everyday lives: "I will probably get a B on the test." "The odds are even for the UCLA—USC game this year." "The Cubs have a chance to win the pennant." "I'll bet two to one that it rains tomorrow." A contemporary mathematics program should provide an opportunity for children to learn more about the subject of probability and to use it in effective and meaningful ways to assist in the decision-making processes they so often face. Probability is a familiar part of the business world, and, when presented properly, children will find it to be an important part of their future lives.

The mathematics of probability can be complex—but need not be. The material in this chapter is intended as a foundational introduction for teachers, but intermediate pupils should be led to discover intuitively many of the basic and fundamental aspects of probability. The topic is much too important to be considered as "just enrichment material" at any grade level.

EXPERIMENTAL PROBABILITY

Today, mathematics programs at all grade levels should include an examination of probability. To be successful, such an introduction should be accompanied by experimentation with physical objects. By examining the results of their experiments and comparing these results with theoretical data, children can develop a greater understanding of probability—and often be quite surprised by variations from expectations due to chance.

We suggest that you use an experimental approach to this topic and interpret the results in light of our discussion of theoretical data. We will use checkers in our discussion, but you can use any objects (coins, for example) that can be easily flipped and have a different pattern on each side so that you can easily distinguish which side falls facing up.

Consider a checker that has a star on one side and circles on the other.

If we flip the checker in the air and let it fall on a table, will the "star" side or the "circle" side be facing up? Clearly, there are only two possibilities: Either the star will be facing up or the circle will be facing up. (We assume throughout that the checker or coin does not land on its edge and that the object used is balanced fairly, or "is honest.") Because only one of two possible results can be obtained by flipping a checker once, a star or a circle, we can express this by the ratio $\frac{1}{2}$. This ratio states that there is one chance out of two possibilities that the star will come up (or, equally likely, one chance out of two possibilities that the circle will come up). The ratio $\frac{1}{2}$ is an expression of the probability that a star (or a circle) will be obtained by flipping the checker once. (You might find it interesting to note that while the *probability* of getting a star is $\frac{1}{2}$, the *odds* of getting a star is $\frac{1}{1}$. This difference is because "odds" are defined as the ratio of the number of possible ways something will occur to the number of possible ways that it won't occur, while "probability" is defined as the ratio of the number of ways something can occur compared to all of the possible occurrences.)

In speaking of probabilities, obtaining a star is one "event," and obtaining a circle is another "event." In one toss of the checker, only one of these two events can occur, and the two possible events are equally probable. On one toss, the probability of obtaining a star is $\frac{1}{2}$ (one chance out of two possibilities), and the probability of obtaining a circle is $\frac{1}{2}$ (one chance out of two possibilities).

Probability, then, is a numerical measure of the chance that a particular event will occur, compared with the total number of events that could possibly occur. The probability of a particular event occurring is the ratio of the number of ways that particular event can occur to the total number of possible events. We can express the ratio mathematically as follows:

$$\text{Probability of a particular event occurring} = \frac{\text{Number of ways the event can occur}}{\text{Total number of possible events}}$$

When a checker is flipped once, the total number of possible events is two. Since the probability of obtaining a star is $\frac{1}{2}$ and the probability of obtaining a circle is $\frac{1}{2}$, what conclusion can we make about the nature of probability from our experiment? The sum of the probabilities of all the possible events is always 1—in this case, $\frac{1}{2} + \frac{1}{2}$ or $\frac{2}{2}$, or 1. This agrees with our common sense: If we flip a checker, it has to result in one of the possible events (since we have barred the possibility of the checker landing on its edge).

To illustrate another aspect of this situation, imagine that you have a checker with a star on both sides. What is the probability of obtaining a circle by flipping the checker?

$$\text{Probability of a particular event occurring} = \frac{\text{Number of ways the event can occur}}{\text{Total number of possible events}} = \frac{0}{2} = 0$$

In short, this event cannot happen. If the checker had a circle on both sides however, then the probability of obtaining a circle by flipping the checker would be $\frac{2}{2}$ or 1, meaning this event would happen without fail.

By performing experiments, we can test whether our theoretical data seem to hold true. However, all experimental data on probability are based on a "long run"—that is, a large number of trials. The greater the number of trials we make (the "longer the run"), the more likely it is that our experimental data will approximate our expected theoretical data. For example, the familiar expression "fifty–fifty chance" simply means that out of 100 trials (for example, flipping a checker 100 times), the number of stars (or circles) we are likely to see will be close to 50. However, this is one of the most misunderstood points about experimental versus theoretical probability. It *could* happen (though it is highly *unlikely*) that we would get 99 stars consecutively.

If we were "lucky enough" to have gotten 99 stars in a row, what would be the probability of obtaining a star on the *next* toss? It would still be one-half. The probability of obtaining a star is one-half on *each* flip. If, instead, you asked what the probability would be of getting 99 stars in a row (before having made your first toss), then the answer is quite small indeed: 1 divided by 2 raised to the ninety-ninth power! But even if we did obtain 99 stars and 1 circle out of 100 tosses, it is likely that in a run of 1000 trials, we would still come close to 500 stars and 500 circles. Students are often fascinated with the comparison of experimental results to "expected" theoretical results.

THEORETICAL PROBABILITY

There are some other aspects about probability that we must be familiar with before we can properly interpret our data. We can obtain theoretical probability by computation. For example, we have said that the probability of obtaining a star by flipping a checker once is $\frac{1}{2}$ (or one out of two possibilities). Suppose we flip the checker twice in succession. What are the possible outcomes for this two-flip experiment? Four results are possible, as shown in the table that follows:

FIRST TOSS	SECOND TOSS	POSSIBLE RESULTS
S	S	Star on first toss Star on second toss
C	S	Circle on first toss Star on second toss
S	C	Star on first toss Circle on second toss
C	C	Circle on first toss Circle on second toss

The table shows that the probability of getting a star and a circle is greater than that of getting two stars or two circles. What are the chances that flipping one checker two times will turn up a star both times? One out of four chances, or $\frac{1}{4}$. What are the chances that the two tosses will turn up a circle both times? One out of four chances, or $\frac{1}{4}$. What are the chances that the two tosses will turn up one star and one circle? Two out of four chances, or $\frac{2}{4}$. However, suppose we designated *order* as a part of the event? Suppose we had one red checker and one black checker and then asked, "What is the probability of obtaining a star on the red checker and a circle on the black checker?"

Red Checker	Black Checker
Star	Star
Star	Circle
Circle	Star
Circle	Circle

Clearly, there is a probability of $\frac{1}{4}$, or one out of four chances, of obtaining this combination. Notice that when we use one red checker and one black checker, the event of one red star and one black circle is different from the event of one red circle and one black star.

PERMUTATIONS AND COMBINATIONS

You may have heard the terms *permutation* and *combination* in other discussions about probability. The preceding discussion represents an application of a *permutation* because the order in which events occur is important. If we remove order from consideration, then it can be said that there are only three different *combinations*, or outcomes, that are possible, namely, two stars, two circles, or a star and a circle; but if order is important, then there are four different outcomes that are possible, namely, two stars, two circles, a star and a circle, or a circle and a star.

Consider this distinction in terms of dice. A single die has six sides, representing values from 1 through 6. What is the probability of obtaining a 3 if you roll a die once? One chance out of six, or $\frac{1}{6}$.

If you roll two dice, one red die and one blue die, what is the probability that you will roll a 5 on the red die and a 6 on the blue die?

We see from the diagram at the top of the next column, often referred to as a *tree diagram*, that there are six possible outcomes for one roll of a single die. But when rolling two dice, we see that there are 36 possible outcomes.

For example, if we roll a 1 on the red die, there are still six possibilities for the blue die. If we roll a 2 on the red die, there are still six possibilities for the blue die. In other words, for each possible outcome of the red die, there are six possibilities for the blue die. Because there are six possibilities for the red die, there are 6×6, or 36, possibilities for the two dice together.

The dice are independent of each other, so the number that comes up on one die does not affect the

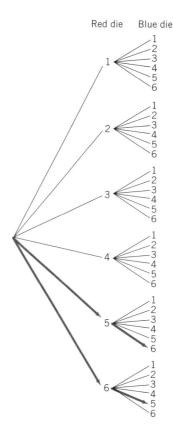

Red die   Blue die

number that will come up on the other die. Therefore, the probability of a 5 appearing on the red die is $\frac{1}{6}$, and the probability that a 6 will come up on the blue die is also $\frac{1}{6}$. The combined probability that the red die will have a 5 and the blue die a 6 is the product of the two probabilities, or $\frac{1}{6} \times \frac{1}{6} = \frac{1}{36}$. If order does not matter, the probability that on a roll of two dice one die will be 5 and the other die a 6 is $\frac{2}{36}$.

We can also examine the possibilities resulting from tossing a single checker twice. Note that tossing one checker two times in a row is the same as tossing two checkers at one time. In both situations the same combinations occur (as long as order does not matter).

1. One checker tossed twice gives the possible outcomes we have already examined.

FIRST TOSS	SECOND TOSS
star	star
circle	star
star	circle
circle	circle

2. Two checkers tossed at once can land in only the same four possible ways (when order matters).

First	☆	☆
Second	◎	☆
Third	☆	◎
Fourth	◎	◎

3. Now flip three checkers at once. What are the possible ways the checkers might land (when order matters)?

	First Checker	Second Checker	Third Checker
A	Circle	Circle	Circle
B	Circle	Circle	Star
C	Circle	Star	Circle
D	Circle	Star	Star
E	Star	Circle	Circle
F	Star	Circle	Star
G	Star	Star	Circle
H	Star	Star	Star

How many possible ways can the three checkers land? Eight. What are the chances that all three checkers will be circles (row A)? One out of eight chances, or $\frac{1}{8}$. What are the chances that two will be circles and one will be a star (rows B, C, and E)? Three out of eight chances, or $\frac{3}{8}$. What are the chances that two will be stars and one will be a circle (rows D, F, and G)? Three out of eight chances, or $\frac{3}{8}$. What are the chances that all three will be stars (row H)? One out of eight chances, or $\frac{1}{8}$. Taking 3 checkers at a time, there are four possible combinations, or ways they can be put together. Notice that again the sum of the probabilities is 1. (As we have noted, this will always be the case.)

$$\frac{1}{8} + \frac{3}{8} + \frac{3}{8} + \frac{1}{8} = \frac{8}{8}, \quad \text{or} \quad 1$$

Now flip a single checker 10 times, and record the results. Then try 20 times, 50 times, 100 times. Record your results in a table like the one at the top of the next column. (One hundred trials can be considered a long run for this experiment.)

What are your experimental results? How many circles did you get? How many stars? Your long-run results *should* be very close to the theoretical probabilities we have already examined. It would be interesting if each student in the class would flip a checker 20 or 25 times. You could then combine the results obtained

Number of Trials	Circle	Star
1		
2		
3		
⋮	⋮	⋮
100		

by all the students into one set of data. This would give a long run in the least amount of time.

MODELS FOR EXPLORING PROBABILITY

Probability has long fascinated mathematicians and others. Blaise Pascal, a seventeenth-century French mathematician, made use of a diagram of probability that is known today as *Pascal's Triangle*. To answer the questions of a friend who was a gambler, Pascal spent some time exploring the mathematics of gambling (which, of course, is based on probability). Pascal's Triangle is a means of representing the probability of the occurrence of a particular event.

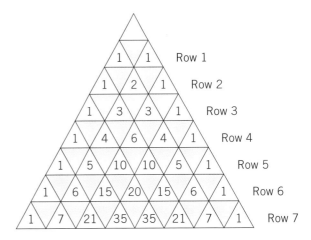

In examining the patterns in the triangle, you will notice that a given number in any row can be determined by adding the numbers named in the two adjacent triangles in the row above the given number. For example, look at the numeral 6 in row 4. The two numbers named in the triangles adjacent to 6 in the preceding row are 3 and 3, and 3 + 3 = 6. Since the triangle could be continued in the same manner, you should be able to use this pattern to name the numbers that should appear in the eighth row. (1, 8, 28, 56, 70, 56, 28, 8, 1)

Let's review the information that we obtained from a long run of testing. When 2 checkers are flipped, the probability is that $\frac{1}{4}$ of the total events are circles, $\frac{2}{4}$ (or $\frac{1}{2}$) are a circle and a star, and $\frac{1}{4}$ are stars. These ratios are read, "one out of four," "two out of four," and so on. When 3 checkers are flipped, $\frac{1}{8}$ of the total events are circles, $\frac{3}{8}$ are two circles and one star, $\frac{3}{8}$ are one circle and two stars, and $\frac{1}{8}$ are stars.

In the following table, the center column names the numerator of the probability ratios, and the right-hand column names the denominator of the probability ratios. For example, when 4 checkers are tossed, the probability ratios of the five different ways the checkers could fall are $\frac{1}{16}$, $\frac{4}{16}$, $\frac{6}{16}$, $\frac{4}{16}$, and $\frac{1}{16}$.

Number of Checkers Tossed	Combinations	Number of Combinations
1	1, 1	2
2	1, 2, 1	4
3	1, 3, 3, 1	8
4	1, 4, 6, 4, 1	16
5	1, 5, 10, 10, 5, 1	32
6	1, 6, 15, 20, 15, 6, 1	64
7	1, 7, 21, 35, 35, 21, 7, 1	128
8	1, 8, 28, 56, 70, 56, 28, 8, 1	256

Notice that our table is arranged in the form of Pascal's Triangle. Look at the table and consider the meaning of the rows. Assume that we are tossing a coin. Let's correlate the possible combinations (heads or tails) with the number patterns in the table.

- Row 1: 1 coin, 1 toss
  2 possible combinations

  (1 + 1 = 2)

H	T

  Heads: $\frac{1}{2}$ or 1 out of 2 chances
  Tails: $\frac{1}{2}$ or 1 out of 2 chances

- Row 2: 1 coin, 2 tosses
  4 possible combinations

  (1 + 2 + 1 = 4)

H H	T H
H T	T T

  2 heads: $\frac{1}{4}$ or 1 out of 4 chances
  1 head and 1 tail: $\frac{2}{4}$ or 2 out of 4 chances
  2 tails: $\frac{1}{4}$ or 1 out of 4 chances

- Row 3: 1 coin, 3 tosses
  8 possible combinations

  (1 + 3 + 3 + 1 = 8)

H H H	T T T
H H T	T T H
H T H	T H H
H T T	T H T

3 heads: $\frac{1}{8}$ or 1 out of 8 chances
2 heads and 1 tail: $\frac{3}{8}$ or 3 out of 8 chances
2 tails and 1 head: $\frac{3}{8}$ or 3 out of 8 chances
3 tails: $\frac{1}{8}$ or 1 out of 8 chances

Each row can be examined in much the same way to determine all of the possible combinations, and new rows could be added to the table indefinitely.

The data in the previous discussion can also be explored using geometric probability. That is, *geometric probability* arguments organize the data set in such a way that visual geometric interpretations help us make sense of the likelihood of an event. For example, consider a random drive from south to north in a valley that has three villages you might wish to visit: Kurlee, Moe, and Lar-ee. There are roads leading into the valley, and you decide to choose which one to take by flipping a coin (when you have two choices) and spinning a fair spinner (when you have three choices). What is the probability that you'll end up at the village of Moe?

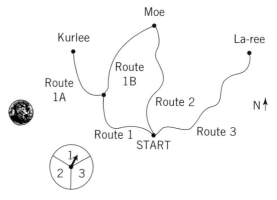

At the start of your trip you have three possible directions in which you could go, two of which *could* lead you to the village of Moe; therefore, you have a $\frac{2}{3}$ probability of heading that direction on your random drive. (The chance of picking the "direct" route is $\frac{1}{3}$ and the chance of picking the other possible route to Moe is also $\frac{1}{3}$.) If we let the entire shape below represent the probability of reaching any village, then the probability of reaching Moe *directly* at this point can be shown by shading a total of one-third of the shape.

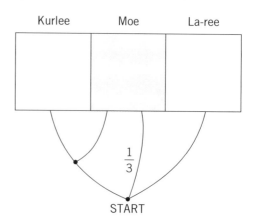

If the spin of the spinner does not result in the direct route, but instead sends you to the fork in the road, then you have only two options available, one of which leads you to Moe. So, *at this point*, you have a probability of $\frac{1}{2}$ that you'll choose the road that takes you to Moe. This can be shown by shading one-half of the one-third representing that route.

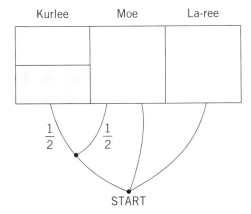

What is the overall probability *before you begin your drive* of choosing roads that allow you to reach Moe? The answer to this question can be found by "combining" the two shaded pieces that represent reaching Moe and interpreting the geometric representation of these probabilities as $\frac{1}{3} + \left(\frac{1}{2} \text{ of } \frac{1}{3}\right)$. That is, $\frac{1}{3} + \frac{1}{6}$ or $\frac{3}{6}$.

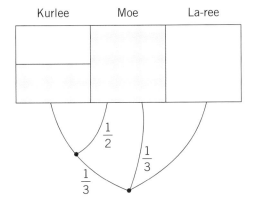

The diagram shows that the probability of reaching Moe on a random drive from south to north is $\frac{1}{2}$, since one-half of the entire region has been shaded. Use a similar argument to determine the probability of ending up at the village of Kurlee.

CLOSURE

Both statistics and probability are intertwined with the data analysis that we must undertake if we are to rationally interpret events that occur in our daily lives. In fact, "daily" may be too weak of a descriptor for the frequency with which we encounter these topics. A glance at nearly any section of the newspaper will readily reveal the degree to which we are influenced by the need to understand data and "weigh" the evidence. The exploration of topics such as those described in this chapter are not diversions from the mathematics curriculum; they are, in fact, essential to the development of a mathematically literate society that creates thoughtful arguments and makes reasoned decisions.

Terminology, Symbols, and Procedures

Box-and-Whisker Plot. Box-and-whisker plots are a visual means of displaying the range, quartiles, mean, and distribution of a data set. The "box" represents the two middle quartiles, and the "whiskers" are the lower and upper quartiles.

Circle Graph. A graph in which sectors of a circle show proportions of data represented is a circle graph.

Data. Data are collections of numerical facts.

Frequency. In a collection of data, the frequency of a measure is the number of times the measure occurs.

Frequency Polygon (or **Line Graph**). A line graph uses line segments to illustrate the change in continuous data.

Graph. Essentially, a graph is a picture designed to show relationships among data in such a way that the reader can easily summarize and interpret the data.

Histogram (or **Bar Graph**). A bar graph uses either vertical or horizontal bars to indicate relationships among data.

Mean (**Arithmetic Mean** or **Average**). The mean for a collection of data is the arithmetic average of the measures. One way to find the mean of a set of data is to calculate the sum of the measures and divide by the number of measures.

Median. If the measures in a set of data are recorded in order, from greatest to least or least to greatest, the median is the measure listed at the middle. If there is no middle measure, as would be the case if an even number of measures were listed in order, then the median is defined to be the average of the two measures that would have bounded the median.

Mode. The mode for a collection of data is the measure that appears with the greatest frequency (is the most repeated).

Pictograph. A pictograph is a graph in which pictures are used to represent values.

Probability. Probability is the numerical measure of the chance that a particular event will occur, depending on the possible events. The probability that an event will occur is expressed as a ratio between the number of ways a particular event can occur and the number of possible events.

$$\text{Probability of a particular event occurring} = \frac{\text{Number of ways the event can occur}}{\text{Total number of possible events}}$$

Range. The range for a collection of data is the difference between the greatest and least measures in the set of data. Sometimes, the range is described by listing the two most extreme values in the set of data.

Statistics. Statistics is the study of numerical data to determine the relationships that exist among the data (such as central tendencies, dispersion, or scatter).

Stem-and-Leaf Plot. Stem-and-leaf plots are an efficient way of displaying and comparing raw data. Stem-and-leaf plotting is a variation from using frequency distributions to organize data. Individual measures are preserved in the display of a stem-and-leaf plot, but the shape of the associated "histogram" is retained.

Practice Exercises for Teachers

These exercises are designed for the reader of this book. While some are suitable for use in the elementary classroom, these examples should not necessarily be given to children in this form. Ideas for classroom activities on the concepts and ideas discussed in this chapter can be found in Part 2 of *Today's Mathematics*, the Student Resource Book.

1. If you flip 4 pennies at one time, what is the probability that all 4 coins will show heads? If you flip 5 pennies, what is the probability that all 5 pennies will show heads? If you flip 6 pennies, what is the probability that all 6 pennies will show heads?

2. What different combinations are possible for 10 pennies flipped at one time? Indicate the ratio for each combination. (Use Pascal's Triangle.)

3. Take three slips of paper. On one write the numeral 1, on the second the numeral 2, and on the third the numeral 3. Place all three slips of paper in a hat or box.
   a) What is the probability that you will draw the 1 on the first draw?
   b) On the second draw, what is the probability that you will draw the 2 if you drew the 3 on the first draw and did not replace it?
   c) What is the probability that you will draw the 3 on the first draw, the 2 on the second draw, and the 1 on the third draw?
   d) What is the probability that you will draw an odd number on the first draw?
   e) What is the probability that you will draw an even number on the first draw?

4. a) If you toss a die, what is the probability that you will roll a 6? A 4? A 3?
   b) What is the probability that either a 1 or a 6 will be rolled?
   c) What is the probability that a 2, 4, or 6 will be rolled?
   d) What is the probability that a 1, 2, 3, or 4 will be rolled?
   e) What is the probability that a 1, 2, 3, 4, or 5 will be rolled?

5. If you place 5 red marbles, 2 blue marbles, and 1 white marble in a bag, what is the probability that on the first draw you will draw a red marble? A blue marble? A white marble?

6. Suppose you toss 4 pennies 32 times. Each time you record the number of heads, and obtain the following frequency table.

Number of Heads	Tally	Frequency
0	||	2
1	⊞⊞ ||	7
2	⊞⊞ ⊞⊞ |||	13
3	⊞⊞ |	6
4	||||	4

   a) What is the mean for this collection of data?
   b) What is the median? The mode? The range?
   c) Make a frequency polygon for this collection of data.

7. Your piggy bank contains 7 quarters, 10 dimes, and 5 nickels. You turn the piggy bank upside down to shake out a coin. (Assume that the size and weight of the coins do not affect this experiment.)

   a) What is the probability of getting a quarter?
   b) What is the probability of getting a dime?
   c) What is the probability of getting a nickel?

8. A regular dodecahedron (a space figure with 12 faces) has a calendar printed on it such that one month is printed on each face. If you roll the dodecahedron, what are the chances of rolling each of the following?

   a) the month of January
   b) a winter month
   c) a month between January and August

9. Use a deck of 52 regular playing cards without the jokers. What are the chances that if you draw one card it will be one of the following?

   a) the ace of spades   b) a jack   c) a diamond
   d) a face card   e) between 3 and 9

10. A drawer contains 12 navy blue socks and 12 black socks. You wish to get either a pair of navy blue socks or a pair of black socks. If you are reaching into the drawer without looking, how many socks must you remove to be sure you have one matched pair?

11. Draw a circle graph based on the following results of rolling a die 100 times; show proportionately how many times each number was rolled.

Number Rolled	Number of Times Number Was Rolled
1	14
2	5
3	15
4	32
5	24
6	10

12. Construct a pictogram using the following data concerning the number of years 5 retired players of the Kansas City Chiefs played in the National Football League.

Player	Years
Jim Lynch, linebacker	8
Mo Moorman, guard	7
Ed Podolak, running back	6
Willie Lanier, linebacker	8
Elmo Wright, wide receiver	4

Teaching Competencies and Self-Assessment Tasks

1. Create a data set in which the mean, median, mode, and range are all identical. Adjust the data set so that the mean, median, mode, and range are all different. Create a new data set in which the range is 20, a mean is 15, a median is 18, and the modes are 21 and 16.
2. Discuss the nature of data most appropriate for display in each type of graph discussed in this chapter.
3. Design a single data set representing a real-life situation that can be convincingly displayed on either a bar graph, line graph, or circle graph. What issues and questions are raised as you create this data set?
4. Identify a real-life data set that is suitable for a stem-and-leaf plot and create such a display. Indicate the mode and range. Identify a real-life data set that is suitable for a box-and-whisker plot and create such a display. Indicate the median, range, and the upper and lower quartiles.
5. Conduct an experiment to determine how frequently a paper cup dropped from a height of 5 feet will land upside down. Express your result as a probability and test it over a larger sample. Make any appropriate revisions in your conclusion. Adjust the height of the drop and examine changes in the result.
6. Identify at least ten situations where we might encounter statistics and/or probability in our daily lives. In what ways are these situations alike? Different?
7. Objects are frequently used to represent amounts in pictographs. In this chapter, for example, pictures of cars were used to represent sales of 100 cars. Suppose a pictograph were drawn using pictures of cereal boxes to represent sales of 1000 boxes. If sales were to double, should the number of pictures of boxes be doubled? Should the size of the boxes (volume) be doubled? Should only the height or width be doubled? Do all of these accurately represent the situation?
8. Research the literature to find uses of Pascal's Triangle, other than probability, in elementary mathematics. Discuss your findings with the class.
9. Discuss appropriate graphing experiences in the kindergarten and/or first-grade classroom.
10. What aspects of probability should be included in the primary mathematics program?

Related Readings and Teacher Resources

For related readings on topics found in this chapter, see the corresponding chapter in Part 2 of *Today's Mathematics*, the Student Resource Book.

Chapter 15

Measurement

Teaching Competencies

Upon completing this chapter, you will be able to:

■ Describe various characteristics and applications of nonstandard and standard units of measure.

■ Relate some of the historical development of measures and measurement.

■ Describe various aspects of the metric and the U.S. customary systems of measurement.

■ Describe the relationship among and between different measuring units and different measurement instruments.

■ Add, subtract, multiply, and divide using denominate numbers.

■ Enumerate steps in children's acquisition of money concepts.

■ Describe an effective and efficient approach for teaching time concepts to children.

■ Prepare lessons reflecting the NCTM *Principles and Standards for School Mathematics* through integrating measurement with other topics within mathematics and with other subject areas in the elementary school curriculum.

ome people feel that measurement is just something you do with a ruler, a scale, or a container. Maybe there's more to it. Consider the following situation as described by a seventh grader:

> It was 10 minutes to two on Friday, May 23rd. Me and my 4 friends were on the way to the third floor to our social studies class to take a test. I got a score of 85 on my last test so I needed to get at least a score of 95 on this one to keep my A average. I wasn't as worried as last time because I knew I could improve.
>
> Last week I tried to talk my parents into giving me a $5.00 raise in my allowance if I earned an A in this class. They said they would consider it if I would agree to save half of it each week.
>
> When I got within 10 feet of the classroom door, I could feel the tension begin to build. I reminded myself that I knew the material, but it was almost 80 degrees in the classroom that day—how could I concentrate? At least I drank a 12-ounce can of pop before class to keep from dehydrating! (It wasn't sugar-free—I needed all the energy I could get.)

The sentences of this story have a common thread. Did you notice that each and every sentence included some sort of reference to a measure or to a measurement? Some references are more obvious than others. For example, the reference to "sugar-free" is a measure showing the lack of sugar content in a soft drink, and the reference to "within 10 feet of the classroom door" is clearly an example of measuring approximate distance. The statement about needing "at least a score of 95" on the test is a measure, of sorts, of the student's knowledge. What about the statements "10 minutes to two," "May 23rd," "last week," and "$5.00 raise"? These are measures of time and money. The comment about saving "half of it" is a comparative form of measuring an amount of money. The reference to the "third floor" is a measure of location, and the comment about "4 friends" is a measure of numberness. Finally, even the sentence in the first paragraph "I wasn't as worried . . . because I knew I could improve" is a measure, albeit subjective, of the student's confidence. The point? Measurement is pervasive in our lives. Take a moment to consider, and perhaps list, all the forms of measurement in which you engage during a single day.

Because measurement is so important due to its practicality and pervasiveness in so many aspects of everyday life, the National Council of Teachers of Mathematics has included the study of measurement as one of the five content standards put forth in the *Principles and Standards for School Mathematics* (2000). The preK–12 measurement standards reads:

Instructional programs from pre-kindergarten through grade 12 should enable all students to—

■ understand measurable attributes of objects and the units, systems, and processes of measurement;

■ apply appropriate techniques, tools, and formulas to determine measurements.

The study of measurement, if effectively structured, also serves as a connector to other related areas of the mathematics curriculum. For example, the study of measurement provides a context for visiting and/or reviewing such topics as number operations, geometric concepts, statistical concepts, algebraic concepts, and general problem-solving situations. "Measurement is an important vehicle for highlighting mathematical connections—not only within mathematics itself, but to areas too often viewed as 'outside of mathematics' such as social studies, science, art, physical education, and the student's own interests and experiences" (NCTM, 1998, p. 70).

THE HISTORICAL DEVELOPMENT OF MEASUREMENT SYSTEMS

One of the first mathematical needs of any society is a system of standard measurement. Even primitive people developed some rudimentary way to mark the passage of time or to describe the distance from one place to another—for example, the distance from the tribe's camp to a herd of animals that could provide food and clothing.

Ancient Egyptian and Babylonian civilizations developed the first recorded systems of measurement in the Western world. The Egyptians were concerned with agriculture, particularly along the fertile Nile River. Consequently, they developed an elaborate system of land measurement for laying out crops and for marking the annual loss and subsequent restoration of land resulting from the great floods of the Nile. They also developed a system for measuring volume—for them, the amount of grain in a container—but this system of volume measurement was extremely complex and awkward to use.

The Babylonians advanced the science of measurement. For example, the Babylonians calculated the length of the sidereal year to be 365 days, 6 hours, and 11 minutes—a figure that is within 3 minutes of the modern calculation. (The sidereal year is computed from the apparent movement of the stars, which gives a more accurate measurement of time than the earth's movement around the sun. Even today, such astronomical observations and scientific measurements help to standardize the measure of time to a high degree of precision.)

The development of systems of measure by peoples of the ancient world was closely tied to the creation of the science of geometry. The English word *geometry* is derived from the Greek *geo*, meaning "earth," and *metron*, meaning "measure," and thus *geometry* means "earth measure." This suggests that the practical activity of measurement was critical to the origin of the abstract discipline of geometry.

The Egyptians and the Babylonians, as well as the ancient Greeks and Romans, used units of measure that, for the most part, were derived from dimensions of the human body. For example, the length of the forearm, called a *cubit*, was used in measurement by the Babylonians and other early peoples. Some of the units early civilizations used for measuring length were the length of a foot, the width of a finger, the width of the palm of a hand, and the length of a soldier's stride. For centuries after the Greeks, units of measure continued to be derived from the human body. In the early Middle Ages, the following units of length were commonly used:

fathom: the distance between a person's hands with arms outstretched
cubit: the distance from the elbow to the tip of the middle finger
hand: the width of the hand
digit: the width of the index finger
foot: the distance from the heel of the foot to the tip of the great toe
yard: the length of the arm from the shoulder to the tip of the middle finger

The limitations of these units of measure should become evident with a little thought. The distance from the elbow to the tip of the middle finger varies from person to person. The width of the hand is greater for a large person than for a small person. Not all people have feet of the same length. In short, these units of measure were inconsistent in that they varied from person to person, and these differences in references were responsible for errors in communicating measures. Measurement would not be invariant until people devised a system of **standard measure**—units of measure that would be the same reference for everyone.

During the late medieval period, attempts were made to establish some standard units of measure. The length of a standard yard was originally determined in the following way: The length of 3 barleycorns was to be an inch; 12 inches were to be a foot; 3 feet were to be a yard. Later, Henry I of England (1068–1135) decreed that the distance from his nose to the thumb of his outstretched arm would be one yard. Edward I of England (1239–1307) established the first fixed standard—one that didn't change based on who happened to be king at the time—an iron rod whose length was defined as one yard.

During the last three centuries, with the evolution of machine tools and more accurate instruments, measurement has become an extremely, but not completely, precise science. So much so, in fact, that in the nineteenth century, England, France, and the United States established bureaus of standards to maintain fixed units of standard measure. Not only the units of linear measurement, but also those of weight and time, have been standardized by defining standard units.

CONTEMPORARY MEASUREMENT SYSTEMS

There are two commonly used systems of measurement today, the *U.S. customary system* and the *metric system*. The U.S. customary system, with which many of us are somewhat familiar, is the system most used by laypersons in the United States and in very few other places in the world. The United Kingdom began conversion to the metric system in 1965; Australia followed in 1970; and Canada, in 1971. The metric system is used throughout other countries of the world and in the scientific work of all nations.

The U.S. customary system of measurement is, in many cases, difficult to work with because of the odd relations between the various units. This confusion is primarily due to the long historical development of the system, which has its roots in units of measure that were in use before the development of standard measure.

Even standardized measurement presents difficulties; for instance, a dry quart is larger than a liquid quart, and a British quart is smaller than either the dry quart or the liquid quart. An ounce that measures liquid is not the same as an ounce that is used to measure dry material; also, the avoirdupois ounce (which we normally use) is lighter than the troy ounce or the apothecaries' ounce.

The accompanying table shows some of the principal units of the U.S. customary system that you might recognize. As we examine the table, we are unable to identify a clear and logical pattern of relations among the various units. This accounts for the awkwardness of the U.S. customary system. The growth of science and industry in the eighteenth century, however, required an efficient and convenient way to measure length, weight, and volume. The *metric system* of measurement was created to satisfy this need.

Length
12 inches = 1 foot
3 feet = 1 yard
$5\frac{1}{2}$ yards = 1 rod
40 rods = 1 furlong
8 furlongs = 1 mile

Area
144 square inches = 1 square foot
9 square feet = 1 square yard
4840 square yards = 1 acre
640 acres = 1 square mile

Volume
3 teaspoons = 1 tablespoon
16 tablespoons = 1 cup
2 cups = 1 pint
2 pints = 1 quart
4 quarts = 1 gallon
2 gallons = 1 peck
4 pecks = 1 bushel

Weight
$437\frac{1}{2}$ grains = 1 ounce
16 ounces = 1 pound
100 pounds = 1 hundredweight
20 hundredweights = 1 ton

The metric system did not evolve out of the capricious customs of the ancient and medieval worlds but was first suggested by various French scientists in the eighteenth century. A number of countries, including France, came to adopt this system. In 1875, the International Bureau of Weights and Measures was established in an attempt to create a uniform and efficient system of measurement. The system that was adopted by the bureau is the metric system. Almost all countries of the world have adopted the metric system and made it the official system of measurement. Moreover, most scientists throughout the world, including those of the United States, do their work with metric units. Consequently, as American society becomes more scientifically and technologically oriented, it becomes necessary, even critical, for us to understand and make use of the metric system. For this reason, the metric system continues to be an important part of the mathematics programs in the elementary schools.

It's interesting to note that the United States officially adopted the metric system in 1875, but it was little-used by the citizenry. In 1975, Gerald Ford, then president, signed the Metric Conversion Act, which called for a *voluntary* conversion to the metric system and established the U.S. Metric Board to handle the coordination of the conversion. Immediately after the passage of the act, there was enthusiasm for change, but the momentum waned, primarily because conversion was not made mandatory. Many today feel that the "metric movement" in the United States is dead, but a great many changes have occurred, and will continue to occur, in how we measure our world. For example, the U.S. military uses metric measures, as does the medical profession. Many sporting events use metric units to measure distance and mass. A large number of major businesses, such as those in the automobile and high-tech industries, are heavily metricated. Products in our stores are labeled metrically; the film we buy is measured in millimeters; and our weather reports and our road signs often reflect both metric and U.S. customary measures. So, although we have not had what might be termed an "overnight explosion of metric" measurements thrust on us, we have adapted well and continue to expand our use of the metric system to include those areas that have traditionally been measured using the U.S. customary system. The simple fact is that if a company (or a society) is to be competitive in a global economy, then it must adapt to metric measurement.

The metric system has evolved over the decades and has been modified into what it is today. The metric system, called *le système international d'unités*, is known today as SI. SI provides eight basic units, listed in the table at the top of the next column.

In elementary school we commonly teach only length, capacity, mass, temperature, and time. The temperature we teach, however, is usually Celsius or Fahrenheit, not the Kelvin scale.

The basic unit of linear measurement (length) in the metric system is the *meter*. Originally, the standard meter was based on a calculation of one ten-millionth

Measurement	Standard Unit	Symbol
Length	meter	m
Capacity	liter	l
Mass	gram	g
Temperature	Kelvin	K
Time	second	s
Electric current	ampere	A
Amount of substance	mole	mol
Luminous intensity	candela	cd

of the distance between the North Pole and the equator, through Paris. Today, having more precise instruments of measurement, we know that this measurement is slightly inaccurate.

The meter has been redefined as the distance between two microscopic lines engraved on a particular platinum-iridium bar maintained under specified conditions at the International Bureau of Weights and Measures at Sèvres, France. A meter was alternatively defined as the length of 1,553,164.13 wavelengths of red cadmium light waves under specified conditions. In 1969, members of the General Conference on Weights and Measures defined the meter as 1,650,763.73 wavelengths of the orange-red line of krypton 86. A more recent definition of a meter is the distance traveled by light in .000000003335640952 second. These modern definitions serve to determine the length of the meter to a phenomenally high degree of precision. (Of course, this information is provided only for the teacher's understanding of continued attempts to increase the level of precision—it is not intended that children be exposed to such formal definitions.) Teachers are reminded of the variability and uncertainty of "the distance from a king's nose to his outstretched thumb" as compared to the scientific definitions given here.

The other units of length in the metric system are related to the meter by powers of ten, as shown in the accompanying table. The names of the units of length based on the meter are composed of two parts, the base *meter* and a prefix that indicates the relation of the unit to the meter. For example, *kilo-* is a prefix meaning "one thousand," so the term *kilometer* designates a unit of length equal to one thousand meters. Most foreign automobile speedometers measure speed in kilometers per hour, just as ours measure speed in miles per hour. (In fact, almost all speedometers are calibrated in both systems.) Similarly, *centi-* is a prefix meaning "one-hundredth," so the term *centimeter* designates a unit of length equal to one-hundredth of a meter. Notice the clear and logical pattern of relations among the various units; this makes for ease and efficiency in scientific work. (See the chart at the top of the next page.)

We do not teach children all the prefixes—there is no need to do so at this stage of development. In elementary school, we usually teach only *kilo-*, *deci-*, *centi-*,

EM	1 exameter	= 1 000 000 000 000 000 000.		meters
Pm	1 petameter	=	1 000 000 000 000 000.	meters
Tm	1 terameter	=	1 000 000 000 000.	meters
Gm	1 gigameter	=	1 000 000 000.	meters
Mm	1 megameter	=	1 000 000.	meters
km	1 kilometer	=	1 000.	meters
hm	1 hectometer	=	100.	meters
dam	1 dekameter	=	10.	meters
m	**1 meter**	**=**	**1.**	**meter**
dm	1 decimeter	=	.1	meter
cm	1 centimeter	=	.01	meter
mm	1 millimeter	=	.001	meter
um	1 micrometer	=	.000 001	meter
nm	1 nanometer	=	.000 000 001	meter
pm	1 picometer	=	.000 000 000 001	meter
fm	1 femtometer	=	.000 000 000 000 001	meter
am	1 attometer	=	.000 000 000 000 000 001	meter

and *milli-*. The existing prefixes are listed in the table solely to familiarize you with the complete system of naming measures. You should *not* find it necessary to memorize the entire table. We sometimes forget that we do not memorize all the measures in the U.S. customary system of measurement, either.

From the eight basic units of the SI, all other measurements are developed. The accompanying table shows the most commonly used measurements:

Quantity	Common Units	Symbol
Length	kilometer meter centimeter millimeter	km m cm mm
Area	square kilometer square meter square centimeter square millimeter	km^2 m^2 cm^2 mm^2
Volume	cubic meter cubic decimeter cubic centimeter	m^3 dm^3 cm^3
Mass	kilogram gram	kg g
Temperature	degree Celsius	°C

Now let us examine some of these different metric measures. Units of area measure in the metric system are based on the convenient relation of powers of ten. Area measure involves the use of squares. For example, one square meter is the amount of area covered by a square one meter on a side.

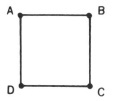

$$\overset{\bullet \rightarrow \bullet}{AB} = \overset{\bullet \rightarrow \bullet}{BC} = \overset{\bullet \rightarrow \bullet}{CD} = \overset{\bullet \rightarrow \bullet}{DA} = 1 \text{ meter}$$
Area of square ABCD = 1 square meter

Thus, we can arrange a table to show square metric units.

sq km	1 square kilometer	=	(1000.)^2	square meters
sq m	**1 square meter**	**=**	**1.**	**square meter**
sq dm	1 square decimeter	=	(.1)^2	square meter
sq cm	1 square centimeter	=	(.01)^2	square meter
sq mm	1 square millimeter	=	(.001)^2	square meter

It is advisable to suggest (or have children identify) some real-world approximations for the various units of measure that are being discussed. These referents are intended only as approximations that will help the children relate an otherwise abstract expression, such as "three square meters," with something very real to them. For this reason, it is important that such referents be clearly understood and not interpreted as "equal to." For instance, an example that might prove helpful when discussing a square meter would be an area similar to that covered by half of a "typical" classroom door or, perhaps, a card table.

The metric system uses the kilogram and gram instead of the U.S. customary units of pounds, ounces, and so forth. Originally, the gram was defined as the weight of one cubic centimeter of pure water under specified conditions (a cubic centimeter being the volume contained by a cube one centimeter on a side). Today, using more precise instruments, scientists have redefined the gram as one-thousandth of the weight of a particular platinum-iridium cylinder maintained under specified conditions. This is an absolute measurement; therefore it has the same value in outer space or on other planets or moons that it does on earth. The *gram* is the basic unit of weight in the metric system. The other units of weight are related to the gram by powers of ten as shown in the following table. (From this point on, we will show only the most commonly used units. You may expand the tables as necessary.)

km	kilogram	=	1000	grams
g	**1 gram**	**=**	**1.**	**gram**

The names of the units of weight other than the gram are composed of two parts, the base *gram* and a prefix that indicates the relation of the unit to the gram. For example, *mega-* is a prefix meaning "one million," so the term *megagram* names a unit equal to one million grams. Similarly, the prefix *micro-* means "one-millionth," so the term *microgram* designates a unit of weight equal to one-millionth of a gram. Again, a clear and logical pattern exists in the relations among the various units.

A representation that is often used as a referent for a gram is a single M&M's® candy or a nickel. A referent model to use for a kilogram might be a classroom dictionary or some other appropriate classroom object, such as a box of manipulatives. Whatever is selected, weigh it ahead of time to be certain that it is reasonably close to a kilogram in weight.

The basic unit of volume in the metric system is the *liter*, which is defined as the volume of one kilogram of pure water under specified conditions. The standard liter was originally intended to equal one-thousandth of a cubic meter, or one cubic decimeter, but because of the inaccuracy in fixing the units of weight, this equality is only approximate. As shown in the accompanying table, the other units of volume in the metric system are related to the liter by powers of ten. (Again, we will not complete the entire table; you can complete additional parts of the table as necessary.)

l	1 liter	=	1.	liter
cl	1 centiliter	=	.01	liter
ml	1 milliliter	=	.001	liter

The names of the other units of volume have two parts, the base *liter* and a prefix indicating the relation of the unit to the liter. For example, *deka-* is a prefix meaning "ten," so the term *dekaliter* names a unit of volume equal to ten liters. Similarly, the prefix *deci-* means "tenth," so the term *deciliter* names a unit of volume equal to one-tenth of a liter. Notice, once more, the clear and logical pattern of relations among the various units.

Many children are familiar with two-liter bottles of soda. You can also use a quart container to represent and demonstrate that it is "a little bit" less than a liter.

The relations among the metric units of length, weight, and volume are summarized in the table at the top of the next column.

Because the units of the metric system are related in a simple and logical way by powers of ten, it is very easy to change from one unit to another. We need only to multiply or divide by the appropriate power of ten. Consider, for example, 2 farmhouses that are 1300 meters apart. Suppose we want to express this distance in kilometers. We know that 1000 meters is equal to 1 kilometer and that each meter is equal to $\frac{1}{1000}$ of a kilometer. Therefore we can multiply 1300 by $\frac{1}{1000}$ (or .001) and obtain 1.3, which is the distance between the 2 farmhouses in kilometers.

Prefix	Linear Measure	Weight	Volume or Capacity
10^3 × base	kilometer	kilogram	kiloliter
10^2 × base	hectometer	hectogram	hectoliter
10^1 × base	dekameter	dekagram	dekaliter
10^0 × base	**meter**	**gram**	**liter**
10^{-1} × base	decimeter	decigram	deciliter
10^{-2} × base	centimeter	centigram	centiliter
10^{-3} × base	millimeter	milligram	milliliter

1300 meters = 1.3 kilometers

(Of course, we could have solved this by dividing 1300 by 1000—a process equivalent to multiplying 1300 by $\frac{1}{1000}$.) Clearly, by using appropriate powers of ten, it is quite easy to change units in the metric system.

In the U.S. customary system, however, it is much more cumbersome to change units. Suppose, for example, that the 2 farmhouses are 1.3 miles apart and that we wish to express this distance in feet. There are 5280 feet in one mile. So, we must multiply 1.3 by 5280 to find the distance in feet between the 2 farmhouses.

$$1 \text{ mile} = 5280 \text{ feet}$$
$$1.3 \text{ miles} = 1.3 \times 5280$$
$$= 6864 \text{ feet}$$

$$\begin{array}{r} 5280 \\ \times \quad 1.3 \\ \hline 1584.0 \\ 5280 \quad\;\; \\ \hline 6864.0 \end{array}$$ (.3 × 5280) (1 × 5280)

Therefore, 1.3 miles is equal to 6864 feet, so the 2 farmhouses are 6864 feet apart.

At this point we can begin to appreciate the efficiency of the metric system. To convert 1.3 miles into 6864 feet, we had to perform a three-step mathematical operation. Even if we had memorized the fact that there are 5280 feet in 1 mile, we would still have had to multiply 1.3 by 5280. But to convert 1300 meters into 1.3 kilometers, we had only to multiply 1300 by $\frac{1}{1000}$ (or divide 1300 by 1000). Converting one metric measure to another metric measure is a process that often requires only a minimal amount of mental mathematics.

If a measurement is expressed in metric units, a computation can be performed to express the same measurement in U.S. customary units. Similarly, if a measurement is expressed in U.S. customary units, a computation can be performed to convert the measurement into metric units. The most common relations between metric and U.S. customary units are listed in the accompanying table. While these relations are only approximate, they are adequate for most practical purposes. The symbol ≈ is read "approximately equal to."

Linear Measure		
1 meter	≈ 39.37 inches	1 centimeter ≈ .3937 inch
1 meter	≈ 3.28 feet	1 centimeter ≈ .0328 foot
1 meter	≈ 1.09 yards	1 centimeter ≈ .0109 yard
1 kilometer ≈ .62 mile		
1 inch ≈ 2.54 centimeters ≈ .0254 meter		
1 foot ≈ 30.48 centimeters ≈ .3048 meter		
1 yard ≈ 91.44 centimeters ≈ .9144 meter		
1 mile ≈ 1609 meters ≈ 1.609 kilometers		

Weight
1 gram   ≈ .035 ounce ≈ .0022 pound
1 kilogram ≈ 2.2 pounds
1 pound   ≈ 453.6 grams ≈ .4536 kilogram
1 ounce   ≈ 28.35 grams ≈ .02835 kilogram

Volume
1 liter   ≈ 61.025 inches
1 liter   ≈ .264 gallon
1 liter   ≈ 1.057 quarts
1 gallon ≈ 231 cubic inches ≈ 3.785 liters
1 quart ≈ 57.75 cubic inches ≈ .946 liter

While the conversion of measurements within a given system of measure is essential, conversion of measurements from one system to a different system is *not* normally taught as part of the elementary school mathematics program. Students need only an understanding of the relative sizes of the measures. Usually, if a measure is given in metric units, the calculating will also be done in metric measure. While *comparison* is certainly appropriate, do not ask children to *convert* from one system of measurement to another.

THE PROCESS OF MEASUREMENT

Throughout this chapter we have been talking about measurement in ways that we all recognize, but we have avoided an explanation of what we mean by the term. What is measurement? **Measurement** is the determination of the size of a thing, or a comparison between some aspect of a thing and a standard unit. When we determine the height of a building, we are using measurement. When we determine the time it takes to run a race, we are using measurement. When we count the number of students in a classroom, we are using measurement. In each of these situations our measurement is expressed by a combination of two things:

1. the measure, which shows us "how many"
2. a standard unit, which shows us the unit of measurement with which the quantity to be measured is compared

For instance, consider these examples:

The building is 350 feet high.
The racetrack is 100 meters long.
The race took 17 seconds.

In the first example, the unit of measurement is feet and the measure is 350; in the second, the unit of measure-

ment is meters and the measure is 100; in the third, the unit of measurement is seconds and the measure is 17.

Let's develop the idea of measurement with respect to linear measurement. Linear measurement, as the name suggests, is concerned with measurement of length. Children in the primary grades can begin to develop some concept of linear measurement by using any suitable object as a measuring device. A child could measure a desk using a pencil, an eraser, a book, or a card, for example. One child might measure the desk as "7 pencils long," and another child might measure it as "14 erasers long." Through a discussion and comparison of such measurements, children will soon realize the need for standard units of measurement to communicate results. Each class might develop its own standard unit of measurement; one class might use a Popsicle stick, for example. They will soon discover that if 2 children use the same measuring instrument carefully, they will arrive at the same (or very nearly the same) measurement of a given object. Each pupil might find that his or her desk is 6 Popsicle sticks long.

After spending a considerable amount of time manipulating familiar objects, children are ready for the more abstract level of comparing line segments, choosing one line segment as a standard unit. Children should be asked to compare the lengths of the following two line segments.

They can do this by tracing $\overleftrightarrow{AB}$ on another sheet of paper and then placing this tracing on top of $\overleftrightarrow{YZ}$. Clearly, $\overleftrightarrow{AB}$ is shorter than $\overleftrightarrow{YZ}$, or $m(\overleftrightarrow{AB}) < m(\overleftrightarrow{YZ})$. The letter m in front of $(\overleftrightarrow{AB})$ is read "the measure of." We can therefore read the sentence $m(\overleftrightarrow{AB}) < m(\overleftrightarrow{YZ})$ as, "The measure of line segment $\overleftrightarrow{AB}$ is less than the measure of line segment $\overleftrightarrow{YZ}$." In the same manner the following two line segments can be compared in length:

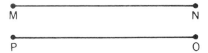

This time the two line segments are of equal length: $m(\overleftrightarrow{MN}) = m(\overleftrightarrow{PQ})$. Children should be encouraged to make a number of such comparisons so that they can gain an understanding of relative (or comparative) lengths.

Now let's introduce a standard unit of length. Let the distance between points S and T, the length of $\overleftrightarrow{ST}$, be called a *unit length*.

Children can compare the length of the following line segment, $\overleftrightarrow{GH}$, with this standard unit:

They should trace $\overleftrightarrow{ST}$ on another sheet of paper and label the tracing $\overleftrightarrow{S'T'}$. Then they should place $\overleftrightarrow{S'T'}$ on the top of $\overleftrightarrow{GH}$ so that points G and S' coincide. The point on $\overleftrightarrow{GH}$ that coincides with point T' can be labeled A.

Children should then place $\overleftrightarrow{S'T'}$ on top of $\overleftrightarrow{GH}$ so that points A and S' coincide and so that point T' coincides with a point to the right of point A (that is, between points A and H). The point that coincides with T' can be labeled E.

Then, by placing $\overleftrightarrow{S'T'}$ on top of $\overleftrightarrow{GH}$ so that points E and S' coincide, children will discover that points H and T' also coincide. Children can thus see that the length of $\overleftrightarrow{GH}$ is three times the length of $\overleftrightarrow{S'T'}$. Since we have defined the length of $\overleftrightarrow{ST}$ to be a unit length, we can say that the length of $\overleftrightarrow{GH}$ is 3 unit lengths.

The process just described for measuring the length of $\overleftrightarrow{GH}$ is, admittedly, a bit awkward. It would be much easier if we had a line segment such as the following:

For this diagram, we set the lengths of $\overleftrightarrow{KL}$, $\overleftrightarrow{LM}$, $\overleftrightarrow{MN}$, and $\overleftrightarrow{NP}$ each equal to 1 unit length. Children should trace $\overleftrightarrow{KP}$ on another sheet of paper and then label the points coinciding with points K, L, M, N, and P as K', L', M', N', and P', respectively. They should then place $\overleftrightarrow{K'P'}$ on top of $\overleftrightarrow{GH}$ so that points G and K' coincide. Clearly, that part of the tracing labeled $\overleftrightarrow{K'N'}$ coincides with $\overleftrightarrow{GH}$. Since the length of $\overleftrightarrow{K'P'}$ is 3 unit lengths, the length of $\overleftrightarrow{GH}$ must also be 3 unit lengths. This measurement can be seen more clearly if $\overleftrightarrow{KP}$ and its tracing are relabeled as follows:

The distance in unit lengths between the point labeled 0 and any other labeled point on the line segment is equal to the number naming the "other" point. For example, the distance between the points labeled 0 and 2 is 2 unit lengths, the distance between the points labeled 0 and 4 is 4 unit lengths, and so on. If we place the relabeled $\overleftrightarrow{K'P'}$ on top of $\overleftrightarrow{GH}$ so that point G and the point labeled 0 coincide, point H coincides with the point labeled 3. The distance between the points labeled 0 and 3 is 3 unit lengths. Therefore, the length of $\overleftrightarrow{GH}$ is also 3 unit lengths.

We have now developed a standard unit for measuring distance—the unit length. We can measure the distance between any two points and the dimensions of any object by comparing the appropriate distances to this standard unit of measure. Such measurements have meaning because the unit length is a fixed unit of measure—it has the same length today as it did yesterday and will have the same length tomorrow—and because a quantitative relation exists between any dis-

tance and the unit length. For example, the height of a particular building is equal to 2300 unit lengths.

We use a number of different units for measuring length or distance. We have already discussed the most important of these—the inch, the foot, the meter, and so on. An understanding of these units can be developed in much the same way that understanding of the unit length was developed. For example, children can construct a line segment AB such that the distance between the end points is 1 inch:

Then they can construct a line segment such as the following, which is composed of three smaller segments, each 1 inch long:

Each of these smaller segments is congruent to $\overleftrightarrow{AB}$. If $\overleftrightarrow{TW}$ is matched with the whole numbers 0 through 3, as in the following illustration, then we can use it to measure distance in inches, just as we used a similar line segment 3 unit lengths long to measure distances in unit lengths.

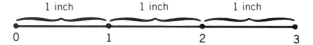

Let's create a line segment, XY, that is 1 centimeter long, another standard unit of measurement. If we use line segment XY four consecutive times, we say that the line segment is 4 centimeters long.

By developing the idea of measure in this way, we can enable children to understand much more clearly what they are doing when they use a ruler marked off in inches or centimeters to measure an object. Other units of length can now be developed in terms of this understanding. For example, having gained an understanding of what inches are, children will be better prepared to comprehend the meaning of feet, yards, miles, and so on. Their understanding of the metric units of linear measurement (centimeter, meter, millimeter, and kilometer) can be developed in much the same manner. (It is interesting to note that this process of converting within a given measurement system provides an effective example of the concept of function discussed in algebra. That is, every yard Y of measure is equal to 3 feet F. The algebraic equation $Y = 3 \times F$ describes this function relationship.)

When measuring a distance with a ruler, we are making a **direct measurement**, which is any measurement that is obtained by placing a measuring instrument directly on the object whose dimensions are to be measured. When we move a yardstick or a meterstick along the floor to find the length and width of a room, we are making a direct measurement. When we compare the dimensions of two windows by applying a tape measure to each of them, we are again making a direct measurement. An **indirect measurement**, on the other hand, is any measurement that is not a direct measurement. For example, if we wish to determine the distance across a wide river, we may have to employ scientific instruments or a mathematical technique; we cannot simply place a yardstick, meterstick, or tape measure on the surface of the water.

Children in grade 1 should be introduced to inches, feet, centimeters, and meters as standard units of linear measure. Rulers in this grade should have only the points marking inches or centimeters. Units smaller than an inch (for example, half inches and quarter inches) will probably only confuse young children at this level. If the number line has been used to develop basic number concepts, children should easily be able to apply these concepts to linear measurement. In fact, a ruler really is simply a concrete number line. Both yardsticks and metersticks can be considered extended number lines.

The teacher should provide many opportunities for children to measure objects in the classroom. First, the children should be asked to estimate the measure of the object. Not only does estimating provide them with the experience of "guessing and checking"; it also provides a very real reason for measuring—to verify the estimate.

In measuring a line segment, we place the edge of the ruler along the line segment as illustrated in the following drawing:

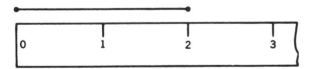

A common mistake made by children is to place the ruler on the segment to be measured in such a way that the left end of the segment lines up with the 1 on the ruler as opposed to the left end of the ruler itself. Some rulers are even made in such a way that the zero point is indented and written on the ruler. For example:

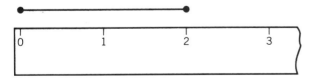

The measurement we have just made is only an *approximation*. In fact, it is impossible to measure any distance exactly. Any ruler or tape measure cannot be other than an imperfect instrument. The marks on a ruler or tape measure are physical marks (that is, they have length and width), and a geometric point cannot be exactly represented by a mark that has dimensions. Moreover, the human eye is incapable of perceiving the

precise points at which an object to be measured begins and ends. Even if we used the most precise and perfect tool to measure, it would still be our human frailty that would cause the measurement to be approximate rather than exact.

In addition to these barriers to exact measurement, there is another difficulty. Examine the following drawing:

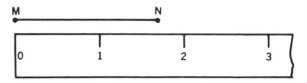

The length of $\overrightarrow{MN}$ is greater than 1 inch, but it is less than 2 inches. There is no whole number of inches that represents exactly the length of $\overrightarrow{MN}$. The best estimate we can make is that the length of $\overrightarrow{MN}$ is approximately 2 inches—that is, it is closer to 2 inches than to any other whole number of inches. This is hardly an exact measurement, but most of the measurements that children make are obviously approximate in this same manner.

As children progress through elementary school and are introduced to fractional numbers on the number line, they should also be introduced to partial units of linear measure. The half inch can be introduced in grade 2, the quarter inch in grade 3, and the eighth inch and sixteenth inch whenever the children have developed a sufficient understanding of the number line and rational numbers.

In the metric system, measures of centimeter and meter can be presented in grade 1. Millimeters can be introduced in grade 2. The units should be used independently: Other metric units should not be presented until children have had some experience with decimals.

Now let's return to the measurement of $\overrightarrow{MN}$. When we measured this line segment before, we found that its length was approximately 2 inches. Once children have become familiar with half inches, however, they can measure $\overrightarrow{MN}$ again, this time with a ruler that is marked to indicate half inches. For example:

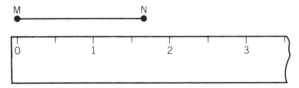

In this ruler, the long lines labeled with numerals indicate inches, while the unlabeled short lines indicate half inches. For example, the distance between the zero mark and the line labeled 2 is 2 inches, and the distance between the end of the ruler and the unlabeled short line just to the left of the line labeled 2 is $1\frac{1}{2}$ inches. Clearly, the length of $\overrightarrow{MN}$ cannot be expressed exactly in terms of whole inches and half inches. However, it is closer to $1\frac{1}{2}$ inches than to 2 inches. Therefore we can say that the length of $\overrightarrow{MN}$ is approximately $1\frac{1}{2}$ inches.

But this poses a problem. Our first measurement indicates that the length of $\overrightarrow{MN}$ is approximately

2 inches, whereas our second measurement indicates that this same length is approximately $1\frac{1}{2}$ inches. How can we reconcile these two measurements? The key to answering this question is the difference in the *precision* of the measurements. The first measurement was made in terms of whole inches, the second in terms of half inches. The second measurement is more precise than the first, although both are approximately correct. To the nearest inch, the length of $\overleftrightarrow{MN}$ is 2 inches. To the nearest half inch, the length of $\overleftrightarrow{MN}$ is $1\frac{1}{2}$ inches.

Now, let's measure the length of $\overleftrightarrow{MN}$ to the nearest quarter inch. This time we must use a ruler, such as the following one, with each 1-inch interval divided into four equivalent parts.

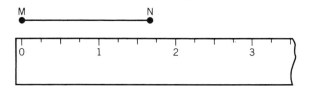

Each small interval is therefore one-quarter of an inch long. Examining this drawing, we see that the length of $\overleftrightarrow{MN}$ is less than $1\frac{3}{4}$ inches but greater than $1\frac{1}{2}$ $\left(\text{or } 1\frac{2}{4}\right)$ inches and that it is closer to $1\frac{3}{4}$ than it is to $1\frac{1}{2}$. Thus the length of $\overleftrightarrow{MN}$ is approximately $1\frac{3}{4}$ inches. This is more precise than either of the other two measurements.

Let's now measure the length of $\overleftrightarrow{MN}$ to the nearest eighth inch.

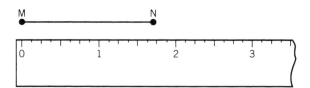

Clearly, of all the lengths indicated in the preceding drawings, $1\frac{3}{4}$ $\left(\text{or } 1\frac{6}{8}\right)$ inches best approximates the length of $\overleftrightarrow{MN}$. To the nearest eighth inch, $\overleftrightarrow{MN}$ is $1\frac{6}{8}$ inches long. The smaller the unit of measure used, the more precise the measurement.

At this point we should note that the first step in the measurement process is to select the units to be used. A measurement is always made in terms of units. It is therefore impossible for children to measure something until they have decided whether they are going to use inches or meters or days or dollars or something else. It is also important that the units be appropriate for the situation. It would be ridiculous to use inches for finding the distance between New York and Los Angeles. It would be equally ridiculous to weigh a small bag of candy on the scales at a truck weighing station. The first step, therefore, is to select a unit of measurement appropriate for the situation at hand.

Another step in the measurement process is to analyze the reasonableness of the measure. We may, for example, determine that the appropriate unit to use to measure the distance from Los Angeles to New York as being miles (or kilometers), but it is certainly unreason-

able to suggest that the distance is 200 miles (or, say, 320 kilometers).

Many children have a tendency to be careless in naming units of measure. In solving a word problem, they may want to give the answer as a measure (a number) without naming the units. For example, consider the following problem:

> If John weighs 89 pounds and Peter weighs 82 pounds, how much do John and Peter weigh together?

When asked the answer to this problem, children may reply, "171." But this is not an appropriate response. Do they mean "171 yards," "171 days," "171 apples," or what? The reply "171" is insufficient because a measurement is always made in terms of some unit. A measurement therefore must always be expressed as a measure and a unit of measure. The numerical answer to this word problem is thus "171 pounds." ("171" shows the measure; "pounds" shows the unit of measurement.) This point must be emphasized. Remember, as discussed in Chapter 5, that a word problem should be answered with a complete sentence. Therefore the complete answer to this particular story problem would be, "Together, John and Peter weigh 171 pounds."

COMPUTING WITH DENOMINATE NUMBERS

Quantities expressed with a numeral and a unit of measure are called **denominate numbers**. Some people criticize work with denominate numbers on the grounds that we cannot perform operations on measurements, only on numbers. In a sense, this argument is correct. Yet, if we look at the real world, we see many practical situations in which we must deal with measurements and hence with denominate numbers. Denominate numbers are not numbers in the mathematical sense: They are measurements of physical attributes of objects, and we use operations on numbers to help us compare and operate with these measurements.

Children should be given the opportunity to work many problems involving units of measure. These may or may not be in the form of word problems, such as the preceding example. Consider the following addition example:

$$\begin{array}{r} 1 \text{ foot } 5 \text{ inches} \\ + 1 \text{ foot } 2 \text{ inches} \\ \hline \end{array}$$

This example is not expressed in terms of a single unit. Rather, the measurements have been made in two units—feet and inches. This is, of course, quite acceptable. We can solve this example by adding the numbers expressed in the feet column and then adding the numbers expressed in the inches column separately.

$$\begin{array}{r} 1 \text{ foot } 5 \text{ inches} \\ + 1 \text{ foot } 2 \text{ inches} \\ \hline 2 \text{ feet } 7 \text{ inches} \end{array}$$

The sum, in this case, is clearly 2 feet 7 inches.

Here is another example, this time using metric measures:

$$\begin{array}{r} 3 \text{ meters } 34 \text{ centimeters} \\ + 2 \text{ meters } 27 \text{ centimeters} \\ \hline 5 \text{ meters } 61 \text{ centimeters} \end{array}$$

Using metric measures, consider how easy it would be to rewrite the example all in one unit and then add the numbers. We can change 3 meters 34 centimeters to 334 centimeters, and we can change 2 meters 27 centimeters to 227 centimeters. Now the example becomes:

$$\begin{array}{r} 334 \text{ centimeters} \\ + 227 \text{ centimeters} \\ \hline 561 \text{ centimeters} \end{array}$$

Note that the addition of metric measure can conveniently be changed to an addition example that is quite familiar to most children. Adding denominate numbers is usually much easier using metric measure than U.S. customary measure.

Now let's consider another example:

$$\begin{array}{r} 4 \text{ pounds } 10 \text{ ounces} \\ + 3 \text{ pounds } \ \ 9 \text{ ounces} \end{array}$$

The answer here is 7 pounds 19 ounces. But 19 ounces is equal to 1 pound 3 ounces. The answer can therefore be expressed as 8 pounds 3 ounces.

$$\left.\begin{array}{r} 7 \text{ pounds} \\ 19 \text{ ounces} \end{array}\right\} \begin{aligned} &= 7 \text{ pounds} + 19 \text{ ounces} \\ &= 7 \text{ pounds} + (1 \text{ pound} + 3 \text{ ounces}) \\ &= (7 \text{ pounds} + 1 \text{ pound}) + 3 \text{ ounces} \\ &= 8 \text{ pounds} + 3 \text{ ounces} \\ &= 8 \text{ pounds } 3 \text{ ounces} \end{aligned}$$

Note that the concept of regrouping as used with place value can be applied to regrouping here: Because 16 ounces equals 1 pound, 19 ounces becomes 1 pound 3 ounces. In general, as a matter of convenience, when a measurement is expressed in two or more units, the larger unit is written with as great a number as possible. The answer to the preceding example can be written in a number of different ways. For example:

8 pounds   3 ounces
7 pounds 19 ounces
6 pounds 35 ounces
and so on

It is more convenient, however, to write the answer as 8 pounds 3 ounces. If we write the answer with a lesser number of pounds, the expression for ounces would necessarily be more cumbersome.

Children often have a difficult time regrouping measurements, even if they normally can regroup in base ten effectively. One technique that seems to help is to provide them with concrete opportunities. For example, students can use gallon and quart containers, along with some rice or sand, to actually carry out the process of regrouping in an exercise such as the following:

$$\begin{array}{r} 2 \text{ gallons } 3 \text{ quarts} \\ + 1 \text{ gallon } \ \ 2 \text{ quarts} \end{array}$$

Three more examples follow in which the answers have been expressed in the most convenient form:

a)
$$\begin{array}{r} 4 \text{ yards } \ \ 2 \text{ feet } \ \ 5 \text{ inches} \\ \times 5 \\ \hline 20 \text{ yards } 10 \text{ feet } 25 \text{ inches} \end{array}$$

$$\begin{aligned} 20 \text{ yards } &10 \text{ feet } 25 \text{ inches} \\ &= 20 \text{ yards} + 10 \text{ feet} + 25 \text{ inches} \\ &= 20 \text{ yards} + 10 \text{ feet} + (2 \text{ feet} + 1 \text{ inch}) \\ &= 20 \text{ yards} + (10 \text{ feet} + 2 \text{ feet}) + 1 \text{ inch} \\ &= 20 \text{ yards} + 12 \text{ feet} + 1 \text{ inch} \\ &= (20 \text{ yards} + 4 \text{ yards}) + 1 \text{ inch} \\ &= 24 \text{ yards} + 1 \text{ inch} \\ &= 24 \text{ yards } 1 \text{ inch} \end{aligned}$$

(*Note:* It is not intended that children write the chain of equations seen here. These are presented to illustrate to the teacher the equivalence between the initial and final answers.)

b)
$$8 \times 77¢ = \square \qquad \begin{array}{r} \$ \ .77 \\ \times \ \ 8 \\ \hline \$6.16 \end{array}$$
$$8 \times 77¢ = \$6.16$$

c)
$$\begin{array}{r} 7 \text{ grams } \ \ 4 \text{ decigrams} \\ \times 6 \\ \hline 42 \text{ grams } 24 \text{ decigrams} \end{array}$$

$$= 44 \text{ grams } \ \ 4 \text{ decigrams}$$

OR, more conveniently, use 7.4 (since 7 grams 4 decigrams = 7.4 grams)

$$\begin{array}{r} 7.4 \\ \times 6 \\ \hline 44.4 \text{ grams (or 444 decigrams)} \end{array}$$

Notice that in Example c), 7 grams 4 decigrams is rewritten as 7.4 grams before the indicated multiplication is performed. This is not necessary, but computation is generally easier in that form. Such simplification is possible because the metric system is based on powers of ten. The expression "4 decigrams" can be rewritten as ".4 gram"; the sum of 7 grams and .4 gram can be expressed as 7.4 grams.

MONEY AND TIME AS MEASURES

Money represents a countable system of measurement of value or worth. Children should be introduced to the concept of measuring money early—usually beginning in kindergarten. First have the children sort attribute blocks according to different characteristics; then have them separate a collection of coins into piles that are alike. Successfully separating the coins into different piles indicates that the child can identify those that are alike and those that are different. Have the children examine each of the different coins and discuss the similarities and the differences with other coins.

The next stage requires the children to recognize the relative value of the coins. How many pennies does it take to have the same value as a nickel? (*Note:* Do not say to young children, "How many pennies are there in a nickel?" We are interested in the relative value of the coins—there are no pennies *in* a nickel, strictly speaking. Instead, a nickel *has the same value* as 5 pennies.) The children can construct a table such as the following:

Nickel	Dime	Quarter	
5 pennies	10 pennies	25 pennies	3 nickels
			1 dime
	2 nickels	5 nickels	
			3 nickels
	5 pennies	2 dimes	10 pennies
	1 nickel	1 nickel	
			2 nickels
		1 dime	15 pennies
		15 pennies	
			1 dime
			2 nickels
		1 dime	5 pennies
		1 nickel	
		10 pennies	
		(and so on)	

Next, children need to recognize the various combinations of coins that are equivalent in value. Ask the children, "What different combinations of coins have the same value as 25 cents?" A variety of numberness skills will come into play as children do this. For example, they will need to practice grouping, counting, addition, subtraction, trading, and renaming.

The concept of making change should be presented next. Use real objects with price tags on them and have the children pretend to buy and sell them. The prices should be realistic so that the children also begin to develop a concept of value. Money notation with the use of ¢ and $ can then be introduced. Additional concepts involving money are addressed in Chapters 5, 6, 13, and 14, where you will find discussions of how money notation provides an excellent forum for examining whole-number and decimal-place value. Money also serves as a motivating denominate context for exploring operations in word problems. Consequently, developmentally appropriate problem-solving experiences that involve money should be present throughout the elementary school curriculum.

Another aspect of measurement that children should be familiar with is time. Children generally have some knowledge of time when they enter school. Time has regulated their lives since birth, so they have developed an intuitive understanding of it; for example, they may seldom miss their favorite television shows.

Readiness activities necessary for an understanding of how time is measured and how to read a clock should begin in kindergarten. By the end of the primary grades, all children should be able to read an analog (circular) clock to the nearest minute.

Informal development of time concepts usually begins in pre-kindergarten and continues more formally each year thereafter through the elementary grades. Begin to develop an understanding of *day* and *week*

through conversation with the children. In grades 1 and 2, *month* and *year* can be developed, and "A.M.," "P.M.," and the calendar can be introduced.

After children have some understanding of numbers, the teacher can begin to use a clock to show times to do certain activities. At this point, it is better to use "even hours," such as two o'clock or three o'clock, rather than two-thirty or four-fifteen.

Do not rush children into reading clocks—it can be a very abstract and difficult task for some. Do not teach "quarter after," "half past," or "quarter to" until the later grades. A young child knows a "quarter" as *twenty-five* cents; and suddenly the teacher wants the child to know a quarter as *fifteen* minutes. So as not to confuse children, reserve the word "quarter" for money at this point. Also, since young children have not been formally introduced to rational numbers, they cannot easily comprehend "one half" as "half past an hour."

Children should be exposed to both the traditional circular clock with "hands" as well as the digital clock. Teaching children how to read a digital clock is relatively straightforward: They read the numerals left to right as either a one- or a two-digit number with the ":" as a break followed by the next number. That is, "10:34" is read, of course, as "ten thirty-four." The only real difficulty occurs with a time such as "2:03" where the zero must be read as "oh."

A child is not ready to learn to read a standard analog clock until he or she can:

1. understand a number line segment from 0 to 60;
2. visualize number lines; and
3. count by fives from 0 to 60.

With these prerequisites in hand, the following paragraphs describe an outstanding method for helping children learn to read a standard clock.

Cut twelve 2-inch-by-5-inch rectangles from colored cardboard or acetate. From the same color of cardboard, cut an arrow-shaped "hand" for the clock. With a paper punch, punch holes in the lower left-hand and right-hand corners of each rectangle. Use brass fasteners to hook the twelve cards together. Write one numeral on the upper left-hand corner of each card. Thus, you have a flexible number line segment from 1 to 12.

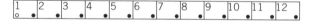

Introduce the children to the number line segment in a horizontal position by laying it on the floor, in the chalk trough, or on a flannel board. Place the arrow so that it points directly at a numeral, and have the children read the numeral.

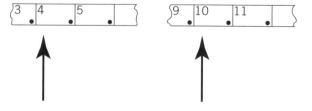

Now place the arrow so that it is pointing somewhere between two numerals.

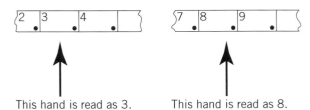

This hand is read as 3.   This hand is read as 8.

The children need to be lead to agree that when the arrow is pointing between two numerals then the number is read as the least value until the hand reaches the next number.

After the children are successful in reading the arrow pointing to the horizontal number line segment, connect the two ends with a brass fastener to make a circular shape, and place it on the floor or on a flannel board. Place the arrow, perhaps now referred to as a "hand," in the center, and have the children practice reading what numeral the hand is pointing toward. You may need to make another set of cards with the numerals 4–8 oriented correctly.

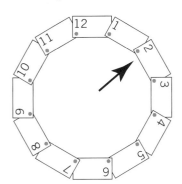

For the next step in teaching how to read a clock, introduce counting by fives beginning with 5 and counting to 55. Cut twelve more 2-inch-by-5-inch cards from a different color of cardboard. Punch holes in their lower left-hand corners, and fasten them with brass fasteners. Print the numerals 5, 10, 15, . . . , 55 on the upper left-hand corner of the cards, and place five equally spaced marks on each card. Cut a longer arrow (hand) out of the same color of cardboard as this number line segment.

Give the children practice in reading the number the arrow is pointing toward.

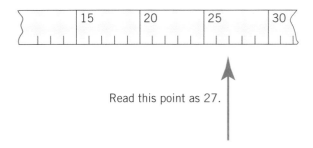

Read this point as 27.

Continue having the children practice reading the arrow as it points toward marks between the numerals

---

Research Snapshot

How can the concept of elapsed time be incorporated into problem-solving situations?

Carpenter, Fennema, Franke, Levi, and Empson (1999) classified rate problems that involve elapsed time as special types of multiplication and division problems.

For example: A baby elephant gains 5 pounds each day. How many pounds will the baby elephant gain in 7 days?

In this problem, the 7 days are not really groups, and the student solving the problem would use 5 counters to represent the 5 pounds gained after one day has passed. It is important to provide your students opportunities to solve problems that involve different kinds of quantities.

What other contexts with measurement could be used to write similar problems?

Carpenter, T. P., Fennema, E., Franke, M. L., Levi, L., & Empson, S. B. (1999). *Children's mathematics: Cognitively guided instruction.* Portsmouth, NH: Heinemann.

For additional research briefs, "ERIC Digests" lets you search more than 2,000 short syntheses of research on a range of education topics. The syntheses were produced by the Educational Resources Information Center (ERIC). Check http://ed.gov/databases/ERIC_Digests/index/

written on the number line segment. After the children are successful in reading the number line segment horizontally, change the arrangement to a circular one.

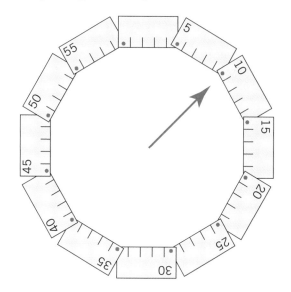

Place the long arrow, now referred to as a hand, in the middle of the clock and have the children practice reading what number the hand is pointing toward.

Now place the number line segment with numerals from 1 to 12 on top of the segment that has numerals from 5 to 55. Place the two arrows or hands together, and discuss how they are different. The hands are not "big" and "little"; one is called the *short hand* and the other the *long hand*. Read the short hand first with the top number line segment; then read the long hand using the number line segment that is underneath. If the children have difficulty, permit them to check by looking at the number line segment underneath. For example, this clock is read as 5:10:

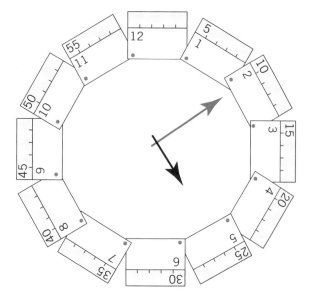

Now the children have developed all the necessary skills they need to read a clock. Continually provide opportunities for them to tell time.

After they have become efficient in reading the clock, the idea of "to the hour" may be introduced. It is much more difficult for children to understand this, so wait until they are proficient in reading "after the hour" before introducing "to the hour."

One other aspect of time that should be explored is the notion of elapsed time. For example, if the students go to school from 9:00 A.M. to 3:15 P.M., how many hours and minutes are they in school? There are a number of mental strategies that they can incorporate here. For example, they can determine how long until noon determine how long after noon, and then add the two results together.

CLOSURE

In this chapter we have concentrated on linear measurement. However, all the most common types of measurement—length, area, volume, weight, time, and money—should be developed in the elementary and middle grades. For the most effective teaching, these concepts should be developed with real materials. Ideas can then be discovered and understood rather than superficially learned and mechanically applied. Time must be provided for children to explore and discover the basic concepts of measurement and the relations that exist among the various units of measurement. The time spent here is an important investment as we will revisit measurement through many applications and in many contexts (such as through perimeter, area, and volume in the next chapters).

Terminology, Symbols, and Procedures

Denominate Number. A quantity expressed by an ordinary numeral in combination with a unit of measurement is a denominate number. For example, if one measures one's height with a yardstick, the measurement might be expressed by one of the following denominate numbers: 67 inches, 5 feet 7 inches, or 1 yard 2 feet 7 inches.

Direct Measurement. A measurement obtained by placing a standard unit next to an object to be measured is a direct measurement. For example, a metric ruler is laid next to a textbook, and the length is measured in centimeters.

Indirect Measurement. A measurement in which the measuring instrument cannot be placed directly next to or on the object to be measured is an indirect measurement. For instance, the distance to the moon or the distance across a river is an indirect measurement.

Measurement. A measurement is a comparison with a known unit. It often involves a determination of the size of something or a comparison of some aspect of an object with a unit accepted as a standard. A measurement is always expressed in two parts:

1. a unit of measure (standard or nonstandard) with which the quantity to be measured is compared
2. the measure, a number comparing the quantity to be measured with an accepted unit of measurement

For example, if a river is 100 feet wide, "100" shows the measure and "feet" shows the unit of measure. If a book is 7 paper clips long, "7" shows the measure, and "paper clips" shows the unit of measure.

Standard Measure. A measure generally accepted by everyone is a standard measure. Examples of standard measures are the kilogram, second, nickel, day, inch, meter, square centimeter, and year.

Practice Exercises for Teachers

These exercises are designed for the reader of this book. While some are suitable for use in the elementary classroom, these examples should not necessarily be given to children in this form. Ideas for classroom activities on the concepts and ideas discussed in this chapter can be found in Part 2 of *Today's Mathematics*, the Student Resource Book.

1. Measure each of the following line segments to the nearest half inch, then to the nearest centimeter.

   a) A————B

   b) M————————N

   c) X————Y

   d) C————D

2. Place the <, =, or > symbol in the two statements to make each of the following statements true.

   a) 5 centimeters _____ 52 millimeters
   b) 1 meter _____ 99 centimeters
   c) 1 yard _____ 36 feet
   d) 4 liters _____ 401 milliliters
   e) 1 mile _____ 5280 feet
   f) 4 kilograms _____ 453.6 grams
   g) 23 centimeters _____ 2.3 millimeters
   h) 7 decimeters _____ 1 meter
   i) 1 bushel _____ 2 pecks
   j) 8 pints _____ 1 gallon
   k) 9 pounds _____ 140 ounces
   l) 2 feet _____ .5 yard
   m) 3 meters _____ 300 centimeters

3. Write each of the following measures in meters. Use the reference chart in this chapter to help you.

   a) 72 decimeters
   b) 41 dekameters
   c) 5000 centimeters
   d) .0672 hectometer
   e) .8 decimeter
   f) .04 hectometer
   g) 92 centimeters
   h) 1241 millimeters
   i) 824 hectometers

4. Write the equivalent of 720 milliliters in each unit as indicated. Use the reference chart in this chapter to help you.

   a) liters
   b) centiliters
   c) deciliters
   d) dekaliters
   e) hectoliters
   f) kiloliters

5. Solve each of the following examples using denominate numbers. Rewrite the metric examples to make them easier to solve. For example, in Part h), 3 cm 8 mm = 38 mm; thus the example should be written as 3×38 mm. (What happens when you try to do the same for those written in U.S. customary units?)

   a)   3 ft 4 in.
        7 ft 9 in.
    +6 ft 5 in.

   b)   8 hr 43 min
    +1 hr 39 min

   c)   4$\overline{)6\text{ m }8\text{ cm}}$

   d)   2 rd 9 ft
       $\times$ 6

   e)   17 ft 7 in.
      -6 ft 9 in.

   f)   5 m 23 cm
      -1 m 67 cm

   g)   7 yd 3 in.
      -2 yd 8 in.

   h)   3 cm 8 mm
      $\times$ 3

   i)   5$\overline{)12\text{ gal }3\text{ pt}}$

   j)   4 m 54 cm
        6 m 63 cm
        9 m 37 cm
    +1 m 52 cm

6. Express each of the following measurements in the units indicated.

   a) 17 feet = _____ yards
   b) $1\frac{3}{4}$ yards = _____ inches
   c) 20 pints = _____ gallons
   d) $1\frac{3}{8}$ pounds = _____ ounces
   e) 3 cups = _____ tablespoons
   f) 7 miles = _____ feet
   g) 1815 square yards = _____ acre
   h) 43 cups = _____ pints
   i) 49 square yards = _____ square feet
   j) 3 gallons = _____ cups

7. Express each of the following measurements in the units indicated. Use the reference chart in this chapter to help you.

   a) 5.4 meters = _____ centimeters
   b) 81 kilometers = _____ meters
   c) 1 megaliter = _____ microliters
   d) 5497 grams = _____ kilograms
   e) 72 liters = _____ microliters
   f) 524 milliliters = ____ deciliters
   g) 2473 micrograms = _____ grams
   h) 7 meters = _____ decimeters

8. Answer each of the following statements true or false.

   a) Most countries of the world use the U.S. customary system of measurement.
   b) The metric system is a base ten system.
   c) The metric system is compatible with our place-value system.
   d) The metric system is much older than the U.S. customary system.
   e) All linear measurement is approximate.
   f) The smaller the unit of measure, the more precise the measure.

9. List all the possible combinations of coins that will make 50 cents if only dimes, nickels, and quarters are used.

10. List all possible combinations of coins that will make one dollar if only dimes, nickels, and quarters are used.

11. Use a metric ruler calibrated in millimeters to calculate the thickness of a penny. (*Hint:* You might want to develop a strategy that uses more than one penny.)

12. Use a metric ruler calibrated in millimeters to calculate the thickness of a dime.

13. What is the greatest amount of money you could have in U.S. coins and still not have change for a dollar?

Teaching Competencies and Self-Assessment Tasks

1. Discuss measurement situations in which standard units of measure are typically NOT used.

2. Develop your own linear measurement system and discuss the difficulties you might encounter as you use this system.

3. Discuss the advantages and disadvantages of the United States adopting the metric system.

4. Discuss measurement situations where fractions are most useful and situations where decimals are most useful.

5. Discuss appropriate measuring instruments for each grade level range—preK–2, 3–5, 6–8.

6. Discuss the similarities and differences between addition of whole numbers and addition of denominate numbers.

7. Compare and contrast addition of measures in U.S. customary units and addition of measures in metric units.

8. Discuss and compare operations using U.S. customary measurement with those using the metric system.

9. Describe two models you might create to help convince a child of the relative values of coins and groups of coins.

10. Examine how several elementary school mathematics textbooks teach children how to tell time. Discuss the similarities and differences between methods used by other elementary textbooks and the method used in this text to introduce the concepts of time.

11. In what ways would you integrate measurement topics with other subjects explored at the preK–2, 3–5, and 6–8 grade levels?

12. Identify and discuss the uses of a metric interest center (mathematics metric lab) within the classroom.

Related Readings and Teacher Resources

For related readings on topics found in this chapter, see the corresponding chapter in Part 2 of *Today's Mathematics*, the Student Resource Book.

Chapter 16

Geometry: Basic Concepts and Structures

Teaching Competencies

Upon completing this chapter, you will be able to:

- Offer reasons for incorporating geometry in the elementary and middle school level.

- Use correct terminology and mathematical notation for figures such as lines, line segments, rays, and angles.

- Classify angles according to their measures and according to their relationship to each other.

- Identify and describe various models and materials that can be used with children to explore geometric concepts.

- Use a straightedge and compass to produce basic geometric constructions.

- Describe fundamental concepts and properties of symmetry.

- Describe fundamental concepts and properties of transformational geometry.

- Prepare lessons reflecting the NCTM *Principles and Standards for School Mathematics* that focus on the development of foundational geometric concepts, structures, and terminology for children.

onsider the following excerpt, adapted from the IDEAS section of an issue of NCTM's journal *Teaching Children Mathematics*:

A child lives at the corner of First Avenue and Elm Street. The school is at Fourth and Oak. In order to walk to school the child needs to follow the streets shown on the map below. Because of houses, fences, and other obstacles it isn't possible to take any short-cuts through the blocks. There are lots of different ways to go, but a direct route from home to school always goes east or south, never west or north.

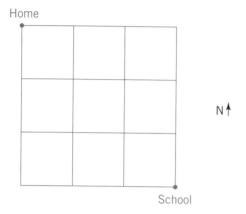

Find a direct route and determine how many blocks long it is. How many different direct routes are there? Is there one direct route that is shorter than any other?

The next day the child decides to take the school bus. The figure below shows the locations of the bus stops between the child's home and the school. Luckily, the last stop the bus makes before heading back to school is right in front of the child's house! Trace any route that goes from the school through all of the bus stops and back to school. (The bus can travel north, south, east, or west.)

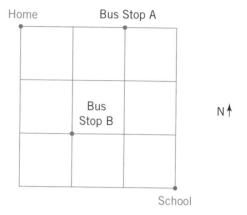

Is the route you traced the shortest route? Describe the shortest route that goes through each stop. What is the minimum length of a school bus route that goes through each stop, but goes through stop A first?

What does the above activity have to do with basic geometric concepts? You may recognize the street maps as grids made up of line segments. The house, school, and bus stops can all be represented by points on these segments. The routes can be thought of as

Research Snapshot

In Chapter 1, the van Hiele model, a theory that identifies five levels of thinking in geometry, was introduced. As you read about the geometric concepts in Chapters 16 and 17, think about how you might use the van Hiele model in your classroom.

van Hiele characterized his model as hierarchical. That is, thinking at level 2 is not possible without level 1.

In a study of 309 students, ages 11 to 18, Gutierrez and Jaime (1998) identified different processes of reasoning as characteristics of several van Hiele levels: Use of definitions, formulation of definitions, classification, and proof.

Results showed that students were not at specific van Hiele levels but could show progress in some ability at higher levels without complete acquisition of lower levels. So, instead of the classical belief that a student was at either level 1 or level 2, students were assessed in the study using some of the processes that underlie the van Hiele levels. What sort of activities might you structure to assist you in identifying the van Hiele levels of children in the classroom?

Gutierrez, A., & Jaime, A. (1998). On the assessment of the van Hiele levels of reasoning. *Focus on Learning Problems in Mathematics, 20,* 27–46.

For additional research briefs, "ERIC Digests" lets you search more than 2,000 short syntheses of research on a range of education topics. The syntheses were produced by the Educational Resources Information Center (ERIC). Check http://ed.gov/databases/ERIC_Digests/index/

paths or networks that traverse these grids and form either simple or nonsimple, closed or open curves. In fact, network theory is one branch of the important field of discrete mathematics that deals with such practical concerns as optimizing schedules and routes for airlines, trucking companies, and the like. Most young children are familiar with the underlying concepts of network theory through such informal activities as finding different ways to walk or ride to a friend's house or a mall. It has been found that children develop a sense of their world by observing geometric concepts and shapes around them; they learn by observation and intuitive processes rather than by complex or formal analysis. According to the NCTM *Principles and Standards for School Mathematics*, the development of geometric and spatial knowledge begins before schooling and is stimulated by exploration of shapes and structures in the child's environment. Foundational geometric ideas discussed in this chapter help children to represent, describe, and communicate an understanding of the mathematics of their world.

EARLY EXPERIENCES IN GEOMETRY

Children have had many experiences with geometry before they enter school. The blocks that children play with are often forms of cubes, prisms, and cylinders. Children develop informal, intuitive understandings about geometry from their own play and observation, but they usually do not have ample opportunities, and, sometimes, are not developmentally ready to verbalize their discoveries. For instance, when building something, children often select an appropriate block for their immediate building needs and yet may not be able to use even unsophisticated geometric vocabulary to explain the reasons for their choice.

In the following drawing on the left, the top block is unstable; on the right, it is stable. Children usually perceive this and choose the configuration of blocks on the right as a base on which they continue to build. Intuitively, with experience manipulating various objects, children learn to compare blocks and develop the ability to visualize the geometric shapes.

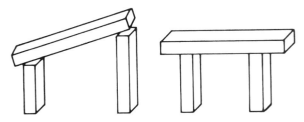

In addition to helping children develop the vocabulary needed to describe their observations and actions, teachers also need to help children develop spatial perception. The development of spatial perception seems a logical component of elementary mathematics curricula since, according to Piagetian theory, many elementary-aged children are still in the sensorimotor or concrete operational stages: They learn by interacting with their environment. Several skills or abilities have been identified

as being components of spatial perception. Those which seem to have a particular relevance to the study of geometry are eye-motor coordination, figure-ground perception, perceptual constancy, position-in-space perception, visual discrimination, visual memory, and perception of spatial relationships. A description and example of each follow.

Eye-motor coordination involves the ability to integrate visual inputs and motor responses. In the activity described above where children place a block across the top of two other blocks, children with poor eye-motor coordination would find balancing the crossbar laborious, even if the upright blocks are the same height. These students often have difficulty focusing on geometric concepts since they use working memory to concentrate on motor skills and movements rather than the geometric concepts that may be embedded within the activity.

Figure-ground perception is the ability to locate figures hidden within a complex background. An example of an activity that uses this skill is the hidden figures puzzles that appear in children's magazines or the puzzles that ask children to determine, for example, how many triangles are in a given figure.

Perceptual constancy refers to the ability to recognize a shape regardless of size, shadings, or orientation in space. Until about age 8, many children recognize a square when one edge is in a horizontal position, but claim it is no longer a square when it has been rotated so that it "stands on a point" as in the figure below:

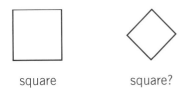

square   square?

Position-in-space perception is the ability to relate an object's position to one's own position. Terms such as *before/behind*, *left/right*, and *above/below* involve position-in-space perception. Primary-aged children who demonstrate reversals in reading or writing words or numerals typically have poor position-in-space perception. Perception of spatial relationships is a more advanced ability. It involves not only the ability to relate objects to one's own position, but also the ability to relate the positions of two or more objects to each other. Both of these spatial abilities come into play when children work with manipulative materials and may even affect their learning of nongeometric topics, such as place value or computational algorithms.

Visual discrimination is the ability to perceive similarities and differences, while visual memory is the ability to accurately recall objects no longer in view. Children's activity books often have games and puzzles that develop these skills. For example, visual discrimination is involved when children are shown several pictures, two of which are identical, and asked to find the matching pair. In a game involving visual memory, children are shown a tray filled with common objects and given one or two minutes to memorize the objects on the tray. While the children are not looking, an object is then removed from the tray, and they must determine which object was removed.

To help children develop spatial perception, let them make use of three blocks, such as a cube, a prism, and a pyramid, and provide them with directions to follow in arranging the blocks—for example:

Place the pyramid in front of the cube. Place the cube on top of the prism. Place the prism behind the cube.

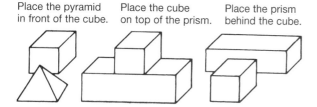

Using blocks or pictures of common items, illustrate words of position and spatial arrangement for the children. A suggested list of contrasting descriptors might include the following:

under/over	above/below	first/last
in front of/behind	high/low	far/near
right/left	inside/outside	

Also include positional situations that have more than two descriptors, such as *beside/by/next to* and *bottom/ middle/top*.

While generally defined and discussed in isolation, activities designed to develop one particular spatial skill often serve to enhance others. Development of these skills also provides teachers opportunities to integrate mathematics with other content areas, such as art or physical education. Even though many of the spatial skills discussed here are considered most appropriate for the early childhood curriculum, upper elementary and middle-grade teachers should include them in their curricula since spatial thinking may be related to success in higher-level mathematics, such as high school geometry and calculus. Provide children with many formal and informal experiences in sorting, classifying, and playing with materials such as attribute pieces, pattern blocks, and geo-blocks. Check teachers' manuals and articles in journals such as *Teaching Children Mathematics* for precise instructions for using these materials.

THE "BUILDING BLOCKS" OF GEOMETRY

Certain basic concepts of geometry—such as point, space, curve, line, line segment, ray, angle, and numerous polygons and polyhedra—must be learned before students are ready for the formal study of geometry that occurs in high school. There are at least two sequences that might be followed to introduce students to these concepts. One sequence, which relies heavily on child development, begins with three-dimensional shapes since they can be represented by concrete materials, builds understanding of two-dimensional shapes through studying the faces of the three-dimensional figures, and concludes with the abstract concepts of one-dimensional and zero-dimensional figures—that is, line, line segment, ray, and point. Another sequence, based more on mathematical structure and logic and less on child development, begins with the abstract concept of point. Under this organization, one-dimensional figures are studied as a collection of points. Two-dimensional and three-dimensional figures logically follow. It is the opinion of the authors of this text that a developmentally appropriate organization is best used with children. However, since this text is designed for preservice and in-service teachers, rather than children directly, the more mathematical sequence (beginning with point and progressing to three-dimensional figures) is the one followed in this text. We highly recommend that teachers in the primary grades consider initiating the exploration of geometric concepts with young children by beginning with three-dimensional figures and, eventually, "working backward" to point.

Some fundamental geometric concepts, such as point, are undefined terms. Such terms are "starting points" for the development of the language of geometry and the foundation off of which conjectures can grow. We can attach meaning to these undefined terms only by assuming particular properties about them. Basic statements, assumed to be true, that express these foundational assumptions in geometry are called *axioms* or *postulates*.

As mentioned earlier, the term *point* is an example of an undefined term in geometry. Although this is not a definition, a geometric **point** can be thought of as an immovable or fixed location in geometric space. Similarly, geometric **space**, which is also undefined, can be thought of as the set of all points. Geometric space and geometric points, like numbers, are abstractions—they don't physically exist in the real world.

A geometric point is a precise, fixed location in geometric space. We cannot see a geometric point because, unlike a pencil or chalk mark, a geometric point has no physical length, width, or thickness—only position. When we "pinpoint" the location of an object, we are specifying its position as precisely as we know how. We can think of a geometric point as providing the most precise way possible of specifying a position.

Geometric points and geometric space are ideas with no physical existence. In constructing figures, however, we often represent geometric ideas by physical representations—dots and lines drawn on paper or the chalkboard. Just as a number is an idea, physically represented by a numeral, so is a geometric point an idea, physically represented by a dot. The dot we draw is a convenient representation. No matter how small we make our dot, it still "covers" infinitely many geometric points; nevertheless, a dot is the most satisfactory way we have of representing the concept of a geometric point. Points represented by dots are usually labeled with capital letters, as in the following example:

■ •A (read, "point A")

What is a plane? To understand the concept of a geometric **plane**, think of a flat tabletop. Imagine the surface of the tabletop extending horizontally in all directions limitlessly.

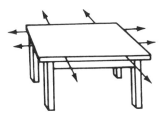

The flat surface of this table extended horizontally in all directions without end suggests a model of a geometric plane. Like all other geometric figures, a plane is a set of points. A plane is a subset of space. A flat surface, such as a classroom wall, contains an infinite number of geometric points. If the wall is removed, can you still imagine the set of points that the flat surface of the wall represented? Now imagine this set of points extended in all directions (left, right, up, and down) indefinitely. This exercise should help you develop an understanding of a geometric plane. If your classroom has a large window, you might make use of it as a starting model of a plane region and have children note that if it was removed, the place (points) where it was still remains.

The primary school child is best introduced to the concept of plane through physical representations of parts of planes. The simplest representations for a child to understand are the surfaces of a desk, a wall, a chalkboard, a sheet of paper, a book cover, the floor of a basketball court, and so on. It should be emphasized that these objects are physical representations of parts of planes. If the child imagines the set of points occupied by a desk top, or by the floor of a basketball court, "going on forever," the child is imagining a geometric plane. This geometric plane is a subset of space; it is a particular set of points representing fixed locations. The set of points occupied by a chalkboard remains when the chalkboard is removed.

A small sheet of cardboard, even an index card, can also be used to represent a part of a plane. Have two pupils each hold a sharpened pencil with the point up. Attempts to balance the cardboard (representing a plane) on the two pencil points (representing two points) will not be successful. But if another pupil holds a third pencil relatively near the other two (but not in line with them), the cardboard will rest steadily on the three pencils.

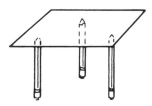

Teachers can reinforce this fact by asking why a three-legged stool never wobbles, even if each of the three legs has a different length. If you have access to a photographic tripod, you might also demonstrate this property. Each of these situations emphasizes an important geometric fact: *Any three points not in a straight line determine a plane.*

If three points are not in a straight line, how many planes can be passed through them? Only one. For example, any other sheet of cardboard resting on the three pencil points would lie in the same plane as the first sheet of cardboard.

The shortest or most direct path between two given points in space is called a *line segment*. A **line segment** is a set of points in a plane that represents the shortest distance between two given points. A line segment has a first (or initial) point and a last (or terminal) point. These are called the *end points*. A line segment has a definite length—the distance between the two end points.

A •————————————————————• B

The symbol for the line segment from point A to point B (with the end points included) is $\overline{AB}$ and is read "line segment AB." A tightly stretched string is a good *physical representation* of a line segment. Many students will recognize the "line segments" drawn on roadways that separate traffic lanes. Other models include the points where two walls intersect, the edges of a chalkboard, the edges of a page, and so on. What others can you think of?

The concept of **line** is also undefined in geometry. A line is a set of points and therefore a subset of space. If we draw a representation of a line segment on paper with pencil and straightedge and imagine that this representation is extended endlessly in opposite directions, the result can be thought of as a geometric line. To help children understand the concept of a line, ask them to imagine line segments extending from their pencil points to:

1. the doorknob (have the end points named in each case)
2. the top of the school flagpole
3. the top of the Washington Monument, the Empire State Building, or some other prominent (and *pointed*) landmark they know
4. a distant star

Having stretched their imaginations to envision the two end points of an imaginary line segment, the children should now be ready for the broader concept of line.

A line has no end points but continues endlessly in each of two opposite directions. To represent a line, we draw a line segment and place arrowheads at each end to show that the line has no end points but extends endlessly in both directions.

ℓ

We often name a line by using a lowercase letter, as above, or by labeling two points on the line. In the drawing on the previous page we can refer to the figure as "line ℓ." We can refer to the figure in the drawing below as "line RS" or "line SR."

Line RS is also indicated by the symbol $\overleftrightarrow{RS}$. When we name two points on a line, we have also named a line segment—in this case, line segment RS, or $\overline{RS}$. Every line segment is a subset of a line. It would be helpful to explain to children that *segment* means "part." Line segment RS is a subset, or part, of line RS.

Suppose we name several points on a line as follows:

Since we can name a line with any two points on the line, what names can we give this line?

$\overleftrightarrow{CE}$	$\overleftrightarrow{ED}$		$\overleftrightarrow{GD}$	$\overleftrightarrow{DE}$
$\overleftrightarrow{CF}$	$\overleftrightarrow{EG}$		$\overleftrightarrow{GF}$	$\overleftrightarrow{DC}$
$\overleftrightarrow{CD}$	$\overleftrightarrow{FD}$	as well as	$\overleftrightarrow{GE}$	$\overleftrightarrow{FE}$
$\overleftrightarrow{CG}$	$\overleftrightarrow{FG}$		$\overleftrightarrow{GC}$	$\overleftrightarrow{FC}$
$\overleftrightarrow{EF}$	$\overleftrightarrow{DG}$		$\overleftrightarrow{DF}$	$\overleftrightarrow{EC}$

Note that when we have named a line with two points, for example, $\overleftrightarrow{EC}$ above, the same line is named by $\overleftrightarrow{CE}$.

EXTENDING THE BASICS—CURVES, REGIONS, AND RAYS

We have established that a line segment consists of a set of points in a plane, and is therefore a subset of space. As mentioned, a line segment is also described as the shortest path between two points in a plane.

There are other paths, however, between points A and B. Some of these are illustrated in the following diagram:

Paths between any two given points are examples of curves. In the previous diagram, the curves that are represented are called *simple curves* because the curve doesn't pass through the same point twice. A **simple curve** is defined as a curve that passes through no point more than once. A line segment is a special kind of simple curve. The mathematical term *curve* is different than the everyday use of the word. A mathematical curve might be a straight line or line segment, while, for example, a highway curve brings a different image to mind.

A **closed curve** is a curve that returns to its starting point. A closed curve has no end points. A **simple closed**

curve, then, is a curve that returns to its starting point without crossing itself at any point. Is a triangle a simple closed curve? Yes. Some other examples of simple closed curves are represented in the following diagram:

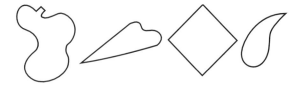

Students should practice drawing simple closed curves, including simple closed curves that pass through one, two, three, or more given points.

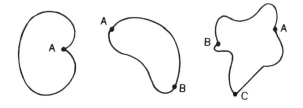

The possibilities are limitless.

Careful notice should be taken of the fact that a curve that crosses itself does not form a simple closed curve. None of the following is a simple closed curve:

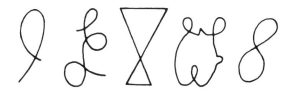

Any curve that forms a simple closed curve separates the plane in which it lies into three sets of points:

1. the set of points comprising the simple closed curve itself
2. the set of points comprising the interior of the simple closed curve
3. the set of points comprising the exterior of the simple closed curve

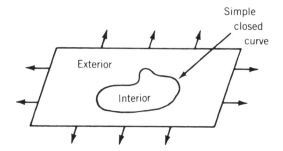

The set of points formed by the union of a simple closed curve and its interior is referred to as a **simple closed region**.

A **ray** is another subset of a line. It consists of a point on the line and all points on the line extending in one direction from that point.

End point of ray ⟶ Ray

The point from which the ray extends is part of the ray and is called the *end point*, or the *initial point*, of the ray. For example, on the following line, we have marked point A:

A

This point is the end point (or initial point) of two rays, one beginning at point A and extending endlessly to the right, the other beginning at point A and extending endlessly to the left. Obviously, an infinite number of rays are contained in a line, since any point on the line can be selected as an end point and there are an infinite number of points on the line.

By naming a point on either side of point A, we can now name the two rays (sometimes referred to as *opposite* rays) that extend from this point.

C   A   B

We can name a ray with two letters, representing two points, as $\overrightarrow{AB}$. This name represents the ray that starts at point A and extends endlessly to the right (through point B). The bar with one arrowhead on it indicates that a ray is being named, and the fact that there is no arrowhead above the A indicates that point A is the end point of the ray. Similarly, $\overleftarrow{AC}$ represents the ray that starts at point A and extends endlessly to the left (through point C). It is interesting to note that the two rays, ray AB and ray AC, have only one point in common, point A.

A commonly used *physical representation* of a ray is a flashlight or searchlight beam. A child can readily imagine a beam of light beginning at the flashlight and continuing endlessly in space in one direction.

With these concepts in mind, children's intuitive perception can be developed. With pencil and straightedge they can practice drawing "lines" on paper and, as symbols are introduced, add these to their drawings. Note that the lines do not always have to be drawn horizontally—in fact, doing so may give a false impression—any direction is, of course, satisfactory.

Remember that when a student uses a straightedge to draw a line segment (or any other geometric figure), the student is only *picturing* a representation of the abstract geometric figure. It is no more correct to say that what has been drawn is a line segment than it is to say that a sketch of a person is a human being. Again, the distinction between words in mathematical language and words in everyday language must be made. At what developmental level should we try to make this distinction clear to children?

Next, children should practice drawing lines through a given point. They may discover that there is (theoretically) no limit to the number of lines that they can draw through any one point. An interesting discussion may ensue by having children draw several lines through a point, first using a blunt crayon, then using a dull pen-

cil, and finally an ultrafine point pen. This activity should help them realize that their ability to draw many lines through a point is influenced by the thickness of the instrument used. Infinitely many abstract lines can be drawn through a given point since abstract lines have no thickness.

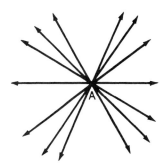

At this stage, children are ready to examine a line through two distinct points. Have them mark two points on a sheet of paper and label them. Then have them draw lines through the two points. They soon realize that only one straight line can be drawn through two points. Because they are marking dots with a pencil to represent points, children may try to draw two or more lines through two points. Remind them that their pencil-drawn dots should be as small as possible (they will still cover many geometric points) so that only one line will pass through two points.

In these exercises, the line children draw through two points should extend beyond the points. The children can then be introduced to the concept of a line segment by drawing a figure that does not extend beyond two points. When drawn this way, it is evident that the segment has a definite length (between the end points). The children can emphasize this fact by drawing more line segments between any two marked points. Practice in drawing geometric figures should be given through exercises such as the following:

1. Draw a line, mark and name four points on the line, and use these points to name the line in several different ways.

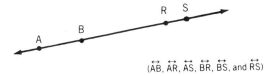

($\overleftrightarrow{AB}$, $\overleftrightarrow{AR}$, $\overleftrightarrow{AS}$, $\overleftrightarrow{BR}$, $\overleftrightarrow{BS}$, and $\overleftrightarrow{RS}$)

2. Given point A, draw lines through point A.

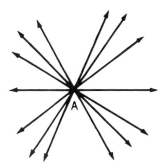

3. Given two points, A and B, draw a line through them.

4. Draw a line segment, name seven points on the line segment, and then use these points to name different line segments.

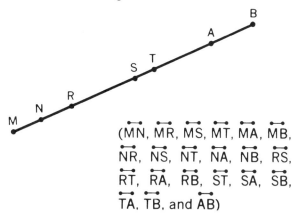

(MN, MR, MS, MT, MA, MB, NR, NS, NT, NA, NB, RS, RT, RA, RB, ST, SA, SB, TA, TB, and AB)

5. Given point R, draw a ray with point R as the end point, and name the ray by naming any other point on the ray.

Do ⋅RT⃗ and ⋅TR⃗ both name this ray we have drawn? No, they don't. RT⃗ names this ray, but TR⃗ names a ray (not drawn here) whose end point is T. The first letter always indicates the end point of a ray.

If children understand what these drawings represent, they will have no difficulty with later drawings and concepts. All figures are "built" with the basic building blocks that we have studied so far in this chapter. They are illustrated in the following diagram:

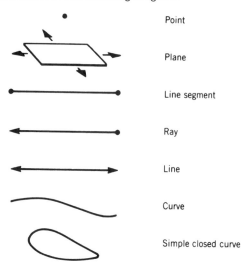

By way of review, while books differ on the subject, this text leaves the concepts of space and point as undefined. **Space** is understood to be the set of all points. Conversely, **points** are understood to be locations in space. A **line segment** is defined as a set of points that is the shortest path between two points. A geometric line is undefined. It extends endlessly in opposite directions. A **ray** is defined as part of a line consisting of a point on the line and all the points on the line extending endlessly in one direction from the initial point.

ANGLES AND ANGLE MEASURE

An **angle** is defined in most mathematics programs as the union of two rays that have a common end point. The common end point of the two rays is called the **vertex** of the angle, and each of the two rays is called a **side** of the angle. To name an angle, we usually name three points on the angle—the vertex and a point on each of the two sides. In the following diagram, the angle is named by the three points C, A, and B:

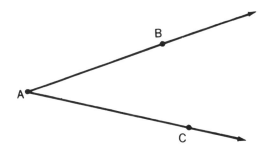

In symbols, we can name the angle as ∠BAC. Notice that the vertex, labeled A, is the second point named in the expression ∠BAC. When we name any angle this way, the vertex is always listed between two other points.

Any angle divides the plane in which it lies into three sets of points:

1. the set of points comprising the angle itself.
2. the set of points comprising the interior of the angle.
3. the set of points comprising the exterior of the angle.

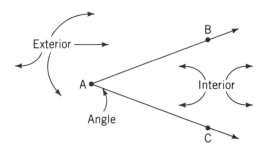

One standard unit of angle measure is called a *degree*. The number of degrees measures the amount of rotation between the sides of an angle. In more advanced mathematics, this rotation may be clockwise or counterclockwise and may range from 0 to 360 degrees (and even more). In the elementary grades, we most commonly measure angles as counterclockwise rotations from an initial ray to a terminal ray with angle measure ranging from greater than 0 degrees to less than or equal to 180 degrees. For example:

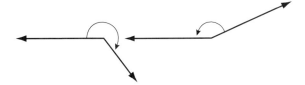

The instrument most commonly used to determine the measures of angles is called a *protractor*.

The primary school student, perceiving geometric shapes and relations intuitively, will not typically be concerned with the measurement of angles. By grades 4 or 5, however, the student should be able to use a simple protractor to draw angles of a given measure or to determine angle measure. The use of a protractor with a "double scale" (as in the figure below) may be inappropriate at this point due to confusion over which scale to use—counterclockwise or clockwise. It is probably best to make a single scale protractor with counterclockwise measures. When using this single scale protractor it is positioned so that the initial ray of the angle to be measured is set on the "zero mark." To determine the measure of an angle, place the protractor with its horizontal center point on the vertex of the angle (B) and its base parallel to one of the sides ($\overleftrightarrow{BC}$). In the following diagram, the measure of ∠ABC (50°) is read directly on the inside semicircular scale:

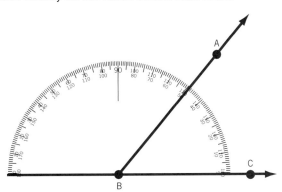

The symbol *m*∠ABC represents the measure of ∠ABC. Thus *m*∠ABC = 50°.

Since many primary school children have an intuitive understanding of the concept of angle, they should practice drawing angles of all sizes. To learn that an angle is the union of two rays with a common end point, they should practice by naming a point and then drawing any two rays from that point. For example:

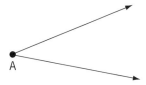

Again, encourage the children to draw in any direction. Teachers tend to draw angles on chalkboards with a horizontal ray or base. Teachers should give them-

selves the same freedom to draw angles in many positions on the chalkboard.

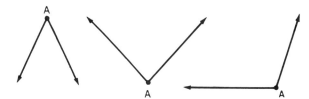

The only discipline to be observed is that drawings such as the following are incorrect (by our definition of *angle*) and should be discouraged. These are not two rays sharing a common endpoint.

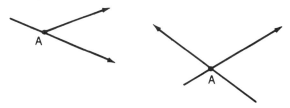

Suppose we have two angles such as the following and we wish to compare them to see whether they have the same "size":

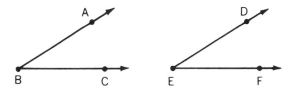

On another sheet of paper, trace ∠ABC and call it ∠A'B'C' (read "angle A prime, B prime, C prime"). We can compare ∠ABC with ∠DEF by putting the tracing ∠A'B'C' on top of ∠DEF. If we place the tracing ∠A'B'C' on ∠DEF so that $\overleftrightarrow{B'C'}$ falls on $\overleftrightarrow{EF}$ we can decide whether ∠ABC has the same measure as ∠DEF. If, after we have placed point B' over point E and $\overleftrightarrow{B'C'}$ over $\overleftrightarrow{EF}$, we find that $\overleftrightarrow{B'A'}$ coincides with $\overleftrightarrow{ED}$, then we know that the two angles have the same measure. If ∠ABC and ∠DEF have the same measure, we say that they are **congruent** or that ∠ABC "is congruent to" ∠DEF.

The symbol ≅ is used to indicate congruence, so we can write ∠ABC ≅ DEF. That is, *m*∠ABC = *m*∠DEF. This is read, "Angle ABC is congruent to angle DEF." If B'A' does not fall on ED, then angle ABC is not congruent to angle DEF. This relation can be written as follows: ∠ABC ≇ ∠DEF. That is, *m*∠ABC ≠ *m*∠DEF.

Angles are sometimes classified according to their properties, some of which we will now examine. Consider $\overleftrightarrow{AB}$ and point D not on $\overleftrightarrow{AB}$. Point C on $\overleftrightarrow{AB}$ is marked directly under point D.

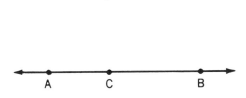

Now draw ray CD.

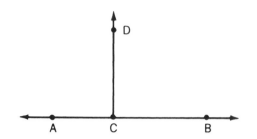

Ray CD determines two angles, ∠ACD and ∠BCD. If these two angles are congruent, then they are called **right angles**, and $\overrightarrow{CD}$ is said to be **perpendicular** to $\overleftrightarrow{AB}$ (in mathematical symbols, CD ⊥ AB). A right angle has a measure of 90°.

Consider $\overleftrightarrow{XY}$, point Z on $\overleftrightarrow{XY}$, and point O not on $\overleftrightarrow{XY}$. Ray ZO is drawn.

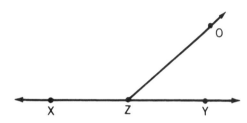

Trace ∠YZO on another sheet of paper, and label the tracing ∠Y'Z'O'. Then compare the tracing ∠Y'Z'O' with ∠BCD (the right angle in the previous example). Place the tracing so that point Z' falls on point C and $\overrightarrow{Z'Y'}$ falls on $\overrightarrow{CB}$. Clearly, ∠Y'Z'O' ≇ ∠BCD; therefore ∠YZO ≇ ∠BCD. Since angle YZO is less than a right angle, we call angle YZO an **acute angle**, which can be defined as an angle that is less than a right angle, or an angle whose measure is less than 90°. Using symbols, we can compare the measures of angle BCD and angle YZO in the following way: $m(∠YZO) < m(∠DCB)$. This is read "The measure in degrees of angle YZO is less than the measure in degrees of angle DCB" or simply "Angle YZO is less than angle DCB."

Now let's examine another situation in which we have line MN and point E on $\overleftrightarrow{MN}$. Another point, G, not on $\overleftrightarrow{MN}$ is marked, and $\overrightarrow{EG}$ is drawn.

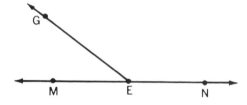

Trace ∠NEG on another sheet of paper, and label the tracing ∠N'E'G'. Compare ∠N'E'G' with ∠BCD (the right angle in the earlier example) by placing point E' on point C and $\overrightarrow{E'N'}$ on $\overrightarrow{CB}$. Clearly, ∠N'E'G' ≇ ∠BCD, and therefore ∠NEG ≇ ∠BCD. Since angle NEG has a measure greater than a right angle but less than 180°, we call angle NEG an *obtuse angle*. Using symbols, we

can compare the measures of angle NEG and angle BCD as follows: $m(∠NEG) > m(∠BCD)$. This is read, "The measure in degrees of angle NEG is greater than the measure in degrees of angle BCD" or simply "Angle NEG is greater than angle BCD." An **obtuse angle** can be defined as an angle whose measure is greater than 90° but less than 180°. (An angle with a measure of exactly 180 is usually called a *straight angle*. Consequently, a line is a representation of a straight angle.)

We can point out *physical representations* of right angles in the classroom. The corner of the room, for example, suggests several right angles.

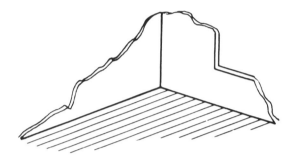

The corners of a window or a chalkboard are also convenient representations of right angles. An excellent representation of a right angle is the corner of a sheet of paper such as a page of this book. Children will probably see the notion of right angle best as the "square corner" of some object. They should be able to draw approximate representations of right angles using any object with a rigid "square corner."

Let's consider names for angle relationships that are based on their relative positions and measures. What statements can we make about the following angles, ∠DOC and ∠COB?

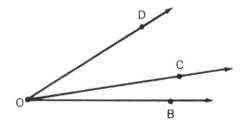

We see that angle DOC and angle COB have a common vertex, point O. The two angles also have a common ray, $\overrightarrow{OC}$, between them. Two angles with a common vertex and a common ray (or side) between them are called **adjacent angles**. In the preceding diagram, angle DOC is adjacent to angle COB.

If the sum of the measures of two angles is equal to the measure of a right angle (90°), the two angles are said to be **complementary angles**. In the following diagram, if $\overrightarrow{OU}$ is perpendicular to $\overleftrightarrow{ST}$, ($\overrightarrow{OU}$ ⊥ $\overleftrightarrow{ST}$)—that is, if ∠SOU and ∠UOT are right angles, then ∠UOV and ∠VOT are complementary angles, since the sum of the measures of ∠UOV and ∠VOT is equal to the measure of the right angle UOT.

$$m(\angle UOV) + m(\angle VOT) = m(\angle UOT)$$

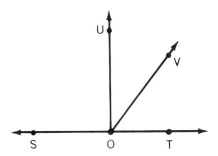

Two angles do not have to be adjacent (as angle UOV and angle VOT are) to be complementary angles. In the following diagram, angle JEK and angle LEM are complementary, because the sum of their measures is 90°:

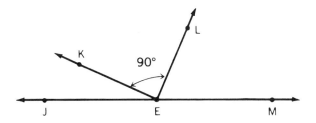

If the sum of the measures of *two* angles is equal to 180°, the two angles are said to be **supplementary angles**. In the following diagram, angle BEC and angle CED are supplementary, because the sum of their measures is equal to 180°.

$$m(\angle BEC) + m(\angle CED) = 180°$$

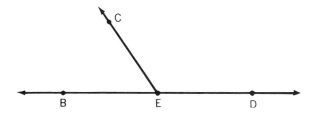

In this case, angle BEC and angle CED are also adjacent angles, but two angles that are not adjacent can also be supplementary. In the following diagram, angle NUP and angle QUR are supplementary, because the sum of their measures is 180°:

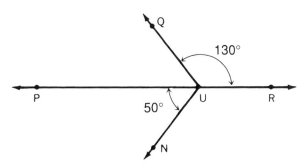

In some instances, adjacent angles are congruent. For example, consider the following diagram:

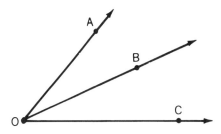

Clearly, angle AOB and angle BOC are adjacent angles. Trace ∠AOB and label the tracing ∠A'O'B'. Place the tracing so that O' falls on point O and ray O'B' falls on ray OC. We see that angle AOB is congruent to angle BOC. Since ∠AOB ≅ ∠BOC, ray OB is said to bisect ∠AOC. To *bisect* means to divide in half. Since ∠AOB ≅ ∠BOC, the measures of these two angles are equal. Therefore $\overrightarrow{OB}$ bisects angle AOC.

EXPLORING GEOMETRIC CONSTRUCTIONS

As well as knowing the vocabulary related to lines and angles, older elementary school children should examine basic procedures for constructing lines and angles. This examination should occur in two distinct ways—one way is to make use of the technology at hand to perform these procedures, and the other should include the exploration of the use of more classical tools. There are several excellent, relatively inexpensive computer software packages available that incorporate elements of computer-assisted design to perform these constructions (see Chapter 4 in Part 2 on computer software). For example, the Geometric preSupposer series, Geometer's Sketchpad, and Elastic Lines include, among other things, the capabilities of constructing parallels, perpendiculars, and angles of various sizes and types. These programs are tools that alleviate the potential drudgery of some constructions and allow the user to concentrate on the underlying problem or concept.

Consider the following question:

■ What is the definition of a median of a triangle?

A student might locate a mathematics text and discover that, in that book, at least, a median is defined as a segment joining a vertex of a triangle to the midpoint of the opposite side.

However, as an alternative to "looking up" the answer to the question, the student might use one of the software packages mentioned to explore the meaning by directing the computer to draw a median in triangle DEF from angle E. The student could then use the features of the software to measure the side cut by the median and note that it is divided into two equivalent segments. Furthermore, the student might then discover that the two new triangles formed by the construction of the median have equal areas. Will this always be the case? A major advantage to such software packages is that they create an environment that encourages formulating hypotheses and making conjectures. Each of the software packages can generate a given construction many times over. Through the use of this repetitive feature, the student can easily re-create this process and measurement on various triangles to discover that, indeed, it appears that a median cuts a triangle into two triangles of equal area. The student has discovered an apparently alternative definition of median that would not have been found if only the textbook had been consulted. This is an example of an informal approach to geometry in the elementary grades that provides a base for a more structured look at proof in later grades.

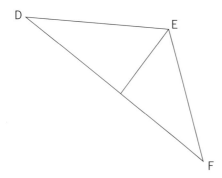

While it is possible to model geometric constructions with dynamic drawing software packages, the classical tools for geometric constructions are the straightedge, the compass, and a *sharp* pencil. (A straightedge is simply a ruler without numerals or other marks on it. A compass is a scribing device of adjustable radius used for drawing arcs.) A challenge in constructing geometric models in this manner lies in trying to draw accurate models without the use of a ruler (to measure lengths) or protractor (to measure angles).

Given the benefits derived from the use of technology in modeling the construction indicated in the example on medians, you may wonder why a student would ever resort to the use of traditional tools. The reason lies in the purpose. The technology performs the process for the user and allows the user the freedom to explore consequences. The use of a straightedge and compass focuses attention on the process itself and allows the student the opportunity to encounter basic structures as emerging concepts.

Let's begin with a simple exercise. Use a straightedge to construct a line segment, $\overleftrightarrow{AB}$.

Using the straightedge, construct another line segment, $\overleftrightarrow{XY}$, longer than $\overleftrightarrow{AB}$. Label any point C on the line segment.

Now, adjust your compass so that the metal point is at point A on $\overleftrightarrow{AB}$ and the pencil of the compass falls on B. The arc made by the compass should pass exactly

through point B. Move the compass point to point C, and draw an arc so that it intersects the line segment containing point C. Label this point of intersection point D.

We can say now that $\overleftrightarrow{CD} \cong \overleftrightarrow{AB}$.

Now let's construct an angle, $\angle JEF$, congruent to a given angle, $\angle ABC$.

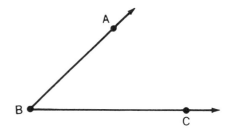

First, draw a ray and label it $\overleftrightarrow{EF}$.

With the metal point on point B, set the compass at any convenient radius and draw an arc through the sides of angle ABC. Label the points of intersection of this arc and the sides of the angle as G and H.

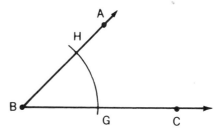

Using this same radius, set the metal compass point on E, and draw an arc that intersects ray EF.

Label the point of intersection of the arc with $\overleftrightarrow{EF}$ as point I. With the compass, measure the distance from point G to point H. Using this measurement, draw an arc from point I that intersects the first arc we drew on this diagram. Label this intersection point J, and draw ray EJ with a straightedge and pencil.

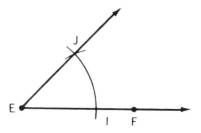

We can now say that ∠JEF ≅ ∠ABC. (Note that arc GH in the earlier figure defines how "wide" the angle is "open" in much the same way as arc IJ does for the figure above.) For practice in construction, use this procedure to draw several other angles congruent to given angles.

Now let's consider the following angle, ∠RST, and construct the bisector of ∠RST:

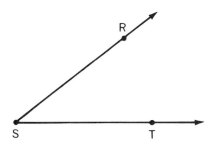

Placing the metal point of the compass at point S, draw an arc so that it intersects rays SR and ST. Label the two points of intersection U and V.

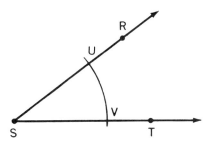

Placing the metal point of the compass at point U, draw an arc between $\overleftrightarrow{ST}$ and $\overleftrightarrow{SR}$. Then, using the same setting on the compass, draw an arc from point V that intersects the arc made from point U. Label the intersection point M. Connect points S and M by means of a straightedge and pencil. The ray SM is the bisector of angle RST.

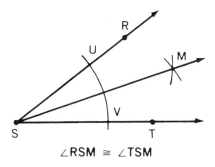

∠RSM ≅ ∠TSM

Exploring basic geometric constructions can provide students with a view of geometry that will serve them well in later studies. The structural nature of classic constructions can help them recognize the logic and connections applied in building paths from the simple to the complex—a foundational component of any axiomatic system.

SYMMETRY AND TRANSFORMATIONAL GEOMETRY

In elementary school, geometry is usually presented in an intuitive manner. As such, elementary and middle school geometry rely heavily on a visual approach. In high school, the student has the opportunity to study geometry as a deductive mathematical system in which results are obtained through careful step-by-step logical reasoning, starting from basic assumptions called *axioms* or *postulates*. In the elementary and middle grades, we often take a more informal approach to geometry. We want the students to become acquainted with some of the terminology of geometry, and we want them to perceive various kinds of relationships and properties between and among geometric figures.

An excellent way to help students develop in these areas is to introduce some of the basic ideas of symmetry and geometric transformations. These ideas are helpful in exploring the properties of geometric figures. According to the NCTM *Principles and Standards for School Mathematics*, instructional programs should include attention to geometry and spatial sense so that all students recognize the usefulness of transformations and symmetry in analyzing mathematical situations (NCTM, 2000, p. 61).

Most of us are familiar with figures that are **symmetric about a line**. In each of the following figures, the given figure is symmetric about the dotted line. The dotted line is called a **line of symmetry** for the figure.

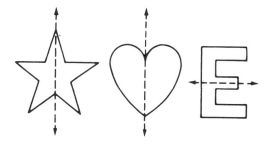

Have the children place a mirror on the line of symmetry of a figure and compare the figure and its reflection.

The Mira Math device is another excellent aid to use when introducing both geometric constructions and symmetry. "Mira" is the commercial name for a red plastic device that has a reflective quality as well as a transparent quality. It can be held in such a way as to display a reflection of a figure drawn on paper. For example,

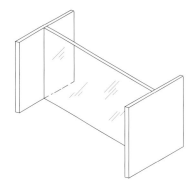

A Mira is especially helpful in studying transformational geometry—the geometry of flips (reflections), slides (translations), turns (rotations), and scaling (dilation). A Mira can also be used for the study of congruence, line segments, angles, geometric shapes, and other geometric concepts, such as parallel and perpendicular lines. Consult the Mira Math teachers' manual for detailed instructions for teaching geometry with this unique device.

A Mira can also be used as an alternative to a straightedge and compass for numerous traditional construction activities. In that context, this device is used to verify constructions by reflections, rotations, and translations. For example, place a Mira vertical to the paper in many different places; how do you know when you have placed the Mira on a line of symmetry? If you were to trace any one of these figures, cut the figure out, and fold it along the dotted line, you would find that the parts on either side of the dotted line match perfectly. The part of the figure on one side of the dotted line is the "mirror image" of the part on the other side.

Symmetry with respect to a line can be described in mathematical terms. A figure is *symmetric with respect to a line ℓ* if each point P of the figure (where P is not on the line ℓ) has a matching point P' on the other side of ℓ such that the line ℓ bisects $\overleftrightarrow{PP'}$ and is perpendicular to $\overleftrightarrow{PP'}$.

For example, consider the following heart-shaped figure:

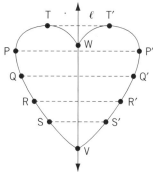

The point P' is called the *image* of P in line ℓ (or the image of P under **reflection** in line ℓ). Similarly, the image of Q is Q', the image of R is R', and so on. We could also think of P as the image of P', of Q as the image of Q', and so on. The point V at the tip of the figure can be thought of as its own image; so can the point W labeled at the top of the figure. The word **flip** is often used in discussing the image or reflection of a figure about a line.

Now, look at the following diagram:

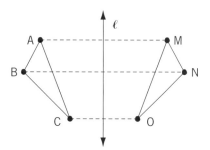

If we flip triangle ABC over line ℓ, point A will fall on point M, point B will fall on point N, and point C will fall on point O. Thus we can speak of triangle MNO as the *flip image* of triangle ABC. The operation of flipping triangle ABC over line ℓ to obtain triangle MNO is an example of a *geometric transformation*. For each point of the original figure, there is a matching point in the flip image.

Another kind of geometric transformation is known as a **translation**. Consider the following rectangle ABCD. Suppose we transform ABCD by matching each vertex with a point 2 inches farther down on the page.

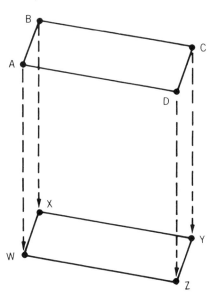

In a similar fashion, we can match every point on ABCD with a point 2 inches lower. The resulting figure, WXYZ, is called the *image of ABCD under a translation*. When we use a translation of a figure, we are finding the figure that we would obtain if it were possible to give the rectangle a straight shove in a given direction and through a given distance. Some authors recommend that translations simply be called **slides**. This word suggests the intuitive meaning of the concept.

We can use an arrow to indicate both the direction and the distance of a translation. For example, we can indicate a translation of $1\frac{1}{2}$ inches to the right by an arrow $1\frac{1}{2}$ inches in length and pointing to the right. If we use such a translation on the following polygon ABCDEF, we get polygon RSTUVW as the image under the translation:

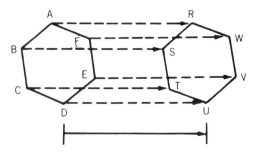

Each point of the image polygon is $1\frac{1}{2}$ inches to the right of its corresponding point in the given polygon.

The arrow below the diagrams of the two polygons indicates how far and in what direction ABCDEF moves under the translation.

Another transformation we can use on a geometric figure is a **rotation**, sometimes simply called a **turn**. If we apply a counterclockwise one-quarter turn to the triangle ABC, as shown in the following diagram, we get AB'C' as the image figure:

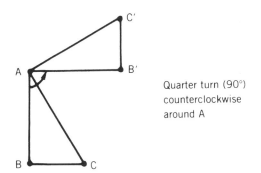

Quarter turn (90°) counterclockwise around A

The point about which the given figure is turned is called the *center* of the turn. The curved arrow indicates the direction of the rotation.

Here are some more diagrams that show a given figure and its image under a turn transformation. Because all points of the original figure remain at the same distance from the center of rotation after rotation, the image figure has the same size and shape as the original.

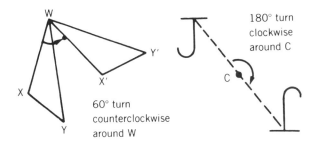

60° turn counterclockwise around W

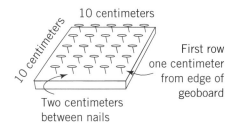

180° turn clockwise around C

Flips, slides, and turns are connected with the important geometric concept of congruence—in fact, these actions can be used to generate an alternative definition of the concept of congruence. Namely, if one figure is the image of another with respect to one of these motions or a combination of these motions, then the figures are congruent. Also, if two figures are congruent, then you can get "from" one figure "to" the other by a flip, a slide, or a turn, or a combination of these motions. That is, one figure is the image of the other through some combination of flips, slides, and/or turns.

To see this, you might ask students to model shapes on dot or graph paper. Have the students form two congruent triangles, one on each of two separate sheets of paper. Then have the children rotate, slide, and even flip the triangles to show that the two triangles are actually congruent. You may need a mirror to show the flip, or you can physically cut out one shape and actually flip it to match the other.

Flips, slides, and turns move figures from one position to another, but they do not change them in any

other way. Figures stay the same size and shape, which is exactly what congruence means. For this reason, flips, slides, and turns are called *rigid motions*. Another type of transformation, scaling (or dilation), uses a scaling factor other than 1 and is a nonrigid motion. This transformation changes the relative size of the figure being transformed by stretching or shrinking it. The resulting figure will be similar to the initial figure. That is, the resulting figure will be the same shape but a different size than the original.

Basic ideas of geometric transformations can be presented to children to help them understand a variety of ideas in geometry. This approach provides many opportunities for children to manipulate cutouts and tracings of geometric figures. A formal development of the ideas of geometric transformations, however, should not be the goal at the elementary level—informal, intuitive experiences with these concepts is more beneficial.

OTHER DEVICES FOR EXPLORING GEOMETRIC CONCEPTS

An excellent device for presenting basic geometric concepts to children is the geoboard. A geoboard is usually a square piece of material in which an array of nails or pegs has been placed. Very often a geoboard is made from a square piece of plywood in which an array of nails has been driven partway into the wood. The nails should protrude about 1 centimeter.

10 centimeters

10 centimeters

First row one centimeter from edge of geoboard

Two centimeters between nails

To make the nails a uniform height, use pliers to hold the nails, and drive the nails in until they hit the top of the pliers. Since the first row of nails is positioned 1 centimeter from the edge and the nails are 2 centimeters apart, several geoboards can be placed side by side to make a large board or to be used as a model for the *x-y* coordinate plane.

Geoboards for the primary grades should probably have a total of 25 or 36 pegs (5 by 5 or 6 by 6). Upper-grade students can use boards with more pegs to model more complex figures and designs.

By placing rubber bands around the nails driven into the geoboard, the students can represent line segments, squares, rectangles, triangles, and angles. Ask students to perform various tasks and answer questions using the geoboard. Examples of more open-ended questions and activities follow:

1. Have the children show a line segment on their geoboards. Using the nails, see who can make the longest line segment and who can make the shortest line segment. In a class discussion, have

different children show why they think their line segment is the longest or shortest.

2. After the children have had time to experiment with making angles on the geoboard, ask them to make an angle with the fewest number of degrees. Have different children show why their angle contains the fewest degrees. Will you accept an angle of 0°?

3. Have the children make an angle with the greatest number of degrees. Will you accept an angle that a child says contains 390°? 190°?

4. Have the children make an acute angle that contains the greatest number of degrees.

5. Have the children make an obtuse angle that contains the greatest number of degrees. Does a 360° angle fit the request?

6. After making open and closed curves, have the children make a closed curve that has the greatest interior and a closed curve that has the smallest interior.

Tangrams are excellent for children to work with when developing concepts of spatial relations. A set of tangrams has 7 pieces that fit together as shown:

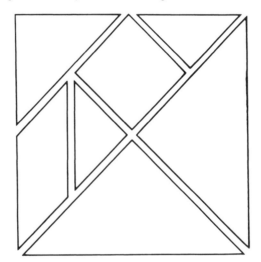

The 7 pieces can be put together in hundreds of different ways. Often it is useful to give the students an outline of a figure and ask them to put the 7 pieces inside the outline. Tangrams can help teach children abut whole-part relationships, spatial relationships, congruence, similarity, perimeter, and area.

CLOSURE

Familiarity with basic geometric concepts is an essential component of how a child comes to know and relate to his or her physical environment. The basic terminology encountered and developed through the exploration of geometry provides a foundation for the communication of ideas, hypotheses, and connections. To analyze, generalize, and convey relationships, characteristics, and properties among and between made observations, it is critical that students be engaged in activities outlined in this chapter and reinforced in Part 2 of this text.

These basic concepts and structures of geometry—the "building blocks" of geometry—are expanded and extended in the next chapter as we explore polygons (two-dimensional figures) and polyhedra (three-dimensional figures).

Terminology, Symbols, and Procedures

Acute Angle. An acute angle is any angle that is less than a right angle. An acute angle has a measure of less than 90°.

Adjacent Angles. Any two angles with a common vertex and a common ray (side) between them are called *adjacent angles*.

Angle. An angle is the union of two rays that have a common end point. If $\overrightarrow{AB}$ and $\overrightarrow{AC}$ are rays, then their union is an angle, which can be denoted by ∠BAC or ∠CAB.

Closed Curve. A closed curve is a curve that returns to its starting point.

Complementary Angles. Two angles are complementary angles if the sum of their measures is equal to the measure of a right angle (90°).

Congruent. Two angles whose measures are equal are said to be congruent and are called *congruent angles*.

Line. The term *line* is an undefined term in geometry. Intuitively, a line is the figure one obtains by extending a line segment through each of its end points so that the figure extends endlessly in opposite directions. If A and B are any two points on a line, then the line can be denoted by $\overleftrightarrow{AB}$ or $\overleftrightarrow{BA}$. Alternatively, a single lowercase letter can be used to label a line.

Line Segment. A segment can be thought of as a set of points that forms the shortest path between two points. The segment from point A to point B can be denoted by $\overrightarrow{AB}$ or $\overrightarrow{BA}$. Points A and B are called the *end points* of the line segment.

Obtuse Angle. An obtuse angle is any angle that has a measure between 90° and 180°.

Perpendicular. Two lines or line segments that intersect at 90° (or at right) angles are said to be perpendicular to each other.

Plane. A plane is an undefined concept in geometry. It can be thought of as the set of points suggested by a flat surface extending endlessly in the directions established by any portion of the surface.

Point. A point in geometry is undefined. A geometric point is considered to be a particular location in geometric space. A point does not have length, width, or depth. A point can be represented by a small dot and is often named with capital letters.

Ray. A subset of a line formed by a given point on the line and all points on the line extending in one direction from the given point is called a *ray*. The given point is called the *end point* of the ray. If C is the end point of a ray that passes through a second point D, then the ray can be denoted by $\overrightarrow{CD}$.

Reflection (or **Flip**). A reflection is a transformation that carries every point A into its image A' with respect to a given line. The given line is a perpendicular bisector of a line joining points A and A'. Consequently, point A and point A' are equidistant from the given line and are on opposite sides of that line.

Right Angle. If a given line is intersected by another line so that the two angles formed on one side of the given line are congruent, then the two angles are said to be right angles. The measure of a right angle is 90°.

Rotation (or **Turn**). A rotation is a transformation that carries every point A into a point A' whose distance from a fixed point O is the same as that of A from O. Under a rotation, every point moves through a given number of degrees around the point O.

Sides of an Angle. The two rays that form an angle are called the *sides* of the angle. The measure of an angle is determined by measuring the rotation from the initial side of the angle to the terminal side.

Simple Closed Curve. A simple closed curve is a closed curve that does not cross itself at any point. Any simple closed curve divides a plane into the following three sets of points:

1. the set of points comprising the simple closed curve itself
2. the set of points comprising the interior of the simple closed curve
3. the set of points comprising the exterior of the simple closed curve

Simple Closed Region. The union of a simple closed curve and its interior is called a *simple closed region*.

Space. Space is considered to be the set of all points (locations).

Supplementary Angles. Two angles are supplementary angles if the sum of their measures is equal to the measure of a straight angle (180°).

Translation (or **Slide**). A translation is a geometric transformation that matches with any point P a point Q that lies at a given distance and in a given direction from P.

Vertex. The vertex of an angle is the common end point of the rays that form the angle.

Practice Exercises for Teachers

These exercises are designed for the reader of this book. While some are suitable for use in the elementary classroom, these examples should not necessarily be given to children in this form. Ideas for classroom activities on the concepts and ideas discussed in this chapter can be found in Part 2 of *Today's Mathematics*, the Student Resource Book.

Note: Obtain or make a geoboard, or use dot paper, to perform the first four exercises.

1. Model some line segments of different lengths.

2. Model some open curves and some curves that are not open.

3. Model the following types of angles.

    a) an acute angle   b) a right angle
    c) an obtuse angle   d) a pair of adjacent angles
    e) supplementary angles

4. Model two perpendicular line segments. Must these be vertical and horizontal?

5. a) Draw a representation of a point. Name it A. How many lines can be drawn through point A?
    b) Draw a representation for another point about 3 centimeters from point A. Name the second point B. Draw line segment AB. How many line segments can be drawn between points A and B?

6. a) Make a tracing of angle PEN below. Name your angle P'E'N'. Using a compass and straightedge, bisect angle P'E'N'. Since both angles have the same measure, we say that the two angles are (congruent) or (equivalent).

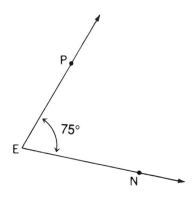

    b) Since angle PEN has a measure of less than 90°, we say that ∠PEN is an (acute) or (right) or (obtuse) angle.

7. Write the number of degrees for the complementary angle of each of the following angles.

    a) $m(\angle MAC) = 25°$ b) $m(\angle DEC) = 45°$ c) $m(\angle CAT) = 80°$
    d) $m(\angle LOT) = 73°$ e) $m(\angle HAT) = 3°$ f) $m(\angle CAP) = 86°$

8. Write the number of degrees for the supplementary angle of each of the following angles.

    a) $m(\angle NOT) = 40°$ b) $m(\angle TOP) = 90°$ c) $m(\angle BUT) = 150°$
    d) $m(\angle LOW) = 170°$ e) $m(\angle INA) = 45°$ f) $m(\angle SAC) = 109°$

9. Make a drawing that represents an acute angle, labeling it ∠XYZ. Construct an angle congruent to ∠XYZ, and label it ∠X'Y'Z'.

10. Identify the geometric concept suggested by each of the following drawings. If the figure can be represented by a symbol, write the symbol.

    a)   A
            •

    b)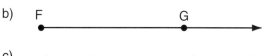

    c)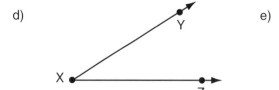

    d)   e)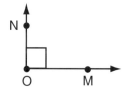

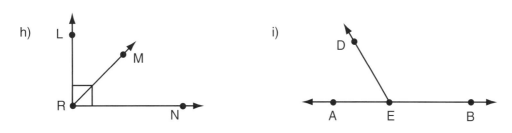

11. Determine whether each of the following statements is true or false.

    a) Line segments, rays, and angles are sets of points.
    b) A line is an infinite set of points.
    c) A line segment is a finite set of points.
    d) Two perpendicular lines form four right angles.
    e) If you make diagrams to represent two lines, line AB and line CD, and the pencil lines you draw do not cross in the diagram, then the two lines cannot intersect.
    f) If two angles are supplementary angles, then they are also adjacent angles.

12. Name all the line segments marked in this picture.

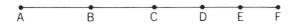

13. Draw a square. Use dotted lines to show all lines of symmetry of the square.

14. Suppose that polygon A'B'C'D'E' is the image of polygon ABCDE under a translation (slide). What can you say about the following?

    a) the relationship between lines AA', BB', CC', DD', and EE'
    b) the lengths of line segments AA', BB', CC', DD', and EE'
    c) the sizes and shapes of ABCDE and A'B'C'D'E'

15. Trace the following figure on a sheet of paper. Then sketch the image of ABCDE under a quarter turn (that is, a turn of 90°) in a counterclockwise direction with respect to point O.

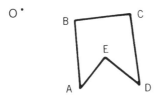

16. Draw each of the following figures after a rotation around point P as suggested under each drawing.

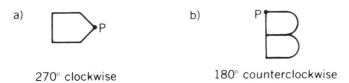

a) 270° clockwise

b) 180° counterclockwise

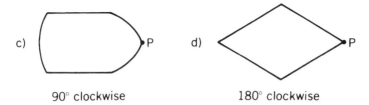

c)		d)	
90° clockwise		180° clockwise	

17. Draw all the lines of symmetry for each of the following figures.

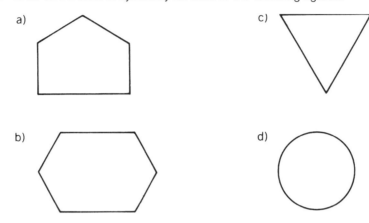

a)

c)

b)

d)

18. Trace each of the following figures on a sheet of paper. Then flip the figure over a line.

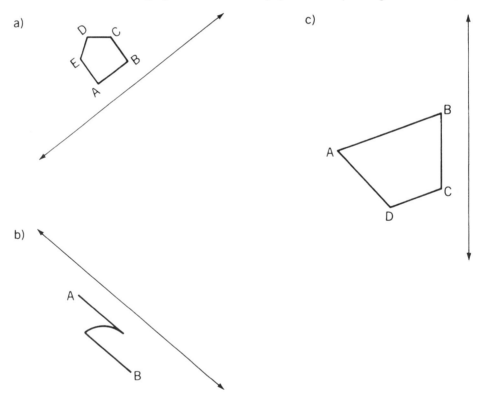

a)

c)

b)

Teaching Competencies and Self-Assessment Tasks

1. Why is the study of geometry essential for elementary and middle school children? What are the benefits of such study to other topics in mathematics and to other subject areas?

2. Examine elementary mathematics textbooks to determine what percent of each program is devoted to geometry. Is the geometric content of these mathematics programs adequate, or should it be increased or decreased? Is the geometry integrated with other mathematical subject matter?

3. Conduct a geometric scavenger hunt around your school by searching for physical representations of basic geometric concepts discussed in this chapter. Find at least three distinct examples of each concept and draw a sketch that correctly names and labels the concept represented.

4. Locate a copy of the computer software Geometric Supposer or Geometer's Sketchpad. Explore the capabilities of these programs and the ways in which they represent and label basic geometric concepts.

5. Make a list of at least ten examples of angles in our environment, such as those suggested by intersecting roads, and classify your examples by angle types and angle relationships.

6. Research the literature, and then discuss the merits of using geoboards to teach the basic concepts of geometry such as those outlined in this chapter.

7. Locate information about the Mira Math aid discussed in this chapter and compare and contrast this device with traditional techniques for teaching geometry.

8. Use a compass and straightedge to construct a square. Describe the process to a friend and defend (justify) each stage of the construction.

9. Use a compass and straightedge to create an abstract design that has several lines of symmetry. Color the design to emphasize the symmetry.

10. Compare and contrast Euclidean geometry and transformational geometry.

11. Discuss how the extensive technical vocabulary of geometry should be handled in an elementary geometry program.

12. Since the child's world is three-dimensional (blocks, balls, and so on), should a geometry program begin with solid geometry (three-dimensional) and then move to plane geometry (two-dimensional)? Argue both sides of this issue.

Related Readings and Teacher Resources

For related readings on topics found in this chapter, see the corresponding chapter in Part 2 of *Today's Mathematics*, the Student Resource Book.

Chapter 17

Geometry: Polygons and Polyhedra

Teaching Competencies

Upon completing this chapter, you will be able to:

- Classify polygons according to the number of sides they contain.

- Classify triangles according to the measures of their angles and/or according to the measures of their sides.

- Calculate perimeters and areas of squares, rectangles, parallelograms, and triangles and calculate the circumference and area of a circle, given its radius or diameter.

- Apply the Pythagorean theorem to find the length of any side of a right triangle, given the measures of the other two sides.

- Recognize and classify three-dimensional shapes such as prisms, pyramids, cylinders, cones, and spheres.

- Calculate the volume and surface area of three-dimensional shapes, given the necessary information about the dimensions of the shape.

- Prepare lessons that combine basic geometric concepts with the exploration of polygons and polyhedra and that integrate geometry with other topics of the mathematics curriculum and the broader elementary school curriculum.

hildren live in a geometric world—the buildings they see on the way to school, the food containers in the kitchen at home, and their toys (especially blocks, balls, and the boxes the toys come in) are geometric. In fact, almost every interaction with their world is in some way couched in geometry. Because of this geometric environment, it is logical that geometry should be emphasized at every grade level, but many teachers either skip or downplay geometry in their teaching programs. There are two probable reasons for this: (1) elementary teachers, in general, may not have sound geometry backgrounds, and (2) teachers may feel that basic operations and computational skill are more important. In today's world, however, we must reevaluate the significance of geometry in the elementary mathematics program. Geometry must not be viewed as a subject relegated to study in grades 9 or 10. Primary and upper elementary school children should be provided opportunities to explore geometric concepts through such processes as locating, orienting, measuring, drawing, modeling, classifying, and sorting. Readers are reminded of an important discussion in Chapter 2 that illustrates ways in which geometry might serve as a lens for studying other mathematical content in the elementary school. Your attention is also drawn to Chapter 18 in Part 2 of this text for valuable information on the scope and sequence of geometry concepts across the grades.

According to the NCTM *Principles and Standards for School Mathematics*:

Instructional programs from pre-kindergarten through grade 12 should enable all students to—

■ analyze characteristics and properties of two- and three-dimensional geometric shapes and develop mathematical arguments about geometric relationships;

■ specify locations and describe spatial relationships using coordinate geometry and other representational systems;

■ apply transformations and use symmetry to analyze mathematical situations;

■ use visualization, spatial reasoning, and geometric modeling to solve problems.

In Chapter 15 we discussed measurement, and in Chapter 16 we considered some of the basic concepts of geometry, including symmetry and transformations. In this chapter we will expand on these concepts and relate measurement to geometry. We are now ready to use the fundamental concepts and structure developed in Chapter 16 to examine a variety of geometric shapes and relations.

DEFINING POLYGONS

Simple closed curves composed of three or more line segments (referred to as sides) are called **polygons**. "Poly" comes from the Greek word *polys*, meaning "many"; and "gon" comes from the Greek word *gonia*, meaning "angle." Therefore, a polygon is, literally, a shape with many angles. The following shapes are examples of polygons:

Polygons are simple closed curves formed by the union of three or more line segments that lie in the same

---

Research Snapshot

What does research say about children's early conceptions of geometric shapes?

Clements, Swaminathan, Hannibal, & Sarama (1999) interviewed 97 children, ages 3 to 6, to investigate the criteria they used to identify and describe shapes. The preschool children exhibited working knowledge of simple geometric forms such as circles, squares, and, to a lesser degree, triangles and rectangles. The children tended to focus on the visual features of the shapes, rather than on the properties of the shapes.

The authors recommend that to help develop more explicit knowledge of the components and properties of shapes, teachers should encourage their students to describe why a figure belongs or does not belong to a shape category.

How else could you help your students discover the properties of shapes?

Clements, D. H., Swaminathan, S., Hannibal, M. A. Z., & Sarama, J. (1999). Young children's concepts of shape. *Journal for Research in Mathematics Education*, 30, 192–212.

For additional research briefs, "ERIC Digests" lets you search more than 2,000 short syntheses of research on a range of education topics. The syntheses were produced by the Educational Resources Information Center (ERIC). Check http://ed.gov/databases/ERIC_Digests/index/

plane and touch only at their end points. Remember that the interior of a polygon is not a part of the polygon itself. A polygon with its interior is referred to as a **polygonal region**.

Polygons have special names according to the number of sides or angles they have. A three-sided (or three-angled) polygon, for example, is called a *triangle*, while a four-sided (or four-angled) polygon is called a *quadrilateral*. If all the sides of a polygon are congruent (that is, have the same length) and all its angles are of equal measure, then it is called a *regular polygon*. Since segments with the same length are congruent, and angles with the same measure are congruent, we can say that a regular polygon is a polygon with congruent sides and congruent angles. If the sides of a polygon are not all congruent or if the angles are not all equal in measure, the polygon is referred to as an **irregular polygon**. Polygons can also be classified as either convex or concave. A polygon is called *convex* if all of its interior angles are less than 180°. If at least one interior angle of a polygon is greater than 180°, then the polygon is *concave*.

The accompanying table names the more familiar polygons. We present this table to illustrate techniques used for naming polygons. It is not necessary that you require students to memorize all these names; require them to know only those names you determine are appropriate for them.

Number of Sides	Prefix	Name of Polygon	Name of Region
3	tri-	triangle	triangular region
4	quad-	quadrilateral	quadrilateral region
5	penta-	pentagon	pentagonal region
6	hexa-	hexagon	hexagonal region
7	hepta-	heptagon	heptagonal region
8	octa-	octagon	octagonal region
9	nona-	nonagon	nonagonal region
10	deca-	decagon	decagonal region
11	undeca-	undecagon	undecagonal region
12	dodeca-	dodecagon	dodecagonal region
⋮	⋮	⋮	⋮
many	poly-	polygon	polygonal region

The geoboard can be a useful tool for exploring basic geometric shapes (see Chapter 16). Each student should have his or her own geoboard with a supply of rubber bands. As each of the different geometric shapes is discussed, the student should be given ample opportunity to experiment and make the shape on the geoboard. Few children (or college students, for that matter) have enough experience creating polygons. After students have each constructed a given polygon, compare them and see how many different ways a given polygon can be made on a geoboard.

A **quadrilateral** is a polygon with four sides. It is a simple closed curve composed of four line segments, none of which lies on the same line.

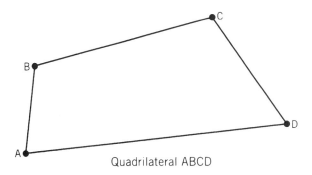

Quadrilateral ABCD

A **pentagon** is a polygon with five sides. It has five line segments lying in a plane and forming a simple closed curve.

Pentagon ABCDE

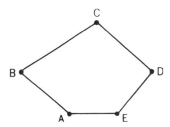

Children may be familiar with the Pentagon building across the Potomac River in Washington, D.C.

A **hexagon** is a polygon with six sides. It has six line segments lying in a plane and forming a simple closed curve.

Hexagon ABCDEF

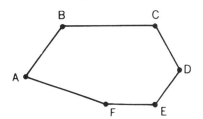

The heads of bolts are often, but not always, hexagonal.

An **octagon** is a polygon with eight sides. It has eight line segments lying in a plane and forming a simple closed curve.

Octagon ABCDEFGH

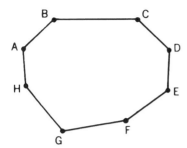

A stop sign, for example, is a regular octagon.

A CLOSER LOOK AT TRIANGLES

Mark any three points that are not on the same line, and connect the three points with line segments. The shape formed is a **triangle**. Let's look at triangles in detail.

We have said that an *angle* is two rays that have a common end point but do not lie on the same line. For example, in the following diagram, the two rays, $\overrightarrow{AB}$ and $\overrightarrow{AC}$, determine the angle CAB (or angle BAC). This can be written as ∠CAB (or ∠BAC). Since there is only one angle represented in the figure with a vertex at A, you can also name this angle ∠A.

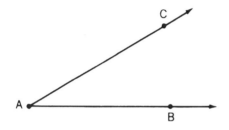

Now, suppose that B is selected as the end point of another ray that passes through (or contains) point C. Then extend $\overrightarrow{BA}$ with B as an end point.

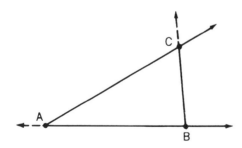

Clearly, we have formed another angle. What can we name this angle whose vertex is point B? We can name it ∠CBA or ∠ABC.

A *closed plane region* is a set of points in one plane that is bounded by a closed curve (but not necessarily a *simple* closed curve). The boundary of the closed plane region formed in the preceding diagram is a triangle. The triangles discussed in this chapter are all planar triangles—that is, each triangle is considered to lie entirely within a plane. (Interestingly, there are other

defined geometries in which this is not the case. You might find it worthwhile, for example, to explore the geometry of the sphere. How does the definition of a "triangle" change when it is drawn on a spherical object?)

Color the following triangle, △ABC (read "triangle ABC"):

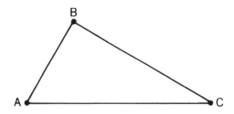

When you colored △ABC, you should have colored only the line segments—$\overrightarrow{AB}$, $\overrightarrow{BC}$, and $\overrightarrow{CA}$—because it is the union of line segments that forms a triangle. When we use the term *triangle*, we mean only the set of points that comprise the closed curve. When we use the term *triangular region*, we mean the union of the closed curve and the interior. If you were to color the triangular region bounded by $\overrightarrow{AB}$, $\overrightarrow{BC}$, and $\overrightarrow{CA}$, you would color both the line segments (the sides) and the interior of △ABC.

A triangle, then, can be seen as the boundary of a particular kind of closed plane region. A triangle partitions, or separates, a plane into three sets of points:

1. the set of points that make up the line segments forming the sides of the triangle
2. the set of points that make up the interior of the triangle
3. the set of points that make up the exterior of the triangle

Since every triangle is made up of three line segments (called sides), we can name certain kinds of triangles according to the relations among the sides.

■ **Equilateral triangle**: A triangle in which the sides are equal in length is called an *equilateral triangle*. Since line segments that are equal in length are said to be congruent, we can also say that an equilateral triangle is a triangle with three congruent sides. For example, the following is an equilateral triangle:

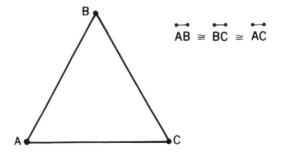

The statement is read, "Line segment AB is congruent to line segment BC, and line segment BC is congruent to line segment AC."

■ **Isosceles triangle:** A triangle in which at least two sides are congruent is called an *isosceles triangle*.

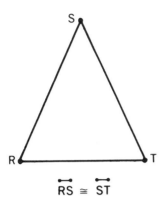

$$\overleftrightarrow{RS} \cong \overleftrightarrow{ST}$$

Are all equilateral triangles also isosceles triangles? Yes, because an isosceles triangle has *at least* two congruent sides, and, so, could have all three congruent. (Be warned that some programs define isosceles triangles as having *exactly* two equal sides. In such cases, obviously, equilateral triangles are not considered to be isosceles.)

■ **Scalene triangle:** If no two sides of a triangle are congruent, we call the triangle a *scalene triangle*.

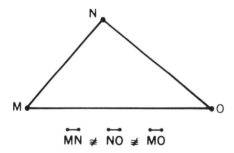

$$\overleftrightarrow{MN} \neq \overleftrightarrow{NO} \neq \overleftrightarrow{MO}$$

When we describe a triangle as being equilateral, isosceles, or scalene, we are describing it according to the relations that exist among its sides. We can also name triangles according to the relations that exist among the angles suggested by the line segments bounding the triangles. Consider the following definitions:

■ **Right triangle:** A right triangle is a triangle that has a "square corner," referred to as a 90° angle or a right angle. Examples of this triangle are common in our environment.

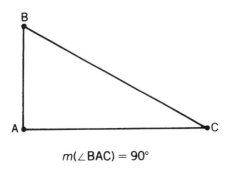

$$m(\angle BAC) = 90°$$

Unfortunately, right triangles are too frequently drawn on a horizontal base with the right angle on the left (as in the illustration shown). However, teachers should take care to show right triangles in many positions or orientations. For example, use an overhead projector with a right triangle drawn on a transparency. After the triangle has been identified, move it to many different positions by rotating or flipping it; have the students explain why it is still a right triangle.

■ **Equiangular triangle:** A triangle whose three angles are congruent is called an *equiangular triangle*.

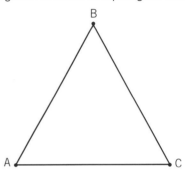

$$m\angle ABC = m\angle BCA = m\angle CAB$$

If we examine any equiangular triangle, we find that not only are its angles all equal in measure but that its sides are also all congruent. Consequently, any equiangular triangle is also an equilateral triangle.

■ **Acute triangle:** We have already learned that an angle with a measure of less than 90° is called an acute angle. If all three of the angles of a triangle are acute, the triangle is called an *acute triangle*.

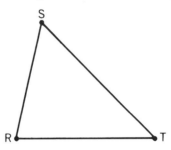

$$m\angle RST < 90°, \; m\angle STR < 90°, \; m\angle TRS < 90°$$

■ **Obtuse triangle:** We have also learned that if an angle has a measure of more than 90° but less than 180°, it is called an obtuse angle. A triangle that has one obtuse angle is called an *obtuse triangle*.

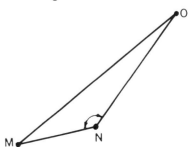

Can any triangle have more than one obtuse angle? Remember that an obtuse angle has a measure of more than 90° but less than 180°. In a triangle the sum of the measures of the three angles is 180°. If the measure of one angle is more than 90°, then the sum of the measures of the other two angles must be less than 90°. Consequently, the answer to the question is, "No, a triangle cannot have more than one obtuse angle."

To verify that the sum of the angles of a triangle is 180°, have upper elementary school children draw several large triangles on a sheet of paper and then use a protractor to find the measures of the angles of the triangles. Ask them to take each triangle separately and add its angle measures. The results will depend on the accuracy with which the children use their protractors. But generally they will find that the sum of the measures of the angles of a triangle is 180°. Because of inaccuracy in their measurements, they may be off a few degrees, but they will be close enough to make the appropriate generalization. We should be able to generalize through inductive reasoning that, in any plane triangle ABC, the sum of the measures of the angles is 180°. In mathematical symbols, we can write, in △ABC:

$$m\angle A + m\angle B + m\angle C = 180°$$

Another way to show that a triangle contains angles measuring 180° is to use a pencil "lying" on a side of a triangle.

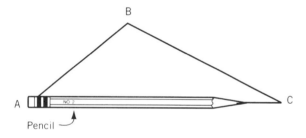

Rotate the pencil through the angle CAB.

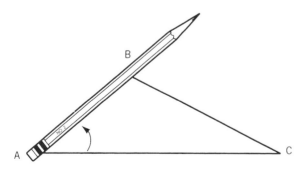

Then, holding it fixed at B, rotate it through angle ABC.

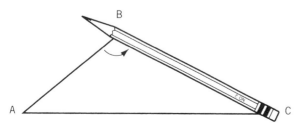

Finally, holding it fixed at C, rotate it through angle BCA.

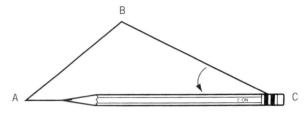

Note that the pencil, having rotated through all three angles of △ABC, has reversed direction—that is, it has turned through 180°.

Younger children can also discover through their own efforts at a "cut-and-paste" activity that the sum of the measures of the angles represented by any triangle is 180°. Have children draw triangles of many different sizes and types on paper. If they cut these triangles out and tear off the corners

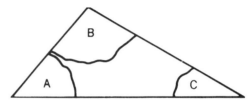

they will discover that the three angles of any one triangle, when placed together as shown here, form a straight line (sometimes thought of as a straight "angle" or an "angle" of 180°).

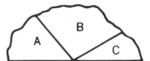

After several trials, children will discover that this is true for any triangle, no matter what its sides or angles measure.

The ancient Egyptian culture developed an extensive practical use for triangles. The Egyptians made use of geometry in surveying the land after the annual spring floods of the Nile river. The floods washed away landmarks, and some method of reestablishing boundaries was necessary. Historians have noted that one surveying tool used by the Egyptians was a rope with thirteen equally spaced knots. If the first and thirteenth knots are joined and a stake is placed at the fourth, the eighth, and the thirteenth knot, a right triangle is constructed.

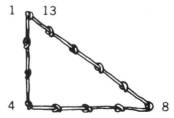

We also know that triangles of this kind were studied by a Greek geometer, Pythagoras, in the sixth century B.C. His statement on the relation between the lengths of the sides of right triangles is known as the

Pythagorean theorem. Consider the following triangle, ABC, in which ∠ACB has the measure of a right angle. In the diagram of this right triangle, we can mark the right angle by making a small square, as shown.

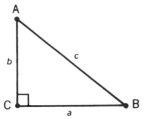

Because we label the vertices of a triangle with capital letters, we sometimes use lowercase letters to name the sides. By custom, the side opposite a given angle is named with the same letter as the angle, but using a lowercase letter. For example, in the preceding diagram, the side opposite angle A is labeled a. The longest side of a right triangle (the side opposite the right angle) is called the *hypotenuse*. The other two sides are called *legs*. The Pythagorean theorem states that the square of the measure of one leg of a right triangle added to the square of the measure of the other leg is equal to the square of the measure of the hypotenuse. (Or, alternatively, the square of the measure of the hypotenuse of a right triangle is equal to the sum of the squares of the measures of the other two sides.) By the time they complete elementary school, students need to understand the meaning of this theorem and be able to state it in words. Committing the "usual" formula to memory makes little sense without knowing what it represents. Nevertheless, using this drawing, we can state the theorem of Pythagoras mathematically as follows:

$$a^2 + b^2 = c^2$$
$$\text{or}$$
$$m(BC)^2 + m(AC)^2 = m(AB)^2$$

Suppose we assign the following unit lengths to the sides of right triangle ACB:

$$a = 4 \text{ units}$$
$$b = 3 \text{ units}$$
$$c = 5 \text{ units}$$

Substituting these values in the mathematical statement of the theorem and performing the indicated computation, we can illustrate the Pythagorean theorem.

$$a^2 + b^2 = c^2$$
$$(4 \times 4) + (3 \times 3) = (5 \times 5)$$
$$16 + 9 = 25$$
$$25 = 25$$

There are literally hundreds of proofs of the Pythagorean theorem. We will not attempt to give a general proof of this theorem, but we will verify and discuss in detail an example that illustrates the theorem.

Consider right triangle ABC.

Using $\overleftrightarrow{AC}$ as one leg, construct the square ACMN.
Using $\overleftrightarrow{CB}$ as one leg, construct the square CBOP.
Using $\overrightarrow{AB}$ as the hypotenuse, construct the square ABRS.

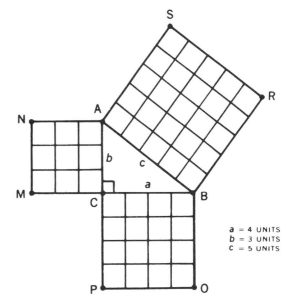

$$a = 4 \text{ UNITS}$$
$$b = 3 \text{ UNITS}$$
$$c = 5 \text{ UNITS}$$

Each of the three square regions we have just constructed is subdivided into unit squares, as shown in the diagram. The number of small square regions along a particular side of the triangle indicates the length of that side. So, the number of small square regions in a particular square region on a side represents the square (a^2 or b^2) of the length of the side next to that particular square region. For example, the hypotenuse AB (named c) has a length of 5 units, so the square (c^2) of the hypotenuse is 25; and the square region ABRS is divided into 25 smaller square regions. It can be observed visually that the number of small squares in square CBOP (16) added to the number of small squares in square ACMN (9) is equal to the number of small squares in square ABRS (25).

$$a^2 + b^2 = c^2$$
$$4^2 + 3^2 = 5^2$$
$$16 + 9 = 25$$
$$25 = 25$$

The regions can be cut out and pasted together to demonstrate even to very young children the physical principle underlying the Pythagorean theorem.

Let's examine the following right triangles in light of the Pythagorean theorem.

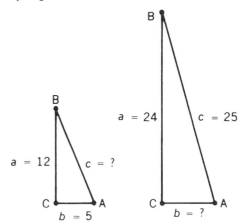

$$a = 12 \qquad c = ?$$
$$b = 5$$

$$a = 24 \qquad c = 25$$
$$b = ?$$

If you know the lengths of the legs of a right triangle, can you find the length of the hypotenuse? Yes, by applying the Pythagorean theorem. If you know the lengths of the hypotenuse and one of the legs of a right triangle, can you find the length of the other leg? Yes, in much the same way. The computations are illustrated in the following diagrams:

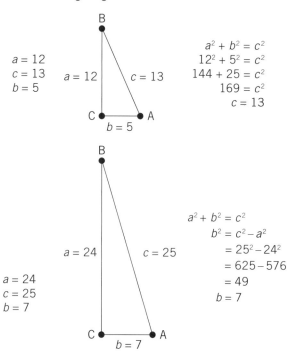

$a = 12$
$c = 13$
$b = 5$

$$a^2 + b^2 = c^2$$
$$12^2 + 5^2 = c^2$$
$$144 + 25 = c^2$$
$$169 = c^2$$
$$c = 13$$

$a = 24$
$c = 25$
$b = 7$

$$a^2 + b^2 = c^2$$
$$b^2 = c^2 - a^2$$
$$= 25^2 - 24^2$$
$$= 625 - 576$$
$$= 49$$
$$b = 7$$

You might discuss how the figure could be interpreted as a wall 24 feet high with a ladder 25 feet long placed 7 feet from the base of the wall. Alternatively, you might think of a person at point B throwing a ball to a person at point C (a distance of 24 feet). How far would he have to throw the ball to get it to the person at point A? What other applications or interpretations of the Pythagorean theorem can you devise that would prove to be useful with elementary school children?

The term *congruent* was defined earlier with respect to angles. Let's see how we can apply the concept of congruence to triangles. **Congruent triangles** are defined as triangles that have the same size and shape. That is, their corresponding sides are congruent, and their corresponding angles are congruent. We define **similar triangles** as triangles that have the same shape but not necessarily the same size. Only the corresponding angles must be congruent; the corresponding sides may have equal or different lengths.

Compare the following three triangles:

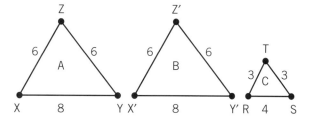

In the triangles pictured, the corresponding sides are as follows:

$\overleftrightarrow{XZ}$ corresponds to $\overleftrightarrow{X'Z'}$ corresponds to $\overleftrightarrow{RT}$.
$\overleftrightarrow{YZ}$ corresponds to $\overleftrightarrow{Y'Z'}$ corresponds to $\overleftrightarrow{ST}$.
$\overleftrightarrow{XY}$ corresponds to $\overleftrightarrow{X'Y'}$ corresponds to $\overleftrightarrow{RS}$.

Triangle A is congruent to triangle B because the corresponding sides of triangles A and B are congruent and the corresponding angles are congruent. Triangle C is similar to triangles A and B because it has the same shape but not the same size. The angles of triangle C are congruent to the corresponding angles of triangle B (and triangle A), but the corresponding sides are not congruent (that is, they do not have the same length).

We can express these relations in the following manner. Triangle A is congruent to triangle B.

$$\triangle A \cong \triangle B$$

Therefore,

$$m(\overleftrightarrow{XZ}) = m(\overleftrightarrow{X'Z'}) \qquad m\angle X = \angle mX'$$
$$m(\overleftrightarrow{XY}) = m(\overleftrightarrow{X'Y'}) \qquad m\angle Y = \angle mY'$$
$$m(\overleftrightarrow{YZ}) = m(\overleftrightarrow{Y'Z'}) \qquad m\angle Z = \angle mZ'$$

Triangle C is similar to triangle B (and to triangle A).

$\triangle C \sim \triangle B$ (The symbol $\sim$ means "is similar to.")

Therefore,

$$m\angle X' = m\angle R$$
$$m\angle Y' = m\angle S$$
$$m\angle Z' = m\angle T$$

Let's compare the similar triangles ABC and DEF, pictured in the following diagram:

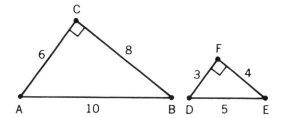

The line segment DF corresponds to $\overleftrightarrow{AC}$. The lengths of these two sides can be compared by a ratio, $\frac{3}{6} = \frac{1}{2}$. That is, the length of side $\overleftrightarrow{DF}$ is to the length of side $\overleftrightarrow{AC}$ as 3 is to 6 (or as 1 is to 2). The ratio of the lengths is $\frac{1}{2}$. Compare the length of side $\overleftrightarrow{EF}$ with that of side $\overleftrightarrow{BC}$. This ratio is $\frac{4}{8} = \frac{1}{2}$. Similarly, comparing the lengths of $\overleftrightarrow{DE}$ and $\overleftrightarrow{AB}$, we find that $\frac{5}{10} = \frac{1}{2}$. If two triangles are similar to each other, the lengths of their corresponding sides will have the same ratio. Applying this idea to triangles DEF and ABC, we see that the ratios of the lengths of corresponding sides is, in each case, $\frac{1}{2}$.

$$\frac{m(\overline{DF})}{m(\overline{AC})} = \frac{m(\overline{EF})}{m(\overline{BC})} = \frac{m(\overline{DE})}{m(\overline{AB})} = \frac{1}{2}$$

If we are given two similar triangles and are told the lengths of three sides of one of the triangles and the length of one side of the other triangle, we can easily find the lengths of the other two sides of the second triangle. This is an application of the concepts of ratio and proportion, which were discussed in Chapter 13. For example, suppose we are given the following two similar triangles:

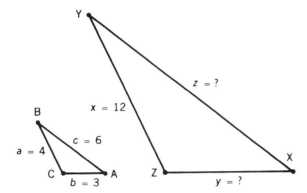

If we know that a and x are corresponding sides, then we know that the ratio of corresponding sides must be $\frac{1}{3}$ (since $\frac{a}{x} = \frac{4}{12} = \frac{1}{3}$, and since the corresponding sides of similar triangles all have the same ratio). Therefore $y = 9$ and $z = 18$.

$$\frac{1}{3} = \frac{3}{y} \qquad y = 9 \quad \left(\text{since } \frac{1 \times 3}{3 \times 3} = \frac{3}{9}\right)$$
$$\frac{1}{3} = \frac{6}{z} \qquad z = 18 \left(\text{since } \frac{1 \times 6}{3 \times 6} = \frac{6}{18}\right)$$

A CLOSER LOOK AT QUADRILATERALS

Before we discuss quadrilaterals, let's take a look at parallel lines. **Parallel lines** can be defined as two lines in the same plane that never intersect. Similarly, we can call two line segments parallel if they are subsets of parallel lines.

In the following diagram, $\overleftrightarrow{AB}$ is parallel to $\overleftrightarrow{CD}$, so the two lines never intersect. This is written $\overleftrightarrow{AB} \parallel \overleftrightarrow{CD}$, which is read, "Line AB is parallel to line CD."

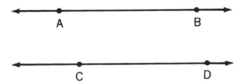

We can also write $\overline{AB} \parallel \overline{CD}$, which is read, "Line segment AB is parallel to line segment CD."

With this in mind, we can now discuss an important class of geometric shapes called quadrilaterals. A **quadrilateral** was defined earlier as a simple closed curve composed of four line segments, none of which lies on the same line. A quadrilateral should not be confused with a *quadrilateral region*, which is defined as a quadrilateral and its interior.

We classified triangles according to angle measure and according to relative length of sides. Quadrilaterals are also classified according to the relations among

their sides and angles. We can name several different kinds of quadrilaterals according to these relations.

■ **Square**: A square is a quadrilateral having four congruent sides and four angles of equal measure. All the angles of a square are right angles—that is, each angle has a measure of 90°. Opposite sides of a square are always parallel.

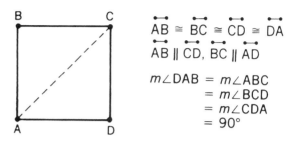

A line segment joining any two opposite vertices of square ABCD divides the square into two right triangles. In fact, a line segment that joins any two non-adjacent vertices of a polygon is called a *diagonal* of the polygon. In square ABCD, we have marked diagonal $\overleftrightarrow{AC}$, forming right triangles ABC and ADC.

■ **Rectangle**: A rectangle is a quadrilateral in which sides opposite each other are both congruent (equal in length) and parallel, and each angle has a measure of 90°.

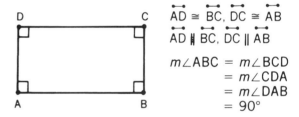

Notice that, since all squares have opposite sides that are congruent and parallel, and since each angle has a measure of 90°, then all squares are also rectangles. However, not all rectangles are squares.

■ **Parallelogram**: A parallelogram is a quadrilateral in which the opposite sides are congruent and parallel. Notice that the parallelogram differs from the rectangle in that the angles of a parallelogram are not necessarily 90°. A parallelogram whose angles are all 90° is also a rectangle. Thus all rectangles are parallelograms, but not all parallelograms are rectangles.

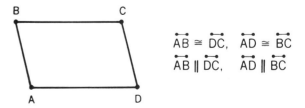

■ **Rhombus**: A rhombus is a quadrilateral in which all four sides are congruent and the opposite sides are parallel. Notice that the rhombus differs from the square in that the angles of a rhombus are not necessarily 90°. A rhombus whose angles are all 90° is a square. Thus all squares are rhombuses, but not all rhombuses are squares. A rhombus is a special kind of parallelogram—a parallelogram in which all four sides are congruent.

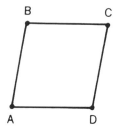

$$\overleftrightarrow{AB} \cong \overleftrightarrow{BC} \cong \overleftrightarrow{CD} \cong \overleftrightarrow{DA}$$

$$\overleftrightarrow{AB} \parallel \overleftrightarrow{DC}$$

$$\overleftrightarrow{AD} \parallel \overleftrightarrow{BC}$$

■ **Trapezoid**: A trapezoid is a quadrilateral in which one and only one pair of sides is parallel. Some mathematics programs change this to read "at least one pair of parallel sides." How does this definition differ from the initial one given?

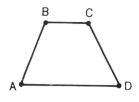 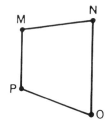

In trapezoid ABCD, $\overleftrightarrow{AD} \parallel \overleftrightarrow{BC}$.
In trapezoid MNOP, $\overleftrightarrow{PM} \parallel \overleftrightarrow{ON}$.

The relations among the various kinds of quadrilaterals can be shown clearly and quickly by means of a diagram. Suppose we consider all quadrilaterals and then name the subsets of this collection of all quadrilaterals.

U = the set of all quadrilaterals
A = the set of all parallelograms
B = the set of all rectangles
C = the set of all rhombuses
D = the set of all squares
E = the set of all trapezoids
F = the set of all other quadrilaterals

Then we can draw the following diagram:

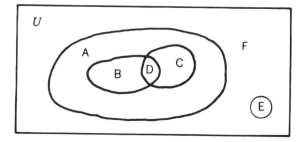

From this diagram we can make a number of observations:

1. All rectangles, rhombuses, and squares are also parallelograms.
2. All squares are both rhombuses of a special type and rectangles of a special type.
3. There are no squares that cannot also be called both rhombuses and rectangles; however, there are rectangles and rhombuses that are not squares.
4. There are rhombuses that are not rectangles.
5. There are rectangles that are not rhombuses.
6. There are no trapezoids that can be called parallelograms, rectangles, rhombuses, or squares.
7. The set of all other quadrilaterals includes all those plane figures formed by four line segments of various lengths.

Understanding the interrelationships of polygons (e.g., that squares are "special" rectangles as well as being "special" rhombuses) involves class inclusion—a characteristic of someone operating at van Hiele's third stage (see Chapter 1). This ability should emerge by the upper elementary grades, but many high school students still lack this ability—possibly due to a lack of emphasis of geometry in their early grades.

A CLOSER LOOK AT CIRCLES

Another important simple closed curve is the circle. A **circle** is not usually thought of as a polygon although some programs refer to it as a polygon with infinitely many sides. A more common definition of a circle is that it is the set of all points in one plane that are an equal distance from a given point, called the *center*. A line segment from the center to any point on the circle is called a **radius** (the plural of radius is *radii*). A line segment extending from any point on the circle to another point on the circle, and passing through the center of the circle, is called a **diameter**. A diameter can therefore be thought of as two radii lying on the same line.

 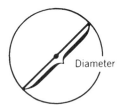

The distance around a circle is called the **circumference** of the circle. Any two points of a circle divide the circle into two parts. Either of these two parts is called an *arc*.

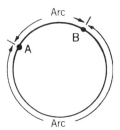

Remember that a circle, like any other geometric shape, is an abstract concept, and the model drawn on paper is merely a representation of a circle. There are three sets of points formed by a circle—the points forming the interior, the points forming the exterior, and the simple closed curve that forms the circle itself.

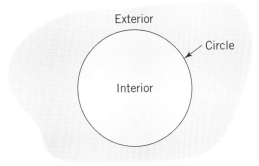

A **circular region** is the simple closed region formed by a circle and its interior—that is, by the points forming a circle *and* the points forming its interior.

There is an important relation between the diameter of a circle and its circumference—the ratio of circumference to diameter is always the same, no matter what size the circle. Children exploring concepts of area need to develop an understanding of this ratio, referred to as **pi**, or π. Often, π is introduced to children as a numerical value that they then mechanically use in a formula to find the circumference and area of a circle without understanding anything of its derivation or meaning. Programs today, however, often introduce the concept of π through experiences that provide children with the opportunity to discover what π represents. We will now describe a simple approach to this topic.

Provide a large circular object, such as a cardboard disk or pie pan, and a ruler. Use the ruler to measure the diameter of the circular object. We can then measure the approximate circumference (the distance around the rim or edge) of the circular object by rolling the circular object through one complete turn and measuring the linear distance traveled. To do this, mark a dot at some point on the circumference, and place this dot on the table at point A. Then roll the circular object until the dot is again on the table, this time at point B. The distance between A and B (just over three full revolutions of the object) approximates the circumference of the object.

Another method would be to use a piece of string to measure around the object. A cloth tape measure would be very helpful in getting accurate measurements. We can compare the diameter with this measured circumference by means of the following ratio: $\frac{\text{circumference}}{\text{diameter}}$. This ratio, expressed as a decimal, should be approximately 3.1. By comparing the circumferences of many circular objects with their diameters, children should draw the

conclusion that π, the ratio of the circumference to the diameter, is "a little more than 3," regardless of the size of the circular object. Children should be encouraged to use the calculator for dividing the circumference by the diameter to avoid clouding the important concept with needlessly tedious paper-and-pencil computations. When students have reached this conclusion, they can then be told that mathematicians have a special symbol for this relationship, the Greek letter π.

Students sometimes wonder what the "exact" value of π is. Mathematicians have proved that π is an irrational number. Thus any fraction or decimal that we may write for π is only an approximation for the actual value of π. Commonly used rational approximations for π are 3.14, 3.1416, and $\frac{22}{7}$. Computers have been able to calculate approximations of π to many millions of decimal places.

AREA, PERIMETER, AND CIRCUMFERENCE MEASUREMENT

Another marriage of geometry and measurement that should be investigated is the concept of area. **Area** gives us a two-dimensional measure of a plane region. Area, like any other measure, is always expressed by a number value and an appropriate unit of measure. The object to be measured is compared with a standard unit measure. An area might be expressed, for example, as 6 square inches (or 6 sq in.). The standard unit of measure in this example is square inches, and the number value is 6, which indicates how many square inches.

The standard units for measuring area are square inches, square feet, square yards, square miles, square meters, square centimeters, and so forth. A square inch, by definition, is that area represented by a square region 1 inch on each side. Similarly, a square centimeter is that area represented by a square region 1 centimeter on each side.

In finding the area of a region we ask, "How many square units are there in the given region?" Children could be asked to place square tiles, such as color tiles, on a shape and count how many tiles it takes to fill the shape. As an example, consider a rectangular region that is 4 units wide and 6 units long. How can we find the area of this region?

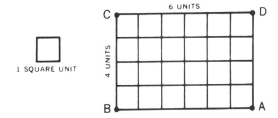

Geoboards can also be useful in exploring area. Since most geoboard pegs split the board into square regions, the children can count the number of squares within a shape. The children can compare their calculated area with the counted area. The two answers should, of course, be the same.

A simple method for determining the area of a rectangular region is to use a ratio. There are 6 square units in one row. This fact can be stated by means of a ratio: $\frac{6}{1}$, or "six square units per row." So, if there are 6 units per row, how many square units are there in 4 rows? This can be expressed as a proportion, using two equivalent ratios.

$$\frac{6}{1} = \frac{\square}{4}$$

The missing numerator is clearly 24.

$$\frac{6 \times 4}{1 \times 4} = \frac{\square}{4}$$
$$\square = 24$$

The denominator of the first ratio is multiplied by 4, so the numerator must also be multiplied by 4. We see that there are 24 square units in the rectangular region. We can verify this fact by counting the number of square units in the region. If the unit is centimeters, then the area is 24 square centimeters; if the unit is inches, then the area is 24 square inches.

To obtain 24 square units, we did not multiply 4 units by 6 units. Instead, we multiplied the number of square units in one row by the number of rows. Thus, 6 square units is multiplied by 4: 4×6 square units = 24 square units.

Consider another region.

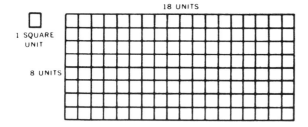

If there are 18 square units in one row, how many square units are there in 8 rows?

$$\frac{18}{1} = \frac{\square}{8}$$
$$\frac{18 \times 8}{1 \times 8} = \frac{\square}{8}$$
$$\square = 144$$

There are 144 square units in 8 rows. Again, we can verify the answer by counting the number of square units in the region.

After children have found the areas of several rectangular regions, they should be able to generalize their findings. The number of units in the length times the number of units in the width gives the number of square units in the area. This fact can be expressed by the following formula:

$$A = \ell \times w$$

In this formula, A stands for area, ℓ stands for length, and w stands for width.

Now, let's use the concepts of area and ratio to determine the area bounded by a parallelogram.

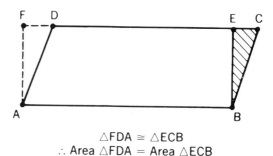

$$\triangle FDA \cong \triangle ECB$$
$$\therefore \text{Area } \triangle FDA = \text{Area } \triangle ECB$$

Cut off the triangular region BEC, and place it on the other end of the parallelogram. The area within the parallelogram ABCD is exactly the same as the area within the rectangle ABEF that is formed. Thus we can determine the area within parallelogram ABCD by determining the area of the rectangular region ABEF.

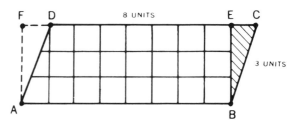

In the rectangular region ABEF, if there are 8 square units in one row, how many units are there in 3 rows?

$$\frac{8}{1} = \frac{\square}{3} \qquad A = \ell \times w$$
$$\frac{8 \times 3}{1 \times 3} = \frac{\square}{3} \qquad A = 8 \times 3$$
$$\square = 24 \qquad A = 24 \text{ square units}$$

The area within the parallelogram is therefore 24 square units.

We can generalize from this last example. If $\overleftrightarrow{AB}$ is called the *base* of the parallelogram (b), and if $\overleftrightarrow{BE}$ is called the *height* of the parallelogram (h), then the number of square units in the area (A) within the parallelogram is indicated by the product of the number of units in the base and the number of units in the height. We can express this fact by means of the following formula:

$$A = b \times h$$

Let's apply these concepts to finding the area of a triangular region.

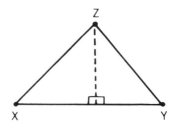

Make a tracing of triangle XYZ, and label it X'Y'Z'. Place $\triangle X'Y'Z'$ next to $\triangle XYZ$, as in the following diagram:

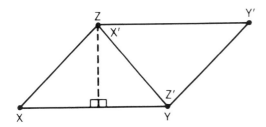

The area of one of the triangular regions is clearly one-half the area within the parallelogram. The formula for the area within the parallelogram is $A = b \times h$. Then the formula for finding the area of a triangle (one-half of a parallelogram) is

$$A = \tfrac{1}{2}(bh)$$

(Notice that this formula has been written without the multiplication symbol "×." This is acceptable notation. The multiplication sign between two factors in a formula can always be omitted, provided the meaning of the expression or sentence remains clear.)

Consider the following triangular region RST, and find its area:

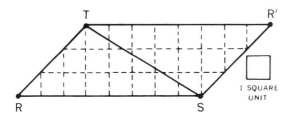

$$
\begin{aligned}
A &= \tfrac{1}{2}bh \\
&= \tfrac{1}{2} \times 8 \times 3 \\
&= \left(\tfrac{1}{2} \times 8\right) \times 3 \\
&= 4 \times 3 \\
&= 12 \text{ square units}
\end{aligned}
$$

The area of the triangular region is 12 square units. These basic principles can also be applied to finding the areas of other triangular regions.

The process of finding the area of a circular region is much more difficult than finding the area of a polygonal region. One method, which will give only an estimate, is to place the circular region on a square grid and count the number of square units covered by the circular region.

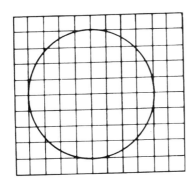

If we count all of the squares that fall completely within the boundary of the circle and compare that number to the number of squares that fall within or cross the boundary, we will have an approximation of the circle's area as between those two numbers. The smaller the square unit, the more accurately the area of the circular region can be estimated.

A second method is to think of the circular region as being made up of many small congruent "triangles," approximated by drawing a large number of radii to form many small regions that are approximately triangular. Notice that the radii must be drawn so that the resulting arcs of the circle are all equal in length if the small "triangular" regions are to be congruent.

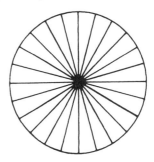

Let's consider this second method of determining the area of a circular region. Examine one of the small regions that has been formed.

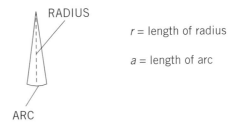

$r = $ length of radius

$a = $ length of arc

We can use the formula $A = \tfrac{1}{2}(ra)$ to find the approximate area of this region. The shape of the region is very nearly triangular, with the arc as a base and the radius as a height. The area within a triangle, remember, is equal to one-half the product of the base and the height. Then, multiplying the area of this region by the total number of regions, we obtain an approximation of the area of the circular region. If we consider each small region a triangle (which is approximately the case), we can state that the area of the circular region (A) is equal to the area within the first triangle $\tfrac{1}{2}(ra_1)$ added to the area within the second triangle $\tfrac{1}{2}(ra_2)$ added to the area within the third triangle $\tfrac{1}{2}(ra_3)$ added to the area within the fourth triangle $\tfrac{1}{2}(ra_4)$, and so on.

$$A = \tfrac{1}{2}(ra_1) + \tfrac{1}{2}(ra_2) + \tfrac{1}{2}(ra_3) + \ldots + \tfrac{1}{2}(ra_n)$$

The term $\tfrac{1}{2}(ra_n)$ represents the area within the last triangle.

The sum of the lengths of the bases of the triangles is approximately equal to $a_1 + a_2 + a_3 + a_4 + \ldots + a_n$, which is the same length as that of the circumference of the circle. So the area within the circle can be expressed by the following equation:

$$A = \frac{1}{2}[r(a_1 + a_2 + a_3 + a_4 + \ldots + a_n)]$$
$$= \frac{1}{2}[r(\text{circumference})]$$

But we know that the circumference of a circle is used to calculate the value of π (pi). The value of π has been defined as the ratio of the circumference to the diameter.

$$\pi = \frac{\text{circumference}}{\text{diameter}}$$

Hence the circumference of a circle is equal to π times its diameter, or 2π times its radius (*r*).

$$\text{circumference} = \pi \times \text{diameter}$$
$$= \pi \times (2 \times \text{radius})$$
$$= 2\pi \times \text{radius}$$
$$= 2\pi r$$

Thus we can calculate the area within a circle to be equal to π times the square of its radius.

$$A = \frac{1}{2}[r(\text{circumference})]$$
$$= \frac{1}{2}[r(2\pi r)]$$
$$= \frac{1}{2} \times 2 \times (\pi \times r \times r)$$
$$= \pi r^2$$

Now, let's use this formula to find the approximate area of a circular region with a radius of 10 units.

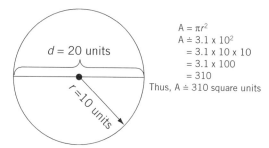

$$A = \pi r^2$$
$$A \doteq 3.1 \times 10^2$$
$$= 3.1 \times 10 \times 10$$
$$= 3.1 \times 100$$
$$= 310$$
Thus, $A \doteq 310$ square units

The area of a circular region with a radius of 10 units is approximately 310 square units. Now determine the approximate circumference of the same circular region.

$$C = \pi \times d$$
$$= 3.1 \times 20$$
$$= 62 \text{ linear units}$$

The circumference is approximately 62 linear units.

The sum of the measures of the line segments that form a polygon is called the **perimeter** (*P*) of the polygon. We can determine the perimeter of a polygon, such as the following scalene triangle, by adding the lengths of the sides.

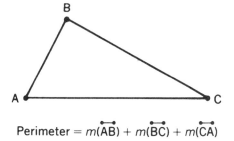

Perimeter $= m(\overleftrightarrow{AB}) + m(\overleftrightarrow{BC}) + m(\overleftrightarrow{CA})$

The length of each side can be approximated by direct measurement with a ruler. The measure of a side can be expressed in symbols. For example, $m(\overrightarrow{AB})$ is read "the measure of the segment AB."

The perimeter of an equilateral triangle is equal to three times the measure of one side, since the three sides are all congruent (equal in measure).

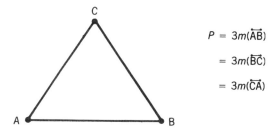

$$P = 3m(\overrightarrow{AB})$$
$$= 3m(\overrightarrow{BC})$$
$$= 3m(\overrightarrow{CA})$$

We can express this fact in symbols by writing $P = 3s$, where *s* stands for any of the three sides.

The perimeter of a square is equal to four times the measure of one side, since all four sides are congruent.

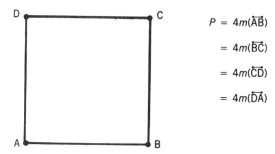

$$P = 4m(\overrightarrow{AB})$$
$$= 4m(\overrightarrow{BC})$$
$$= 4m(\overrightarrow{CD})$$
$$= 4m(\overrightarrow{DA})$$

This fact can also be expressed in symbols as $P = 4s$, where *s* stands for the length of any of the four sides.

The perimeter of a rectangle is equal to twice the measure of one of the sides representing the length added to twice the measure of one of the sides representing the width. Let ℓ equal the measure of the length and *w* equal the measure of the width.

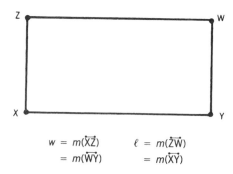

$w = m(\overrightarrow{XZ})$ $\ell = m(\overrightarrow{ZW})$
$= m(\overrightarrow{WY})$ $= m(\overrightarrow{XY})$

The perimeter, then, can be determined according to the following formula:

$$P = 2\ell + 2w$$

Note, however, that the formula is not as important as the concept. Children that wish to simply add the lengths of the sides to determine the perimeter should not be criticized.

DEFINING POLYHEDRA

So far, in our discussion of geometry we have considered only shapes lying entirely in one plane. Now, we will examine shapes in three dimensions. Three-dimensional shapes, sometimes called *spatial shapes*, are geometric shapes that do not lie entirely in one plane. Since the environment in which we live is three-dimensional, children are more likely to be familiar with representations of three-dimensional shapes than they are with representations of plane shapes. Just as sheets of paper and chalkboards can be used to represent planes, so can shoe boxes, rooms, skyscrapers, silos, and basketballs be used to represent various kinds of three-dimensional shapes.

The most effective introductory approach to the topic of three-dimensional shapes is to lead children to become even more aware of familiar physical shapes around them and to associate these physical shapes with the geometric shapes that they suggest. For example, it is quite likely that the children are in a classroom with a floor, a ceiling, and four walls and that one pair of opposite walls is longer than the other pair. A room like this represents a particular kind of geometric three-dimensional shape.

Early in our study of plane shapes, we defined what is meant by a simple closed curve. Let's begin our study of three-dimensional shapes by defining a simple closed surface. A *simple closed curve*, we remember, consists of the points in a plane that divide the plane into three sets of points—the points forming the simple closed curve itself, the points forming the interior of the curve, and the points forming the exterior of the curve.

Analogously, a **simple closed surface** consists of the points in space that divide space into three sets of points—the points forming the simple closed surface itself, the points forming the interior of the three-dimensional shape, and the points forming the exterior of the three-dimensional shape. For example:

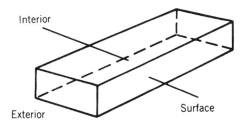

When discussing plane regions, we defined the union of a simple closed curve and its interior as a *plane region*. In spatial geometry, we define the union of a simple closed surface and its interior as a three-dimensional region or **space region**.

If we examine the walls of a room, we see that the intersection of two walls can be thought of as representing a line segment. If we think of the two walls as representing or determining planes (remember that planes extend endlessly, without bounds), the intersection of these two planes is clearly a line. We can generalize by noting that the intersection of any two planes is always a line, as shown in the following diagram:

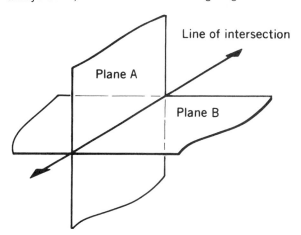

But planes do not always intersect. If we examine the opposite walls of most rooms, we see that they do not meet and would not meet if the walls were extended indefinitely. If we consider the planes that the two walls can be thought of as representing, we see that the planes do not intersect. Two planes that have no intersection (that never intersect) are called **parallel planes**.

We are now prepared to consider a very important kind of simple closed surface, the prism. A **prism** can be defined as a simple closed surface formed by two congruent polygonal regions in parallel planes and three or more quadrilateral regions joining the two congruent polygonal regions so as to enclose the space between them completely. The following diagram illustrates one kind of prism.

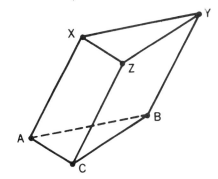

The triangular regions ABC and XYZ are the two congruent polygonal regions in parallel planes; AXZC, CZYB, and BYXA are the quadrilateral regions joining triangular regions ABC and XYZ and enclosing completely the space between them.

The two congruent parallel polygonal regions are called the *bases* of the prism. In the prism pictured above, the triangular regions ABC and XYZ are the bases. The quadrilateral regions of a prism that join the two bases are called *lateral faces* or *sides*. In this prism the quadrilateral regions AXZC, CZYB, and BYXA are the faces. All of the polygonal regions that form the prism (the lateral faces and the two bases) are called the *faces*. The line segment formed by the intersection of two sides (faces) is called an *edge*. Each point where three edges (or three faces) intersect is called a *vertex* (the plural of vertex is *vertices*). The preceding prism above has five faces (ABC, AXZC, CZYB, BYXA, and XYZ), nine edges ($\overrightarrow{AB}$, $\overrightarrow{BC}$, $\overrightarrow{CA}$, $\overrightarrow{XZ}$, $\overrightarrow{YZ}$, $\overrightarrow{XY}$, $\overrightarrow{AX}$, $\overrightarrow{BY}$, and $\overrightarrow{CZ}$), and six vertices (points A, B, C, X, Y, and Z).

Many different kinds of three-dimensional shapes can be classified as prisms, and each is named according to the polygonal regions forming the bases. The accompanying table shows some of the principal types of prisms.

NAME OF PRISM	POLYGONAL REGIONS FORMING THE BASES	NUMBER OF FACES	NUMBER OF EDGES	NUMBER OF VERTICES
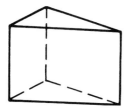 TRIANGULAR PRISM	TRIANGULAR REGIONS	5	9	6
QUADRILATERAL PRISM	QUADRILATERAL REGIONS	6	12	8
HEXAGONAL PRISM	HEXAGONAL REGIONS	8	18	12

You may be interested in examining the columns displaying the number of faces (*f*), edges (*e*), and vertices (*v*) to see if you can find a relationship between these values. Leonhard Euler, a Swiss mathematician of the eighteenth century, derived a now-famous formula expressing this relationship:

$$f + v = e + 2$$

Many prisms are shaped so that if we could imagine setting them horizontally on one of their bases, their sides and the edges joining the two bases would be perpendicular to the bases. (Because all the lateral edges of a prism are parallel, we need to know only that one of the lateral edges is perpendicular to the bases.) Such prisms are called **right prisms**. The prisms pictured in the preceding table and in the following shape are right prisms.

Other prisms are shaped so that if they are placed horizontally on one of their bases, their sides and the edges joining the bases are not all perpendicular to the bases.

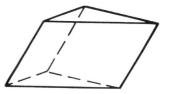

These prisms are not right prisms. The prisms we examine in this chapter are all right prisms.

A quadrilateral prism with rectangular bases is called a **rectangular prism**. The following diagram pictures a rectangular prism:

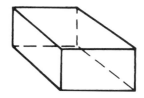

Like any other quadrilateral prism, it has six sides, twelve edges, and eight vertices. A rectangular prism that is also a right prism is referred to as a **right rectangular prism**. Children often refer to this shape as a box. The use of informal language should not be discouraged, but students in the upper elementary grades should begin to encounter and use more sophisticated terminology and vocabulary when discussing geometry.

Let's look at a particular kind of right rectangular prism. The sides of this particular prism are all congruent square regions, and all the edges of the prism are congruent. This three-dimensional shape is called a **cube**—a quadrilateral prism in which the six faces are all congruent square regions. The following diagram shows a cube:

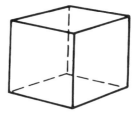

Just as area is an important measurement concept in two-dimensional geometry, an important measurement concept in spatial geometry is that of volume. **Volume** is a measure of the space occupied by a space region. The volume of an object is named by a numeral and an appropriate unit name—for example, 3 cubic feet or 4 cubic centimeters. Notice that the unit name is "cubic" feet or centimeters. We always use cubic units in measuring volume—cubic inches, cubic feet, cubic centimeters, and so on. What does "cubic feet" mean? Consider a cube whose edges are each 1 foot long.

(Remember that the edges of a cube are all congruent, or equal in length.) The measure of the space enclosed by such a cube is defined as 1 cubic foot. We can define cubic inches or any other unit of volume in a similar way. What does "cubic centimeters" mean? A cube whose edges are each 1 centimeter in length is called a *cubic centimeter*. The unit cube from a set of base ten blocks or Cuisenaire rods is a cubic centimeter.

Now, let's examine the following right rectangular prism:

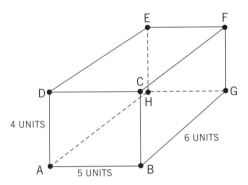

Let's see how we can determine the volume of this rectangular prism. To do this, we must determine how many cubic units can be fitted into the prism. How many cubic units can be placed end-to-end along the edge $\overrightarrow{AB}$?

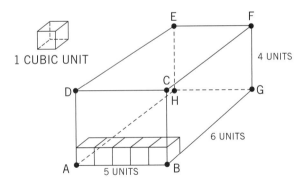

Five cubic units can be placed end-to-end along edge AB. How many cubic units can we place end-to-end along edge $\overrightarrow{BG}$?

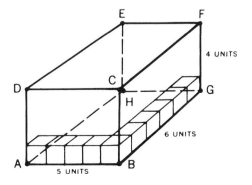

The answer is 6. How many cubic units can be placed on the lower base, rectangle ABGH? If there are 5 cubic units in one row, how many are there in 6 rows?

$$\frac{5}{1} = \frac{\Box}{6}$$

$$\frac{5 \times 6}{1 \times 6} = \frac{\Box}{6}$$

$$\Box = 30$$

Thus, 30 cubic units can be placed on the lower base.

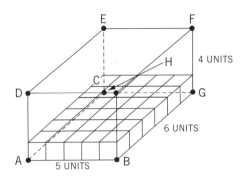

Since the prism is 4 units high, it can hold 4 layers of these cubic units. If there are 30 cubic units in 1 layer, 4 layers contain 120 (or 4×30) cubic units.

After solving a number of similar exercises involving right rectangular prisms, both concretely with cubes and boxes and pictorially as shown here, children should be able to make a generalization about finding the volume of such spatial shapes. Their generalization might be written as a formula. The volume, V, within a right rectangular prism is equal to the number of cubic units that can be placed along the length of the prism, ℓ, times the number of cubic units that can be placed along the width, w, times the number of cubic units that can be placed along the height, h.

$$V = \ell \times w \times h$$
$$\text{or}$$
$$V = \ell wh$$

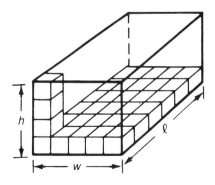

Using this formula, find the volume of a right rectangular prism 6 units wide, 15 units long, and 7 units high.

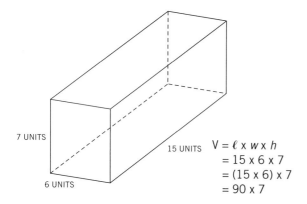

$V = \ell \times w \times h$
$= 15 \times 6 \times 7$
$= (15 \times 6) \times 7$
$= 90 \times 7$

The volume of this prism is 630 cubic units.

The following formula is another way of expressing the volume within a right rectangular prism:

$$V = b \times h$$
or
$$V = bh$$

Using this formula, the volume, V, of a right rectangular prism is equal to the number of cubic units that can be placed on one of the bases, b, times the number of cubic units that can be placed along the height, h.

This formula is equivalent to the first formula, $V = \ell wh$, since the number of cubic units that can be placed on one of the bases of the prism (b) is determined by the product of the number of cubic units that can be placed along the length of the prism (ℓ) and the number of cubic units that can be placed along the width (w). In the formula $V = \ell \times w \times h$, we simply replace $\ell \times w$ with its equivalent, b, to obtain:

$$V = \ell \times w \times h$$
or
$$V = b \times h$$

An advantage of the formula $V = bh$ is that it is valid for any right prism. It is not restricted to right rectangular prisms as is the other formula. For example, consider the following right triangular prism:

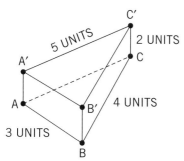

We know that the area of one of the bases (triangular region ABC or triangular region A'B'C') is 6 square units. (Triangles ABC and A'B'C' are right triangles, so the area of the triangular region ABC or A'B'C' is one-half the product of its legs: $\frac{1}{2} \times 3 \times 4$, or 6.) Therefore, we can fit 6 cubic units on one of the bases of the prism. But there are 2 layers of these cubic units because the

height of the prism is 2 units. Consequently, 6×2, or 12, cubic units can be placed in the prism, so the volume of the right triangular prism is 12 cubic units. The same result can be obtained by using our second formula.

$$V = bh$$
$$= \left(\frac{1}{2} \times 3 \times 4\right) \times 2$$
$$= 6 \times 2$$
$$= 12 \text{ cubic units}$$

In a similar manner we can determine the volume within any right prism.

A **pyramid** is a simple closed surface formed by a simple closed region, a point not in the plane of the region, and triangular regions joining the simple closed region and the point outside the region, completely enclosing the space between them. In the pyramid shown here, ABCD is the simple closed region, E is the point not in the plane of ABCD, and the triangular regions joining ABCD and point E are ABE, BCE, CDE, and DAE.

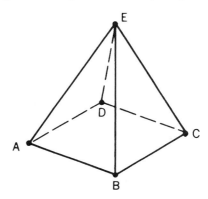

The simple closed region ABCD is called the *base* of the pyramid, and the triangular regions ABE, BCE, CDE, and DAE are called *lateral faces*. The naming of the parts of a pyramid is consistent with that of prisms. In the diagram of the pyramid, the plane regions ABCD, ABE, BCE, CDE, and DAE are the *faces*; $\overrightarrow{AB}$, $\overrightarrow{BC}$, $\overrightarrow{CD}$, $\overrightarrow{DA}$, $\overrightarrow{AE}$, $\overrightarrow{BE}$, $\overrightarrow{CE}$, and $\overrightarrow{DE}$ are the *edges*; and points A, B, C, D, and E are the *vertices*.

Pyramids are classified and named according to the polygonal region forming the base. For example, a quadrilateral pyramid whose base is formed by a rectangular region is called a *rectangular pyramid*. In the following diagram, the quadrilateral region WXYZ (the base) is rectangular; thus the three-dimensional shape represented is a rectangular pyramid. A rectangular pyramid, like any other quadrilateral pyramid, has five faces, eight edges, and five vertices.

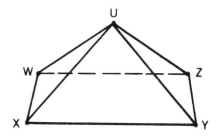

The accompanying table shows some of the principal kinds of pyramids. (Note that Euler's formula, faces + vertices = edges + 2, mentioned earlier in this chapter, also applies to pyramids.)

NAME OF PYRAMID	POLYGONAL REGION FORMING BASE	NUMBER OF FACES	NUMBER OF EDGES	NUMBER OF VERTICES
TRIANGULAR PYRAMID	TRIANGULAR REGION	4	6	4
QUADRILATERAL PYRAMID	QUADRILATERAL REGION	5	8	5
HEXAGONAL PYRAMID	HEXAGONAL REGION	7	12	7

Another simple closed surface that children have often seen is the cylinder. A **cylinder** is a simple closed surface formed by two congruent simple closed regions (not polygonal regions) in parallel planes and one or more surfaces (at least one of which is curved) formed by the union of the line segments that join corresponding points of the curves that bound the two congruent regions. The following drawings illustrate various kinds of cylinders:

The simple closed regions at the ends of a cylinder are called the *bases* of the cylinder. The surface or surfaces that join the two bases are called the *lateral faces*. The bases and lateral faces of a cylinder are illustrated in the following drawing:

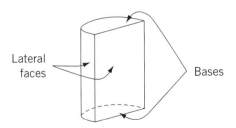

Lateral faces   Bases

A few of the shapes that the bases of a cylinder might have are indicated in the following diagram:

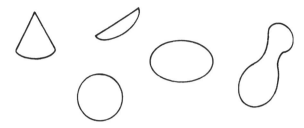

If the bases are polygonal regions, the simple closed surface is a prism rather than a cylinder. (Remember that a polygon is a simple closed curve formed by the union of line segments and that a polygonal region is formed by the union of a polygon and its interior.) If a simple closed surface is a prism, the edges of its two bases are all line segments; but if a simple closed surface is a cylinder, the sides of its bases are not all line segments. This is the essential difference between a prism and a cylinder.

If the line segment joining the centers of the bases of a cylinder is perpendicular to the bases, then the cylinder is a **right cylinder**. A cylinder whose bases are circular regions is called a **circular cylinder**. Elementary school children often refer to this shape informally as a can.

In a **right circular cylinder**, the line segment joining the centers of the bases is perpendicular to both bases and parallel to the sides of the cylinder.

A cone is another three-dimensional shape that is familiar to most children. A **cone** is a simple closed surface having a base, a vertex, and one or more lateral faces joining the base and the vertex. The following drawings illustrate various kinds of cones:

The *base* of a cone is a simple closed nonpolygonal plane region. The *vertex* is a point not in the plane of the base. The *lateral face* or *faces* consist of all those line segments joining the vertex and the simple closed curve bounding the base. The base, vertex, and lateral faces of a cone are illustrated in the following drawing:

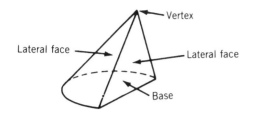

Some of the shapes that the base of a cone might have are indicated in the following drawings:

If a polygonal region forms the base, the simple closed surface is a pyramid rather than a cone. If a simple closed surface is a pyramid, the edges of the base are all line segments; if a simple closed surface is a cone, the edges of the base are not all line segments. This is the essential difference between a pyramid and a cone.

A cone whose base is a circular region is referred to as a **circular cone**. If the line segment joining the center of the base with the vertex of the cone is perpendicular to the base, then the circular cone is called a **right circular cone**.

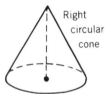
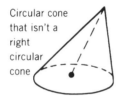

Another simple closed surface that is familiar to all children is the sphere. Young children have all played with balls or other toys that have suggested spheres, and they are therefore familiar with physical representations, or models, of spheres. A **sphere** is a simple closed surface and is the set of all points in space that are the same distance from a given point, called the *center*. A sphere divides space into three sets of points—the points forming the sphere itself, the points forming the interior of the sphere, and the points forming the exterior of the sphere.

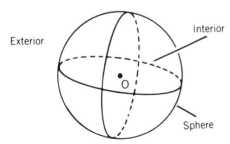

Any line that passes through the interior of a sphere intersects the sphere at two points. In the following diagram, A and B represent the points of intersection of a sphere with a line passing through the center, O, of the sphere:

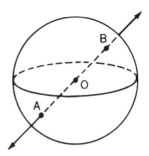

A line segment that passes through the center of a sphere and whose end points are points on the sphere is called a *diameter* of the sphere. Hence, $\overleftrightarrow{AB}$ is a diameter of the preceding sphere. A line segment whose end points are a point on a sphere and the center of the sphere is called a *radius* of the sphere. In the preceding sphere, $\overleftrightarrow{OA}$ and $\overleftrightarrow{OB}$ are radii.

Another important aspect of the measure of three-dimensional shapes is the concept of surface area. The *surface area* of a simple closed surface is the total area of the surfaces that form the shape. Consider the following right rectangular prism:

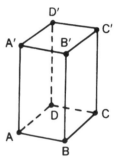

Imagine a physical model of this prism. If we cut the model along edges AA', A'B', B'C', C'D', AB, BC, and CD and flattened it out, it would look something like this:

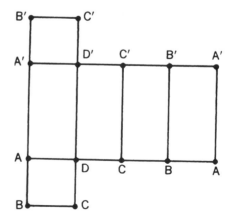

(Perhaps you should model this with an empty cracker box.) We can see now that the surface area of a prism is the sum of the areas of all of the sides—in this case, the sum of the areas of the two congruent bases added to the areas of the four lateral faces.

Children need to have experiences that help them see the meaning of surface area. This is more important than memorizing a formula. Nevertheless, how can we derive a formula that could be used to calculate the total surface area? Every prism has two congruent bases, so the surface area must contain the area of one base multiplied by 2 ($2b$, where b stands for the area of a base). It must also contain the area of the lateral faces. In the preceding right rectangular prism, the area of the lateral faces is calculated as follows:

$$\text{area} = (AB \times AA') + (BC \times BB')$$
$$+ (CD \times CC') + (DA \times DD')$$

In this formula we use AB, AA', BC, and so on, as abbreviations for the longer notation $m(\overset{\bullet}{AB})$, $m(\overset{\bullet}{AA'})$, $m(\overset{\bullet}{BC})$, and so on. Since the prism is a right prism, we know that $AA' = BB' = CC' = DD' = h$, so area $= (AB \times h) + (BC \times h) + (CD \times h) + (DA \times h)$. By applying the distributive property, we can state:

$$\text{area} = (AB + BC + CD + DA) \times h$$

Then, since (AB + BC + CD + DA) is equal to the perimeter of a base of the prism:

$$\text{area} = \text{perimeter of a base} \times \text{height of the prism}$$
$$= Ph$$

Since we are looking for the total surface area of the prism, we must include the area of the two bases as well as the area of the four vertical sides. Thus:

$$\text{area} = \text{area of two bases} + \text{area of four sides}$$
$$= 2 \times (AB \times BC) + Ph$$
$$= 2b + Ph$$

Now, let's calculate the surface area of the following right rectangular prism, in which rectangular regions ABCD and A'B'C'D' are the bases. (Can you see why we don't need to label the lengths of all of the sides?)

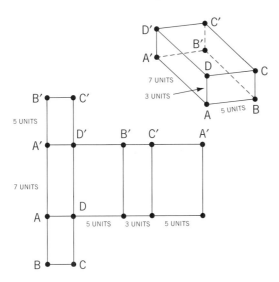

surface area = (2 × area of a base)
$$+ (\text{perimeter of a base} \times \text{height})$$
$$= 2b + Ph$$
$$= [2 \times (3 \times 5)] + [(3 + 5 + 3 + 5) \times 7]$$
$$= [2 \times 15] + [16 \times 7]$$
$$= 30 + 112$$
$$= 142$$

The surface area is 142 square units.

We can use this same method to determine a formula for finding the surface area of a right triangular prism. Imagine cutting and flattening a physical model of the following right triangular prism:

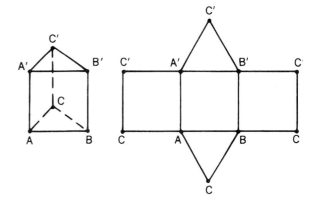

The surface area of this three-dimensional shape must contain the areas of the two bases—the area of the triangular region ABC plus the area of the triangular region A'B'C' (ABC is congruent to A'B'C')—which can be represented by $2b$, where b stands for the area of either of the two bases. It must also contain the area of the lateral faces, which are rectangular regions.

$$\text{area} = (AB \times AA') + (BC \times BB') + (CA \times CC')$$

Since $AA' = BB' = CC' = h$, we can write

$$\text{area} = (AB \times h) + (BC \times h) + (CA \times h)$$
$$= (AB + BC + CA) \times h$$

Since the perimeter (P) of the base is equal to AB + BC + CA, we can write

$$\text{area} = Ph$$

Therefore:

$$\text{surface area} = (2 \times \text{area of a base}) + (\text{perimeter}$$
$$\text{of a base} \times \text{height})$$
$$= 2b + Ph$$

We can generalize from this by noting that the surface area (SA) of any right triangular prism is equal to the sum of the areas of its two bases ($2b$) and the product of the perimeter of one of the bases and the height of the prism (Ph).

$$SA = 2b + Ph$$

Let's use this formula to find the surface area of the following right triangular prism:

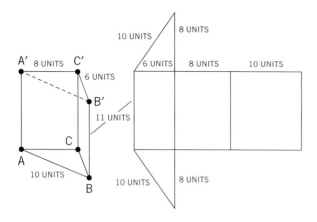

$$SA = 2b + Ph$$
$$= [2 \times (\tfrac{1}{2} \times 6 \times 8)] + [(6 + 8 + 10) \times 11]$$
$$= [2 \times 24] + [24 \times 11]$$
$$= 48 + 264$$
$$= 312$$

The surface area is 312 square units.

CLOSURE

Young children need ample opportunity to play with blocks that are cubes, rectangular prisms, pyramids, cones, and spheres. Older children need experiences cutting paper models and pasting them together to make solid three-dimensional shapes. Use clear plastic for the faces of three-dimensional shapes and use a strong glue to fasten Velcro (which can be purchased at a fabric store) along the edges. The pieces then may easily be put together and taken apart. For example, make six equivalent square regions out of clear plastic, and glue Velcro around each edge as follows:

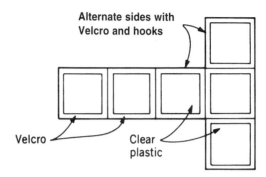

Now fold the square regions into a cube. An interesting variation would be to arrange the six pieces on a table-top in a number of different ways that would each yield a cube if folded into a three-dimensional shape. (By making faces of different shapes you should be able to collect enough pieces to model a wide variety of prisms and pyramids.)

Geometry provides an opportunity to explore a different view of mathematics that aids in the development of a spatial sense. Through knowledge of geometry, we can solve problems from other topics in mathematics and from other fields, even within such disciplines as art and physical education. To gain full advantage and transfer of knowledge, be certain to integrate geometry into other curricular areas.

Terminology, Symbols, and Procedures

Area. Area is a measure that expresses the size of a plane region in some surface measuring unit, usually square units.

Circle. A circle is the set of all points in a plane that are a given (equal) distance from a given point in the plane. The given point is called the *center* of the circle and is not part of the circle.

Circular Region. A circular region is the union of a circle and its interior.

Circumference. The circumference of a circle is the distance from a point on the circle along an arc, in either a clockwise or a counterclockwise direction, back to the starting point.

Cone. A cone is a simple closed surface formed by a simple closed region (not a polygon), a point that is not in the plane of this region (the *vertex*), and one or more surfaces (at least one of which is curved) formed by the union of those line segments that join the vertex to the curve that bounds the simple closed region. The simple closed region is called the *base* of the cone. The surface or surfaces that join the base with the vertex are called *lateral faces*.

   Circular Cone. A cone with a circular region forming its base is called a circular cone.

   Right Circular Cone. If the line segment joining the center of the base with the vertex of the cone is perpendicular to the base, the cone is called a right circular cone.

Cube. A cube is a right rectangular prism whose faces are all congruent square regions. By definition, all the edges of a cube are congruent.

Cylinder. A cylinder is a simple closed surface formed by two congruent simple closed regions in parallel planes (not polygonal regions) and one or more surfaces (at least one of which is curved) formed by the union of the line segments that join corresponding points of the curves that bound the two congruent regions. The simple closed regions at the ends of a cylinder are called the *bases* of the cylinder. The surface or surfaces that join the two bases are called *lateral faces*.

Circular Cylinder. A cylinder with circular regions forming its bases is a circular cylinder.

Right Circular Cylinder. If the line segment joining the centers of the bases of a circular cylinder is perpendicular to the bases, then the cylinder is a right circular cylinder.

Right Cylinder. If the line segment joining the centers of the bases of a cylinder is perpendicular to the bases, then the cylinder is a right cylinder.

Diameter. A line segment extending from one point on a circle to another point on the circle and passing through the center is called a diameter.

Formula for Finding the Volume of Any Right Prism. The volume (V) of a right prism is equal to the area of one of its bases (AREA b) times its height (h).

$$V = (\text{AREA } b)h$$

Formula for Finding the Volume of a Right Rectangular Prism. The volume (V) of a right rectangular prism is equal to its length (ℓ) times its width (w) times its height (h).

$$V = \ell \times w \times h \quad \text{or} \quad V = \ell wh$$

Hexagon. A polygon with six sides.

Image of a Point with Respect to a Line. If ℓ is any line, then the image of a point P that is not in ℓ is the unique point P' such that ℓ bisects $\overleftrightarrow{PP'}$ and $\ell \perp \overleftrightarrow{PP'}$. If P is a point on ℓ, then we say that P is its own image.

Irregular Polygon. A polygon with incongruent sides or angles that are not equal in measure.

Line of Symmetry. A shape is symmetric with respect to a line ℓ if for any point P of the shape not on ℓ there is a corresponding point P' on the shape such that ℓ bisects $\overleftrightarrow{PP'}$ and ℓ is perpendicular to $\overleftrightarrow{PP'}$.

Octagon. A polygon with eight sides.

Parallel Lines. Parallel lines are lines in the same plane that never intersect.

Parallel Planes. Two planes that have no common points are called parallel planes.

Pentagon. A polygon with five sides.

Perimeter. The sum of the measures of the line segments that form a polygon is called the perimeter of the polygon.

Pi (π). The ratio of the circumference of a circle to its diameter is called pi (π). Pi is an irrational number. Some rational-number approximate values commonly used to represent π are 3.1, 3.14, and $\frac{22}{7}$.

Polygon. A polygon is a simple closed curve formed by the union of three or more line segments (*sides*). If the sides of a polygon are all equal (congruent) and if the angles suggested are all equal in measure, the polygon is called a *regular polygon*.

Prism. A prism is a simple closed surface formed by two congruent polygonal regions in parallel planes and quadrilateral regions joining the two congruent polygonal regions, completely enclosing the space between them.

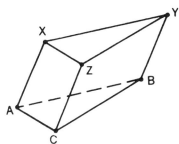

The polygonal regions of the prism pictured (ABC and XYZ) are called the *bases* of the prism. The quadrilateral regions (ABYX, BCZY, and CAXZ) that join together the two bases are called *lateral faces*, or *sides*. The faces of a prism are the polygonal regions that form the prism (ABC, XYZ, ABYX, BCZY, and CAXZ). A line segment formed by the intersection of two sides ($\overline{AB}$, $\overline{BC}$, $\overline{CA}$, $\overline{XY}$, $\overline{YZ}$, $\overline{ZX}$, $\overline{AX}$, $\overline{BY}$, and $\overline{CZ}$) is called an *edge*. The point formed by the intersection of three edges or by the intersection of three faces is called a *vertex* (plural, *vertices*). The vertices in this prism are A, B, C, X, Y, and Z. Prisms are classified according to the polygonal regions that form the bases. For example, if a prism has rectangular regions forming its two bases, it is called a rectangular prism.

Right Prism. If a prism is shaped so that the edges joining the two bases are perpendicular to the bases, then the prism is a right prism.

Right Rectangular Prism. A rectangular prism that is also a right prism is a right rectangular prism.

Pyramid. A pyramid is a simple closed surface formed by a simple closed region, a point (vertex) not in the plane of the region, and triangular regions joining the simple closed region and the vertex, completely enclosing the space between them.

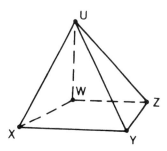

The simple closed region (WXYZ) is called the *base* of the pyramid. The triangular regions (WXU, XYU, YZU, and ZWU) that join the base with the point U not in the plane of the base are called *lateral faces*. The faces of the pyramid are the polygonal regions that form the prism (WXYZ, WXU, XYU, YZU, and ZWU). A line segment formed by the intersection of two faces ($\overline{WX}$, $\overline{XY}$, $\overline{YZ}$, $\overline{ZW}$, $\overline{UW}$, $\overline{UX}$, $\overline{UY}$, and $\overline{ZY}$) is called an *edge*. A point formed by the intersection of three or more edges, or by the intersection of three or more faces, is a *vertex* of the pyramid (U, W, X, Y, and Z). Pyramids are classified according to the polygonal region forming the base. For example, if a pyramid has a rectangular region forming its base, it is called a *rectangular pyramid*.

Pythagorean Theorem. The Pythagorean theorem states that in a right triangle, the square of the measure of the hypotenuse is equal to the sum of the squares of the measures of the other two sides.

Quadrilateral. A quadrilateral is a polygon with four sides, formed by a simple closed curve of four line segments.

Parallelogram. A quadrilateral with opposite sides that are congruent and parallel is called a parallelogram.

Rectangle. A quadrilateral that has four right angles and opposite sides that are congruent is called a rectangle.

Rhombus. A quadrilateral with all four sides congruent is called a rhombus.

Square. A quadrilateral that has four right angles and four congruent sides is called a square.

Trapezoid. A quadrilateral with exactly two parallel sides is called a trapezoid.

Radius. A line segment extending from the center of a circle to any point on the circle itself is called a radius (plural, *radii*).

Radius of a Sphere. A line segment whose end points are a point on a sphere and the center of the sphere is called a radius (plural, *radii*) of the sphere.

Simple Closed Surface. A simple closed surface is a set of points in space that divides space into three sets of points—the points forming the simple closed surface itself, the points forming the interior of the three-dimensional shape, and the points forming the exterior of the three-dimensional shape.

Space Region. The union of a simple closed surface and its interior is called a space region.

Sphere. A sphere is a simple closed surface consisting of all points in space that are the same distance from a given point, called the *center*. A sphere divides space into three sets of points—the points forming the sphere itself, the points forming the interior of the sphere, and the points forming the exterior of the sphere.

Triangle. A triangle is a polygon with three sides, formed by a simple closed curve of three line segments.

Acute Triangle. If all three of the angles of a triangle are acute angles, the triangle is an acute triangle.

Congruent Triangles. Triangles whose corresponding sides and angles are congruent are congruent triangles.

Equiangular Triangle. If the three angles of a triangle are all equal in measure, the triangle is an equiangular triangle.

Equilateral Triangle. If all three sides of a triangle are congruent, the triangle is an equilateral triangle.

Isosceles Triangle. If at least two sides of a triangle are congruent, the triangle is an isosceles triangle.

Obtuse Triangle. If one of the three angles of a triangle is an obtuse angle, the triangle is an obtuse triangle.

Right Triangle. If one of the angles of a triangle is a right angle, the triangle is a right triangle.

Scalene Triangle. If no two sides of a triangle are congruent, the triangle is a scalene triangle.

Similar Triangles. Triangles whose corresponding angles are congruent but whose corresponding sides are not necessarily congruent are similar triangles.

Volume. Volume is a measure of the space occupied by a three-dimensional region. Volume is measured in cubic units—for example, cubic inches. One cubic inch of space is the amount of space enclosed by a cube having edges 1 inch long.

Practice Exercises for Teachers

These exercises are designed for the reader of this book. While some are suitable for use in the elementary classroom, these examples should not necessarily be given to children in this form. Ideas for classroom activities on the concepts and ideas discussed in this chapter can be found in Part 2 of *Today's Mathematics*, the Student Resource Book.

1. Classify each of the following triangular regions according to its sides. Classify each according to its angles. Then, determine its area and perimeter.

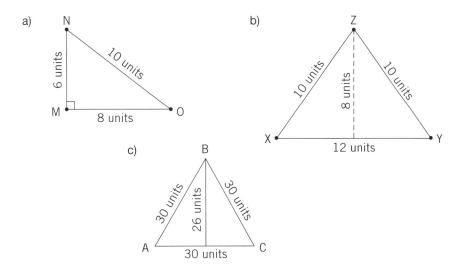

2. Use your knowledge of the area of a parallelogram to develop a formula for the area of a trapezoid. Use b_1 for the length of the lower base, b_2 for the length of the upper base (the bases are the parallel sides), and h for the height of the trapezoid.

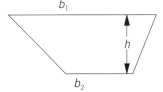

3. Classify each of the following quadrilaterals; then determine its area and perimeter.

a)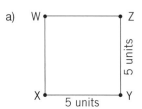

b)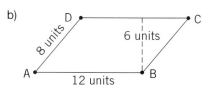

c)

d)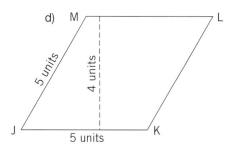

e)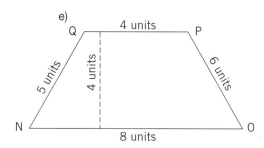

4. Construct a polygon congruent to each of the following shapes.

a)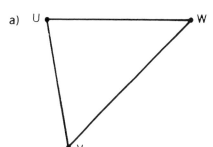

b)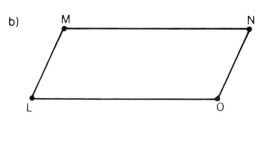

5. Determine the area and circumference of each of the following circles.

a)

b)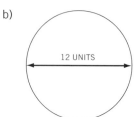

6. Use the Pythagorean theorem to determine the measure of the indicated side in each of the following shapes.

   a) Find the measure of side *a*.

   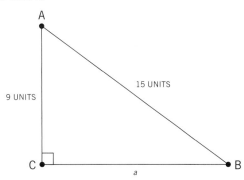

   b) Find the measure of side *b*.

   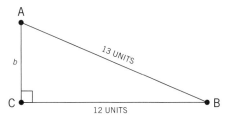

   c) Find the measure of side *c*.

   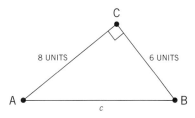

7. The measures of two angles of a triangle are 63° and 46°. What is the measure of the third angle?

8. Identify each of the following space regions, and list the bases, edges, and vertices for each region.

   a)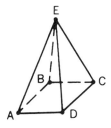

   c)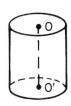

   b)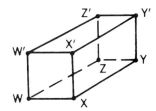

   d)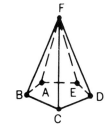

9. Find the volume of each of the following space regions.

a)

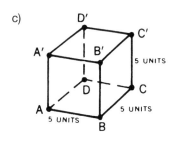

b)

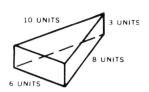

c)

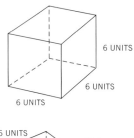

10. Calculate the surface area (*SA*) of each of the following space regions.

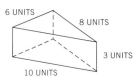

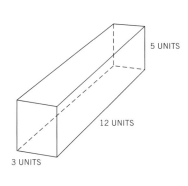

(The bases are right triangles.)

11. For each of the following descriptions listed, match the geometric three-dimensional shape or shapes.

   a) The formula for the volume of   Sphere
      this three-dimensional shape is $V = bh$.
   b) A three-dimensional shape with all points   Pyramid
      equally distant from a single point
   c) A three-dimensional shape whose lateral   Prism
      faces are rectangles
   d) A three-dimensional shape with four faces   Cone
   e) A three-dimensional shape whose lateral
      faces are triangles   Cylinder

12. If each of the regions found below and on page 337 were cut along the outer boundary and folded together, what three-dimensional shape could it make?

a)

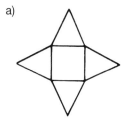

b)

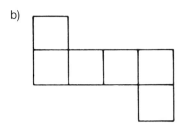

c) 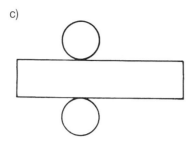   d)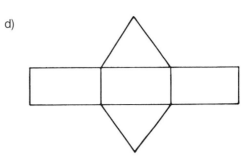

13. Complete the following table.

Space Figure	Area of Base	Height	Volume
Cylinder	42 sq in.	10 in.	
Cube			125 cu cm
Triangular prism	37 sq in.		518 cu in.
Cylinder	24 sq m	50 dm	
Rectangular prism	27 sq mm		243 cu mm
Square prism	6 sq ft	18 in.	

Teaching Competencies and Self-Assessment Tasks

1. Go on a shape scavenger hunt around your neighborhood! Find different examples of distinctly different polygons and polyhedrons, make sketches, and sort the shapes in more than one way.

2. Keep a tally of triangular shapes that you see in your surroundings during a given day. Which types of triangles are more prevalent than others? Why?

3. Explain what we mean when we say that all linear measurements are approximate.

4. Describe a number of real-life applications of the Pythagorean theorem that children can explore. Be sure to include examples involving both indirect and direct measurement, as discussed in Chapter 15.

5. Raid your kitchen! Locate a number of products that are packaged in prisms, cylinders, and other spatial shapes. Check your local grocery store for other polyhedra.

6. Discuss the role of formulas in a geometry program. Should formulas be memorized? Should formulas be developed or should they be presented as fact to children?

7. Locate and discuss the recommendations for teaching geometry in elementary school as reported in the *Principles and Standards for School Mathematics* published by the National Council of Teachers of Mathematics. Include a discussion of the degree of emphasis that should be placed on geometry in an elementary mathematics program.

Related Readings and Teacher Resources

For related readings on topics found in this chapter, see the corresponding chapter in Part 2 of *Today's Mathematics*, the Student Resource Book.

Chapter 18

A Look Back as You Move Ahead

Overview

This chapter might have used "∞," the infinity symbol, as a chapter identifier. In this context, it would represent the process of continuing professional development that every dedicated teacher recognizes as essential. This "final chapter" is actually located in Part 2 of this text. It is undoubtedly a chapter that will prove to be an invaluable resource both during and after this course and that will serve you well in your efforts to become an effective teacher.

In this chapter, we examine FOUR EXTREMELY USEFUL RESOURCES for any teacher:

■ a COMPREHENSIVE GRADE-LEVEL DISCUSSION of the elementary and middle school mathematics curriculum

■ a HIERARCHICALLY ARRANGED CHECKLIST OF MATHEMATICAL CONCEPT CLUSTERS to help you identify prerequisite knowledge, skills, and processes

■ a thorough set of THEMATIC MATHEMATICS ACTIVITIES that show the application of the NCTM *Principles and Standards for School Mathematics* to the zoo, to the grocery store, to health, to transportation, and to geography.

This special chapter closes with

■ a CLASSROOM VIGNETTE SUPPORTING THE NCTM STANDARDS OF CURRICULUM, TEACHING, AND ASSESSMENT illustrating the vision of teaching mathematics supported by this text.

The completion of this text and this course is not a finish line—it is a starting line. The process of becoming a teacher is lifelong and, consequently, professional development is a part of the job that cannot be ignored. As you set out on this journey, it is to your advantage to familiarize yourself with any and all resources that may help you become a master teacher. We sincerely believe that *Today's Mathematics* is such a resource for you now and in the future. We hope you feel the same.

It is our sincere wish that *Today's Mathematics* will assist YOU with tomorrow's challenges!

Appendix

Answers to Practice Exercises, Chapters 5-17

Chapter 5: Problem Solving, Decision Making, and Communicating in Mathematics

1. You may desire to use more precision than we have. To the nearest half inch, the box would measure $1\frac{1}{2}$ in. by $5\frac{1}{2}$ in. by 8 in. The volume would be 66 cu. in.

2. There are two distinct rectangles that meet the criteria: a rectangle 4 by 4 and a rectangle 3 by 6. Units are immaterial.

3. There are ten distinct arrangements.

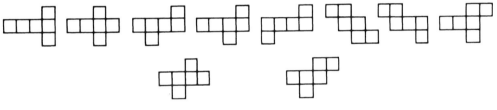

4. a) False statement   b) True statement   c) True statement
   d) Open sentence   e) Open sentence   f) False statement
   g) Open sentence   h) False statement   i) True statement
   j) Not a sentence   k) Open sentence   l) Not a sentence

5. a) $59 + 14 = \square$ b) $42 + 13 = \square$ c) $2 \times \square = 234$ d) $130 - 20 = \square$

6. a) $\square = 14$ b) $\square = 11$ c) $\square = 4$ d) $\square = 7$
   e) $\square = 7$ f) $\square = 6$ g) $\square = 0$ h) $\square = 4$

7. $\square + (\square + 3) = 29$ Lila is age 13 and Mike is age 16.

8. Mary is 9 years of age, Tammy is 2 years of age, and Kelly, as given in the problem, is 27 years of age.

9. a) Multiplication   b) Addition
   c) Subtraction   d) Division

10. a) $32 \times .25 = \square$ b) $72 \div 29 = \square$ c) $1.00 - .87 = \square$

11. a) Compound, disjunction   b) Simple   c) Compound, conditional
    d) Compound, conjunction   e) Simple   f) Simple

12. a) T   b) T   c) F   d) T   e) F
    f) F   g) F   h) T   i) T   j) F

13. a) Ray is a good student and John is a good student.
    b) I tried the car and it wouldn't start.
    c) If you try, then you will succeed.
    d) Judy will call before noon or Susan will call before noon.

14. a) Some   b) Some   c) All
    d) All   e) Some   f) None

15. a) F   b) T   c) F   d) T   e) F
    f) T   g) F   h) F   i) T   j) F

16. a) You can conclude that Figure C has four sides.
    b) You can conclude that Jeff does not do his schoolwork.
    c) You can conclude that we might go on a picnic.
    d) You can conclude that we will shovel the sidewalk.

17. a) Promise not broken   b) Promise broken
    c) Promise not broken   d) Promise not broken

Chapter 6: Number Sense, Numeration, and Place Value

1. a) Concrete   b) Semiabstract   c) Semiconcrete
   d) Concrete   e) Semiabstract   f) Abstract

2. Group of seven   X   X   X   X   X   X   X
              ↕   ↕   ↕   ↕   ↕   ↕   ↕
   Group of nine   X   X   X   X   X   X   X   X   X

3.

4. a) 4 red rods = 1 brown rod   b) 7 white rods = 1 black rod
   c) 3 light green rods = 1 blue rod   d) $3\frac{1}{2}$ red rods = 1 black rod
   e) 5 red rods = 1 orange rod

5. a) 4 hundreds, 42 tens, 423 ones   b) 0 hundreds, 7 tens, 79 ones
   c) 3 hundreds, 38 tens, 382 ones   d) 13 hundreds, 136 tens, 1365 ones
   e) 0 hundreds, 3 tens, 37 ones   f) 9 hundreds, 96 tens, 963 ones

6. 7 is the digit in the tens place, but there are 57 tens in 578.

7. 4 is the digit in the hundreds place, but there are 24 hundreds in 2481.

8. 6 is the digit in the ones place, but there are 386 ones in 386.

9. a) 7 pieces will be necessary: 2 flats, 1 long, 4 cubes.
   b) 21 pieces will be necessary: 2 blocks, 4 flats, 9 longs, 6 cubes.
   c) 9 pieces will be necessary: 6 longs, 3 cubes.
   d) 14 pieces will be necessary: 5 flats, 6 longs, 3 cubes.
   e) 11 pieces will be necessary: 7 flats, 3 longs, 1 cube.
   f) 24 pieces will be necessary: 3 blocks, 8 flats, 6 longs, 7 cubes.

10. Answers may vary. Some possible responses include:
    Base ten has ten symbols.
    Each place to the left is ten times greater than the place to its immediate right.
    There is a symbol for the empty set.
    There is a decimal point used as a reference point to locate the different places.

11. a) 1 hundred, 9 tens, 7 ones; $(1 \times 10^2) + (9 \times 10^1) + (7 \times 10^0)$; $100 + 90 + 7$
    b) 2 thousands, 4 hundreds, 9 tens, 6 ones; $(2 \times 10^3) + (4 \times 10^2) + (9 \times 10^1) + (6 \times 10^0)$;
       $2000 + 400 + 90 + 6$
    c) 6 tens, 3 ones; $(6 \times 10^1) + (3 \times 10^0)$; $60 + 3$

12. 1 flat, 23 cubes
    1 flat, 2 longs, 3 cubes
    1 flat, 1 long, 13 cubes
    12 longs, 3 cubes
    11 longs, 13 cubes

10 longs, 23 cubes
9 longs, 33 cubes
8 longs, 43 cubes
7 longs, 53 cubes
6 longs, 63 cubes
5 longs, 73 cubes
4 longs, 83 cubes
3 longs, 93 cubes
2 longs, 103 cubes
1 long, 113 cubes
123 cubes

13. a) 235   b) 27   c) 4271   d) 1279   e) 134,958   f) 35   g) 2849

14. a) three-five, base eight
    b) eight-seven, base nine
    c) four-zero, base five
    d) four-three-two, base ten (432 in base ten could also be read "four hundred thirty-two.")

Remember that number names such as "twenty," "thirteen," and "forty-five" are all base ten names for numbers and cannot be used when discussing bases other than ten. This is why names such as "three-five" are used in other bases.

15. "One hundred twenty-five, base twelve" might be misunderstood as an abbreviated way of saying "one hundred twenty-five in base twelve," which would mean the base twelve numeral for 125. "One hundred twenty-five" is so closely connected to our base ten system that it would be misleading to use it in naming numerals in other systems.

16. a) 26_{eight} b) IT_{twelve} c) 10110_{two} d) 42_{five} e) 24_{nine} f) 112_{four}

17. a) Sixteen different symbols   b) Answers will vary.

A set of symbols could be:

Symbol	Value	Symbol	Value
0	0		
1	1	E	11
2	2	T	12
3	3	N	13
4	4	F	14
5	5	f	15
6	6	10	16
7	7	11	17
8	8	12	18
9	9	13	19
t	10	14	20

18. In base ten, each place value to the left has a value ten times as great as the value of the place to its immediate right. Each place to the right has a value of one-tenth of the place to its immediate left. In this example we are comparing 40 with 800. $\frac{40}{800}$ can be simplified to $\frac{1}{20}$. So, the 4 represents a value that is $\frac{1}{20}$ of the value of the 8 in 9843.

19. Base two

2^4	2^3	2^2	2^1	2^0
16	8	4	2	1

Base three

3^4	3^3	3^2	3^1	3^0
81	27	9	3	1

Base four

4^4	4^3	4^2	4^1	4^0
256	64	16	4	1

Base five	5^4	5^3	5^2	5^1	5^0
	625	125	25	5	1

Base six	6^4	6^3	6^2	6^1	6^0
	1296	216	36	6	1

Base seven	7^4	7^3	7^2	7^1	7^0
	2401	343	49	7	1

Base eight	8^4	8^3	8^2	8^1	8^0
	4096	512	64	8	1

Base nine	9^4	9^3	9^2	9^1	9^0
	6561	729	81	9	1

Base twelve	12^4	12^3	12^2	12^1	12^0
	20736	1728	144	12	1

20. b^9, b^8, b^7, b^6, b^5, b^4, b^3, b^2, b^1, b^0

21. a) 22_{nine}, 23_{nine}, 24_{nine}, 25_{nine}, 26_{nine}
    b) 20_{five}, 21_{five}, 22_{five}, 23_{five}, 24_{five}
    c) 110_{two}, 111_{two}, 1000_{two}, 1001_{two}, 1010_{two}
    d) $E0_{twelve}$, $E1_{twelve}$, $E2_{twelve}$, $E3_{twelve}$, $E4_{twelve}$
    e) 1006_{seven}, 1010_{seven}, 1011_{seven}, 1012_{seven}, 1013_{seven}
    f) 536_{eight}, 537_{eight}, 540_{eight}, 541_{eight}, 542_{eight}
    g) 1100_{nine}, 1101_{nine}, 1102_{nine}, 1103_{nine}, 1104_{nine}
    h) 1220_{three}, 1221_{three}, 1222_{three}, 2000_{three}, 2001_{three}
    i) 300_{four}, 301_{four}, 302_{four}, 303_{four}, 310_{four}

22.

Standard Notation	Expanded Notation	Exponential Notation
101101_{two}	$(1 \times 100000)_{two} + (1 \times 1000)_{two}$ $+ (1 \times 100)_{two} + (1 \times 1)_{two}$	$(1 \times 10^5)_{two} + (1 \times 10^3)_{two}$ $+ (1 \times 10^2)_{two} + (1 \times 10^0)_{two}$
1234_{five}	$(1 \times 1000)_{five} + (2 \times 100)_{five}$ $+ (3 \times 10)_{five} + (4 \times 1)_{five}$	$(1 \times 10^3)_{five} + (2 \times 10^2)_{five}$ $+ (3 \times 10^1)_{five} + (4 \times 10^0)_{five}$
3765_{eight}	$(3 \times 1000)_{eight} + (7 \times 100)_{eight}$ $+ (6 \times 10)_{eight} + (5 \times 1)_{eight}$	$(3 \times 10^3)_{eight} + (7 \times 10^2)_{eight}$ $+ (6 \times 10^1)_{eight} + (5 \times 10^0)_{eight}$
212_{three}	$(2 \times 100)_{three} + (1 \times 10)_{three}$ $+ (2 \times 1)_{three}$	$(2 \times 10^2)_{three} + (1 \times 10^1)_{three}$ $+ (2 \times 10^0)_{three}$
6045_{seven}	$(6 \times 1000)_{seven} + (4 \times 10)_{seven}$ $+ (5 \times 1)_{seven}$	$(6 \times 10^3)_{seven} + (4 \times 10^1)_{seven}$ $+ (5 \times 10^0)_{seven}$
5214_{six}	$(5 \times 1000)_{six} + (2 \times 100)_{six}$ $+ (1 \times 10)_{six} + (4 \times 1)_{six}$	$(5 \times 10^3)_{six} + (2 \times 10^2)_{six}$ $+ (1 \times 10^1)_{six} + (4 \times 10^0)_{six}$
212_{four}	$(2 \times 100)_{four} + (1 \times 10)_{four}$ $+ (2 \times 1)_{four}$	$(2 \times 10^2)_{four} + (1 \times 10^1)_{four}$ $+ (2 \times 10^0)_{four}$
$12TE_{twelve}$	$(1 \times 1000)_{twelve} + (2 \times 100)_{twelve}$ $+ (T \times 10)_{twelve} + (E \times 1)_{twelve}$	$(1 \times 10^3)_{twelve} + (2 \times 10^2)_{twelve}$ $+ (T \times 10^1)_{twelve} + (E \times 10^0)_{twelve}$
8640_{nine}	$(8 \times 1000)_{nine} + (6 \times 100)_{nine}$ $+ (4 \times 10)_{nine}$	$(8 \times 10^3)_{nine} + (6 \times 10^2)_{nine}$ $+ (4 \times 10^1)_{nine}$

23.

Base Ten	Base Nine	Base Eight	Base Seven	Base Six	Base Five	Base Four	Base Three	Base Two
1	1	1	1	1	1	1	1	1
2	2	2	2	2	2	2	2	10
3	3	3	3	3	3	3	10	11
4	4	4	4	4	4	10	11	100
5	5	5	5	5	10	11	12	101
6	6	6	6	10	11	12	20	110
7	7	7	10	11	12	13	21	111
8	8	10	11	12	13	20	22	1000
9	10	11	12	13	14	21	100	1001
10	11	12	13	14	20	22	101	1010
11	12	13	14	15	21	23	102	1011
12	13	14	15	20	22	30	110	1100
13	14	15	16	21	23	31	111	1101
14	15	16	20	22	24	32	112	1110
15	16	17	21	23	30	33	120	1111
16	17	20	22	24	31	100	121	10000
17	18	21	23	25	32	101	122	10001
18	20	22	24	30	33	102	200	10010
19	21	23	25	31	34	103	201	10011
20	22	24	26	32	40	110	202	10100
21	23	25	30	33	41	111	210	10101
22	24	26	31	34	42	112	211	10110
23	25	27	32	35	43	113	212	10111
24	26	30	33	40	44	120	220	11000
25	27	31	34	41	100	121	221	11001

24. a) place-value   b) base
    c) 1   d) standard notation, expanded notation, exponential notation
    e) digits

25. a) Three thousand, three
    b) Six hundred six thousand, sixty
    c) Seven hundred seven thousand, seven hundred
    d) Three hundred forty-five million, seven hundred sixty-eight thousand, two hundred thirty-one
    e) One trillion, one billion, one million, one thousand, one
    f) Twenty-one million, four hundred seventy-eight thousand

26. Each place in the base nine numeral occupies two places in the base three numeral. Each digit in the base nine numeral is then connected to its respective base three representation, thus providing the quick conversion.

Chapter 7: Addition and Subtraction of Whole Numbers

1.
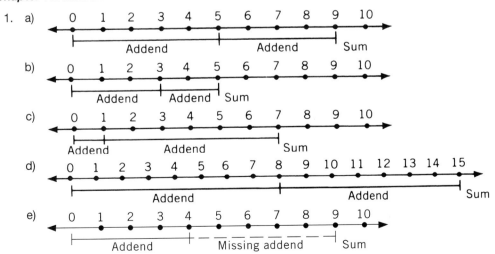

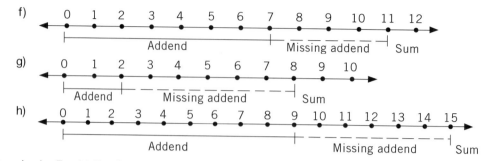

2. a) 4 + 7 = 11, 7 + 4 = 11, 11 − 4 = 7, 11 − 7 = 4
    b) 2 + 7 = 9, 7 + 2 = 9, 9 − 7 = 2, 9 − 2 = 7
    c) 6 + 7 = 13, 7 + 6 = 13, 13 − 7 = 6, 13 − 6 = 7
    d) 31 + 44 = 75, 44 + 31 = 75, 75 − 44 = 31, 75 − 31 = 44

3. a) □ − 9 = 8, □ − 8 = 9   b) □ − 4 = 9, □ − 9 = 4
    c) □ − 53 = 39, □ − 39 = 53   d) □ − 7 = 6, □ − 6 = 7

4. a) 8 + 1 = 9, 1 + 3 = 4, 10 + 30 = 40   b) 6 + 1 = 7, 2 + 3 = 5, 20 + 30 = 50
    c) 3 + 5 = 8, 7 + 1 = 8, 70 + 10 = 80   d) 2 + 5 = 7, 5 + 4 = 9, 50 + 40 = 90

5. a)   1 tens 8 ones
           +4 tens 1 one
            5 tens 9 ones = 59

    b)   2 hundreds 4 tens 7 ones
           +5 hundreds 3 tens 2 ones
            7 hundreds 7 tens 9 ones = 779

    c)   7 tens 3 ones
           +2 tens 5 ones
            9 tens 8 ones = 98

    d)   3 hundreds 6 tens 4 ones
           +2 hundreds 1 tens 3 ones
            5 hundreds 7 tens 7 ones = 577

6. There are several different methods for recording the steps. Your method may be different from the one shown.

    a)   37 = 3 tens   7 ones
           +49 = +4 tens   9 ones
                  7 tens 16 ones
                  7 tens (1 ten 6 ones)
                  (7 tens 1 ten) 6 ones
                  8 tens 6 ones = 86

    b)   61 =   6 tens 1 ones
           +54 = + 5 tens 4 ones
                  11 tens 5 ones
                   1 hundred 1 ten 5 ones = 115

    c)   73 =   7 tens   3 ones
           +88 = + 8 tens   8 ones
                  15 tens 11 ones
                  15 tens (1 ten 1 one)
                  (15 tens 1 ten) 1 one
                  16 tens 1 one
                   1 hundred 6 tens 1 one = 161

    d)   219 = 2 hundreds 1 tens   9 ones
           +466 = +4 hundreds 6 tens   6 ones
                   6 hundreds 7 tens 15 ones
                   6 hundreds 7 tens (1 ten 5 ones)
                   6 hundreds (7 tens 1 ten) 5 ones
                   6 hundreds 8 tens 5 ones = 685

e) $\quad$ 378 = $\quad$ 3 hundreds 7 tens 8 ones
$\quad$ +154 = +1 hundreds 5 tens 4 ones
$\qquad\qquad$ 4 hundreds 12 tens 12 ones
$\qquad\qquad$ 4 hundreds 12 tens (1 ten 2 ones)
$\qquad\qquad$ 4 hundreds (12 tens 1 ten) 2 ones
$\qquad\qquad$ 4 hundreds (13 tens) 2 ones
$\qquad\qquad$ 4 hundreds (1 hundred 3 tens) 2 ones
$\qquad\qquad$ (4 hundreds 1 hundred) 3 tens 2 ones
$\qquad\qquad$ 5 hundreds 3 tens 2 ones = 532

f) $\quad$ 56 = 5 tens 6 ones = 4 tens 16 ones
$\quad$ −29 = −2 tens 9 ones = −2 tens 9 ones
$\qquad\qquad\qquad\qquad\qquad\quad$ 2 tens 7 ones = 27

g) $\quad$ 346 = 3 hundreds 4 tens 6 ones = 2 hundreds 14 tens 6 ones
$\quad$ − 83 = −$\qquad\qquad$ 8 tens 3 ones = −$\qquad\qquad$ 8 tens 3 ones
$\qquad\qquad\qquad\qquad\qquad\qquad$ 2 hundreds 6 tens 3 ones = 263

h) $\quad$ 459 = 4 hundreds 5 tens 9 ones = 3 hundreds 15 tens 9 ones
$\quad$ −272 = −2 hundreds 7 tens 2 ones = −2 hundreds 7 tens 2 ones
$\qquad\qquad\qquad\qquad\qquad\qquad$ 1 hundreds 8 tens 7 ones = 187

i) $\quad$ 521 = 5 hundreds 2 tens 1 ones = 4 hundreds 11 tens 11 ones
$\quad$ −146 = −1 hundred 4 tens 6 ones = −1 hundred $\quad$ 4 tens 6 ones
$\qquad\qquad\qquad\qquad\qquad\qquad$ 3 hundreds 7 tens 5 ones = 375

j) $\quad$ 832 = 8 hundreds 3 tens 2 ones = 7 hundreds 12 tens 12 ones
$\quad$ −398 = −3 hundreds 9 tens 8 ones = −3 hundreds 9 tens 8 ones
$\qquad\qquad\qquad\qquad\qquad\qquad$ 4 hundreds 3 tens 4 ones = 434

7. a) $\quad$ 37 + 28 = (30 + 7) + (20 + 8) $\qquad$ Renaming
$\qquad\qquad\qquad$ = 30 + (7 + 20) + 8 $\qquad\quad$ Associative property
$\qquad\qquad\qquad$ = 30 + (20 + 7) + 8 $\qquad\quad$ Commutative property
$\qquad\qquad\qquad$ = (30 + 20) + (7 + 8) $\qquad$ Associative property
$\qquad\qquad\qquad$ = 50 + 15 $\qquad\qquad\qquad\quad$ Addition
$\qquad\qquad\qquad$ = 50 + (10 + 5) $\qquad\qquad$ Renaming
$\qquad\qquad\qquad$ = (50 + 10) + 5 $\qquad\qquad$ Associative property
$\qquad\qquad\qquad$ = 60 + 5 $\qquad\qquad\qquad\quad$ Addition
$\qquad\qquad\qquad$ = 65 $\qquad\qquad\qquad\qquad$ Renaming

$\quad$ b) $\quad$ 276 + 49 = (200 + 70 + 6) + (40 + 9) $\qquad$ Renaming
$\qquad\qquad\qquad$ = 200 + 70 + (6 + 40) + 9 $\qquad\quad$ Associative property
$\qquad\qquad\qquad$ = 200 + 70 + (40 + 6) + 9 $\qquad\quad$ Commutative property
$\qquad\qquad\qquad$ = 200 + (70 + 40) + (6 + 9) $\qquad$ Associative property
$\qquad\qquad\qquad$ = 200 + 110 + 15 $\qquad\qquad\qquad$ Addition
$\qquad\qquad\qquad$ = 200 + (100 + 10) + (10 + 5) $\quad$ Renaming
$\qquad\qquad\qquad$ = (200 + 100) + (10 + 10) + 5 $\quad$ Associative property
$\qquad\qquad\qquad$ = 300 + 20 + 5 $\qquad\qquad\qquad$ Addition
$\qquad\qquad\qquad$ = 325 $\qquad\qquad\qquad\qquad\quad$ Renaming

$\quad$ c) $\quad$ 48 + 75 = (40 + 8) + (70 + 5) $\qquad$ Renaming
$\qquad\qquad\qquad$ = 40 + (8 + 70) + 5 $\qquad\quad$ Associative property
$\qquad\qquad\qquad$ = 40 + (70 + 8) + 5 $\qquad\quad$ Commutative property
$\qquad\qquad\qquad$ = (40 + 70) + (8 + 5) $\qquad$ Associative property
$\qquad\qquad\qquad$ = 110 + 13 $\qquad\qquad\qquad\quad$ Addition
$\qquad\qquad\qquad$ = (100 + 10) + (10 + 3) $\qquad$ Renaming
$\qquad\qquad\qquad$ = 100 + (10 + 10) + 3 $\qquad$ Associative property
$\qquad\qquad\qquad$ = 100 + 20 + 3 $\qquad\qquad\quad$ Addition
$\qquad\qquad\qquad$ = 123 $\qquad\qquad\qquad\qquad$ Renaming

8. a) $\quad$ 500 = 50 tens 0 ones = 49 tens 10 ones
$\quad$ −273 = −27 tens 3 ones = −27 tens 3 ones
$\qquad\qquad\qquad\qquad\qquad\quad$ 22 tens 7 ones = 227

b) $802 = \;$ 80 tens 2 ones $= \;$ 79 tens 12 ones
$\underline{-367} = \underline{-36 \text{ tens 7 ones}} = \underline{-36 \text{ tens } \;\; 7 \text{ ones}}$
  43 tens   5 ones $= 435$

c) $900 = \;$ 90 tens 0 ones $= \;$ 89 tens 10 ones
$\underline{-258} = \underline{-25 \text{ tens 8 ones}} = \underline{-25 \text{ tens } \;\; 8 \text{ ones}}$
  64 tens 2 ones $= 642$

9. Addend + Addend = Sum   Sum = Addend + Addend
   Sum − Addend = Addend   Addend = Sum − Addend

10. The take-away situation can be illustrated by setting up a single collection of objects representing 54 and then literally taking away 18 from this collection to leave 36. The comparison situation can be illustrated by setting up two collections, one with 54 objects and the other with 18 objects, and then comparing the two collections on a one-to-one basis, showing that the larger set has 36 more (or the smaller has 36 less). The missing addend model can be illustrated by setting up one collection of the lesser amount (18) and then answering the question of how many more you need to get the larger amount (54) by adding onto the collection of 18.

Chapter 8: Multiplication and Division of Whole Numbers

1. a)

Three groups of 4 triangles equals twelve triangles; thus $3 \times 4 = 12$.

b) • • • •   Three rows of 4 dots
    • • • •   is 12 dots; thus
    • • • • $3 \times 4 = 12$

c) 0 1 2 3 4 5 6 7 8 9 10 11 12

Three segments of 4 units each equals 12 units; thus $3 \times 4 = 12$.

d)
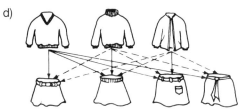

The set of ordered pairs of 3 sweaters and 4 skirts equals 12 outfits; thus $3 \times 4 = 12$.

2. a) • •   b) • • • • • •   c) • • •   d) • • •
      • •   • • • • • •   • • •   • • •
      • •   • • • • • •   • • •
      • •   • • •
                                                   • • •

   e) $4 + 4 + 4 = 12$

3. The array on the left is a 3-by-6 array, and the one on the right is a 6-by-3 array.

Since both arrays contain 18 objects, we can see that $3 \times 6 = 6 \times 3$.

4. a) $5 \times 4 = 20$ b) $3 \times 7 = 21$ c) $3 \times 12 = 36$

5.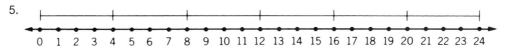

6. $\begin{array}{r} 5 \\ + 5 \\ \hline 10 \\ + 5 \\ \hline 15 \\ + 5 \\ \hline 20 \end{array}$ Four 5s are added to make 20.

7. a) $3 \times 7 = 21$ b) $4 \times 8 = 32$
   $21 \div 3 = 7$ or $21 \div 7 = 3$ $32 \div 4 = 8$ or $32 \div 8 = 4$

8. a)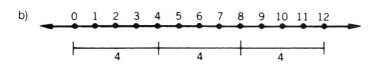
   There are 6 groups of 3 in 18.

   b)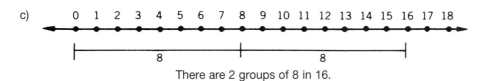
   There are 3 groups of 4 in 12.

   c)
   There are 2 groups of 8 in 16.

   d)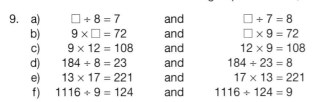
   There are 3 groups of 3 in 11, with 2 left over.

9. a) $\square \div 8 = 7$ and $\square \div 7 = 8$
   b) $9 \times \square = 72$ and $\square \times 9 = 72$
   c) $9 \times 12 = 108$ and $12 \times 9 = 108$
   d) $184 \div 8 = 23$ and $184 \div 23 = 8$
   e) $13 \times 17 = 221$ and $17 \times 13 = 221$
   f) $1116 \div 9 = 124$ and $1116 \div 124 = 9$

10.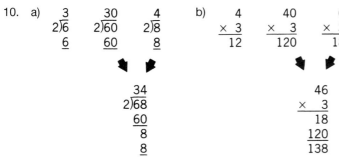

11. a) $6 \times 97 = 6 \times (100 - 3) = (6 \times 100) - (6 \times 3) = 600 - 18 = 582$
    b) $7 \times 48 = 7 \times (50 - 2) = (7 \times 50) - (7 \times 2) = 350 - 14 = 336$
    c) $4 \times 98 = 4 \times (100 - 2) = (4 \times 100) - (4 \times 2) = 400 - 8 = 392$
    d) $3 \times 1998 = 3 \times (2000 - 2) = (3 \times 2000) - (3 \times 2) = 6000 - 6 = 5994$

12. $48 - 6 = 42$, $42 - 6 = 36$, $36 - 6 = 30$, $30 - 6 = 24$, $24 - 6 = 18$, $18 - 6 = 12$, $12 - 6 = 6$, $6 - 6 = 0$

6 has been subtracted from 48 eight times; thus $48 \div 6 = 8$

13.

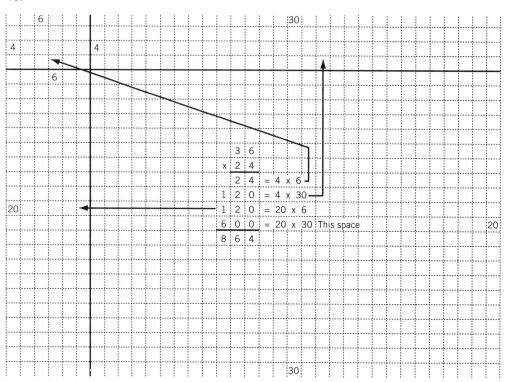

14.

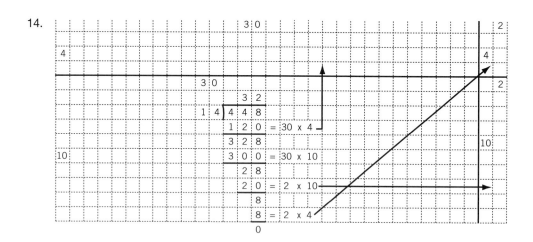

Chapter 9: Number Theory and Number Systems

1. a) 1, 2, 4, 8   b) 1, 17
    c) 1, 2, 3, 4, 6, 8, 12, 24   d) 1, 2, 4, 5, 10, 20, 25, 50, 100
    e) 1, 2, 5, 10

2. a) 1×12, 2×6, 3×4, 12×1, 6×2, 4×3
    b) 1×27, 3×9, 27×1, 9×3
    c) 1×48, 2×24, 3×16, 4×12, 6×8, 48×1, 24×2, 16×3, 12×4, 8×6
    d) 1×100, 2×50, 4×25, 5×20, 10×10, 100×1, 50×2, 25×4, 20×5
    e) 1×10, 2×5, 10×1, 5×2

3. Your answers should show the following kinds of rectangular arrays.
   a) 9-by-1, 3-by-3, and 1-by-9　　　　　　　b) 1-by-11, and 11-by-1
   c) 1-by-10, 2-by-5, 5-by-2, and 10-by-1　　d) 1-by-4, 2-by-2, and 4-by-1

4. a) 2　　b) 2, 7　　c) 2, 3　　d) 2, 5　　e) 41

5. a) $2 \times 2 \times 7$　　b) $2 \times 3 \times 13$　　c) 2×19　　d) $2 \times 2 \times 23$　　e) $2 \times 5 \times 11$

6. a) Divisible by 3　　　　　　b) Divisible by 3　　c) Divisible by 3 and 5
   d) Divisible by 2 and 3 and 5　　e) Divisible by 2

7. 5 and 7, 11 and 13, 17 and 19, 29 and 31, 41 and 43, 59 and 61, 71 and 73

8. a) 6　　b) 42　　c) 10　　d) 4

9. a) $2 \times 2 \times 3 \times 3 \times 5 = 180$　　b) $2^2 \times 3 \times 5 \times 7 = 420$
   c) $2 \times 2 \times 2 \times 7 = 56$　　d) $3 \times 3 \times 5 = 45$

10. Composite. Yes. The conjecture that the data were suggesting was first formulated by Goldbach in 1742. He hypothesized that all even numbers greater than 2 can be written as the sum of a pair of prime numbers.

11. 1, 13, 169. Any number that can be expressed as a prime number squared has exactly three divisors: 1, the number itself, and its positive square root.

12. $28 = 1 + 2 + 4 + 7 + 14$

13.

Number System	Subsets
Counting numbers	Counting numbers
Whole numbers	Counting numbers, whole numbers
Rational numbers	Integers, whole numbers, counting numbers, rational numbers
Irrational numbers	Irrational numbers
Real numbers	Rational numbers, irrational numbers, integers, whole numbers, counting numbers, real numbers
Integers	Whole numbers, counting numbers, integers

14. a) $^-2$　　b) $^+3$　　c) 0　　d) $\frac{^+1}{4}$　　e) $\frac{^+2}{3}$　　f) $^-217$
    g) $^+43$　　h) $^+47$　　i) $^-73$　　j) $^+49$　　k) $\frac{^+7}{8}$　　l) $\frac{^+14}{23}$

15. a)

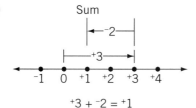

$^+3 + {}^-2 = {}^+1$

b)

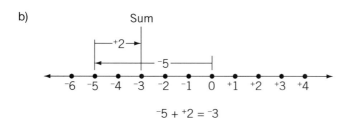

$^-5 + {}^+2 = {}^-3$

c)

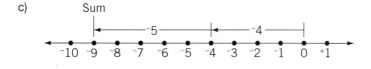

$^-4 + {}^-5 = {}^-9$

d)

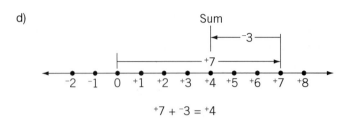

$$^+7 + {}^-3 = {}^+4$$

e)

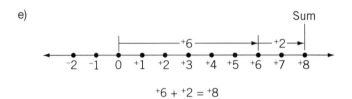

$$^+6 + {}^+2 = {}^+8$$

f)

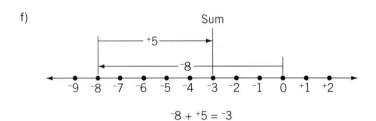

$$^-8 + {}^+5 = {}^-3$$

g)

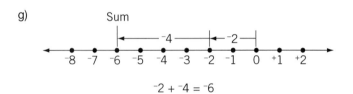

$$^-2 + {}^-4 = {}^-6$$

h)

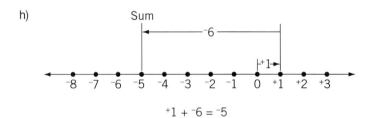

$$^+1 + {}^-6 = {}^-5$$

16. a) $^-43 + {}^+17 = {}^-26$ b) $^-57 + {}^-78 = {}^-135$ c) $^+61 + {}^-56 = {}^+5$

    d) $^-83 + {}^+69 = {}^-14$ e) $^+47 + {}^+34 = {}^+81$ f) $^-92 + {}^-89 = {}^-181$

    g) $^-68 + {}^+73 = {}^+5$ h) $^-37 + {}^-53 = {}^-90$ i) $^+48 + {}^-84 = {}^-36$

17. a) $\square + {}^-8 = {}^+7$

Missing addend   Sum

Addend $^-8$

$$^+7 - {}^-8 = {}^+15$$

b) $^-3 + \square = ^-4$

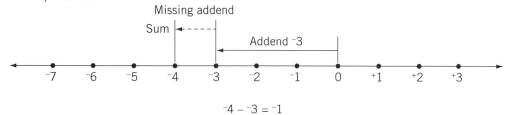

$$^-4 - ^-3 = ^-1$$

c) $^+2 + \square = ^+6$

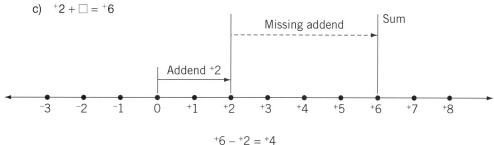

$$^+6 - ^+2 = ^+4$$

d) $^+3 + \square = ^-9$

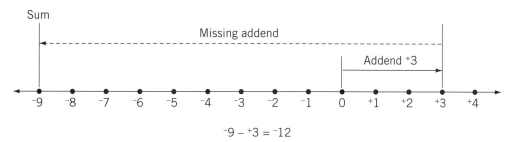

$$^-9 - ^+3 = ^-12$$

e) $^-8 + \square = ^-1$

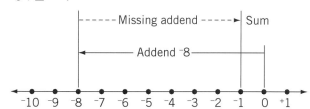

$$^-1 - ^-8 = ^+7$$

f) $^-7 + \square = ^+4$

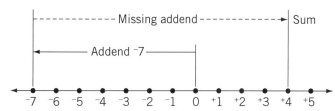

$$^+4 - ^-7 = ^+11$$

18. a) $^-24 - ^-42 = ^+18$ b) $^-51 - ^+68 = ^-119$ c) $^+23 - ^-19 = ^+42$
     d) $^-73 - ^+91 = ^-164$ e) $^+86 - ^-27 = ^+113$ f) $^+39 - ^+93 = ^-54$

19. a) $^-7 \times {}^-9 = {}^-63$ b) $^-8 \times {}^+6 = {}^-48$ c) $^-9 \times {}^-6 = {}^+54$
    d) $^-43 \times {}^-17 = {}^+731$ e) $^+32 \times {}^-23 = {}^-736$ f) $^-47 \times {}^-18 = {}^+846$
    g) $^-68 \times {}^+42 = {}^-2856$ h) $^+53 \times {}^+65 = {}^+3445$ i) $^-85 \times {}^-19 = {}^+1615$
    j) $^-39 \times {}^+17 = {}^-663$ k) $^+74 \times {}^-51 = {}^-3774$ l) $^-67 \times {}^+37 = {}^-2479$

20. a) $^-48 \div {}^+6 = {}^-8$ b) $^+72 \div {}^+9 = {}^+8$ c) $^-63 \div {}^-7 = {}^+9$
    d) $^-42 \div {}^-7 = {}^+6$ e) $^-69 \div {}^-3 = {}^+23$ f) $^-144 \div {}^+6 = {}^-24$
    g) $^-72 \div {}^-4 = {}^+18$ h) $^+84 \div {}^-12 = {}^-7$ i) $^+98 \div {}^-14 = {}^-7$
    j) $^-204 \div {}^-34 = {}^+6$ k) $^-208 \div {}^+26 = {}^-8$ l) $^+378 \div {}^-42 = {}^-9$

21. a) $\frac{{}^+3}{4} \times \frac{{}^-7}{8} = \frac{{}^-21}{32}$ b) $\frac{{}^-5}{6} \div \frac{{}^-2}{3} = \frac{{}^+5}{4} = {}^+1\frac{1}{4}$ c) $^-.8 \times {}^-.06 = {}^-.048$

    d) $^-.96 \div {}^+1.2 = {}^-.8$ e) $\frac{{}^-3}{5} + \frac{{}^-5}{9} = \frac{{}^-52}{45} = {}^-1\frac{7}{45}$ f) $^+7.8 - {}^-.21 = {}^+8.01$

    g) $\frac{{}^+7}{8} - \frac{{}^+2}{3} = \frac{{}^+5}{24}$ h) $^-3.41 + {}^+2.9 = {}^-.51$ i) $\frac{{}^-5}{8} \times \frac{{}^-4}{15} = \frac{{}^+1}{6}$

    j) $^-1.84 \div {}^+2.3 = {}^-.8$ k) $^+2.03 - {}^+1.45 = {}^+.58$ l) $\frac{{}^+9}{13} + \frac{{}^-2}{7} = \frac{{}^+37}{91}$

22. a) G   b) F
    c) G (and E, since every set contains itself as a subset)   d) A, B, C, D, and E
    e) E, D, and G   f) None

Chapter 10: Algebraic Reasoning: Generalizing Patterns and Relationships

1. a) $x = {}^-4$ b) $x = {}^-7$ c) $x = 3$ d) $x = \frac{{}^-1}{2}$ e) $x = \frac{{}^-1}{4}$

2. a) $x + 5 = y$ (linear)   b) $2x + 1 = y$ (linear)   c) $x^2 + 1 = y$ (nonlinear)

3. a)

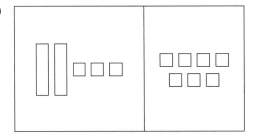

   b)

   c)

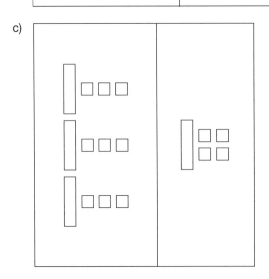

d)

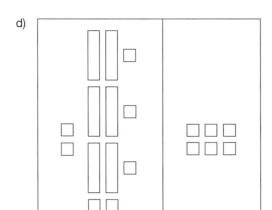

e)

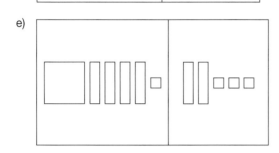

4. Let x = birth month; then, following the steps of the problem, we have

    $10x$
    $10x + 20$
    $10(10x + 20)$ or $100x + 200$
    $100x + 200 + 165$ or $100x + 365$
    Say you happen to be 21 years old; then,
    $100x + 365 + 21$
    $100x + 365 + 21 - 365$ or $100x + 21$

The $100x$ term multiplies your birth month by 100, putting your birth month in the hundreds and thousands place, leaving your age in the tens and ones place.

5. a)

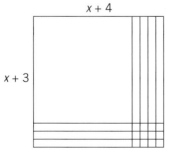

$x + 4$

$x + 3$

$x^2 + 7x + 12$

    b)

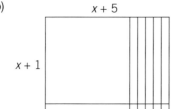

$x + 5$

$x + 1$

$x^2 + 6x + 5$

c)

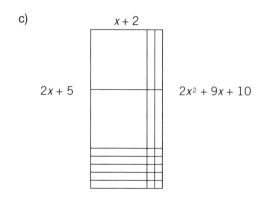

d)

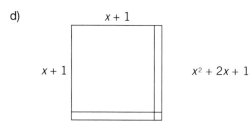

e)

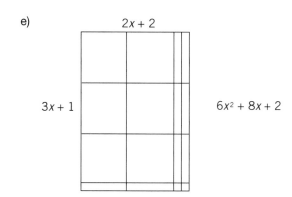

6. a) 19
    b) If there are only 2 teams, there is only 1 game (A plays B). If there are 3 teams, there are 3 games (A plays B, B plays C, and A plays C). If there are 4 teams, there are 6 games (A plays B, B plays C, C plays D, D plays A, C plays A, and B plays D). A table helps us to see a pattern.

# of teams	# of games
2	1
3	3
4	6
5	?

The pattern suggests that each new entry in the games column of the table is the sum of the previous entries in the two columns. That is, the ? above should be replaced by 10 (4 + 6).

    c) $y = \frac{(x + 1)(x + 2)}{2}$

    d) The independent variable is the number of teams. The dependent variable is the number of games.

7. a) $14,974.45   b) $100,626.52   c) $32,207.73
    d) $17,292.52   e) $2779.96

8. a) Approximately 120 feet   b) The launch pad must be at a height of 5 feet.
    c) 50 seconds   d) Approximately 75 feet
    e) Answers will vary.

9. Plan A can be thought of as $y = 20 + 1.5x$, where x represents the number of rentals and y is the total amount spent. Plan B can be thought of as $y = 2.75x$. If we set $2.75x = 20 + 1.5x$ and solve for x, we see that $x = 16$. This means that the two plans are the same if we rent 16 videos. If we rent fewer than 16, then plan B will be better.

10. a) $2x - 1$, where x is the number of the term
     b) x^2, where x is the number of the term
     c) Beginning with the first term, add 5 and then subtract 2 and continue this pattern.
     d) This sequence of numbers is reminiscent of the prime numbers. The next term would be the next prime in the order, 17.
     e) Beginning with the first term, add 5; then add the double of 5 (10); then add the double of 10 (20); then add the double of 20 (40). The next term, according to this pattern, would be 157 (77 add the double of 40).

11. a) $D = T + 4$ or $D - 4 = T$ b) $D = T + 3.5$ or $D - 3.5 = T$
     c) $\frac{D}{2} = T$ or $D = 2T$ d) $2D = 3T + 1$ or $2D - 1 = 3T$
     e) $4T + D = 43$

Chapter 11: Rational Numbers Expressed as Fractions: Concepts

1. Answers may vary.

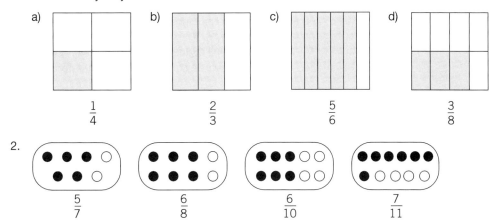

2.

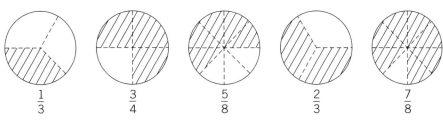

3. Answers may vary.

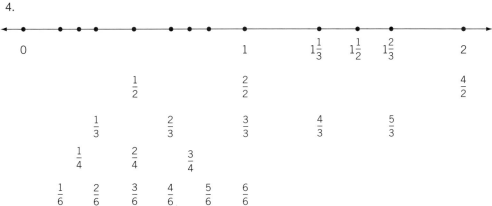

4.

5. a) $\frac{1}{9}, \frac{1}{8}, \frac{1}{7}, \frac{1}{6}, \frac{1}{5}, \frac{1}{4}, \frac{1}{3}, \frac{1}{2}$ b) $\frac{1}{5}, \frac{2}{5}, \frac{3}{5}, \frac{4}{5}, \frac{5}{5}, \frac{6}{5}$

   c) $\frac{1}{6}, \frac{1}{3}, \frac{3}{6}, \frac{4}{6}, \frac{5}{6}, \frac{3}{3}$ d) $\frac{1}{8}, \frac{1}{4}, \frac{1}{3}, \frac{3}{8}, \frac{5}{8}, \frac{2}{3}, \frac{3}{4}, \frac{4}{4}$

6. a) $\frac{1}{10} = \frac{2}{20}$ b) $\frac{3}{4} > \frac{3}{8}$ c) $\frac{3}{8} < \frac{2}{3}$ d) $\frac{1}{2} > \frac{5}{12}$

   e) $\frac{2}{3} < \frac{5}{6}$ f) $\frac{11}{8} > \frac{5}{4}$ g) $\frac{5}{8} < \frac{3}{4}$ h) $\frac{3}{14} = \frac{6}{28}$

7. a) $\frac{2}{3}$ b) $\frac{1}{4}$ c) $\frac{9}{16}$ d) $\frac{5}{6}$

   e) $\frac{2}{3}$ f) $\frac{13}{23}$ g) 25 h) $\frac{2}{3}$

8. a) $\frac{18}{5}$ b) $\frac{53}{10}$ c) $\frac{15}{8}$ d) $\frac{22}{7}$

   e) $\frac{9}{2}$ f) $\frac{131}{8}$ g) $\frac{27}{5}$ h) $\frac{50}{7}$

9. a) $\frac{1}{2}, \frac{2}{4}, \frac{3}{6}, \frac{4}{8}, \frac{5}{10}, \frac{6}{12}, \frac{7}{14}$

   b) $\frac{3}{8}, \frac{6}{16}, \frac{9}{24}, \frac{12}{32}, \frac{15}{40}, \frac{18}{48}, \frac{21}{56}$

   c) $\frac{5}{7}, \frac{10}{14}, \frac{15}{21}, \frac{20}{28}, \frac{25}{35}, \frac{30}{42}, \frac{35}{49}$

10. 3; 7, 3; $\frac{3 \times 7}{5 \times 7}$; equivalent

11. If a rectangular region is divided into 7 regions of the same size, then we can represent $\frac{4}{7}$ by shading 4 of these regions. If each of the 7 regions into which the original was divided is itself divided into 100 smaller regions (all the same size), then the original region will have been divided into 7×100 or 700 equivalent regions. Since each shaded region will also get divided into 100 smaller regions (all the same size), the shaded portion of the original rectangular region will consist of 4×100 or 400 small regions. Thus the portion of the original rectangular region that is shaded can be represented by $\frac{4 \times 100}{7 \times 100}$ or $\frac{400}{700}$. Therefore $\frac{4}{7} = \frac{400}{700}$.

12. a) $5\frac{4}{5}$ b) $4\frac{1}{4}$ c) $5\frac{2}{7}$ d) $2\frac{2}{3}$ e) $3\frac{7}{12}$

   f) $7\frac{3}{4}$ g) $8\frac{1}{6}$ h) $3\frac{4}{5}$ i) $1\frac{12}{13}$ j) $4\frac{8}{9}$

13. a) F   b) F   c) T   d) T
   e) F   f) F   g) T   h) T

Chapter 12: Rational Numbers Expressed as Fractions: Operations

1. a) $\frac{5}{7} + \frac{4}{7} = \frac{9}{7} = 1\frac{2}{7}$ b) $\frac{7}{5} + \frac{11}{5} = \frac{18}{5} = 3\frac{3}{5}$ c) $\frac{5}{4} + \frac{3}{4} = \frac{8}{4} = 2$

2.

                                 Addends

+	$\frac{5}{12}$	$\frac{1}{12}$	$\frac{7}{12}$	$\frac{11}{12}$	$\frac{1}{4}$	$\frac{17}{12}$	$\frac{2}{3}$	$\frac{5}{6}$	$\frac{2}{5}$	$\frac{1}{2}$	$\frac{1}{3}$	$\frac{3}{4}$	$\frac{1}{7}$
$\frac{3}{12}$	$\frac{2}{3}$	$\frac{1}{3}$	$\frac{5}{6}$	$1\frac{1}{6}$	$\frac{1}{2}$	$1\frac{2}{3}$	$\frac{11}{12}$	$1\frac{1}{12}$	$\frac{13}{20}$	$\frac{3}{4}$	$\frac{7}{12}$	1	$\frac{11}{28}$
$\frac{3}{4}$	$1\frac{1}{6}$	$\frac{5}{6}$	$1\frac{1}{3}$	$1\frac{2}{3}$	1	$2\frac{1}{6}$	$1\frac{5}{12}$	$1\frac{7}{12}$	$1\frac{3}{20}$	$1\frac{1}{4}$	$1\frac{1}{12}$	$1\frac{1}{2}$	$\frac{25}{28}$

(Row labels on the left: A d d e n d s)

3. a) $\frac{3}{16} + \frac{7}{16} = \frac{10}{16} = \frac{10 \div 2}{16 \div 2} = \frac{5}{8}$

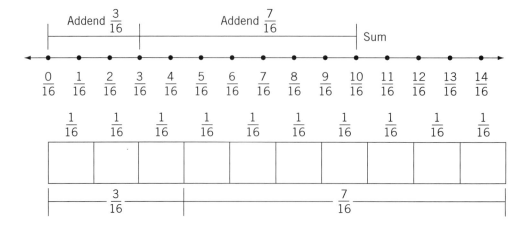

b) $\frac{6}{7} + \frac{5}{7} = \frac{11}{7} = \frac{7}{7} + \frac{4}{7} = 1\frac{4}{7}$

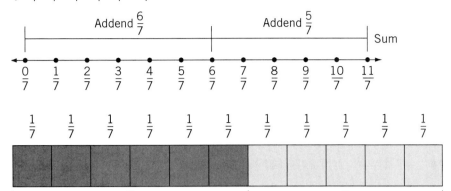

c) $\frac{7}{8} + \frac{3}{8} = \frac{10}{8} = \frac{8}{8} + \frac{2}{8} = 1 + \frac{2}{8} = 1\frac{1}{4}$

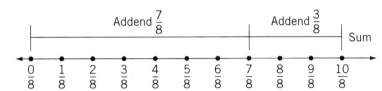

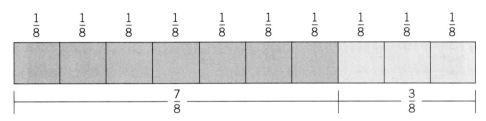

d) $\frac{2}{9} + \frac{7}{9} = \frac{9}{9} = 1$

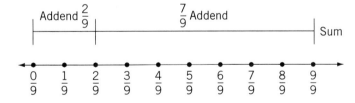

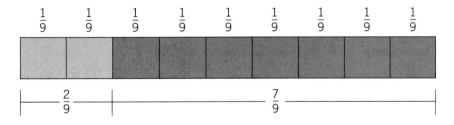

4. a) 12   b) 60   c) 24   d) 45   e) 30

5. a) $1\frac{2}{5} - \frac{4}{5} = \frac{7}{5} - \frac{4}{5} = \frac{3}{5}$

   b) $1 - \frac{1}{6} = \frac{6}{6} - \frac{1}{6} = \frac{5}{6}$

   c) $\frac{5}{3} - \frac{5}{9} = \frac{15}{9} - \frac{5}{9} = \frac{10}{9} = 1\frac{1}{9}$ or $1\frac{2}{3} - \frac{5}{9} = \frac{15}{9} - \frac{5}{9} = \frac{10}{9} = 1\frac{1}{9}$

6. Note that circular regions could be used instead of rectangular ones.

a) $\frac{4}{5} - \frac{3}{10} = \frac{8}{10} - \frac{3}{10} = \frac{5}{10} = \frac{1}{2}$

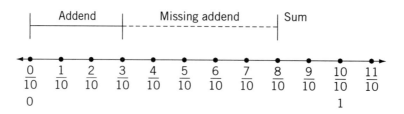

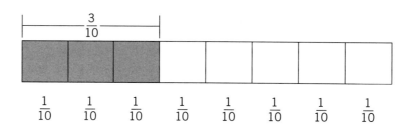

b) $\frac{7}{8} - \frac{3}{4} = \frac{7}{8} - \frac{6}{8} = \frac{1}{8}$

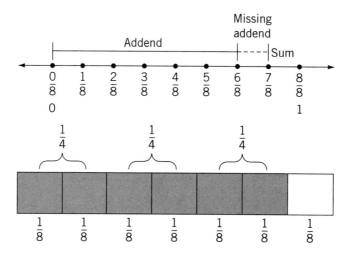

c) $\frac{5}{6} - \frac{1}{3} = \frac{5}{6} - \frac{2}{6} = \frac{3}{6} = \frac{1}{2}$

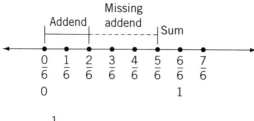

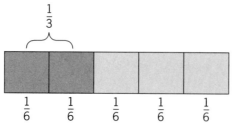

d) $\frac{2}{3} - \frac{1}{4} = \frac{8}{12} - \frac{3}{12} = \frac{5}{12}$

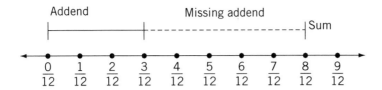

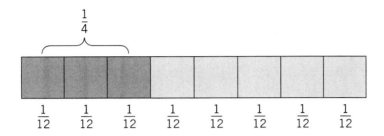

7. a)

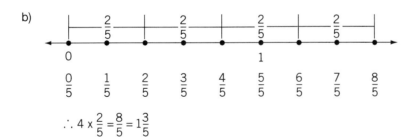

$\therefore 3 \times \frac{1}{4} = \frac{3}{4}$

b)

$\therefore 4 \times \frac{2}{5} = \frac{8}{5} = 1\frac{3}{5}$

c)

$\therefore 5 \times \frac{2}{3} = \frac{10}{3} = 3\frac{1}{3}$

d)

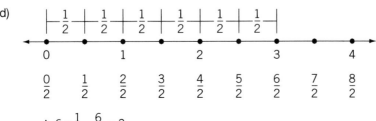

$\therefore 6 \times \frac{1}{2} = \frac{6}{2} = 3$

e)

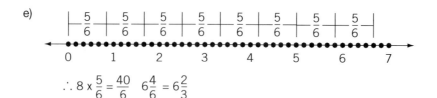

$$\therefore 8 \times \frac{5}{6} = \frac{40}{6} \quad 6\frac{4}{6} = 6\frac{2}{3}$$

f)

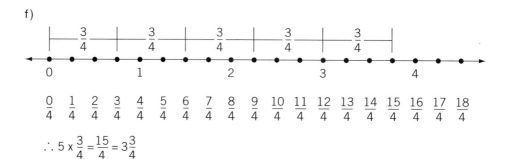

$$\frac{0}{4} \quad \frac{1}{4} \quad \frac{2}{4} \quad \frac{3}{4} \quad \frac{4}{4} \quad \frac{5}{4} \quad \frac{6}{4} \quad \frac{7}{4} \quad \frac{8}{4} \quad \frac{9}{4} \quad \frac{10}{4} \quad \frac{11}{4} \quad \frac{12}{4} \quad \frac{13}{4} \quad \frac{14}{4} \quad \frac{15}{4} \quad \frac{16}{4} \quad \frac{17}{4} \quad \frac{18}{4}$$

$$\therefore 5 \times \frac{3}{4} = \frac{15}{4} = 3\frac{3}{4}$$

8. a) $\frac{1}{2} \times \frac{3}{4} =$

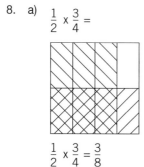

$$\frac{1}{2} \times \frac{3}{4} = \frac{3}{8}$$

b) $\frac{2}{3} \times \frac{1}{4} =$

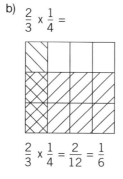

$$\frac{2}{3} \times \frac{1}{4} = \frac{2}{12} = \frac{1}{6}$$

c) $\frac{2}{5} \times \frac{1}{6} =$

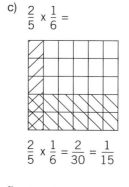

$$\frac{2}{5} \times \frac{1}{6} = \frac{2}{30} = \frac{1}{15}$$

d) $\frac{5}{6} \times \frac{1}{8} =$

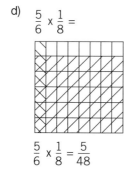

$$\frac{5}{6} \times \frac{1}{8} = \frac{5}{48}$$

e) $\frac{3}{8} \times \frac{4}{5} =$

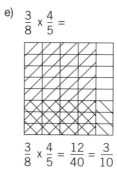

$$\frac{3}{8} \times \frac{4}{5} = \frac{12}{40} = \frac{3}{10}$$

f) $\frac{2}{3} \times \frac{4}{5} =$

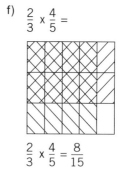

$$\frac{2}{3} \times \frac{4}{5} = \frac{8}{15}$$

9. a) How many groups of $\frac{2}{9}$ are there in $\frac{8}{9}$?

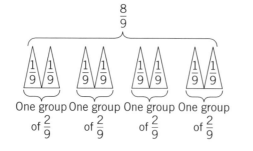

$$2\frac{9}{\smash{\big)}\,\dfrac{8}{9}} \quad \dfrac{4}{}$$

$$-\frac{8}{9}$$

b)   How many groups of $\frac{1}{4}$ are there in $\frac{3}{4}$?

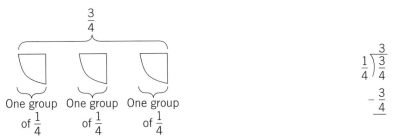

$$\frac{1}{4}\overline{)\begin{array}{c}3\\[2pt]\frac{3}{4}\\[2pt]-\frac{3}{4}\\\hline\end{array}}$$

c)   How many groups of $\frac{5}{11}$ are there in $\frac{10}{11}$?

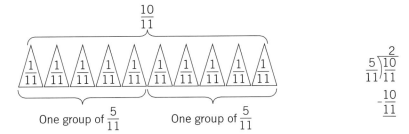

$$\frac{5}{11}\overline{)\begin{array}{c}2\\[2pt]\frac{10}{11}\\[2pt]-\frac{10}{11}\\\hline\end{array}}$$

d)   How many groups of $\frac{1}{4}$ are there in $\frac{3}{8}$?

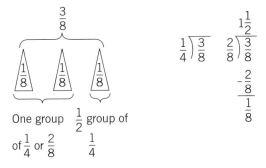

$$\frac{1}{4}\overline{)\ \frac{3}{8}}\qquad \frac{2}{8}\overline{)\begin{array}{c}1\frac{1}{2}\\[2pt]\frac{3}{8}\\[2pt]-\frac{2}{8}\\\hline\frac{1}{8}\end{array}}$$

e)   How many groups of $\frac{2}{3}$ are there in $\frac{5}{6}$?

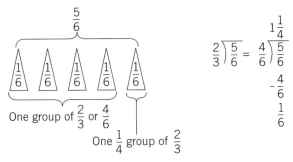

$$\frac{2}{3}\overline{)\ \frac{5}{6}}\ =\ \frac{4}{6}\overline{)\begin{array}{c}1\frac{1}{4}\\[2pt]\frac{5}{6}\\[2pt]-\frac{4}{6}\\\hline\frac{1}{6}\end{array}}$$

f) How many groups of $\frac{4}{5}$ are there in $\frac{4}{3}$?

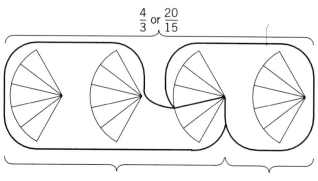

$$\frac{4}{3} \text{ or } \frac{20}{15}$$

$$1\frac{8}{12} = 1\frac{2}{3}$$

$$\frac{4}{5}\overline{\smash{\big)}\frac{4}{3}} = \frac{12}{15}\overline{\smash{\big)}\frac{20}{15}}$$

$$\frac{12}{15}$$

$$\frac{8}{15}$$

One group of $\frac{4}{5}$ or $\frac{12}{15}$ $\frac{8}{12}$

$$1\frac{8}{12}$$
or
$$1\frac{2}{3}$$

10. a) $\frac{5}{3}$ b) 4 or $\frac{4}{1}$ c) $\frac{6}{5}$ d) $\frac{8}{7}$ e) $\frac{5}{9}$

   f) $\frac{4}{9}$ g) $\frac{1}{17}$ h) $\frac{9}{31}$ i) $\frac{8}{55}$

11. a) $\dfrac{\frac{2}{9}}{\frac{8}{9}} = \dfrac{\frac{2}{9} \times \frac{9}{8}}{\frac{8}{9} \times \frac{9}{8}} = \dfrac{\frac{2}{9} \times \frac{9}{8}}{1} = \frac{18}{72} = \frac{2}{8} = \frac{1}{4}$

   b) $\dfrac{\frac{3}{4}}{\frac{1}{4}} = \dfrac{\frac{3}{4} \times \frac{4}{1}}{\frac{1}{4} \times \frac{4}{1}} = \dfrac{\frac{12}{4}}{1} = \frac{12}{4} = 3$

   c) $\dfrac{\frac{10}{11}}{\frac{5}{11}} = \dfrac{\frac{10}{11} \times \frac{11}{5}}{\frac{5}{11} \times \frac{11}{5}} = \dfrac{\frac{110}{55}}{1} = 2$

   d) $\dfrac{\frac{3}{8}}{\frac{1}{4}} = \dfrac{\frac{3}{8} \times \frac{4}{1}}{\frac{1}{4} \times \frac{4}{1}} = \dfrac{\frac{12}{8}}{1} = \frac{12}{8} = 1\frac{4}{8} = 1\frac{1}{2}$

   e) $\dfrac{\frac{5}{6}}{\frac{2}{3}} = \dfrac{\frac{5}{6} \times \frac{3}{2}}{\frac{2}{3} \times \frac{3}{2}} = \dfrac{\frac{15}{12}}{1} = 1\frac{3}{12} = 1\frac{1}{4}$

   f) $\dfrac{\frac{4}{3}}{\frac{4}{5}} = \dfrac{\frac{4}{3} \times \frac{5}{4}}{\frac{4}{5} \times \frac{5}{4}} = \dfrac{\frac{20}{12}}{1} = \frac{5}{3} = 1\frac{2}{3}$

12. a) <   b) =   c) >

13. a) $\frac{13}{27} < \frac{27}{55}$ b) $\frac{18}{21} < \frac{71}{81}$ c) $\frac{23}{67} < \frac{6}{17}$

14. a) $\left(\frac{3}{4} \times \frac{5}{6}\right) \div \frac{2}{3} = \frac{15}{24} \div \frac{2}{3}$
$$= \frac{15}{\cancel{24}_8} \times \frac{\cancel{3}^1}{2}$$
$$= \frac{15}{16}$$

   b) $\left(\frac{7}{8} \div \frac{4}{5}\right) \times \frac{1}{2} = \left(\frac{7}{8} \times \frac{5}{4}\right) \times \frac{1}{2}$
$$= \frac{35}{32} \times \frac{1}{2}$$
$$= \frac{35}{64}$$

   c) $\frac{2}{5} \times \left(\frac{2}{3} \div \frac{3}{4}\right) = \frac{2}{5} \times \left(\frac{2}{3} \times \frac{4}{3}\right)$
$$= \frac{2}{5} \times \frac{8}{9}$$
$$= \frac{16}{45}$$

   d) $\frac{5}{7} \div \left(\frac{4}{9} \times \frac{2}{5}\right) = \frac{5}{7} \div \frac{8}{45}$
$$= \frac{5}{7} \times \frac{45}{8}$$
$$= \frac{225}{56}$$
$$= 4\frac{1}{56}$$

15. a) $\frac{7}{\cancel{9}_3} \times \frac{\cancel{3}^1}{8} = \frac{7 \times 1}{3 \times 8} = \frac{7}{24}$

   b) $\frac{\cancel{4}^3}{\cancel{9}_1} \times \frac{\cancel{16}^3}{\cancel{28}_7} = \frac{1 \times 3}{1 \times 7} = \frac{3}{7}$

   c) $\frac{6}{7} \div \frac{4}{5} = \frac{\cancel{6}^3}{7} \times \frac{5}{\cancel{4}_2} = \frac{15}{14} = 1\frac{1}{14}$

   d) $\frac{8}{9} \div \frac{4}{18} = \frac{\cancel{8}^2}{\cancel{9}_1} \times \frac{\cancel{18}^2}{\cancel{4}_1} = \frac{2 \times 2}{1 \times 1} = \frac{4}{1} = 4$

   e) $\frac{5}{6} \div \frac{20}{21} = \frac{\cancel{5}^1}{\cancel{6}_2} \times \frac{\cancel{21}^7}{\cancel{20}_4} = \frac{1 \times 7}{2 \times 4} = \frac{7}{8}$

   f) $\frac{3}{11} \times 2\frac{4}{9} = \frac{\cancel{3}^1}{\cancel{11}_1} \times \frac{\cancel{22}^2}{\cancel{9}_3} = \frac{1 \times 2}{1 \times 3} = \frac{2}{3}$

   g) $2\frac{5}{6} \div 3\frac{1}{4} = \frac{17}{6} \div \frac{13}{4} = \frac{17}{\cancel{6}_3} \times \frac{\cancel{4}^2}{13} = \frac{34}{39}$

   h) $1\frac{3}{8} \times 4\frac{2}{3} = \frac{11}{\cancel{8}_4} \times \frac{\cancel{14}^7}{3} = \frac{77}{12} = 6\frac{5}{12}$

16. $12\frac{1}{2} \times 11\frac{3}{4} = \frac{25}{2} \times \frac{47}{4} = \frac{1175}{8} = 146\frac{7}{8}$ square feet.

Change $146\frac{7}{8}$ square feet to square yards by dividing by 9, because there are 9 square feet in 1 square yard. It will require $16\frac{23}{72}$ square yards. A realistic answer would be 17 square yards.

Chapter 13: Rational Numbers Expressed as Decimals: Concepts and Operations

1. $300 + 40 + 6 + .1 + .02 + .008$ or

    $(3 \times 100) + (4 \times 10) + (6 \times 1) + \left(1 \times \frac{1}{10}\right) + \left(2 \times \frac{1}{100}\right) + \left(8 \times \frac{1}{1000}\right)$ or

    $(3 \times 10^2) + (4 \times 10^1) + (6 \times 10^0) + (1 \times 10^{-1}) + (2 \times 10^{-2}) + (8 \times 10^{-3})$

2. a) $2\frac{1896}{10,000}$ b) $\frac{3201}{1,000,000}$ c) $\frac{12}{99} = \frac{4}{33}$ d) $\frac{46}{99}$

    e) $\frac{8}{9}$ f) $\frac{1}{4}$ g) $\frac{71}{198}$ h) $\frac{72}{999} = \frac{8}{11}$

3. a) $.\overline{571428}$ b) $1.\overline{923076}$ c) $.7\overline{2}$ d) $.91\overline{6}$ e) $.3\overline{3}$ f) $.6\overline{6}$

4. No. Every fractional number can be written as a terminating decimal or as a repeating decimal. Suppose that $\frac{a}{b}$ is any fraction with a whole-number numerator and a counting-number denominator. To rewrite $\frac{a}{b}$ as a decimal, we can go through the usual division process after rewriting $\frac{a}{b}$ in the form $b\overline{)a}$. Suppose that we are going through the division algorithm. Each time we go through the subtraction stage, one of two things could happen: We get a difference of zero or we get a difference not equal to zero. If we ever get a difference of zero, the division algorithm is at an end, and the quotient we have obtained is a terminating decimal. What happens if we never do get a difference of zero? Because of the way the division algorithm operates, there are only a limited number of possible differences we can obtain at the subtraction stage (these differences are 0, 1, 2, 3, . . . , and $b - 1$). If the division algorithm never yields a difference of zero, then at some point one of the other possible differences occurs a second time. If we are already to the right of the decimal point when this occurs, then we will soon come again to this same difference. Once these differences begin to repeat, the digits in the quotient repeat also.

5. a)
    ```
        2.34
       17.1
        .0234
     +  .123
       19.5864
    ```

    b)
    ```
      43.7      =   43.700
     −12.684    = −12.684
                    31.016
    ```

    c)
    ```
       7.43
     × 2.1
        .743
      14.86
      15.603
    ```

    d) $6.2\overline{)8.928}$

    Multiply both divisor and dividend by 10.

    ```
          1.44
     62)89.28
        62.00  ← (1 × 62)
        27.28
        24.80  ← (.4 × 62)
         2.48
         2.48  ← (.04 × 62)
            0
    ```

6. a) $\frac{3}{97} = \frac{12}{\Box}$ Since $3 \times 4 = 12$ and $97 \times 4 = 388$, $\Box = 388$, and 12 cans of tomato juice cost 388 cents, or $3.88.

    b) $\frac{5}{1} = \frac{35}{\Box}$ $\Box = 7$ Seven cars are needed.

    c) $\frac{100}{1} = \frac{\Box}{3}$ $\Box = 300$ Three hundred centimeters are needed.

    d) $\frac{1}{.6} = \frac{\Box}{1}$ $\Box = 1.666\ldots$ Approximately 1.67 kilometers measure the same length as 1 mile.

7. a) $\frac{\Box}{100} = \frac{50}{150}$ $\Box = 33\frac{1}{3}$ The chair is discounted (marked down) by $33\frac{1}{3}\%$.

    b) $\frac{\Box}{100} = \frac{13}{112.9}$ $\Box = 11.5$ Gasoline has increased at the rate of 11.5%.

c) $\frac{10}{100} = \frac{33}{\square}$ $\square = 330$ The test was taken by 330 children.

d) $\frac{56}{100} = \frac{\square}{500}$ $\square = 280$ 280 children walk to school.

e) $\frac{17}{100} = \frac{391}{\square}$ $\square = 2300$ The total number of children is 2300.

8. a) $r \times b = p$

    $\square \times \$150 = \$50$

    $\square = \frac{50}{150} = \frac{1}{3}$

    $\square = 33\frac{1}{3}\%$ discount

    b) $r \times b = p$

    $\square \times 61.9 = 37$

    $\square = \frac{37}{61.9}$

    $\square = 59.7\%$ or about a 60% increase

    c) $r \times b = p$

    $.10 \times \square = 33$

    $\square = \frac{33}{.10}$

    $\square = 330$

    330 students took the test.

    d) $r \times b = p$

    $.56 \times 500 = \square$

    $280 = \square$

    280 students walk to school.

    e) $r \times b = p$

    $.17 \times \square = 391$

    $\square = \frac{391}{.17}$

    $\square = 2300$

    2300 children attend Greenspun.

9. a) 938,000   b) 23,700   c) 4,660,000,000   d) 5,300,000
    e) .0831   f) .000003641   g) .0022   h) .00004681

10. a) 7.3×10^3 b) 2.4×10^7 c) 8.9×10^9
    d) 1.23×10^2 e) 1.6432×10^4 f) 4.3756×10^2

11. $\frac{1}{3} = .333\ldots$ (repeats beginning after the first decimal place).

    $\frac{5}{7} = .71428571428\ldots$ (repeats beginning after the sixth decimal place).

    $\frac{6}{13} = .4615384615384\ldots$ (repeats beginning after the sixth decimal place).

12. $\frac{1}{2}$ can be represented by shading 50 of the 100 squares. Since 1% is $\frac{1}{100}$, 1 square out of the 100 would be shaded. Clearly, $\frac{1}{2}\%$ would be a shading of half of the square that represents 1%.

13. a) 87.5% or $87\frac{1}{2}\%$ b) $81.\overline{81}\%$ or $81\frac{9}{11}\%$ c) 20%
    d) $53.\overline{846153}\%$ or $53\frac{11}{13}\%$ e) 75%   f) $88.\overline{8}\%$ or $88\frac{8}{9}\%$

Chapter 14: Data Analysis: Graphs, Statistics, and Probability

1. $\frac{1}{16}, \frac{1}{32}, \frac{1}{64}$

2. There are eleven possible combinations.

    a) all tails $\frac{1}{1024}$ b) 1 head and 9 tails $\frac{5}{512}$

    c) 2 heads and 8 tails $\frac{45}{1024}$ d) 3 heads and 7 tails $\frac{15}{128}$

    e) 4 heads and 6 tails $\frac{105}{512}$ f) 5 heads and 5 tails $\frac{63}{256}$

    g) 6 heads and 4 tails $\frac{105}{512}$ h) 7 heads and 3 tails $\frac{15}{128}$

    i) 8 heads and 2 tails $\frac{45}{1024}$ j) 9 heads and 2 tails $\frac{5}{512}$

    k) all heads $\frac{1}{1024}$

3. a) $\frac{1}{3}$ b) $\frac{1}{2}$ c) $\frac{1}{6}$ d) $\frac{2}{3}$ e) $\frac{1}{3}$

4. a) $\frac{1}{6}, \frac{1}{6}, \frac{1}{6}$ b) $\frac{1}{3}$ c) $\frac{1}{2}$ d) $\frac{2}{3}$ e) $\frac{5}{6}$

5. red marble $\frac{5}{8}$, blue marble $\frac{2}{8}$ or $\frac{1}{4}$, white marble $\frac{1}{8}$

6. a) mean $= \frac{67}{32}$ or about 2 heads per toss   b) median = 2; mode = 2; range = 4

c)

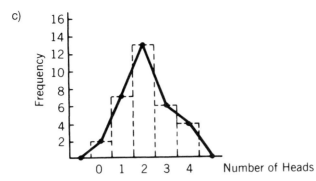

7. a) $\frac{7}{22}$ b) $\frac{10}{22}$ or $\frac{5}{11}$ c) $\frac{5}{22}$

8. a) $\frac{1}{12}$ b) $\frac{3}{12}$ or $\frac{1}{4}$ c) $\frac{6}{12}$ or $\frac{1}{2}$

9. a) $\frac{1}{52}$ b) $\frac{4}{52}$ or $\frac{1}{13}$ c) $\frac{13}{52}$ or $\frac{1}{4}$ d) $\frac{12}{52}$ or $\frac{3}{13}$ e) $\frac{20}{52}$ or $\frac{5}{13}$

10. Three socks. Since there are only two colors possible, a total of three socks MUST produce a pair of like color.

11. Results of 100 rolls of a die:

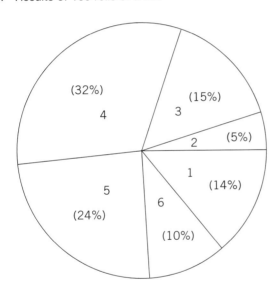

12. Number of years five Kansas City Chiefs played in NFL:

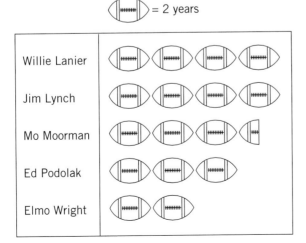

Chapter 15: Measurement

1. a) $m(\overset{\leftrightarrow}{AB}) \approx 2\frac{1}{2}$ inches   b) $m(\overset{\leftrightarrow}{MN}) \approx 4\frac{1}{2}$ inches
          ≈ 7 centimeters ≈ 11 centimeters

   c) $m(\overset{\leftrightarrow}{XY}) \approx 1\frac{1}{2}$ inches   d) $m(\overset{\leftrightarrow}{CD}) \approx 2$ inches
          ≈ 4 centimeters ≈ 6 centimeters

2. a) 5 centimeters < 52 millimeters   b) 1 meter > 99 centimeters
   c) 1 yard < 36 feet   d) 4 liters > 401 milliliters
   e) 1 mile = 5280 feet   f) 4 kilograms > 453.6 grams
   g) 23 centimeters > 2.3 millimeters   h) 7 decimeters < 1 meter
   i) 1 bushel > 2 pecks   j) 8 pints = 1 gallon
   k) 9 pounds > 140 ounces   l) 2 feet > .5 yard
   m) 3 meters = 300 centimeters

3. a) 7.2 meters   b) 410 meters   c) 50 meters
   d) 6.72 meters   e) .08 meter   f) 4 meters
   g) .92 meter   h) 1.241 meters   i) 82,400 meters

4. a) .72 liter   b) 72 centiliters   c) 7.2 deciliters
   d) .072 dekaliter   e) .0072 hectoliter   f) .00072 kiloliter

5. a) 16 ft 18 in. or 17 ft 6 in. or $17\frac{1}{2}$ ft   b) 10 hrs 22 min
   c) 1 m 52 cm or 152 cm   d) 12 rd 54 ft or 15 rd $4\frac{1}{2}$ ft
   e) 10 ft 10 in.   f) 3 m 56 cm or 356 cm
   g) 4 yd 31 in. or 4 yd 2 ft 7 in.   h) 11 cm 4 mm or 114 cm
   i) 2 gal $3\frac{4}{5}$ pt   j) 22 m 6 cm or 2206 cm

6. a) $5\frac{2}{3}$ yards   b) 63 inches   c) $2\frac{1}{2}$ gallons   d) 22 ounces
   e) 48 tablespoons   f) 36,960 feet   g) $\frac{3}{8}$ acre   h) $21\frac{1}{2}$ pints
   i) 441 square feet   j) 48 cups

7. a) 540 centimeters   b) 81,000 meters
   c) 10^{12} (or 1,000,000,000,000 microliters)   d) 5.497 kilograms
   e) 72,000,000 microliters   f) 5.24 deciliters
   g) .002473 gram   h) 70 decimeters

8. a) F   b) T   c) T   d) F   e) T   f) T

9. 2 quarters; 1 quarter, 5 nickels; 1 quarter, 1 dime, 3 nickels; 1 quarter, 2 dimes, 1 nickel; 5 dimes; 4 dimes, 2 nickels; 3 dimes, 4 nickels; 2 dimes, 6 nickels; 1 dime, 8 nickels; 10 nickels.

10.

Quarters	Dimes	Nickels	Quarters	Dimes	Nickels
4	0	0	1	2	11
3	2	1	1	1	13
3	1	3	1	0	15
3	0	5	0	10	0
2	5	0	0	9	2
2	4	2	0	8	4
2	3	4	0	7	6
2	2	6	0	6	8
2	1	8	0	5	10
2	0	10	0	4	12
1	7	1	0	3	14
1	6	3	0	2	16
1	5	5	0	1	18
1	4	7	0	0	20
1	3	9			

11. Approximately 27 stacked pennies measure about 4 cm; therefore 1 penny is about .15 mm in thickness.

12. Approximately 8 stacked dimes measure about 1 cm; thus 1 dime is about .125 mm in thickness.

13. $1.19 [1 half-dollar and 1 quarter (or 3 quarters) and 4 dimes and 4 pennies]

Chapter 16: Geometry: Basic Concepts and Structures

Answers to the examples that relate to the geoboard will vary. Some possible answers are given.

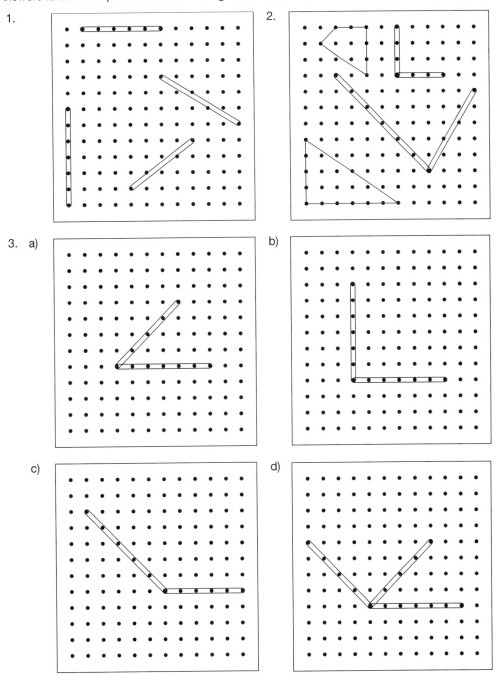

e)

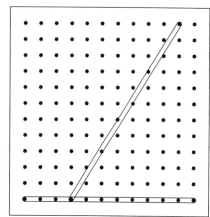

4.

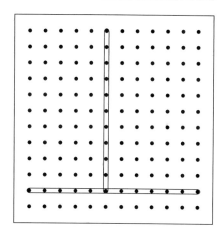

5. a) an infinite number of lines
   b) one line segment

6. a) congruent   b) acute

7. a) 65°   b) 45°   c) 10°   d) 17°   e) 87°   f) 4°

8. a) 140°   b) 90°   c) 30°   d) 10°   e) 135°   f) 71°

9. Answers will vary, depending on the given figure. But the results should appear this way:

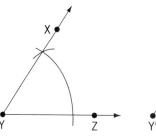 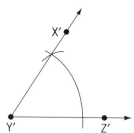

10. a) point   (A)
    b) ray   ($\overrightarrow{FG}$)
    c) line   ($\overleftrightarrow{HK}$) or ($\overleftrightarrow{KH}$)
    d) acute angle   (∠ZXY or ∠YXZ)
    e) right angle   (∠NOM or ∠MON)
    f) line segment   ($\overline{ST}$ or $\overline{TS}$)
    g) obtuse angle   (∠PQR or ∠RQP)
    h) adjacent angles, or complementary angles [$m(∠LRM) + m(∠MRN) = 90°$]
    i) adjacent angles, or supplementary angles [$m(∠AED) + m(∠DEB) = 180°$]

11. a) T   b) T   c) F   d) T   e) F   f) F

12. $\overleftrightarrow{AB}$ $\overleftrightarrow{AC}$ $\overleftrightarrow{AD}$ $\overleftrightarrow{AE}$ $\overleftrightarrow{AF}$

   $\overleftrightarrow{BC}$ $\overleftrightarrow{BD}$ $\overleftrightarrow{BE}$ $\overleftrightarrow{BF}$

   $\overleftrightarrow{CD}$ $\overleftrightarrow{CE}$ $\overleftrightarrow{CF}$

   $\overleftrightarrow{DE}$ $\overleftrightarrow{DF}$

   $\overleftrightarrow{EF}$

13. Every square has four lines of symmetry.

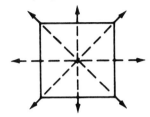

14. a) Each line coincides with or is parallel to each of the others.
     b) They are all the same length.
     c) Polygon ABCDE is the same size and shape as polygon A'B'C'D'E'; in other words, the two polygons are congruent.

15.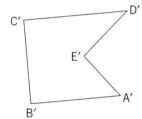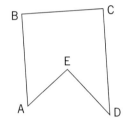

16. a) 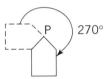   b)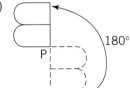

     c) 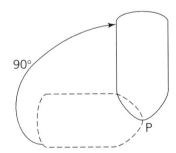   d)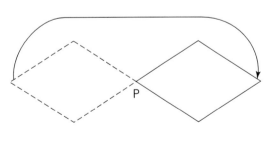

17. a)   b)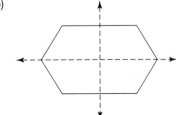

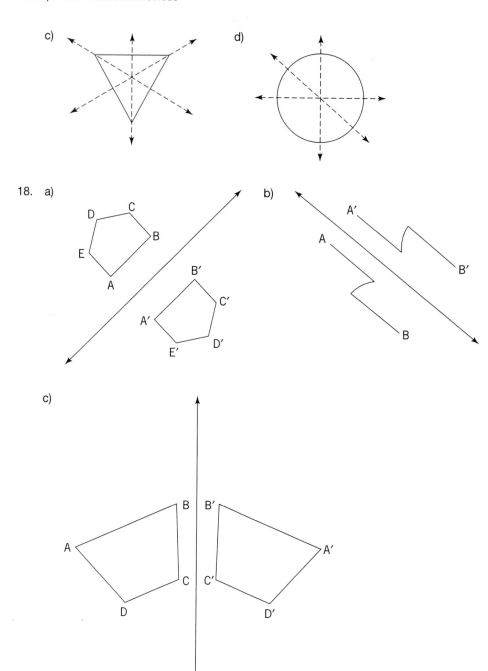

c)

d)

18. a)

b)

c)

Chapter 17: Geometry: Polygons and Polyhedra

1. a) scalene triangle; right triangle

$A = \frac{1}{2}bh$

$\quad = \frac{1}{2} \times 8 \times 6$

$\quad = \left(\frac{1}{2} \times 8\right) \times 6$

$\quad = 4 \times 6$

$\quad = 24$

The area is 24 square units.

$P = m(\overleftrightarrow{MO}) + m(\overleftrightarrow{ON}) + m(\overleftrightarrow{NM})$

$\quad = 8 + 10 + 6$

$\quad = 24$

The perimeter is 24 units.

b)   isosceles triangle; acute triangle

$A = \frac{1}{2}bh$

$= \frac{1}{2} \times 12 \times 8$

$= \left(\frac{1}{2} \times 12\right) \times 8$

$= 6 \times 8$

$= 48$

The area is 48 square units.

$P = m(\overleftrightarrow{XY}) + m(\overleftrightarrow{YZ}) + m(\overleftrightarrow{ZX})$

$= 12 + 10 + 10$

$= 32$

The perimeter is 32 units.

c)   equilateral triangle; equiangular triangle

$A = \frac{1}{2}bh$

$= \frac{1}{2} \times 30 \times 26$

$= \left(\frac{1}{2} \times 30\right) \times 26$

$= 15 \times 26$

$= 390$

The area is 390 square units.

$P = 3s$

$= 3 \times 30$

$= 90$

The perimeter is 90 units.

2. If we cut out two copies of the trapezoid shown on the left, we can place the pieces together to form the figure shown on the right.

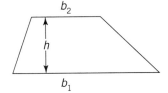
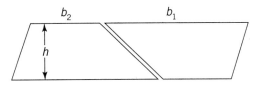

The figure on the right has area $h(b_1 + b_2)$, so the trapezoid has area $\frac{1}{2}[h(b_1 + b_2)]$.

3. a)   square

$A = s^2$

$= 5 \times 5$

$= 25$

The area is 25 square units.

$P = m(\overleftrightarrow{WX}) + m(\overleftrightarrow{XY}) + m(\overleftrightarrow{ZW})$

$= 4s$

$= 4 \times 5$

$= 20$

The perimeter is 20 units.

b)   parallelogram

$A = bh$

$= 12 \times 6$

$= 72$

The area is 72 square units.

$P = 2\ell + 2w$

$= (2 \times 12) + (2 \times 8)$

$= 24 + 16$

$= 40$

The perimeter is 40 units.

c)   rectangle

$A = \ell w$

$= 27 \times 8$

$= 216$

The area is 216 square units.

$P = 2\ell + 2w$

$= (2 \times 27) + (2 \times 8)$

$= 54 + 16$

$= 70$

The perimeter is 70 units.

d)   rhombus

$A = bh$

$= 5 \times 4$

$= 20$

The area is 20 square units.

$P = 4s$

$= 4 \times 5$

$= 20$

The perimeter is 20 units.

e) trapezoid

$A = \frac{1}{2}(b_1 + b_2)h$ $P = a + b + c + d$

$\quad = \frac{1}{2}(8 + 4) \times 4$ $\quad = (8 + 6) + (4 + 5)$

$\quad = 6 \times 4$ $\quad = 14 + 9$

$\quad = 24$ $\quad = 23$

The area is 24 square units.   The perimeter is 23 units.

4. a) 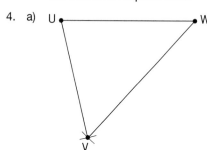   b)

5. a) $A \cong \pi r^2$ $C \cong \pi d$

$\quad = 3.1 \times (4 \times 4)$ $\quad = 3.1 \times (4 + 4)$

$\quad = 3.1 \times 16$ $\quad = 3.1 \times 8$

$\quad = 49.6$ $\quad = 24.8$

The area of the circle is   The circumference is
approximately 49.6 square units.   approximately 24.8 units.

b) $A \cong \pi r^2$ $C \cong \pi d$

$\quad = 3.1 \times (6 \times 6)$ $\quad = 3.1 \times 12$

$\quad = 3.1 \times 36$ $\quad = 37.2$

$\quad = 111.6$

The area is approximately   The circumference is
111.6 square units.   approximately 37.2 units.

6. a) $c^2 = a^2 + b^2$ b) $c^2 = a^2 + b^2$ c) $c^2 = a^2 + b^2$

$225 = a^2 + 81$ $169 = 144 + b^2$ $c^2 = 36 + 64$

$\quad a^2 = 144$ $\quad b^2 = 25$ $c^2 = 100$

$\quad a = 12$ $\quad b = 5$ $\quad c = 10$

Side a is 12 units long.   Side b is 5 units long.   Side c is 10 units long.

7. Since the sum of the measures of the angles of any triangle is 180°, the measure of the third angle must be 71°.

8. a) rectangular pyramid
       base: the rectangular region ABCD
       edges: $\overrightarrow{AB}$, $\overrightarrow{BC}$, $\overrightarrow{CD}$, $\overrightarrow{DA}$, $\overrightarrow{AE}$, $\overrightarrow{BE}$, $\overrightarrow{CE}$, $\overrightarrow{DE}$
       vertices: A, B, C, D, E

   b) rectangular prism
       bases: any one of the following pairs of rectangular regions—WXYZ and W'X'Y'Z', XX'Y'Y and WW'Z'Z, WW'X'X and ZZ'Y'Y
       edges: $\overrightarrow{WW'}$, $\overrightarrow{XX'}$, $\overrightarrow{YY'}$, $\overrightarrow{ZZ'}$, $\overrightarrow{WX}$, $\overrightarrow{XY}$, $\overrightarrow{YZ}$, $\overrightarrow{ZW}$, $\overrightarrow{W'Z'}$, $\overrightarrow{X'Y'}$, $\overrightarrow{Y'Z'}$, $\overrightarrow{W'X'}$
       vertices: W, X, Y, Z, W', X', Y', Z'

   c) right circular cylinder
       bases: the two circular regions with centers O and O'
       edges: (We haven't defined the edges of a cylinder.)
       vertices: (We haven't defined the vertices of a cylinder.)

   d) pentagonal pyramid
       base: the pentagonal region ABCDE
       edges: $\overrightarrow{AB}$, $\overrightarrow{BC}$, $\overrightarrow{CD}$, $\overrightarrow{DE}$, $\overrightarrow{EA}$, $\overrightarrow{AF}$, $\overrightarrow{BF}$, $\overrightarrow{CF}$, $\overrightarrow{DF}$, $\overrightarrow{EF}$
       vertices: A, B, C, D, E, F

9. a) $V = \ell wh$ $V = bh$

           $= 14 \times 7 \times 3$ or $= (14 \times 7) \times 3$

           $= 294$ $= 98 \times 3$

                               $= 294$

The volume is 294 cubic units.

b)   The polygons forming the bases of this prism are right triangles. The area of each base is therefore equal to one-half the product of the legs of the right triangle bounding the base.

$V = bh$

    $= \left(\frac{1}{2} \times 6 \times 8\right) \times 3$

    $= 24 \times 3$

    $= 72$

The volume is 72 cubic units

c) $V = \ell wh$ $V = bh$

           $= 5 \times 5 \times 5$ or $= (5 \times 5) \times 5$

           $= 125$ $= 25 \times 5$

                               $= 125$

The volume is 125 cubic units.

10. a) $SA = 2b + ph$

         $= [2 \times (6 \times 6)] + [(6 + 6 + 6 + 6) \times 6]$

         $= [2 \times 36] + [24 \times 6]$

         $= 72 + 144$

         $= 216$

The surface area is 216 square units.

b) $SA = 2b + ph$

         $= [2 \times (3 \times 12)] + [(12 + 3 + 12 + 3) \times 5]$

         $= [2 \times 36] + [30 \times 5]$

         $= 72 + 150$

         $= 222$

The surface area is 222 square units.

c)   The polygons forming the bases of this prism are right triangles. The area of each base is therefore equal to one-half the product of the legs of the right triangle bounding the bases.

$SA = 2b + ph$

    $= [2 \times \left(\frac{1}{2} \times 6 \times 8\right)] + [(6 + 8 + 10) \times 3]$

    $= [2 \times 24] + [24 \times 3]$

    $= 48 + 72$

    $= 120$

The surface area is 120 square units.

11. a)   prism, cylinder   b)   sphere
      c)   cylinder, prism   d)   triangular pyramid
      e)   pyramid

12. a)   rectangular pyramid   b)   cube
      c)   cylinder   d)   triangular prism

13.

Space Figure	Area of Base	Height	Volume
Cylinder	42 sq in.	10 in.	420 cu in.
Cube	25 sq cm	5 cm	125 cu cm
Triangular prism	37 sq in.	14 in.	518 cu in.
Cylinder	24 sq m	50 dm	120 cu m
Rectangular prism	27 sq mm	9 mm	243 cu mm
Square prism	6 sq ft	18 in.	9 cu ft

Index